Penguin Education

Penguin Critical Anthologies
General Editor: Christopher Ric

William Wordsworth

Edited by Graham McMaster

William Wordsworth
A Critical Anthology

Edited by
Graham McMaster
Penguin Books

Penguin Books Ltd, Harmondsworth,
Middlesex, England
Penguin Books Inc, 7110 Ambassador Road,
Baltimore, Md 21207, USA
Penguin Books Australia Ltd,
Ringwood, Victoria, Australia

First published 1972
This selection copyright © Graham McMaster, 1972
Introduction and notes copyright © Graham McMaster, 1972

Made and printed in Great Britain by
Hazell Watson & Viney Ltd,
Aylesbury, Bucks
Set in Monotype Bembo

Contents

6 Contents

7 Contents

8 Contents

9 Contents

Part Three **Modern Views**

10   Contents

Preface

A collection as generous as the present one might be expected to be comprehensive enough to be self-sufficient. This, alas, is not the case. There are books on Wordsworth which do aim at completeness. The titles of some of them are to be found in the final bibliography, and I hope that those who have not yet tried them will be encouraged to do so. Obviously enough, the chief advantage of such a collection as this is its variousness. It is every scholar's business to convince us that his approach is the true one. In the context of so many endeavours, we can be both more grateful and more sceptical.

Although the work is made up of many heterogeneous parts, it is hoped that it does make a whole, and that its sense best unfolds read as a whole from start to finish. For those who have not the time for this, however, the index attempts to plot the course of some of the most important controversies in the history of Wordsworth criticism.

A large part of the book was prepared in Poland, where Words-worthiana are in fairly short supply. That it has appeared at all is due to the help of Christopher Ricks, Martin Lightfoot, John Harvey, Ivor Kemp and the staff of the British Council Library in Warsaw.

Table of Dates

1793   Stays in London, with visits to the Isle of Wight (July), Denbighshire via the Wye Valley (August) and Keswick. *An Evening Walk* and *Descriptive Sketches* published by J. Johnson, St Paul's Churchyard. *Guilt and Sorrow* (first version) and *A Letter to the Bishop of Llandaff* written.

1794   Joins Dorothy, who has been brought up separately. They visit Wordsworth's friends the Hutchinsons, Keswick and Whitehaven. Spends some time with Raisley Calvert in Keswick and Penrith.

1795   *January* Raisley Calvert dies and leaves Wordsworth a legacy.
        September Wordsworth settles down at Racedown Lodge, Dorset, with Dorothy and the son of Basil Montagu. Meets Coleridge who, in 1794, was impressed by *Descriptive Sketches*.

1796   During this and the following year, Wordsworth writes *The Borderers*. At Racedown most of the time except for a summer journey to London.

1797   Mary Hutchinson pays a long visit to Racedown and Coleridge stays there in June. *The Ruined Cottage* in composition. Wordsworth and Dorothy lease Alfoxden House, Somerset.
        November Wordsworth, Dorothy and Coleridge go on two short walking tours. Wordsworth visits Bristol. *The Old Cumberland Beggar* and *Animal Tranquillity and Decay* written.

1798   Many *Lyrical Ballads* written, and the first version of *Peter Bell*. After an expedition to Cheddar with Dorothy and Coleridge, Wordsworth goes to Bristol and returns to Alfoxden with Cottle.
        June The Alfoxden lease expires and the Wordsworths

spend a week with Coleridge in Nether Stowey, afterwards moving to Bristol.

10–13 July Wordsworth and Dorothy go on an excursion to Tintern Abbey, and *Lines* composed.

September Lyrical Ballads published, ostensibly anonymously, by Biggs & Cottle of Bristol, in one volume. They were reissued by Arch of London later in 1798.

September Wordsworth, Dorothy and Coleridge arrive in Hamburg.

October Wordsworth and Dorothy in Goslar, Saxony. Most of *The Prelude*, Book I written; also 'Lucy' and 'Matthew' Poems.

1799   *23 February* Wordsworth and Dorothy leave Goslar and walk through central Germany.

April They join Coleridge in Göttingen and arrive back in England at the end of the month. Wordsworth, Coleridge and John Wordsworth go on a walking tour in the Lakes.

21 December Wordsworth and Dorothy take up residence at Dove Cottage, Townend, Grasmere. Most of *The Prelude*, Book II written this autumn.

1800   *Lyrical Ballads, with Other Poems* published in two volumes by Longman and Rees. The first volume is called 'second edition'. Wordsworth is given as the author. The volumes actually appeared in January 1801.

1802   *August* Wordsworth visits Calais and meets Annette and Caroline.

4 October Wordsworth marries Mary Hutchinson.

Lyrical Ballads, with Pastoral and Other Poems (volume 1, third edition; volume 2 second edition). A great number of short poems written this year, including the first half of *Intimations of Immortality*.

1803   First tour in Scotland. Wordsworth meets Walter Scott.

1804   *4 January* Wordsworth reads *The Prelude*, Book II to
         Coleridge.
         January–March Intimations completed, *Ode to Duty* and
         The Prelude, Books III, IV, V composed.
         April The Prelude, Book VI, and part of Book IX written.
         16 August Wordsworth's daughter Dora is born.
         October–December The Prelude, Books VII, VIII, IX, X
         written.

1805   *The Prelude*, Book XII.
         5 February Wordsworth's brother John dies at sea.
         May The Prelude, Books XIII, XIV. (*The Prelude*
         completed.)

1806   *January The Waggoner* written.
         March–May Wordsworth visits London and meets
         Godwin and Charles James Fox.
         June Thomas Wordsworth born.
         July–September Wordsworth is working on what later
         became *The Excursion*.
         October Reunion with Coleridge who has been in Italy.
         A long winter visit to Sir George Beaumont at
         Coleorton, Leicestershire.

1807   *May Poems in Two Volumes* published by Longman.
         Wordsworth begins to pay more attention to regular
         church-going.
         April Visit to London.
         July Wordsworth takes the tenancy of Allan Bank,
         Grasmere.
         October The White Doe of Rylstone started.
         November De Quincey visits Townend.
         December The Wordsworths visit Stockton-on-Tees.

1808   *January* The White Doe of Rylstone finished.
February–April Wordsworth in London and meets
Henry Crabb Robinson. Decides against publishing
The White Doe of Rylstone. Wordsworth's friendship with
Coleridge starts to cool.
May The Wordsworths move to Allan Bank. Coleridge
pays a visit in September.
September Catharine Wordsworth born.
November–February Visit from De Quincey.
Wordsworth writes the tract on the Convention of Cintra.
December and January Parts of it appear in the *Courier*.

1809   *May–June* The tract on the *Convention of Cintra*
published. Wordsworth writes *Guide to the Lakes,*
A Reply to Mathetes, Essay upon Epitaphs.

1810   *Guide to the Lakes* published anonymously as an
introduction to a series of views of the Lake District
published by the Rev. Joseph Wilkinson. Work resumed
on *The Excursion* in Spring, and Books V, VI and VII
written. In summer, Wordsworth starts to be troubled
with the eye-disease, trachoma, which affected him
intermittently for the rest of his life.

1811   Wordsworth becomes interested in education and teaches
in Grasmere school. Books VIII and IX of *The Excursion*
written. The coolness between Wordsworth and
Coleridge begins to turn into hostility.
June The Wordsworths move to Grasmere Vicarage.

1812   Coleridge visits Grasmere without calling on
Wordsworth. When Wordsworth visits London in April,
a reconciliation is partly patched up between them.
June Wordsworth's daughter Catharine dies.
December His son Thomas dies. His grief is partly
expressed in additions made to *The Excursion*, Book III.

1813   *May* The Wordsworths move to Rydal Mount. Relations
with De Quincey, now living at Townend, deteriorate.
March Wordsworth appointed Distributor of Stamps
for Westmorland, a present from the Lonsdale interest.

1814   *July* Tour in Scotland. Wordsworth visits Scott and
Hogg. *The Excursion, Being a Portion of The Recluse:
A Poem* published by Longman in 500 copies.

1815   Wordsworth prepares collected edition of poems. By
March, 300 copies of *The Excursion* have been sold.
March Poems, including Lyrical Ballads first collective
edition of poems published in two volumes, according
to Wordsworth's new principles of arrangement.
Wordsworth is disturbed by Coleridge's criticisms of
The Excursion.
May In London, makes an enemy of Hazlitt. *The
White Doe of Rylstone* published, quarto, at a price of
one guinea.

1816   *February* Wordsworth begins writing a series of patriotic
poems on the downfall of Napoleon. Caroline
Wordsworth marries in February.
May Pamphlet *A Letter to a Friend of Burns* published,
and attacked by Wilson (Christopher North) in
Blackwood's Magazine.
May Wordsworth's brother Richard dies.

1818   Winter visit to London; a meeting with Coleridge
marked by coolness and sarcasm. Meets Keats.
Wordsworth campaigns for the Lowther (Lonsdale)
interest in Westmorland against Henry Brougham. A
number of short prose political pieces written and *Two
Addresses to the Freeholders of Westmorland* published as a
pamphlet.
November Nineteen of the *Duddon* sonnets written.

1819   *April* Publication of *Peter Bell: A Tale in Verse*.
        Burlesques on Wordsworth printed including *Peter Bell;
        A Lyrical Ballad* and *The Dead Asses: A Lyrical Ballad*.
        Peter Bell; A Tale in Verse, second edition.
        June The Waggoner published.
        October Publication of Shelley's *Peter Bell the Third*.
        More *Duddon* poems written, and the third volume of
        Miscellaneous Poems prepared.

1820   Wordsworth engages in more election work.
        May The River Duddon: a Series of Sonnets published.
        Miscellaneous Poems in four volumes (second collected
        edition, revised) and *The Excursion* (second edition,
        revised).
        May–October Tour on the Continent. Wordsworth
        visits Annette and Caroline in Paris.
        December Visits his brother Christopher, now Master
        of Trinity, in Cambridge, and the idea for
        Ecclesiastical Sketches begins to take shape.

1821   Wordsworth reading for *Ecclesiastical Sketches*, and in
        March begins to write them.
        July An attack of eye trouble.
        November Hazlitt delivers a personal attack on
        Wordsworth in the *London Magazine*.
        November–December Wordsworth writes the *Continental
        Tour* poems.

1822   *March* Publication of *Ecclesiastical Sketches* and *Memorials
        of a Tour on the Continent, 1820*.

1823   Visits to London, Belgium and Holland.

1824   *September* Tour in Wales.
        June The Excursion second edition, sold out.

1825   Visit to Rydall by Scott and J. G. Lockhart.

1827   Death of Sir George Beaumont.
May publication of *Poetical Works*, five volumes (third collected edition, revised).

1828   Rhineland Tour. A pirated one-volume edition of *Poems* published in Paris.

1829   Tour in Ireland.

1831   Third tour in Scotland; visits Scott at Abbotsford before his departure for Italy.

1832   Wordsworth begins revising *The Prelude*. Despair at the prospect of the Reform Bill. *Poetical Works*, four volumes (fourth collected edition, revised) published.

1833   Wordsworth visits the Isle of Man, Staffa and Iona. The Arnold family rents Allan Bank.

1834   *Postscript* to *Yarrow Revisited* written, a political autobiography.

1835   *January* *Yarrow Revisited and Other Poems* published.
June Sara Hutchinson dies. Dorothy Wordsworth begins to lose her mental faculties. *Extempore Effusion on the death of James Hogg* written.

1837   In this and the previous year publication of *Poetical Works*, six volumes (fifth collected edition, revised). For the first time a portrait of the poet; *Alice Fell* restored to the canon. On a tour with H. C. Robinson in Italy. Poems from this tour were written over the next few years. Criminal law reforms move Wordsworth to write the sonnets on capital punishment.

1838   *Sonnets* published in one volume. Honorary degree from University of Durham.

1839   Honary degree from the University of Oxford. *The Prelude* revised again.

1841   Declines to stand as a candidate for Parliament for Ayr
        Boroughs. Dora Wordsworth marries.

1842   *Poems, Chiefly of Early and Late Years* published, including
        a number of poems from the Racedown years, extensively
        revised, and *The Borderers*. Wordsworth resigns the
        Distributorship of Stamps and receives a Civil List pension
        of £300 a year. Isabella Fenwick comes to live in Rydall
        Mount.

1843   Accepts the Poet Laureateship on the death of Southey.

1845   *Poems*, one volume (sixth collected edition, revised)
        published.
        April Attends Court. *Kendal and Windermere Railway,
        Two Letters reprinted from the Morning Post.*

1847   Dora Wordsworth dies.

1849–50 *Poetical Works*, six volumes (with final corrections)
        published.

1850   *23 April* Wordsworth dies.
        July The Prelude published by Mary Wordsworth, who
        chose the title.

Part One Contemporaneous Criticism

Introduction

Up to 1820 the name of Wordsworth was trampled under foot: from 1820 it was militant: from 1830 to 1835 it has been triumphant.

De Quincey's claim is bold and attractively neat: but in many respects Wordsworth's public success some thirty years earlier had been less ambiguous and qualified. By 1820, public opinion, establishing a precedent for later generations, had already decided on its favourites and its idea of the true Wordsworthian canon. Wordsworth was thought of as a 'wild but unequal genius, throwing off ... by accident, poems of exquisite beauty ... not sufficient ... to redeem the great mass of careless and absurd writing of which he has been the author' (*British Critic*, 1821). An essential precondition of the extent of Wordsworth's popularity before his death was a programme of selection and tacit forgetfulness, dulling the sharpness of the Wordsworthian experience, in which the poet himself connived and to a certain extent led. The mass of adulatory writing which appeared after 1819 has for us, consequently, a severely limited usefulness. To find really live and illuminating responses, we have to return to the time of *Lyrical Ballads*, or, paradoxically to those critiques of the middle years which stung Wordsworth the most.

1798, the year of the first volume of *Lyrical Ballads*, is a landmark of literary history, full of revolutionary significance. It would be wrong to make little of the originality of that volume and false, in general tendency and implication, if accurate in certain details, to suggest that its real place in literary history is with the eighteenth century, not with the romantics. Nevertheless, the impression of a deliberate, revolutionary intention, a desire to mend English verse overnight, and an eagerness to shock and offend, came somewhat later and was fostered by Wordsworth's critical apparatus, the essays and appendices with which he protected his verse. In R. D. Mayo's essay, the ballads can be seen to be as much the conclusion and justification of one convention as the start of a new one. The contemporary notices bear out Mayo's analysis with only few qualifications. The critics felt obliged to dissent from the utterances of the young radical in Wordsworth, but they were disposed to recognize the truth of his claims that the poems were experimental in employing the simplicity of the convention for serious purposes. Like Wordsworth himself, the reviewers were sufficiently bored by the trivial subjects to which poetry had been applied by the followers of Erasmus Darwin, the dominant influence at that time. The notices of the first volume are indeed brief and mostly confined to quotations, which make them uneconomical to reprint. Their lengthy excerpts were however very significant for Wordsworth, for the reviews and magazines entered many more homes than did volumes of poetry. One important fact arises from these reviews: that there is little to suggest that the sympathies of these critics were being expanded too fast to be tolerable, or too greatly. Also significant is the fact that the most highly esteemed poem was *Goody Blake and Harry Gill*, closely followed by *The Idiot Boy* and the other seemingly naïve and rude rhymes which disappeared from favour a few years later, and which, to this day, are seldom read with anything but dismay and impatience. Here was an audience with which Wordsworth achieved a genuine rapport. But it was an audience which had been fed by the eighteenth century; one to which neither Wordsworth's sentiment nor his humour was unacceptable. Its place would soon be taken by another which had quite different standards and expectations. We find that the Whig politician Charles James Fox enjoyed *The Idiot Boy*: his death may be thought of as the close of the era.

The most sympathetic – and the most overtly Wordsworthian – review, appeared in the *British Critic*, written by Wordsworth's friend Francis Wrangham. The support of people like Wrangham was, over the years, a great consolation and support to

Wordsworth, who would not have scrupled to have had more
friends and partisans in the public reviews could he have
managed it. It was a considerable grievance to him that Southey
had been unfavourable to the ballads in a review (*Critical Review*,
October 1798): if Southey had not felt that he could help the
volume to sell, Wordsworth wrote, he should have left the task
to some who did. Dorothy Wordsworth was once shocked by an
unfavourable notice of *Ecclesiastical Sketches* which appeared in
the *Literary Gazette*, for both were published by the same firm.
But the days of unscrupulous puffing by publishers, using reviews
chiefly to push their own stock, were over, and had largely been
buried by the rise of the *Edinburgh Review*.

Southey had criticized Wordsworth for the triviality of his
subjects – anticipating later comments; but, as the popularity of
the *Lyrical Ballads* increased, he came to change his mind about
them. Not only did the poems go through four editions by 1805,
but many of them were anthologized and pirated countless times.

Wordsworth, before 1807, does not have the sound of a
disappointed man. He speaks of being able to 'command [his]
price with the booksellers' and the letter containing the 'harmonies
of criticism' (see p. 88) gives us an unexpected glimpse of his
buoyant and assertive sense of his own powers and stature during
the vital years in which *The Prelude* and the 1807 poems were
composed. Above all, he was confident that he had an audience,
and was able to accept with equanimity any adverse criticism,
content that the better sort were with him. Most important of all
was the inner circle of his friends and relations: the women of his
household, his brother John, Coleridge, Lamb and Thomas Poole.
The solidity of their support was vital for Wordsworth's self
confidence. They were not, however, merely passive and uncritical.
The letter that Wordsworth sent to the Hutchinson girls (see p. 84),
while it shows beautifully the studied care behind each word in
the poem, and makes the typically Wordsworthian demand that

the sisters see and feel as the poet does, actually proves his
responsiveness to criticism; for all the things that Mary and Sara
had disapproved of actually disappeared in the published version
of *The Leech-Gatherer*.

Wordsworth had yet more friends to depend on than this small
family circle: his poetry was winning him golden opinions from
all sorts of people: the ardent discipleship of Wilson and De
Quincey, praise from Charles James Fox. Wilson's letter on *The
Idiot Boy*, as we can see from the extraordinary (for Wordsworth)
length of the reply, must especially have charmed him and
confirmed him in his sense of his own sanity and representative
humanity.

The first discordant note was sounded by Jeffrey in his mention
of Wordsworth in a review (1802) of Southey's *Thalaba*. It was
Jeffrey who first made articulate, and continued to mould, the
opposition to Wordsworth's 'new modes of feeling'. The
Edinburgh's lead in condemning the 1807 poems was followed by
almost all of its competitors, decisively halting the spread of his
reputation. Jeffrey's famous dismissal of *The Excursion* (most
reviews were rather favourable) must have been responsible
single-handed for its slow sales.

Contemporary Edinburgh gossip accused Jeffrey of hypocrisy,
for, it was claimed, Jeffrey had been seen in tears over a volume
of the *Lyrical Ballads* he had condemned so roundly. But Jeffrey's
criticism was not generally dishonest or malicious, although what
he called the 'vivacities' of his style were certainly composed with
an eye to his own sales. Jeffrey based his criticism on principles
and trusted his own private feelings no more than he did
Wordsworth's. While lesser critics delighted in showing how little
Wordsworth's poetic theory corresponds with his practice (an
easy target which still receives a few tired feints), Jeffrey met him
fairly and squarely on the basic and intransigent part of the
doctrine: that the poet's own feelings, be what they might, were

valuable as long as they were reported faithfully. Poet and critic shared the common language of eighteenth-century psychology. But while Wordsworth was convinced that his 'associations' (that is, the feelings of pleasure or pain he was accustomed to link to certain actions) were healthful and such as might be profitable to all men, Jeffrey found in them too much that was eccentric and obscure.

He was not alone in disapproving, although his voice was crucial in being both public and confident. Southey, Anna Seward and even Coleridge very early had thought that some of Wordsworth's emotions were too private and *fortuitous* to have a wider human reference. Not only were his readers puzzled by Wordsworth's emotions, but repelled by the arrogance with which he demanded they be *controlled* by his feelings. A story which Walter Scott wrote in his diary illustrates, with typical charity, both reactions:

Wordsworth told Anne and me a story the object of which was to show that Crabbe had not imagination. He, Sir George Beaumont and Wordsworth, were sitting in Murray the bookseller's back room. Sir George, after sealing a letter, blew out the candle which had enabled him to do so, and, exchanging a look with Wordsworth, began to admire in silence the undulating thread of smoke which slowly arose from the expiring wick when Crabbe put on the extinguisher. ... The error is not in yourself receiving deep impressions from slight hints, but in supposing that precisely the same sort of impression must arise in the minds of men otherwise of kindred feeling, or that the commonplace folks of the world can derive such inductions at any time or under any circumstances (3 January 1827).

Wordsworth's confidence that he could find 'a tale in everything', and his attentive and reverential brooding over the slightest

incidents in his own emotional life, resulted in the really
revolutionary *Poems in Two Volumes* of 1807. The warm confidence
in which they had been composed, inspired by the reaction to
Lyrical Ballads, was shattered by the attention the poems received
from an incredulous and derisive world. Most significantly for
Wordsworth's future development, the nature lyrics and the section
called 'moods of my own mind' (including poems like *Daffodils*,
the *Cuckoo*, *The Small Celandine*) were universally condemned,
while the most highly admired portion of the two volumes was
the series of 'Sonnets dedicated to liberty'. Even professed
Wordsworthians concurred implicitly by being even more
vociferous than usual on behalf of the sonnets. Most reviewers
made a particular point of lamenting the absence of any blank
verse of the *Tintern Abbey* mould, for that poem had already
become a classic.

The results for Wordsworth's poetry were unhappy. The
question of the 'great decade', endlessly canvassed in
Wordsworthian studies, has usually posited some loss of power or
deadening of the sensibilities. But whether this is true or not, it is
clear that by 1807–8 Wordsworth must have realized that he had
no significant audience for his great work – a fact of great
importance for a poet who felt that his mission was above all to
be a great moral teacher. Nor was he encouraged to return to the
style of *Lyrical Ballads*, for when *Peter Bell* and *The Waggoner*
(both essentially early work) were published in 1818, they were
met with a cry of derision the loudest to date.

The inner-circle audience also melted away almost to nothing.
John Wordsworth died in 1805, and it was not long before
Wordsworth was not on speaking terms with Coleridge, Wilson
and De Quincey. The younger generation, represented by Keats
or Shelley, were much further from him, and were in any case
very qualified in their enthusiasm for him; for with Wordsworth's
acceptance of a government place, and his Tory electioneering,

political differences had begun to intervene.

Wordsworth's extreme and relatively novel sensitivity to adverse criticism, in spite of his frequently asserted indifference to it, is very apparent in his altered demeanour in the second decade of the nineteenth century. Observers and friends found him dogmatic and conceited, alternately pompous and sulky. Haydon in his diary for 27 March 1821, contrasted him with Scott:

It is singular how success and the want of it operate on two extraordinary men. Scott enters a room and sits at a table with a coolness and self-possession of conscious fame; Wordsworth with an air of mortified elevation of head as if fearful he was not esteemed as he deserved. Scott is always cool and amusing; Wordsworth often egotistical and overbearing. Scott can afford to talk of trifles because he knows the World will think him a great man who condescends to trifle; Wordsworth must always be eloquent and profound because he knows he is considered childish and puerile. Scott seems to wish to seem less than he is; Wordsworth struggles to be thought at the moment greater than he is suspected to be.

It was typical of this obstinacy of Wordsworth's that he published *The White Doe of Rylestone* at the price of one guinea 'to show [his] opinion of it'. By contrast, in the late 1830s when his works were selling well and he was making upwards of five hundred a year by them, his pet project was a cheap edition which would reach all classes.

The poems of 'old age', or indeed any composed in part or wholly after 1807, books like *The Excursion, Duddon, Memorials of a Tour*, show Wordsworth's intention to speak directly to his audience. In spite of his frequent laments about the state of public taste, he knew – from their approval of his sonnets and *Tintern Abbey* – what they would find acceptable in both subject and manner, and did not hesitate to offer it to them.

This, for Wordsworth, necessitated the adoption of an external rhetoric. Some poetry thrives on the employment of a particular rhetoric. But as its successful use depends very largely on a measure of common agreement about a fitting language and suitable materials, it is an instrument ill suited to the expression of new modes of feeling. In making his meaning clearer, Wordsworth began to make it less than it was. He communicated across readily understandable concepts such as patriotism, moral imperatives, the picturesque enjoyment of landscape and the pleasures of retirement – the stock in trade of much poetry of the later eighteenth century.

There is abundant evidence of the compromise reached between Wordsworth and his public in his activities of the later years: the reclassification and revision of his earlier poems; the only just frustrated impulse to drop poems like *Alice Fell* from the canon; and the entire lack in the later letters of those intimate revelations of himself in the act of composition which are so important a part of the letters of the early years. No longer do we watch the poet observing himself fascinatedly – that sense of the mind watching its own motions which is so much a part of the content of his earlier verse.

The reviews became in general much more favourable and condescending to Wordsworth for abandoning his early errors. Jeffrey, however, was even more critical of Wordsworth's grand than his simple style, frequently detecting its windy emptiness.

After 1820, Wordsworth's reputation grew steadily, especially in Oxford and Cambrige, which both had strong Wordsworthian cliques. Perceptive criticism continued to appear in print – by Wrangham, by T. N. Talfourd or John Scott, the editor of the *London Magazine*. Judged by the mere number of lines, what was by common consent dropped from the body of great work appears trivial compared to what remained. But with the suspicion that Wordsworth was not fully in control of his poetry-making there remained the reading public's assumption of the right to feel superior, to refuse to have their feelings 'controlled' by those of the poet, to select and excise at will. In the years to come anything a little odd or disturbing, or deliberately comic, could be simply consigned to the pile of rejects, aiding the process of simplification and smoothing out, paving the way for the Victorian Sage of Rydal. His well-known crankiness and unevenness relieved everyone of the obligation to take seriously whatever was at all unusual.

In the selection that follows, I have attempted to choose only those passages which are valuable as criticism in their own right. This seems to me to be especially true of all Wordsworth's own comments, of all the informal comments recorded in the diaries and letters of his friends, and of the full-length treatments by Jeffrey, Hazlitt and Wrangham. It is a pity not to include more: a complete review perhaps, because in spite of their habit of including pages of quotations, the early reviewers are most impressive at their leisure.

Some of the problems they faced are bound to suggest themselves to modern readers – the relevance, for instance, of all of Wordsworth's experiences and his modes of feeling. The attempts of his contemporaries to estimate the importance to themselves of the obscurely sensed but seemingly irresponsible and certainly unaccountable power of Wordsworth, while the experiences were still raw and unfamiliar, with a 'harshness and acerbity connected and combined with words and images all aglow' (Coleridge of *Descriptive Sketches*), make these early accounts uniquely valuable.

William Wordsworth

Autobiographical Memoranda 1847 (dictated; first appeared in print in *Memoirs of William Wordsworth* by Christopher Wordsworth in 1851)

I was born at Cockermouth, in Cumberland, on 7 April 1770, the second son of John Wordsworth, attorney-at-law, as lawyers of this class were then called, and law-agent to Sir James Lowther, afterwards Earl of Lonsdale. My mother was Anne, only daughter of William Cookson, Mercer, of Penrith, and of Dorothy, born Crackanthorp, of the ancient family of that name, who from the times of Edward III had lived in Newbiggen Hall, Westmorland. My grandfather was the first of the name of Wordsworth who came into Westmorland, where he purchased the small estate of Sockbridge. He was descended from a family who had been settled at Peniston in Yorkshire, near the sources of the Don, probably before the Norman Conquest. Their names appear on different occasions in all the transactions, personal and public, connected with that parish; and I possess, through the kindness of Colonel Beaumont, an almery made in 1525, at the expense of a William Wordsworth, as is expressed in a Latin inscription carved upon it, which carries the pedigree of the family back four generations from himself.

The time of my infancy and early boyhood was passed partly at Cockermouth, and partly with my mother's parents at Penrith, where my mother, in the year 1778, died of a decline, brought on by a cold, the consequence of being put, at a friend's house in London, in what used to be called 'a best bedroom'. My father never recovered his usual cheerfulness of mind after this loss, and died when I was in my fourteenth year, a schoolboy, just returned from Hawkshead, whither I had been sent with my elder brother Richard, in my ninth year.

I remember my mother only in some few situations, one of which was her pinning a nosegay to my breast when I was going to say the catechism in the church, as was customary before Easter. I remember also telling her on one weekday that I had been at church, for our school stood in the churchyard, and we had frequent opportunities of seeing what was going on there. The occasion was, a woman doing penance in the church, in a white sheet. My mother commended my having been present, expressing a hope that I should remember the circumstance for the rest of my life. 'But,' said I, 'Mama, they did not give me a penny as I had been told they would.' 'Oh,' said she, recanting her praises, 'if that was your motive, you were very properly disappointed.'

My last impression was having a glimpse of her on passing the door of her bedroom during her last illness, when she was reclining in her easy chair. An intimate friend of hers, Miss Hamilton by name, who was used to visit her at Cockermouth, told me that she once said to her, that the only one of her five children about whose future life she was anxious, was William; and he, she said, would be remarkable either for good or evil. The cause of this was, that I was of a stiff, moody and violent temper; so much so that I remember going once into the attics of my grandfather's house at Penrith, upon some indignity having been put upon me, with an intention of destroying myself with one of the foils which I knew was kept there. I took the foil in my hand, but my heart failed. Upon another occasion, while I was at my grandfather's house at Penrith, along with my eldest brother Richard, we were whipping tops together in the large drawing-room, on which the carpet was only laid down upon particular occasions. The walls were hung round with family pictures, and I said to my brother, 'Dare you strike your whip through that old lady's petticoat?' He replied 'No, I won't.' 'Then,' said I, 'here goes;' and I struck my lash through her hooped petticoat, for which no doubt, though I have forgotten it, I was properly punished. But possibly, from some want of judgement in punishments inflicted, I had become rather perverse and obstinate in defying chastisement and rather proud of it than otherwise.

Of my earliest days at school I have little to say, but that they were very happy ones, chiefly because I was left at liberty, then and in the vacations, to read whatever books I liked. For example, I read all Fielding's works, *Don Quixote*, *Gil Blas* and any part of Swift that I liked; *Gulliver's Travels*, and the *Tale of a Tub* being both much to my taste. I was very much indebted to one of the ushers of Hawkshead School, by name Shaw, who taught me more of Latin in a fortnight than I had learnt during two preceding years at the School of Cockermouth. Unfortunately for me this excellent master left our school and went to Stafford, where he taught for many years. It may be perhaps as well to mention, that the first verses which I wrote were a task imposed by my master; the subject, 'The Summer Vacation'; and of my own accord I added others upon 'Return to School'. There was nothing remarkable in either poem; but I was called upon, among other scholars, to write verses upon the completion of the second centenary from the foundation of the school in 1585, by Archbishop Sandys. These verses were much admired, far more than they deserved, for they were but a tame imitation of Pope's versification, and a little in his style. This exercise, however, put it into my head to compose verses from the impulse of my own mind, and I wrote, while yet a schoolboy, a long poem running upon my own adventures, and the scenery of the country in which I was brought up. The only part of that poem which has been preserved is the conclusion of it, which stands at the beginning of my collected Poems.[1]

In the month of October 1787, I was sent to St John's College, Cambridge, of which my uncle, Dr Cookson, had been a fellow. The master, Dr Chevallier, died very soon after; and, according to the custom of the time, after being placed in the coffin, was removed to the hall of the college, and the pall, spread over the coffin, was stuck over by copies of verses, English or Latin, the composition of the students of St John's. My uncle seemed mortified when upon inquiry he learnt that none of these verses were from my pen, 'because,' said he, 'it would have been a fair opportunity for distinguishing yourself'. I did not, however, regret that I had been silent on this occasion, as I felt no interest in the deceased person, with whom I had had no intercourse, and whom I had never seen but during his walks in the college grounds.

When at school, I, with the other boys of the same standing, was put upon reading the first six books of Euclid, with the exception of the fifth; and also in algebra I learnt simple and quadratic equations; and this was for me unlucky, because I had a full twelve-month's start of the freshmen of my year, and accordingly got in a rather idle way; reading nothing but classic authors according to my fancy, and Italian poetry. My Italian master was named Isola, and had been well acquainted with Gray the poet. As I took to these studies with much

1 *Dear Native Regions.*

interest, he was proud of the progress I made. Under his correction I translated the Vision of Mirza and two or three other papers of the Spectator, into Italian. In the month of August 1790, I set off for the Continent, in companionship with Robert Jones, a Welshman, a fellow-collegian. We went staff in hand, without knapsacks, and carrying each his needments tied up in a pocket handkerchief, with about twenty pounds apiece in our pockets. We crossed from Dover and landed at Calais on the eve of the day when the king was to swear fidelity to the new constitution; an event which was solemnized with due pomp at Calais. On the afternoon of that day we started, and slept at Ardres. For what seemed best to me worth recording in this tour, see the Poem of my own Life.

After taking my degree in January 1791, I went to London, stayed there for some time, and then visited my friend Jones, who resided in the Vale of Clwyyd, North Wales. Along with him I made a pedestrian tour through North Wales, for which also see the Poem.

In the autumn of 1791 I went to Paris, where I stayed some little time, and then went to Orleans, with a view to being out of the way of my own countrymen, that I might learn to speak the language fluently. At Orleans, and Blois, and Paris, on my return, I passed fifteen or sixteen months. It was a stirring time. The king was dethroned when I was at Blois, and the massacres of September took place when I was at Orleans. But for these matters see also the Poem. I came home before the execution of the king and passed the subsequent time among my friends in London and elsewhere, till I settled with my only sister at Racedown in Dorsetshire, in the year 1796.

Here we were vitsied by Mr Coleridge, then residing at Bristol; and for the sake of being near him when he had removed to Nether Stowey, in Somersetshire, we removed to Alfoxden, three miles from that place. This was a very pleasant and productive time of my life. Coleridge, my sister, and I, set off on a tour to Linton and other places in Devonshire; and in order to defray his part of the expense, Coleridge on the same afternoon commenced his poem of the *Ancient Mariner*, in which I was to have borne my part, and a few verses were written by me, and some assistance in planning the poem; but our styles agreed so little, that I withdrew from the concern, and he finished it himself.

In the course of that spring I composed many poems, most of

which were printed at Bristol, in one volume, by my friend Joseph Cottle, along with Coleridge's *Ancient Mariner*, and two or three other of his pieces.

In the autumn of 1798, Mr Coleridge, a friend of his Mr Chester, my sister and I, crossed from Yarmouth to Hamburg, where we remained a few days, and saw, several times, Klopstock the poet. Mr Coleridge and his friend went to Ratzburg, in the north of Germany, and my sister and I preferred going southward; and for the sake of cheapness, and the neighbourhood of the Hartz Mountains, we spent the winter at the old imperial city of Goslar. The winter was perishingly cold – the coldest of this century; and the good people with whom we lodged told me one morning, that they expected to find me frozen to death, my little sleeping room being immediately over an archway. However, neither I nor my sister took any harm.

We returned to England in the following spring, and went to visit our friends the Hutchinsons, at Sockburn-on-Tees, in the county of Durham, with whom we remained till 19 December. We then came, on St Thomas's Day, the 21st, to a small cottage at Townend, Grasmere, which, in the course of a tour some months previously with Mr Coleridge, I had been pleased with, and had hired. This we furnished for about a hundred pounds, which sum had come to my sister by a legacy from her uncle Crackanthorp.

I fell to composition immediately, and published, in 1800, the second volume of the *Lyrical Ballads*.

In the year 1802 I married Mary Hutchinson, at Brompton, near Scarborough, to which part of the country the family had removed from Sockburn. We had known each other from childhood, and had practised reading and spelling under the same old dame at Penrith, a remarkable personage, who had taught three generations, of the upper classes principally, of the town of Penrith and its neighbourhood.

After our marriage we dwelt, together without sister, at Townend, where three of our children were born. In the spring of 1808, the increase of our family caused us to remove to a larger house, then just built, Allan Bank, in the same vale; where our two younger children were born, and who died at the rectory, the house we afterwards occupied for two years. They died in 1812, and in 1813 we came to Rydal Mount, where we have since lived with no further sorrow till 1835, when my sister became a confirmed invalid, and our sister Sara Hutchinson died. She lived alternately with her brother and with us.

William Wordsworth

Preface to *Lyrical Ballads* 1800, 1802
[The 1800 text is given here, with notes of the major additions and changes made in 1802.]

The First Volume of these Poems has already been submitted to general perusal. It was published, as an experiment which, I hoped, might be of some use to ascertain, how far, by fitting to metrical arrangement a selection of the real language of men in a state of vivid sensation, that sort of pleasure and that quantity of pleasure may be imparted, which a Poet may rationally endeavour to impart.

I had formed no very inaccurate estimate of the probable effect of those poems: I flattered myself that they who should be pleased with them would read them with more than common pleasure: on the other hand I was well aware that by those who should dislike them they would be read with more than common dislike. The result has differed from my expectation in this only, that I have pleased a greater number, than I ventured to hope I should please.

For the sake of variety and from a consciousness of my own weakness I was induced to request the assistance of a Friend, who furnished me with the Poems of the *Ancient Mariner*, the *Foster Mother's Tale*, the *Nightingale*, the *Dungeon* and the Poem entitled *Love*. I should not, however, have requested this assistance, had I not believed that the poems of my Friend would in great measure have the same tendency as my own, and that, though there would be found a difference, there would be found no discordance in the colours of our style; as our opinions on the subject of poetry do almost entirely coincide.

Several of my Friends are anxious for the success of these Poems from a belief, that if the views, with which they were composed, were indeed realized, a class of Poetry would be produced, well adapted to interest mankind permanently, and not unimportant in the multiplicity and in the quality of its moral relations: and on this account they have advised me to prefix a systematic defence of the theory, upon which the poems were written. But I was unwilling to undertake the task, because I knew that on this occasion the Reader would look coldly upon my arguments, since I might be suspected of having been principally influenced by the selfish and foolish hope of *reasoning* him into an approbation of these particular Poems: and I was still more unwilling to undertake the task, because adequately to display my opinions and fully to enforce my arguments would require a space wholly disproportionate to the nature of a preface. For to treat the subject with the clearness and coherence, of which I believe it susceptible, it would be necessary to give a full account of the present state of the public taste in this country, and to determine how far this taste is healthy or depraved; which again could not be determined, without pointing out, in what manner language and the human mind act and react on each other, and without retracing the revolutions not of literature alone but likewise of society itself. I have therefore altogether declined to enter regularly upon this defence; yet I am sensible, that there would be some impropriety in abruptly obtruding upon the Public, without a few words of introduction, Poems so materially different from those, upon which general approbation is at present bestowed.

It is supposed, that by the act of writing in verse an Author makes a formal engagement that he will gratify certain known habits of association, that he not only thus apprizes the Reader that certain classes of ideas and expressions will be found in his book, but that others will be carefully excluded. This exponent or symbol held forth by metrical language must in different eras of literature have excited very different expectations: for example, in the age of Catullus Terence and Lucretius, and that of Statius or Claudian, and in our own country, in the age of Shakespeare and Beaumont and Fletcher, and that of Donne and Cowley, or Dryden, or Pope. I will not take upon me to determine the exact import of the promise which by the act of writing in verse an Author in the present day makes to his Reader; but I am certain it will appear to many persons that I have not fulfilled the terms of an engagement thus voluntarily contracted.[1] I hope therefore the Reader will not censure me, if I attempt to state what I have proposed to myself to perform, and also (as far as the limits of a preface will permit) to explain some of the chief reasons which have determined me in my purpose: that at least he may be spared any unpleasant feeling of disappointment, and that I myself may be protected from the most dishonourable accusation which can be brought against an author, namely, that of an indolence which prevents him from endeavouring to ascertain what is his duty, or when his duty is ascertained prevents him from performing it.

The principal object then which I proposed to myself in these Poems was to make the incidents of common life interesting by[2] tracing in them, truly though not ostentatiously, the primary laws of our nature: chiefly as far as regards the manner in which we associate ideas in a state of excitement. Low and rustic life was generally chosen because in that situation the essential passions of the heart find a better soil in which they can attain their maturity, are less under restraint, and speak a plainer and more emphatic language; because in that situation our elementary feelings exist in a state of greater simplicity and consequently may be more accurately contemplated and more forcibly communicated; because the manners of rural life germinate from those elementary feelings; and from the necessary character of rural occupations are more easily comprehended; and are more durable; and lastly, because in that situation the passions of men are incorporated with the beautiful and permanent forms of

1 *1802* adds, after 'contracted':
They who have been accustomed to the gaudiness and inane phraseology of many modern writers, if they persist in reading this book to its conclusion, will, no doubt, frequently have to struggle with feelings of strangeness and awkwardness: they will look around for poetry, and will be induced to inquire by what species of courtesy these attempts can be permitted to assume that title.

2 In *1802* the phrase 'to make the incidents of common life interesting by' is expanded to:
to choose incidents and situations from common life, and to relate or describe them, throughout, as far as was possible, in a selection of language really used by men; and, at the same time, to throw over them a certain colouring of the imagination, whereby ordinary things should be presented to the mind in an unusual way: and further, and above all, to make these incidents and situations interesting by

nature. The language too of these men is adopted (purified indeed from what appear to be its real defects, from all lasting and rational causes of dislike or disgust) because such men hourly communicate with the best objects from which the best part of language is originally derived; and because, from their rank in society and the sameness and narrow circle of their intercourse, being less under the action of social vanity they convey their feelings and notions in simple and unelaborated expressions. Accordingly such a language arising out of repeated experience and regular feelings is a more permanent and far more philosophical language than that which is frequently substituted for it by Poets, who think that they are conferring honour upon themselves and their art in proportion as they separate themselves from the sympathies of men, and indulge in arbitrary and capricious habits of expression in order to furnish food for fickle tastes and fickle appetites of their own creation.

I cannot be insensible of the present outcry against the triviality and meanness both of thought and language, which some of my contemporaries have occasionally introduced into their metrical compositions; and I acknowledge that this defect where it exists, is more dishonourable to the Writer's own character than false refinement or arbitrary innovation, though I should contend at the same time that it is far less pernicious in the sum of its consequences. From such verses the Poems in these volumes will be found distinguished at least by one mark of difference, that each of them has a worthy *Purpose*. Not that I mean to say, that I always write with a distinct purpose formally conceived; but I believe that my habits of meditation have so formed my feelings, as that my descriptions of such objects as strongly excite those feelings, will be found to carry along with them a *purpose*. If in this opinion I am mistaken I can have little right to the name of a Poet. For all good poetry is the spontaneous overflow of powerful feelings; but though this be true, Poems to which any value can be attached, were never produced on any variety of subjects but by a man who being possessed of more than usual organic sensibility had also thought long and deeply. For our continued influxes of feeling are modified and directed by our thoughts, which are indeed the representatives of all our past feelings; and as by contemplating the relation of these general representatives to each other, we discover what is really important to men, so by the repetition and continuance of this act feelings connected with important subjects will be nourished, till at length, if we be originally possessed of much organic sensibility, such habits of mind will be produced that by obeying blindly and mechanically the impulses of those habits we shall describe objects and utter sentiments of such a nature and in such connection with each other, that the understanding of the being to whom we address ourselves, if he be in a healthful state of association, must necessarily be in some degree enlightened, his taste exalted, and his affections ameliorated.

I have said that each of these poems has a purpose. I have also informed my Reader what this purpose will be found principally to be: namely to illustrate the manner in which our feelings and ideas are associated in a state of excitement. But speaking in less general language,[1] it is to follow the fluxes and refluxes of the mind when agitated by the great and simple affections of our nature. This object I have endeavoured in these short essays to attain by various means; by tracing the maternal passion through many of its more subtle windings, as in the poems of *The Idiot Boy* and the *Mad Mother*; by accompanying the last struggles of a human being at the approach of death, cleaving in solitude to life and society, as in the Poem of *The Forsaken Indian*; by showing, as in the Stanzas entitled *We are Seven*, the perplexity and obscurity which in childhood attend our notion of death, or rather our utter inability to admit that notion; or by displaying the strength of fraternal, or to speak more philosophically, of moral attachment when early associated with the great and beautiful objects of nature, as in *The Brothers*; or, as in the Incident of *Simon Lee*, by placing my Reader in the way of receiving from ordinary moral sensations another and more salutary impression than we are accustomed to receive from them. It has also been part of my general purpose to attempt to sketch characters under the influence of less impassioned[2] feelings, as in the *Old Man Travelling*, *The Two Thieves*, etc., characters of which the elements are simple, belonging rather to nature than to manners, such as exist now and will probably always exist, and which from their constitution may be distinctly and profitably contemplated. I will not abuse the indulgence of my Reader by dwelling longer upon this subject; but it is proper that I

1 But, speaking in language somewhat more appropriate
2 feelings, as in the *Two April mornings*, *The Fountain*, the

should mention one other circumstance which distinguishes these Poems from the popular Poetry of the day; it is this, that the feeling therein developed gives importance to the action and situation and not the action and situation to the feeling. My meaning will be rendered perfectly intelligible by referring my Reader to the Poems entitled *Poor Susan* and *The Childless Father*, particularly to the last Stanza of the latter Poem.

I will not suffer a sense of false modesty to prevent me from asserting, that I point my Reader's attention to this mark of distinction far less for the sake of these particular Poems than from the general importance of the subject. The subject is indeed important! For the human mind is capable of excitement without the application of gross and violent stimulants; and he must have a very faint perception of its beauty and dignity who does not know this, and who does not further know that one being is elevated above another in proportion as he possesses this capability. It has therefore appeared to me that to endeavour to produce or enlarge this capability is one of the best services in which, at any period, a Writer can be engaged; but this service, excellent at all times, is especially so at the present day. For a multitude of causes unknown to former times are now acting with a combined force to blunt the discriminating powers of the mind, and unfitting it for all voluntary exertion to reduce it to a state of almost savage torpor. The most effective of these causes are the great national events which are daily taking place, and the increasing accumulation of men in cities, where the uniformity of their occupations produces a craving for extraordinary incident which the rapid communication of intelligence hourly gratifies. To this tendency of life and manners the literature and theatrical exhibitions of the country have conformed themselves. The invaluable works of our elder writers, I had almost said the works of Shakespeare and Milton, are driven into neglect by frantic novels, sickly and stupid German Tragedies, and deluges of idle and extravagant stories in verse. When I think upon this degrading thirst after outrageous stimulation I am almost ashamed to have spoken of the feeble effort with which I have endeavoured to counteract it; and reflecting upon the magnitude of the general evil, I should be oppressed with no dishonourable melancholy, had I not a deep impression of certain inherent and indestructible qualities of the human mind, and likewise of certain powers in the great and permanent objects that act upon it which are equally inherent and indestructible; and did I not further add to this impression a belief that the time is approaching when the evil will be systematically opposed by men of greater powers and with far more distinguished success.

Having dwelt thus long on the subjects and aim of these Poems, I shall request the Reader's permission to apprise him of a few circumstances relating to their *style*, in order, among other reasons, that I may not be censured for not having performed what I never attempted. Except in a very few instances the Reader will find no personifications of abstract ideas in these volumes, not that I mean to censure such personifications: they may be well fitted for certain sorts of composition, but in these Poems I propose to myself to imitate, and, as far as possible, to adopt the very language of men, and I do not find that such personifications make any regular or natural part of that language. I wish to keep my Reader in the company of flesh and blood, persuaded that by so doing I shall interest him. Not but that I believe that others who pursue a different track may interest him likewise:[1] I do not interfere with their claim, I only wish to prefer a different claim of my own. There will also be found in these volumes little of what is usually called poetic diction; I have taken as much pains to avoid it as others ordinarily take to produce it; this I have done for the reason already alleged, to bring my language near to the language of men, and further, because the pleasure which I have proposed to myself to impart is of a kind very different from that which is supposed by many persons to be the proper object of

---

1 The passage from 'Except . . .' to '. . . likewise.' becomes in *1802*:

The Reader will find that personifications of abstract ideas rarely occur in these volumes; and, I hope, are utterly rejected as an ordinary device to elevate the style and raise it above prose. I have proposed to myself to imitate, and, as far as is possible, to adopt the very language of men; and assuredly such personifications do not make any natural or regular part of that language. They are, indeed, a figure of speech occasionally prompted by passion, and I have made use of them as such; but I have endeavoured utterly to reject them as a mechanical device of style, or as a family language which Writers in metre seem to lay claim to by prescription. I have wished to keep my Reader in the company of flesh and blood, persuaded that by doing so I shall interest him. I am, however, well aware that others who pursue a different track may interest him likewise;

poetry. I do not know how without being culpably particular I can give my Reader a more exact notion of the style in which I wished these poems to be written than by informing him that I have at all times endeavoured to look steadily at my subject, consequently I hope it will be found that there is in these Poems little falsehood of description, and that my ideas are expressed in language fitted to their respective importance. Something I must have gained by this practice, as it is friendly to one property of all good poetry, namely good sense; but it has necessarily cut me off from a large portion of phrases and figures of speech which from father to son have long been regarded as the common inheritance of Poets. I have also thought it expedient to restrict myself still further, having abstained from the use of many expressions, in themselves proper and beautiful, but which have been foolishly repeated by bad Poets till such feelings of disgust are connected with them as it is scarcely possible by any art of association to overpower.

If in a Poem there should be found a series of lines, or even a single line, in which the language, though naturally arranged and according to the strict laws of metre, does not differ from that of prose, there is a numerous class of critics who, when they stumble upon these prosaims as they call them, imagine that they have made a notable discovery, and exult over the Poet as over a man ignorant of his own profession. Now these men would establish a canon of criticism which the Reader will conclude he must utterly reject if he wishes to be pleased with these volumes. And it would be a most easy task to prove to him that not only the language of a large portion of every good poem, even of the most elevated character, must necessarily, except with reference to the metre, in no respect differ from that of good prose, but likewise that some of the most interesting parts of the best poems will be found to be strictly the language of prose when prose is well written. The truth of this assertion might be demonstrated by innumerable passages from almost all the poetical writings, even of Milton himself. I have not space for much quotation; but, to illustrate the subject in a general manner I will here adduce a short composition of Gray, who was at the head of those who by their reasonings have attempted to widen the space of separation betwixt Prose and Metrical composition, and was more than any other man curiously elaborate in the structure of his own poetic diction.

In vain to me the smiling mornings shine,
And reddening Phoebus lifts his golden fire:
The birds in vain their amorous descant join,
Or chearful fields resume their green attire:
These ears alas! for other notes repine;
A different object do these eyes require;
My lonely anguish melts no heart but mine;
And in my breast the imperfect joys expire;
Yet Morning smiles the busy race to cheer,
And new-born pleasure brings to happier men;
The fields to all their wonted tribute bear;
To warm their little loves the birds complain.
I fruitless mourn to him that cannot hear
And weep the more because I weep in vain.
(*Sonnet on the Death of Richard West*)

It will easily be perceived that the only part of this Sonnet which is of any value is the lines printed in Italics; it is equally obvious that except in the rhyme, and in the use of the single word 'fruitless' for fruitlessly, which is so far a defect, the language of these lines does in no respect differ from that of prose.

Is there then, it will be asked, no essential difference between the language of prose and metrical composition?[1] I answer that there neither is nor can be any essential difference. We are fond of tracing the resemblance between Poetry and Painting, and, accordingly, we call them Sisters: but where shall we find bonds of connection sufficiently strict to typify the affinity between metrical and prose composition? They both speak by and to the same organs; the bodies in which both of them are clothed may be said to be of the same substance, their affections are kindred and almost identical, not

1 In *1802* this sentence is expanded to:
By the foregoing quotation I have shown that the language of Prose may yet be well adapted to Poetry; and I have previously asserted that a large portion of the language of every good poem can in no respect differ from that of good Prose. I will go further. I do not doubt that it may be safely affirmed, that there neither is, nor can be, any essential difference between the language of prose and metrical composition.

necessarily differing even in degree; Poetry[1] sheds no tears 'such as Angels weep,' but natural and human tears; she can boast of no celestial Ichor that distinguishes her vital juices from those of prose; the same human blood circulates through the veins of them both.

If it be affirmed that rhyme and metrical arrangement of themselves constitute a distinction which overturns what I have been saying on the strict affinity of metrical language with that of prose, and paves the way for other distinctions[4] which the mind voluntarily admits, I answer that[5] the distinction of rhyme and metre is

1 I here use the word 'Poetry' (though against my own judgement) as opposed to the words Prose, and synonomous with metrical composition. But much confusion has been introduced into criticism by this contradistinction of Poetry and Prose, instead of the more philosophical one of Poetry and Science.[2] The only strict antithesis to Prose is Metre.[3] [Wordsworth's footnote.]

2 of Poetry and Matter of fact, or Science.

3 is Metre; nor is this, in truth, a *strict* antithesis; because lines and passages of metre so naturally occur in writing prose, that it would be scarcely possible to avoid them, even if it were desirable.

4 for other artificial distinctions

5 Here a long passage is inserted in *1802*:
I answer that the language of such Poetry as I am recommending is, as far as is possible, a selection of the language really spoken by men; that this selection, wherever it is made with true taste and feeling, will of itself form a distinction far greater than would at first be imagined, and will entirely separate the composition from the vulgarity and meanness of ordinary life; and, if metre be superadded thereto, I believe that a dissimilitude will be produced altogether sufficient for the gratification of a rational mind. What other distinction would we have? Whence is it to come? And where is it to exist? Not, surely, where the Poet speaks through the mouths of his characters: it cannot be necessary here, either for elevation of style, or any of its supposed ornaments: for, if the Poet's subject be judiciously chosen, it will naturally, and upon fit occasion, lead him to passions the language of which, if selected truly and judiciously, must necessarily be dignified and variegated, and alive with metaphors and figures. I forbear to speak of an incongruity which would shock the intelligent Reader, should the Poet interweave any foreign splendour of his own with that which the passage naturally suggests: it is sufficient to say that such addition is unnecessary. And, surely, it is more probable that those passages, which with propriety abound with metaphors and figures, will have their due effect, if, upon other occasions where the passions are of a milder character, the style also be subdued and temperate.

But, as the pleasure which I hope to give by the Poems I now present to the Reader must depend entirely on just notions upon this subject, and, as it is in itself of the highest importance to our taste and moral feelings, I cannot content myself with these detached remarks. And if, in what I am about to say, it shall appear that my labour is unnecessary, and that I am like a man fighting a battle without enemies, I would remind such persons, that, whatever may be the language outwardly holden by men, a practical faith in the opinions I am wishing to establish is almost unknown. If my conclusions are admitted, and carried as far as they must be carried if admitted at all, our judgements concerning the works of the greatest Poets both ancient and modern will be far different from what they are at present, both when we praise and when we censure: and our moral feelings influencing, and influenced by these judgements will, I believe, be corrected and purified.

Taking up the subject, then, upon general grounds, I ask what is meant by the word Poet? What is a Poet? To whom does he address himself? And what language is to be expected from him? He is a man speaking to men: a man, it is true, endued with more lively sensibility, more enthusiasm and tenderness, who has a greater knowledge of human nature, and a more comprehensive soul, than are supposed to be common among mankind; a man pleased with his own passions and volitions, and who rejoices more than other men in the spirit of life that is in him; delighting to contemplate similar volitions and passions as manifested in the goings on of the Universe, and habitually impelled to create them where he does not find them. To these qualities he has added a disposition to be affected more than other men by absent things as if they were present; an ability of conjuring up in himself passions, which are indeed far from being the same as those produced by real events, yet (especially in those parts of the general sympathy which are pleasing and delightful) do more nearly resemble the passions produced by real events, than anything which, from the motions of their own minds merely, other men are accustomed to feel in themselves; whence, and from practice, he has acquired a greater readiness and power in expressing what he thinks and feels, and especially those thoughts and feelings which, by his own choice, or from the structure of his own mind, arise in him without immediate external excitement.

But, whatever portion of this faculty we may suppose even the greatest Poet to possess, there cannot be a doubt but that the language which it will suggest to him, must, in liveliness and truth, fall far short of that which is uttered by men in real life, under the actual pressure of those passions, certain shadows of which the Poet thus produces, or feels to be produced, in himself. However exalted a notion we would wish to cherish of the character of a Poet, it is obvious, that, while he describes and imitates passions, his situation is altogether slavish and mechanical, compared with the freedom and power of real and substantial action and suffering. So that it will be the wish of the Poet to bring his feelings near to those of the persons whose feelings he describes, nay, for short spaces of time perhaps, to let himself slip into an entire delusion, and even confound and identify his own feeling with theirs; modifying only the language which is thus suggested to him, by a consideration that he describes for a particular purpose, that of giving pleasure. Here, then, he will apply the principle on which I have so much insisted, namely that of selection;

on this he will depend for removing what would otherwise be painful or disgusting in the passion; he will feel that there is no necessity to trick out or to elevate nature: and, the more industriously he applies this principle, the deeper will be his faith that no words, which his fancy or imagination can suggest, will be to be compared with those which are the emanations of reality and truth.

But it may be said by those who do not object to the general spirit of these remarks, that, as it is impossible for the Poet to produce upon all occasions language as exquisitely fitted for the passion as that which the real passion itself suggests, it is proper that he should consider himself as in the situation of a translator, who deems himself justified when he substitutes excellences of another kind for those which are unattainable by him; and endeavours occasionally to surpass his original, in order to make some amends for the general inferiority to which he feels that he must submit. But this would be to encourage idleness and unmanly despair. Further, it is the language of men who speak of what they do not understand; who talk of Poetry, as if it were a thing as indifferent as a taste for Rope-dancing, or Frontiniac or Sherry. Aristotle, I have been told, hath said, that Poetry is the most philosophic of all writing: it is so: its object is truth, not individual and local, but general, and operative; not standing upon external testimony, but carried alive into the heart by passion; truth which is its own testimony, which gives strength and divinity to the tribunal to which it appeals, and receives them from the same tribunal. Poetry is the image of man and nature. The obstacles which stand in the way of the fidelity of the Biographer and Historian, and of their consequent utility, are incalculably greater than those which are to be encountered by the Poet who has an adequate notion of the dignity of his art. The Poet writes under one restriction only, namely, that of the necessity of giving immediate pleasure to a human Being possessed of that information which may be expected from him, not as a lawyer, a physician, a mariner, an astronomer or a natural philosopher, but as a Man. Except this one restriction, there is no object standing between the Poet and the image of things; between this, and the Biographer and Historian there are a thousand.

Nor let this necessity of producing immediate pleasure be considered as a degradation of the Poet's art. It is far otherwise. It is an acknowledgement of the beauty of the universe, an acknowledgement the more sincere, because it is not formal, but indirect; it is a task light and easy to him who looks at the world in the spirit of love: further, it is a homage paid to the native and naked dignity of man, to the grand elementary principle of pleasure, by which he knows, and feels, and lives, and moves. We have no sympathy but what is propagated by pleasure: I would not be misunderstood; but wherever we sympathize with pain it will be found that the sympathy is produced and carried on by subtle combinations with pleasure. We have no knowledge, that is, no general principles drawn from the contemplation of particular facts, but what has been built up by pleasure, and exists in us by pleasure alone. The Man of Science, the Chemist and Mathematician, whatever difficulties and disgusts they may have had to struggle with, know and feel this. However painful may be the objects with which the Anatomist's knowledge is connected, he feels that his knowledge is pleasure; and where he has no pleasure he has no knowledge. What then does the Poet? He considers man and the objects that surround him as acting and reacting upon each other, so as to produce an infinite complexity of pain and pleasure; he considers man in his own nature and in his ordinary life as contemplating this with a certain quantity of immediate knowledge, with certain convictions, intuitions and deductions which by habit become of the nature of intuitions; he considers him as looking upon this complex scene of ideas and sensations, and finding everywhere objects that immediately excite in him sympathies which, from the necessities of his nature, are accompanied by an overblance of enjoyment.

To this knowledge which all men carry about with them, and to these sympathies in which without any other discipline than that of our daily life we are fitted to take delight, the Poet principally directs his attention. He considers man and nature as essentially adapted to each other, and the mind of man as naturally the mirror of the fairest and most interesting qualities of nature. And thus the Poet, prompted by this feeling of pleasure which accompanies him through the whole course of his studies, converses with general nature with affections akin to those, which, through labour and length of time, the Man of Science has raised up in himself, by conversing with those particular parts of nature which are the objects of his studies. The knowledge both of the Poet and the Man of Science is pleasure; but the knowledge of the one cleaves to us as a necessary part of our existence, our natural and unalienable inheritance; the other is a personal and individual acquisition, slow to come to us, and by no habitual and direct sympathy connecting us with our fellow beings. The Man of Science seeks truth as a remote and unknown benefactor; he cherishes and loves it in his solitude: the Poet, singing a song in which all human beings join with him, rejoices in the presence of truth as our visible friend and hourly companion. Poetry is the breath and finer spirit of all knowledge: it is the impassioned expression which is in the countenance of all Science. Emphatically may it be said of the Poet, as Shakespeare hath said of man, 'that he looks before and after'. He is the rock of defence of human nature; an upholder and preserver, carrying everywhere with him relationship and love. In spite of difference of soil and climate, of language and manners, of laws and customs, in spite of things silently gone out of mind and things violently destroyed, the Poet binds together by passion and knowledge the vast empire of human society, as it is spread over the whole earth and over all time. The objects of the Poet's thoughts are everywhere; though the eyes and senses of man are, it is true, his favourite guides, yet he will follow wheresoever he can find an atmosphere of sensation in which to move his wings. Poetry is the first and last of all knowledge – it is as immortal as the heart of man. If the labours of men of Science should ever create any material revolution, direct or indirect, in our condition, and in the impressions which we habitually receive, the Poet will sleep then no more than at present, but he will be ready to follow the steps of the Man of Science, not only in those general indirect effects, but he will be at his side, carrying sensation into the midst of the objects of the Science itself. The remotest discoveries of the Chemist, the Botanist or Mineralogist, will be as proper objects of the Poet's art as any upon which it can be employed, if the time should ever come when these things shall be familiar to us, and the relations under which they are contemplated by the followers of these respective Sciences shall be manifestly and palpably material to us as enjoying and suffering beings. If the time should ever come when what is now called Science, thus familiarized to men, shall be ready to put on, as it were, a form of flesh and blood, the Poet will lend his divine spirit to aid the transfiguration, and will welcome the Being thus produced, as a dear and genuine inmate of the household of man. It is not, then, to be supposed that any one, who holds that sublime notion of Poetry which I have attempted to convey, will break in upon the sanctity and truth of his pictures by transitory and accidental ornaments, and endeavour to excite admiration of himself by arts, the necessity of which must manifestly depend upon the assumed meanness of his subject.

What I have thus far said applies to Poetry in general; but especially to those parts of composition where the Poet speaks through the mouths of his characters; and upon this point it appears to have such weight that I will conclude, there are few persons of good sense, who would not allow that the dramatic parts of composition are defective, in proportion as they deviate from the real language of nature, and are coloured by a diction of the Poet's own, either peculiar to him as an individual Poet, or belonging simply to Poets in general, to a body of men who, from the circumstance of their compositions being in metre, it is expected will employ a particular language.

It is not, then, in the dramatic parts of composition that we look for this distinction of language; but still it may be proper and necessary where the Poet speaks to us in his own person and character. To this I answer by referring my Reader to the description which I have before given of a Poet. Among the qualities which I have enumerated as principally conducing to form a Poet, is implied nothing differing in kind from other men, but only in degree. The sum of what I have there said is that the Poet is chiefly distinguished from other men by a greater promptness to think and feel without immediate external excitement, and a greater power in expressing such thoughts and feelings as are produced in him in that manner. But these passions and thoughts are the general passions and thoughts and feelings of men. And with what are they connected? Undoubtedly with our moral sentiments and animal sensations, and with the causes which excite these; with the operations of the elements and the appearance of the visible universe; with storm and sunshine, with the revolutions of the seasons, with cold and heat, with loss of friends and kindred, with injuries and resentments, gratitude and hope, with fear and sorrow. These, and the like, are the sensations and objects which the Poet describes, as they are the sensations of other men, and the objects which interest them. The Poet thinks and feels in the spirit of the passions of men. How, then, can his language differ in any material degree from that of all other men who feel vividly and see clearly? It might be *proved* that it is impossible. But supposing this were not the case, the Poet might then be allowed to use a peculiar language regular[1] and uniform, and not, like that which is produced by what is usually called poetic diction, arbitrary and subject to infinite caprices upon which no calculation whatever can be made. In the one case the Reader is utterly at the mercy of the Poet respecting what imagery or diction he may choose to connect with the passion, whereas in the other the metre obeys certain laws, to which the Poet and Reader both willingly submit because they are certain, and because no interference is made by them with the passion but such as the concurring testimony of ages has shown to heighten and improve the pleasure which co-exists with it.

It will now be proper to answer an obvious question, namely, why, professing these opinions have I written in verse? To this in the first place I reply,[2] because, however I may have restricted myself, there is still left open to me what confessedly constitutes the most valuable object of all writing whether in prose or verse, the great and universal passions of men, the most general and interesting of their occupations, and the entire world of nature, from which I am at liberty to supply myself with endless combinations of forms and imagery. Now, granting for a moment that whatever is interesting in these objects may be as vividly described in prose, why am I to be condemned if to such description I have endeavoured to superadd the charm which by the consent of all nations is acknowledged to exist in metrical language? To this it will be answered,[3] that a very small part of the pleasure given by Poetry depends upon the metre, and

when expressing his feelings for his own gratification, or for that of men like himself. But Poets do not write for Poets alone, but for men. Unless therefore we are advocates for that admiration which depends upon ignorance, and that pleasure which arises from hearing what we do not understand, the Poet must descend from this supposed height, and, in order to excite rational sympathy, he must express himself as other men express themselves. To this it may be added, that while he is only selecting from the real language of men, or, which amounts to the same thing, composing accurately in the spirit of such selection, he is treading upon safe ground, and we know what we are to expect from him. Our feelings are the same with respect to metre; for, as it may be proper to inform the Reader,

1 the distinction of metre is regular
2 To this, in addition to such answer as is included in what I have already said, I reply in the first place, because,
3 To this, by such as are unconvinced by what I have already said, it may be answered,

that it is injudicious to write in metre unless it be accompanied with the other artificial distinctions of style with which metre is usually accompanied, and that by such a deviation more will be lost from the shock which will be thereby given to the Reader's associations than will be counterbalanced by any pleasure which he can derive from the general power of numbers. In answer to those who thus contend for the necessity of accompanying metre with certain appropriate colours of style in order to the accomplishment of its appropriate end, and who also, in my opinion, greatly underrate the power of metre in itself, it might perhaps be almost sufficient to observe that poems are extant, written upon more humble subjects, and in a more naked and simple style than what I have aimed at, which poems have continued to give pleasure from generation to generation. Now, if nakedness and simplicity be a defect, the fact here mentioned affords a strong presumption that poems somewhat less naked and simple are capable of affording pleasure at the present day, and[1] all that I am now attempting is to justify myself for having written under the impression of this belief.

But I might point out various causes why, when the style is manly, and the subject of some importance, words metrically arranged will long continue to impart such a pleasure to mankind as he who is sensible of the extent of that pleasure will be desirous to impart. The end of Poetry is to produce excitement in coexistence with an over-balance of pleasure. Now, by the supposition, excitement is an unusual and irregular state of the mind; ideas and feelings do not in that state succeed each other in accustomed order. But if the words by which this excitement is produced are in themselves powerful or the images and feelings have an undue proportion of pain connected with them, there is some danger that the excitement may be carried beyond its proper bounds. Now the co-presence of something regular, something to which the mind has been accustomed when in an unexcited state or a less excited state, cannot but have great efficacy in temper-ing and restraining the passion by an intertexture of ordinary feeling.[2]

1 and, what I wished *chiefly* to attempt, at present, was to justify
2 intertexture of ordinary feeling, and of feeling not strictly and necessarily connected with the passion. This is unquestionably true, and hence, though the opinion will at first appear paradoxical, from the tendency of metre to divest language in a certain degree of its reality, and thus to throw a sort of half consciousness of unsubstantial existence over the whole composition,

This[1] may be illustrated by appealing to the Reader's own experience of the reluctance with which he comes to the re-perusal of the distressful parts of Clarissa Harlowe or the Gamester. While Shakespeare's writings, in the most pathetic scenes, never act upon us as pathetic beyond the bounds of pleasure – an effect[2] which is in a great degree to be ascribed to the small, but continual and regular impulses of pleasurable surprise from the metrical arrangement. – On the other hand (what it must be allowed will much more frequently happen) if the Poet's words should be incommensurate with the passion, and inadequate to raise the Reader to a height of desirable excitement, then (unless the Poet's choice of his metre has been grossly injudicious) in the feelings of pleasure which the Reader has been accustomed to connect with metre in general, and in the feeling, whether cheerful or melancholy, which he has been accustomed to connect with that particular movement of metre, there will be found something which will greatly contribute to impart passion to the words, and to effect the complex end which the Poet proposes to himself.

If I had undertaken a systematic defence of the theory upon which these poems are written, it would have been my duty to develop the various causes upon which the pleasure received from metrical language depends. Among the chief of these causes is to be reckoned a principle which must be well known to those who have made any of the Arts the object of accurate reflection; I mean the pleasure which the mind derives from the perception of similitude in dissimilitude. This principle is the great spring of the activity of our minds and their chief feeder. From this principle the direction of the sexual appetite, and all the passions connected with it take their origin: It is the life of our ordinary conversation; and upon the accuracy with which similitude in dissimilitude, and dissimilitude in similitude are

---

there can be little doubt but that more pathetic situations and sentiments, that is, those which have a greater proportion of pain connected with them, may be endured in metrical composition, especially in rhyme, than in prose. The metre of the old ballads is very artless; yet they contain many passages which would illustrate this opinion, and, I hope, if the following Poems be attentively perused, similar instances will be found in them.

1 This opinion may be further illustrated
2 an effect which, in a much greater degree than might at first be imagined, is to be ascribed

perceived, depend our taste and our moral feelings. It would not have been a useless employment to have applied this principle to the consideration of metre, and to have shown that metre is hence enabled to afford much pleasure, and to have pointed out in what manner that pleasure is produced. But my limits will not permit me to enter upon this subject and I must content myself with a general summary.

I have said that Poetry is the spontaneous overflow of powerful feelings: it takes its origin from emotion recollected in tranquillity: the emotion is contemplated till by a species of reaction the tranquillity gradually disappears, and an emotion, similar to[1] that which was before the subject of contemplation, is gradually produced, and does itself actually exist in the mind. In this mood successful composition generally begins, and in a mood similar to this it is carried on; but the emotion, of whatever kind and in whatever degree, from various causes is qualified by various pleasures, so that in describing any passions whatsoever, which are voluntarily described, the mind will upon the whole be in a state of enjoyment. Now if Nature be thus cautious in preserving in a state of enjoyment a being thus employed, the Poet ought to profit by the lesson thus held forth to him, and ought especially to take care, that whatever passions he communicates to his Reader, those passions, if his Reader's mind be sound and vigorous, should always be accompanied with an overbalance of pleasure. Now the music of harmonious metrical language, the sense of difficulty overcome, and the blind association of pleasure which has been previously received from works of rhyme or metre of the same or similar construction,[2] all these imperceptibly make up a complex feeling of delight, which is of the most important use in tempering the painful feeling which will always be found intermingled with powerful descriptions of the deeper passions. This effect is always produced in pathetic and impassioned poetry; while in lighter compositions the ease and gracefulness with which the Poet manages his numbers are themselves confessedly a principal source of the gratification of the Reader. I might perhaps include all

1 an emotion, kindred to that which
2 similar construction, an indistinct perception perpetually renewed of language closely resembling that of real life, and yet, in the circumstances of metre, differing from it so widely, all these

which it is *necessary* to say on this subject by affirming what few persons will deny, that of two descriptions either of passions, manners or characters, each of them equally well executed, the one in prose and the other in verse, the verse will be read a hundred times where the prose is read once. We see that Pope by power of verse alone, has contrived to render the plainest common sense interesting, and even frequently to invest it with the appearance of passion. In consequence of these convictions I related in metre the Tale of *Goody Blake and Harry Gill*, which is one of the rudest of this collection. I wished to draw attention to the truth that the power of the human imagination is sufficient to produce such changes even in our physical nature as might almost appear miraculous. The truth is an important one; the fact (for it is a *fact*) is a valuable illustration of it. And I have the satisfaction of knowing that it has been communicated to many hundreds of people who would never have heard of it, had it not been narrated as a Ballad, and in a more impressive metre than is usual in Ballads.

Having thus adverted to a few[1] of the reasons why I have written in verse, and why I have chosen subjects from common life, and endeavoured to bring my language near to the real language of men, if I have been too minute in pleading my own cause, I have at the same time been treating a subject of general interest; and it is for this reason that I request the Reader's permission to add a few words with reference solely to these particular poems, and to some defects which will probably be found in them. I am sensible that my associations must sometimes have been particular instead of general, and that, consequently, giving to things a false importance, sometimes from diseased impulses I may have written upon unworthy subjects; but I am le s apprehensive on this account, than that my language may frequently have suffered from those arbitrary connections of feelings and ideas with particular words,[2] from which no man can altogether protect himself. Hence I have no doubt that in some instances feelings even of the ludicrous may be given to my Readers by expressions which appeared to me tender and pathetic. Such faulty expressions, were I convinced they were faulty at present, and that they must necessarily continue to be so, I would willingly

1 Having thus explained a few
2 with particular words and phrases, from which

take all reasonable pains to correct. But it is dangerous to make these alterations on the simple authority of a few individuals, or even of certain classes of men; for where the understanding of an Author is not convinced, or his feelings altered, this cannot be done without great injury to himself: for his own feelings are his stay and support, and if he sets them aside in one instance, he may be induced to repeat this till his mind loses all confidence in itself and becomes utterly debilitated. To this it may be added, that the Reader ought never to forget that he is himself exposed to the same errors as the Poet, and perhaps in a much greater degree: for there can be no presumption in saying that it is not probable he will be so well acquainted with the various stages of meaning through which the words have passed, or with the fickleness or stability of the relations of particular ideas to each other; and above all, since he is so much less interested in the subject, he may decide lightly and carelessly.

Long as I have detained my Reader, I hope he will permit me to caution him against a mode of false criticism which has been applied to Poetry in which the language closely resembles that of life and nature. Such verses have been triumphed over in parodies of which Dr Johnson's Stanza is a fair specimen.

I put my hat upon my head,
And walk'd into the Strand,
And there I met another man
Whose hat was in his hand.

Immediately under these lines I will place one of the most justly admired stanzas of the *Babes in the Wood*.

These pretty Babes with hand in hand
Went wandering up and down;
But never more they saw the Man
Approaching from the Town.

In both of these stanzas the words, and the order of the words, in no respect differ from the most unimpassioned conversation. There are words in both, for example, 'the Strand', and 'the Town', connected with none but the most familiar ideas; yet the one stanza we admit as admirable, and the other as a fair example of the superlatively contemptible. Whence arises this difference? Not from the metre, not from the language, not from the order of the words; but the *matter* expressed in Dr Johnson's stanza is contemptible. The proper method of treating trivial and simple verses to which Dr Johnson's stanza would be a fair parallelism is not to say this is a bad kind of poetry, or this is not poetry, but this wants sense; it is neither interesting in itself, nor can lead to anything interesting; the images neither originate in that sane state of feeling which arises out of thought, nor can excite thought or feeling in the Reader. This is the only sensible manner of dealing with such verses: Why trouble yourself about the species till you have previously decided upon the genus? Why take pains to prove that an Ape is not a Newton when it is self-evident that he is not a man.

I have one request to make of my Reader, which is, that in judging these Poems he would decide by his own feelings genuinely, and not by reflection upon what will probably be the judgement of others. How common is it to hear a person say, 'I myself do not object to this style of composition or this or that expression, but to such and such classes of people it will appear mean or ludicrous.' This mode of criticism so destructive of all sound unadulterated judgement is almost universal: I have therefore to request that the Reader would abide independently by his own feelings, and that if he finds himself affected he would not suffer such conjectures to interfere with his pleasure.

If an Author by any single composition has impressed us with respect for his talents, it is useful to consider this as affording a presumption, that, on other occasions where we have been displeased, he nevertheless may not have written ill or absurdly; and, further, to give him so much credit for this one composition as may induce us to review what has displeased us with more care than we should otherwise have bestowed upon it. This is not only an act of justice, but in our decisions upon poetry especially, may conduce in a high degree to the improvement of our own taste: for an *accurate* taste in Poetry and in all the other arts, as Sir Joshua Reynolds has observed, is an *acquired* talent, which can only be produced by thought and long continued intercourse with the best models of composition. This is mentioned not with so ridiculous a purpose as to prevent the most inexperienced Reader from judging for himself (I have already said that I wish him to judge for himself;) but merely to temper the rashness of decision, and to suggest that if Poetry be a subject on which much time has not been bestowed, the judgement may be erroneous, and that in many cases it necessarily will be so.

I know nothing would have so effectually contributed to further the end which I have in view as to have shown of what kind the pleasure is, and how the pleasure is produced which is confessedly produced by metrical composition essentially different from what I have here endeavoured to recommend; for the Reader will say that he has been pleased by such composition and what can I do more for him? The power of any art is limited and he will suspect that if I propose to furnish him with new friends it is only upon condition of his abandoning his old friends. Besides, as I have said, the Reader is himself conscious of the pleasure which he has received from such composition, composition to which he has peculiarly attached the endearing name of Poetry; and all men feel an habitual gratitude, and something of an honourable bigotry for the objects which have long continued to please them: we not only wish to be pleased, but to be pleased in that particular way in which we have been accustomed to be pleased. There is a host of arguments in these feelings; and should be the less able to combat them successfully, as I am willing to allow, that, in order entirely to enjoy the Poetry which I am recommending, it would be necessary to give up much of what is ordinarily enjoyed. But would my limits have permitted me to point out how this pleasure is produced, I might have removed many obstacles, and assisted my Reader in perceiving that the powers of language are not so limited as he may suppose; and that it is possible that poetry may give other enjoyments, of a purer, more lasting, and more exquisite nature. But this part of my subject I have been obliged altogether to omit: as it has been less my present aim to prove that[1] the interest excited by some other kinds of poetry is less vivid, and less worthy of the nobler powers of the mind, than to offer reasons for presuming, that, if the object which I have proposed to myself were adequately attained, a species of poetry would be produced which is genuine poetry; in its nature well adapted to interest mankind permanently, and likewise important in the multiplicity and quality of its moral relations.

1 This part of my subject I have not altogether neglected; but it has been less my present aim to prove, that

From what has been said, and from a perusal of the Poems, the Reader will be able clearly to perceive the object which I have proposed to myself: he will determine how far I have attained this object; and, what is a much more important question, whether it be worth attaining; and upon the decision of these two questions will rest my claim to the approbation of the public.

Appendix on Poetic Diction
added by Wordsworth to the 1802 edition of *Lyrical Ballads*

As perhaps I have no right to expect from a Reader of an Introduction to a volume of Poems that attentive perusal without which it is impossible, imperfectly as I have been compelled to express my meaning, that what I have said in the Preface should throughout be fully understood, I am the more anxious to give an exact notion of the sense in which I use the phrase *poetic diction*; and for this purpose I will here add a few words concerning the origin of the phraseology which I have condemned under that name. The earliest Poets of all nations generally wrote from passion excited by real events; they wrote naturally, and as men: feeling powerfully as they did, their language was daring, and figurative. In succeeding times, Poets, and men ambitious of the fame of Poets, perceiving the influence of such language, and desirous of producing the same effect, without having the same animating passion, set themselves to a mechanical adoption of those figures of speech, and made use of them, sometimes with propriety, but much more frequently applied them to feelings and thoughts with which they had no natural connection whatsoever. A language was thus insensibly produced, differing sensibly from the real language of men in *any situation*. The Reader or Hearer of this distorted language found himself in a perturbed and unusual state of mind: when affected by the genuine language of passion he had been in a perturbed and unusual state of mind also: in both cases he was willing that his common judgement and understanding should be laid asleep, and he had no instinctive and infallible perception of the true to make him reject the false; the one served him as a passport for the other. The agitation and confusion of mind were in both cases delightful, and no wonder if he confounded the one with the other, and believed them both to be produced by the same, or similar causes. Besides, the Poet spake to him in the character of a man to be looked up to, a man of genius and authority. Thus, and from a variety of other causes, this distorted language was received with admiration; and Poets, it is probable, who had before contented themselves for the most part with misapplying only expressions which at first had been dictated by real passion, carried the abuse still further, and introduced phrases composed apparently in the spirit of the original figurative language of passion, yet altogether of their own invention, and distinguished by various degrees of wanton deviation from good sense and nature.

It is indeed true that the language of the earliest Poets was felt to differ materially from ordinary language, because it was the language of extraordinary occasions; but it was really spoken by men, language which the Poet himself had uttered when he had been affected by the events which he described, or which he had heard uttered by those around him. To this language it is probable that metre of some sort or other was early superadded. This separated the genuine language of Poetry still further from common life, so that whoever read or heard the poems of these earliest Poets felt himself moved in a way in which he had not been accustomed to be moved in real life, and by causes manifestly different from those which acted upon him in real life. This was the great temptation to all the corruptions which have followed: under the protection of this feeling succeeding Poets constructed a phraseology which had one thing, it is true, in common with the genuine language of poetry, namely, that it was not heard in ordinary conversation; that it was unusual. But the first Poets, as I have said, spake a language which, though unusual, was still the language of men. This circumstance, however, was disregarded by their successors; they found that they could please by easier means: they became proud of a language which they themselves had invented, and which was uttered only by themselves; and, with the spirit of a fraternity, they arrogated it to themselves as their own. In process of time metre became a symbol or promise of this unusual language, and whoever took it upon him to write in metre, according as he possessed more or less true poetic genius, introduced less or more of this adulterated phraseology into his compositions, and the true and the false became so inseparably interwoven that the taste of men was gradually perverted and this language was received as a natural language: and at length, by the influence of books upon men, did to a certain degree really become so. Abuses of this kind were imported from one nation to another, and with the progress of refinement this diction became daily more and more currupt, thrusting out of sight the plain humanities of nature by a motley masquerade of tricks, quaintnesses, hieroglyphics and enigmas.

It would be highly interesting to point out the causes of the pleasure given by this extravagant and absurd language; but this is not the place; it depends upon a great variety of causes, but upon none perhaps more than its influence in impressing a notion of the peculiarity and exaltation of the Poet's character, and in flattering the Reader's self-love by bringing him nearer to a sympathy with that character; an effect which is accomplished by unsettling ordinary habits of thinking, and thus assisting the Reader to approach to that perturbed and dizzy state of mind in which if he does not find himself, he imagines that he is *balked* of a peculiar enjoyment which poetry can and ought to bestow.

The sonnet which I have quoted from Gray, in the Preface, except the lines printed in Italics, consists of little else but this diction, though not of the worse kind; and indeed, if one may be permitted to say so, it is far too common in the best writers both ancient and modern. Perhaps I can in no way, by positive example, more easily give my Reader a notion of what I mean by the phrase *poetic diction* than by referring him to a comparison between the metrical paraphrases which we have of passages in the Old and New Testament, and those passages as they exist in our common Translation. See Pope's *Messiah* throughout, Prior's 'Did sweeter sounds adorn my flowing tongue,' etc., 'Though I speak with the tongues of men and of angels,' etc. etc. See 1 Corinthians, xiii. By way of immediate example, take the following of Dr Johnson:

Turn on the prudent Ant thy heedless eyes,
Observe her labours, Sluggard, and be wise;
No stern command, no monitory voice,
Prescribes her dutie:, or directs her choice;
Yet, timely provident, she hastes away
To snatch the blessings of a plenteous day;
When fruitful Summer loads the teeming plain,
She crops the harvest and she stores the grain.

How long shall sloth usurp they useless hours,
Unnerve thy vigour, and enchain thy powers?
While artful shades thy downy couch enclose,
And soft solicitation courts repose,
Amidst the drowsy charms of dull delight,
Year chases year with unremitted flight,
Till want now following, fraudulent and slow,
Shall spring to seize thee, like an ambushed foe.

From this hubbub of words pass to the original.

Go to the Ant, thou Sluggard, consider her ways, and be
wise: which having no guide, overseer, or ruler, provideth her
meat in the summer, and gathereth her food in the harvest.
How long wilt thou sleep, O Sluggard? when wilt thou
arise out of thy sleep? Yet a little sleep, a little slumber, a
little folding of the hands to sleep. So shall thy poverty
come as one that travaileth, and thy want as an armed man
(Proverbs, vi).

One more quotation and I have done. It is from Cowper's verses
supposed to be written by Alexander Selkirk:

Religion! what treasure untold
Resides in that heavenly word!
More precious than silver and gold,
Or all that this earth can afford.
But the sound of the church-going bell
These valleys and rocks never heard,
Ne'er sighed at the sound of a knell,
Or smiled when a sabbath appeared.

Ye winds, that have made me your sport
Convey to this desolate shore
Some cordial endearing report
Of a land I must visit no more.
My friends, do they now and then send
A wish or a thought after me?
O tell me I yet have a friend,
Though a friend I am never to see.

I have quoted this passage as an instance of three different styles of composition. The first four lines are poorly expressed; some Critics would call the language prosaic; the fact is it would be bad prose, so bad that it is scarcely worse in metre. The epithet 'church-going' applied to a bell, and that by so chaste a writer as Cowper, is an instance of the strange abuses which Poets have introduced into their language till they and their Readers take them as matters of course, if they do not single them out expressly as objects of admiration. The two lines 'Ne'er sighed at the sound,' etc., are, in my opinion, an instance of the language of passion wrested from its proper use, and, from the mere circumstance of the composition being in metre, applied upon an occasion that does not justify such violent expressions; and I should condemn the passage, though perhaps few Readers will agree with me, as vicious poetic diction. The last stanza is throughout admirably expressed: it would be equally good whether in prose or verse, except that the Reader has an exquisite pleasure in seeing such natural language so naturally connected with metre. The beauty of this stanza tempts me here to add a sentiment which ought to be the pervading spirit of a system, detached parts of which have been imperfectly explained in the Preface – namely, that in proportion as ideas and feelings are valuable, whether the composition be in prose or in verse, they require and exact one and the same language.

Francis Wrangham

from '*Lyrical Ballads* in Two Volumes by William Wordsworth', *British Critic*   February 1801

Mr Wordsworth has, indeed, appeared before the public some years ago, as author of *Descriptive Sketches* and of *An Evening Walk*; compositions in which were discoverable the fire and fancy of a true poet, though obscured by diction often and intentionally inflated. His style is now wholly changed, and he has adopted a purity of expression, which, to the fastidious ear, may sometimes sound poor and low, but which is infinitely more correspondent with true feeling than what, by the courtesy of the day, is usually called poetical language.

Whatever may be thought of these poems, it is evident that they are not to be confounded with the flood of poetry which is poured forth in such profusion by the modern Bards of Science, or their brethren the Bards of Insipidity. The author has thought for himself; he has deeply studied human nature, in the book of human action; and has adopted his language from the same sources as his feelings. Aware that his poems are so materially different from those upon which general approbation is at present bestowed, he has now defended them in a Preface of some length; not with the foolish hope of reasoning his readers into the approbation of these particular Poems, but as a necessary justification of the species of poetry to which they belong. This Preface, though written in some parts with a degree of metaphysical obscurity, conveys much penetrating judicious observation, important at all times but especially when, as it is well observed

the invaluable works of our elder writers are driven into
neglect by frantic novels, sickly and stupid German
tragedies and deluges of idle and extravagant stories in verse.

Perhaps it would be expecting too much from any one but Shakespeare, were we to demand that he should be the poet of human nature. It would be no mean, and indeed it would be very lofty praise, to assert of a writer that he is able to pour into other bosoms powerful feelings of a particular class, or belonging to a particular order of men. To this praise Mr Wordsworth lays a well-supported claim. He declares himself the poet chiefly of low and rustic life (some specimens of ability he has given in other lines but this is evidently his excellence) and he portrays it, not under its disgusting forms, but in situations affording, as he thinks, the best soil for the essential passions of the heart, incorporated with an elementary and durable state of manners and with the beautiful and permanent forms of nature. Each separate poem has, as its distinct *purpose*, the development of a feeling, which gives importance to the action and situation, and not the action or situation to the feeling. Whether the particular purpose is, in every case, *worthy* of a poet, will perhaps admit of some doubt. We have no hesitation in saying, that it is generally interesting, often invaluable.

As to the subjects it must be owned that their worth does not always appear at first sight but, judging from our own feelings, we must assert that it generally grows upon the reader by subsequent perusal. The following remarks may perhaps illustrate the cause of this improving interest.

1. It is not requisite that the poetic feeling should be strictly referable to any of those known and powerful classes, called the sublime, the terrible, the pathetic, etc. It may sometimes consist in a gentle agitation of the contending emotions, from which a preponderance of pleasure is ultimately produced, as from the melancholy recollections of a cheerful old man, in the *Two April Mornings*, and *The Fountain*; sometimes it may arise from the mixture of lively imagery with various feelings, as with exultation and pity, in the two parts of *Hartleap Well*; sometimes it may be founded on the soft and almost insensible affections which we receive from natural scenery, aided perhaps, by some accidental associations in our minds. Of this kind are the different *Poems on the Naming of Places, Lines Written with a Slate Pencil*, etc., *Rural Architecture* and some others. Even where the feeling called forth is of a rich and noble character, such as we may recur to, and feed upon, it may yet be wrought up so gradually, including so many circumstances of appropriate manners, of local description, of actual events, etc., that the subtle uniting thread will be lost, without a persevering effort towards attention on the part of the reader. Who that has studied Shakespeare, must not be conscious how often the connection of minute and trifling incidents with the main story has eluded his observation until after repeated perusals. Something of this kind will probably occur to the readers of *The Brothers, The Cumberland Beggar* and more particularly of the Poem entitled *Michael*; yet these three are of the highest order of Poems in the volume. The interest, especially of the first, is so dramatically wrought up, the minute touches are so accurately studied, the general effect is so insensibly produced, and appeals so forcibly to the heart, as to rank its author far beyond the reach of common-place praise or censure.

Perhaps the English language can boast few instances of descriptive poetry, enlivened with a happier variety of imagery, than the fanciful echo in the *Poem inscribed to Joanna*. The lady's laugh, to be sure, is loud, but it is not unpleasing.

But the two most singular specimens of unpretending yet irresistible pathos are the two songs, page 50 and 52. In artlessness they strongly remind us of Burns; but perhaps go beyond him in delicacy. As they have a secret connection we shall insert both.[1]

When the art of poetry has long been cultivated among a polished people, and brought to a state of great refinement, the natural operation of an ill-judged ambition, to excel even those who have most successfully adorned the language, leads writers either to employ an affected and over laboured style, or at least, to keep always on the high stilts of elegance, to the exclusion of nature and simplicity. In such a state of poetic art, that man may be considered as a public benefactor, who, with talents equal to the task, which is arduous, recalls attention to the moral natural style, and shows what may be effected by simple language, expressive of human passions, and genuine, not artificial feelings. In this character Mr Wordsworth appears, and appears with success, to which we could by no means refuse our approbation. We will not deny that sometimes he goes so far in his pursuit of simplicity as to become flat or weak; but, in general, he sets an example which the full dressed poet of affectation might wish, but wish in vain, to follow. He who would correct Mr Wordsworth as the dancing master of Hogarth would correct the attitude of Antinous.

Charles Lamb

from a letter to William Wordsworth   February 1801

What most pleases me is *The Song of Lucy*. *Simon's Sickly daughter*, in the *Sexton*, made me cry. Next to these are the descriptions of these continuous echoes in the story of *Joanna's Laugh*, where the mountains, and all the scenery absolutely seem alive; and that fine Shakespearian character of the happy man, in *The Brothers*,

1 'Strange fits of passion' and 'She dwelt among the untrodden ways' are quoted in full here.

that creeps about the fields
Following his fancies by the hour, to bring
Tears down his cheek, or solitary smiles
Into his face, until the setting sun
Write Fool upon his forehead.

I will mention one more – the delicate and curious feeling in the wish for *The Cumberland Beggar*, that he may have about him the melody of the birds, although he hear them not. Here the mind knowingly passes a fiction upon herself, first substituting her own feelings for the Beggar's, and in the same breath detecting the fallacy, will not part with the wish. *The Poet's Epitaph* is disfigured, to my taste, by common satire upon parsons and lawyers in the beginning and the coarse epithet of 'pin-point' in the sixth stanza. All the rest is eminently good, and your own. I will just add that it appears to me a fault in the *Beggar*, that the instructions conveyed in it are too direct and like a lecture; they don't slide into the mind while he is imagining no such matter. An intelligent reader finds a sort of insult in being told, 'I will teach you how to think upon this subject.' This fault, if I am right, is in a ten thousandth worse degree to be found in Sterne, and in many novelists and modern poets, who put up a sign-post to show you where to feel. . . . To sum up a general opinion of the second volume, I do not feel any one poem in it so forcibly as the *Ancient Mariner* and *The Mad Mother* and the *Lines at Tintern Abbey* in the first.

William Wordsworth

from a letter to Thomas Poole   9 April 1801

In the last poem of my second volume[1] I have attempted to give a picture of a man, of strong mind and lively sensibility, agitated by two of the most powerful affections of the human heart; the parental affection, and the love of property, landed property, including the feelings of inheritance, home, and personal and family independence. This poem has, I know, drawn tears from the eyes of more than one

1 *Michael.*

– persons well acquainted with the manners of the Statesmen, as they are called, of this country; and, moreover, persons who never wept, in reading verse, before. This is a favourable augury for me. But nevertheless I am anxious to know the effect of this poem upon you, on many accounts; because you are yourself the inheritor of an estate which has long been in possession of your family; and, above all, because you are so well acquainted, nay, so familiarly conversant with the language, manners and feeling of the middle order of people who dwell in the country. Though from the comparative infrequency of small landed properties in your neighbourhood, your situation has not been altogether so favourable as mine, yet your daily and hourly intercourse with these people must have far more than counter-balanced any disadvantage of this kind; so that all things considered, perhaps there is not in England a more competent judge than you must be, of the skill and knowledge with which my pictures are drawn.

William Wordsworth

from a letter to Miss Taylor 9 April 1801
[She had requested from Wordsworth 'an account of such events in [his] life as may have had an influence in forming [his] present opinions'.]

In what I have said I am afraid there will be little which will throw any light on my writings, or gratify the wish which you entertain, to know how I came to adopt the opinions which I have expressed in my Preface; and to write in the style in which my poems are written: but in truth my life has been unusually barren of events, and my opinions have grown slowly, and I may say insensibly.

You ask me if I have always thought so independently. To this question I am able to give you a satisfactory answer by referring you to two poems, which I published in the beginning of the year 1793. The one is entitled *Descriptive Sketches made during a Pedestrian Tour in the Italian, Grison, Swiss and Savoyard Alps*, the other *An evening Walk, an Epistle addressed to a Young Lady*, both published, with my name, by Johnson, St Paul's Churchyard. They are juvenile productions, inflated and obscure, but they contain many new images, and vigorous lines; and they would perhaps interest you, by showing how very widely different my former opinions must have been from those which I hold at present. It would have given me great pleasure to have sent you copies of these poems, if I had been possessed of them. Johnson has told some of my friends who have called for them, that they were out of print: this must have been a mistake. Unless he has sent them to the trunk-maker's they must be lying in some corner of his warehouse, for I have reason to believe that they never sold much.

You flatter me, Madam, that my style is distinguished by a genuine simplicity. Whatever merit I may have in this way I have attained solely by endeavouring to look, as I have said in my Preface, steadily at my subject. If you read over carefully the poem of *The Female Vagrant*, which was the first written of the Collection (indeed it was written several years before the others) you will see that I have not formerly been conscious of the importance of this rule. The diction of that poem is often vicious, and the descriptions are often false, giving a mind inattentive to the true nature of the subject on which it was employed. Hoping that it may afford you some amusement I will write down a few corrections of this poem in which I have endeavoured to bring the language nearer to truth. I think, if you will take the trouble of comparing these corrections with the correspondent passages in the printed poem, you will perceive in what manner I have attempted gradually to purify my diction.

Omit the first stanza entirely and begin the poem with the second, omit the third and fourth stanzas. Page 70 the line 'His little range of water was denied' must have another substituted for it which I have not written. Page 72. For, 'With proud parade' read, 'day after day', the next line for '*to sweep* the streets' read '*and clear'd* the streets'. Page 73 read the first stanza thus

There long were we neglected; and we bore
Much sorrow ere the fleet its anchor weigh'd.
Green fields before us, and our native shore,
We breathed a pestilential air that made
Ravage for which no knell was heard – We pray'd
For our departure; wish'd and wish'd, nor knew

71 William Wordsworth

'Mid that long sickness, and those hopes delay'd,
That happier &c. . . . Omit the first stanza of page 74

Page 75 after fourth line read thus

I was too calm – though heavily distress'd!
O me! how quiet sky and ocean were!
My heart was heal'd within me, I was bless'd
And look'd, and look'd &c &c

Page 76 read first stanza thus

At midnight once a storming army came:
Yet do I see the miserable sight,
The bayonet, the Soldier, and the flame
That followed us, and fac'd us, in our flight:
When rape and Murder by the ghastly light
Seized their joint prey, the Mother and the child!
But I must leave these thoughts – From night to night
From day to day the air breath'd soft and mild
And on the gliding vessel heaven and ocean smil'd.

Page 77 read the first stanza thus

And oft I thought, (my fancy was so strong)
That I at last a resting place had found:
Here will I dwell said I, my whole life long
Roaming the illimitable waters round;
Here will I live: of every friend disown'd,
Here will I roam about the ocean flood –
To break my dream &c &c

In the next stanza of the same page for 'How dismal toll'd' read
'Dismally toll'd'.[1]

1 See R. L. Brett & A. R. Jones edition of *Lyrical Ballads*, Methuen, 1963.

Henry Crabb Robinson

from a letter to Thomas Robinson   6 June 1802

A few days since I received Wordsworth's *Lyrical Ballads*. . . . I am at present in danger of becoming unjust to English Literature being absorbed in the beauties of the German. These exquisite Volumes were enough to bring me back to justice. There are a few ballads – *The Thorn, The Idiot Boy, Goody Blake and Harry Gill*, which will rank with the first rate compositions in the Language. . . . Wordsworth has the art . . . of doing much with simple means. His repetition of simple phrases, and his dwelling on simple but touching Incidents, his skill in drawing the deepest moral, and tenderest interest out of trifles, evince a great master, a Talent truly Shakespearian, for instance in *Goody Blake*:

And fiercely by the arm he took her
   And by the arm he held her fast
And fiercely by the arm he shook her
   And cried I've caught you then at last.

How cunning is this delay! This dwelling on so slight a circumstance. . . . The following stanza, 'Oh joy for her' is exquisite as well as the whole a most pathetically poetical display of poverty. Wordsworth is equally happy in his expression of moral sentiments:

Oh reader, had you in your Mind,
   Such stores as silent thought can bring,
Oh gentle reader, you will find
   A tale in everything.

There is in my mind more Genius and Merit in such Reflections and such descriptions unostentatious as they are; than in many an admired ode. I would rather have written *The Thorn* than all the tinsel gaudy lines of Darwin's botanic garden. The one is an artificial versifier, the other is a feeler and painter of feelings. But all the pieces have not this superior merit. *The Female Vagrant*, etc. are cold and trite – Wordsworth's excellence appears greatest when he is most original.

Henry Crabb Robinson

from his diary   25 July 1802

Wordsworth's *Ballads* have infinite metrical beauty. . . . I consider Wordsworth as our first living poet; he will certainly attain very great eminence. . . . Low life is generally more fit than high life for poetical description because there we see human nature in its greater purity.

Samuel Taylor Coleridge

from a letter to Robert Southey   29 July 1802

Although Wordsworth's Preface is half a child of my own brain and arose out of conversations so frequent that with few exceptions, we could scarcely either of us, perhaps, positively say which first stated a particular thought (I am speaking of the Preface as it stood in the second volume), yet I am far from going all lengths with Wordsworth. He has written lately a number of poems (thirty-two in all) some of them of considerable length (the longest 160 lines), the greatest number of these, to my feelings, very excellent compositions, but here and there, a daring humbleness of language and versification, and a strict adherence to matter of fact, even to prolixity, that startled me. His alterations, likewise, in *Ruth* perplexed me,[1] and I have thought again and have not had my doubts solved by Wordsworth. On the contrary I rather suspect that somewhere or other there is a radical difference in our opinions respecting poetry; this I shall endeavour to go to the bottom of, and, acting the arbitrator between the old school and the new school, hope to lay down some plain and conspicuous, though not superficial, canons of criticism respecting poetry. . . . In the new edition of the *Lyrical Ballads* there is a valuable appendix which I am sure you must like, and in the Preface itself considerable additions; one on the dignity and nature of the office and character of a poet that is very grand, and a sort of Verulamian[2] power and majesty, but it is, in parts (and this is the fault, *me judice*, of

1 See *Poetical Works*, vol. II, pp. 227–35.
2 i.e. Baconian.

all the latter half of that *Preface*) obscure beyond any necessity, and the extreme elaboration and almost constrainedness of the diction contrasted (to my feelings) somewhat harshly with the general style of these *Poems* to which the *Preface* is an introduction.

Robert Southey

from a letter to Samuel Taylor Coleridge   4 August 1802

We shall probably agree together some day upon Wordsworth's lyrical poems. Does he not associate more feeling with particular phrases, and you also with him, than those phrases can convey to any one else?

John Wilson

from a letter to William Wordsworth   24 May 1802

That luxury, sir, I have enjoyed; that luxury your poems have afforded me, and for this reason I now address you. Accept my thanks for the raptures you have occasioned me; and however much you may be inclined to despise me, know at least that these thanks are sincere and fervent. To you, sir, mankind are indebted for a species of poetry which will continue to afford pleasure while respect is paid to virtuous feelings. The flimsy ornaments of language, used to conceal meanness of thought and want of feeling, may captivate for a short time the ignorant and unwary, but true taste will discover the imposture, and expose the authors of it to merited contempt. The real feelings of human nature, expressed in simple and forcible language, will, on the contrary, please those only who are capable of entertaining them, and in proportion to the attention which we pay to the faithful delineation of such feelings, will be the enjoyment derived from them. That poetry, therefore, which is the language of nature, is certain of immortality, provided circumstances do not occur to pervert the feelings of humanity, and occasion a complete revolution in the government of the mind.

That your poetry is the language of nature, in my opinion, admits of no doubt. Both the thoughts and expressions may be tried by that standard. You have seized upon those feelings that most deeply interest the heart, and that also come within the sphere of common observation. You do not write merely for the pleasure of philosophers and men of improved taste, but for all who think – for all who feel. If we have ever known the happiness arising from parental or fraternal love; if we have ever known that delightful sympathy of souls connecting persons of different sex; if we have ever dropped a tear at the death of friends, or grieved for the misfortunes of others; if, in short, we have ever felt the more amiable emotions of human nature – it is impossible to read *your* poems without being greatly interested and frequently in raptures; your sentiments, feelings and thoughts are therefore exactly such as ought to constitute the subject of poetry, and cannot fail of exciting interest in every heart. But, sir, your merit does not solely consist in delineating the real features of the human mind under those different aspects it assumes, when under the influence of various passions and feelings; you have, in a manner truly admirable, explained a circumstance, very important in its effects upon the soul when agitated, that has indeed been frequently alluded to, but never generally adopted by any author in tracing the progress of emotions – I mean that wonderful effect which the appearances of external nature have upon the mind when in a state of strong feeling. . . . But your poems may not be considered merely in a philosophical light, or even as containing refined and natural feelings; they present us with a body of morality of the purest kind. They represent the enjoyment resulting from the cultivation of the social affections of our nature; they inculcate a conscientious regard to the rights of our fellow-men; they show that every creature on the face of the earth is entitled in some measure to our kindness. They prove that in every mind, *however* depraved, there exist some qualities deserving our esteem. They point out the proper way to happiness. They show that such a thing as perfect misery does not exist. They flash on our souls conviction of immortality. Considered therefore in this view, *Lyrical Ballads* is, to use your own words, the book which I value next to my Bible; and though I may, perhaps, never have the happiness of seeing you, yet I will always consider you as a friend, who has by his instructions done me a service which it can never be in my power to repay. Your instructions have afforded me inexpressible pleasure; it will be my own fault if I do not reap from them much advantage.

I have said, sir, that in all your poems you have adhered strictly to natural feelings, and described what comes within the range of every person's observation. It is from following out this plan that, in my estimation, you have surpassed every poet both of ancient and modern times. But to me it appears that in the execution of this design you have inadvertently fallen into an error, the effects of which are, however, exceedingly trivial. No feeling, no state of mind ought, in my opinion, to become the subject of poetry, that does not please. Pleasure may, indeed, be produced in many ways, and by means that at first sight appear calculated to accomplish a very different end. Tragedy of the deepest kind produces pleasure of a high nature. To point out the causes of this would be foreign to the purpose. But we may lay this down as a general rule, that no description can please, where the sympathies of our soul are not excited, and no narration interest, where we do not enter into the feelings of some of the parties concerned. On this principle, many feelings which are undoubtedly natural, are improper subjects of poetry, and many situations, no less natural, incapable of being described so as to produce the grand effect of poetical composition. This, sir, I would apprehend, is reasonable, and founded on the constitution of the human mind. There are a thousand occurrences happening every day, which do not in the least interest an unconcerned spectator, though they no doubt occasion various emotions in the breast of those to whom they immediately relate. To describe these in poetry would be improper. Now, sir, I think that in several cases you have fallen into this error. You have described feelings with which I cannot sympathize, and situations in which I take no interest. I know that I can relish your beauties, and that makes me think that I can also perceive your faults. But in this matter I have not trusted wholly to my own judgement, but heard the sentiments of men whose feelings I admired, and whose understanding I respected. In a few cases, then, I think that even you have failed to excite interest. In the poem entitled *The Idiot Boy*, your intention, as you inform us in your preface, was to trace the maternal passion through its more subtle windings. This design is no doubt accompanied with much difficulty, but, if properly executed, cannot fail of interesting the heart. But sir, in my opinion, the manner in which you have executed this plan has frustrated the end you intended to produce by it; the affection of Betty Foy has nothing in it to excite interest. It exhibits merely the effects of that instinctive feeling inherent in the constitution of every animal. The excessive fondness of the mother disgusts us, and prevents us from sympathizing with her. We are unable to enter into her feelings; we cannot conceive ourselves actuated by the same feelings, and consequently take little or no interest in her situation. The object of her affection is indeed her son, and in that relation much consists, but then he is represented as totally destitute of any attachment towards her; the state of his mind is represented as perfectly deplorable, and, in short, to me it appears almost unnatural that a person in a state of complete idiotism should excite the warmest feelings of attachment in the breast even of his mother. This much I know, that among all the people ever I knew to have read this poem, I never met one who did not rise rather displeased from the perusal of it, and the only cause I could assign for it was the one now mentioned. This inability to receive pleasure from descriptions such as that of *The Idiot Boy*, is, I am convinced, founded upon established feelings of human nature, and the principle of it constitutes, as I daresay you recollect, the leading feature of Smith's *Theory of Moral Sentiments*. I therefore think that, in the choice of this subject, you have committed an error. You never deviate from nature; in you that would be impossible; but in this case, you have delineated feelings which, though natural, do not please, but which create a certain degree of disgust and contempt. With regard to the manner in which you have executed your plan, I think too great praise cannot be bestowed upon your talents. You have most admirably delineated the idiotism of the boy's mind, and the situations in which you place him are perfectly calculated to display it. The various thoughts that pass through the mother's mind are highly descriptive of her foolish fondness, her extravagant fears, and her ardent hopes. The manner in which you show how bodily sufferings are frequently removed by mental anxieties or pleasures, in the description of the cure of Betty Foy's female friend, is excessively well managed, and serves to establish a very curious and important truth. In short, everything you proposed to execute has been executed in a masterly manner. The fault, if there be one, lies in

the plan, not in the execution. This poem we heard recommended as
one in your best manner, and accordingly it is frequently read in
this belief. The judgement formed of it is, consequently, erroneous.
Many people are displeased with the performance; but they are not
careful to distinguish faults in the plan from faults in the execution,
and the consequence is, that they form an improper opinon of your
genius. In reading any composition, most certainly the pleasure we
receive arises almost wholly from the sentiment, thoughts and descriptions contained in it. A secondary pleasure arises from admiration
of those talents requisite to the production of it. In reading *The Idiot
Boy*, all persons who allow themselves to think, must admire your
talents, but they regret that they have been so employed, and while
they esteem the author, they cannot help being displeased with his
performance. I have seen a most excellent painting of an idiot, but it
created in me inexpressible disgust. I admired the talents of the artist,
but I had no other source of pleasure. The poem of *The Idiot Boy*
produced upon me an effect in every respect similar.

William Wordsworth

Letter to John Wilson   June 1802

My dear Sir

Had it not been for a very amiable modesty you would not have
imagined that your letter could give me any offence. It was on many
accounts highly grateful to me. I was pleased to find that I had given
so much pleasure to an ingenuous and able mind, and I further
considered the enjoyment which you had had from my Poems as an
earnest that others might be delighted with them in the same, or a
like manner. It is plain from your letter that the pleasure which I have
given you has not been blind or unthinking; you have studied the
poems, and prove that you have entered into the spirit of them. They
have not given you a cheap or vulgar pleasure; therefore I feel that
you are entitled to my kindest thanks for having done some violence
to your natural diffidence in the communication which you have
made to me.

There is scarcely any part of your letter that does not deserve particular notice; but partly from some constitutional infirmities, and partly from certain habits of mind, I do not write any letters unless upon business, not even to my dearest friends. Except during absence from my own family I have not written five letters of friendship during the last five years. I have mentioned this in order that I may retain your good opinion, should my letter be less minute than you are entitled to expect. You seem to be desirous of my opinion on the influence of natural objects in forming the character of Nations. This cannot be understood without first considering their influence upon men in general, first, with reference to such subjects as are common to all countries; and, next, such as belong exclusively to any particular country, or in a greater degree to it than to another. Now it is manifest that no human being can be so besotted and de-based by oppression, penury or any other evil which unhumanizes man as to be utterly insensible to the colours, forms or smell of flowers, the [? voices] and motions of birds and beasts, the appearances of the sky and heavenly bodies, the general warmth of a fine day, the terror and uncomfortableness of a storm, etc., etc. How dead soever many full-grown men may outwardly seem to these things, all are more or less affected by them; and in childhood, in the first practice and exercise of their senses, they must have been not the nourishers merely, but often the fathers of their passions. There cannot be a doubt that in tracts of country where images of danger, melancholy and grandeur, or loveliness, softness and ease prevail, they will make themselves felt powerfully in forming the characters of the people, so as to produce a uniformity of national character, where the nation is small and is not made up of men who, inhabiting different soils, climates, etc., by their civil usages and relations, materially interfere with each other. It was so formerly, no doubt, in the Highlands of Scotland; but we cannot perhaps observe it in our own island at the present day, because, even in the most sequestered places, by manufactures, traffic, religion, law, interchange of inhabitants, etc., distinctions are done away which would otherwise have been strong and obvious. This complex state of society does not, however, prevent the characters of individuals from frequently receiving a strong bias, not merely from the impressions of general nature, but also from local objects and images. But it seems that to produce these effects, in the degree in which we frequently find them to be produced, there must be a peculiar sensibility of original organization combining with moral accidents, as is exhibited in *The Brothers* and in *Ruth*; I mean, to produce this in a marked degree; not that I believe that any man was ever brought up in the country without loving it especially in his better moments, or in a district of particular grandeur or beauty, without feeling some stronger attachment to it on that account than he would otherwise have felt. I include, you will observe, in these considerations, the influence of climate, changes in the atmosphere and elements, and the labours and occupations which particular districts require.

You begin what you say upon *The Idiot Boy* with this observation, that nothing is a fit subject for poetry which does not please. But here follows a question, Does not please whom? Some have little knowledge of natural imagery of any kind, and, of course, little relish for it; some are disgusted with the very mention of the words 'pastoral poetry', 'sheep' or 'shepherds'; some cannot tolerate a poem with a ghost or any supernatural agency in it; others would shrink from an animated description of the pleasures of love, as from a thing carnal and libidinous; some cannot bear to see delicate and refined feelings ascribed to men in low conditions of society, because their vanity and self-love tell them that these belong only to themselves and men like themselves in dress, station and way of life; others are disgusted with the naked language of some of the most interesting passions of men, because either it is indelicate, or gross, or vulgar; as many fine ladies could not bear certain expressions in *The Mother* and *The Thorn*, and as in the instance of Adam Smith, who, we are told, could not endure the ballad of *Clym of the Clough*, because the author had not written like a gentleman. Then there are professional and national prejudices for evermore. Some take no interest in the description of a particular passion or quality, as love of solitariness, we will say, genial activity of fancy, love of nature, religion, and so forth, because they have [little or] nothing of it in themselves; and so on without end. I return then to [the] question, please whom? or what? I answer, human nature, as it has been [and ever] will be. But where are we to find the best measure of this? I answer, [from with]in; by stripping our own hearts naked, and by looking out of ourselves to[wards men] who lead the simplest lives, and those most according to nature; men who have never known false refinements, wayward and artificial desires, false criticisms, effeminate habits of thinking and feeling, or who, having known these things, have out-grown them. This latter class is the most to be depended upon, but it is very small in number. People in our rank in life are perpetually falling into one sad mistake, namely, that of supposing that human nature and the persons they associate with are one and the same thing. Whom do we generally associate with? Gentlemen, persons of fortune, professional men, ladies, persons who can afford to buy, or can easily procure, books of half-a-guinea price, hot-pressed, and printed upon superfine paper. These persons are, it is true, a part of human nature, but we err lamentably if we suppose them to be fair representatives of the vast mass of human existence. And yet few ever consider books but with reference to their power of pleasing these persons and men of a higher rank; few descend lower, among cottages and fields, and among children. A man must have done this habitually before his judgement upon *The Idiot Boy* would be in any way decisive with me. I *know* I have done this myself habitually; I wrote the poem with exceeding delight and pleasure, and whenever I read it I read it with pleasure. You have given me praise for having reflected faithfully in my Poems the feelings of human nature. I would fain hope that I have done so. But a great Poet ought to do more than this: he ought, to a certain degree, to rectify men's feelings, to give them new compositions of feeling, to render their feelings more sane, pure and permanent, in short, more consonant to nature, that is, to eternal nature, and the great moving spirit of things. He ought to travel before men occasionally as well as at their sides. I may illus-trate this by a reference to natural objects. What false notions have prevailed from generation to generation as to the true character of the Nightingale. As far as my Friend's Poem in the *Lyrical Ballads* is read, it will contribute greatly to rectify these. You will recollect a passage in Cowper, where, speaking of rural sounds, he says,

> And *even* the boding owl
> That hails the rising moon has charms for me.

Cowper was passionately fond of natural objects, yet you see he mentions it as a marvellous thing that he could connect pleasure with the cry of the owl. In the same poem he speaks in the same manner of that beautiful plant, the gorse; making in some degree an amiable boast of his loving it, *unsightly* and unsmooth as it is. There are many aversions of this kind, which, though they have some foundation in nature, have yet so slight a one that, though they may have prevailed hundreds of years, a philosopher will look upon them as accidents. So with respect to many moral feelings, either of love or dislike. What excessive admiration was paid in former times to personal prowess and military success; it is so with the latter even at the present day, but surely not nearly so much as heretofore. So with regard to birth, and innumerable other modes of sentiment, civil and religious. But you will be inclined to ask by this time how all this applies to *The Idiot Boy*. To this I can only say that the loathing and disgust which many people have at the sight of an idiot, is a feeling which, though having some foundation in human nature, is not necessarily attached to it in any virtuous degree, but is owing in a great measure to a false delicacy, and, if I may say it without rudeness, a certain want of comprehensiveness of thinking and feeling. Persons in the lower classes of society have little or nothing of this: if an idiot is born in a poor man's house, it must be taken care of, and cannot be boarded out, as it would be by gentlefolks, or sent to a public or private asylum for such unfortunate beings. [Poor people,] seeing frequently among their neighbours such objects, easily [forget] whatever there is of natural disgust about them, and have [therefore] a sane state, so that without pain or suffering they [perform] their duties towards them. I could with pleasure pursue this subject, but I must now strictly adopt the plan which I proposed to myself when I began to write this letter, namely, that of setting down a few hints or memorandums, which you will think of for my sake.

I have often applied to idiots, in my own mind, that sublime expression of Scripture, that *their life is hidden with God*. They are worshipped, probably from a feeling of this sort, in several parts of the East. Among the Alps, where they are numerous, they are considered, I believe, as a blessing to the family to which they belong. I have, indeed, often looked upon the conduct of fathers and mothers of the lower classes of society towards idiots as the great triumph of the human heart. It is there that we see the strength, disinterestedness and grandeur of love; nor have I ever been able to contemplate an object that calls out so many excellent and virtuous sentiments without finding it hallowed thereby, and having something in me which bears down before it, like a deluge, every feeble sensation of disgust and aversion.

There are, in my opinion, several important mistakes in the latter part of your letter which I could have wished to notice; but I find myself much fatigued. These refer both to the Boy and the Mother. I must content myself simply with observing that it is probable that the principle cause of your dislike to this particular poem lies in the *word* Idiot. If there had been any such word in our language *to which we had attached passion*, as lack-wit, half-wit, witless, etc., I should have certainly employed it in preference; but there is no such word. Observe (this is entirely in reference to this particular poem), my 'Idiot' is not one of those who cannot articulate, or of those that are usually disgusting in their persons:

Whether in cunning or in joy,
And then his words were not a few, etc.

and the last speech at the end of the poem. The boy whom I had in my mind was by no means disgusting in his appearance, quite the contrary; and I have known several with imperfect faculties who are handsome in their persons and features. There is one, at present, within a mile of my own house, remarkably so, though [he has something] of a stare and vacancy in his countenance. A friend of mine knowing that some persons had a dislike to the poem, such as you have expressed, advised me to add a stanza, describing the person of the boy [so as] entirely to separate him in the imaginations of my readers from that class of idiots who are disgusting in their persons; but the narration in the poem is so rapid and impassioned, that I could not find a place in which to insert the stanza without checking the progress of the poem and [so leaving] a deadness upon the feeling. This poem has, I know, frequently produced the same effect as it did upon you and your friends; but there are many also to whom it affords exquisite delight, and who, indeed, prefer it to any other of my poems. This proves that the feelings there delineated are such as men *may* sympathize with. This is enough for my purpose. It is not enough for me as a Poet, to delineate merely such feelings as all men *do* sympathize with; but it is also highly desirable to add to these others, such as all men *may* sympathize with, and such as there is reason to believe they would be better and more moral beings if they did sympathize with.

I conclude with regret, because I have not said one half of [what I intended] to say; but I am sure you will deem my excuse sufficient, [when I] inform you that my head aches violently, and I am in other respects unwell. I must, however, again give you my warmest thanks for your kind letter. I shall be happy to hear from you again, and do not think it unreasonable that I should request a letter from you when I feel that the answer which I may make to it will not perhaps be above three or four lines. This I mention to you with frankness, and you will not take it ill after what I have before said of my remissness in writing letters. I am, dear sir, with great respect,

Yours sincerely,

W. Wordsworth

William Wordsworth

Letter to Sara and Mary Hutchinson   14 June 1802

My dear Mary

I shall say nothing about your letter and Sara's because Dorothy in expressing her feelings will express mine also. Your objection to the word *view* is ill-founded; substitute the word *see*, and it does not express my feeling. I speak as having been much impressed, and for a length of time, by the sight of the old man[1] – view is used with propriety because there is continuousness in the thing – for example had I seen a man shoot at a bird with the point of his gun behind his back, the action being instantaneous, I should say, The like I never did see – I speak in this place with the feeling upon me of having been and being absolutely then, *viewing* the old man. 'Sickness had by him', I know not why you object to – the poem is throughout written in the language of men – 'I suffered much by a sickness had by me long ago' is a phrase which anybody might use, as well as 'a sickness which I had long ago'.

1 The letter refers to *Resolution and Independence*.

In the poem on leaving Grasmere[1] is a stanza which I am sure none of you have understood. I find neither D[orothy] nor C[oleridge] understand it. But first correct the first stanza thus:

Farewell, thou little nook of mountain ground
Thou rocky corner in the lowest stair
Of that magnificent Temple which doth bound
One side of our whole Vale with grandeur rare.

After the words 'blessed life which we lead here' insert the following stanza

Dear spot! which we have watched
And oh most constant, yet most fickle Place
That hast a wayward heart, as thou dost shew
To them who look not daily on thy face,
Who, being loved, in love no bounds dost know,
And say'st when we forsake thee, let them go etc.,

I have been obliged to alter the last stanza thus for both C., and D., supposed the word 'scorner' not to apply to myself, as I meant it, but any casual visitor, tourist, for example. This idea is as wretchedly mean as the other is beautiful. I have no doubt however that you certainly understood it as C. and D. have done, as my idea was not developed as it ought to have been, and as I hope it is now. I am for the most part uncertain about my success in *altering* poems; but in this case by the additional stanza I am sure I have produced a great improvement – Tell me your opinion – 'Primrose Vest' cannot stand. I should never have thought of such an expression but in a Spenserian poem, Spenser having many such expressions – But here it cannot stand, if it were only on account of 'saffron coat', an expression beautiful and appropriate. Let it stand thus:

Here with its primroses the steep rock's breast
Glittered at evening like a starry sky –

and thus the beautiful line is preserved.[2]

W.W.

1 *A Farewell*, composed in 1802 but first published in 1815, even further revised.
2 'Glittered at evening like a starry sky' is the beautiful line referred to and did stand in the published version.

My dear Sara

I am exceedingly sorry that the latter part of *The Leech-Gatherer* has displeased you, the more so because I cannot take to myself (that being the case) much pleasure or satisfaction in having pleased you in the former part. I will explain to you in prose my feeling in writing that poem, and then you will be better able to judge whether the fault be mine or yours or partly both. I describe myself as having been exalted to the highest pitch of delight by the joyousness and beauty of Nature and then as depressed, even in the midst of those beautiful objects, to the lowest dejection and despair. A young Poet in the midst of the happiness of Nature is described as overwhelmed by the thought of the miserable reverses which have befallen the happiest of all men, viz. Poets – I think of this till I am so deeply impressed by it, that I consider the manner in which I was rescued from my dejection and despair almost as an interposition of Providence. 'Now whether it was by peculiar grace leading from above' – A person reading this poem with feelings like mine will have been awed and controlled, expecting almost something spiritual or supernatural – What is brought forward? 'A lonely place, a Pond', 'by which an old man *was*, far from all house or home' – not stood or sat, but '*was*' – the figure presented in the most naked simplicity possible. This feeling of spirituality or supernaturalness is again referred to as being strong in my mind in this passage – '*How came he here* thought I or what can he be doing?' I then describe him whether ill or well is not for me to judge with perfect confidence, but this I can *confidently* affirm, that, though I believe that God has given me a strong imagination, I cannot conceive a figure more impressive than that of an old Man like this, the survivor of a Wife and ten children, travelling alone among the mountains and all lonely places, carrying with him his own fortitude, and the necessities which an unjust state of society has entailed upon him. You say and Mary (that is you can say no more than that) the Poem is *very well* after the introduction of the old man; this is not true, if it is not more than very well it is very bad, there is no intermediate state. You speak of his speech as tedious: everything is tedious when one does not read with the feelings of the author – *The Thorn* is tedious to hundreds; and so is *The Idiot Boy* to hundreds. It is the character of the old man to tell his story in a manner which an impatient reader must necessarily feel as tedious. But Good God! Such a figure in such a place, a pious self-respecting, miserably infirm, and [?   ] Old Man telling such a tale!

My dear Sara, it is not a matter of indifference whether you are pleased with this figure and his employment; it may be comparatively so, whether you are pleased or not with *this poem*; but it is of the utmost importance that you should have had pleasure from contemplating the fortitude, independence, persevering spirit and the general moral dignity of this old man's character. Your feelings upon the Mother, and the Boys with the Butterfly,[1] were not indifferent: it was an affair of whole continents of moral sympathy. I will talk more with you on this when we meet – at present, farewell and Heaven for ever bless you!

W.W.

William Wordsworth

from a letter to Richard Wordsworth   26 June 1803

A few days ago I had a letter from Mr Fox in which he says that he read the poems with great pleasure especially those in rhyme, he is not partial to blank verse. He mentioned *Goody Blake* etc., *The Mad Mother, The Idiot Boy* and *We are Seven* as having given him particular pleasure. I have had high encomiums on the poems from the most respectable quarters, indeed the highest authorities, both in literature, good sense, and people of consequence in the State. There is no doubt but that if my health should enable me to go on writing I shall be able to command my price with the Booksellers.

1 *Beggars.*

William Wordsworth

A footnote appended by Wordsworth on a letter of Dorothy's
to Sara Hutchinson 1801

For Coleridge's entertainment I send the following harmonies of
criticism

Nutting
Mr C. Wordsworth
worth its weight in gold

Nutting
Mr Stoddart
can make neither head nor tail
of it

To Joanna
Mr John Wordsworth
the finest poem of its length
you have written

To Joanna
Mr Stoddart
takes the description of the
echoes as a thing regularly to
be believed, of course can make
nothing of the poem

A Poet's Epitaph
Mr Charles Lamb
the latter part eminently good
and your own

A Poet's Epitaph
Mr Stoddart
The latter part I don't like, it is
very ill written

The Cumberland Beggar
Mr John Wordsworth
Indeed everybody seems
delighted with *Cumberland
Beggar*

The Cumberland Beggar
Mr Charles Lamb
The instructions too direct. You
seem to presume your readers
are stupid etc.

The Idiot Boy
Mr John Wordsworth
To a Lady, a friend of mine, I
gave the two volumes: they
were both new to her. The
Idiot Boy of all the poems her
delight: could talk of nothing
else.
But here comes the *Waggon*.

The Idiot Boy
Mr Stoddart
Thrown into a *fit* almost with
disgust, cannot *possibly* read it.

Anonymous

from a review of *Poems in Two Volumes, Critical Review*
August 1807

Had Mr Wordsworth set any bounds whatever to the excesses of
sentiment, had he given any admission to the suggestions of reason
and experience, had he resisted the overweening impulses of vanity,
and estimated properly the poor and wretched affectation of singularity, he had that within him which might have insured him a high
and distinguished literary reputation. He is gifted by nature with
pure and noble feelings, with a mind capable of admiring and enjoying all her charms, and a heart alive to the impressions of benevolence
and virtue. He has acquired the command of language and the power
of harmony. He possesses a warm imagination and all the enthusiasm
of genuine poetry.

  We are not among the numbers of his injudicious friends and
flatterers; yet our memory has often dwelt with delight on his
Tintern Abbey, his *Evening Sail to Richmond,* his *Michael,* and a few
more of his pieces contained in his first publication of *Lyrical Ballads.*
Even in our magisterial chair we are not ashamed to confess that he
has had the power to draw iron tears from our stony hearts. We wish
that we could say as much of any one of the numerous specimens
now before us. But, alas, we fear the mind of Mr W. has been too
long accustomed to the enervating debauchery of taste for us to
entertain much hope of his recovery. . . . He must undergo a certain
term of rigid penance and inward fortification, before he can become
what he once promised to be, the poet of the heart, and not the
capricious minion of a debasing affectation. But when the man to
whom in early youth, 'Nature was all in all: who cannot paint what
then he was,'; when that man is found in his ripe years, drivelling to
the redbreast, . . . and to a common pile-wort; . . . how can we
sufficiently lament the infatuation of self-conceit and our own
disappointed hopes?

  Is it possible for Mr Wordsworth not to feel that while he is pouring out his nauseous and nauseating sensibilities to weeds and insects,
he debases himself to a level with his idiot boy, infinitely below his
pretty Celandine and little butterfly?

Above all things we would entreat Mr Wordsworth to spend more time in his library and less in company with the moods of his own mind. If he is not too proud to be taught he may yet derive instruction and amendment from books; but in his present diseased state, he is the very worst companion for himself.

We have said that the present volumes contain no poems which will bear comparison with the best of his *Lyrical Ballads*. Yet there are a few which, though not free from affectation, would do credit to a poet of less acknowledged abilities. We here and there discover symptoms of reason and judgement, which we gladly hail as a proof that his mind is not yet irrecoverably lost in the vortex of false taste and puerile conceit.

William Wordsworth

from a letter to Francis Wrangham   November 1807

I am told that there has appeared in the said journal [*Critical Review*] an article purporting to be a review of those poems which is a miserable heap of spiteful nonsense, even worse than anything that has appeared hitherto, in these disgraceful days. I have not seen it, for I am only a chance-reader of reviews, but from what I have heard of the contents of this precious piece, I feel not so much inclined to accuse the author of malice as of sheer, honest insensibility and stupidity.

. . . I am much pleased that Mrs Wrangham and yourself have been gratified by these breathings of simple nature, the more so because I conclude, from the character of the poems which you have particularized, that the volumes cannot but improve upon you. I see that you have entered into the spirit of them. You mention the Daffodils; you know [a Mr Butler]; . . . when I was in Town in spring he happened to see the volumes lying upon Montagu's mantlepiece and to glance his eye upon this very poem of the daffodils; 'aye', says he, 'a fine morsel this for the Reviewers'. When this was told me, for I was not present, I observed that there were two lines in that little poem which if thoroughly felt would annihilate nine-tenths

of the Reviews of the Kingdom, as they would find no readers; the
lines I alluded to were those

They flash upon that inward eye,
Which is the bliss of Solitude.

Samuel Taylor Coleridge

'To William Wordsworth: Composed on the Night after his
Recitation of a Poem on the Growth of a Poet's Mind'
January 1807

Friend of the wise! and Teacher of the Good!
Into my heart have I received that Lay
More than historic, that prophetic Lay
Wherein (high theme by thee first sung aright)
Of the foundations and the building up
Of a Human Spirit thou hast dared to tell
What may be told, to the understanding mind
Revealable; and what within the mind
By vital breathings secret as the soul
Of vernal growth, oft quickens in the heart
Thoughts all too deep for words! –

            Theme hard as high!
Of smiles spontaneous, and mysterious fears
(The first-born they of Reason and twin-birth),
Amid the howl of more than wintry storms,
The Halcyon hears the voice of vernal hours
Already on the wing.

            Eve following eve,
Dear tranquil time, when the sweet sense of Home
Is sweetest! moments for their own sake hailed
And more desired, more precious, for thy song,
In silence listening, like a devout child,
My soul lay passive, by thy various strain
Driven as in surges now beneath the stars,
With momentary stars of my own birth,

Fair constellated foam, still darting off
Into the darkness; now a tranquil sea,
Outspread and bright, yet swelling to the moon.

And when – O Friend! my comforter and guide!
Strong in thyself, and powerful to give strength! –
Thy long sustained Song finally closed,
And thy deep voice had ceased – yet thou thyself
Wert still before my eyes, and round us both
That happy vision of beloved faces –
Scarce conscious, and yet conscious of its close
I sate, my being blended in one thought
(Thought was it? or aspiration? or resolve?)
Absorbed, yet hanging still upon the sound –
And when I rose, I found myself in prayer.

Francis Jeffrey

from a review of *Poems in Two Volumes* (1807),
Edinburgh Review   October 1807

The *Lyrical Ballads* were unquestionably popular; and, we have no
hesitation in saying, deservedly popular; for, in spite of their occasional vulgarity, affectation and silliness, they were undoubtedly
characterized by a strong spirit of originality, of pathos, and natural
feeling; and recommended to all good minds by the clear impression
which they bore of the amiable dispositions and virtuous principles
of the author. By the help of these qualities, they were enabled, not
only to recommend themselves to the indulgence of many judicious
readers, but even to beget among a pretty numerous class of persons,
a sort of admiration of the very defects by which they were attended.
It was upon this account chiefly, that we thought it necessary to set
ourselves against this alarming innovation. Childishness, conceit and
affectation, are not of themselves very popular or attractive; and
though mere novelty has sometimes been found sufficient to give
them a temporary currency, we should have had no fear of their
prevailing to any dangerous extent, if they had been graced with no
more seductive accompaniments. It was precisely because the per-

verseness and bad taste of this new school was combined with a great deal of genius and of laudable feeling, that we were afraid of their spreading and gaining ground among us, and that we entered into the discussion with a degree of zeal and animosity which some might think unreasonable towards authors, to whom so much merit had been conceded.[1] There were times and moods, in which we were led to suspect ourselves of unjustifiable severity, and to doubt whether a sense of public duty had not carried us rather too far in reprobation of errors, that seemed to be atoned for by excellences of no vulgar description. At other times the magnitude of these errors – the disgusting absurdities into which they led their feebler admirers, and the derision and contempt which they drew from the more fastidious, even upon the merits with which they were associated, made us wonder more than ever at the perversity by which they were retained, and regret that we had not declared ourselves against them with still more formidable and decided hostility. In this temper of mind we read the *annonce* of Mr Wordsworth's publication with greater anxiety, than he or his admirers will probably give us credit for.

We have been greatly disappointed as to the quality of the poetry; but we doubt whether the publication has afforded so much satisfaction to any of his other readers: it has freed us from all doubt or hesitation as to the justice of our former censures, and has brought the matter to a test, which we cannot help hoping may be convincing to the author himself.

Mr Wordsworth, we think, has now brought the question, as to the merits of his new school of poetry, to a very fair and decisive issue. The volumes before us are much more strongly marked by all its peculiarities than any former publication of the fraternity. In our apprehension, they are on this very account, infinitely less interesting or meritorious; but it belongs to the public, and not to us, to decide upon their merit, and we will confess, that so strong is our conviction of their obvious inferiority, and the grounds of it, that we are willing for once to waive our right of appealing to posterity, and to take the judgement of the present generation of readers, and even of Mr Wordsworth's former admirers, as conclusive on this occasion. If

1 Jeffrey is referring to his review of Southey's *Thalaba, Edinburgh Review*, October 1802.

these volumes, which have all the benefits of the author's former popularity, turn out to be nearly as popular as the *Lyrical Ballads* – if they sell to nearly the same extent, or are quoted and imitated among half as many individauls, we shall admit that Mr Wordsworth has come much nearer the truth in his judgement of what constitutes the charm of poetry, than we had previously imagined – and shall institute a more serious and respectful inquiry into his principles of composition than we have yet thought necessary. . . .

The end of poetry, we take it, is to please – and the name, we think, is strictly applicable to every metrical composition from which we receive pleasure, without any laborious exercise of the understanding. This pleasure may, in general, be analysed into three parts – that which we derive from the excitement of Passion or emotion – that which is derived from the play of Imagination, or the easy exercise of Reason – and that which depends on the character and qualities of the Diction. . . . The last has been alternately overrated and under-valued by the professors of the poetical art, and is in such low estima-tion with the author now before us, that it is necessary to say a few words in explanation of it.

One great beauty of diction exists only for those who have some degree of scholarship or critical skill. This is what depends on the exquisite *propriety* of the words employed, and the delicacy with which they are adapted to the meaning which is to be expressed. Many of the finest passages in Virgil and Pope derive their principal charm from the fine propriety of their diction. Another source of beauty, which extends only to the more instructed class of readers, is that which consists in the judicious or happy application of expressions which have been sanctified by the use of famous writers, or which bear the stamp of a simple or venerable antiquity. There are other beauties of diction, however, which are perceptible by all – the beauties of sweet sound and pleasant associations. The melody of words and verses is indifferent to no reader of poetry; but the chief recommendation of poetical language is certainly derived from those general associations, which give it a character of dignity or elegance, sublimity or tenderness. Everyone knows that there are low and mean expressions, as well as lofty and grave ones; and that some words bear the impression of coarseness and vulgarity, as clearly as others do of refinement and affection. We do not mean, of course, to

say anything in defence of the hackneyed common-places of ordinary
versemen. Whatever might have been the original character of these
unlucky phrases, they are now associated with nothing but ideas of
schoolboy imbecility and vulgar affectation. But what we do maintain is, that much of the most popular poetry in the world owes its
celebrity chiefly to the beauty of its diction; and that no poetry can
be long or generally acceptable, the language of which is coarse,
inelegant or infantine.

From this great source of pleasure, we think the readers of Mr
Wordsworth are in a great measure cut off. His diction has nowhere
any pretensions to elegance or dignity; and he has scarcely ever
condescended to give the grace of correctness or melody to his versification. If it were merely slovenly and neglected, however, all this
might be ignored. Strong sense and powerful feeling will ennoble
any expressions; or, at least, no one who is capable of estimating
those higher merits, will be disposed to mark these little defects. But,
in good truth, no man, nowadays, composes verse for publication
with a slovenly neglect of their language. It is a fine and laborious
manufacture, which can scarcely ever be made in a hurry; and the
faults which it has, may, for the most part, be set down to bad taste
or incapacity, rather than to carelessness or oversight. With Mr
Wordsworth and his friends, it is plain that their peculiarities of
diction are things of choice, and not of accident. They write as they
do, upon principle and system; and it evidently costs them much
pains to keep *down* to the standard which they have proposed to
themselves. They are, to the full, as much mannerists, too, as the
poetasters who ring changes on the commonplaces of magazine
versification; and all the difference between them is, that they borrow
their phrases from a different and a scantier *gradus ad Parnassum*. If
they were, indeed, to discard all imitation and set phraseology, and to
bring in no words merely for show or for metre – as much, perhaps,
might be gained in freedom and originality, as would infallibly be
lost in allusion and authority; but, in point of fact, the new poets are
just as great borrowers as the old; only that, instead of borrowing
from the more popular passages of their illustrious predecessors, they
have preferred furnishing themselves from vulgar ballads and plebeian
nurseries.

Their peculiarities of diction alone, are enough, perhaps, to render them ridiculous; but the author before us really seems anxious to court this literary martyrdom by a device still more infallible – we mean, that of connecting his most lofty, tender, or impassioned conceptions, with objects and incidents, which the greater part of his readers will probably persist in thinking low, silly, or uninteresting. Whether this is done from affectation and conceit alone, or whether it may not arise, from the self-illusion of a mind of extraordinary sensibility, habituated to solitary meditation, we cannot undertake to determine. It is possible enough, we allow, that the sight of a friend's garden spade, or a sparrow's nest, or a man gathering leeches might really have suggested to such a mind a train of powerful impressions and interesting reflections; but it is certain, that, to most minds, such associations will always appear forced, strained and unnatural; and that the composition in which it is attempted to exhibit them will always have the air of parody, or ludicrous and affected singularity. All the world laughs at Elegiac stanzas to a sucking-pig – a Hymn on Washing-day – Sonnets to one's grand-mother – or Pindarics on gooseberry-pie; and yet, we are afraid, it will not be quite easy to convince Mr Wordsworth, that the same ridicule must infallibly attach to most of the pathetic pieces in these vol-umes. . . .

All English writers of sonnets have imitated Milton, and, in this way, Mr Wordsworth, when he writes sonnets escapes again from the trammels of his own unfortunate system; and the consequence is, that his sonnets are as much superior to the greater part of his other poems, as Milton's sonnets are superior to his.

Francis Jeffrey

from a review on George Crabbe, *Edinburgh Review* April 1808

Mr Crabbe exhibits the common people of England pretty much as they are, and as they must appear to every one who will take the trouble of examining into their condition; at the same time that he renders his sketches in a very high degree interesting and beautiful – by selecting what is most fit for description – by grouping them into such forms as must catch the attention or awake the memory – and by scattering over the whole, such traits of moral sensibility, of sarcasm and of useful reflection, as every one must feel to be natural, and own to be powerful. The gentlemen of the new school, on the other hand, scarcely ever condescend to take their subjects from any description of persons that are at all known to the common inhabitants of the world; but invent for themselves certain whimsical and unheard of beings, to whom they impute some fantastical combination of feelings, and labour to excite our sympathy for them, either by placing them in incredible situations, or by some strained and exaggerated moralization of a vague and tragical description. Mr Crabbe, in short, shows us something which we have all seen, or may see, in real life; and draws from it such feelings and such reflections as every human being must acknowledge that it is calculated to excite. He delights us by the truth, and vivid and picturesque beauty of his representations, and by the force and pathos of the sensations with which we feel that they ought to be connected. Mr Wordsworth and his associates show us something that mere observation never yet suggested to any one. They introduce us to beings whose existence was not previously suspected by the acutest observers of nature; and excite an interest for them, more by an eloquent and refined analysis of their own capricious feelings, than by any obvious or very intelligible ground of sympathy in their situation. The common sympathies of our nature, and our general knowledge of human character, do not enable us either to understand, or to enter into the feelings of their characters. They are unique specimens and varieties of our kind, and must be studied under a separate classification. They have an idiosyncrasy, upon which all common occurrences operate in a peculiar manner; and those who are best acquainted with human nature, and with other poetry, are at a loss to comprehend the new system of feeling and of writing which is here introduced to their notice. Instead of the men and women of ordinary humanity, we have certain moody and capricious personages, made after the poet's own heart and fancy – acting upon principles, and speaking in a language of their own. Thus, instead of employing the plain vulgar character, which may be read by all the world, these writers make use of a sort of cypher, which can only be learned with pains and study; and, dressing up all their persons in a kind of grotesque masquerade habit, they have given birth to a species of composition more fantastic and unnatural than a pastoral or an opera. Into this unnatural composition, however, they have introduced a great deal of eloquence and beauty, and have put many natural thoughts and touching expressions into the mouths of their imaginary persons. By this means, and by the novelty of their manner, they have seduced many into a great admiration of their genius, and even made some willing to believe, that their conception of character is in itself just and natural, and that all preceding writers have been in an error with regard to that great element of poetry. Many, to be sure, found it impossible to understand either their precepts or their example; and, unable to recognize the traits of our common nature in the strange habiliments with which these ingenious persons had adorned it, gave up the attempt in despair and, recurring to easier authors, looked on, with mixed wonder and contempt, while they were collecting the suffrages of their admirers. Many, however, did understand a part; and, in their raised imaginations, fancied that they admired the whole: while others, who only guessed at a passage here and there, laboured, by their encomiums, to have it thought that there was nothing which passed their comprehension.

Those who are acquainted with the *Lyrical Ballads*, or the more recent publication of Mr Wordsworth, will scarcely deny the justice of this representation; but in order to vindicate it to such as do not enjoy that inestimable advantage, we must beg leave to make a few hasty references to the former, and by far the least exceptionable of these productions.

A village schoolmaster, for instance, is a pretty common poetical character. Goldsmith has drawn him inimitably; so has Shenstone, with the slight change of sex; and Mr Crabbe, in two passages, has followed their footsteps. Now, Mr Wordsworth has a village schoolmaster also – a personage who makes no small figure in three or four of his poems. But by what traits is this worthy old gentleman delineated by the new poet? No pedantry – no innocent vanity of learning – no mixture of indulgence with the pride of power, and of poverty with the consciousness of rare acquirements. Every feature which belongs to the situation, or marks the character in common apprehension, is scornfully discarded by Mr Wordsworth, who represents this grey-haired rustic pedagogue as a sort of half crazy, sentimental person, overrun with fine feelings, constitutional merriment, and a most humorous melancholy. Here are the two stanzas in which this consistent and intelligible character is portrayed. The diction is at least as new as the conception.

> The sighs which Mathew heard were sighs
>   Of one tired out with *fear* and *madness*;
> The tears which came to Mathew's eyes
>   Were tears of light – *the oil of gladness*.
>
> Yet sometimes, when the secret cup
>   Of still and serious thought went round,
> He seemed as if he *drank it up*,
>   He felt with spirit so profound.
> Thou *soul*, of God's best *earthly mould*,[1] &c.

A frail damsel is a character common enough in all poems; and one upon which many fine and pathetic lines have been expended. Mr Wordsworth has written more than three hundred lines on that subject: but, instead of new images of tenderness, or delicate representation of intelligible feelings, he has contrived to tell us nothing whatever of the unfortunate fair one, but that her name is Martha Ray; and that she goes up to the top of a hill, in a red cloak, and cries 'O misery!' All the rest of the poem is filled with a description of an old thorn and a pond, and of the silly stories which the neighbouring old women told about them.

The sports of childhood, and the untimely death of promising youth, is also a common topic of poetry. Mr Wordsworth has made some blank verse about it; but, instead of the delightful and picturesque sketches with which so many authors of moderate talents have presented us on this inviting subject, all that he is pleased to communicate of the rustic child, is, that he used to amuse himself with shouting to the owls, and hearing them answer. To make amends for this brevity, the process of his mimicry is most accurately described.

> With fingers interwoven, both hands
> Press'd closely, palm to palm, and to his mouth
> Uplifted, he, as through an instrument,

1 Jeffrey misquotes in l.1: Wordsworth wrote Matthew not Mathew; heaved not heard; l.2: fun not fear; in 1815 Wordsworth revised *oil* to *dew* (l.4); there is no comma after *soul* (l.9) (*Matthew*, ll. 21–9).

Blew mimic hootings to the silent owls,
That they might answer him.[1]

This is all we hear of him; and for the sake of this one accomplishment, we are told, that the author has frequently stood mute, and gazed on his grave for half an hour together!

Love, and the fantasies of lovers, have afforded an ample theme to poets of all ages. Mr Wordsworth, however, has thought fit to compose a piece, illustrating this copious subject by one single thought. A lover trots away to see his mistress one fine evening, staring all the way at the moon: when he comes to her door,

O mercy! to myself I cried,
If Lucy should be dead!

And there the poem ends!

Now, we leave it to any reader of common candour and discernment to say, whether these representations of character and sentiment are drawn from that eternal and universal standard of truth and nature, which every one is knowing enough to recognize, and no one great enough to depart from with impunity; or whether they are not formed, as we have described them, upon certain fantastic and affected peculiarities in the mind or fancy of the author, into which it is most improbable that many of his readers will enter, and which cannot, in some cases, be comprehended without much effort and explanation. Instead of multiplying instances of these wide and wilful aberrations from ordinary nature, it may be more satisfactory to produce the author's own admission of the narrowness of the plan upon which he writes, and of the very extraordinary circumstances which he himself sometimes thinks it necessary for his readers to keep in view, in order to understand the beauty or propriety of his delineations.

A pathetic tale of guilt or superstition may be told, we are apt to fancy, by the poet himself, in his general character of poet, with full as much effect as by any other person. An old nurse, at any rate, or a monk or parish clerk, is always at hand to give grace to such a narration. None of these, however, would satisfy Mr Wordsworth. He has written a long poem of this sort, in which he thinks it indispens-

1 'There was a boy', ll. 7–11.

ably necessary to apprise the reader, that he has endeavoured to represent the language and sentiments of a particular character – of which character, he adds,

the reader will have a general notion, if he has ever known a man, *a captain of a small trading vessel*, for example, who, being *past the middle age of life*, has retired upon *an annuity, or small independent income*, to some *village* or country town, of which he was *not a native*, or in which he had not been accustomed to live.

Now, we must be permitted to doubt, whether, among all the readers of Mr Wordsworth, there is a single individual who has had the happiness of knowing a person of this very peculiar description; or who is capable of forming any sort of conjecture of the particular disposition and turn of thinking which such a combination of attributes would be apt to produce. To us, we will confess, the *annonce* appears as ludicrous and absurd as it would be in the author of an ode or an epic to say,

of this piece the reader will necessarily form a very erroneous judgement, unless he is apprised, that it was written by a pale man in a green coat, sitting cross-legged on an oaken stool, with a scratch on his nose, and a spelling dictionary on the table.[1]

1 Some of our readers may have a curiosity to know in what manner this old annuitant captain expresses himself in the village of his adoption. For their gratification, we annex the two first stanzas of his story, in which, with all the attention we have been able to bestow, we have been utterly unable to detect any characteristic traits, either of a seaman, an annuitant or a stranger in a country town. It is a style, on the contrary, which we should ascribe, without hesitation, to a certain poetical fraternity in the West of England, and which, we verily believe, never was, and never will be, used by any one out of that fraternity.

William Wordsworth

from a letter to Richard Sharp　29 September 1808

After all, if the Picture (... about *The Apothecary*[1]) were true to nature, what claim would it have to be called Poetry? At the best, it is the meanest kind of satire, except the merely personal. The sum of all is, that nineteen out of twenty of Crabbe's Pictures are mere matters of fact; with which the Muses have just about as much to do as they have with a collection of medical reports, or law cases.

Francis Jeffrey

from an article on Robert Burns, *Edinburgh Review*　January 1809

Our other remark is of a more limited application; and is addressed chiefly to the followers and patrons of that new school of poetry, against which we have thought it our duty to neglect no opportunity of testifying. Those gentlemen are outrageous for simplicity; and we beg leave to recommend to them the simplicity of Burns. He has copied the spoken language of passion and affection, with infinitely more fidelity than they have ever done, on all occasions which properly admitted of such adaptation: but he has not rejected the helps of elevated language and habitual associations; nor debased his composition by an affectation of babyish interjections, and all the puling expletives of an old nurserymaid's vocabulary. They may look long enough among his nervous and manly lines, before they find any 'Good lacks!' – 'Dear hearts!' – or 'As a body may say,' in them; or any stuff about dancing daffodils and sister Emmelines. Let them think, with what infinite contempt the powerful mind of Burns would have perused the story of Alice Fell and her duffle cloak, of Andrew Jones and the half-crown, or of Little Dan without breeches, and his thievish grandfather.[2] Let them contrast their own fantastical personages of hysterical schoolmasters and sentuous leechgatherers,

---

1 Referring to the portrait in George Crabbe's *The Borough*.
2 *The Two Thieves*.

with the authentic rustics of Burns's *Cotters's Saturday Night*, and his inimitable songs; and reflect on the different reception which these personifications have met with from the public. Though they will not be reclaimed from their puny affectations by the example of their learned predecessors, they may, perhaps, submit to be admonished by a self-taught and illiterate poet, who drew from Nature far more directly than they can do, and produced something so much like the admired copies of the masters whom they have abjured.

James Montgomery

from a review of *Poems in Two Volumes*, *Eclectic Review*
January 1808

His *Cumberland Beggar*, *Tintern Abbey*, his *Verses on the Naming of Places*, and some other pieces in his former volumes, have taught us new sympathies, the existence of which in our nature has scarcely been intimated to us by any preceding poet. But Mr Wordsworth must be reminded that in these his most successful pieces, he has attired his thoughts in diction of transcendent beauty. We will quote two brief passages from *Tintern Abbey*:

For I have learned
To look on nature, not as in the hour
Of thoughtless youth, but hearing oftentimes
The still sad music of humanity,
Nor harsh nor grating, though of ample power
To chasten and subdue. And I have felt
A presence that disturbs me with the joy
Of elevated thoughts; a sense sublime
Of something far more deeply interfused,
Whose dwelling is the light of setting suns,
And the round ocean, and the living air,
And the blue sky, and in the mind of man:
A motion and a spirit, that impels
All thinking things, all objects of all thought,
And rolls through all things.

Therefore let the moon
Shine on thee in thy solitary walk;
And let the misty mountain winds be free
To blow against thee; and in after years,
When these wild ecstasies shall be matured
Into a sober pleasure, when thy mind
Shall be a mansion for all lovely forms,
Thy memory be as a dwelling place
For all sweet sounds and harmonies; Oh! then,
If solitude, or fear, or pain, or grief,
Should be thy portion, with what healing thoughts
Of tender joy wilt thou remember me,
And these my exhortations!

This is no more the language than these are the thoughts of men in general in a state of excitement; language more exquisitely elaborate and thoughts more patiently worked out of the very marble of the mind, we rarely met with in any writer of either prose or verse. For such tales as *Andrew Jones, The Last of the Flock, Goody Blake and Harry Gill* etc., 'the real language of men' may be employed with pleasing effect; but when Mr Wordsworth would 'Present ordinary things in an unusual way, by casting over them a certain colouring of imagination', he is compelled very frequently to resort to splendid, figurative and amplifying language. ... These volumes are distinguished by the same blemishes and beauties as were found in their predecessors, but in an inverse proportion; the defects of the poet, in this performance, being as much greater than his merits as they were less in his former publication. It is remarkable that we have not, among all the piebald miscellanies before us, a single example of that species of poetry, for which the author's theory of diction and his habits of thinking peculiarly qualify him. The blank verse was the glory of his former volumes and in these there is not a trace of it. But songs we have, and sonnets, and stories of every length and form of versification and of every style and character from sublimity to silliness. Most of these are reveries in rhyme, in which the Poet's mind seems to be delightfully dreaming while his thoughts are romping at random, and playing all manner of mischievous pranks about him; assuming at pleasure the most antic shapes, tricking themselves with the gaudiest colours, sporting at large in every field of fancy and spurning with gallant independence every rule of art and every sanction of precedent for the government of licentious genius. It would be in vain to attempt to characterize all the contents of these incomparable and almost incomprehensible volumes. A more rash and injudicious speculation on the weakness or the depravity of the public taste has seldom been made, and we trust that its inevitable failure will bring back Mr Wordsworth himself to a sense of his own dignity.

A specimen of Mr Wordsworth's finest talent – that of *personal description* – may be found in a poem which we have not room to quote, though we consider it the best in the volume, entitled *Resolution and Independence*.

William Wordsworth

from a letter to Sir George Beaumont   January/February 1808

I am quite delighted to hear of your picture for *Peter Bell*; I was much pleased with the sketch, and I have no doubt that the picture will surpass it as far as a picture ought to do. I long much to see it. I should approve of any engraver approved of by you. But remember that no poem of mine will ever be popular; and I am afraid that the sale of Peter would not carry the expense of the engraving, and that the poem, in the estimation of the public, would be a weight upon the print. I say not this in modest disparagement of the poem, but in sorrow for the sickly taste of the public in verse. The *People* would love the poem of *Peter Bell*, but the *public* (a very different being) will never love it. Thanks for dear Lady B.'s transcript of your friend's letter; it is written with candour, but I must say a word or two not in praise of it. 'Instances of what I mean,' says your friend, 'are to be found in a poem on a daisy' (by the bye, it is on *the* Daisy, a mighty difference!) 'and on the Daffodils *reflected in the water*!' . . . what shall we think of criticism or judgement founded upon, and exemplified by, a poem which must have been so inattentively perused? My language is precise; and, therefore, it would be false modesty to charge myself with blame.

>   Beneath the trees
> Ten thousand dancing in the *breeze*.
> The *waves beside* them danced, but they
> Outdid the *sparkling waves* in glee.

Can expression be more distinct? And let me ask your friend how it is possible for flowers to be *reflected* in water where there are waves? They may indeed in *still* water; but the very object of my poem is the trouble or agitation, both of the flowers and the water. I must needs respect the understanding of every one honoured by your friendship; but sincerity compels me to say that my poems must be more nearly looked at before they can give rise to any remarks of much value, even from the strongest minds. . . .

A letter was also sent to me, addressed to a friend of mine, and by him communicated to me, in which this identical poem was singled out for fervent approbation. What then shall we say? Why, let the poet first consult his own heart, as I have done, and leave the rest to posterity; to, I hope, an improving posterity. The fact is, the English *Public* are at this moment in the same state of mind with respect to my poems, if small things may be compared with great, as the French are in respect to Shakespeare; and not the French alone, but almost the whole Continent. In short, in your friend's letter, I am condemned for the very thing for which I ought to have been praised; viz., that I have not written down to the level of superficial observers and un-thinking minds. Every great poet is a teacher: I wish either to be considered as a teacher, or as nothing.

William Wordsworth

from a letter to Lady Beaumont   21 May 1807

It is impossible that any expectations can be lower than mine concerning the immediate effect of this little work upon what is called the Public. I do not here take into consideration the envy and malevolence and all the bad passions which always stand in the way of a work of any merit from a living poet; but merely think of the pure absolute honest ignorance, in which all worldlings of every rank and situation must be enveloped, with respect to the thoughts, feelings and images, on which the life of my poems depends. The things which I have taken, whether from within or without – what have they to do with routs, dinners, morning calls, hurry from door to door, from street to street, on foot or in carriage; with Mr Pitt or Mr Fox, Mr Paul or Sir Francis Burdett, the Westminster Election or the Borough of Honiton; in a word, for I cannot stop to make my way through the hurry of images that present themselves to me, what have they to do with endless talking about things nobody cares for except as far as their own vanity is concerned, and this with persons they care nothing for but as their vanity or *selfishness* is concerned; what have they to do (to say all at once) with a life without love? In such a life there can be no thought; for we have no thought (save thoughts of pain) but as far as we have love and admiration. It is an awful truth, that there neither is, nor can be, any genuine enjoyment of Poetry among nineteen out of twenty of those persons who live, or wish to live, in the broad light of the world – among those who either are, or are striving to make themselves, people of consideration in society. This is a truth, and an awful one, because to be incapable of a feeling of Poetry in my sense of the word is to be without love of human nature and reverence for God.

Upon this I shall insist elsewhere; at present let me confine myself to my object, which is to make you, my dear Friend, as easy-hearted as myself with respect to these Poems. Trouble not yourself upon their present reception; of what moment is that compared with what I trust is their destiny, to console the afflicted, to add sunshine to daylight by making the happy happier, to teach the young and the gracious of every age, to see, to think and feel, and therefore to become more actively and securely virtuous; this is their office, which I trust they will faithfully perform long after we (that is, all that is mortal of us) are mouldered in our graves. I am well aware how far it would seem to many I overrate my own exertions when I speak in this way, in direct connection with the Volumes I have just made public.

I am not, however, afraid of such censure, insignificant as probably the majority of those poems would appear to very respectable persons; I do not mean London wits and witlings, for these have too many bad passions about them to be respectable even if they had more intellect than the benign laws of providence will allow to such a heartless existence as theirs is; but grave, kindly-natured, worthy persons, who would be pleased if they could. I hope that these Volumes are not without some recommendations, even for Readers of this class, but their imagination has slept; and the voice which is the voice of my Poetry without Imagination cannot be heard.

Leaving these, I was going to say a word to such Readers as Mr Rogers. Such! – how would he be offended if he knew I considered him only as a representative of a class, and not an unique! 'Pity,' says Mr R., 'that so many trifling things should be admitted to obstruct the view of those that have merit;' now, let this candid judge take, by way of example, the sonnets, which, probably, with the exception of two or three other Poems for which I will not contend appear to him the most trifling, as they are the shortest, I would say to him, omitting things of higher consideration, there is one thing which must strike you at once if you will only read these poems – that those to Liberty, at least, have a connection with, or a bearing upon, each other, and therefore, if individually they want weight, perhaps, as a Body, they may not be so deficient, at least this ought to induce you to suspend your judgement, and qualify it so far as to allow that the writer aims at least at comprehensiveness. But dropping this, I would boldly say at once, that these Sonnets, while they each fix the attention upon some important sentiment separately considered, do at the same time collectively make a Poem on the subject of civil Liberty and national independence, which, either for simplicity of style or grandeur of moral sentiment, is, alas! likely to have few parallels in the Poetry of the present day. Again, turn to the 'Moods of my own Mind'. There is scarcely a Poem here of above thirty Lines, and very trifling these poems will appear to many; but, omitting to speak of them individually, do they not, taken collectively, fix the attention upon a subject eminently poetical, viz., the interest which objects in nature derive from the predominance of certain affections more or less permanent, more or less capable of salutary renewal in the mind of the being contemplating these objects? This is poetic, and essentially poetic, and why? Because it is creative.

But I am wasting words, for it is nothing more than you know, and if said to those for whom it is intended, it would not be understood.

I see by your last Letter that Mrs Fermor has entered into the spirit of these 'Moods of my own Mind'. Your transcript from her Letter gave me the greatest pleasure; but I must say that even she has something yet to receive from me. I say this with confidence, from her thinking that I have fallen below myself in the Sonnet beginning— 'With ships the sea was sprinkled far and nigh.' As to the other which she objects to, I will only observe that there is a misprint in the last line but two, 'And *though* this wilderness' for 'And *through* this wilderness' – that makes it unintelligible. This latter Sonnet for many reasons, though I do not abandon it, I will not now speak of; but upon the other, I could say something important in conversation, and will attempt now to illustrate it by a comment which I feel will be very inadequate to convey my meaning. There is scarcely one of my Poems which does not aim to direct the attention to some moral sentiment, or to some general principle, or law of thought, or of our intellectual constitution. For instance in the present case, who is there that has not felt that the mind can have no rest among a multitude of objects, of which it either cannot make one whole, or from which it cannot single out one individual, whereupon may be concentrated the attention divided among or distracted by a multitude? After a certain time we must either select one image or object, which must put out of view the rest wholly, or must subordinate them to itself while it stands forth as a Head:

> Now glowed the firmament
> With living sapphires! Hesperus, that *led*
> The starry host, rode brightest; till the Moon,
> Rising in clouded majesty, at length,
> Apparent *Queen*, unveiled *her peerless* light,
> And o'er the dark her silver mantle threw.[1]

Having laid this down as a general principle, take the case before us. I am represented in the Sonnet as casting my eyes over the sea, sprinkled with a multitude of Ships, like the heavens with stars, my mind may be supposed to float up and down among them in a kind of dreamy indifference with respect either to this or that one, only in a pleasurable state of feeling with respect to the whole prospect. 'Joyously it showed,' this continued till that feeling may be supposed

[1] *Paradise Lost*, iv, 604–9.

to have passed away, and a kind of comparative listlessness or apathy
to have succeeded, as at this line, 'Some veering up and down, one
knew not why.' All at once, while I am in this state, comes forth an
object, an individual, and my mind, sleepy and unfixed, is awakened
and fastened in a moment. 'Hesperus, that *led* The starry host,' is a
poetical object, because the glory of his own nature gives him the
preeminence the moment he appears; he calls forth the poetic faculty,
receiving its exertions as a tribute; but this Ship in the Sonnet may,
in a manner still more appropriate, be said to come upon a mission
of the poetic Spirit, because in its own appearance and attributes it is
barely sufficiently distinguish[ed] to rouse the creative faculty of the
human mind; to exertions at all times welcome, but doubly so when
they come upon us when in a state of remissness. The mind being
once fixed and roused, all the rest comes from itself; it is merely a
lordly Ship, nothing more:

This ship was nought to me, nor I to her,
Yet I pursued her with a lover's look.

My mind wantons with grateful joy in the exercise of its own powers,
and, loving its own creation,

This ship to all the rest I did prefer,

making her a sovereign or a regent, and thus giving body and life to
all the rest; mingling up this idea with fondness and praise

where she comes the winds must stir;

and concluding the whole with

On went She, and due north her journey took.

Thus taking up again the Reader with whom I began, letting him
know how long I must have watched this favourite vessel, and inviting him to rest his mind as mine is resting.

Having said so much upon a mere fourteen lines, which Mrs
Fermor did not approve, I cannot but add a word or two upon my
satisfaction in finding that my mind has so much in common with
hers, and that we participate so many of each other's pleasures. I
collect this from her having singled out the two little Poems, the
Daffodils, and the Rock crowned with snowdrops. I am quite sure

that whoever is pleased with either of these quiet and tender delineations must be fitted to walk through the recesses of my poetry with delight, and will there recognize, at every turn, something or other in which, and over which, it has that property and right which knowledge and love confer. The line 'Come, blessed barrier, etc.' in the sonnet upon Sleep, which Mrs F. points out, had before been mentioned to me by Coleridge, and indeed by almost everybody who had heard it, as eminently beautiful. My letter (as this second sheet, which I am obliged to take, admonishes me) is growing to an enormous length; and yet, saving that I have expressed my calm confidence that these Poems will live, I have said nothing which has a particular application to the object of it, which was to remove all disquiet from your mind on account of the condemnation they may at present incur from that portion of my contemporaries who are called the Public. I am sure, my dear Lady Beaumont, if you attach any importance [to it] it can only be from an apprehension that it may affect me, upon which I have already set you at ease, or from a fear that this present blame is ominous of their future or final destiny. If this be the case, your tenderness for me betrays you; be assured that the decision of these persons has nothing to do with the Question; they are altogether incompetent judges. These people in the senseless hurry of their idle lives do not *read* books, they merely snatch a glance at them that they may talk about them. And even if this were not so, never forget what I believe was observed to you by Coleridge, that every great and original writer, in proportion as he is great or original, must himself create the taste by which he is to be relished; he must teach the art by which he is to be seen; this, in a certain degree even to all persons, however wise and pure may be their lives, and however unvitiated their taste; but for those who dip into books in order to give an opinion of them, or talk about them to take up an opinion – for this multitude of unhappy, and misguided, and misguiding beings, an entire regeneration must be produced; and if this be possible, it must be a work *of time*. To conclude, my ears are stone-dead to this idle buzz, and my flesh as insensible as iron to these petty stings; and after what I have said I am sure yours will be the same. I doubt not that you will share with me an invincible confidence that my writings (and among them these little Poems) will cooperate with the benign tendencies in human nature and society, wherever found;

and that they will, in their degree, be efficacious in making men wiser, better and happier. Farewell; I will not apologize for this Letter, though its length demands an apology. Believe me, eagerly wishing for the happy day when I shall see you and Sir George here, most affectionately yours,

Wm Wordsworth

Robert Southey

from a letter to Anna Seward   December 1807

It is the vice of Wordsworth's intellect to be always upon the stretch and strain – to look at pile-worts and daffodowndillies through the same telescope which he applies to the moon and stars, and to find fit subjects for philosophizing and fine feeling in every peasant and vagabond he meets. Had I been his adviser, a great part of his last volume should have been suppressed. ... *The Lyrical Ballads* have failed not because the language of conversation is little adapted to the purpose of poetic pleasure, but because it has been tried upon uninteresting subjects.

Henry Crabb Robinson

from a letter to Thomas Robinson   March 1808

He expatiated with warmth on them. And spoke of them with that unaffected zeal which pleased me, though the customs of life do not authorize it. He explained some of the most exceptionable and I was flattered to find his own opinion of them so correspondent with my own. The sonnet which he is most anxious to have popular because he says, were it generally admired, it would evince an elevation of mind and a strength and purity of fancy which we have not yet witnessed. It is the admirable 'Two voices are there'; you will recollect this was my favourite. He explained the *Beggars* as I understood it. It is a poetical exhibition of the power of physical beauty and the charm of health and vigour even in the state of the greatest moral

depravity. 'Once in a lonely hamlet':[1] ... displays, he says, more
than any other of his poems a profound knowledge of Woman's
heart. He could feel no respect for the Mother who could read it
without emotion and admiration. Wordsworth quotes his own verses
with pleasure and seems to attach to the approbation of them a
greater connection with moral worth which others may deem the
effect of vanity. I think myself there is a danger of his not allowing
enough for the influence of unconventional and habitual taste in
making those dislike his poems as poems whose sensibility is yet
awake to the moral truths and sentiments they teach and exhibit. He
also speaks with a contempt for others which I think very censurable.

Francis Jeffrey

from a review of John Wilson's *The Isle of Palms*,
Edinburgh Review 1812

Mr Wilson is not free from some of the faults of diction which we
think belong to his school [i.e. of Wordsworth and Southey]. He is
occasionally mystical and not seldom childish. But he has less of these
peculiarities than most of his associates: and there is one more important fault from which, we think, he has escaped altogether. We
allude now to the offensive assumption of exclusive taste, judgement
and morality which pervades most of the writings of this tuneful
brotherhood. There is a tone of tragic, keen and intolerant reprobation in all the censures they bestow, that is not a little alarming to
ordinary sinners. Everything they do not like is accursed, and pestilent,
and inhuman; and they can scarcely differ from any body upon a point
of criticism, politics or metaphysics, without wondering what a heart
he must have; and expressing, not merely dissent, but loathing and
abhorrence. Neither is it very difficult to perceive, that they think it
barely possible for anyone to have any just notion of poetry, any
genuine warmth of affection or philanthropy, or any large views as
to the true principles of happiness and virtue, who does not agree
with them in most of their vagaries, and live a life very nearly akin
to that which they have elected for themselves. The inhabitants of

1 *The Emigrant Mother.*

towns, therefore, and most of those who are engaged in the ordinary business or pleasures of society, are cast off without ceremony as *demoralized* or *denatured* beings; and it would evidently be a considerable stretch of charity in these new apostles of taste and wisdom, to believe that any one of this description could have a genuine relish for the beauties of nature – could feel any ardent or devoted attachment to another – or even comprehend the great principles upon which private and public virtue must be founded.

William Hazlitt

from a review of *The Excursion, Examiner*   21, 28 August, 2 October 1814

In power of intellect, in lofty conception, in the depth of feeling, at once simple and sublime, which pervades every part of it, and which gives to every object an almost preternatural and preterhuman interest, this work has seldom been surpassed. The poem of *The Excursion* resembles that part of the country in which the scene is laid. It has the same vastness and magnificence, overwhelming, oppressive power. It excites or recalls the same sensations which those who have traversed that wonderful scenery must have felt. We are surrounded with the constant sense and superstitious awe of the collective power of matter, of the gigantic and eternal forms of nature, on which, from the beginning of time, the hand of man has made no impression. Here are no dotted lines, no hedgerow beauties, no box-tree borders, no gravel walks, no square mechanic enclosures; all is left loose and irregular in the rude chaos of aboriginal nature. The boundaries of hill and valley are the poet's only geography, and we wander with him incessantly over deep beds of moss and waving fern, amidst the troops of red deer and wild animals. Such is the severe simplicity of Mr Wordsworth's taste that I doubt whether he would not reject a druidical temple, or time hallowed ruin, as too modern or artificial for his purpose. He only familiarizes himself or his readers with a stone, covered with lichens, which has slept on the same spot of ground from the creation of the world, or with the rocky fissure between two mountains caused by thunder, or with a cavern scooped out by the sea. His mind is, as it were, coeval with the primary forms of things; his imagination holds immediately from nature and 'owes no allegiance' but 'to the elements'.

The Excursion may be considered as a philosophical pastoral poem, as a scholastic romance. It is less a poem on the country than on the love of country. It is not so much a description of natural objects as of the feelings associated with them; not an account of the manners of rural life, but the result of the poet's reflections on it. He does not present the reader with a lively succession of images or incidents, but paints the outgoings of his own heart, the shapings of his own fancy. He may be said to create his own materials; his thoughts are his real subjects. His understanding broods over that which is 'without form and void' and 'makes it pregnant'. He sees all things in himself. He hardly ever avails himself of remarkable objects or situations, but, in general, rejects them as interfering with the workings of his own mind, as disturbing the smooth, deep, majestic current of his own feelings. Thus his descriptions of natural scenery are not brought home distinctly to the naked eye by forms and circumstances, but every object is seen through the medium of innumerable recollections, is clothed with the haze of imagination like the glittering vapour, is obscured with the excess of glory, has the shadowy brightness of a waking dream. The image is lost in the sentiment, as sound in the multiplication of echoes,

And visions, as prophetic eyes avow,
Hang on each leaf, and cling to every bough.

In describing human nature, Mr Wordsworth equally shuns the common vantage-grounds of popular story, of striking incident or fatal catastrophe, as cheap and vulgar modes of producing an effect. He scans the human race as the naturalist measures the earth's zone, without attending to the picturesque points of view, the abrupt inequalities of the surface. He contemplates the passions and habits of men, not in their extremes but the first elements; their follies and vices, not at their height, with all their embossed seeds upon their heads, but as lurking in embryo, the seeds of the disorder inwoven with our very constitution. He only sympathizes with those simple forms of feeling which mingle at once with his own identity, or with the stream of general humanity. To him the great and small are the same; the near and the remote; what appears and what only is. The general and the permanent, like the Platonic ideas, are his only realities. All accidental varieties and individual contrasts are lost in an endless continuity of feeling, like drops of water in the ocean stream. An intense intellectual egotism swallows up everything. Even the dialogues introduced in the present volume are soliloquies of the same character, taking three different views of one subject. The recluse, the pastor and the pedlar, are three persons in one poet. We ourselves disapprove of these interlocutions between Lucius and Caius as impertinent babbling, where there is no dramatic distinction of character. But the evident scope and tendency of Mr Wordsworth's mind is the reverse of dramatic. It resists all change of character, all variety of scenery, all the hustle, machinery, and pantomime of the stage or of real life – whatever might relieve or relax or change the direction of its own activity, jealous of all competition. The power of his mind preys upon itself. It is as if there were nothing but himself and the universe. He lives in the busy solitude of his own heart; in the deep silence of thought. His imagination lends life and feeling only to the 'bare trees and mountains bare', peoples the viewless tracts of air, and converses with the silent clouds.

We could have wished that our author had given to his work the form of a didactic poem altogether, with only occasional digressions or allusions to particular instances. But he has chosen to encumber himself with a load of narrative and description, which sometimes hinders the progress and effect of the general reasoning, and which, instead of being interwoven with the text, would have come in better as plain prose notes at the end of the volume. Mr Wordsworth, indeed, says finely, and perhaps as truly as finely:

Exchange the shepherds frock of native grey
For robes with regal purple tinged; convert
The crook into a sceptre; give the pomp
Of circumstance; and here the tragic Muse
Shall find apt subjects for her highest art.
Amid the groves, beneath the shadowy hills,
The generations are prepared; the pangs,
The internal pangs, are ready; the dead strife
Of poor humanity's afflicted will
Struggling in vain with ruthless destiny.[1]

But he immediately declines availing himself of these resources of the rustic moralist: for the priest who officiates as the 'sad historian of the pensive plain' says in reply:

Our system is not fashioned to preclude
That sympathy which you for others ask:
And I could tell, not travelling for my theme
Beyond the limits of these humble graves,
Of strange disasters; but I pass them by,
Loth to disturb what Heaven hath hushed to peace.[2]

There is, in fact, in Mr Wordsworth's mind, an evident repugnance to admit anything that tells for itself, without the interpretation of the poet – a fastidious antipathy to immediate effect – a systematic unwillingness to share the palm with his subject. Where, however, he has a subject presented to him 'such as the meeting soul may pierce' and to which he does not grudge to lend the aid of his fine genius, his powers of description and fancy seem to be little inferior to those of his classical predecessor, Akenside. Among several others which we might select, we give the following passage, describing the religion of ancient Greece:

In that fair clime the lonely herdsman stretch'd
On the soft grass through half a summer's day,
With music dulled his indolent repose:
And in some fit of weariness, if he,
When his own breath was silent, chanc'd to hear etc.[3]

The foregoing is one of a succession of splendid passages equally enriched the philosophy and poetry, tracing the fictions of Eastern mythology to the immediate intercourse of the imagination with Nature, and to the habitual propensity of the human mind to endow the outward forms of being with life and conscious motion. With this expansive and animating principle Mr Wordsworth has forcibly, but somewhat severely, contrasted the cold, narrow, lifeless spirit of modern philosophy:

1 The Excursion, vi, ll. 548–57.
2 ll. 567–72.
3 ll. 851–5.

Now shall our great discoverers obtain
From sense and reason less than these obtained

From the chemists and metaphysicians our author turns to the laughing sage of France, Voltaire: 'Poor gentleman, it fares no better with him, for he is a wit.' We cannot, however, agree with Mr Wordsworth that *Candide* is dull. It is, if our author pleases, 'the production of a scoffer's pen', but it is anything but dull. It may not be proper in a grave, discreet, orthodox, promising young divine, who studies his opinions in the contraction or distension of his patron's brow, to allow any merit to a work like *Candide*; but we conceive that it would have been more manly in Mr Wordsworth, nor do we think it would have hurt the cause he espouses, if he had blotted out the epithet after it had peevishly escaped him. Whatsoever savours of a little, narrow, inquisitorial spirit does not sit well on a poet and a man of genius. The prejudices of a philosopher are not natural. There is a frankness and sincerity of opinion which is a paramount obligation in all questions of intellect, though it may not govern the decisions of the spiritual courts, who may, however, be solely left to take care of their own interests. There is a plain directness and simplicity of understanding, which is the only security against the evils of levity on the one hand or of hypocrisy on the other. A speculative bigot is a solecism in the intellectual world. We can assure Mr Wordsworth that we should not have bestowed so much consideration on a single voluntary perversion of language, but that our respect for his character makes us jealous of his smallest faults. . . .

Mr Wordsworth's writings exhibit all the internal power without any of the external form of poetry. He has scarcely any of the pomp and decoration and scenic effect of poetry; no gorgeous palaces or solemn temples awe the imagination; nor cities rise with 'glistering spires and pinnacles adorned'; we meet no knights pricking forth on air steeds; no hair-breadth scapes and perilous accidents by flood or field. Either from the predominant habit of his mind not requiring the stimulus of outward impressions, or from the want of an imagination teeming with various forms, he takes the common everyday events and objects of nature, or rather seeks those that are the most simple and barren of effect; but he adds to them a weight of interest from the resources of his mind which makes the most insignificant things serious and even formidable. All other interests are absorbed in the deeper interests of his own thoughts, and find the same level. His mind magnifies the littleness of his subject and raises the meanness; lends it his strength, and clothes it with borrowed grandeur. With him a molehill covered with wild thyme assumes the importance of the 'great vision of the guarded mount'; a puddle is filled with preternatural forces and agitated with the fiercest storms of passion.

The extreme simplicity which some persons have objected to in Mr Wordsworth's poetry, is to be found only in the subject and style; the sentiments are subtle and profound. In the latter respect, his poetry is as much above the common standard or capacity, as in the other it is below it. His poems bear a distant resemblance to some of Rembrandt's landscapes, who, more than any other painter, created the medium through which he saw nature, and out of the stump of an old tree, a break in the sky and a bit of water, could produce an effect almost miraculous.

Mr Wordsworth's poems in general are the history of a refined and contemplative mind, conversant only with itself and nature. An intense feeling of the associations of this kind is the peculiar and characteristic feature of all his productions. He has described the love of nature better than any other poet. This sentiment, mainly felt in all its force and sometimes carried to an excess, is the source both of his strength and of his weakness. However we may sympathize with Mr Wordsworth in his attachment to groves and fields we cannot extend the same admiration to their inhabitants, or to the manners of country life in general. We go along with him when he makes pedlars and ploughmen his heroes and the interpreters of his sentiments. It is, we think, getting into low company, and company besides which we do not like. We take Mr Wordsworth himself for a great poet, a fine moralist, and a deep philosopher; but if he insists on introducing us to a friend of his, a parish clerk or the barber of the village, who is as wise as himself, we must be excused if we draw back with some little want of cordial faith. We are satisfied with the friendship which subsisted between Parson Adams and Joseph Andrews. The author himself lets out occasional hints that all is not as it should be amongst these northern Arcadians. Though, in general he professes to soften the harsher features of rustic vice, he has given us one picture of the depraved and inveterate selfishness which we apprehend could only be found among the inhabitants of these boasted mountain districts.

To conclude, if the skill with which the poet had chosen his materials had been equal to the power which he has undeniably exerted over them – if the objects (whether persons or things) which he makes use of as the vehicle of his sentiments had been such as to convey them to all their depth and force, then the production before us might indeed 'have proved a monument' as he himself wishes it, worthy of the author and his country. Whether, as it is, this very original and powerful performance may not rather remain like one of those stupendous but half finished structures which have been suffered to moulder into decay, because the cost and labour attending them exceeded their use or beauty, we feel that it would be presumptuous in us to determine.[1]

Dorothy Wordsworth

from a letter to Catherine Clarkson   11 November 1814

I saw two sections of Hazlitt's review at Rydale, and did not think them nearly so well written as I should have expected from him – though he praised more than I should have expected. His opinion that all the characters are but one character, I cannot but think utterly false – there seems to me an astonishing difference considering that the primary elements are the same – fine talents and a strong imagination. He says that the narratives are a clog upon the poem. I was sorry to hear that for I am sure with common readers those parts of the poem will be by far the most interesting. Mary tells me that they have seen the last part of Hazlitt's review which is more a criticism upon country life and its effects than upon the poem, and amongst other evils he has the audacity to complain that there are no courtesans to be found in the country. He makes another bold assertion that all people living in retirement hate each other.

1 This was Hazlitt's first formal treatment of Wordsworth. He had set out to do justice to one whom he regarded as the great poet of the age, although he despised his politics. It was reprinted in *The Spirit of the Age*, 1825, but with the final part more prominent and the whole more severe. Hazlitt and Wordsworth quarrelled soon after and personal hostility intervened in their literary relations.

Benjamin Robert Haydon

from his diary   29 March 1824

He [Wordsworth] was relating to me with great horror Hazlitt's licentious conduct to the girls of the Lake and that no woman could walk after dark, for his 'satyr and *beastly* appetites'. Some girl called him a black-faced rascal, when Hazlitt enraged pushed her down, 'and because, Sir', said Wordsworth, 'she refused to gratify his abominable and devilish propensities, he lifted up her petticoats and *smote* her on *the bottom*'.

Josiah Conder

from a review of *The Excursion*, *Eclectic Review*   January 1815

Nothing can be more artless than the narrative, or externally more unpretending than the characters of *The Excursion*; nor would any thing be more easy (according to the fashionable practice of reviewers) than, with that insidious candour, which tells the truth so as to insinuate a lie, and secure a false impression, to detail the story, and exhibit the persons in such a manner as to cast unmerited ridicule both on the Author and on his subject. With us, however, it is no self-denial to forego the occasion of attempting to shine at the expense of genius such as Mr Wordsworth's. Selecting men of low estate, and incidents of everyday occurrence, he throws around both such a colouring of imagination as to exalt them far above the stalking heroes, and monstrous adventures of romance. His powers are peculiar; his descriptions, his figures, his similes and his reflections, are all homogeneous and *unique*. He writes almost as if he had never read, and while he unperceivedly avails himself of the experience and wisdom of others, he seems to utter only his own observations from his own knowledge. Corresponding with this originality of mind, he has invented a style more intellectual than that of any of his contemporaries, and in contradiction to his own theory (see the Preface to *Lyrical Ballads*, &c.), as different from the most energetic language of ordinary minds in excitement, as the strain of his argument is elevated above vulgar reasoning. Hence this poem is not more distinguished by depth, compass and variety of speculation, than by exquisite choice of ornament, and inimitably appropriate diction. The poet possesses the rare felicity of seizing the evanescent forms of thought, at any moment of their change, and fixing them in any point of view, in phraseology so perfect, that the words seem rather the thoughts themselves made palpable, than the symbols of thoughts. No difficulty of mastering his conceptions ever discourages him from attempting the full expression of them; he resolutely faces his subject, fastens on it, wrestles with it, and never quits it till he has won his whole purpose. This may be the true secret of his superiority; others, his equals perhaps in genius, are sooner weary of labour, or impatient of delay, and content themselves with less than the highest attainable reward; Mr Wordsworth seems always to do his best; he is not satisfied with conquering, he must also triumph.

Francis Jeffrey

from a review of *The Excursion, Edinburgh Review*   November 1814

This will never do. It bears no doubt the stamp of the author's heart and fancy; but unfortunately not half so visibly as that of his peculiar system. His former poems were intended to recommend that system, and to bespeak favour for it by their individual merit; but this, we suspect, must be recommended by the system – and can only expect to succeed where it has been previously established. It is longer, weaker and tamer, than any of Mr Wordsworth's other productions; with less boldness of originality, and less even of that extreme simplicity and lowliness of tone which wavered so prettily, in the *Lyrical Ballads*, between silliness and pathos. We have imitations of Cowper, and even of Milton here, engrafted on the natural drawl of the Lakers – and all diluted into harmony by that profuse and irrepressible wordiness which deluges all the blank verse of this school of poetry, and lubricates and weakens the whole structure of their style.

Though it fairly fills 420 good quarto pages, without note, vignette, or any sort of extraneous assistance, it is stated in the title – with something of an imprudent candour – to be but 'a portion' of a larger work; and in the preface, where an attempt is rather unsuccessfully made to explain the whole design, it is still more rashly disclosed, that it is but 'a part of the second part of a *long* and laborious work' – which is to consist of three parts.

What Mr Wordsworth's ideas of length are, we have no means of accurately judging; but we cannot help suspecting that they are liberal, to a degree that will alarm the weakness of most modern readers. As far as we can gather from the Preface, the entire poem – or one of them, for we really are not sure whether there is to be one or two – is of a biographical nature; and is to contain the history of the author's mind, and of the origin and progress of his poetical powers, up to the period when they were sufficiently matured to qualify him for the great work on which he has been so long employed. Now, the quarto before us contains an account of one of his youthful rambles in the vales of Cumberland, and occupies precisely the period of three days; so that, by the use of a very powerful *calculus*, some estimate may be formed of the probable extent of the entire biography.

This small specimen, however, and the statements with which it is prefaced, have been sufficient to set our minds at rest in one particular. The case of Mr Wordsworth, we perceive, is now manifestly hopeless; and we give him up as altogether incurable, and beyond the power of criticism. We cannot indeed altogether omit taking precautions now and then against the spreading of the malady; but for himself, though we shall watch the progress of his symptoms as a matter of professional curiosity and instruction, we really think it right not to harass him any longer with nauseous remedies, but rather to throw in cordials and lenitives, and wait in patience for the natural termination of the disorder. In order to justify this desertion of our patient, however, it is proper to state why we despair of the success of a more active practice.

A man who has been for twenty years at work on such matter as is now before us, and who comes complacently forward with a whole quarto of it after all the admonitions he has received, cannot reasonably be expected to 'change his hand, or check his pride,' upon the suggestion of far weightier monitors than we can pretend to be. Inveterate habit must now have given a kind of sanctity to the errors of early taste; and the very powers of which we lament the perversion, have probably become incapable of any other application. The very quantity, too, that he has written, and is at this moment working up for publication upon the old pattern, makes it almost hopeless to look for any change of it. All this is so much capital already sunk in the concern; which must be sacrificed if it be abandoned: and no man likes to give up for lost the time and talent and labour which he has embodied in any permanent production. We were not previously aware of these obstacles to Mr Wordsworth's conversion; and, considering the peculiarities of his former writings merely as the result of certain wanton and capricious experiments on public taste and indulgence, conceived it to be our duty to discourage their repetition by all the means in our power. We now see clearly, however, how the case stands; and, making up our minds, though with the most sincere pain and reluctance, to consider him as finally lost to the good cause of poetry, shall endeavour to be thankful for the occasional gleams of tenderness and beauty which the natural force of his imagination and affections must still shed over all his productions, and to which we shall ever turn with delight, in spite of the affection and mysticism and prolixity, with which they are so abundantly contrasted.

Long habits of seclusion, and an excessive ambition of originality, can alone account for the disproportion which seems to exist between this author's taste and his genius; or for the devotion with which he has sacrificed so many precious gifts at the shrine of those paltry idols which he has set up for himself among his lakes and his mountains. Solitary musings, amidst such scenes, might no doubt be expected to nurse up the mind to the majesty of poetical conception – (though it is remarkable, that all the greater poets lived, or had lived, in the full current of society). – But the collision of equal minds – the admonition of prevailing impressions – seems necessary to reduce its redundancies, and repress that tendency to extravagance or puerility, into which the self-indulgence and self-admiration of genius is so apt to be betrayed, when it is allowed to wanton, without awe or restraint, in the triumph and delight of its own intoxication. That its flights should be graceful and glorious in the eyes of men, it seems almost to be necessary that they should be made in the consciousness that men's eyes are to behold them, and that the inward transport and vigour by which they are inspired, should be tempered by an occasional reference to what will be thought of them by those ultimate dispensers of glory. An habitual and general knowledge of the few settled and permanent maxims, which form the canon of general taste in all large and polished societies – a certain tact, which informs us at once that many things, which we still love and are moved by in secret, must necessarily be despised as childish, or derided as absurd, in all such societies – though it will not stand in the place of genius, seems necessary to the success of its exertions; and though it will never enable any one to produce the higher beauties of art, can alone secure the talent which does produce them, from errors that must render it useless. Those who have most of the talent, however, commonly acquire this knowledge with the greatest facility; and if Mr Wordsworth, instead of confining himself almost entirely to the society of the dalesmen and cottagers, and little children, who form the subjects of his book, had condescended to mingle a little more with the people that were to read and judge of it, we cannot help thinking, that its texture would have been considerably improved. At least it appears to us to be absolutely impossible, that any one who had lived or mixed familiarly with men of literature and ordinary judgement in poetry (of course we exclude the coadjutors and disciples of his own school), could ever have fallen into such gross faults, or so long mistaken them for beauties. His first essays we looked upon in a good degree as poetical paradoxes, maintained experimentally, in order to display talent, and court notoriety; and so maintained, with no more serious belief in their truth, than is usually generated by an ingenious and animated defence of other paradoxes. But when we find, that he has been for twenty years exclusively employed upon articles of this very fabric, and that he has still enough of raw material on hand to keep him so employed for twenty years to come, we cannot refuse him the justice of believing that he is a sincere convert to his own system, and must ascribe the peculiarities of his composition, not to any transient affectation, or accidental caprice of imagination, but to a settled perversity of taste or understanding, which has been fostered, if not altogether created, by the circumstances to which we have already alluded.

The volume before us, if we were to describe it very shortly, we should characterize as a tissue of moral and devotional ravings, in which innumerable changes are rung upon a few very simple and familiar ideas: but with such an accompaniment of long words, long sentences, and unwieldy phrases – and such a hub-bub of strained raptures and fantastical sublimities, that it is often extremely difficult for the most skilful and attentive student to obtain a glimpse of the author's meaning – and altogether impossible for an ordinary reader to conjecture what he is about. Moral and religious enthusiasm, though undoubtedly poetical emotions, are at the same time but dangerous inspirers of poetry; nothing being so apt to run into interminable dullness or mellifluous extravagance, without giving the unfortunate author the slightest intimation of his danger. His laudable zeal for the efficacy of his preachments, he very naturally mistakes for the ardour of poetical inspiration; and, while dealing out the high words and glowing phrases which are so readily supplied by themes of this description, can scarcely avoid believing that he is eminently original and impressive. All sorts of commonplace notions and expressions are sanctified in his eyes, by the sublime ends for which they are employed; and the mystical verbiage of the Methodist pulpit is repeated, till the speaker entertains no doubt that he is the elected organ of divine truth and persuasion. But if such be the common hazards of seeking inspiration from those potent fountains, it may easily be conceived what chance Mr Wordsworth had of escaping their enchantment – with his natural propensities to wordiness, and his unlucky habit of debasing pathos with vulgarity. The fact accordingly is, that in this production he is more obscure than a Pindaric poet of the seventeenth century; and more verbose 'than even himself of yore'; while the wilfulness with which he persists in choosing his examples of intellectual dignity and tenderness exclusively from the lowest ranks of society, will be sufficiently apparent, from the circumstance of his having thought fit to make his chief prolocutor in this poetical dialogue, and chief advocate of Providence and Virtue, *an old Scotch Pedlar* – retired indeed from business – but still rambling about in his former haunts, and gossiping among his old customers, without his pack on his shoulders. The other persons of the drama are, a retired military chaplain, who has grown half an atheist and half a misanthrope – the wife of an unprosperous weaver – a servant girl with her infant – a parish pauper, and one or two other personages of equal rank and dignity.

William Wordsworth

from a letter to Catherine Clarkson   December 1814

To you I will whisper that *The Excursion* has one merit if it has no other, viz., variety of musical effect. Tell Patty Smith[1] this. . . . Exhort her to study with her fingers till she has learned to confess it to herself. Miss S.'s notion of poetical imagery is probably taken from *The Pleasures of Hope*, or *Gertrude of Wyoming*; see, for instance stanza first of said poems. There is very little imagery of that kind in *The Excursion*; but I am very far from subscribing to your concession that there is little imagery in the poem; either collateral, in the way of metaphor colouring the style; illustrative, in the way of simile; or directly under the shape of description or incident. There is a great deal, though not quite so much as will be found in the other parts of the poem, where the subjects are more lyrically treated, and where there is less narration or description turning upon manners, and those repeated actions which constitute habits, or a course of life. Poetic passion (Dennis has well observed) is of two kinds; imaginative and enthusiastic, and merely human and ordinary. Of the former it is only to be feared that there is too great a proportion. But all this must inevitably be lost upon Miss P.S.

The soul, dear Mrs Clarkson, may be regiven, when it has been taken away. My own 'Solitary' is an instance of this; but a soul that has been dwarfed by a course of bad culture cannot, after a certain age, be expanded into one of even ordinary proportion. Mere error of opinion, mere apprehension of ill consequences from supposed mistaken views on my part, could never have rendered your correspondent blind to the innumerable analogies and types of infinity, or insensible to the countless awakenings to noble aspirations, which I have transfused into that poem from the Bible of the Universe, as it speaks to the ear of the intelligent, and as it lies open to the eyes of the humble-minded.

I have alluded to the lady's errors of opinion. She talks of my being a worshipper of Nature. A passionate expression, uttered incautiously in the poem upon the Wye, has led her into this mistake; she, reading in cold-heartedness, and substituting the letter for the spirit. Unless I

1 The daugher of William Smith, MP for Norwich.

am greatly mistaken there is nothing of this kind in *The Excursion*. There is indeed a passage towards the end of the fourth book, where the Wanderer introduces the simile of the Boy and the Shell and what follows, that has something ordinarily (but absurdly) called *Spinosistic*. But the intelligent reader will easily see the dramatic propriety of the passage. The Wanderer, in the beginning of the book, had given vent to his own devotional feelings, and announced in some degree his own creed. He is here preparing the way for more distinct conceptions of the Deity by reminding the Solitary of such religious feelings as cannot but exist in the minds of those who affect atheism. She condemns me for not distinguishing between Nature as the work of God, and God himself. But where does she find this doctrine inculcated? Whence does she gather that the author of *The Excursion* looks upon Nature and God as the same? He does not indeed consider the Supreme Being as bearing the same relation to the Universe as the watchmaker bears to a watch. In fact there is nothing in the course of the religious education adopted in this country, and in the use made by us of the Holy Scriptures, that appears to me so injurious as perpetually talking about *making* by God. . . . I have done little or nothing towards your request of furnishing you with arguments to cope with my antagonist. Read the book if it pleases you; the construction of the language is uniformly perspicuous; at least I have taken every possible pains to make it so, therefore you will have no difficulty there. The impediments you may meet with will be of two kinds, such as exist in the *Ode* which concluded my second volume of poems. The poem rests upon two recollections of childhood; on that of a splendour in the objects of sense which is passed away, and the other an indisposition to bend to the law of death, as applying to our own particular case. A reader who has not had a vivid recollection of these feelings having existed in his mind in childhood cannot understand that poem. So also with regard to some of the elements of the human soul whose importance is insisted upon in *The Excursion*, and some of those images of sense which are dwelt upon as holding that relation to Immortality and Infinity which I before alluded to. If a person has not been in the way of receiving these images, it is not likely that he can form such an adequate conception of them as will bring him into vivid sympathy with the poet. For instance, one who has never heard the echoes of the flying Raven's voice in a mountainous country, as described at the close of the fourth book, will not perhaps be able to relish that illustration; yet every one must have been in the way of perceiving similar effects from different causes – but I have tired myself and must have tired you. One word upon ordinary or popular passion. Could your correspondent read the description of Robert and the fluctuations of hope and fear in Margaret's mind and the gradual decay of herself and her dwelling without a bedimmed eye then I pity her. Could she read the distress of the Solitary after the loss of his family and the picture of his quarrel with his own conscience (though this tends more to meditative passion) without some agitation then I envy her not her tranquility. Could the anger of Ellen before she sat down to weep over her Babe, tho' she were but a poor serving maid, be found in a book, and that book said to be without passion, then, thank Heaven! that the person so speaking is neither my wife nor my sister, nor one upon whom (unless I could work in her a great alteration) I am forced daily to converse with. . . .

As to the *Edinburgh Review* I hold the Author of it in entire contempt. And therefore shall not pollute my fingers with the touch of it. There is one sentence in the *Ex.* ending in 'Sublime attractions of the Grave', which, if the poem had contained nothing else that I valued, would have made it almost a matter of religion with me to keep out of the way of the best stuff which so mean a mind as Mr Jeffrey's could produce in connection with it. . . .

. . . your friend's remarks were monstrous. To talk of the offence of writing *The Excursion* and the difficulty of forgiving the author is carrying audacity and presumption to a height of which I did not think any *woman* was capable. Had my poem been much coloured by books, as many parts of what I have to write must be, I should have been accused (as Milton has been) of pedantry and of having a mind which could not support itself but by other men's labours. Do not you perceive that my conversations almost all take place out of doors and all with grand objects of Nature, surrounding the speakers, for the express purpose of their being alluded to in illustration of the subjects treated of? *Much* imagery from books would have been an impertinence and an incumbrance; where it was required, it is found.

As to passion, it is never to be lost sight of that *The Excursion* is *part* of a work; that in its plan it is conversational; and that if I had introduced stories exciting curiosity, and filled with violent conflicts of passion and a rapid interchange of striking incidents, these things could never have harmonized with the rest of the work; and all further discourse, comment, or reflection must have been put a stop to.

Samuel Taylor Coleridge

from a letter to Lady Beaumont 3 April 1815

Of *The Excursion*, excluding the tale of the *Ruined Cottage*, which I have ever thought the finest poem in our language, comparing it with any of the same or similar length, I can truly say that one half of the number of its beauties would make all the beauties of all his contemporary poets collectively mount to the balance: – but yet – the fault may be in my own mind. – I do not think, I did not feel, it equal to the work on the growth of his own spirit [i.e. *The Prelude*]. As proofs meet me in every part of *The Excursion* that the poet's genius has not flagged, I have sometimes fancied that, having by the conjoint operation of his own experience, feelings and reason, *himself* convinced *himself* of truths, which the generality of persons have either taken for granted from their infancy, or at least adopted in early life, he has attached all their own depth and weight to doctrines and words, which come almost as truisms or commonplaces to others. From this state of mind, in which I was comparing Wordsworth with myself, I was roused by the infamous *Edinburgh Review* of the poem. If ever guilt lay on a writer's hand, and if malignity, slander, hypocrisy and self-contradictory baseness can constitute guilt, I dare openly, and openly (please God) I will, impeach the writer of that article of it. These are awful times – a dream of dreams. To be a prophet is, and ever has been, an unthankful office.

William Wordsworth

from *Essay, Supplementary to the Preface* 1815

[The *Essay, Supplementary* was much commented on when it first appeared and was the real reason for much of the hostility shown

towards the *Collected Poems* of 1815. Wordsworth's friends
tended to regret its inclusion. The portion here omitted contains
a brief sketch of English poetical taste from the time of
Shakespeare.]

By this time, I trust that the judicious Reader, who has now first
become acquainted with these poems, is persuaded that a very senseless outcry has been raised against them and their Author. Casually,
and very rarely only, do I see any periodical publication, except a
daily newspaper; but I am not wholly unacquainted with the spirit in
which my most active and persevering Adversaries have maintained
their hostility; nor with the impudent falsehoods and base artifices to
which they have had recourse. These, as implying a consciousness on
their parts that attacks honestly and fairly conducted would be un-
availing, could not but have been regarded by me with triumph; had
they been accompanied with such display of talents and information
as might give weight to the opinions of the Writers, whether favourable or unfavourable. But the ignorance of those who have chosen
to stand forth as my enemies, as far as I am acquainted with their
enmity, has unfortunately been still more gross than their disin-
genuousness, and their incompetence more flagrant than their malice.
The effect in the eyes of the discerning is indeed ludicrous: yet,
contemptible as such men are, in return for the forced compliment
paid me by their long-continued notice (which, as I have appeared so
rarely before the public, no one can say has been solicited) I entreat
them to spare themselves. The lash, which they are aiming at my
productions, does, in fact, only fall on phantoms of their own brain;
which, I grant, I am innocently instrumental in raising. By what
fatality the orb of my genius (for genius none of them seem to deny
me) acts upon these men like the moon upon a certain description of
patients, it would be irksome to inquire; nor would it consist with
the respect which I owe myself to take further notice of opponents
whom I internally despise.

  With the young, of both sexes, Poetry is, like love, a passion; but,
for much the greater part of those who have been proud of its power
over their minds, a necessity soon arises of breaking the pleasing
bondage; or it relaxes of itself; the thoughts being occupied in domestic cares, or the time engrossed by business. Poetry then becomes only

an occasional recreation; while to those whose existence passes away in a course of fashionable pleasure it is a species of luxurious amusement. In middle and declining age, a scattered number of serious persons resort to poetry, as to religion, for a protection against the pressure of trivial employments, and as a consolation for the afflictions of life. And lastly, there are many, who, having been enamoured of this art in their youth, have found leisure, after youth was spent, to cultivate general literature; in which poetry has continued to be comprehended *as a study*.

Into the above Classes the Readers of poetry may be divided; Critics abound in them all; but from the last only can opinions be collected of absolute value, and worthy to be depended upon, as prophetic of the destiny of a new work. The young, who in nothing can escape delusion, are expecially subject to it in their intercourse with poetry. The cause, not so obvious as the fact is unquestionable, is the same as that from which erroneous judgements in this art, in the minds of men of all ages, chiefly proceed; but upon Youth it operates with peculiar force. The appropriate business of poetry (which, nevertheless, if genuine is as permanent as pure science) her appropriate employment, her privilege and her *duty*, is to treat of things not as they *are*, but as they *appear*; not as they exist in themselves, but as they *seem* to exist to the senses and to the *passions*. What a world of delusion does this acknowledged principle prepare for the inexperienced! what temptations to go astray are here held forth for those whose thoughts have been little disciplined by the understanding, and whose feelings revolt from the sway of reason! When a juvenile Reader is in the height of his rapture with some vicious passage, should experience throw in doubts, or common-sense suggest suspicions, a lurking consciousness that the realities of the Muse are but shows, and that her liveliest excitements are raised by transient shocks of conflicting feeling and successive assemblages of contradictory thoughts – is ever at hand to justify extravagance, and to sanction absurdity. But, it may be asked, as these illusions are unavoidable, and no doubt eminently useful to the mind as a process, what good can be gained by making observations the tendency of which is to diminish the confidence of youth in its feelings, and thus to abridge its innocent and even profitable pleasures? The reproach implied in the question could not be warded off, if Youth were incapable of being delighted with what is truly excellent; or if these errors always terminated of themselves in due season. But, with the majority, though their force be abated, they continue through life. Moreover, the fire of youth is too vivacious an element to be extinguished or damped by a philosophical remark; and, while there is no danger that what has been said will be injurious or painful to the ardent and the confident, it may prove beneficial to those who, being enthusiastic, are, at the same time, modest and ingenuous. The intimation may unite with their own misgivings to regulate their sensibility, and to bring in, sooner than it would otherwise have arrived, a more discreet and sound judgement.

If it should excite wonder that men of ability, in later life, whose understandings have been rendered acute by practice in affairs, should be so easily and so far imposed upon when they happen to take up a new work in verse, this appears to be the cause; that, having discontinued their attention to poetry, whatever progress may have been made in other departments of knowledge, they have not, as to this art, advanced in true discernment beyond the age of youth. If then a new poem fall in their way, whose attractions are of that kind which would have enraptured them during the heat of youth, the judgement not being improved to a degree that they shall be disgusted, they are dazzled; and prize and cherish the faults for having had power to make the present time vanish before them, and to throw the mind back, as by enchantment, into the happiest season of life. As they read, powers seem to be revived, passions are regenerated, and pleasures restored. The Book was probably taken up after an escape from the burthen of business, and with a wish to forget the world, and all its vexations and anxieties. Having obtained this wish, and so much more, it is natural that they should make report as they have felt.

If Men of mature age, through want of practice, be thus easily beguiled into admiration of absurdities, extravagances and misplaced ornaments, thinking it proper that their understandings should enjoy a holiday, while they are unbending their minds with verse, it may be expected that such Readers will resemble their former selves also in strength of prejudice, and an inaptitude to be moved by the unostentatious beauties of a pure style. In the higher poetry, an enlightened Critic chiefly looks for a reflection of the wisdom of the heart and the grandeur of the imagination. Wherever these appear, simplicity accompanies them; Magnificence herself, when legitimate, depending upon a simplicity of her own, to regulate her ornaments. But it is a well known property of human nature that our estimates are ever governed by comparisons, of which we are conscious with various degrees of distinctness. Is it not, then, inevitable (confining these observations to the effects of style merely) that an eye, accustomed to the glaring hues of diction by which such Readers are caught and excited, will for the most part be rather repelled than attracted by an original Work the colouring of which is disposed according to a pure and refined scheme of harmony? It is in the fine arts as in the affairs of life, no man can *serve* (i.e. obey with zeal and fidelity) two Masters.

As Poetry is most just to its own divine origin when it administers the comforts and breathes the spirit of religion, they who have learned to perceive this truth, and who betake themselves to reading verse for sacred purposes, must be preserved from numerous illusions to which the two Classes of Readers, whom we have been considering, are liable. But, as the mind grows serious from the weight of life, the range of its passions is contracted accordingly; and its sympathies become so exclusive that many species of high excellence wholly escape, or but languidly excite, its notice. Besides, Men who read from religious or moral inclinations, even when the subject is of that kind which they approve, are beset with misconceptions and mistakes peculiar to themselves. Attaching so much importance to the truths which interest them, they are prone to overrate the Authors by whom these truths are expressed and enforced. They come prepared to impart so much passion to the Poet's language, that they remain unconscious how little, in fact, they receive from it. And, on the other hand, religious faith is to him who holds it so momentous a thing, and error appears to be attended with such tremendous consequences, that, if opinions touching upon religion occur which the Reader condemns, he not only cannot sympathize with them however animated the expression, but there is, for the most part, an end put to all satisfaction and enjoyment. Love, if it before existed, is converted into dislike; and the heart of the Reader is set against the Author and his book. To these excesses, they, who from their professions ought to be the most guarded against them, are perhaps the most liable; I mean those sects whose religion, being from the calculating understanding, is cold and formal. For when Christianity, the religion of humility, is founded upon the proudest faculty of our nature, what can be expected but contradictions? Accordingly, believers of this cast are at one time contemptuous; at another, being troubled as they are and must be with inward misgivings, they are jealous and suspicious; and at all seasons, they are under temptation to supply, by the heat with which they defend their tenets, the animation which is wanting to the constitution of the religion itself.

Faith was given to man that his affections, detached from the treasures of time, might be inclined to settle upon those of eternity: the elevation of his nature, which this habit produces on earth, being to him a presumptive evidence of a future state of existence; and giving him a title to partake of its holiness. The religious man values what he sees chiefly as an 'imperfect shadowing forth' of what he is incapable of seeing. The corners of religion refer to indefinite objects, and are too weighty for the mind to support them without relieving itself by resting a great part of the burthen upon words and symbols. The commerce between Man and his Maker cannot be carried on but by a process where much is represented in little, and the infinite Being accommodates himself to a finite capacity. In all this may be perceived the affinities between religion and poetry; between religion – making up the deficiencies of reason by faith, and poetry – passionate for the instruction of reason; between religion – whose element is infinitude, and whose ultimate trust is the supreme of things, submitting herself to circumscription and reconciled to substitutions; and poetry – ethereal and transcendent, yet incapable to sustain her existence without sensuous incarnation. In this community of nature may be perceived also the lurking incitements of kindred error; so that we shall find that no poetry has been more subject to distortion, than that species the argument and scope of which is religious; and no lovers of the art have gone further astray than the pious and the devout.

Wither then shall we turn for that union of qualifications which must necessarily exist before the decisions of a critic can be of absolute value? For a mind at once poetical and philosophical; for a critic whose affections are as free and kindly as the spirit of society, and whose understanding is severe as that of dispassionate government?

Where are we to look for that initiatory composure of mind which no selfishness can disturb? For a natural sensibility that has been tutored into correctness without losing any thing of its quickness; and for active faculties capable of answering the demands which an Author of original imagination shall make upon them, associated with a judgement that cannot be duped into admiration by aught that is unworthy of it? Among those and those only, who, never having suffered their youthful love of poetry to remit much of its force, have applied, to the consideration of the laws of this art, the best power of their understandings. At the same time it must be observed – that, as this Class comprehends the only judgements which are trustworthy, so does it include the most erroneous and perverse. For to be mistaught is worse than to be untaught; and no perverseness equals that which is supported by system, no errors are so difficult to root out as those which the understanding has pledged its credit to uphold. In this Class are contained Censors, who, if they be pleased with what is good, are pleased with it only by imperfect glimpses, and upon false principles; who, should they generalize rightly to a certain point, are sure to suffer for it in the end; who, if they stumble upon a sound rule, are fettered by misapplying it, or by straining it too far; being incapable of perceiving when it ought to yield to one of higher order. In it are found Critics too petulant to be passive to a genuine Poet, and too feeble to grapple with him; Men, who take upon them to report of the course which *he* holds whom they are utterly unable to accompany, confounded if he turn quick upon the wing, dismayed if he soar steadily into 'the region'; Men of palsied imaginations and indurated hearts; in whose minds all healthy action is languid, who, therefore, feed as the many direct them, or, with the many, are greedy after vicious provocatives; Judges, whose censure is auspicious, and whose praise ominous! In this Class meet together the two extremes of best and worst.

The observations presented in the foregoing series are of too ungracious a nature to have been made without reluctance; and were it only on this account I would invite the Reader to try them by the test of comprehensive experience. If the number of judges who can be confidently relied upon be in reality so small, it ought to follow that partial notice only, or neglect, perhaps long continued, or attention wholly inadequate to their merits – must have been the fate of most works in the higher departments of poetry; and that, on the other hand, numerous productions have blazed into popularity, and have passed away, leaving scarcely a trace behind them: it will be, further, found that when Authors have at length raised themselves into general admiration and maintained their ground errors and prejudices have prevailed concerning their genius and their works, which the few who are conscious of those errors and prejudices would deplore; if they were not recompensed by perceiving that there are select Spirits for whom it is ordained that their fame shall be in the world an existence like that of Virtue, which owes its being to the struggles it makes, and its vigour to the enemies whom it provokes; a vivacious quality ever doomed to meet with opposition, and still triumphing over it; and, from the nature of its dominion, incapable of being brought to the sad conclusion of Alexander, when he wept that there were no more worlds for him to conquer. . . .

If there be one conclusion more forcibly pressed upon us than another by the review which has been given of the fortunes and fate of Poetical Works, it is this, that every Author, as far as he is great and at the same time *original*, has had the task of *creating* the taste by which he is to be enjoyed: so has it been, so will it continue to be. This remark was long since made to me by the philosophical Friend for the separation of whose Poems from my own I have previously expressed my regret. The predecessors of an original Genius of a high order will have smoothed the way for all that he has in common with them; and much he will have in common; but, for what is peculiarly his own, he will be called upon to clear and often to shape his own road: he will be in the condition of Hannibal among the Alps.

And where lies the real difficulty of creating that taste by which a truly original Poet is to be relished? Is it in breaking the bonds of custom, in overcoming the prejudices of false refinement, and displacing the aversions of inexperience? Or, if he labour for an object which here and elsewhere I have proposed to myself, does it consist in divesting the Reader of the pride that induces him to dwell upon those points wherein Men differ from each other, to the exclusion of those in which all Men are alike, or the same; and in making him ashamed of the vanity that renders him insensible of the appropriate excellence which civil arrangements, less unjust than might appear, and Nature illimitable in her bounty, have conferred on Men who stand below him in the scale of society? Finally, does it lie in establishing that dominion over the spirits of Readers by which they are to be humbled and humanized, in order that they may be purified and exalted?

If these ends are to be attained by the mere communication of *knowledge*, it does *not* lie here. TASTE, I would remind the Reader, like IMAGINATION, is a word which has been forced to extend its services far beyond the point to which philosophy would have confined them. It is a metaphor, taken from a *passive* sense of the human body, and transferred to things which are in their essence *not* passive, to intellectual *acts* and *operations*. The word, imagination, has been over-strained, from impulses honourable to mankind to meet the demands of the faculty which is perhaps the noblest of our nature. In the instance of taste, the process has been reversed, and from the prevalence of dispositions at once injurious and discreditable, being no other than that selfishness which is the child of apathy, which, as Nations decline in productive and creative power, makes them value themselves upon a presumed refinement of judging. Poverty of language is the primary cause of the use which we make of the word, Imagination; but the word, Taste, has been stretched to the sense which it bears in modern Europe by habits of self-conceit, inducing that inversion in the order of things whereby a passive faculty is made paramount among the faculties conversant with the fine arts. Proportion and congruity, the requisite knowledge being supposed, are subjects upon which taste may be trusted; it is competent to this office; for in its intercourse with these the mind is *passive*, and is affected painfully or pleasurably as by an instinct. But the profound and the exquisite in feeling, the lofty and universal in thought and imagination; or in ordinary language the pathetic and the sublime; are neither of them accurately speaking, objects of a faculty which could ever without a sinking in the spirit of Nations have been designated by the metaphor – *Taste*. And why? Because without the exertion of a cooperating *power* in the mind of the Reader, there can be no adequate sympathy with either of these emotions: without this auxiliar impulse elevated or profound passion cannot exist.

Passion, it must be observed, is derived from a word which

signifies *suffering*; but the connection which suffering has with effort, with exertion, and *action*, is immediate and inseparable. How strikingly is this property of human nature exhibited by the fact, that, in popular language, to be in a passion, is to be angry! But,

Anger in hasty *words* or *blows*
Itself discharges on its foes.

To be moved, then, by a passion, is to be excited, often to external and always to internal, effort; whether for the continuance and strengthening of the passion, or for its suppression, accordingly as the course which it takes may be painful or pleasurable. If the latter, the soul must contribute to its support, or it never becomes vivid, and soon languishes, and dies. And this brings us to the point. If every great Poet with whose writings men are familiar, in the highest exercise of his genius, before he can be thoroughly enjoyed, has to call forth and to communicate *power*, this service, in a still greater degree, falls upon an original Writer, at his first appearance in the world. Of genius the only proof is, the act of doing well what is worthy to be done, and what was never done before. Of genius, in the fine arts, the only infallible sign is the widening the sphere of human sensibility, for the delight, honour and benefit of human nature. Genius is the introduction of a new element into the intellectual universe: or, if that be not allowed, it is the application of powers to objects on which they had not before been exercised, or the employment of them in such a manner as to produce effects hitherto unknown. What is all this but an advance, or a conquest, made by the soul of the Poet? Is it to be supposed that the Reader can make progress of this kind, like an Indian Prince or General – stretched on his Palanquin, and borne by his Slaves? No, he is invigorated and inspirited by his Leader, in order that he may exert himself, for he cannot proceed in quiescence, he cannot be carried like a dead weight. Therefore to create taste is to call forth and bestow power, of which knowledge is the effect; and *there* lies the true difficulty.

As the pathetic participates of an *animal* sensation, it might seem – that, if the springs of this emotion were genuine, all men, possessed of competent knowledge of the facts and circumstances, would be instantaneously affected. And, doubtless, in the works of every true Poet will be found passages of that species of excellence, which is proved by effects immediate and universal. But there are emotions of the pathetic that are simple and direct, and others – that are complex and revolutionary; some – to which the heart yields with gentleness, others – against which it struggles with pride: these varieties are infinite as the combinations of circumstance and the constitutions of character. Remember, also, that the medium through which, in poetry, the heart is to be affected – is language; a thing subject to endless fluctuations and arbitrary associations. The genius of the Poet melts these down for his purpose; but they retain their shape and quality to him who is not capable of exerting, within his own mind, a corresponding energy. There is also a meditative, as well as a human, pathos; an enthusiastic, as well as an ordinary, sorrow; a sadness that has its seat in the depths of reason, to which the mind cannot sink gently of itself – but to which it must descend by treading the steps of thought. And for the sublime, if we consider what are the cares that occupy the passing day, and how remote is the practice and the course of life from the sources of sublimity, in the soul of Man, can it be wondered that there is little existing preparation for a Poet charged with a new mission to extend its kingdom, and to augment and spread its enjoyments?

Away, then, with the senseless iteration of the word, *popular*, applied to new works in Poetry, as if there were no test of excellence in this first of the fine arts but that all Men should run after its productions, as if urged by an appetite, or constrained by a spell! The qualities of writing best fitted for eager reception are either such as startle the world into attention by their audacity and extravagance; or they are chiefly of a superficial kind, lying upon the surfaces of manners; or arising out of a selection and arrangement of incidents, by which the mind is kept upon the stretch of curiosity, and the fancy amused without the trouble of thought. But in everything which is to send the soul into herself, to be admonished of her weakness or to be made conscious of her power; wherever life and nature are described as operated upon by the creative or abstracting virtue of the imagination; wherever the instinctive wisdom of antiquity and her heroic passions uniting, in the heart of the Poet, with the meditative wisdom of later ages, have produced that accord of sublimated humanity, which is at once a history of the remote past and a prophetic annunciation of the remotest future, *there*, the Poet must reconcile himself for a season to few and scattered hearers. Grand thoughts (and Shakespeare must often have sighed over this truth), as they are most naturally and most fitly conceived in solitude, so can they not be brought forth in the midst of plaudits without some violation of their sanctity. Go to a silent exhibition of the productions of the Sister Art, and be convinced that the qualities which dazzle at first sight, and kindle the admiration of the multitude, are essentially different from those by which permanent influence is secured. Let us not shrink from following up these principles as far as they will carry us, and conclude with observing – that there never has been a period, and perhaps never will be, in which vicious poetry, of some kind or other, has not excited more zealous admiration, and been far more generally read, than good; but this advantage attends the good, that the *individual*, as well as the species, survives from age to age: whereas, of the depraved, though the species be immortal the individual quickly *perishes*; the object of present admiration vanishes, being supplemented by some other as easily produced; which, though no better, brings with it at least the irritation of novelty, with adaptation, more or less skilful, to the changing humours of the majority of those who are most at leisure to regard poetical works when they first solicit their attention.

It is the result of the whole that, in the opinion of the Writer, the judgement of the People is not to be respected? The thought is most injurious; and could the charge be brought against him, he would repel it with indignation. The People have already been justified, and their eulogium pronounced by implication, when it was said, above – that, of *good* Poetry, the *individual*, as well as the species, *survives*. And how does it survive but through the People? what preserves it but their intellect and their wisdom?

Past and future, are the wings
On whose support, harmoniously conjoined,
Moves the great Spirit of human knowledge
MS

The voice that issues from this Spirit is that *Vox populi* which the Deity inspires. Foolish must he be who can mistake for this a local acclamation, or a transitory outcry – transitory though it be for years, local though from a Nation. Still more lamentable is his error, who can believe that there is anything of divine infallibility in the clamour of that small though loud portion of the community, ever governed by factitious influence, which, under the name of the PUBLIC, passes itself, upon the unthinking, for the PEOPLE. Towards the Public, the Writer hopes that he feels as much deference as it is intitled to: but to the People, philosophically characterized, and to the embodied spirit of their knowledge, so far as it exists and moves, at the present, faithfully supported by its two wings, the past and the future, his devout respect, his reverence, is due. He offers it willingly and readily; and, this done, takes leave of his Readers, by assuring them – that, if he were not persuaded that the Contents of these Volumes, and the Work to which they are subsidiary, evinced something of the 'Vision and the Faculty divine', and that, both in words and things, they will operate in their degree, to extend the domain of sensibility for the delight, the honour and the benefit of human nature, notwithstanding the many happy hours which he has employed in their composition, and the manifold comforts and enjoyment they have procured to him, he would not, if a wish could do it, save them from immediate destruction; from becoming at this moment, to the world, as a thing that had never been.

Lord Byron

from a letter to Leigh Hunt   30 October 1815

I take leave to differ with you on Wordsworth, as freely as I once agreed with you; at that time I gave him credit for a promise, which is unfulfilled. I still think his capacity warrants all you say of *it* only, but that his performances since *Lyrical Ballads* are miserably inadequate to the ability which lurks within him: there is undoubtedly much natural talent spilt over *The Excursion*; but it is rain upon rocks – where it stands and stagnates, or rain upon sands, where it falls without fertilizing. Who can understand him? Let those who do, make him intelligible. Jacob Behmen, Swedenborg and Joanna Southcote, are mere types of this apostle of mystery and mysticism. But I have done – no, I have not done, for I have two petty and perhaps unworthy objections in small matters to make to him, which, with his pretensions to accurate observation, and fury against Pope's false translation of 'the Moonlight scene in Homer', I wonder he should have fallen into; – these be they: – He says of Greece in the body of his book – that it is a land of

Rivers, fertile plains and *sounding* shores,
Under a *cope* of variegated sky[1]

The rivers are dry half the year, the plains are barren, and the shores still and tideless as the Mediterranean can make them; the sky is anything but variegated, being for months and months but 'darkly, deeply, beautifully blue'. The next is in his notes where he talks of our 'Monuments crowded together in the busy etc., of a large town' as compared with the 'still seclusion' of a Turkish cemetery in some *remote* place'. This is pure stuff; for *one* monument in our churchyard there are *ten* in the Turkish, and so crowded, that you cannot walk between them. . . .

These things I was struck with, as coming peculiarly in my own way; and in both of these he is wrong, yet I should have noticed neither but for his attack on Pope for a like blunder, and a peevish affectation about him of despising a popularity which he will never attain.

Henry Crabb Robinson

from his diary   9 May 1815

Wordsworth, in answer to the common reproach that his sensibility is excited by objects which produce no effect on others, admits the fact, and is proud of it. He says that he cannot be accused of being insensible to the real concerns of life. He does not waste his feelings on unworthy objects, for he is alive to the actual interests of society. I think the justification complete. If Wordsworth expected immediate popularity, he would betray his ignorance of public taste, reproachful to a man of character. Wordsworth spoke of the changes in his new poems. He has substituted 'ebullient' for 'fiery' speaking of the

1 Rivers and fertile plains, and sounding shores
under a cope of sky more variable
The Excursion, iv, ll. 719–20.

nightingale; and 'jocund' for 'laughing' applied to the daffodils; but he will probably restore the original epithets.[1] We agreed in preferring the original reading; but on my gently alluding to the lines 'Three foot long by two foot wide' and confessing that I dared not read them aloud in company, he said, 'They ought to be liked.' Wordsworth particularly recommended to me among his poems of Imagination, *Yew-Trees* and a description of *Night*. These are, he says, amongst the best for the imaginative power displayed in them. I have since read them. They are fine; but I believe I do not understand in what their excellence consists. Wordsworth himself, as Hazlitt has well observed, has a pride in deriving no aid from his subject. It is the mere power, which he is conscious of exerting, in which he delights; not the production of a work in which men rejoice, on account of the sympathies and sensibilities it excites in them. Hence he does not much esteem his *Laodamia* as it belongs to the inferior class of poems founded on the affections. Yet in this, as in other peculiarities of Wordsworth, there is a German bent in his mind.

Henry Crabb Robinson

from his diary   10 September 1816

If this were the place, and if my memory were good, I could enrich my journal by retailing Wordsworth's conversation. He is an eloquent speaker, and he talked upon his own art, and his own works, very feelingly and very profoundly; but I cannot venture to state more than a few intelligible results, for I own that much of what he said was above my comprehension.

He stated, what I had before taken for granted, that most of his lyrical ballads were founded on some incident he had witnessed, or heard of. He mentioned the origin of several poems.

Lucy Gray, that tender and pathetic narrative of a child mysteriously lost on a common, was occasioned by the death of a child who fell into the lock of a canal. His object was to exhibit poetically entire

1 'Fiery' was restored to later versions of 'O Nightingale!' but 'jocund' remained.

solitude, and he represents the child as observing the day-moon, which no town or village girl would even notice.

The Leech-Gatherer he did actually meet near Grasmere, except that he gave to his poetic character powers of mind which his original did not possess.

The fable of *The Oak and the Broom* proceeded from his beholding a rose in just such a situation as he described the broom to be in. Perhaps, however, all poets have had their works suggested in like manner. What I wish I could venture to state after Wordsworth, is his conception of the manner in which mere fact is converted into poetry by the power of the imagination.

He represented, however, much as, unknown to him, the German philosophers have done, that by the imagination the mere fact is exhibited as connected with that infinity without which there is no poetry.

He spoke of his tale of the dog, called *Fidelity*. He says he purposely made the narrative as prosaic as possible, in order that no discredit might be thrown on the truth of the incident. In the description at the beginning, and in the moral at the end, he has alone indulged in a poetic vein; and these parts, he thinks, he has peculiarly succeeded in.

He quoted some of the latter poem, and also from *The Kitten and Falling Leaves*, to show he had connected even the kitten with the great, awful and mysterious powers of nature. But neither now, nor in reading the Preface to Wordsworth's new edition of his poems, have I been able to comprehend his ideas concerning poetic imagination. I have not been able to raise my mind to the subject, farther than this, that imagination is the faculty by which the poet conceives and produces – that is, images – individual forms, in which are embodied universal ideas or abstractions. This I do comprehend, and I find the most beautiful and striking illustrations of this faculty in the works of Wordsworth himself.

The incomparable twelve lines, 'She dwelt among the untrodden ways,' ending, 'The difference to me!' are finely imagined. They exhibit the powerful effect of the loss of a very obscure object upon one tenderly attached to it. The opposition between the apparent strength of the passion and the insignificance of the object is delight-fully conceived, and the object itself well portrayed.

Samuel Taylor Coleridge

from *Biographia Literaria*, chapter 22   1817

In a comparatively small number of poems he chose to try an experiment; and this experiment we will suppose to have failed. Yet even in these poems it is impossible not to perceive that the natural *tendency* of the poet's mind is to great objects and elevated conceptions. The poem entitled *Fidelity* is for the greater part written in language, as unraised and naked as any perhaps in the two volumes. Yet take the following stanza and compare it with the preceding stanzas of the same poem.

There sometimes does a leaping fish
Send through the tarn a lonely cheer;
The Crags repeat the Raven's croak,
In symphony austere;
Thither the rainbow comes – the Cloud –
And mists that spread the flying shroud;
And sunbeams; and the sounding blast,
That, if it could, would hurry past;
But that enormous barrier holds it fast.

Or compare the four last lines of the concluding stanza with the former half:

Yes, proof was plain that, since the day
On which the Traveller thus had died,
The Dog had watched about the spot,
Or by his Master's side:
How nourish'd here through such long time
He knows, who gave that love sublime,
And gave that strength of feeling, great
Above all human estimate.

Can any candid and intelligent mind hesitate in determining, which of these best represents the tendency and native character of the poet's genius? Will he not decide that the one was written because the poet *would* so write, and the other because he could not so entirely repress the force and grandeur of his mind, but that he must in some part or other of *every* composition write otherwise? In short, that his only disease is the being out of his element; like the swan, that, having amused himself, for a while, with crushing the weeds on the river's bank, soon returns to his own majestic movements on its reflecting and sustaining surface. Let it be observed that I am here supposing the imagined judge, to whom I appeal, to have already decided against the poet's theory, as far as it is different from the principles of the art, generally acknowledged.

I cannot here enter into a detailed examination of Mr Wordsworth's works; but I will attempt to give the main results of my own judgement, after an acquaintance of many years, and repeated perusals. And though, to appreciate the defects of a great mind it is necessary to understand previously its characteristic excellences, yet I have already expressed myself with sufficient fulness, to preclude most of the ill effects that might arise from my pursuing a contrary arrangement. I will therefore commence with what I deem the prominent *defects* of his poems hitherto published.

The first *characteristic, though only occasional* defect, which I appear to myself to find in these poems is the *inconstancy* of the *style*. Under this name I refer to the sudden and unprepared transitions from lines or sentences of peculiar felicity – (at all events striking and original) – to a style, not only unimpassioned but undistinguished. He sinks too often and too abruptly to that style, which I should place in the second division of language, dividing it into the three species; *first,* that which is peculiar to poetry; *second,* that which is only proper in prose; and *third,* the neutral or common to both. . . .

But in the perusal of works of literary *art,* we *prepare* ourselves for such language; and the business of the writer, like that of a painter whose subject requires unusual splendour and prominence, is so to raise the lower and neutral tints, that what in a different style would be the *commanding* colours, are here used as the means of that gentle *degradation* requisite in order to produce the effect of a *whole.* Where this is not achieved in a poem, the metre merely reminds the reader of his claims in order to disappoint them; and where this defect occurs frequently, his feelings are alternately startled by anticlimax and hyperclimax.

I refer the reader to the exquisite stanzas cited for another purpose from *The Blind Highland Boy;* and then annex, as being in my opinion instances of this *disharmony* in style, the two following:

And one, the rarest, was a shell,
Which he, poor Child, had studied well:
The Shell of a green Turtle, thin
And hollow; – you might sit therein,
    It was so wide, and deep.
Our Highland Boy oft visited
The house which held this prize; and, led
By choice or chance, did thither come
One day, when no one was at home,
    And found the door unbarred.

Or page 172, vol. i.[1]

'Tis gone – forgotten – *let me do*
My best – there was a smile or two,
I can remember them, I see
The smiles, worth all the world to me.
Dear Baby! I must lay thee down:
Thou troublest me with strange alarms;
Smiles hast Thou, sweet ones of thy own;
I cannot keep thee in my arms;
For they confound me: *as it is,*
I have forgot those smiles of his!

Or page 269, vol. i.[2]

Thou hast a nest, for thy love and thy rest
And though little troubled with sloth,
Drunken Lark! thou would'st be loth
To be such a Traveller as I.
    Happy, happy liver!
With a soul as strong as a mountain River
Pouring out praise to th' Almighty Giver,
Joy and jollity be with us both!
Hearing thee, or else some other,
    As merry a Brother
I on the earth will go plodding on,
By myself, cheerfully, till the day is done.

1 The Emigrant Mother [1815], 55–64.
2 To a Sky-Lark [1807–20], 18–29.

The incongruity, which I appear to find in this passage, is that of
the two noble lines in italics with the preceding and following. So
vol. ii. page 30.[1]

Close by a Pond, upon the further side,
He stood alone; a minute's space, I guess,
I watch'd him, he continuing motionless:
To the Pool's further margin then I drew;
He being all the while before me full in view.

Compare this with the repetition of the same image, in the next
stanza but two.

And, still as I drew near with gentle pace,
Beside the little pond or moorish flood
Motionless as a Cloud the Old Man stood,
That heareth not the loud winds when they call;
And moveth altogether, if it move at all.

Or lastly, the second of the three following stanzas, compared both
with the first and the third.

My former thoughts returned; the fear that kills;
And hope that is unwilling to be fed;
Cold, pain, and labour, and all fleshly ills;
And mighty Poets in their misery dead.
But now, perplex'd by what the Old Man had said,
My question eagerly did I renew,
'How is it that you live, and what is it you do?'

He with a smile did then his words repeat;
And said, that, gathering leeches, far and wide
He travelled; stirring thus about his feet
The waters of the Ponds where they abide.
'Once I could meet with them on every side;
But they have dwindled long by slow decay;
Yet still I persevere, and find them where I may.'

While he was talking thus, the lonely place,
The Old Man's shape, and speech, all troubled me:

1 *The Leech-Gatherer*, omitted in final version, see *Works* ed. de Selincourt, II,
p. 237.

In my mind's eye I seemed to see him pace
About the weary moors continually,
Wandering about alone and silently.

Indeed this fine poem is *especially* characteristic of the author. There is scarce a defect or excellence in his writings of which it would not present a specimen. But it would be unjust not to repeat that this defect is only occasional. From a careful reperusal of the two volumes of poems, I doubt whether the objectionable passages would amount in the whole to one hundred lines; not the eighth part of the number of pages. In *The Excursion* the feeling of incongruity is seldom excited by the diction of any passage considered in itself, but by the sudden superiority of some other passage forming the context.

The second defect I can generalize with tolerable accuracy, if the reader will pardon an uncouth and new coined word. There is, I should say, not seldom a *matter-of-factness* in certain poems. This may be divided into, *first*, a laborious minuteness and fidelity in the representation of objects, and their positions, as they appeared to the poet himself; *secondly*, the insertion of accidental circumstances, in order to the full explanation of his living characters, their dispositions and actions; which circumstances might be necessary to establish the probability of a statement in real life, where nothing is taken for granted by the hearer; but appear superfluous in poetry, where the reader is willing to believe for his own sake. . . .

The second division respects an apparent minute adherence to *matter-of-fact* in character and incidents; *a biographical* attention to probability, and an *anxiety* of explanation and retrospect. Under this head I shall deliver, with no feigned diffidence, the results of my best reflection on the great point of controversy between Mr Wordsworth and his objectors; namely, on *the choice of his characters*. I have already declared, and, I trust justified, my utter dissent from the mode of argument which his critics have hitherto employed. To *their* question, – 'Why did you chuse such a character, or a character from such a rank of life?' – the poet might in my opinion fairly retort: why with the conception of my character did you make wilful choice of mean or ludicrous associations not furnished by me, but supplied from your own sickly and fastidious feelings? How was it, indeed, probable, that such arguments could have any weight with an author, whose plan, whose guiding principle, and main object it was to attack and subdue that state of association, which leads us to place the chief value on those things on which man *differs* from man, and to forget or disregard the high dignities, which belong to *Human Nature*, the sense and the feeling, which *may* be, and *ought* to be, found in *all* ranks? The feelings with which, as Christians, we contemplate a mixed congregation rising or kneeling before their common Maker, Mr Wordsworth would have us entertain at *all* times, as men, and as readers; and by the excitement of this lofty, yet prideless impartiality in *poetry*, he might hope to have encouraged its continuance in *real life*. The praise of good men be his! In real life, and, I trust, even in my imagination, I honour a virtuous and wise man, without reference to the presence or absence of artificial advantages. Whether in the person of an armed baron, a laurelled bard, or of an old Pedlar, or still older Leech-gatherer, the same qualities of head and heart must claim the same reverence. And even in poetry I am not conscious, that I have ever suffered my feelings to be disturbed or offended by any thoughts or images, which the poet himself has not presented.

But yet I object, nevertheless, and for the following reasons. First, because the object in view, as an *immediate* object, belongs to the moral philosopher, and would be pursued, not only more appropriately, but in my opinion with far greater probability of success, in sermons or moral essays, than in an elevated poem. It seems, indeed, to destroy the main fundamental distinction, not only between a *poem* and *prose*, but even between philosophy and works of fiction, inasmuch as it proposes *truth* for its immediate object, instead of *pleasure*. ...

Third; an undue predilection for the *dramatic* form in certain poems, from which one or other of two evils result. Either the thoughts and diction are different from that of the poet, and then there arises an incongruity of style; or they are the same and indistinguishable, and then it presents a species of ventriloquism, where two are represented as talking, while in truth one man only speaks.

The fourth class of defects is closely connected with the former; but yet are such as arise likewise from an intensity of feeling disproportionate to *such* knowledge and value of the objects described, as can be fairly anticipated of men in general, even of the most cultivated classes; and with which therefore few only, and those few particularly circumstanced, can be supposed to sympathize: In this class, I comprise occasional prolixity, repetition, and an eddying, instead of progression, of thought. As instances, see pages 27, 28 and 62 of the Poems, volume 1 and the first eighty lines of the Sixth Book of *The Excursion*.[1]

Fifth and last; thoughts and images too great for the subject. This is an approximation to what might be called *mental* bombast, as distinguished from verbal: for, as in the latter there is a disproportion of the expressions to the thoughts so in this there is a disproportion of thought to the circumstance and occasion. This, by the bye, is a fault of which none but a man of genius is capable. It is the awkwardness and strength of Hercules with the distaff of Omphale.

It is a well known fact, that bright colours in motion both make and leave the strongest impressions on the eye. Nothing is more likely too, than that a vivid image or visual *spectrum*, thus originated, may become the link of association in recalling the feelings and images that had accompanied the original impression. But if we describe this in such lines, as

They flash upon that inward eye,
Which is the bliss of solitude![2]

in what words shall we describe the joy of restrospection, when the images and virtuous actions of a whole well-spent life, pass before that conscience which is indeed the *inward* eye: which is indeed '*the bliss of solitude?*' Assuredly we seem to sink most abruptly, not to say burlesquely, and almost as in a medley, from this couplet to –

And then my heart with pleasure fills.
And dances with the *daffodils*.[3]

The second instance is from volume 2, page 12, where the poet having gone out for a day's tour of pleasure, meets early in the morning with a knot of Gipsies, who had pitched their blanket-tents and straw-beds, together with their children and asses, in some field by the road-side. At the close of the day on his return our tourist found them in the same place. 'Twelve hours,' says he,

1 '*Anecdote for Fathers*', stanzas 4–13. Page 62 (1815 *Poems*) is blank.
2 *I wandered lonely as a cloud*, 21–2.
3 23–4.

Twelve hours, twelve bounteous hours are gone, while I
Have been a traveller under open sky,
Much witnessing of change and cheer,
Yet as I left I find them here![1]

Whereat the poet, without seeming to reflect that the poor tawny
wanderers might probably have been tramping for weeks together
through road and lane, over moor and mountain, and consequently
must have been right glad to rest themselves, their children and cattle,
for one whole day; and overlooking the obvious truth, that such
repose might be quite as necessary for *them*, as a walk of the same
continuance was pleasing or healthful for the more fortunate poet;
expresses his indignation in a series of lines, the diction and imagery
of which would have been rather above, than below the mark, had
they been applied to the immense empire of China improgressive for
thirty centuries:

The weary Sun betook himself to rest: –
– Then issued Vesper from the fulgent west,
Outshining, like a visible God,
The glorious path in which he trod.
And now, ascending, after one dark hour,
And one night's diminution of her power,
Behold the mighty Moon! this way
She looks, as if at them – but they
Regard not her: – oh, better wrong and strife,
Better vain deeds or evil than such life!
The silent Heavens have goings on:
The stars have tasks – but *these* have none![2]

The last instance of this defect, (for I know no other than these
already cited) is from the Ode, page 351, volume 2, where, speaking
of a child, 'a six years' Darling of a pigmy size,' he thus addresses
him:

Thou best Philosopher, who yet dost keep
Thy heritage, thou Eye among the blind,
That, deaf and silent, read'st the eternal deep,

1 Gipsies, 9–12.
2 Gipsies [1815], 13–24.

Haunted for ever by the Eternal Mind, –
Mighty Prophet! Seer blest!
On whom those truths do rest,
Which we are toiling all our lives to find;
Thou, over whom thy Immortality
Broods like the Day, a Master o'er a Slave,
A presence which is not to be put by.[1]

Now here, not to stop at the daring sprit of metaphor which connects the epithets 'deaf and silent', with the apostrophized *eye*: or (if we are to refer it to the preceding word, 'Philosopher'), the faulty and equivocal syntax of the passage; and without examining the propriety of making a 'Master *brood* o'er a Slave', or 'the *Day*' brood *at all*; we will merely ask, what does all this mean? In what sense is a child of that age a *Philosopher*? In what sense does he *read* 'the eternal deep'? In what sense is he declared to be 'for *ever haunted*' by the Supreme Being? or so inspired as to deserve the splendid titles of a *Mighty Prophet*, a *blessed Seer*? By reflection? by knowledge? by conscious intuition? or by *any* form of modification of consciousness? These would be tidings indeed; but such as would presuppose an immediate revelation to the inspired communicator, and require miracles to authenticate his inspiration. Children at this age give us no such information of themselves; and at what time were we dipped in the Lethe, which has produced such utter oblivion of a state so godlike? There are many of us that still possess some remembrances, more or less distinct, respecting themselves at six years old; pity that the worthless straws only should float, while treasures, compared with which all the mines of Golconda and Mexico were but straws, should be absorbed by some unknown gulf into some unknown abyss. . . .

In what sense can the magnificent attributes, above quoted, be appropriated to a *child*, which would not make them equally suitable to a *bee*, or a *dog*, or *a field of corn*; or even to a ship, or to the wind and waves that propel it? The omnipresent Spirit works equally in *them*, as in the child; and the child is equally unconscious of it as they. It cannot surely be, that the four lines, immediately following, are to contain the explanation?

1 *Intimations of Immortality* [1815] stanza viii.

>   To whom the grave
> Is but a lonely bed without the sense or sight
>   Of day or the warm light,
> A place of thought where we in waiting lie; –[1]

Surely, it cannot be that this wonder-rousing apostrophe is but a comment on the little poem, *We are Seven*? – that the whole meaning of the passage is reducible to the assertion, that a *child*, who by the by at six years old would have been better instructed in most Christian families, has no other notion of death than that of lying in a dark, cold place? And still, I hope, not as *in a place of thought*! not the frightful notion of lying *awake* in his grave! The analogy between death and sleep is too simple, too natural, to render so horrid a belief possible for children; even had they not been in the habit, as all Christian children are, of hearing the latter term used to express the former. But if the child's belief be only, that 'he is not dead, but sleepeth': wherein does it differ from that of his father and mother, or any other adult and instructed person? To form an idea of a thing's becoming nothing; or of nothing becoming a thing; is impossible to all finite beings alike, of whatever age, and however educated or uneducated. Thus it is with splendid paradoxes in general. If the words are taken in the common sense, they convey an absurdity; and if, in contempt of dictionaries and custom, they are so interpreted as to avoid the absurdity, the meaning dwindles into some bald truism. Thus you must at once understand the words *contrary* to their common import, in order to arrive at any *sense*; and *according* to their common import, if you are to receive from them any feeling of *sublimity* or *admiration*.

Though the instances of this defect in Mr Wordsworth's poems are so few, that for themselves it would have been scarcely just to attract the reader's attention toward them; yet I have dwelt on it, and perhaps the more for this very reason. For being so very few, they cannot sensibly detract from the reputation of an author, who is even characterized by the number of profound truths in his writings, which will stand the severest analysis; and yet few as they are, they are exactly those passages which his *blind* admirers would be most likely, and best able, to imitate. But Wordsworth, where he is indeed Wordsworth, may be mimicked by copyists, he may be plundered by

1 *Intimations of Immortality*, 122–5 (later suppressed by Wordsworth).

plagiarists; but he can not be imitated, except by those who are not born to be imitators. For without his depth of feeling and his imaginative power his *sense* would want its vital warmth and peculiarity; and without his strong sense, his *mysticism* would become *sickly* – mere fog, and dimness!

To these defects which, as appears by the extracts, are only occasional, I may oppose, with far less fear of encountering the dissent of any candid and intelligent reader, the following (for the most part correspondent) excellencies. First, an austere purity of language both grammatically and logically; in short a perfect appropriateness of the words to the meaning. Of how high value I deem this, and how particularly estimable I hold the example at the present day, has been already stated; and in part too the reasons on which I ground both the moral and intellectual importance of habituating ourselves to a strict accuracy of expression. It is noticeable, how limited an acquaintance with the masterpieces of art will suffice to form a correct and even a sensitive taste, where none but masterpieces have been seen and admired: while on the other hand, the most correct notions, and the widest acquaintance with the works of excellence of all ages and countries, will not perfectly secure us against the contagious familiarity with the far more numerous offspring of tastelessness or of a perverted taste. If this be the case, as it notoriously is, with the arts of music and painting, much more difficult will it be, to avoid the infection of multiplied and daily examples in the practice of an art, which uses words, and words only, as its instruments. In poetry, in which every line, every phrase, may pass the ordeal of deliberation and deliberate choice, it is possible, and barely possible, to attain that *ultimatum* which I have ventured to propose as the infallible test of a blameless style; namely; its *untranslatableness* in words of the same language without injury to the meaning. Be it observed, however, that I include in the *meaning* of a word not only its correspondent object, but likewise all the associations which it recalls. For language is framed to convey not the object alone, but likewise the character, mood and intentions of the person who is representing it. In poetry it *is* practicable to preserve the diction uncorrupted by the affectations and misappropriations, which promiscuous authorship, and reading not promiscuous only because it is disproportionally most conversant with the compositions of the day, have rendered general. Yet even to the poet, composing in his own province, it is an arduous work: and as the result and pledge of a watchful good sense, of fine and luminous distinction, and of complete self-possession, may justly claim all the honour which belongs to an attainment equally difficult and valuable, and the more valuable for being rare. It is at *all* times the proper food of the understanding; but in an age of corrupt eloquence it is both food and antidote. . . .

The second characteristic excellence of Mr Wordsworth's works a correspondent weight and sanity of the Thoughts and Sentiments – won, not from books; but – from the poet's own meditative observation. They are *fresh* and have the dew upon them. His muse, at least when in her strength of wing, and when she hovers aloft in her proper element,

Makes audible a linked lay of truth,
Of truth profound a sweet continuous lay,
Not learnt, but native, her own natural notes![1]

Even throughout his smaller poems there is scarcely one, which is not rendered valuable by some just and original reflection.

See page 25, volume 2[2] or the two following passages in one of his humblest compositions.

O Reader! had you in your mind
Such stores as silent thought can bring,
O gentle Reader! you would find
A tale in every thing.

and

I've heard of hearts unkind, kind deeds
With coldness still returning;
Alas! the gratitude of men
Has oftener left *me* mourning.[3]

or in a still higher strain the six beautiful quatrains, page 134.

Thus fares it still in our decay:
And yet the wiser mind

1 Coleridge's *To William Wordsworth*, 58–60.
2 'Stargazers', Stanzas 3–6.
3 *Simon Lee*, 65–8, 85–8.

Mourns less for what age takes away
Than what it leaves behind.

The Blackbird in the summer trees,
The Lark upon the hill,
Let loose their carols when they please,
Are quiet when they will.

With Nature never do *they* wage
A foolish strife; they see
A happy youth, and their old age
Is beautiful and free:

But we are pressed by heavy laws;
And often, glad no more,
We wear a face of joy, because
We have been glad of yore.

If there is one who need bemoan
His kindred laid in earth,
The household hearts that were his own,
It is the man of mirth.

My days, my Friend, are almost gone,
My life has been approved,
And many love me; but by none
Am I enough beloved.[1]

or the sonnet on Buonaparte, page 202, Volume 2; or finally (for a
volume would scarce suffice to exhaust the instances,) the last stanza
of the poem on the withered Celandine, volume 2, page 312.

To be a Prodigal's Favorite – then, worse truth,
A Miser's Pensioner – behold our lot!
O Man! that from thy fair and shining youth
Age might but take the things Youth needed not![2]

   Third (and wherein he soars far above Daniel) the sinewy strength
and originality of single lines and paragraphs: the frequent *curiosa
felicitas* of his diction, of which I need not here give specimens, having

1 *The Fountain*, 33–56.
2 *The Small Celandine*, 21–5.

anticipated them in a preceding page. This beauty, and as eminently
characteristic of Wordsworth's poetry, his rudest assailants have felt
themselves compelled to acknowledge and admire.

Fourth: the perfect truth of nature in his images and descriptions
as taken immediately from nature, and proving a long and genial
intimacy with the very spirit which gives the physiognomic expression
to all the works of nature. Like a green field reflected in a calm and
perfectly transparent lake, the image is distinguished from the reality
only by its greater softness and lustre. Like the moisture or the polish
on a pebble, genius neither distorts nor false-colours its objects; but
on the contrary brings out many a vein and many a tint, which
escape the eye of common observation, thus raising to the rank of
gems what had been often kicked away by the hurrying foot of the
traveller on the dusty high road of custom.

Let me refer to the whole description of skating, volume 1 pages 44
to 47, especially to the lines

So through the darkness and the cold we flew,
And not a voice was idle: with the din
Meanwhile the precipices rang aloud;
The leafless trees and every icy crag
Tinkled like iron; while the distant hills
Into the tumult sent an alien sound
Of melancholy, not unnoticed, while the stars,
Eastward, were sparkling clear, and in the west
The orange sky of evening died away.[1]

Or to the poem on *The Green Linnet*, volume 1 p. 244. What can be
more accurate yet more lovely than the two concluding stanzas?

Upon yon tuft of hazel trees,
That twinkle to the gusty breeze,
Behold him perched in ecstasies,
    Yet seeming still to hover;
There! where the flutter of his wings
Upon his back and body flings
Shadows and sunny glimmerings,
    That cover him all over.

[1] i.e. *The Prelude* [1805], I, 465–73.

While thus before my eyes he gleams,
A Brother of the Leaves he seems;
When in a moment forth he teems
   His little song in gushes:
As if it pleased him to disdain
And mock the Form which he did feign,
While he was dancing with the train
   Of Leaves among the bushes.

Or the description of the blue-cap, and of the noon-tide silence, p. 284; or the poem to the cuckoo, p. 299; or, lastly, though I might multiply the references to ten times the number, to the poem, so completely Wordsworth's, commencing

Three years she grew in sun and shower –

Fifth: a meditative pathos, a union of deep and subtle thought with sensibility; a sympathy with man as man; the sympathy indeed of a contemplator, rather than a fellow-sufferer or co-mate (*spectator, haud particeps*) but of a contemplator, from whose view no difference of rank conceals the sameness of the nature; no injuries of wind or weather, of toil, or even of ignorance, wholly disguise the human face divine. The superscription and the image of the Creator still remain legible to *him* under the dark lines, with which guilt or calamity had cancelled or cross-barred it. Here the Man and the Poet lose and find themselves in each other, the one as glorified, the latter as substantiated. In this mild and philosophic pathos, Wordsworth appears to me without a compeer. Such as he *is*: so he writes. See volume 1 pages 134 to 136,[1] or that most affecting composition. *The Affliction of Margaret — of —*, pages 165 to 168, which no mother, and, if I may judge by my own experience, no parent can read without a tear. Or turn to that genuine lyric, in the former edition, entitled, *The Mad Mother*, pages 174 to 178, of which I cannot refrain from quoting two of the stanzas, both of them for their pathos, and the former for the fine transition in the two concluding lines of the stanza, so expressive of that deranged state, in which, from the increased sensibility, the sufferer's attention is abruptly drawn off by every trifle, and in the same instant plucked back again by the one despotic

1 ' 'Tis said that some have died for Love'

thought, bringing home with it, by the blending, *fusing* power of Imagination and Passion, the alien object to which it had been so abruptly diverted, no longer an alien but an ally and an inmate.

Suck, little Babe, oh suck again!
It cools my blood; it cools my brain;
Thy lips, I feel them, Baby! they
Draw from my heart the pain away.
Oh! press me with thy little hand;
It loosens something at my chest;
About that tight and deadly band
I feel thy little fingers prest.
The breeze I see is in the tree!
It comes to cool my Babe and me.

Thy Father cares not for my breast,
'Tis thine, sweet Baby, there to rest;
'Tis all thine own! – and, if its hue
Be changed, that was so fair to view,
'Tis fair enough for thee, my dove!
My beauty, little Child, is flown,
But thou wilt live with me in love;
And what if my poor cheek be brown?
'Tis well for me, thou canst not see
How pale and wan it else would be.[1]

Last, and pre-eminently I challenge for this poet the gift of *Imagination* in the highest and strictest sense of the word. In the play of *Fancy*, Wordsworth, to my feelings, is not always graceful, and sometimes *recondite*. The *likeness* is occasionally too strange, or demands too peculiar a point of view, or is such as appears the creature of predetermined research, rather than spontaneous presentation. Indeed his fancy seldom displays itself, as mere and unmodified fancy. But in imaginative power, he stands nearest of all modern writers to Shakespeare and Milton; and yet in a kind perfectly unborrowed and his own. To employ his own words, which are at once an instance and an illustration, he does indeed to all thoughts and to all objects

---

1 '*Her eyes are wild*' [1815] or *The Mad Mother* [1798–1805].

> add the gleam,
> The light that never was, on sea or land,
> The consecration, and the poet's dream.[1]

I have advanced no opinion either for praise or censure, other than as texts introductory to the reasons which compel me to form it. Above all, I was fully convinced that such a criticism was not only wanted; but that, if executed with adequate ability, it must conduce, in no mean degree, to Mr Wordsworth's *reputation*. His *fame* belongs to another age, and can neither be accelerated nor retarded. How small the proportion of the defects are to the beauties, I have repeatedly declared; and that no one of them originates in deficiency of poetic genius. Had they been more and greater, I should still, as a friend to his literary character in the present age, consider an analytic display of them as *pure gain*; if only it removed, as surely to all reflecting minds even the foregoing analysis must have removed, the strange mistake, so slightly grounded, yet so widely and industriously propagated, of Mr Wordsworth's turn for *simplicity*!

John Keats

from a letter to John Hamilton Reynolds   May 1818

You say 'I fear there is little chance of anything else in this life'. You seem by that to have been going through with a more painful and acute zest the same labyrinth that I have – I have come to the same conclusion thus far. My Branchings out therefrom have been numerous: one of them is the consideration of Wordsworth's genius and as a help, in the manner of gold being the meridian Line of worldly wealth – how he differs from Milton. And here I have nothing but surmises, from an uncertainty whether Milton's apparently less anxiety for Humanity proceeds from his seeing further or no than Wordsworth: And whether Wordsworth has in truth epic passion, and martyrs himself to the human heart, the main region of his song – In regard to his genius alone – we find what he says true as far as we have experienced and we can judge no further but by

1 *Elegiac Stanzas*, 14–16.

larger experience – for axioms in philosophy are not axioms until they are proved upon our pulses. We read fine things but never feel them to the full until we have gone the same steps as the Author. . . .

I compare human life to a large Mansion of Many Apartments, two of which I can only describe, the doors of the rest being as yet shut upon me. The first we step into we call the infant or thoughtless Chamber, in which we remain as long as we do not think – We remain there a long while, and notwithstanding the doors of the second Chamber remain wide open, showing a bright appearance, we care not to hasten to it; but are at length imperceptibly impelled by the awakening of this thinking principle within us – we no sooner get into the second Chamber, which I call the Chamber of Maiden-Thought, than we become intoxicated with the light and atmosphere, we see nothing but pleasant wonders, and think of delaying there for ever in delight: However among the effects this breathing is father of is that tremendous one of sharpening one's vision into the heart and nature of Man – of convincing one's nerves that the world is full of Misery and Heartbreak, Pain, Sickness and oppression – whereby this Chamber of Maiden Thought becomes gradually darken'd and at the same time on all sides of it many *doors* are set open – but all dark – all leading to dark passages – We see not the balance of good and evil. We are in a Mist. *We* are now in that state – We feel the 'burden of the Mystery'. To this Point was Wordsworth come, as far as I can conceive when he wrote *Tintern Abbey* and it seems to me that his genius is explorative of those dark Passages. Now if we live, and go on thinking, we too shall explore them – he is a Genius and superior to us, in so far as he can, more than we, make discoveries, and shed a light in them – Here I must think Wordsworth is deeper than Milton – though I think it has depended more upon the general and gregarious advance of intellect, than individual greatness of Mind.

Percy Bysshe Shelley

from '*Peter Bell the Third*'   October 1819

He had a mind which was somehow
  At once circumference and centre
Of al l he might feel or know;
Nothing ever went out, although
  Something did ever enter.

He had as much imagination
  As a pint-pot; – he never could
Fancy another situation
From which to dart his contemplation,
  Than that wherein he stood.

Yet his was individual mind,
  And new created all he saw
In a manner, and refined
Those new creations, and combined
  Them by a master-spirit's law.

Thus – though unimaginative –
  An apprehension clear, intense,
Of his mind's work, had made alive
The things it wrought on; I believe
  Wakening a sort of thought in sense.

But from the first 'twas Peter's drift
  To be a kind of moral eunuch,
He touched the hem of Nature's shift,
Felt faint – and never dared uplift
  The closest, all concealing tunic.

At night he oft would start and wake
  Like a lover, and began
In a wild measure songs to make
On moor, and glen, and rocky lake,
  And on the heart of man –

And on the universal sky –
  And on the wide earth's bosom green, –
And on the sweet, strange mystery
Of what beyond these things may lie,
  And yet remain unseen.

For in his thought he visited
  The spots in which, ere dead and damned,
He in his wayward life had led;
Yet know not whence his thoughts were fed
  Which thus his fancy crammed.

And these obscure remembrances
  Stirred such harmony in Peter,
That, whensoever he should please,
He could speak of rocks and trees
  In poetic metre.

For though it was without a sense
  Of memory, yet he remembered well
Many a ditch and quick-set fence;
Of lakes he had intelligence,
  He knew something of heath and fell.

He also had dim recollections
  Of pedlars tramping on their rounds;
Milk pans and pails; and odd collections
Of saws and proverbs; and reflections
  Old parsons make in burying grounds.

But Peter's verse was clear, and came
  Announcing from the frozen hearth
Of a cold age, that none might tame
The soul of that diviner flame
  It augured to the Earth:

Like gentle rains, on the dry plains,
  Making that green which late was gray,
Or like the sudden moon, that strains
Some gloomy chamber's window-panes
  With a broad light like day.

For language was in Peter's hand
  Like clay while he was yet a potter;
And he made songs for all the land,
Sweet both to feel and understand,
  As pipkins late to mountain Cotter.

Anonymous

from a review of *The Waggoner*, *Eclectic Review* July 1819

Mr Wordsworth has one chance of being read by posterity. It rests upon his finding some judicious friend to do for him the kind office which Pope did for Parnell, and which has probably saved his fame. If Wordsworth's best pieces could be collected into one volume, some of his early lyrics, a few of his odes, his noble sonnets, all his landscape sketches, and the best parts of *The Excursion*, while all his idiots and his waggoners were collected into a bonfire on the top of Skiddaw, then 'Sybilline Leaves' would form a most precious addition to our literature, and his name and his poetry would live, when his system and his absurdities and his critics should be forgotten.

Francis Jeffrey

from a review of *Memorials of a Tour on the Continent*,
Edinburgh Review November 1822

His *Peter Bell* and his *Waggoner* put his admirers, we believe, a little to their shifts; but since he has openly taken to the office of a publican, and exchanged the company of leech-gatherers for that of tax-gatherers, he has fallen into a way of writing which is equally dis-tasteful to his friends and his old monitors – a sort of prosy, solemn, obscure, feeble kind of mouthing, sadly garnished with shreds of phrases from Milton and the Bible – but without nature and without passion, and with a plentiful lack of meaning, compensated only by a large allowance of affection and egotism. This is the taste in which a volume of *Sonnets to the River Duddon* is composed and another which he calls *Ecclesiastical Sketches*, and these precious *Memorials of a Tour*.

The great characteristic of these works is a sort of emphatic inanity – a singular barrenness and feebleness of thought, disguised under a sententious and assuming manner and a style beyond example verbose and obscure. Most of the little pieces of which they are composed begin with the promise of some striking image or deep reflection; but end, almost invariably, in disappointment – having, most commonly, no perceptible meaning at all – or one incredibly puerile and poor – and exemplifying nothing but the very worthless art of saying ordinary things in an unintelligible way – and hiding no meaning in a kind of stern and pompous wordiness.

John Wilson

from a review of *Ecclesiastical Sketches* and *Memorials of a Tour on the Continent, Blackwood's Edinburgh Magazine*   August 1822

Wordsworth never comes forth before the public, from his solitude among the mountains, without deeply delighting all true lovers of poetry. – 'His soul is like a star, and dwells apart.' He is the same man in all things now, that he was twenty years ago, when the *Lyrical Ballads* produced such a wonderful sensation, and told that another great poet had been given to England. All the other first-rate writers of the age have, more or less, written directly and expressly for the age; have followed as often as guided the prevalent taste; and have varied their moods and measures according to the fluctuations of popular feeling, sentiment, and opinion. . . . But Wordsworth buries his spirit in the solitary haunts and recesses of nature, and suffers no living thing to intrude there, to disturb the dreams of his own imagination. He is to himself all in all. – He holds communings with the great spirit of human life, and feels a sanctity in all the revelations that are made to him in solitude. Profoundly versed in the knowledge of all sentiments, feelings and passions, that ever dignified, adorned or purified man's heart, Wordsworth broods over them incessantly, and they are to him his own exceeding great reward. He knows that his poetry is good, and he is calmly satisfied. Indeed, his poetry is to him religion; and we venture to say, that it has been felt to be so by thousands.

William Wordsworth

from a letter to John Kenyon   1836

Dear Mrs Kenyon was right as to the *bare*[1] – the contradiction is in the *words* only – bare, as not being covered with smoke or vapour; clothed, as being attired in the beams of the morning. Tell me if you approve of the following alteration, which is the best I can do for the amendment of the fault

The city now doth on her forehead wear
The glorious crown of morning; silent, bare,
Ship towers, etc.

[1] In answer to a letter objecting to a seeming contradiction in *Upon Westminster Bridge*; the amendment which Wordsworth suggests here was never put into print.

Part Two **The Developing Debate**

Introduction

Before his death in 1850, Wordsworth had already taken his place among the classics. In the year following his death, the publication of *The Prelude* and his nephew's *Memoir* provided an occasion for public summary of his reputation, something about which there was a large measure of agreement.

Yet the way in which his reputation was established in his lifetime had resulted in the presentation of his work to the coming generation as a body of belief, the truth of which was independent of those particular, perhaps unrepeatable, experiences which were for him its sole guarantee. For Wordsworth the truths of his work had been 'carried alive into the heart by passion'; but his later audience found it in many cases preferable to ignore the moments of eccentric private vision and hold fast to the sentiment and reflective morality which were sometimes their adjuncts.

John Stuart Mill perhaps expressed more fully than he realized a common feeling when he called Wordsworth the poet of unpoetical natures: he said that Wordsworth himself

never bounding, never ebullient ... never ... *possessed* by any feeling ... has feeling enough to form a decent, graceful, even beautiful decoration to a thought which is in itself interesting and moving (1833, reprinted in *Dissertations and Discussions*).

Here indeed is a turnabout from 1810: the thoughts *themselves* are interesting – all the poet does is to illustrate them gracefully. The poet himself is excessively normative, no longer the wild eccentric. Furthermore, Wordsworth appealed, as Mill stated, to people who would not normally have been interested in poetry but who sensed some deficiency in their own personalities which he alone could repair. Mill himself was rescued from the depression which closed his education by Wordsworth's poetry. Suffering from a nervous breakdown, he read, in 1828, the collected 1815 poems and found there 'the precise thing for [his] mental wants at that particular juncture' and 'felt [himself] at once better and happier as [he] came under their influence' (*Autobiography*).

Wordsworth has in recent times been the object of some critical condescension because he was used as an anodyne in this way, as a form of spiritual convalescence from the inhumanity of Victorian materialism. But it was hardly Wordsworth's fault that his followers drew strength from only a minor part of his achievement. Nevertheless the critics, or rather the interpreters and propagandists of Wordsworthian doctrines, placed too great a strain on the poems from which they drew their systems, whatever might have been the value of the systems.

It is difficult to adduce the name of a representative Wordsworthian; his readers were too many and too various. Something of the range among those who heard his call can be found between Pater and Ruskin. Pater's claim for Wordsworth, made in 1874, is modest and clear eyed. His poetry, according to Pater, was a continued protest against the predominance of machinery in life: and this is its value. But Pater's presentation of Wordsworth as caring for the 'flowers and leaves' of life and not its 'fruits' does tend towards the reduction of Wordsworth to a sentimental recluse unmoved by normal human cares. Ruskin's letter to Brown by contrast indicates how sufficient and completely trustworthy a guide Wordsworth was for him in 1843. Wordsworthianism – poetry, doctrine and visionary experience – was so much a part of the texture of his own life that any criticism of the master must have been in some respects a saddened recognition by the pupil of his own failures. As he grew older, Ruskin noticed more and more things that were for him defects of character in Wordsworth, notably his provinciality and self enclosedness of thought, and his lack of humility in the facet of nature. 'He has also a vague notion that Nature would not be able to get on without Wordsworth; and finds considerable part of his pleasure in looking at himself as well as her' (*Modern Painters*, vol. 3

no. 16, 38). The last bit is brilliantly acute as well as sarcastic. As in the early days, it is essentially hostile criticism which recognizes the truth, even to which it may be antipathetic.

Ruskin's later attack on Wordsworth in *Fiction, Fair and Foul* had much in common with the temper of the times. Too great a load had been placed by Ruskin and his contemporaries on Wordsworth's shoulders; Arnold's phrase of 'poetical baggage' is very apt. The poet himself was likely to disappear or at least to seem punier than he was. For some, the Wordsworthian experience was truly one which had to be guarded from the shocks of the stirring world. By the time Arnold had come to write his preface, the very natural reaction had occurred, and Wordsworth's poems were as much undervalued as, perhaps, their spiritual restorativeness had been exaggerated.

But the insistence of the Wordsworthians upon the doctrine and upon the 'sanative power' of Wordsworth would have been by no means so damaging had they been willing to broaden their understanding of Wordsworth, and indeed of their knowledge of his poems. Instead they were bent on consolidating the unconscious process of selection that had been taking place since the 1820s. Their affection was, it is true, given to *Poems in Two Volumes* and *Lyrical Ballads*, mainly the second volume, and not, after all, to *Duddon* and *Memorials of a Tour*.

What was chiefly missing was any sense at all of the significance of *The Prelude*, published by Mary Wordsworth in 1850 with remarkably little stir. For the Victorians, it was an afterthought: the poet's work was complete in their selection of it. The Wordsworth they saw in it was the one they had come to know (with very mixed feelings) by the time of his death, the same that glimmered dimly from the pages of Christopher Wordsworth's monument of dull piety, the *Memoir*, which appeared at the same time as *The Prelude* and actually took pride of place in the public reviews. The poem was ignored by both *Quarterly* and *Edinburgh*.

A tiny and unflattering notice appeared in the *Westminster*. *Fraser's* indeed praised it as 'a great autobiographical poem', but there are clear signs that the reviewer had read it skimpily. The review is basically a disquisition on Wordsworth's 'pantheism' and doctrine of the imagination based mainly on *Tintern Abbey*, the reviewer merely rehearsing what he had already discovered about Wordsworth. The promised continuation of the article became instead a review of the *Memoir*, with which *Fraser's* was clearly much more at ease.

There was a much more warm and enthusiastic tribute in the *Eclectic* – which offered the only notice of any importance – from which the following is taken:

He has found his mission in the task of faithfully and fully registering his own experiences, recording his own impressions and painting his own images – feeling that these are so peculiar as to be worth everlasting transmission – and that they are so peculiar because they reflect nature in a manner in which it was never reflected before. He loves to draw his own eye not merely because it is bright nor because it is his own, but because the works of God are mirrored on it at an angle and in colours altogether singular. His writings are all confessions of his passionate love to the material universe and of the strange relation in which material objects stand to his mind. And if men pardon the egotism of Montaigne and Rousseau for the sake of the frank and full disclosure of their writings, expressive of two curious and anomalous structures of mind and morale, much more should the innocent shrift of a pure and peculiar spirit like Wordsworth's, whose sole sin lies in loving too well, be accepted, nay welcomed with gladness by every lover of poetry, nature and man (*Eclectic Review*, December 1850).

Although the close of the first sentence begs its own question, and although ideas about religion and the picturesque are getting in the way here and closing the eyes of the reviewer, this suggests a willingness to respond to detail in a way that might have quite altered the Victorian concept of Wordsworth had it been followed up. But it is clear that the poet's revisions and excisions, and the piety of his family and friends, had been only too successful in presenting Wordsworth as the complete and finished product of his own matured doctrines. The *Eclectic* compares Wordsworth to *Sartor Resatrus* – 'the two most interesting and faithful records of the individual experience of men of genius which exist'. But Sartor is 'more human, more representative', while Wordsworth is 'mild and cherubic' in his experience.

This introduces the most important problem for Wordsworthian studies of the next half century. It follows on from the definitive summing up of Wordsworth's character that had occurred a few months earlier in the *Eclectic's* review of the *Memoir*:

We have said that his life, *as a poet*, was far from perfect. Our meaning is that he did not sufficiently sympathize with the doings of society, the fulness of modern life, and the varied passions, unbeliefs, sins and miseries of modern human nature. His soul dwelt apart. He came, like the Baptist, 'neither eating nor drinking' and men said 'he hath a demon'. He saw at morning, from London bridge 'all its mighty heart' lying still: but he did not at noon plunge artistically into the thick of its throbbing life, far less sound the depth of its wild midnight heavings of revel and wretchedness, of hopes and fears, of stifled fury and eloquent despair. Nor, although he sang 'the mighty stream of tendency' of this wondrous age, did he ever launch his poetic craft upon it, nor seem to see the whitherwards of its swift and awful stress. He has upon the whole stood aside from his time – not on a peak of the past – not on an anticipated Alp of the future, but on his own Cumberland highlands – hearing the tumult and remaining still, lifting up his life as a far seen beacon fire, studying the manners of the humble dwellers in the vales below – 'piping a simple song to thinking hearts', and striving to waft to brother spirits the fine infection of his own enthusiasm, faith, hope and devotion (*Eclectic Review*, July 1850).

This was also Arnold's more famous judgement:

But Wordsworth's eyes avert their ken
From half of human fate (*Obermann*, 1848).

Wordsworth's strangeness was beginning to make itself felt once more; but while his contemporaries had thought it an eccentric and dreamy wildness, the Victorians found it an excessive 'normality', an entirely untypical inborn healthiness and simplicity. The central problem for later nineteenth-century critics emerges from this: how best can the reading of Wordsworth be organized so that he should once more communicate, so that the poems and the doctrine, by now so disturbingly out of joint with each other, could once more be seen as one, as rational and intelligible.

One solution to the problem was found by more or less ignoring it. This was the answer of what may truly be considered the Wordsworthian orthodoxy: found in, for instance, J. C. Shairp's *Wordsworth: The Mind and the Poet* and in Aubrey de Vere's *The Wisdom and Truth of Wordsworth's Poetry* and *The Genius and Passion of Wordsworth*. De Vere's essays are not unintelligent or simple minded, but they do attempt to still obstinate questionings by the greatness of the claims for the 'wisdom and truth . . . of its philosophy'. He sets out to examine those qualities successively in connection with (1) the moral relations of man; (2) with their political relations; (3) with poetry, art, science and human progress; (4) with the exterior universe; (5) with a few of those problems which concern the origin and end of man as a spiritual and immortal being.

With such an introduction, there is clearly no question as to Wordsworth's complete sufficiency in all the problems of life. Yet this cannot have been the case for a troubled and intelligent Victorian. He could not have been much impressed when De Vere chose *Laodamia* to illustrate Wordsworth's 'wisdom' in handling 'moral relations' and *Dion* his 'political wisdom'. The modern reader likewise can have little to expect from a handling of Wordsworth's treatment of nature and imagination that fails to cite *The Prelude*.

Clough's *Lecture* is by contrast, and not only by contrast, a brilliant and clear piece of thinking and is in marked opposition to the orthodoxy. It represents a stage which, as far as 'philosophy' is concerned, is half-way between admiration and disbelief. In Arnold, Swinburne and Stephen the debate becomes, retrospectively, modern and recognizable.

Arnold's contribution was primarily a critical one. His clear distinction of the poems of the creative period was a preliminary act of re-focusing which was to be of great influence and value with its bare but authoritative statement. The companion effort to concentrate attention where (he thought) it belonged, represented by the famous statement 'Poetry is the reality; philosophy is the illusion' is of more doubtful usefulness. In the context of Arnold's task at the time it was necessary, to uncover Wordsworth from the embarrassing mound of propaganda which had overwhelmed his poems. Arnold however had no real intention of dismissing Wordsworth's 'application of ideas to life'. The confusion is only apparent. Arnold rightly dismissed the idea that Wordsworth came upon the world with a series of texts which he systematically illustrated poetically, as J. S. Mill would have had it. Then, Arnold adopted a formula which, while fully based on the great poetry he had critically distinguished, would retain Wordsworth's status as a great moral teacher, and yet be less mystic and esoteric, and be capable of communicating more widely with men's ordinary experiences. That this was a deliberate compromise does not appear overtly in the Preface because Arnold did not choose to expound the implications of his formula: 'criticism of life' and 'the power of feeling the joy offered in nature'. However, taken together, they open up a whole new area for systematization, and are responsible for one current critical orthodoxy. The influence of Arnold has been very great. But his approach, emphasizing as it did selection and criticism, was not the only one, nor the most invigorating. Arnold's critical genius really epitomized the nineteenth-century concept of Wordsworth, and ensured its survival.

Arnold singled out Leslie Stephen for special criticism. But it was probably he who provided a liberating impulse. There is much more in his essay on *Wordsworth's Ethics* than the simple-minded system-mongering Arnold holds up for our disapproval. Stephen's answer to the problem which has been isolated here, which could have come only with time and from one of Stephen's background, was to broaden the whole subject. Wordsworth's ideas were taken seriously and were found to have a permanent importance: but they were also seen in a particular historical context, as the products of Wordsworth's time and place. This enabled Stephen to distance Wordsworth's 'thoughts' and so to treat them with unusual tact and delicacy; subscription to or rejection of them not being a matter of urgency. Furthermore, by withdrawing emphasis from Wordsworth's sense of joy and placing it on his power to turn pain and sorrow to account, Stephen brings Wordsworth much closer to common experience. Instead of presenting contemplation, solitude and wise passiveness as the all-in-all of the Wordsworthian experience, he posits a dynamic relation between action, suffering, relationship, withdrawal, solitude and relationship once more. Wordsworth is indeed only a spectator, and occasional critic, of the striving world of his day, but in Stephen's reading he is seen to be at least continuous with it. The respect for Wordsworth's ideas which accompanies an understanding of them as bound to a certain time is also present in the chapter from Whitehead's *Science and the Modern World*.

Finally, there is Bradley's important essay, originally an Oxford lecture on poetry, which offers a third way. In the context of the Victorian debate, it was an astonishing reversal to admit that Wordsworth's poetry took its strength very far from what is usually recognized to be the stuff of ordinary life. This was the beginning of a new problem: how could the peculiar and personal depths of Wordsworth's poetic inspiration be recognized without consigning him to a rather precious mysticism which would once again make him unreadable?

John Ruskin

from a letter to the Rev. Walter Brown   1843

Wordsworth has a grand, consistent, perfectly disciplined, all grasping intellect – for which nothing is too small, nothing too great, arranging everything in due relations, divinely pure in its conceptions of pleasure, majestic in the equanimity of its benevolence – intense as white fire with chastized feeling. Coleridge may be the greater poet but surely it admits of no question which is the greater man. Wordsworth often appears to want energy because he has so much judgement, and because he never enunciates any truth but with full views of many points which diminish the extent of its application, while Coleridge and others say more boldly what they see more partially. I believe Coleridge has very little moral influence on the world: his writings are those of a benevolent man in a fever. Wordsworth may be trusted as a guide in everything, he feels nothing but what we all ought to feel – what every mind in pure moral health must feel, he says nothing but what we all ought to believe – what all strong intellects must believe. He has written some things trifling, some verses which might be omitted – but none to be *regretted*.

[Then he criticizes *Christabel* and continues] How different is [Wordsworth's] *The White Doe of Rylstone*, a poem of equal grace and imagination, but how pure, how just, how chaste in its truth, how high in its end, showing how 'anguish wild as dreams of restless sleep is tempered and allayed by sympathies aloft ascending and descending deep'. . . .[1] Or if you want pure pathos take *The Brothers*, the most really affecting, most perfect piece of natural feeling in the English language. The last two lines of it are, to my mind, the most exquisite close that ever poet wrote. And then read *The Affliction of Margaret* and *The Female Vagrant* and *Lucy Gray* and 'She dwelt. . . .' – and then with the magnificent comprehension and faultless majesty of *The Excursion* to crown all.

1 From stanza 6 of the *Dedication* to *The White Doe of Rylstone*.

Robert Browning

from a letter to Harriet Martineau   16 February 1846

Was ever such a '*great*' poet before? Put one trait with the other –
the theory of rural innocence – alternation of 'vulgar trifles' with
dissertating with style of 'the utmost grandeur that *even you* can
conceive' (speak for yourself, Miss M.) – and that amiable transition
from two o'clock's grief at the death of one's brother to three
o'clock's happiness in the 'extraordinary mesmeric discourse' of
one's friend. All this, and the rest of the serene and happy inspired
daily life which a piece of 'unpunctuality' can ruin, and to which
the guardian 'angel' brings as crowning qualification the knack of
poking the fire adroitly – of this – what can one say but that – no,
best hold one's tongue and read the *Lyrical Ballads* with finger in ear.
Did not Shelley say long ago 'He had no more *imagination* than a
pint-pot' – though in those days he used to walk about France and
Flanders like a man? *Now*, he is 'most comfortable in his worldly
affairs' and just this comes of it! He lives the best twenty years of his
life after the way of his own heart – and when one presses in to see
the result of the rare experiment – what the *one* alchemist whom
fortune has allowed to get all his coveted materials and set to work at
last in earnest with fire and melting pot – what he produces after all
the talk of him and the like of him; why, you get *pulvis et cinis* – a
man at the mercy of tongs and shovel!

Walter Bagehot

from 'Wordsworth, Tennyson and Browning; or, Pure,
Ornate and Grotesque Art in English Poetry'   1864

[The essay quotes in full Wordsworth's two sonnets *The Trosachs*
and *Westminster Bridge* and continues]

Instances of barer style than this may easily be found, instances of
colder style – few better instances of purer style. Not a single expression (the invocation in the concluding couplet of the second

sonnet perhaps excepted[1]) can be spared, yet not a single expression rivets the attention. If indeed we take out the phrase

This City now doth, like a garment, wear
The beauty of the morning;

and the description of the brilliant yellow of autumn

(October's workmanship to rival May)

they have independent value, but they are not noticed in the sonnet when we read it through; they fall into place there, and being in their place, are not seen. The great subject of the two sonnets, the religious aspect of beautiful but grave nature – the religious aspect of a city about to waken and to be alive, are the only ideas left in our mind. To Wordsworth has been vouchsafed the last grace of the self-denying artist; you think neither of him nor his style, but you cannot help thinking of – you *must* recall – the exact phrase, the *very* sentiment he wished.

Arthur Hugh Clough

from 'Lecture on the Poetry of Wordsworth', *Poetry and Prose Remains*, vol. I   1869

It is a curious and yet an undeniable fact that Wordsworth, who began his poetical course with what was, at any rate, understood by most readers to be a disclaimer and entire repudiation of the ornament of style and poetic diction, really derives from his style and his diction his chief and special charm. I shall not venture categorically to assert that his practice is in positive opposition to the doctrine he maintains in the Prefaces, and supplementary remarks, which accompanied his *Lyrical Ballads*, and which, calling down upon him and them the hostility of reviews and the ridicule of satirists, made him notorious as one

Who both by precept and example shows
That prose is verse, and verse is merely prose.

1 'Dear God! the very houses seem asleep. . . .'

Certain it is however that he did bestow infinite toil and labour upon his poetic style; and that in the nice and exquisite felicities of poetic diction he specially surpassed his contemporaries; that his scrupulous and painstaking spirit, in this particular, constitutes one of his special virtues as a poet. The moving accident, as he says, was not his trade; of event and of action his compositions are perfectly destitute; a lyrical and didactic almost exclusively, scarcely ever in any sense a dramatic writer, it is upon beauty of expression that by the very necessity of his position he has to depend. Scott and Byron are mere negligent schoolboys compared with him. . . .

Wordsworth's practice, in all probability, was far more just than his theory. His theory, indeed, as directed not against style in general, but against the then prevalent vices of style, was a very tolerably justifiable and useful theory, but his practice was extremely meritorious; his patience, and conscientious labour deserve all praise. He has not indeed (Nature had not bestowed on him) the vigour and heartiness of Scott, or the force and the sweep and the fervour of Byron; but his poems do more perfectly and exquisitely and unintermittedly express his real meaning and significance and character than do the poems of either Scott or Byron. Lyrical verse is by its nature more fugitive than drama or story; yet I incline to believe that there are passages of Wordsworth which, from the mere perfection of their language will survive when the Marmions and the Laras are deep in dust. As writers for their age, as orators, so to say, as addressing themselves personally to their contemporaries, Byron and Scott, were far more influential men, *are* far greater names. They had more, it may be, to say to their fellows; they entered deeper perhaps into the feelings and life of their time; they received a larger and livelier recognition and a more immediate and tangible reward of popular enthusiasm and praise. It may be, too, that they had something not for their own generation only, but for all ages, which quite as well deserved a permanent record as anything in the mind of Wordsworth.

But that permanent beauty of expression, that harmony between thought and word which is the condition of 'immortal verse', they did not, I think – and Wordsworth did – take pains to attain. There is hardly anything in Byron or Scott which in another generation people will not think they can say over again quite as well, and more agreeably and familiarly for themselves; there is nothing which, it will be plain, has, in Scott's or Byron's way of putting it, attained the one form which of all others truly belongs to it; which any new attempt will, at the very utmost, merely successfully repeat. For poetry, like science, has its final precision; and there are expressions of poetic knowledge which can no more be rewritten than could the elements of geometry. There are pieces of poetic language which, try as men will, they will simply have to recur to, and confess that it has been done before them. I do not say that there is in Wordsworth anything like the same quantity of this supreme result which you find in Shakespeare or Virgil; there is far less of the highest poetry than in Shakespeare; there is far more admixture of the unpoetic than in Virgil. But there is in him a good deal more truly complete and finished poetic attainment than in his other English contemporaries.

And this is no light thing. People talk about style as if it were a mere accessory, the unneeded but pleasing ornament, the mere put-on dress of the substantial being, who without it is much the same as with it. Yet is it not intelligible that by a change of intonation, accent, or it may be, accompanying gesture, the same words may be made to bear most different meanings? What is the difference between good and bad acting but style, and yet how different good acting is from bad. On the contrary, it may really be affirmed that some of the highest truths are only expressible to us by style, only appreciable as indicated by manner. . . .

Had Wordsworth been more capable of discerning his bad from his good, there would, it is likely enough, have been far less of the bad; but the good perhaps would have been very far less good. The consequence is, however, that to prove him a true poet, you have to hunt down a bit here and a bit there, a few lines in a book of the *Prelude on The Excursion*, one sonnet perhaps amongst eighty or ninety, one stanza in a series of *Memorials of Tours in Scotland or on the Continent*; only very occasionally finding the reward of a complete poem, good throughout, and good as a whole.

What is meant when people complain of him as mawkish, is a different matter. It is, I believe, that instead of looking directly at an object, and considering it as a thing in itself, and allowing it to operate upon him as a fact in itself, he takes the sentiment produced by it in his own mind, as the thing, as the important and really real fact. The real thing ceases to be real; the world no longer exists; all that exists is the feeling, somehow generated in the poet's sensibility. This sentimentalizing over sentiment, this sensibility about sensibility, has been carried, I grant, by the Wordsworthians to a far more than Wordsworthian excess. But he has something of it surely. He is apt to wind up his short pieces with reflections upon the way in which, hereafter, he expects to reflect upon his present reflections. Nevertheless this is not by any means attributable to all his writings. . . .

Wordsworth, we have said, succeeded beyond the other poets of the time in giving a perfect expression to his meaning, in making his verse permanently true to his genius and his moral frame. Let us now proceed to inquire the worth of that genius and moral frame, the sum of the real significance of his character and view of life.

> Unless above himself he can
> Erect himself, how poor a thing is Man.

are words which he himself adopts from the Elizabethan poet Daniel, translated by him from Seneca, and introduces into that part of *The Excursion* which gives us what I might call his creed, the statement of those substantive convictions upon which after a certain amount of fluctuation and tossing about in the world he found himself or got himself anchored.

A certain elevation and fixity characterize Wordsworth everywhere. You will not find, as in Byron, an ebullient overflowing life, refusing all existing restrictions, and seeking in vain to create for itself, to own in itself any permanent law or rule. To have attained a law, to exercise a lordship by right divine over passions and desires – this is Wordsworth's preeminence.

Nor do we find, as in Scott, a free vigorous animal nature ready to accept whatever things earth has to offer, eating and drinking and enjoying heartily; . . . a certain withdrawal and separation; a moral and almost religious selectiveness, a rigid refusal and a nice picking and choosing, are essential to Wordsworth's being. It has been not inaptly said by a French critic that you may trace in him, as in Addison, Richardson, Cowper, a spiritual descent from the Puritans.

. . . More rational, certainly, than either Byron's hot career of wilfulness or Scott's active but easy existence amidst animal spirits and out-of-door enjoyments, more dignified, elevated, serious, significant and truly human, was Wordsworth's homely and frugal life in the cottage at Grasmere. While wandering with his dear waggoners round his dearer lakes, talking with shepherds, watching hills and stars, studying the poets and fashioning verses, amidst all this there was really something higher than either wildly crying out to have things as one chose, or cheerfully taking the worldly good things as one found them, working to gain the means and relish for amusement. He did not, it is true, sweep away with him the exulting hearts of youth, 'o'er the glad waters of the dark blue sea'; he did not win the eager and attentive ear of high and low, at home and abroad, with the entertainment of immortal Waverley novels; but to strive not unsuccessfully to build the lofty rhyme, to lay slowly the ponderous foundations of pillars to sustain man's moral fabric, to fix a centre around which the chaotic elements of human impulse and desire might take solid form and move in their ordered ellipses, to originate a spiritual vitality, this was perhaps greater than sweeping over glad blue waters or inditing immortal novels.

> Unless above himself he can
> Erect himself, how poor a thing is Man.

Unless above himself, how poor a thing; yet, if beyond and outside of his world, how useless and purposeless a thing. This also must be remembered. And I cannot help thinking that there is in Wordsworth's poems something of a spirit of withdrawal and seclusion from, and even evasion of, the actual world. In his own quiet rural sphere it is true he did fairly enough look at things as they were; he did not belie his own senses, nor pretend to recognize in outward things what really was not in them. But his sphere was a small one; the objects he lived among unimportant and petty. Retiring early from all conflict and even contact with the busy world, he shut himself from the elements which it was his business to encounter and master. This gives to his writings, compared with those of Scott and Byron, an appearance of sterility and unreality. He cannot indeed, be said, like Cowper, to be an indoors poet; but he is a poet rather of a country house or a picturesque tour, not of life and business, action and fact.

This also sadly lessens the value which we must put on that high moral tone which we have hitherto been extolling. To live in a quiet village, out of the road of all trouble and temptation, in a pure, elevated, high moral sort of manner, is after all no such very great a feat. . . .

There may be, moreover, a further fault in Wordsworth's high morality, consequent on this same evil of premature seclusion, which I shall characterize by the name of arbitrary positiveness. There is such a thing in morals, as well as in science, as drawing your conclusion before you have properly got your premises. It is desirable to attain a fixed point; but it is essential that the fixed point be a right one. We ought to hold fast by what is true; but because you choose to be positive, do not therefore be sure you have the truth.

Another evil consequence is the triviality in many places of his imagery, and the mawkishness, as people say, of his sentiment. I cannot myself heartily sympathize with the *Ode to the Small Celandine*, or repeated poems to the daisy. I find myself a little recoil from the statement that

To me the meanest flower that blows doth give
Thoughts that do often lie too deep for tears.

These phenomena of external nature, which in the old and great poets come forward simply as analogies and similitudes of what is truly great, namely human nature, and as expressions of curious and wonderful relations, are in Wordsworth themselves the truly great, all important and preeminently wonderful things of the universe. Blue sky and white clouds, larks and linnets, daisies and celandines – these, it appears, are 'the proper subject of mankind'; not, as we used to think, the wrath of Achilles, the guilt and remorse of Macbeth, the love and despair of Othello.

This tendency to exaggerate the importance of flowers and fields, lakes and waterfalls, and scenery, I remember myself, when a boy of eighteen, to have heard, not without a shock of mild surprise, the venerable poet correct. People come to the lakes, he said, and are charmed with a particular spot, and build a house, and find themselves discontented, forgetting that these things are only the sauce and the garnish of life. Nevertheless we fear that the exclusive student of Wordsworth may go away with the strange persuasion that it is his business to walk about this world of life and action, and, avoiding life and action, have his gentle thoughts excited by flowers and running waters and shadows on mountain sides.

This we conceive is a grievous inherent error in Wordsworth. The poet of Nature he may be; but this sort of writing does justice to the proper worth and dignity neither of man nor of Nature.

Walter Pater

'Wordsworth' 1874 (first printed in *Fortnightly Review* and reprinted in *Appreciations*, 1889)

Some English critics at the beginning of the present century had a great deal to say concerning a distinction, of much importance, as they thought, in the true estimate of poetry, between the *Fancy*, and another more powerful faculty – the *Imagination*. This metaphysical distinction, borrowed originally from the writings of German philosophers, and perhaps not always clearly apprehended by those who talked of it, involved a far deeper and more vital distinction, which indeed all true criticism more or less directly has to do, the distinction, namely, between higher and lower degrees of intensity in the poet's perception of his subject, and in his concentration of himself upon his work. Of those who dwelt upon the metaphysical distinction between the Fancy and the Imagination, it was Wordsworth who made the most of it, assuming it as the basis for the final classification of his poetical writings; and it is in these writings that the deeper and more vital distinction, which, as I have said, underlies the metaphysical distinction, is most needed, and may be best illustrated.

For nowhere is there so perplexed a mixture as in Wordsworth's own poetry, of work touched with intense and individual power, with work of almost no character at all. He has much conventional sentiment, and some of that insincere poetic diction, against which his most serious critical efforts were directed: the reaction in his political ideas, consequent on the excesses of 1795, makes him, at times, a mere declaimer on moral and social topics; and he seems, sometimes, to force an unwilling pen, and write by rule. By making the most of these blemishes it is possible to obscure the true aesthetic value of his work, just as his life also, a life of much quiet delicacy and independence, might easily be placed in a false focus, and made to appear a somewhat tame theme in illustration of the more obvious parochial virtues. And those who wish to understand his influence and experience his peculiar savour, must bear with patience the presence of an alien element in Wordsworth's work, which never coalesced with what is really delightful in it, nor underwent his special power. Who that values his writings most has not felt the intrusion there, from time to time, of somethihg tedious and prosaic? Of all poets equally great, he would gain most by a skilfully made anthology. Such a selection would show, in truth, not so much what he was, or to himself and others seemed to be, as what, by the more energetic and fertile quality in his writings, he was ever tending to become. And the mixture in his work, as it actually stands, is so perplexed, that one fears to miss the least promising composition even, lest some precious morsel should be lying hidden within – the few perfect lines, the phrase, the single word perhaps, to which he often works up mechanically through a poem, almost the whole of which may be tame enough. He who thought that in all creative work the larger part was *given* passively, to the recipient mind, who waited so dutifully upon the gift, to whom so large a measure was sometimes given, had his times also of desertion and relapse; and he has permitted the impress of these too to remain in his work. And this duality there – the fitfulness with which the higher qualities manifest themselves in it, gives the effect in his poetry of a power not altogether his own, or under his control, which comes and goes when it will, lifting or lowering a matter, poor in itself; so that that old fancy which made the poet's art an enthusiasm, a form of divine possession, seems almost literally true of him.

This constant suggestion of an absolute duality between higher and lower moods, and the work done in them, stimulating one always to look below the surface, makes the reading of Wordsworth an excellent sort of training towards the things of art and poetry. It begets in those, who, coming across him in youth, can bear him at all, a habit of collectedness of mind in the right appreciation of poetry, an expectation of things, in this order, coming to one; by means of a right discipline of the temper as well as of the intellect. He meets us with the promise that he has much, and something very peculiar, to give us, if we will follow a certain difficult way, and seems to have the secret of a special and privileged state of mind. And those who have undergone his influence, and followed this difficult way, are like people who have passed through some initiation, a *disciplina arcani*, by submitting to which they become able constantly to distinguish in art, speech, feeling, manners, that which is organic, animated, expressive, from that which is only conventional, derivative, inexpressive.

But although the necessity of selecting these precious morsels for oneself is an opportunity for the exercise of Wordsworth's peculiar influence, and induces a kind of just criticism and true estimate of it, yet the purely literary product would have been more excellent had the writer himself purged away that alien element. How perfect would have been the little treasury, shut between the covers of how thin a book. Let us suppose the desired separation made, the electric thread untwined, the golden pieces, great and small, lying apart together. What are the peculiarities of this residue? What special sense does Wordsworth exercise, and what instincts does he satisfy? What are the subjects and the motives which in him excite the imaginative faculty? What are the qualities in things and persons which he values, the impression and sense of which he can convey to others, in an extraordinary way?

An intimate consciousness of the expression of natural things, which weighs, listens, penetrates, where the earlier mind passed roughly by, is a large element in the complexion of modern poetry. It has been remarked as a fact in mental history again and again. It reveals itself in many forms; but it is strongest and most attractive in what is strongest and most attractive in modern literature. It is exemplified, almost equally, by writers as unlike each other as Senancour and Theophile Gautier: as a singular chapter in the history of the human mind, its growth might be traced from Rousseau to Chateaubriand, from Chateaubriand to Victor Hugo: it has doubtless some latent connection with those pantheistic theories which locate an intelligent soul in material things, and have largely exercised men's minds in some modern systems of philosophy: it is traceable even in the graver writings of historians: it makes as much difference between ancient and modern landscape art, as there is between the rough masks of an early mosaic and a portrait by Reynolds or Gainsborough. Of this new sense, the writings of Wordsworth are the central and elementary expression: he is more simply and entirely occupied with it than any other poet, though there are fine expressions of precisely the same thing in so different a poet as Shelley. There was in his own character a certain contentment, a sort of inborn religious placidity, seldom found united with a sensibility so mobile as his, which was favourable to the quiet habitual observation of inanimate, or imperfectly animate, existence. His life of eighty years is divided by no very profoundly felt incidents: its changes are almost wholly inward, and it falls into broad, untroubled, perhaps somewhat monotonous spaces. What it most resembles is the life of one of those early Italian or Flemish painters, who, just because their minds were full of heavenly visions, passed, some of them, the better part of sixty years in quiet, systematic industry. This placid life matured a quite unusual sensibility, really innate in him, to the sights and sounds of the natural world – the flower and its shadow on the stone, the cuckoo and its echo. The poem of *Resolution and Independence* is a storehouse of such records: for its fulness of imagery it may be compared to Keats's *Saint Agnes' Eve*. To read one of his longer pastoral poems for the first time, is like a day spent in a new country: the memory is crowded for a while with its precise and vivid incidents –

The pliant harebell swinging in the breeze
On some grey rock; –

The single sheep and the one blasted tree
And the bleak music from that old stone wall; –

In the meadows and the lower ground
Was all the sweetness of a common dawn; –

And that green corn all day is rustling in thine ears.[1]

Clear and delicate at once, as he is in the outlining of visible imagery, he is more clear and delicate still, and finely scrupulous, in the noting of sounds; so that he conceives of noble sound as even moulding the human countenance to nobler types, and as something

1 'As a light
And pliant harebell, swinging in the breeze
On some grey rock'
is an image of Wordsworth's state of mind in *The Prelude* [1850], X, 276–8; 'This single sheep', XII, 319–20; 'In the meadows', IV, 329–30; 'And that green corn ... in *thy* ears', *The Pet Lamb*, 28.

actually 'profaned' by colour, by visible form, or image. He has a power likewise of realizing and conveying to the consciousness of the reader, abstract and elementary impressions – silence, darkness, absolute motionlessness: or, again, the whole complex sentiment of a particular place, the abstract expression of desolation in the long white road, of peacefulness in a particular folding of the hills. In the airy building of the brain, a special day or hour even, comes to have for him a sort of personal identity, a spirit or angel given to it, by which, for its exceptional insight, or the happy light upon it, it has a presence in one's history, and acts there, as a separate power or accomplishment; and he has celebrated in many of his poems the 'efficacious spirit', which, as he says, resides in these 'particular spots' of time.

It is to such a world, and to a world of congruous meditation thereon, that we see him retiring in his but lately published poem of *The Recluse* – taking leave, without much count of costs, of the world of business, of action and ambition, as also of all that for the majority of mankind counts as sensuous enjoyment.

And so it came about that this sense of a life in natural objects, which in most poetry is but a rhetorical artifice, is with Wordsworth the assertion of what for him is almost literal fact. To him every natural object seemed to possess more or less of a moral or spiritual life, to be capable of a compansionship with man, full of expression, of inexplicable affinities and delicacies of intercourse. An emanation, a particular spirit, belonged, not to the moving leaves or water only, but to the distant peak of the hills arising suddenly, by some change of perspective, above the nearer horizon, to the passing space of light across the plain, to the lichened Druidic stone even, for a certain weird fellowship in it with the moods of men. It was like a 'survival', in the peculiar intellectual temperament of a man of letters at the end of the eighteenth century, of that primitive condition, which some philosophers have traced in the general history of human culture, wherein all outward objects alike, including even the works of men's hands, were believed to be endowed with animation, and the world was 'full of souls' – that mood in which the old Greek gods were first begotten, and which had many strange aftergrowths.

In the early ages, this belief, delightful as its effects on poetry often are, was but the result of a crude intelligence. But, in Wordsworth, such power of seeing life, such perception of a soul, in inanimate

things, came of an exceptional susceptibility to the impressions of
eye and ear, and was, in its essence, a kind of sensuousness. At least, it
is only in a temperament exceptionally susceptible on the sensuous
side, that this sense of the expressiveness of things comes to be so large
a part of life. That he awakened 'a sort of thought in sense', is
Shelley's just estimate of this element in Wordsworth's poetry.

And it was through nature, thus ennobled by a semblance of passion
and thought, that he thus approached the spectacle of human life.
Human life, indeed, is for him, at first, only an additional grace of
an expressive landscape. When he thought of man, it was of man as in
the presence and under the influence of these effective natural objects,
and linked to them by many associations. The close connection of
man with natural objects, the habitual association of his thoughts and
feelings with a particular spot of earth, has sometimes seemed to
degrade those who are subject to its influence, as if it did but reinforce that physical connection of our nature with the actual lime and
clay of the soil, which is always drawing us nearer to our end. But
for Wordsworth, these influences tended to the dignity of human
nature, because they tended to tranquillize it. By raising nature to
the level of human thought he gives it power and expression: he
subdues man to the level of nature, and gives him thereby a certain
breadth and coolness and solemnity. The leech-gatherer on the moor,
the woman 'stepping westward', are for him natural objects, almost
in the same sense as the aged thorn, or the lichened rock on the
heath. In this sense the leader of the 'Lake School', in spite of an
earnest preoccupation with man, his thoughts, his destiny, is the
poet of nature. And of nature, after all, in its modesty. The English
lake country has, of course, its grandeurs. But the peculiar function
of Wordsworth's genius, as carrying in it a power to open out the
soul of apparently little or familiar things, would have found its
true test had he become the poet of Surrey, say! and the prophet of
its life. The glories of Italy and Switzerland, though he did write a
little about them, had too potent a material life of their own to serve
greatly his poetic purpose.

Religious sentiment, consecrating the affections and natural regrets
of the human heart, above all, that pitiful awe and care for the perish-
ing human clay, of which relic-worship is but the corruption, has
always had much to do with localities, with the thoughts which

attach themselves to actual scenes and places. Now what is true of it everywhere, is truest of it in those secluded valleys where one generation after another remains in the same abiding-place; and it was on this side, that Wordsworth apprehended religion most strongly. Consisting, as it did so much, in the recognition of local sanctitites, in the habit of connecting the stones and trees of a particular spot of earth with the great events of life, till the low walls, the green mounds, the half-obliterated epitaphs seemed full of voices, and a sort of natural oracles, the very religion of these people of the dales appeared but as another link between them and the earth, and was literally a religion of nature. It tranquillized them by bringing them under the placid rule of traditional and narrowly localized observances. 'Grave livers', they seemed to him, under this aspect, with stately speech, and something of that natural dignity of manners which underlies the highest courtesy.

And, seeing man thus as a part of nature, elevated and solemnized in proportion as his daily life and occupations brought him into companionship with permanent natural objects, his very religion forming new links for him with the narrow limits of the valley, the low vaults of the church, the rough stones of his home, made intense for him now with profound sentiment, Wordsworth was able to appreciate passion in the lowly. He chooses to depict people from humble life, because, being nearer to nature than others, they are on the whole more impassioned, certainly more direct in their expression of passion, than other men: it is for this direct expression of passion, that he values their humble words. In much that he said in exaltation of rural life, he was but pleading indirectly for that sincerity, that perfect fidelity to one's own inward presentations, to the precise features of the pictures within, without which any profound poetry is impossible. It was not for their tameness, but for this passionate sincerity, that he chose incidents and situations from common life, 'related in a selection of language really used by men'. He constantly endeavours to bring his language near to the real language of men: to the real language of men, however, not on the dead level of their ordinary intercourse, but in select moments of vivid sensation, when this language is winnowed and ennobled by excitement. There are poets who have chosen rural life as their subject, for the sake of its passionless repose, and times when Wordsworth himself extols the mere calm and dispassionate survey of things as the highest aim of poetical culture. But it was not for such passionless calm that he preferred the scenes of pastoral life; and the meditative poet, sheltering himself, as it might seem, from the agitations of the outward world, is in reality only clearing the scene for the great exhibitions of emotion, and what he values most is the almost elementary expression of elementary feelings.

And so he has much for those who value highly the concentrated presentment of passion, who appraise men and women by their susceptibility to it, and art and poetry as they afford the spectacle of it. Breaking from time to time into the pensive spectacle of their daily toil, their occupations near to nature, come those great elementary feelings, lifting and solemnizing their language and giving it a natural music. The great, distinguishing passion came to Michael by the sheepfold, to Ruth by the wayside, adding these humble children of the furrow to the true aristocracy of passionate souls. In this respect, Wordsworth's work resembles most that of George Sand, in those of her novels that depict country life. With a penetrative pathos, which puts him in the same rank with the masters of the sentiment of pity in literature, with Meinhold and Victor Hugo, he collects all the traces of vivid excitement which were to be found in that pastoral world – the girl who rung her father's knell; the unborn infant feeling about its mother's heart; the instinctive touches of children; the sorrows of the wild creatures, even – their home-sickness, their strange yearnings; the tales of passionate regret that hang by a ruined farm-building, a heap of stones, a deserted sheepfold; that gay, false, adventurous, outer world, which breaks in from time to time to bewilder and deflower these quiet homes; not 'passionate sorrow' only, for the overthrow of the soul's beauty, but the loss of, or carelessness for personal beauty even in those whom men have wronged – their pathetic wanness; the sailor 'who, in his heart, was half a shepherd on the stormy seas'; the wild woman teaching her child to pray for her betrayer; incidents like the making of the shepherd's staff, or that of the young boy laying the first stone on the sheepfold; – all the pathetic episodes of their humble existence, their longing, their wonder at fortune, their poor pathetic pleasures, like the pleasures of children, won so hardly in the struggle for bare existence; their yearning towards each other, in their darkened houses, or at their early toil. A sort of biblical depth and solemnity hangs over this strange, new, passionate, pastoral world, of which he first raised the image, and the reflection of which some of our best modern fiction has caught from him.

He pondered much over the philosophy of his poetry, and reading deeply in the history of his own mind, seems at times to have passed the borders of a world of strange speculations, inconsistent enough, had he cared to note such inconsistencies, with those traditional beliefs, which were otherwise the object of his devout acceptance. Thinking of the high value he set upon customariness, upon all that is habitual, local, rooted in the ground, in matters of religious sentiment, you might sometimes regard him as one tethered down to a world, refined and peaceful indeed, but with no broad outloook, a world protected, but somewhat narrowed, by the influence of received ideas. But he is at times also something very different from this, and something much bolder. A chance expression is overheard and placed in a new connection, the sudden memory of a thing long past occurs to him, a distant object is relieved for a while by a random gleam of light – accidents turning up for a moment what lies below the surface of our immediate experience – and he passes from the humble graves and lowly arches of 'the little rock-like pile' of a Westmorland church, on bold trains of speculative thought, and comes, from point to point, into strange contact with thoughts which have visited, from time to time, far more venturesome, perhaps errant, spirits.

He had pondered deeply, for instance, on those strange reminiscences and forebodings, which seem to make our lives stretch before and behind us, beyond where we can see or touch anything, or trace the lines of connections. Following the soul, backwards and forwards, on these endless ways, his sense of man's dim, potential powers became a pledge to him, indeed, of a future life, but carried him back also to that mysterious notion of an earlier state of existence – the fancy of the Platonists – the old heresy of Origen. It was in this mood that he conceived those oft-reiterated regrets for a half-ideal childhood, when the relics of Paradise still clung about the soul – a childhood, as it seemed, full of the fruits of old age, lost for all, in a degree, in the passing away of the youth of the world, lost for each one, over again, in the passing away of the actual youth. It is this ideal childhood which he celebrates in his famous *Ode on the Recollections of Childhood*, and some other poems which may be grouped around it, such as the lines on *Tintern Abbey*, and something like what he describes was actually truer of himself than he seems to have understood; for his own most delightful poems were really the instinctive production of earlier life, and most surely for him, 'the first diviner influence of this world' passed away, more and more completely, in his contact with experience.

Sometimes as he dwelt upon those moments of profound, imaginative power, in which the outward object appears to take colour and expression, a new nature almost, from the prompting of the observant mind, the actual world would, as it were, dissolve and detach itself, flake by flake, and he himself seemed to be the creator, and when he would the destroyer, of the world in which he lived – that old isolating thought of many a brain-sick mystic of ancient and modern times.

At other times, again, in those periods of intense susceptibility, in which he appeared to himself as but the passive recipient of external influences, he was attracted by the thought of a spirit of life in outward things, a single, all-pervading mind in them, of which man, and even the poet's imaginative energy, are but moments – that old dream of the *anima mundi*, the mother of all things and their grave, in which some had desired to lose themselves, and others had become indifferent to the distinctions of good and evil. It would come, sometimes, like the sign of the *macrocosm* to Faust in his cell: the network of man and nature was seen to be pervaded by a common, universal life: a new, bold thought lifted him above the furrow, above the green turf of the Westmorland churchyard, to a world altogether different in its vagueness and vastness, and the narrow glen was full of the brooding power of one universal spirit.

And so he has something, also, for those who feel the fascination of bold speculative ideas, who are really capable of rising upon them to conditions of poetical thought. He uses them, indeed, always with a very fine apprehension of the limits within which alone philosophical imaginings have any place in true poetry; and using them only for poetical purposes, is not too careful even to make them consistent with each other. To him, theories which for other men bring a world of technical diction, brought perfect form and expression, as in those two lofty books of *The Prelude*, which describe the decay and the restoration of Imagination and Taste. Skirting the borders of this world of bewildering heights and depths, he got but the first exciting influence of it, that joyful enthusiasm which great imaginative theories prompt, when the mind first comes to have an understanding of them; and it is not under the influence of these thoughts that his poetry becomes tedious or loses its blitheness. He keeps them, too, always within certain ethical bounds, so that no word of his could offend the simplest of those simple souls which are always the largest part of mankind. But it is, nevertheless, the contact of these thoughts, the speculative boldness in them, which constitutes, at least for some minds, the secret attraction of much of his best poetry – the sudden passage from the lowly thoughts and places to the majestic forms of philosophical imagination, the play of these forms over a world so different, enlarging so strangely the bounds of its humble churchyards, and breaking such a wild light on the graves of christened children. . . .

The office of the poet is not that of the moralist, and the first aim of Wordsworth's poetry is to give the reader a peculiar kind of pleasure. But through his poetry, and through this pleasure in it, he does actually convey to the reader an extraordinary wisdom in the things of practice. One lesson, if men must have lessons, he conveys more clearly than all, the supreme importance of contemplation in the conduct of life.

Contemplation – impassioned contemplation – that is with Wordsworth the end-in-itself, the perfect end. We see the majority of mankind going most often to definite ends, lower or higher ends, as their own instincts may determine; but the end may never be attained, and the means not be quite the right means, great ends and little ones alike being, for the most part, distant, and the ways to them, in this dim world, somewhat vague. Meantime, to higher or lower ends, they move too often with something of a sad countenance, with hurried and ignoble gait, becoming, unconsciously, something like thorns, in their anxiety to bear grapes; it being possible for people in the pursuit even of great ends, to become themselves thin and impoverished in spirit and temper, thus diminishing the sum of perfection in the world, at its very sources. . . .

Yet, for most of us, the conception of means and ends covers the whole of life, and is the exclusive type or figure under which we represent our lives to ourselves. Such a figure, reducing all things to machinery, though it has on its side the authority of that old Greek moralist who has fixed for succeeding generations the outline of the theory of right living, is too like a mere picture or description of men's lives as we actually find them, to be the basis of the higher ethics. It covers the meanness of men's daily lives, and much of the dexterity and the vigour with which they pursue what may seem to them the good of themselves or of others; but not the intangible perfection of those whose ideal is rather in *being* than *doing* – not those *manners* which are, in the deepest as in the simplest sense, *morals*, and without which one cannot so much as offer a cup of water to a poor man without offence – not the part of 'antique Rachel', sitting in the company of Beatrice; and even the moralist might well endeavour rather to withdraw men from the too exclusive consideration of means and ends, in life.

Against this predominance of machinery in our existence, Wordsworth's poetry, like all great art and poetry, is a continual protest. Justify rather the end by the means, it seems to say: whatever may become of the fruit, make sure of the flowers and leaves. It was justly said, therefore, by one who had meditated very profoundly on the true relation of means to ends in life, and on the distinction between what is desirable in itself and what is desirable only as machinery, that when the battle which he and his friends were waging had been won, the world would need more than ever those qualities which Wordsworth was keeping alive and nourishing.[1]

That the end of life is not action but contemplation – *being* as distinct from *doing* – a certain disposition of the mind: is, in some shape or other, the principle of all the higher morality. In poetry, in art, if you enter into their true spirit at all, you touch this principle, in a measure: these, by their very sterility, are a type of beholding for the mere joy of beholding. To treat life in the spirit of art, is to make life a thing in which means and ends are identified: to encourage such treatment, the true moral significance of art and poetry. Wordsworth, and other poets who have been like him in ancient or more recent times, are the masters, the experts, in this art of impassioned contemplation. Their work is, not to teach lessons, or enforce rules, or even to stimulate us to noble ends; but to withdraw the thoughts for a little while from the mere machinery of life, to fix them, with

1 [John Stuart Mill]

appropriate emotions, on the spectacle of those great facts in man's existence which no machinery affects, 'on the great and universal passions of men, the most general and interesting of their occupations and the entire world of nature,' – on 'the operations of the elements and the appearances of the visible universe, on storm and sunshine, on the revolutions of the seasons, on cold and heat, on loss of friends and kindred, on injuries and resentments, on gratitude and hope, on fear and sorrow'. To witness this spectacle with appropriate emotions is the aim of all culture; and of these emotions poetry like Wordsworth's is a great nourisher and stimulant. He sees nature full of sentiment and excitement; he sees men and women as parts of nature, passionate, excited, in strange grouping and connection with the grandeur and beauty of the natural world: images, in his own words, 'of man suffering, amid awful forms and powers'.

Such is the figure of the more powerful and original poet, hidden away, in part, under those weaker elements of Wordsworth's poetry, which for some minds determine their entire character; a poet some- what bolder and more passionate than might at first sight be supposed, but not too bold for true poetical taste; an unimpassioned writer, you might sometimes fancy, yet thinking the chief aim, in life and art alike, to be a certain deep emotion; seeking most often the great elementary passions in lowly places; having at least this condition of all impassioned work, that he aims always at an absolute sincerity of feeling and diction, so that he is the true forerunner of the deepest and most passionate poetry of our day; yet going back also, with some- thing of a protest against the conventional fervour of much of the poetry popular in his own time, to those older English poets, whose unconscious likeness often comes out in him.

Leslie Stephen

from 'Wordsworth's Ethics', *Hours in a Library*, Third Series   1879

The great aim of moral philosophy is to unite the disjoined element, to end the divorce between reason and experience, and to escape from the alternative of dealing with empty but symmetrical formulae or concrete and chaotic facts. No hint can be given here as to the direction in which a final solution must be sought. Whatever the true method, Wordsworth's mode of conceiving the problem shows how powerfully he grasped the questions at issue. If his doctrines are not systematically expounded, they all have a direct bearing upon the real difficulties involved. They are stated so forcibly in his noblest poems that we might almost express a complete theory in his own language. But, without seeking to make a collection of aphorisms from his poetry, we may indicate the cardinal points of his teaching.[1]

The most characteristic of all his doctrines is that which is embodied in the great ode upon the *Intimations of Immortality*. The doctrine itself – the theory that the instincts of childhood testify to the preexistence of the soul – sound fanciful enough; and Wordsworth took rather unnecessary pains to say that he did not hold it as a serious dogma. We certainly need not ask whether it is reasonable or orthodox to believe that 'our birth is but a sleep and a forgetting'. The fact symbolized by the poetic fancy – the glory and freshness of our childish instincts – is equally noteworthy, whatever its cause. Some modern reasoners would explain its significance by reference to a very different kind of preexistence. The instincts, they would say, are valuable, because they register the accumulated and inherited experience of past generations. Wordsworth's delight in wild scenery is regarded by them as due to the 'combination of states that were organized in the race during barbarous times, when its pleasurable activities were amongst the mountains, woods and waters'. In childhood we are most completely under the dominion of these inherited impulses. The correlation between the organism and its medium is then most perfect, and hence the peculiar theme of childish communion with nature.

Wordsworth would have repudiated the doctrine with disgust. He would have been 'on the side of the angels'. No memories of the savage and the monkey, but the reminiscences of the once-glorious soul could explain his emotions. Yet there is this much in common between him and the men of science whom he denounced with too

1 J. S. Mill and Whewell were, for their generation, the ablest exponents of two opposite systems of thought upon such matters. Mill has expressed his obligations to Wordsworth in his *Autobiography*, and Whewell dedicated to Wordsworth his *Elements of Morality* in acknowledgement of his influence as a moralist.

little discrimination. The fact of the value of these primitive instincts is admitted, and admitted for the same purpose. Man, it is agreed, is furnished with sentiments which cannot be explained as the result of his individual experience. They may be intelligible, according to the evolutionist, when regarded as embodying the past experience of the race; or, according to Wordsworth, as implying a certain mysterious faculty imprinted upon the soul. The scientific doctrine, whether sound or not, has modified the whole mode of approaching ethical problems; and Wordsworth, though with a very different purpose, gives a new emphasis to the facts, upon a recognition of which, according to some theorists, must be based the reconciliation of the great rival schools – the intuitionists and the utilitarians. The parallel may at first sight seem fanciful; and it would be too daring to claim for Wordsworth the discovery of the most remarkable phenomenon which modern psychology must take into account. There is, however, a real connection between the two doctrines, though in one sense they are almost antithetical. Meanwhile we observe that the same sensibility which gives poetical power is necessary to the scientific observer. The magic of the ode, and of many other passages in Wordsworth's poetry, is due to his recognition of this mysterious efficacy of our childish instincts. He gives emphasis to one of the most striking facts of our spiritual experience, which had passed with little notice from professed psychologists. He feels what they afterwards tried to explain.

The full meaning of the doctrine comes out as we study Words-worth more thoroughly. Other poets – almost all poets – have dwelt fondly upon recollections of childhood. But not feeling so strongly, and therefore not expressing so forcibly, the peculiar character of the emotion, they have not derived the same lessons from their observation. The Epicurean poets are content with Herrick's simple moral –

Gather ye rosebuds while ye may –

and with his simple explanation –

That age is best which is the first,
When youth and blood are warmer.

Others more thoughtful look back upon the early days with the passionate regret of Byron's verses:

There's not a joy the world can give like that it takes away,
When the glow of early thought declines in feeling's dull
  decay;
'Tis not on youth's smooth cheek the blush alone which fades
  so fast,
But the tender bloom of heart is gone, ere youth itself be
  past.

Such painful longings for the 'tender grace of a day that is dead' are
spontaneous and natural. Every healthy mind feels the pang in
proportion to the strength of its affections. But it is also true that the
regret resembles too often the maudlin meditation of a fast young
man over his morning's soda-water. It implies, that is, a non-
recognition of the higher uses to which the fading memories may
still be put. A different tone breathes in Shelley's pathetic but rather
hectic moralizings, and his lamentations over the departure of the
'spirit of delight'. Nowhere has it found more exquisite expression
than in the marvellous *Ode to the West Wind*. These magical verses –
his best, as it seems to me – describe the reflection of the poet's own
mind in the strange stir and commotion of a dying winter's day. They
represent, we may say, the fitful melancholy which oppresses a noble
spirit when it has recognized the difficulty of forcing facts into conformity with the ideal. He still clings to the hope that his 'dead
thoughts' may be driven over the universe,

Like withered leaves to quicken a new birth.

But he bows before the inexorable fate which has cramped his
energies:

A heavy weight of years has chained and bowed
One too like thee; tameless and swift and proud.

Neither Byron nor Shelley can see any satisfactory solution, and
therefore neither can reach a perfect harmony of feeling. The world
seems to them to be out of joint, because they have not known how
to accept the inevitable, nor to conform to the discipline of facts.
And, therefore, however intense the emotion, and however exquisite
its expression, we are left in a state of intellectual and emotional
discontent. Such utterances may suit us in youth, when we can afford
to play with sorrow. As we grow older we feel a certain emptiness in

them. A true man ought not to sit down and weep with an exhausted debauchee. He cannot afford to confess himself beaten with the idealist who has discovered that Rome was not built in a day, nor revolutions made with rose-water. He has to work as long as he has strength; to work in spite of, even by strength of, sorrow, disappointment, wounded vanity, and blunted sensibilities; and therefore he must search for some profounder solution for the dark riddle of life.

This solution it is Wordsworth's chief aim to supply. In the familiar verses which stand as a motto to his poems –

The child is father to the man,
And I could wish my days to be
Bound each to each by natural piety –

the great problem of life, that is, as he conceives it, is to secure a continuity between the period at which we are guided by half-conscious instincts, and that in which a man is able to supply the place of these primitive impulses by reasoned convictions. This is the thought which comes over and over again in his deepest poems, and round which all his teaching centred. It supplies the great moral, for example, of *The Leech-Gatherer*:

My whole life I have lived in a pleasant thought,
    As if life's business were a summer mood;
As if all needful things would come unsought
    To genial faith, still rich in genial good.

When his faith is tried by harsh experience, the leech-gatherer comes,

Like a man from some far region sent,
To give me human strength by apt admonishment;

for he shows how the 'genial faith' may be converted into permanent strength by resolution and independence. The verses most commonly quoted, such as –

We poets in our youth begin in gladness,
But therefore come in the end despondency and sadness,

give the ordinary view of the sickly school. Wordsworth's aim is to supply an answer worthy not only of a poet, but a man. The same sentiment again is expressed in the grand *Ode to Duty*, where the

Stern daughter of the voice of God

is invoked to supply that 'genial sense of youth' which has hitherto
been a sufficient guidance; or in the majestic morality of *The Happy
Warrior*; or in the noble verses on *Tintern Abbey*; or, finally, in the
great ode which gives most completely the whole theory of that
process by which our early intuitions are to be transformed into
settled principles of feeling and action.

Wordsworth's philosophical theory, in short, depends upon the
asserted identity between our childish instincts and our enlightened
reason. The doctrine of a state of preexistence as it appears in other
writers – as, for example, in the Cambridge Platonists[1] – was
connected with an obsolete metaphysical system, and the doctrine –
exploded in its old form – of innate ideas. Wordsworth does not
attribute any such preternatural character to the 'blank misgivings'
and 'shadowy recollections' of which he speaks. They are invaluable
data of our spiritual experience; but they do not entitle us to lay
down dogmatic propositions independently of experience. They are
spontaneous products of a nature in harmony with the universe in
which it is placed, and inestimable as a clear indication that such a
harmony exists. To interpret and regulate them belongs to the
reasoning faculty and the higher imagination of later years. If he does
not quite distinguish between the province of reason and emotion –
the most difficult of philosophical problems – he keeps clear of the
cruder mysticism, because he does not seek to elicit any definite
formulae from those admittedly vague forebodings which lie on the
borderland between the two sides of our nature. With his invariable
sanity of mind, he more than once notices the difficulty of distinguishing between that which nature teaches us and the interpretations which
we impose upon nature.[2] He carefully refrains from pressing the
inference too far.

The teaching, indeed, assumes that view of the universe which is
implied in his pantheistic language. The Divinity really reveals
Himself in the lonely mountains and the starry heavens. By contemplating them we are able to rise into that 'blessed mood' in which for a

1 The poem of Henry Vaughan, to which reference is often made in this
connection, scarcely contains more than a pregnant hint.
2 As, for example, in the lines on *Tintern Abbey*: 'If this be but a vain belief.'

time the burden of the mystery is rolled off our souls, and we can 'see into the life of things'. And here we must admit that Wordsworth is not entirely free from the weakness which generally besets thinkers of this tendency. Like Shaftesbury in the previous century, who speaks of the universal harmony as emphatically though not as poetically as Wordsworth, he is tempted to adopt a too facile optimism. He seems at times to have overlooked that dark side of nature which is recognized in theological doctrines of corruption, or in the scientific theories about the fierce struggle for existence. Can we in fact say that these early instincts prove more than the happy constitution of the individual who feels them? Is there not a teaching of nature very apt to suggest horror and despair rather than a complacent brooding over soothing thoughts? Do not the mountains which Wordsworth loved so well, speak of decay and catastrophe in every line of their slopes? Do they not suggest the helplessness and narrow limitations of man, as forcibly as his possible exaltation? The awe which they strike into our souls has its terrible as well as it amiable side; and in moods of depression the darker aspect becomes more conspicuous than the brighter. Nay, if we admit that we have instincts which are the very substance of all that afterwards becomes ennobling, have we not also instincts which suggest a close alliance with the brutes? If the child amidst his newborn blisses suggests a heavenly origin, does he not also show sensual and cruel instincts which imply at least an admixture of baser elements? If man is responsive to all natural influences, how is he to distinguish between the good and the bad, and, in short, to frame a conscience out of the vague instincts which contain the germs of all the possible developments of the future?

To say that Wordsworth has not given a complete answer to such difficulties, is to say that he has not explained the origin of evil. It may be admitted, however, that he does to a certain extent show a narrowness of conception. The voice of nature, as he says, resembles an echo; but we 'unthinking creatures' listen to 'voices of two different natures'. We do not always distinguish between the echo of our lower passions and the 'echoes from beyond the grave'. Wordsworth sometimes fails to recognize the ambiguity of the oracle to which he appeals. The 'blessed mood' in which we get rid of the burden of the world, is too easily confused with the mood in which we simply refuse to attend to it. He finds lonely meditation so inspiring that he is too indifferent to the troubles of less self-sufficing or clear-sighted human beings. The ambiguity makes itself felt in the sphere of morality. The ethical doctrine that virtue consists in conformity to nature becomes ambiguous with him, as with all its advocates, when we ask for a precise definition of nature. How are we to know which natural forces make for us and which fight against us?

The doctrine of the love of nature, generally regarded as Wordsworth's great lesson to mankind, means, as interpreted by himself and others, a love of the wilder and grander objects of natural scenery; a passion for the 'sounding cataract', the rock, the mountain and the forest; a preference, therefore, of the country to the town, and of the simpler to the more complex forms of social life. But what is the true value of this sentiment? The unfortunate Solitary in *The Excursion* is beset by three Wordsworths; for the Wanderer and the Pastor are little more (as Wordsworth indeed intimates) than reflections of himself, seen in different mirrors. The Solitary represents the anti-social lessons to be derived from communion with nature. He has become a misanthrope, and has learnt from *Candide* the lesson that we clearly do not live in the best of all possible worlds. Instead of learning the true lesson from nature by penetrating its deeper meanings, he manages to feed

Pity and scorn and melancholy pride

by accidental and fanciful analogies, and sees in rock pyramids or obelisks a rude mockery of human toils. To confute this sentiment, to upset *Candide*,

This dull product of a scoffer's pen,

is the purpose of the lofty poetry and versified prose of the long dialogues which ensue. That Wordsworth should call Voltaire dull is a curious example of the proverbial blindness of controversialists; but the moral may be equally good. It is given most pithily in the lines –

We live by admiration, hope, and love;
And even as these are well and wisely fused,
The dignity of being we ascend.

'But what is Error?' continues the preacher; and the Solitary replies by saying, 'somewhat haughtily', that love, admiration, and hope are 'mad fancy's favourite vassals'. The distinction between fancy and imagination is, in brief, that fancy deals with the superficial resemblances, and imagination with the deeper truths which underlie them. The purpose, then, of *The Excursion*, and of Wordsworth's poetry in general, is to show how the higher faculty reveals a harmony which we overlook when, with the Solitary, we

Skim along the surfaces of things.

The rightly prepared mind can recognize the divine harmony which underlines all apparent disorder. The universe is to its perceptions like the shell whose murmur in a child's ear seems to express a mysterious union with the sea. But the mind must be rightly prepared. Everything depends upon the point of view. One man, as he says in an elaborate figure, looking upon a series of ridges in spring from their northern side, sees a waste of snow, and from the south a continuous expanse of green. That view, we must take it, is the right one which is illuminated by the 'ray divine'. But we must train our eyes to recognize its splendour; and the final answer to the Solitary is therefore embodied in a series of narratives, showing by example how our spiritual vision may be purified or obscured. Our philosophy must be finally based, not upon abstract speculation and metaphysical arguments, but the diffused consciousness of the healthy mind. As Butler sees the universe by the light of conscience, Wordsworth sees it through the wider emotions of awe, reverence and love, produced in a sound nature.

The pantheistic conception, in short, leads to an unsatisfactory optimism in the general view of nature, and to an equal tolerance of all passions as equally 'natural'. To escape from this difficulty we must establish some more discriminative mode of interpreting nature. Man is the instrument played upon by all impulses, good or bad. The music which results may be harmonious or discordant. When the instrument is in tune, the music will be perfect; but when is it in tune, and how are we to know that it is in tune? That problem once solved we can tell which are the authentic utterances and which are the accidental discords. And by solving it, or by saying what is the right constitution of human beings, we shall discover which is the true philosophy of the universe, and what are the dictates of a sound moral sense. Wordsworth implicitly answers the question by explaining, in his favourite phrase, how we are to build up our moral being.

The voice of nature speaks at first in vague emotions, scarcely distinguishable from mere animal buoyancy. The boy, hooting in mimicry of the owls, receives in his heart the voice of mountain torrents and the solemn imagery of rocks, and woods, and stars. The sportive girl is unconsciously moulded into stateliness and grace by the floating clouds, the bending willow, and even by silent sympathy with the motions of the storm. Nobody has ever shown, with such exquisite power as Wordsworth, how much of the charm of natural objects in later life is due to early associations, thus formed in a mind not yet capable of contemplating its own processes. As old Matthew says in the lines which, however familiar, can never be read without emotion –

My eyes are dim with childish tears,
  My heart is idly stirred;
For the same sound is in my ears
  Which in those days I heard.

And the strangely beautiful address to the cuckoo might be made into a text for a prolonged commentary by an aesthetic philosopher upon the power of early association. It curiously illustrates, for example, the reason of Wordsworth's delight in recalling sounds. The croak of the distant raven, the bleat of the mountain lamb, the splash of the leaping fish in the lonely tarn, are specially delightful to him, because the hearing is the most spiritual of our senses; and these sounds, like the cuckoo's cry, seem to convert the earth into an 'unsubstantial fairy place'. The phrase 'association' indeed implies a certain arbitrariness in the images suggested, which is not quite in accordance with Wordsworth's feeling. Though the echo depends partly upon the hearer, the mountain voices are specially adapted for certain moods. They have, we may say, a spontaneous affinity for the nobler affections. If some early passage in our childhood is associated with a particular spot, a house or a street will bring back the petty and accidental details: a mountain or a lake will revive the deeper and more permanent elements of feeling. If you have made love in a palace, according to Mr Disraeli's prescription, the sight of it will recall the splendour of the object's dress or jewellery; if, as Wordsworth would prefer, with a background of mountains, it will appear in later days as if they had absorbed, and were always ready again to radiate forth, the tender and hallowing influences which then for the first time entered your life. The elementary and deepest passions are most easily associated with the sublime and beautiful in nature.

The primal duties shine aloft like stars;
The charities that soothe, and heal, and bless,
Are scattered at the feet of man like flowers.

And therefore if you have been happy enough to take delight in these natural and universal objects in the early days, when the most permanent associations are formed, the sight of them in later days will bring back by preordained and divine symbolism whatever was most ennobling in your early feelings. The vulgarising associations will drop off of themselves, and what was pure and lofty will remain.

From this natural law follows another of Wordsworth's favourite precepts. The mountains are not with him a symbol of anti-social feelings. On the contrary, they are in their proper place as the background of the simple domestic affections. He loves his native hills, not in the Byronic fashion, as a savage wilderness, but as the appropriate framework in which a healthy social order can permanently maintain itself. That, for example, is, as he tells us, the thought which inspired *The Brothers*, a poem which excels all modern idylls in weight of meaning and depth of feeling, by virtue of the idea thus embodied. The retired valley of Ennerdale, with its grand background of hills, precipitous enough to be fairly called mountains, forces the two lads into closer affection. Shut in by these 'enormous barriers', and undistracted by the ebb and flow of the outside world, the mutual love becomes concentrated. A tie like that of family blood is involuntarily imposed upon the little community of dalesmen. The image of sheep-tracks and shepherds clad in country grey is stamped upon the elder brother's mind, and comes back to him in tropical calms; he hears the tones of his waterfalls in the piping shrouds; and when he returns, recognizes every fresh scar made by winter storms on the mountain sides, and knows by sight every unmarked grave in the little churchyard. The fraternal affection sanctifies the scenery, and the sight of the scenery brings back the affection with overpowering force upon his return. This is everywhere the sentiment inspired in Wordsworth by his beloved hills. It is not so much the love of nature pure and simple, as of nature seen through the deepest human feelings. The light glimmering in a lonely cottage, the one rude house in the deep valley, with its 'small lot of life-supporting fields and guardian rocks', are necessary to point the moral and to draw to a definite focus the various forces of sentiment. The two veins of feeling are inseparably blended. The peasant noble, in the *Song at the Feast of Brougham Castle* learns equally from men and nature:

Love had he found in huts where poor men lie;
  His daily teachers had been woods and hills,
The silence that is in the starry skies,
  The sleep that is among the lonely hills.

Without the love, the silence and the sleep would have had no spiritual meaning. They are valuable as giving intensity and solemnity to the positive emotion.

The same remark is to be made upon Wordsworth's favourite teaching of the advantages of the contemplative life. He is fond of enforcing the doctrine of the familiar lines, that we can feed our minds 'in a wise passiveness', and that

One impulse from the vernal wood
  Can teach you more of man,
Of moral evil and of good,
  Than all the sages can.

And, according to some commentators, this would seem to express the doctrine that the ultimate end of life is the cultivation of tender emotions without reference to action. The doctrine, thus absolutely stated, would be immoral and illogical. To recommend contemplation in preference to action is like preferring sleeping to waking; or saying, as a full expression of the truth, that silence is golden and speech silvern. Like that familiar phrase, Wordsworth's teaching is not to be interpreted literally. The essence of such maxims is to be one-sided. They are paradoxical in order to be emphatic. To have seasons of contemplation, of withdrawal from the world and from books, of calm surrendering of ourselves to the influences of nature, is a practice commended in one form or other by all moral teachers. It is a sanitary rule, resting upon obvious principles. The mind which is always occupied in a multiplicity of small observations, or the regulation of practical details, loses the power of seeing general principles and of associating all objects with the central emotions of 'admiration, hope and love'. The philosophic mind is that which habitually sees the general in the particular, and finds food for the deepest thought in the simplest objects. It requires, therefore, periods of repose, in which the fragmentary and complex atoms of distracted feeling which make up the incessant whirl of daily life may have time to crystallize round the central thoughts. But it must feed in order to assimilate; and each process implies the other as its correlative. A constant interest, therefore, in the joys and sorrows of our neighbours is as essential as quiet, self-centred rumination. It is when the eye 'has kept watch o'er man's mortality', and by virtue of the tender sympathies of 'the human heart by which we live', that to us

The meanest flower which blows can give
Thoughts that do often lie too deep for tears.

The solitude which implies severance from natural sympathies and affections is poisonous. The happiness of the heart which lives alone,

Housed in a dream, an outcast from the kind,

. . . .
Is to be pitied, for 'tis surely blind.

Wordsworth's meditations upon flowers or animal life are impressive because they have been touched by this constant sympathy. The sermon is always in his mind, and therefore every stone may serve for a text. His contemplation enables him to see the pathetic side of the small pains and pleasures which we are generally in too great a hurry to notice. There are times, of course, when this moralizing tendency leads him to the regions of the namby-pamby or sheer prosaic platitude. On the other hand, no one approaches him in the power of touching some rich chord of feeling by help of the pettiest incident. The old man going to the fox-hunt with a tear on his cheek, and saying to himself,

The key I must take, for my Helen is dead;

or the mother carrying home her dead sailor's bird; the village schoolmaster, in whom a rift in the clouds revives the memory of his little daughter; the old huntsman unable to cut through the stump of rotten wood – touch our hearts at once and for ever. The secret is given in the rather prosaic apology for not relating a tale about poor Simon Lee:

O reader! had you in your mind
  Such stores as silent thought can bring,
O gentle reader! you would find
  A tale in everything.

The value of silent thought is so to cultivate the primitive emotions that they may flow spontaneously upon every common incident, and that every familiar object becomes symbolic of them. It is a familiar remark that a philosopher or man of science who has devoted himself to meditation upon some principle or law of nature, is always finding new illustrations in the most unexpected quarters. He cannot take up a novel or walk across the street without hitting upon appropriate instances. Wordsworth would apply the principle to the building up of our 'moral being'. Admiration, hope and love should be so constantly in our thoughts, that innumerable sights and sounds which are meaningless to the world should become to us a language incessantly suggestive of the deepest topics of thought.

This explains his dislike to science, as he understood the word, and his denunciations of the 'world'. The man of science is one who cuts up nature into fragments, and not only neglects their possible significance for our higher feelings, but refrains on principle from taking it into account. The primrose suggests to him some new device in classification, and he would be worried by the suggestion of any spiritual significance as an annoying distraction. Viewing all objects 'in disconnection, dead and spiritless', we are thus really waging

An impious warfare with the very life
Of our own souls.

We are putting the letter in place of the spirit, and dealing with nature as a mere grammarian deals with a poem. When we have learnt to associate every object with some lesson

Of human suffering or of human joy;
when we have thus obtained the 'glorious habit',

> By which sense is made
> Subservient still to moral purposes,
> Auxiliar to divine;

the 'dull eye' of science will light up; for, in observing natural processes, it will carry with it an incessant reference to the spiritual processes to which they are allied. Science, in short, requires to be brought into intimate connection with morality and religion. If we are forced for our immediate purpose to pursue truth for itself, regardless of consequences, we must remember all the more carefully that truth is a whole, and that fragmentary bits of knowledge become valuable as they are incorporated into a general system. The tendency of modern times to specialism brings with it a characteristic danger. It requires to be supplemented by a correlative process of integration. We must study details to increase our knowledge; we must accustom ourselves to look at the detail in the light of the general principles in order to make it fruitful.

The influence of that world which 'is too much with us late and soon' is of the same kind. The man of science loves barren facts for their own sake. The man of the world becomes devoted to some petty pursuit without reference to ultimate ends. He becomes a slave to money, or power, or praise, without caring for their effect upon his moral character. As social organization becomes more complete, the social unit becomes a mere fragment instead of being a complete whole in himself. Man becomes

The senseless member of a vast machine,
Serving as doth a spindle or a wheel.

The division of labour, celebrated with such enthusiasm by Adam Smith,[1] tends to crush all real life out of its victims. The soul of the political economist may rejoice when he sees a human being devoting his whole faculties to the performance of one subsidiary operation in the manufacture of a pin. The poet and the moralist must notice with anxiety the contrast between the old-fashioned peasant who, if he discharged each particular function clumsily, discharged at least many

1 See Wordsworth's reference to *The Wealth of Nations*, in *The Prelude*, Book XIII.

functions, and found exercise for all the intellectual and moral faculties of his nature, and the modern artisan doomed to the incessant repetition of one petty set of muscular expansions and contractions, and whose soul, if he has one, is therefore rather an incumbrance than otherwise. This is the evil which is constantly before Wordsworth's eyes, as it has certainly not become less prominent since his time. The danger of crushing the individual is a serious one according to his view; not because it implies the neglect of some abstract political rights, but from the impoverishment of character which is implied in the process. Give every man a vote, and abolish all interference with each man's private tastes, and the danger may still be as great as ever. The tendency to 'differentiation' – as we call it in modern phraseology – the social pulverization, the lowering and narrowing of the individual's sphere of action and feeling to the pettiest details, depends upon processes underlying all political changes. It cannot, therefore, be cured by any nostrum of constitution-mongers, or by the negative remedy of removing old barriers. It requires to be met by profounder moral and religious teaching. Men must be taught what is the really valuable part of their natures, and what is the purest happiness to be extracted from life, as well as allowed to gratify fully their own tastes; for who can say that men encouraged by all their surroundings and appeals to the most obvious motives to turn themselves into machines, will not deliberately choose to be machines? Many powerful thinkers have illustrated Wordsworth's doctrine more elaborately, but nobody has gone more decisively to the root of the matter.

One other side of Wordsworth's teaching is still more significant and original. Our vague instincts are consolidated into reason by meditation, sympathy with our fellows, communion with nature, and a constant devotion to 'high endeavours'. If life run smoothly, the transformation may be easy, and our primitive optimism turn imperceptibly into general complacency. The trial comes when we make personal acquaintance with sorrow, and our early buoyancy begins to fail. We are tempted to become querulous or to lap ourselves in indifference. Most poets are content to bewail our lot melodiously, and admit that there is no remedy unless a remedy be found in 'the luxury of grief'. Prosaic people become selfish though not sentimental. They laugh at their old illusions, and turn to the solid consolations of comfort. Nothing is more melancholy than to study many biographies, and note – not the failure of early promise which may mean merely an aiming above the mark – but the progressive deterioration of character which so often follows grief and disappointment. If it be not true that most men grow worse as they grow old, it is surely true that few men pass through the world without being corrupted as much as purified.

Now Wordsworth's favourite lesson is the possibility of turning grief and disappointment into account. He teaches in many forms the necessity of 'transmuting' sorrow into strength. One of the great evils is a lack of power,

An agonizing sorrow to transmute.

The Happy Warrior is, above all, the man who in face of all human miseries can

Exercise a power
Which is our human nature's highest dower;
Controls them, and subdues, transmutes, bereaves
Of their bad influence, and their good receives;

who is made more compassionate by familiarity with sorrow, more placable by contest, purer by temptation, and more enduring by distress.[1] It is owing to the constant presence of this thought, to his sensibility to the refining influence of sorrow, that Wordsworth is the only poet who will bear reading in times of distress. Other poets mock us by an impossible optimism, or merely reflect the feelings which, however we may play with them in times of cheerfulness, have now become an intolerable burden. Wordsworth suggests the single topic which, so far at least as this world is concerned, can really be

1 So, too, in *The Prelude*:
  Then was the truth received into my heart,
  That, under heaviest sorrow earth can bring,
  If from the affliction somewhere do not grow
  Honour which could not else have been, a faith,
  An elevation, and a sanctity;
  If new strength be not given, nor old restored,
  The fault is ours, not Nature's.

[1850, X, 464–70. The last line is misquoted, Stephen substituting 'fault' for 'blame'.]

called consolatory. None of the ordinary commonplaces will serve, or serve at most as indications of human sympathy. But there is some consolation in the thought that even death may bind the survivors closer, and leave as a legacy enduring motives to noble action. It is easy to say this; but Wordsworth has the merit of feeling the truth in all its force, and expressing it by the most forcible images. In one shape or another the sentiment is embodied in most of his really powerful poetry. It is intended, for example, to be the moral of *The White Doe of Rylstone*. There, as Wordsworth says, everything fails so far as its object is external and unsubstantial; everything succeeds so far as it is moral and spiritual. Success grows out of failure; and the mode in which it grows is indicated by the lines which give the key-note of the poem. Emily, the heroine, is to become a soul

By force of sorrows high
Uplifted to the purest sky
Of undisturbed serenity.

The White Doe is one of those poems which make many readers inclined to feel a certain tenderness for Jeffrey's dogged insensibility; and I confess that I am not one of its warm admirers. The sentiment seems to be unduly relaxed throughout; there is a want of sympathy with heroism of the rough and active type, which is, after all, at least as worthy of admiration as the more passive variety of the virtue; and the defect is made more palpable by the position of the chief actors. These rough borderers, who recall William of Deloraine and Dandie Dinmont, are somehow out of their element when preaching the doctrines of quietism and submission to circumstances. But, whatever our judgement of this particular embodiment of Words-worth's moral philosophy, the inculcation of the same lesson gives force to many of his finest poems. It is enough to mention *The Leech-gatherer*, *The Stanzas on Peele Castle*, *Michael*, and, as expressing the inverse view of the futility of idle grief, *Laodamia*, where he has succeeded in combining his morality with more than his ordinary beauty of poetical form. The teaching of all these poems falls in with the doctrine already set forth. All moral teaching, I have sometimes fancied, might be summed up in the one formula, 'Waste not'. Every element of which our nature is composed may be said to be good in its proper place; and therefore every vicious habit springs out of the misapplication of forces which might be turned to account by judicious training. The waste of sorrow is one of the most lamentable forms of waste. Sorrow too often tends to produce bitterness or effeminacy of character. But it may, if rightly used, serve only to detach us from the lower motives and give sanctity to the higher. That is what Wordsworth sees with unequalled clearness, and he therefore sees also the condition of profiting. The mind in which the most valuable elements have been systematically strengthened by meditation, by association of deep thought with the most universal presences, by constant sympathy with the joys and sorrows of its fellows, will be prepared to convert sorrow into a medicine instead of a poison. Sorrow is deteriorating so far as it is selfish. The man who is occupied with his own interests makes grief an excuse for effeminate indulgence in self-pity. He becomes weaker and more fretful. The man who has learnt habitually to think of himself as part of a greater whole, whose conduct has been habitually directed to noble ends, is purified and strengthened by the spiritual convulsion. His disappointment, or his loss of some beloved object, makes him more anxious to fix the bases of his happiness widely and deeply, and to be content with the consciousness of honest work, instead of looking for what is called success.

But I must not take to preaching in the place of Wordsworth. The whole theory is most nobly summed up in the grand lines already noticed on the character of the Happy Warrior. There Wordsworth has explained in the most forcible and direct language the mode in which a grand character can be formed; how youthful impulses may change into manly purpose; how pain and sorrow may be transmuted into new forces; how the mind may be fixed upon lofty purposes; how the domestic affections – which give the truest happiness – may also be the greatest source of strength to the man who is

More brave for this, that he has much to lose;

and how, finally, he becomes indifferent to all petty ambition –

Finds comfort in himself and in his cause;
And, while the mortal mist is gathering, draws
His breath in confidence of Heaven's applause.
  This is the Happy Warrior, this is he
  Whom every man in arms should wish to be.

We may now see what ethical theory underlies Wordsworth's teaching of the transformation of instinct into reason. We must start from the postulate that there is in fact a Divine order in the universe; and that conformity to this order produces beauty as embodied in the external world, and is the condition of virtue as regulating our character. It is by obedience to the 'stern lawgiver', Duty, that flowers gain their fragrance, and that 'the most ancient heavens' preserve their freshness and strength. But this postulate does not seek for justification in abstract metaphysical reasoning. The *Intimations of Immortality* are precisely intimations, not intellectual intuitions. They are vague and emotional, not distinct and logical. They are a feeling of harmony, not a perception of innate ideas. And, on the other hand, our instincts are not a mere chaotic mass of passions, to be gratified without considering their place and function in a certain definite scheme. They have been implanted by the Divine hand, and the harmony which we feel corresponds to a real order. To justify them we must appeal to experience, but to experience interrogated by a certain definite procedure. Acting upon the assumption that the Divine order exists, we shall come to recognize it, though we could not deduce it by an *à priori* method.

The instrument, in fact, finds itself originally tuned by its Maker, and may preserve its original condition by careful obedience to the stern teaching of life. The buoyancy common to all youthful and healthy natures then changes into a deeper and more solemn mood. The great primary emotions retain the original impulse, but increase their volume. Grief and disappointment are transmuted into tenderness, sympathy and endurance. The reason, as it develops, regulates, without weakening, the primitive instincts. All the greatest, and therefore most common, sights of nature are indelibly associated with 'admiration, hope and love'; and all increase of knowledge and power is regarded as a means for furthering the gratification of our nobler emotions. Under the opposite treatment, the character loses its freshness, and we regard the early happiness as an illusion. The old emotions dry up at their source. Grief produces fretfulness, misanthropy or effeminacy. Power is wasted on petty ends and frivolous excitement, and knowledge becomes barren and pedantic. In this way the postulate justifies itself by producing the noblest type of character. When the 'moral being' is thus built up, its instincts become its convictions, we recognize the true voice of nature, and distinguish it from the echo of our passions. Thus we come to know how the Divine order and the laws by which the character is harmonized are the laws of morality.

To possible objections it might be answered by Wordsworth that this mode of assuming in order to prove is the normal method of philosophy. 'You must love him,' as he says of the poet,

> Ere to you
> He will seem worthy of your love.

The doctrine corresponds to the *crede ut intelligas* of the divine; or to the philosophic theory that we must start from the knowledge already constructed within us by instincts which have not yet learnt to reason. And, finally, if a persistent reasoner should ask why – even admitting the facts – the higher type should be preferred to the lower, Wordsworth may ask, Why is bodily health preferable to disease? If a man likes weak lungs and a bad digestion, reason cannot convince him of his error. The physician has done enough when he has pointed out the sanitary laws obedience to which generates strength, long life, and power of enjoyment. The moralist is in the same position when he has shown how certain habits conduce to the development of a type superior to its rivals in all the faculties which imply permanent peace of mind and power of resisting the shocks of the world without disintegration. Much undoubtedly remains to be said. Wordsworth's teaching, profound and admirable as it may be, has not the potency to silence the scepticism which has gathered strength since his day, and assailed fundamental – or what to him seemed fundamental – tenets of his system. No one can yet say what transformation may pass upon the thoughts and emotions for which he found utterance in speaking of the Divinity and sanctity of nature. Some people vehemently maintain that the words will be emptied of all meaning if the old theological conceptions to which he was so firmly attached should disappear with the development of new modes of thought. Nature, as regarded by the light of modern science, will be the name of a cruel and wasteful, or at least of a purely neutral and indifferent power, or perhaps as merely an equivalent for the Unknowable, to which the conditions of our intellect prevent us from ever attaching any intelligible predicate. Others would say that in whatever terms we choose to speak of the mysterious darkness which surrounds our little island of comparative light, the emotion generated in a thoughtful mind by the contemplation of the universe will remain unaltered or strengthen with clearer knowledge; and that we shall express ourselves in a new dialect without altering the essence of our thought. The emotions to which Wordsworth has given utterance will remain, though the system in which he believed should sink into oblivion; as, indeed, all human systems have found different modes of symbolizing the same fundamental feelings. But it is enough vaguely to indicate considerations not here to be developed.

It only remains to be added once more that Wordsworth's poetry derives its power from the same source as his philosophy. It speaks to our strongest feelings because his speculation rests upon our deepest thoughts. His singular capacity for investing all objects with a glow derived from early associations; his keen sympathy with natural and simple emotions; his sense of the sanctifying influences which can be extracted from sorrow, are of equal value to his power over our intellects and our imaginations. His psychology, stated systematically, is rational; and, when expressed passionately, turns into poetry. To be sensitive to the most important phenomena is the first step equally towards a poetical or a scientific exposition. To see these truly is the condition of making the poetry harmonious and the philosophy logical. And it is often difficult to say which power is most remarkable in Wordsworth. It would be easy to illustrate the truth by other than moral topics. His sonnet, noticed by De Quincey, in which he speaks of the abstracting power of darkness, and observes that as the hills pass into twilight we see the same sight as the ancient Britons, is impressive as it stands, but would be equally good as an illustration in a metaphysical treatise. Again, the sonnet beginning

With ships the sea was sprinkled far and wide,

is at once , as he has shown in a commentary of his own, an illustration of a curious psychological law – of our tendency, that is, to introduce an arbitrary principle of order into a random collection of objects – and, for the same reason, a striking embodiment of the corresponding mood of feeling. The little poem called *Stepping Westward* is in the same way at once a delicate expression of a specific sentiment and an acute critical analysis of the subtle associations suggested by a single phrase. But such illustrations might be multiplied indefinitely. As he has himself said, there is scarcely one of his poems which does not call attention to some moral sentiment, or to a general principle or law of thought, of our intellectual constitution.

Finally, we might look at the reverse side of the picture, and endeavour to show how the narrow limits of Wordsworth's power are connected with certain moral defects; with the want of quick sympathy which shows itself in his dramatic feebleness, and the austerity of character which caused him to lose his special gifts too early and become a rather commonplace defender of conservatism; and that curious diffidence (he assures us that it was 'diffidence') which induced him to write many thousand lines of blank verse entirely about himself. But the task would be superfluous as well as ungrateful. It was his aim, he tells us, 'to console the afflicted; to add sunshine to daylight by making the happy happier; to teach the young and the gracious of every age to see, to think, and therefore to become more actively and securely virtuous'; and, high as was the aim, he did much towards its accomplishment.

(258–84)

Matthew Arnold

from the Introduction to *Poems of Wordsworth*   1879

Wordsworth has been in his grave for some thirty years, and certainly his lovers and admirers cannot flatter themselves that this great and steady light of glory as yet shines over him. He is not fully recognized at home; he is not recognized at all abroad. Yet I firmly believe that the poetical performance of Wordsworth is, after that of Shakespeare and Milton, of which all the world now recognizes the worth, undoubtedly the most considerable in our language from the Elizabethan age to the present time. Chaucer is anterior; and on other grounds, too, he cannot well be brought into the comparison. But taking the roll of our chief poetical names, besides Shakespeare and Milton, from the age of Elizabeth downwards, and going through it, – Spenser, Dryden, Pope, Gray, Goldsmith, Cowper, Burns, Coleridge, Scott, Campbell, Moore, Byron, Shelley, Keats (I mention those only who are dead), – I think it certain that Wordsworth's name deserves to stand, and will finally stand, above them all. Several of the poets named have gifts and excellences which Wordsworth has not. But taking the performance of each as a whole, I say that Wordsworth seems to me to have left a body of poetical work superior in power, in interest, in the qualities which give enduring freshness, to that which any one of the others has left.

But this is not enough to say. I think it certain, further, that if we take the chief poetical names of the Continent since the death of Molière, and, omitting Goethe, confront the remaining names with that of Wordsworth, the result is the same. Let us take Klopstock, Lessing, Schiller, Uhland, Rückert and Heine for Germany; Filicaia, Alfieri, Manzoni and Leopardi for Italy; Racine, Boileau, Voltaire, André Chenier, Béranger, Lamartine, Musset, M. Victor Hugo (he has been so long celebrated that although he still lives I may be permitted to name him) for France. Several of these, again, have evidently gifts and excellences to which Wordsworth can make no pretension. But in real poetical achievement it seems to me indubitable that to Wordsworth, here again, belongs the palm. It seems to me that Wordsworth has left behind him a body of poetical work which wears, and will wear, better on the whole than the performance of any one of these personages, so far more brilliant and celebrated, most of them, than the homely poet of Rydal. Wordsworth's performance in poetry is on the whole, in power, in interest, in the qualities which gave enduring freshness, superior to theirs.

This is a high claim to make for Wordsworth. But if it is a just claim, if Wordsworth's place among the poets who have appeared in the last two or three centuries is after Shakespeare, Molière, Milton, Goethe, indeed, but before all the rest, then in time Wordsworth will have his due. We shall recognize him in his place, as we recognize Shakespeare and Milton; and not only we ourselves shall recognize him, but he will be recognized by Europe also. Meanwhile, those who recognize him already may do well, perhaps, to ask themselves whether there are not in the case of Wordsworth certain special obstacles which hinder or delay his due recognition by others, and whether these obstacles are not in some measure removable.

The Excursion and *The Prelude*, his poems of greatest bulk, are by no means Wordsworth's best work. His best work is in his shorter pieces, and many indeed are there of these which are of first-rate excellence. But in his seven volumes the pieces of high merit are mingled with a mass of pieces very inferior to them; so inferior to them that it seems wonderful how the same poet should have produced both. Shakespeare frequently has lines and passages in a strain quite false, and which are entirely unworthy of him. But one can imagine his smiling if one could meet him in the Elysian Fields and tell him so; smiling and replying that he knew it perfectly well himself, and what did it matter? But with Wordsworth the case is different. Work altogether inferior, work quite uninspired, flat and dull, is produced by him with evident unconsciousness of its defects, and he presents it to us with the same faith and seriousness as his best work. Now a drama or an epic fill the mind, and one does not look beyond them; but in a collection of short pieces the impression made by one piece requires to be continued and sustained by the piece following. In reading Wordsworh the impression made by one of his fine pieces is too often dulled and spoiled by a very inferior piece coming after it.

Wordsworth composed verses during a space of some sixty years; and it is no exaggeration to say that within one single decade of those years, between 1798 and 1808, almost all his really first-rate work was produced. A mass of inferior work remains, work done before and after this golden prime, imbedding the first-rate work and clogging it, obstructing our approach to it, chilling, not unfrequently, the high-wrought mood with which we leave it. To be recognized far and wide as a great poet, to be possible and receivable as a classic, Wordsworth needs to be relieved of a great deal of the poetical baggage which now encumbers him. To administer this relief is indispensable, unless he is to continue to be a poet for the few only, a poet valued far below his real worth by the world.

There is another thing. Wordsworth classified his poems not according to any commonly received plan of arrangement, but according to a scheme of mental physiology. He has poems of the fancy, poems of the imagination, poems of sentiment and reflexion, and so on. His categories are ingenious but far-fetched, and the result of his employment of them is unsatisfactory. Poems are separated one from another which possess a kinship of subject or of treatment far more vital and deep than the supposed unity of mental origin which was Wordsworth's reason for joining them with others.

The tact of the Greeks in matters of this kind was infallible. We may rely upon it that we shall not improve upon the classification adopted by the Greeks for kinds of poetry; that their categories of epic, dramatic, lyric and so forth, have a natural propriety, and should be adhered to. It may sometimes seem doubtful to which of two categories a poem belongs; whether this or that poem is to be called, for instance, narrative or lyric, lyric or elegiac. But there is to be found in every good poem a strain, a predominant note, which determines the poem as belonging to one of these kinds rather than the other; and here is the best proof of the value of the classification, and of the advantage of adhering to it. Wordsworth's poems will never produce their due effect until they are freed from their present artificial arrangement, and grouped more naturally.

Disengaged from the quantity of inferior work which now obscures them, the best poems of Wordsworth, I hear many people say, would indeed stand out in great beauty, but they would prove to be very few in number, scarcely more than half-a-dozen. I maintain, on the other hand, that what strikes me with admiration, what establishes in my opinion Wordsworth's superiority, is the great and ample body of powerful work which remains to him, even after all his inferior work has been cleared away. He gives us so much to rest upon, so much which communicates his spirit and engages ours!

This is of very great importance. If it were a comparison of single pieces, or of three or four pieces, by each poet, I do not say that Wordsworth would stand decisively above Gray, or Burns, or Keats, or Manzoni, or Heine. It is in his ampler body of powerful work that I find his superiority. His good work itself, his work which counts, is not all of it, of course, of equal value. Some kinds of poetry are in themselves lower kinds than others. The ballad kind is a lower kind; the didactic kind, still more, is a lower kind. Poetry of this latter sort, counts, too, sometimes, by its biographical interest partly, not by its poetical interest pure and simple; but then this can only be when the poet producing it has the power and importance of Wordsworth, a power and importance which he assuredly did not establish by such didactic poetry alone. Altogether, it is, I say, by the great body of powerful and significant work which remains to him, after every reduction and deduction has been made, that Wordsworth's superiority is proved.

To exhibit this body of Wordsworth's best work, to clear away obstructions from around it, and to let it speak for itself, is what every lover of Wordsworth should desire. Until this has been done, Wordsworth, whom we, to whom he is dear, all of us know and feel to be so great a poet, has not had a fair chance before the world. When once it has been done, he will make his way best not by our advocacy of him, but by his own worth and power. We may safely leave him to make his way thus, we who believe that a superior worth and power in poetry finds in mankind a sense responsive to it and disposed at last to recognize it. Yet at the outset, before he has been duly known and recognized, we may do Wordsworth a service, perhaps, by indicating in what his superior power and worth will be found to consist, and in what it will not.

Long ago, in speaking of Homer, I said that the noble and profound application of ideas to life is the most essential part of poetic greatness. I said that a great poet receives his distinctive character of superiority from his application, under the conditions immutably fixed by the laws of poetic beauty and poetic truth, from his application, I say, to his subject, whatever it may be, of the ideas.

On man, on nature, and on human life,

which he has acquired for himself. The line quoted is Wordsworth's own; and his superiority arises from his powerful use, in his best pieces, his powerful application to his subject, of ideas 'on man, on nature and on human life'.

Voltaire, with his signal acuteness, most truly remarked that 'no nation has treated in poetry moral ideas with more energy and depth than the English nation'. And he adds: 'There, it seems to me, is the great merit of the English poets.' Voltaire does not mean, by 'treating in poetry moral ideas', the composing moral and didactic poems; – that brings us but a very little way in poetry. He means just the same thing as was meant when I spoke above 'of the noble and profound application of ideas to life'; and he means the application of these ideas under the conditions fixed for us by the laws of poetic beauty and poetic truth. If it is said that to call these ideas *moral* ideas is to introduce a strong and injurious limitation, I answer that it is to do nothing of the kind, because moral ideas are really so main a part of human life. The question, *how to live*, is itself a moral idea; and it is the question which most interests every man, and with which, in some way or other, he is perpetually occupied. A large sense is of course to be given to the term *moral*. Whatever bears upon the question, 'how to live', comes under it.

Nor love thy life, nor hate; but, what thou liv'st,
Live well; how long or short, permit to heaven.

In those fine lines, Milton utters, as every one at once perceives, a moral idea. Yes, but so too, when Keats consoles the forward-bending lover on the Grecian Urn, the lover arrested and presented in immortal relief by the sculptor's hand before he can kiss, with the line,

For ever wilt thou love, and she be fair –

he utters a moral idea. When Shakespeare says, that

We are such stuff
As dreams are made of, and our little life
Is rounded with a sleep,

he utters a moral idea.

Voltaire was right in thinking that the energetic and profound treatment of moral ideas, in this large sense, is what distinguishes the English poetry. He sincerely meant praise, not dispraise or hint of limitation; and they err who suppose that poetic limitation is a necessary consequence of the fact, the fact being granted as Voltaire states it. If what distinguishes the greatest poets is their powerful and profound application of ideas to life, which surely no good critic will deny, then to prefix to the term ideas here the term moral makes hardly any difference, because human life itself is in so pre-ponderating a degree moral.

It is important, therefore, to hold fast to this: that poetry is at bottom a criticism of life; that the greatness of a poet lies in his powerful and beautiful application of ideas to life, – to the question: How to live. Morals are often treated in a narrow and false fashion, they are bound up with systems of thought and belief which have had their day, they are fallen into the hands of pedants and professional dealers, they grow tiresome to some of us. We find attraction, at times, even in a poetry of revolt against them; in a poetry which might take for its motto Omar Khayam's words: 'Let us make up in the tavern for the time which we have wasted in the mosque.' Or we find attractions in a poetry indifferent to them, in a poetry where the contents may be what they will, but where the form is studied and exquisite. We delude ourselves in either case; and the best cure for our delusion is to let our minds rest upon that great and inexhaustible word *life*, until we learn to enter into its meaning. A poetry of revolt against moral ideas is a poetry of revolt against *life*; a poetry of indifference towards moral ideas is a poetry of indifference towards *life*.

Epictetus had a happy figure for things like the play of the senses, or literary form and finish, or argumentative ingenuity, in comparison with 'the best and master thing' for us, as he called it, the concern, how to live. Some people were afraid of them, he said, or they disliked and undervalued them. Such people were wrong; they were unthankful or cowardly. But the things might also be over-prized, and treated as final when they are not. They bear to life the relation which inns bear to home.

As if a man, journeying home, and finding a nice inn on the road, and liking it, were to stay for ever at the inn! Man, thou hast forgotten thine object; thy journey was not *to* this, but *through* this. 'But this inn is taking.' And how many other inns, too, are taking, and how many fields and meadows! but as places of passage merely. You have an object, which is this: to get home, to do your duty to your family, friends and fellow-countrymen, to attain inward freedom, serenity, happiness, contentment. Style takes your fancy, arguing takes your fancy, and you forget your home and want to make your abode with them and to stay with them, on the plea that they are taking. Who denies that they are taking? but as places of passage, as inns. And when I say this, you suppose me to be attacking the care for style, the care for argument. I am not; I attack the resting in them, the not looking to the end which is beyond them.

Now, when we come across a poet like Théophile Gautier, we have a poet who has taken up his abode at an inn, and never got farther. There may be inducements to this or that one of us, at this or that moment, to find delight in him, to cleave to him; but after all, we do not change the truth about him, – we only stay ourselves in his inn along with him. And when we come across a poet like Wordsworth, who sings,

Of truth, of grandeur, beauty, love and hope,
And melancholy fear subdued by faith,
Of blessed consolations in distress,
Of moral strength and intellectual power,
Of joy in widest commonalty spread –

then we have a poet intent on 'the best and master thing', and who prosecutes his journey home. We say, for brevity's sake, that he deals with *life*, because he deals with that in which life really consists. This is what Voltaire means to praise in the English poets, – this dealing with what is really life. But always it is the mark of the greatest poets that they deal with it; and to say that the English poets are remarkable for dealing with it, is only another way of saying, what is true, that in poetry the English genius has especially shown its power.

Wordsworth deals with it, and his greatness lies in his dealing with it so powerfully. I have named a number of celebrated poets above all of whom he, in my opinion, deserves to be placed. He is to be placed above poets like Voltaire, Dryden, Pope, Lessing, Schiller, because these famous personages, with a thousand gifts and merits, never, or scarcely ever, attain the distinctive accent and utterance of the high and genuine poets –

'Quique pii vates et Phoebo digna locuti,'

at all. Burns, Keats, Heine, not to speak of others in our list, have this accent; who can doubt it? And at the same time they have treasures of humour, felicity, passion, for which in Wordsworth we shall look in vain. Where, then, is Wordsworth's superiority? It is here; he deals with more of *life* than they do; he deals with *life*, as a whole, more powerfully.

No Wordsworthian will doubt this. Nay, the fervent Wordsworthian will add, as Mr Leslie Stephen does, that Wordsworth's poetry is precious because his philosophy is sound; that his 'ethical system is as distinctive and capable of exposition as Bishop Butler's'; that his poetry is informed by ideas which 'fall spontaneously into a scientific system of thought'. But we must be on our guard against the Wordsworthians, if we want to secure for Wordsworth his due rank as a poet. The Wordsworthians are apt to praise him for the wrong things, and to lay far too much stress upon what they call his philosophy. His poetry is the reality, his philosophy, – so far, at least, as it may put on the form and habit of 'a scientific system of thought', and the more that it puts them on – is the illusion. Perhaps we shall one day learn to make this proposition general, and to say: Poetry is the reality, philosophy the illusion. But in Wordsworth's case, at any rate, we cannot do him justice until we dismiss his formal philosophy.

The Excursion abounds with philosophy, and therefore The Excursion is to the Wordsworthian what it never can be to the disinterested lover of poetry – a satisfactory work. 'Duty exists,' says Wordsworth, in The Excursion; and then he proceeds thus:

> Immutably survive,
> For our support, the measures and the forms,
> Which an abstract Intelligence supplies,
> Whose kingdom is, where time and space are not.

And the Wordsworthian is delighted, and thinks that here is a sweet union of philosophy and poetry. But the disinterested lover of poetry will feel that the lines carry us really not a step farther than the proposition which they would interpret; that they are a tissue of elevated but abstract verbiage, alien to the very nature of poetry.

Or let us come direct to the centre of Wordsworth's philosophy, as 'an ethical system, as distinctive and capable of systematical exposition as Bishop Butler's':

> One adequate support
> For the calamities of mortal life
> Exists, one only; – an assured belief
> That the procession of our fate, howe'er
> Sad or disturbed, is ordered by a Being
> Of infinite benevolence and power;
> Whose everlasting purposes embrace
> All accidents, converting them to good.[1]

1 The Excursion, IV, 10–17.

That is doctrine such as we hear in church too, religious and philosophic doctrine; and the attached Wordsworthian loves passages of such doctrine, and brings them forward in proof of his poet's excellence. But however true the doctrine may be, it has, as here presented, none of the characters of *poetic* truth, the kind of truth which we require from a poet, and in which Wordsworth is really strong.

Even the 'intimations' of the famous Ode, those corner-stones of the supposed philosophic system of Wordsworth – the idea of the high instincts and affections coming out in childhood, testifying of a divine home recently left, and fading away as our life proceeds – this idea, of undeniable beauty as a play of fancy, has itself not the character of poetic truth of the best kind; it has no real solidity. The instinct of delight in Nature and her beauty had no doubt extraordinary strength in Wordsworth himself as a child. But to say that universally this instinct is mighty in childhood, and tends to die away afterwards, is to say what is extremely doubtful. In many people, perhaps with the majority of educated persons, the love of nature is nearly imperceptible at ten years old, but strong and operative at thirty. In general we may say of these high instincts of early childhood, the base of the alleged systematic philosophy of Wordsworth, what Thucydides says of the early achievements of the Greek race: 'It is impossible to speak with certainty of what is so remote; but from all that we can really investigate, I should say that they were no very great things.'

Finally the 'scientific system of thought' in Wordsworth gives us at last such poetry as this, which the devout Wordsworthian accepts:

O for the coming of that glorious time
When, prizing knowledge as her noblest wealth
And best protection, this Imperial Realm,
While she exacts allegiance, shall admit
An obligation, on her part, to *teach*
Them who are born to serve her and obey;
Binding herself by statute to secure,
For all the children whom her soil maintains,
The rudiments of letters, and inform
The mind with moral and religious truth.[1]

1 *The Excursion*, IX, 293–302.

Wordsworth calls Voltaire dull, and surely the production of these un-Voltarian lines must have been imposed on him as a judgement! One can hear them being quoted at a Social Science Congress; one can call up the whole scene. A great room in one of our dismal provincial towns; dusty air and jaded afternoon daylight; benches full of men with bald heads and women in spectacles; an orator lifting up his face from a manuscript written within and without to declaim these lines of Wordsworth; and in the soul of any poor child of nature who may have wandered in thither, an unutterable sense of lamentation, and mourning, and woe!

'But turn we,' as Wordsworth says, 'from these bold, bad men,' the haunters of Social Science Congresses. And let us be on our guard, too, against the exhibitors and extollers of a 'scientific system of thought' in Wordsworth's poetry. The poetry will never be seen aright while they thus exhibit it. The cause of its greatness is simple, and may be told quite simply. Wordsworth's poetry is great because of the extraordinary power with which Wordsworth feels the joy offered to us in nature, the joy offered to us in the simple primary affections and duties; and because of the extraordinary power with which, in case after case, he shows us this joy, and renders it so as to make us share it.

The source of joy from which he thus draws is the truest and most unfailing source of joy accessible to man. It is also accessible universally. Wordsworth brings us word, therefore, according to his own strong and characteristic line, he brings us word

Of joy in widest commonalty spread.

Here is an immense advantage for a poet. Wordsworth tells of what all seek, and tells of it at its truest and best source, and yet a source where all may go and draw for it.

Nevertheless, we are not to suppose that everything is precious which Wordsworth, standing even at this perennial and beautiful source, may give us. Wordsworthians are apt to talk as if it must be. They will speak with the same reverence of *The Sailor's Mother*, for example, as of *Lucy Gray*. They do their master harm by such lack of discrimination. *Lucy Gray* is a beautiful success; *The Sailor's Mother* is a failure. To give aright what he wishes to give, to interpret and render successfully, is not always within Wordsworth's own command. It is within no poet's command; here is the part of the Muse, the inspiration, the God, the 'not ourselves'. In Wordsworth's case, the accident, for so it may almost be called, of inspiration, is of peculiar importance. No poet, perhaps, is so evidently filled with a new and sacred energy when the inspiration is upon him; no poet, when it fails him, is so left 'weak as is a breaking wave'. I remember hearing him say that 'Goethe's poetry was not inevitable enough'. The remark is striking and true; no line in Goethe, as Goethe said himself, but its maker knew well how it came there. Wordsworth is right, Goethe's poetry is not inevitable; not inevitable enough. But Wordsworth's poetry, when he is at his best, is inevitable, as inevitable as Nature herself. It might seem that Nature not only gave him the matter for his poem, but wrote his poem for him. He has no style. He was too conversant with Milton not to catch at times his master's manner, and he has fine Miltonic lines; but he has no assured poetic style of his own, like Milton. When he seeks to have a style he falls into ponderosity and pomposity. In *The Excursion* we have his style, as an artistic product of his own creation; and although Jeffrey completely failed to recognize Wordsworth's real greatness, he was yet not wrong in saying of *The Excursion*, as a work of poetic style: 'This will never do.' And yet magical as is that power, which Wordsworth has not, of assured and possessed poetic style, he has something which is an equivalent for it.

Every one who has any sense for these things feels the subtle turn, the heightening, which is given to a poet's verse by his genius for style. We can feel it in the

After life's fitful fever, he sleeps well –

of Shakespeare; in the

though fall'n on evil days,
On evil days though fall'n, and evil tongues –

of Milton. It is the incomparable charm of Milton's power of poetic style which gives such worth to *Paradise Regained*, and makes a great poem of a work in which Milton's imagination does not soar high. Wordsworth has in constant possession, and at command, no style of this kind; but he had too poetic a nature, and had read the great poets too well, not to catch, as I have already remarked, something of it occasionally. We find it not only in his Miltonic lines; we find it in such a phrase as this, where the manner is his own, not Milton's –

>   the fierce confederate storm
> Of sorrow barricaded evermore
> Within the walls of cities;

although even here, perhaps, the power of style, which is undeniable, is more properly that of eloquent prose than the subtle heightening and change wrought by genuine poetic style. It is style, again, and the elevation given by style, which chiefly makes the effectiveness of *Laodamia*. Still the right sort of verse to choose from Wordsworth, if we are to seize his true and most characteristic form of expression, is a line like this from *Michael*:

And never lifted up a single stone.

There is nothing subtle in it, no heightening, no study of poetic style, strictly so called, at all; yet it is expression of the highest and most truly expressive kind.

Wordsworth owed much to Burns, and a style of perfect plainness, relying for effect solely on the weight and force of that which with entire fidelity it utters, Burns could show him.

> The poor inhabitant below
> Was quick to learn and wise to know,
> And keenly felt the friendly glow
>   And softer flame;
> But thoughtless follies laid him low
>   And stain'd his name.

Every one will be conscious of a likeness here to Wordsworth; and if Wordsworth did great things with this nobly plain manner, we must remember, what indeed he himself would always have been forward to acknowledge, that Burns used it before him.

Still Wordsworth's use of it has something unique and unmatchable. Nature herself seems, I say, to take the pen out of his hand, and to write for him with her own bare, sheer, penetrating power. This arises from two causes: from the profound sincereness with which Wordsworth feels his subject, and also from the profoundly sincere and natural character of his subject itself. He can and will treat such a subject with nothing but the most plain, first-hand, almost austere naturalness. His expression may often be called bald, as, for instance, in the poem of *Resolution and Independence*; but it is bald as the bare mountain tops are bald, with a baldness which is full of grandeur.

Wherever we meet with the successful balance, in Wordsworth, of profound truth of subject with profound truth of execution, he is unique. His best poems are those which most perfectly exhibit this balance. I have a warm admiration for *Laodamia* and for the great *Ode*; but if I am to tell the very truth, I find *Laodamia* not wholly free from something artificial, and the great *Ode* not wholly free from something declamatory. If I had to pick out poems of a kind most perfectly to show Wordsworth's unique power, I should rather choose poems such as *Michael, The Fountain, The Highland Reaper.* And poems with the peculiar and unique beauty which distinguishes these, Wordsworth produced in considerable number; besides very many other poems of which the worth, although not so rare as the worth of these, is still exceedingly high.

On the whole, then, as I said at the beginning, not only is Wordsworth eminent by reason of the goodness of his best work, but he is eminent also by reason of the great body of good work which he has left to us. With the ancients I will not compare him. In many respects the ancients are far above us, and yet there is something that we demand which they can never give. Leaving the ancients, let us come to the poets and poetry of Christendom. Dante, Shakespeare, Molière, Milton, Goethe, are altogether larger and more splendid luminaries in the poetical heaven than Wordsworth. But I know not where else, among the moderns, we are to find his superiors.

To disengage the poems which show his power, and to present them to the English-speaking public and to the world, is the object of this volume. I by no means say that it contains all which in Wordsworth's poems is interesting. Except in the case of *Margaret*, a story composed separately from the rest of *The Excursion*, and which belongs to a different part of England, I have not ventured on detaching portions of poems, or on giving any piece otherwise than as Wordsworth himself gave it. But, under the conditions imposed by this reserve, the volume contains, I think, everything, or nearly everything, which may best serve him with the majority of lovers of poetry, nothing which may disserve him.

I have spoken lightly of Wordsworthians: and if we are to get Wordsworth recognized by the public and by the world, we must recommend him not in the spirit of a clique, but in the spirit of disinterested lovers of poetry. But I am a Wordsworthian myself. I can read with pleasure and edification *Peter Bell*, and the whole series of *Ecclesiastical Sonnets*, and the address to Mr Wilkinson's spade, and even the *Thanksgiving Ode*; – everything of Wordsworth, I think, except *Vaudracour and Julia*. It is not for nothing that one has been brought up in the veneration of a man so truly worthy of homage; that one has seen him and heard him, lived in his neighbourhood and been familiar with his country. No Wordsworthian has a tenderer affection for this pure and sage master than I, or is less really offended by his defects. But Wordsworth is something more than the pure and sage master of a small band of devoted followers, and we ought not to rest satisfied until he is seen to be what he is. He is one of the very chief glories of English poetry; and by nothing is England so glorious as by her poetry. Let us lay aside every weight which hinders our getting him recognized as this, and let our one study be to bring to pass, as widely as possible and as truly as possible, his own word concerning his poems: 'They will cooperate with the benign tendencies in human nature and society, and will, in their degree, be efficacious in making men wiser, better and happier.'

John Ruskin

from *Fiction, Fair and Foul*   1880

To contend with this carnal orchestra [Ruskin has just been discussing modern society], the religious world . . . has nothing to oppose but the innocent rather than religious verses of the school recognized as that of the English Lakes; very creditable to them: domestic at once and refined, observing the errors of the world outside of the Lakes with a pitying and tender indignation and arriving in lacustrine seclusion at many valuable principles of philosophy, as pure as the tarns of their mountains and of corresponding depth.

I have lately seen, and with extreme pleasure, Mr Matthew Arnold's arrangement of Wordsworth's poems: and read with sincere interest his high estimate of them. But great poets' work never needs arrangement by other hands: and though it is very proper that Silver How should clearly understand and brightly praise its fraternal Rydal Mount, we must not forget that over there are the Andes, all the while.

Wordsworth's rank and scale among poets were determined by himself, in a single exclamation:

What was the great Parnassus' self to thee,
Mount Skiddaw?

Answer his question faithfully, and you have the relation between the great masters of the Muse's teaching and the pleasant fingerer of his pastoral flute among the reeds of Rydal.

Wordsworth is simply a Westmorland peasant, with considerably less shrewdness than most border Englishmen or Scotsmen inherit; and no sense of humour: but gifted (in this singularly) with vivid sense of natural beauty, and a pretty turn for reflections, not always acute, but, as far as they reach, medicinal to the fever of the restless and corrupted life around him. Water to parched lips may be better than Samian wine, but do not let us therefore confuse the qualities of wine and water. I much doubt there being many inglorious Miltons in our country churchyards; but I am very sure there are many Wordsworths resting there, who were inferior to the renowned one only in caring less to hear themselves talk.

With an honest and kindly heart, a stimulating egoism, a wholesome contentment in modest circumstances, and such sufficient ease, in that accepted state, as permitted the passing of a good deal of time in wishing that daisies could see the beauty of their own shadows [see 'So fair, so sweet, withal so sensitive'], and other such profitable mental exercises, Wordsworth has left us a series of studies of the graceful and happy shepherd life of our lake country, which to me personally, for one, are entirely sweet and precious; but they are only so as the mirror of an existent reality in many ways more beautiful than its picture.

But the other day I went for an afternoon's rest into the cottage of one of our country people of old statesman class; cottage lying nearly midway between two village churches, but more conveniently for downhill walk towards one than the other. I found, as the good housewife made tea for me, that nevertheless she went up the hill to church. 'Why do not you go to the nearer church?' I asked. 'Don't you like the clergyman?' 'Oh no, Sir', she answered, 'it isn't that; but you know I couldn't leave my mother.' 'Your mother! she is buried at H— then?' 'Yes, sir; and you know I couldn't go to church anywhere else.'

That feelings such as these existed among the peasants, not of Cumberland only, but of all the tender earth that gives forth her fruit for the living and receives her dead to peace, might perhaps have been, to our great and endless comfort, discovered before now, if Wordsworth had been content to tell us what he knew of his own village and people, not as the leader of a new and only correct school of poetry, but simply as a country gentleman of sense and feeling, fond of primroses, kind to the parish children, and reverent of the spade with which Wilkinson had tilled his lands: and I am by no means sure that his influence on the stronger minds of his time was anywise hastened or extended by the spirit of tunefulness under whose guidance he discovered that heaven rhymed to seven, and Foy to boy.

Tuneful nevertheless at heart, and of the heavenly choir, I gladly and frankly acknowledge him; and our English literature enriched with a new and singular virtue in the aerial purity and healthful rightness of his quiet song; – but *aerial* only, – not ethereal; and lowly in its privacy of light.

A measured mind, and calm; innocent, unrepentant; helpful to sinless creatures and scatheless, such of the flock as do not stray. Hopeful at least, if not faithful: content with intimations of immortality such as may be in skipping of lambs, and laughter of children – incurious to see in the hands the print of the Nails.

A gracious and constant mind; as the herbage of its native hills, fragrant and pure; – yet, to the sweep and the shadow, the stress and distress, of the greater souls of men, as the tufted thyme to the laurel wilderness of Tempe, – as the gleaming euphrasy to the dark branches of Dodona.

A. C. Swinburne

from 'Wordsworth and Byron', *Miscellanies* 1886.
(first published in 1884)

Devotion to Wordsworth, if it has a tendency to exalt, has also a
tendency to infatuate the judicial sense and spirit of his disciples; to
make them, even as compared with other devotees, unusually prone
to indulgence in such large assertions and assumptions on their
master's behalf as seem at least to imply claims which it may be presumed that their apparent advocates would not seriously advance or
deliberately maintain. It would in some instances be as unreasonable
to suppose that they would do so, as to imagine that Mr Arnold
really considers the dissonant doggerel of Wordsworth's halting lines
to a skylark equal or superior to Shelley's incomparable transfusion
from notes into words of the spirit of the skylark's song. Such an
instance is afforded us by the most illustrious – with a single exception
– of all Wordsworth's panegyrists. After an exposition of his philosophy second only in value, if indeed it be second, to the tribute
offered by Coleridge, Sir Henry Taylor prefixes to some excellent
remarks on the poem of *Michael* the following explanation of his
preference for such work to the work of other poets:

It is an attribute of unusual susceptibility of imagination to
need no extraordinary provocatives; and when this is
combined with intensity of observation and peculiar force of
language, it is the high privilege of the poet so endowed to
rest upon the common realities of life and to dispense with
its anomalies – leaving to less gifted writers – such as
Aeschylus and Sophocles and Shakespeare – the
representation of strange fatalities and of nature 'erring from
itself'.

No better example than this could possibly be chosen of the kind
of writing which has done so much to estrange so many from study
or appreciation of a poet whose most distinguished admirers apparently find it necessary to vindicate their admiration by the attempted
establishment of a principle which if it had any practical significance
or import whatsoever would result, when logically and duly carried

out, in the acceptance of such critical canons as would reject *Othello* and *Oedipus* and the *Oresteia* on the ground of inferiority in subject, from the high station in which they are to be supplanted by such claimants as *Peter Bell*, and *Harry Gill*, and *The Idiot Boy*. If Wordsworth's claims as a poet can only be justified on grounds that would prove him a deeper student of nature, a saner critic of life, a wiser man and a greater poet than Shakespeare, the inference is no less obvious than inevitable: Wordsworth's claims as a poet must in that case go by the board altogether, and at once, and for ever. It is not in any way incompatible with the truest and the deepest admiration for the loftiest of all pastoral poems to enter a respectful protest against this unluckiest of all critical conclusions; and to repeat that protest with some energy when we come upon such a parallel as almost immediately follows it.

[Taylor, according to Swinburne, thinks that most readers misunderstand the nature of the language of passion, which is neither violent nor extravagant, but, preeminently, the language of Wordsworth.]

... The psalms of David or the raptures of the Book of Job, are examples of poetic passion less consonant and less reconcilable in language and in style with the Wordsworthian canon than even the poetry of Aeschylus, of Shakespeare, or of Hugo. 'The enthusiasm which lies in the language of reserve' and which we are bidden to recognize in Wordsworth as a test of poetic superiority, is certainly no distinguishing note of theirs. In the wail of David, in the wail of Cassandra, in the cry of Lear over Cordelia, of Othello over Desdemona, of Triboulet over Blanche and of Fabrice over Isora – in each of these unsurpassable masterpieces of passionate poetry there sounds the same key note of unbridled and self-abandoned agony, the same breathless and burning strain of music wrung forth without reticence or reserve from the uttermost depths of human suffering; though the diversity of style between them is perhaps as wide as may be possible between various forms of equally perfect and equally sublime expression discovered by poets of various ages and countries for equally profound and equally permanent varieties of human emotion. Surely it was not the aim of the great poet so eloquently mispraised, if not sometimes so perversely misinterpreted, by the exponents of his demands on our admirations – surely it was not the aim of Words-

worth to work on the same lines – to rule in the same province as do
these. Meditation and sympathy, not action and passion, were the two
main strings of his serene and stormless lyre. Of these no hand ever
held more gentle yet more sovereign rule than Wordsworth's. His
command of all qualities and powers that are proper to the natural
scope, and adequate to the just application of his genius, was as
perfect as the command of those greater than he – of the greatest
among all great poets – over the worlds of passion and action. And
therefore if his unwary and uncritical disciples would abstain from
forcing the question upon their readers by dint of misapplied or
unqualified eulogy, few or none would care to recall the fact that
when Wordsworth, at the age of twenty-six, made his one attempt to
invade that province of poetry which above all others requires from
its invaders a mastery of such resources as Shelley could command
at the age of twenty-seven – an imaginative grasp and a sympathetic
understanding of action and passion, the result was a tragedy to
which perhaps somewhat less than justice has been done on the score
of literary power, but which in the moral conception and development of its leading idea is, I suppose, unparalleled by any serious
production of the human intellect for morbid and monstrous extravagance of horrible impossibility. [Here follows a discussion of
The Borderers.]

[After quoting Arnold on 'poetical baggage', Swinburne continues]
Here, at length, is the first thoroughly right thing said about Wordsworth, the first thoroughly right note sounded in his praise that ever
if I may venture to speak my mind – has touched the key in which the
final judgement of the future will express its decision in favour and in
honour of this great and misappreciated poet. His earlier disciples or
believers, from the highest to the lowest in point of intelligence –
from a young man like Mr Henry Taylor to a young man like Mr
Frederick Faber – all were misled, as it seems to my humble understanding, by their more or less practical consent to accept Wordsworth's own point of view as the one and only proper or adequate
outlook from which to contemplate the genius and work, the aim and
accomplishment, of Wordsworth. Not that he did wrong to think
of himself as a great teacher; he was a teacher no less benificent than
great; but he was wrong in thinking himself a poet because he was a

teacher. This radical and incurable error vitiated more than half of his theory of poetry, and impaired more than half his practice.

Gerard Manley Hopkins

from a letter to R. W. Dixon   7 August 1886

By the by, why should Wordsworth-worship be 'a difficult thing'? It is a common one now, is it not? Not *the* common, but like soldiers in a crowd, not a numerous but a notable fact. Did you see what Lord Selborne[1] lately said? What I suppose grows on people is that Wordsworth's peculiar grace, his *charisma*, as theologians say, has been granted in equal measure to so very few men since times was – to Plato and who else? I mean his spiritual insight into nature; and this they perhaps think is above all the poet's gift? If it is true, if we sort things, so that art is art and philosophy philosophy, it seems rather the philosopher's than the poet's: at any rate he had it in a sovereign degree. He had a 'divine philosophy' and a lovely gift of verse; but in his work there is nevertheless *beaucoup à redire*: it is due to the universal fault of our literature, its weakness is rhetoric. The strictly poetic insight and inspiration of our poetry seems to me to be of the very finest, finer perhaps than the Greek; but its rhetoric is inadequate – seldom firstrate, mostly only just sufficient, sometimes even below par. By rhetoric I mean all the common and teachable element in literature, what grammar is to speech, what thoroughbase is to music, what theatrical experience gives to playwrights. If you leave out the embroidery (to be sure the principal thing) of for instance *The Excursion* and look only at the groundwork and stuff of the web is it not fairly true to say 'This will never do'? There does seem to be a great deal of dullness, superfluity, aimlessness, poverty of plan. I remember noticing as a boy, it was the discovery of a trade secret, how our poets treat *spirit* and its compounds as one syllable; it is, though founded really on a mistake, the mere change of pronunciation, a beautiful tradition of the poets. Wordsworth had told himself or been told of this trifle: why did he not learn or someone tell him that sonnets have a natural charpente and structure never, or at

1 President of the Wordsworth Society.

least seldom, to be broken through? For want of knowing this his inspired sonnets, εὔμορφι κολοσσοί',[1] suffer from 'hernia', and combine the tiro's blunder with the master's perfection.

Gerard Manley Hopkins

from a letter to R. W. Dixon   23 October 1886

I feel now I am warm and my hand is in for my greater task, Wordsworth's ode; and here, my dear friend, I must earnestly remonstrate with you; must have it out with you. Is it possible that – but it is in black and white; you say that the ode is not, for Wordsworth, good; and much less great [i.e. *Intimations of Immortality*]. . . . There have been in all history, a few, a very few men, whom common repute, even where it did not trust them, has treated as having had something happen to them that does not happen to other men, as having *seen something*, whatever that really was. Plato is the most famous of these. Or to put it as it seems to me I must somewhere have written to you or to somebody, human nature in these men saw something, got a shock; wavers in opinion, looking back, whether there was anything in it or no; but is in a tremble ever since. Now what Wordsworthians mean is, what would seem to be the growing mind of the English speaking world and may perhaps come to be that of the world at large is that in Wordsworth when he wrote that ode human nature got another of those shocks, and the tremble from it is spreading. This opinion I do strongly share; I am, ever since I knew that ode, in that tremble. . . . The ode itself seems to me better than anything else I know of Wordsworth's, so much as to equal or outweigh everything else he wrote: to me it appears so. For Wordsworth was an imperfect artist, as you say: as his matter varied in importance and as he varied in insight (for he had a profound insight of some things and little of others) so does the value of his work vary. Now the interest and importance of the matter were here of the highest, his insight was at its very deepest, and hence to my mind the extreme value of the poem.

1 'Beautiful Statues', Aeschylus, *Agamemnon*, 416.

His powers rose, I hold, with the subject: the execution is so fine. The powers are musically interlaced, the rhythms so happily succeed (surely it is a magical change 'O joy that in our embers'), the diction throughout is so charged and steeped in beauty and yearning (what a stroke 'The moon doth with delight').

A. C. Bradley

from *Oxford Lectures on Poetry*   1909

[Bradley's essay, of which the extract below is the final section, has been concerned to underline Wordsworth's originality and his strangeness.]

After quoting the lines from *A Poet's Epitaph*, and Arnold's lines on Wordsworth, I asked how the man described in them ever came to write the *Ode* on Immortality, or *Yew-Trees*, or why he should say,

For I must tread on shadowy ground, must sink
Deep – and, aloft ascending, breathe in worlds
To which the heaven of heavens is but a veil.

The aspect of Wordsworth's poetry which answers this question forms my last subject.

We may recall this aspect in more than one way. First, not a little of Wordsworth's poetry either approaches or actually enters the province of the sublime. His strongest natural inclination tended there. He himself speaks of his temperament as 'stern', and tells us that

  to the very going out of youth
[He] too exclusively esteemed *that* love,
And sought *that* beauty, which, as Milton says,
Hath terror in it.[1]

This disposition is easily traced in the imaginative impressions of his childhood as he describes them in *The Prelude*. His fixed habit of looking

1 *The Prelude*, XIV, 243–6.

> with feelings of fraternal love
> Upon the unassuming things that hold
> A silent station in this beauteous world,

was only formed, it would seem, under his sister's influence, after his recovery from the crisis that followed the run of his towering hopes in the French Revolution. It was part of his endeavour to find something of the distant ideal in life's familiar face. And though this attitude of sympathy and humility did become habitual, the first bent towards grandeur, austerity, sublimity, retained its force. It is evident in the political poems, and in all those pictures of life which depict the unconquerable power of affection, passion, resolution, patience or faith. It inspires much of his greatest poetry of Nature. It emerges occasionally with a strange and thrilling effect in the serene, gracious, but sometimes stagnant atmosphere of the later poems – for the last time perhaps in that magnificent stanza of the *Extempore Effusion upon the Death of James Hogg* 1835,

> Like clouds that rake the mountain-summits,
>   Or waves that own no curbing hand,
> How fast has brother followed brother
>   From sunshine to the sunless land!

Wordsworth is indisputably the most sublime of our poets since Milton.

We may put the matter, secondly, thus. However much Wordsworth was the poet of small and humble things, and the poet who saw his ideal realized, not in Utopia, but here and now before his eyes, he was, quite as much, what some would call a mystic. He saw everything in the light of 'the visionary power'. He was, for himself

> The transitory being that beheld
> This Vision.

He apprehended all things, natural or human, as the expression of something which, while manifested in them, immeasurably transcends them. And nothing can be more intensely Wordsworthian than the poems and passages most marked by this visionary power and most directly issuing from this apprehension. The bearing of these statements on Wordsworth's inclination to sublimity will be obvious at a glance.

Now we may prefer the Wordsworth of the daffodils to the Wordsworth of the yew-trees, and we may even believe the poet's mysticism to be moonshine; but it is certain that to neglect or throw into the shade this aspect of his poetry is neither to take Wordsworth as he really was nor to judge his poetry truly, since this aspect appears in much of it that we cannot deny to be first rate. Yet there is, I think, and has been for some time, a tendency to this mistake. It is exemplified in Arnold's Introduction and has been increased by it, and it is visible in some degree even in Pater's essay. Arnold wished to make Wordsworth more popular; and so he was tempted to represent Wordsworth's poetry as much more simple and unambitious as than it really was, and as much more easily apprehended than it ever can be. He was also annoyed by attempts to formulate a systematic Wordsworthian philosophy; partly, doubtless, because he knew that, however great the value of a poet's ideas may be, it cannot by itself determine the value of his poetry; but partly also because, having himself but little turn for philosophy, he was disposed to regard it as illusory; and further because, even in the poetic sphere, he was somewhat deficient in that kind of imagination which is allied to metaphysical thought. This is one reason of his curious failure to appreciate Shelley, and of the evident irritation which Shelley produced in him. And it is also one reason why, both in his *Memorial Verses* and in the introduction to his selection from Wordsworth, he either ignores or depreciates that aspect of the poetry with which we are just now concerned. It is not true, we must bluntly say, that the cause of the greatness of this poetry 'is simple and may be told quite simply'. It is true, and it is admirably said, that this poetry 'is great because of the extraordinary power with which Wordsworth feels the joy offered to us in nature, the joy offered to us in the simple primary affection and duties'. But this is only half the truth.

Pater's essay is not thus one-sided. It is, to my mind, an extremely fine piece of criticism. Yet the tendency to which I am objecting does appear in it. Pater says, for example, that Wordsworth is the poet of nature

and of nature, after all, in her modesty. The English Lake country has, of course, it grandeurs. But the peculiar

function of Wordsworth's genius, as carrying in it a power
to open out the soul of apparently little and familiar things,
would have found its true test had he become the poet of
Surrey, say! and the prophet of its life.

This last sentence is, in one sense, doubtless true. The 'function'
referred to could have been exercised in Surrey, and was excercised
in Dorset and Somerset, as well as in the Lake country. And this
function was a 'peculiar function of Wordsworth's genius'. But that
it was *the* peculiar function of his genius, or more peculiar than that
other function which forms our present subject, I venture to deny;
and for the full exercise of this latter function, it is hardly hazardous
to assert, Wordsworth's childhood in a mountain district, and his
subsequent residence there, were indispensable. This will be doubted
for a moment, I believe, only by those readers (and they are not a few)
who ignore *The Prelude* and *The Excursion*. But *The Prelude* and *The
Excursion*, though there are dull pages in both, contain much of
Wordsworth's best and most characteristic poetry. And even in a
selection like Arnold's, which, perhaps wisely, makes hardly any use
of them, many famous poems will be found which deal with nature
but not with nature 'in her modesty'.

My main object was to insist that the 'mystic', 'visionary',
'sublime', aspect of Wordsworth's poetry must not be slighted. I
wish to add a few remarks on it, but to consider it fully would carry
us far beyond our bounds; and, even if I attempted the task, I should
not formulate its results in a body of doctrines. Such a formulation
is useful, and I see no objection to it in princple, as one method of
exploring Wordsworth's mind with a view to the better apprehension of his poetry. But the method has its dangers, and it is another
matter to put forward the results as philosophically adequate, or to
take the position that 'Wordsworth was first and foremost a philosophical thinker, a man whose intention and purpose it was to think
out for himself, faithfully and seriously, the questions concerning
man and nature and human life' (Dean Church). If this were true,
he should have given himself to philosophy and not to poetry; and
there is no reason to think that he would have been eminently successful. Nobody ever was so who was not forced by a special natural
power and an imperious impulsion into the business of 'thinking

out', and who did not develop this power by years of arduous discipline. Wordsworth does not show it in any marked degree; and though he reflected deeply and acutely, he was without philosophical training. His poetry is immensely interesting as an imaginative expression of the same mind which, in his day, produced in Germany great philosophies. His poetic experience, his intuitions, his single thoughts, even his large views, correspond in a striking way, with ideas methodically developed by Kant, Schelling, Hegel, Schopenhauer. They remain admirable material for philosophy; and a philosophy which found itself driven to treat them as moonshine would probably be a very poor affair. But they are like the experience and the utterances of men of religious genius; great truths are enshrined in them, but generally the shrine would have to be broken to liberate these truths in a form which would satisfy the desire to understand. To claim for them the power to satisfy that desire is an error, and it tempts those in whom that desire is predominant to treat them as beautiful illusions.

Setting aside, then, any questions as to the ultimate import of the 'mystic' strain in Wordsworth's poetry, I intend only to call attention to certain traits in the kind of poetic experience which exhibits it most plainly. And we may observe at once that there in this there is always traceable a certain hostility to 'sense'. I do not mean that hostility which is present in *all* poetic experience, and of which Wordsworth was very distinctly aware. The regular action of the senses on their customary material produces, in his view, a 'tyranny' over the soul. It helps to construct that everyday picture of the world, of sensible objects and events 'in disconnection dead and spiritless', which we take for reality. In relation to this reality we become passive slaves; it lies on us with a weight 'heavy as frost and deep almost as life'. It is the origin of our torpor and our superficiality. *All* poetic experience is, broadly speaking, of two different kinds. The perception of the daffodils as dancing in glee, and in sympathy with other gleeful beings, shows us a living, joyous, loving world, and so a 'spiritual' world, not a merely 'sensible' one. But the hostility to sense is no more than a hostility to *mere* sense: this 'spiritual' world is itself the sensible world more fully apprehended: the daffodils do not change or lose their colour in disclosing their glee. On the other hand, in the kind of experience which forms our present subject, there is always some feeling of definite contrast with the limited sensible world. The arresting feature or object is felt in some way *against* this background, or even as in some way a denial of it. Sometimes it is a visionary unearthly light resting on a scene or on some strange figure. Sometimes it is the feeling that the scene or figure belongs to the world of dream. Sometimes it is an intimation of boundlessness, contradicting or abolishing the fixed limits of our habitual view. Sometimes it is the obscure sense of 'unknown modes of being', unlike the familiar modes. This kind of experience, further, comes often with a distinct shock, which may bewilder, confuse or trouble the mind. And, lastly, it is especially, though not invariably, associated with mountains, and again with solitude. Some of these bald statements I will go on to illustrate, only remarking that the boundary between these modes of imagaintion is, naturally, less marked and more wavering in Wordsworth's poetry than in my brief analysis.

We may begin with a poem standing near this boundary, the famous verses *To the Cuckoo*, 'O blithe new-comer'. It stands near the boundary because, like the poem on the Daffodils, it is entirely happy. But it stands unmistakably on the further side of the boundary, and is, in truth, more nearly allied to the *Ode* on Immortality than to the poem on the Daffodils. The sense of sight is baffled, and its tyranny broken. Only a cry is heard, which makes the listener look a thousand ways, so shifting is the direction from which it reaches him. It seems to come from a mere 'voice', 'an invisible thing', 'a mystery'. It brings in him 'a tale of visionary hours' – hours of childhood, when he sought this invisible thing in vain, and the earth appeared to his bewildered but liberated fancy 'an unsubstantial fairy place'. And still, when he hears it, the great globe itself, we may say, fades like an unsubstantial pageant; or, to quote from the Immortality *Ode*, the 'shades of the prison house' melt into air. These words are much more solemn than the Cuckoo poem; but the experience is of the same type, and 'the visionary gleam' of the ode, like the 'wandering voice' of the poem, is the expression through sense of something beyond sense.

Take another passage referring to childhood. It is from *The Prelude*, Book I. Here there is something more than perplexity. There is apprehension, and we are approaching the sublime:

One summer evening (led by her)[1] I found
A little boat tied to a willow tree
Within a rocky cave, its usual home.
Straight I unloosed her chain, and stepping in
Pushed from the shore. It was an act of stealth
And troubled pleasure, nor without the voice
Of mountain echoes did my boat move on;
Leaving behind her still, on either side,
Small circles glittering idly in the moon,
Until they melted all into one track
Of sparkling light. But now, like one who rows,
Proud of his skill, to reach a chosen point
With an unswerving line, I fixed my view
Upon the summit of a craggy ridge,
The horizon's utmost boundary; far above
Was nothing but the stars and the grey sky.
She was an elfin pinnace; lustily
I dipped my oars into the silent lake,
And, as I rose upon the stroke, my boat
Went heaving through the water like a swan;
When, from behind that craggy steep till then
The horizon's bound, a huge peak, black and huge,
As if with voluntary power instinct,
Upreared its head. I struck and struck again,
And growing still in stature the grim shape
Towered up between me and the stars, and still,
For so it seemed, with purpose of its own
And measured motion like a living thing,
Strode after me. With trembling oars I turned,
And through the silent water stole my way
Back to the covert of the willow tree;
There in her mooring place I left my bark, –
And through the meadows homeward went, in grave
And serious mood; but after I had seen
That spectacle, for many days, my brain
Worked with a dim and undetermined sense
Of unknown modes of being; o'er my thoughts

1 Nature.

There hung a darkness, call it solitude
Or blank desertion. No familiar shapes
Remained, no pleasant images of trees,
Of sea or sky, no colours of green fields;
But huge and mighty forms, that do not live
Like living men, moved slowly through the mind
By day, and were a trouble to my dreams.[1]

The best commentary to a poem is generally to be found in the poet's other works. And those last dozen lines furnish the best commentary on that famous passage in the *Ode*, where the poet, looking back to his childhood, gives thanks for it – not however for its careless delight and liberty,

But for those obstinate questionings
Of sense and outward things,
Fallings from us, vanishings;
Blank misgivings of a Creature
Moving about in worlds not realized,
High instincts before which our mortal Nature
Did tremble like a guilty thing surprised.

Whether, or how, these experiences afford 'intimations of immortality' is not in question here; but it will never do to dismiss them so airily as Arnold did. Without them Wordsworth is not Wordsworth.

The most striking recollections of his childhood have not in all cases this manifest affinity to the *Ode*, but wherever the visionary feeling appears in them (and it appears in many), this affinity is still traceable. There is, for instance, in *The Prelude*, Book XII, the description of the crag, from which, on a wild dark day, the boy watched eagerly the two highways below for the ponies that were coming to take him home for the holidays. It is too long to quote, but every reader of it will remember

the wind and sleety rain
And all the business of the elements,
The single sheep, and the one blasted tree,
And the bleak music from that old stone wall,

[1] I, 357–400.

The noise of wood and water, and the mist
That on the line of each of those two roads
Advanced in such indisputable shapes.[1]

Everything here is natural, but everything is apocalyptic. And we
happen to know why. Wordsworth is describing the scene in the
light of memory. In that eagerly expected holiday his father died;
and that scene, as he recalled it, was charged with the sense of contrast
between the narrow world of common pleasures and blind and easy
hopes, and the vast unseen world which encloses it in benificent yet
dark and inexorable arms. The visionary feeling has here a peculiar
tone; but always, openly or covertly, it is the intimation of something
illimitable, over-arching or breaking into the customary 'reality'.
Its character varies; and so sometimes at its touch the soul, suddenly
conscious of its own infinity, melts in rapture into that infinite
being; while at other times the 'mortal nature' stands dumb, incapable of thought, or shrinking from some presence

Not uninformed with Phantasy, and looks
That threaten the profane.

This feeling is so essential to many of Wordsworth's most characteristic poems that it may almost be called their soul; and failure to
understand them frequently arises from obtuseness to it. It appears in
a mild and tender form, but quite openly, in the lines *To a Highland
Girl*, where the child, and the rocks and trees and lake and road by
her home, seem to the poet

Like something fashioned in a dream.

It gives to *The Solitary Reaper* its note of remoteness and wonder;
and even the slight shock of bewilderment due to it is felt in the
opening line of the most famous stanza:

Will no one tell me what she sings?

Its etherial music accompanies every vision of *The White Doe*, and
sounds faintly to us from far away through all the tales of failure and
anguish. Without it such shorter narratives as *Hart-Leap Well* and

Resolution and Independence would lose the imaginative atmosphere which adds mystery and grandeur to the apparently simple 'moral'.

In *Hart-Leap Well* it is conveyed at first by slight touches of contrast. Sir Walter, in his long pursuit of the Hart, has mounted his third horse.

Joy sparkled in the prancing courser's eyes;
The horse and horseman are a happy pair;
But, though Sir Walter like a falcon flies,
There is a doleful silence in the air.

A rout this morning left Sir Walter's hall,
That as they galloped made the echoes roar;
But horse and man are vanished, one and all;
Such race, I think, was never seen before.

At last even the dogs are left behind, stretched one by one among the mountain fern.

Where is the throng, the tumult of the race?
The bugles that so joyfully were blown?
- This chase it looks not like an earthly chase;
Sir Walter and the Hart are left alone.

Thus the poem begins. At the end we have the old shepherd's description of the utter desolation of the spot where the waters of the little spring had trembled with the last deep groan of the dying stag, and where the Knight, to commemorate his exploit, had built a basin for the spring, three pillars to mark the last three leaps of his victim, and a pleasure-house, surrounded by trees and trailing plants, for the summer joy of himself and his paramour. But now 'the pleasure house is dust' and the trees are grey, 'with neither arms nor head':

Now, here is neither grass nor pleasant shade;
The sun on drearier hollow never shone;
So will it be, as I have often said,
Till trees, and stones, and fountain all are gone.

It is only this feeling of the presence of mysterious inviolable Powers, behind the momentary powers of hard pleasure and empty pride, that justifies the solemnity of the stanza:

The Being, that is in the clouds and air,
That is in the green leaves among the groves,
Maintains a deep and reverential care
For the unoffending creatures whom he loves.

Hart-Leap Well is a beautiful poem, but whether it is entirely successful is, perhaps, doubtful. There can be no sort of doubt as to *Resolution and Independence*, probably, if we must choose, the most Wordsworthian of Wordsworth's poems, and the best test of ability to understand him. The story, if given in a brief argument, would sound far from promising. We should expect for it, too, a ballad form somewhat like that of *Simon Lee*. When we read it, we find instead lines of extraordinary grandeur, but, mingled with them, lines more pedestrian than could be found in an impressive poem from another hand – for instance,

And, drawing to his side, to him did say
'The morning gives us promise of a glorious day'.

or,

How is it that you live, and what is it that you do?

We meet also with that perplexed persistence, and that helpless reiteration of a question (in this case one already clearly answered), which in other poems threatens to become ludicrous, and on which a writer with a keener sense of the ludicrous would hardly have ventured. Yet with all this, and by dint of all this, we read with bated breath, almost as if we were in the presence of that 'majestical' Spirit in *Hamlet*, come to 'admonish' from another world, though not this time by terror. And one source of this effect is the confusion, the almost hypnotic obliteration of the habitual reasoning mind, that falls on the poet as he gazes at the leech-gatherer, and hears, without understanding, his plain reply to the inquiry about himself, and the prosaic 'occupation' he 'pursues':

The old man still stood talking by my side;
But now his voice to me was like a stream
Scarce heard; nor word from word could I divide;
And the whole body of the man did seem
Like one whom I had met with in a dream;

Or like a man from some far region sent,
To give me human strength, by apt admonishment.

The same question was asked again, and the answer was repeated.
But

While he was talking thus, the lonely place,
The old man's shape, and speech, all troubled me.

'Trouble' is a word not seldom employed by the poet to denote the
confusion caused by some visionary experience. Here are, again, the
fallings from us, vanishings, blank misgivings, dim fore-feelings of
the soul's infinity.

　　Out of many illustrations I will choose three more. There is in
The Prelude, Book IV, the passage (so strongly resembling *Resolution
and Independence* that I merely refer to it) where Wordsworth describes an old soldier suddenly seen, leaning against a milestone on
the moon-lit road, all alone:

No living thing appeared in earth or air;
And, save the flowing water's peaceful voice,
Sound there was none. . . .
　　　　　　　　　　　. . . still his form
Kept the same awful steadiness – at his feet
His shadow lay, and moved not.

His shadow proves that he was no ghost; but a ghost was never
ghostlier than he. And by him we may place the London beggar of
The Prelude, Book VII:

How oft, amid those overflowing streets,
Have I gone forward with the crowd, and said
Unto myself, 'The face of every one
That passes by me is a mystery!'
Thus have I looked, nor ceased to look, oppressed
By thoughts of what and whither, when and how,
Until the shapes before my eyes became
A second-sight procession, such as glides
Over still mountains, or appears in dreams;
And once, far travelled in such mood, beyond
The reach of common indication, lost

Amid the moving pageant, I was smitten
Abruptly, with the view (a sight not rare)
Of a blind Beggar, who, with upright face,
Stood, propped against a wall, upon his chest
Wearing a written paper, to explain
His story, whence he came, and who he was.
Caught by the spectacle my mind turned round
As with the might of waters; an apt type
This label seemed of the utmost we can know,
Both of ourselves and of the universe;
And, on the shape of that unmoving man,
His steadfast face and sightless eyes, I gazed,
As if admonished from another world.[1]

Still more curious psychologically is the passage in the preceding
book of *The Prelude*, which tells us of a similar shock and leads to the
description of its effects. The more prosaically I introduce the passage,
the better. Wordsworth and Jones ('Jones, as from Calais southward
you and I') set out to walk over the Simplon, then traversed only by
a rough mule-track. They wandered out of the way, and, meeting a
peasant, discovered from his answers to their questions that without
knowing it they '*had crossed the Alps*'. This may not sound important,
and the italics are Wordsworth's not mine. But the next words are
these:

Imagination – here the Power so called
Through sad incompetence of human speech,
That awful Power rose from the mind's abyss
Like an unfathered vapour that enwraps,
At once, some lonely traveller. I was lost;
Halted without an effort to break through;
But to my conscious soul I now can say –
'I recognise thy glory : in such strength
Of usurpation, when the light of sense
Goes out, but with a flash that has revealed
The invisible world, doth greatness make abode,
There harbours; whether we be young or old,
Our destiny, our being's heart and home,

1 626–49.

Is with infinitude, and only there;
With hope it is, hope that can never die,
Effort, and expectation, and desire,
And something evermore about to be.[1]

And what was the result of this shock? The poet may answer for
himself in some of the greatest lines in English poetry. The travellers
proceeded on their way down the Defile of Gondo.

Downwards we hurried
And, with the half-shaped road which we had missed,
Entered a narrow chasm. The brook and road
Were fellow-travellers in this gloomy strait,
And with them did we journey several hours
At a slow pace. The immeasurable height
Of woods decaying, never to be decayed,
The stationary blasts of waterfalls,
And in the narrow rent at every turn
Winds thwarting winds, bewildered and forlorn,
The torrents shooting from the clear blue sky,
The rocks that muttered close upon our ears,
Black drizzling crags that spake by the way-side
As if a voice were in them, the sick sight
And giddy prospect of the raving stream,
The unfettered clouds and region of the Heavens,
Tumult and peace, the darkness and the light –
Were all like workings of one mind, the features
Of the same face, blossoms upon one tree;
Characters of the great Apocalypse,
The types and symbols of Eternity,
Of first, and last, and midst, and without end.[2]

I hardly think that 'the poet of Surrey, say, and the prophet of its
life' could have written thus. And of all the poems to which I have
lately referred, and all the passages I have quoted, there are but two
or three which do not cry aloud that their birth-place was the moor
or the mountain, and that severed from their birth-place they would
perish. The more sublime they are, or the nearer they approach

1 VI, 592–608.
2 VI, 619–40.

sublimity, the more is this true. The cry of the cuckoo in O *blithe new-comer*, though visionary, is not sublime; but, echoed by the mountain, it is

Like – but oh, how different!

It was among the mountains that Wordsworth, as he says of his Wanderer, *felt* his faith. It was there that all things

Breathed immortality, revolving life,
And greatness still revolving; infinite:
There littleness was not; the least of things
Seemed infinite; and there his spirit shaped
Her prospects, nor did he believe, – he *saw*.[1]

And even if we count his vision a mere dream, still he put into words, as no other poet has, the spirit of the mountains.

Two voices are there; one is of the sea,
One of the mountains; each a mighty voice.

And of the second of these we may say that few or none hears it right now he is gone.

   Partly because he is the poet of mountains he is, even more pre-eminently, the poet of solitude. For there are tones in the mountain voice scarcely audible except in solitude, and the reader whom Wordsworth's greatest poetry baffles could have no better advice offered him than to do what he has probably never done in his life – to be on a mountain alone. But for Wordsworth not this solitude only, but all solitude and all things solitary had an extraordinary fascination.

The outward show of sky and earth,
Of hill and valley, he has viewed;
And impulses of *deeper birth*
Have come to him in solitude.

The sense of solitude, it will readily be found, is essential to nearly all the poems and passages we have been considering, and to some of quite a different character, such as the Daffodil stanzas. And it is not merely that the poet is alone; what he sees is so too. If the leech-

[1] *The Excursion*, I, 227–32.

gatherer and the soldier on the moon-lit road had not been solitary
figures, they would not have awakened 'the visionary power'; and
it is scarcely fanciful to add that if the boy who was watching for his
father's ponies had had beside him any more than the *single* sheep
and the *one* blasted tree, the mist would not have advanced along the
roads 'in such indisputable shapes'. With Wordsworth that power
seems to have sprung into life at once on the perception of loneliness.
What is lonely is a spirit. To call a thing lonely or solitary is, with
him, to say that it opens a bright or solemn vista into infinity. He
himself wanders lonely as a cloud: he seeks the souls of lonely places:
he listens in awe to

One voice, the solitary raven. . . .
An iron knell, with echoes from afar:

against the distant sky he describes the shepherd,

A solitary object and sublime,
Above all height! like an aerial cross
Stationed alone upon a spiry rock
Of the Chartreuse, for worship.[1]

But this theme might be pursued for hours, and I will refer
only to two poems more. The editor of *The Golden Treasury*, a book
never to be thought of without gratitude, changed the title of *The
Solitary Reaper* into *The Highland Reaper*. He may have had his
reasons. Perhaps he had met some one who thought that the Reaper
belonged to Surrey. Still the change was a mistake: the solitary in
Wordsworth's title gave the keynote. The other poem is *Lucy Gray*.
'When I was little', a lover of Wordsworth once said, 'I could hardly
bear to read Lucy Gray, it made me feel so lonely'. Wordsworth
called it *Lucy Gray, or Solitude* and this young reader understood
him. But there is too much reason to fear that for half his readers his
solitary child is generalized into a mere little girl, and that they never
receive the main impression he wished to produce. Yet his intention
is announced in the opening lines, and as clearly shown in the lovely
final stanzas, which give even to this ballad the visionary touch
which distinguishes it from *Alice Fell*:

1 *The Prelude*, VIII, 273–6.

Yet some maintain that to this day
She is a living child;
That you may see sweet Lucy Gray
Upon the lonesome wild.

O'er rough and smooth she strips alone,
And never looks behind;
And sings a solitary song
That whistles in the wind.

The solitariness which exerted so potent a spell on Wordsworth
had in it nothing 'Byronic'. He preached in *The Excursion* against
the solitude of 'self-indulging spleen'. He was even aware that he
himself, though free from that weakness, had felt

> perhaps too much
> The self-sufficing power of Solitude.

No poet is more emphatically the poet of community. A great part
of his verse – a part as characteristic and as precious as the part on
which I have been dwelling – is dedicated to the affections of home
and neighbourhood and country, and to that soul of joy and love
which links together all Nature's children and 'steals from earth to
man, from man to earth'. And this soul is for him as truly the presence
of 'the Being that is in the clouds and air' and in the mind of man as
are the power, the darkness, the silence, the strange gleams and
mysterious visitations which startle and confuse with intimations of
infinity. But solitude and solitariness were to him, in the main, one
of these intimations. They had not for him merely the 'eeriness'
which they have at times for everyone, though that was essential to
some of the poems we have reviewed. They were the symbol of power
to stand alone, to be 'self-sufficing', to dispense with custom and
surroundings and aid and sympathy – a self-dependence at once the
image and the communication of 'the soul of all the worlds'. Even
when they were full of 'sounds and sweet airs that give delight and
hurt not', the solitude of the Reaper or of Lucy, they so appealed to
him. But they appealed also to that austerer strain which led him to
love 'bare trees and mountains bare', and lonely places, and the bleak
music of the old stone wall, and to dwell with awe, and yet with
exultation, on the majesty of that 'unconquerable mind' which

through long years holds its solitary purpose, sustains its solitary passion, feeds upon its solitary anguish. For this mind, as for the blind beggar or the leech-gatherer, the 'light of sense' and the sweetness of life have faded or 'gone out'; but in it 'greatness makes abode', and it 'retains its station proud', 'by form or image unprofaned'. Thus, in whatever guise it might present itself, solitariness 'carried far into his heart' the haunting sense of an 'invisible world'; of some Life beyond this 'transitory being' and 'unapproachable by death';

Of Life continuous, Being unimpaired;
That hath been, is, and where it was and is
There shall endure, – existence unexposed
To the blind walk of mortal accident;
From diminution safe and weakening age;
While man grows old, and dwindles, and decays;
And countless generations of mankind
Depart; and leave no vestige where they trod.

For me, I confess, all this is far from being 'mere poetry' – partly because I do not believe that any such thing as 'mere poetry' exists. But whatever kind or degree of truth we may find in all this, everything in Wordsworth that is sublime or approaches sublimity has, directly or more remotely, to do with it. And without this part of his poetry Wordsworth would be 'shorn of his strength', and would no longer stand, as he does stand, nearer than any other poet of the nineteenth Century to Milton.

(125–45)

Part Three Modern Views

Introduction

Bradley's essay, which has clearly initiated a good deal of
contemporary debate, might well have stood at the head of the
present section. But then, if the spread of Victorian views can be
adequately represented by Arnold, Stephen and Bradley, it is
clear that there has been no great critical discontinuity anyway.
Their judgements, or perhaps their interests, are reflected quite
fully by the lines drawn in contemporary criticism. This is not to
say that they sit as guiding presences over the current debate, as
some resemblances between Victorian and contemporary studies
of Wordsworth must be fortuitous. The development of studies of
Wordsworth's intellectual history, and the background to it, owes
much more to the growth of university education and the need of
scholars to conduct research than it does to the influence of
Leslie Stephen. But the critical approaches proposed by the
Victorians have, until quite recently, been absorbing and
provoking enough to occupy most of their successors.

With all the energy poured into criticism in modern years, it
can hardly have sat still; and it is undeniable that the experience
of reading modern criticism is an entirely different experience
from that of reading Pater, Swinburne and Arnold. But with
Wordsworth at least, the differences – the distinctive tone, the
difficulty of intellectual reference and the density of allusion – are
grounded on literary scholarship, which expanded rapidly after
the First World War. This distinction is not a trivial one, for it
means that although the critical response to the work is similar, it
has been filled out by the vastly greater amount of information
that exists about Wordsworth and the writing of his poems, and
by the material which is available from other scholarly
disciplines. For convenience, this may be represented as an
advance along three fronts.

Leslie Stephen, like Arnold, slighted *The Prelude*, but he lived
long enough to write appreciatively of Emile Legouis's *La
Jeunesse de Wordsworth*, first published in English in 1897.

Wordsworth's following in Europe had never been very great:
he had remained a figure of purely English importance, never
arousing the adulation received by Scott and Byron. In
nineteenth-century America too, Wordsworth had been a
respected figure but had not been the subject of an invigorating
criticism, being presumably too far from the central concerns of
American creative writers. Henry James provides a link between
the Americans and the Europeans when he writes, à propos of
Taine's *History of English Literature*:

We are tempted to say that a Frenchman who should have
twisted himself into a relish for Wordsworth would almost
have lost our respect.

Yet it was Legouis's being French which presumably gave an
important stimulus to his researches. It was he who pointed to the
importance of Wordsworth's stay in France, and his connection
with the French Revolution – the early radical days of
Wordsworth having been completely overshadowed by his later
'apostasy'. This in turn necessitated a greater focus of attention on
The Prelude, virtually the only text which deals with those days.
Of considerable importance also was the discovery of
Wordsworth's love affair with Annette Vallon and the birth of
his daughter Caroline. These events, though very open secrets
in the Wordsworth circle, had been totally obscured in the course
of the nineteenth-century – apart from a garbled tradition
which survived in the Coleridge family. In effect, they were
discovered anew by Legouis and the American scholar G. M.
Harper. The results were published stage by stage in Harper's
Life (1916), in an appendix to Legouis's *Early Life* (2nd edition),
in Harper's *Wordsworth's French Daughter* and in some articles on
the Vallon family published in the *Revue des Deux Mondes* in 1922.
A pamphlet published by Legouis entitled *Wordsworth in a new
Light*, which takes a reflective look at the discoveries, although not

reprinted here because of its length, is of great interest. The title is thoroughly justified. Legouis is both studied and moderate: he points up the relationship the whole episode of Annette might have to some of the tales in *Lyrical Ballads*, the *Lucy* poems, *The Prelude*. After such a discovery, the feeling is inevitable that there is a depth of emotion in certain of Wordsworth's poems which has been previously overlooked. R. D. Mayo's discoveries that the theme of forsaken mothers was a common subject in the later eighteenth-century must be regarded as a qualification to but not an overthrow of the importance of this discovery. Legouis does not avoid the less attractive side of Wordsworth's character: writing of the sonnet 'It is a beauteous evening', he writes:

There is indeed a wonderful forgetfulness of contingencies, a rare lack of self-compunction in the father, who transforms himself into a sovereign pontiff.

It is in many ways a model of the tact required from biographical criticism, while it does not give up the right to interpret and even judge where necessary.

There can have been very few critical studies of Wordsworth published in the last ten or fifteen years which have more than mentioned Annette Vallon in passing. Very few now would tolerate the thesis of Herbert Read that the one key to Wordsworth's life and work subsequent to 1792 is his remorse over his seduction and abandonment of Annette. But the joint discovery of Harper and Legouis has had one important enduring effect: it has overturned many of the stereotyped views of Wordsworth as a creature supernaturally asexual and free from common human emotions which had become common even by the time of *The Excursion* – Shelley, we may remember, had made quite free use of it in *Peter Bell the Third*. The discovery of the Annette episode brought Wordsworth in some sense closer to common humanity and reversed the trend of much Victorian myth. Read's, like so many accounts of Wordsworth, is convincing only up to a point. Read ignores the conventionality of the 'guilt and sorrow' in many of the poems; and the private response of Wordsworth to this part of his life was very far from obsessive. It is indeed surprising to discover the calm matter-of-factness with which Wordsworth and the rest of his family accepted his past.

Recent years have seen other rediscoveries of great writers. Our apprehension of Dickens has been completely reshaped by the emphasis placed on his 'blacking-factory' trauma and his secret love affair with Ellen Ternan, so that a Freudian interpretation of Dickens's novels is now the norm. A general reorientation is necessary and valuable with many of the great nineteenth-century writers; and so it is with Wordsworth. But when biographical criticism moves away from this end and seeks to establish very precise correlations, and to interpret particular poems or novels, or whole *oeuvres* according to a psychological model, it becomes tendentious and open to hostile criticism. This is evidenced by the controversy surrounding F. W. Bateson's *Wordsworth – A Reinterpretation*. Bateson's central thesis – though by no means the only thing in the book – that Wordsworth can be best understood in the light of an only half-unconsciously suppressed incestuous feeling for his sister Dorothy, has seemed incredible and repugnant to many of Bateson's critics. Whether one can agree with this interpretation or not the book is a rewarding one because Bateson, in common with almost all modern critics, regards Wordsworth as less a philosopher who wrote in verse than as a troubled spirit whose own disturbances and not his tranquil sense of joy in nature formed the subject of and stimulus for his poems. This is of course only part of a very much more wide ranging change that has taken place in this century, but has clearly been helped by the guidance given by biographical studies. It is the nature of these disturbances that is being investigated at present: is it more helpful to enlist the aid of Freud, Jung or Kierkegaard and Sartre? Perhaps there is at the moment a feeling that the pendulum has swung too far away from the Victorian conception: a poet who is at the mercy of his own complexes has no autonomy; and there have been no recent studies along the same lines as Bateson's.

The second key to Wordsworthian studies was the textual criticism of Ernest de Selincourt and Helen Darbishire. To the critic, the tangled mass of Wordsworth's revisions and erasures, the chronology of the texts, and the circling of his mind around certain central experiences, have been evident in a way not previously feasible. It has been possible to plot Wordsworth's growth as a man and as an artist, an approach which was obviously discouraged by Victorian anthologies, or by Wordsworth's own collected editions of his works. Enid Welsford's *Salisbury Plain*, an account of the successive changes undergone by one poem, is a good representative of what this approach can yield, although there have been fewer of such explicit studies than might have been expected. Nevertheless, a number of studies of the 'development of mind and art' variety are in fact little more than reasoned expansions of de Selincourt's scholarship, with paraphrases of poems for padding. Otherwise, much of the most discriminating criticism of this kind has been focused on *The Prelude*, and has tended to be subsumed into the discussion, which has haunted modern criticism, of the nature of the 'great period': what its true limits were, what was the source of its power and inspiration, and why it failed after 1808 (or some earlier date), if it did fail. The notion of the creative decade is not a new one – it was made explicit in Arnold's *Preface*. But the point was made much more telling and sharp by de Selincourt, who first published a parallel text of two (1805 and 1850) versions of *The Prelude*. Here are laid bare Wordsworth's later evasions of what seems to have beeen the nub of his experience, and his toning down of the uncompromising 'egotism' of his youth. In spite of

expectations, however, the 1805 text has not entirely superseded
the one published by Mary Wordsworth. Mary Burton in *The
One Wordsworth* has argued against the division of Wordsworth,
by analogy with Donne, into radical young Bill and prosy old
Father William. Her conclusions are that Wordsworth became a
more competent craftsman as he grew older, his verse benefiting
from a greater command over syntax, imagery and clarity, and an
avoidance of the prolixity and banality which mark much of his
early verse. The last part of this is of course disputable: many
would argue that the banality is only apparent and is indeed a
part of Wordsworth's dramatic purpose. However, the extract
printed from John Jones's *The Egotistical Sublime* bears out Mrs
Burton's contention in passing. Convincing though much of their
argument is at a certain level, few readers show any enthusiasm
for *The Excursion*, let alone the Duddon poems, the
Ecclesiastical Sketches or the many Memorials of Tours. Studies
which really make serious claims for the later Wordsworth are
uncommon, and indeed to make such claims, one would be really
forced into the position that while Wordsworth's inspiration and
talent for creating new poems disappeared, his skill and
craftsmanship – his sheer power over form and style – increased.
This is of course possible, but it is an unfamiliar and heretical
proposition,
  Of the many theories which account for the absence from the
later verse of the characteristic and unique Wordsworthian
experiences, perhaps the most sophisticated and aesthetically
satisfying are those which, like David Ferry's, present it as the
virtually inevitable end to those finely balanced tensions which
made Wordsworth's verse the subtle thing it is. Most other theories
rely on the positing of some sort of crisis in Wordsworth's life,
psychological or otherwise.
  The major reorientation that has taken place has been the
virtual rediscovery of *The Prelude*. De Selincourt's edition has

been of great importance, but the major part of the work has
been American. Beatty (1922) was the first consciously to deprecate
Arnold and follow Stephen in estimating Wordsworth's doctrine
and art 'in the context of their historical relations'. His study was
followed by that of Havens (1941), another contextual and
comparative study, examining Wordsworth's thought in relation
to the eighteenth century, and by that of Potts (1953) which
discusses analogues and sources. *The Prelude* is the central text in
recent books by Lindenberger, Ferry and Hartman, whose
preoccupation is the unravelling of Wordsworth's vision of reality,
the sense of relation between the inner and outer worlds of his
vision. Many of these later studies owe at bottom a great deal to
Bradley, and, by looking at Wordsworth's poems from unfamiliar
and difficult perspectives, have helped us to step away from a
century of cultural familiarization and so to see poems like
Daffodils and *Nutting* as the records of a very peculiar and personal
experience, very near to the limits of the average reader's
capacity for involvement, or perhaps entirely beyond it. They
have made us much more sympathetic to the responses of
contemporary readers like Anna Seward and Francis Jeffrey.

   In contrast, there has been another critical trend, largely in
Britain, which sees Wordsworth principally as the poet of
community and relationship. His own claims to be a force for
moral health and normality are accepted largely at their face
value. According to John Danby (1960) he was the last great poet
of the Renaissance tradition. Some of the claims seem specious
enough: such as Danby's that Wordsworth in *Michael* shows an
incisive understanding of the nature and value of *work* in an
organic society. Nevertheless, there are truths about Wordsworth,
as regards both intention and achievement, which are not well
handled in those American studies which see Wordsworth as a
lonely figure, brooding intensely over an apocalyptic sense of
mortality. A familiar tradition in British criticism, well

represented by Danby, insists that Wordsworth's landscape is above all, even at its bleakest, *peopled*, and has clear relations with the eighteenth-century and its social poetry. Instead of *The Prelude*, the central poems here are *Michael*, *The Leech-Gatherer*, *The Old Cumberland Beggar* and many of the ballads from the first volume of *Lyrical Ballads*, which are now being read with respect and a genuine effort at understanding – for the first time in more than a century and a half. It is a pity that Wordsworth's most eighteenth-century poem, *The Excursion*, has so far received next to no attention from British critics. However, the poem called *The Ruined Cottage* which eventually became absorbed into *The Excursion* has been read more and more in the last twenty years. Francis Jeffrey found it a rare exception in Wordsworth's works and had to admit to being moved by it; and clearly F. R. Leavis's statement that it is Wordsworth's finest work has been influential. Together with *Michael* and *The Brothers* it is a vital text in a critical position which seeks to deny the old charge that Wordsworth is a mere 'ventriloquist' when he handles the emotions of others.

Jonathan Wordsworth (1969) makes this claim:

[*The Ruined Cottage*] shows in Wordsworth a humanity, an insight into emotions not his own, that is wholly convincing – places him, perhaps unexpectedly, among the very few great English tragic writers.

Mr Wordsworth takes issue with other recent writers[1] who have found Wordsworth callous in his handling of his forlorn or desperate protagonists like *The Old Cumberland Beggar* or *Margaret*. His analysis, however, while insisting on Wordsworth's

1 Cleanth Brooks in 'Wordsworth and Human Suffering: Notes on Two Early Poems', *From Sensibility to Romanticism, Essays Presented to Frederick A. Pottle* edited by Frederick Hilles and Harold Bloom (Oxford University Press, 1965) and Edward E. Bostetter *The Romantic Ventriloquists* (Seattle, 1963).

'humanity', makes it clear that the poet's conception of the value of life and death and the meaning of pain and suffering are not often recognized as normal and comforting by the modern reader.

There have been some celebrated attacks on Wordsworth in this century. Babbitt (1931) censured Wordsworth's doctrines of 'primitivism' and 'wise passiveness' as being irrelevant in a modern scientific context, while Aldous Huxley asked what happened to the doctrine of joy in nature outside the English lake district. Douglas Bush, in an essay strangely enough entitled 'A Minority Report',[1] also rehearsed what was essentially a nineteenth-century complaint – that the poet evaded too much of life to be called great. Salvador de Madariaga attacked the Englishness, or lack of passion and spontaneity, in Wordsworth's verse, which he found cold and over-purposeful.

Yet for most readers these complaints have missed their target, and Wordsworth's reputation as a major poet is not in doubt. It is encouraging too that some commentators have been interested enough by Wordsworth to be able to break new critical ground and to move on from questions posed in the nineteenth-century, and are taking him seriously enough to look closer at his own statements on the nature of his art. One such new interest is represented here very briefly by John Jones on Wordsworth's language. Davie (1955) and Clarke (1962) have also written persuasively on the subject. There is a pleasing symmetry about this, for Wordsworth was far ahead of his time in the penetration of his account of the structure and function of the poet's language. Given the current intellectual climate, language indeed, rather than history or ideas, must now be the growth point in Wordsworthian studies. Indeed, another interest to be

1 In *Wordsworth: Centenary Studies Presented at Cornell and Princeton Universities*, edited by Gilber T. Dunklin (Hamden, 1963).

defined is by no means divorced from this – the concern with Wordsworthian psychology. By this is meant not his own personal psychiatric case history, which is being largely discarded as an effective tool, but his deliberate attempt to write verse which would mirror mental events and, to use his own phraseology, illustrate general laws of the human mind. Something of the subtlety with which he attended to the mind's reactions is available from his own analysis of part of *Resolution and Independence* in the 1815 *Preface* or of the sonnet 'With ships the sea was sprinkled'. Several recent critics have followed up hints from Wordsworth. S. M. Parrish (1957) argues that the centre of *The Thorn* is not the emotions of Martha Ray but the psychological reactions of the garrulous old sea-captain whom Jeffrey found so hard to stomach. There are two important essays in Thomson (1969), by Davie on the *Lyrical Ballads* and Anthony Conran on the Goslar Poems, which, by 'looking steadily' at what Wordsworth actually wrote, and not what it is assumed he meant to write, show us Wordsworth's psychology in some of its depth, precision and occasional quirkiness.

Yet these essays are not very far from the work of Ferry or Hartman. What all these critiques have in common, as has all the best recent work on Wordsworth, is a recognition of the bleak absoluteness of Wordsworth's presentation of his experiences and his claims for it. Whatever the final nature of Wordsworth's philosophy or experience, it is clear that formulae such as 'joy in nature' or dismissive gestures such as 'the sage of Rydal' are not applicable to more than a small fraction of the very large body of important work. If Wordsworth is to be genuinely appreciated now, it can only be with as great an effort of sympathy and imagination as was needed in 1800 and 1807.

Helen Darbishire

'Wordsworth's *Prelude*', *The Nineteenth-Century*   May 1926

Between the years 1798 and 1805, the most fruitful years of his
poetic life, Wordsworth composed a long autobiographical poem,
known to his family and friends as 'the poem on his own early life',
or 'the poem on the growth of his mind', or 'the poem addressed
to Coleridge'. Of that work *The Prelude*, published after his death
in 1850, is a much-revised version. The original poem, preserved in
two manuscript copies made by Dorothy Wordsworth and Sara
Hutchinson in the winter of 1805-6, has since remained in the hands
of the Wordsworth family. Mr Gordon Wordsworth recently
entrusted these manuscripts, together with others relevant to *The
Prelude*, to the careful hands of Professor de Selincourt, whose
edition of *The Prelude*, just published,[1] gives us that early poem intact.
No event so important as this has happened in the literary world for
many years. The original *Prelude* is in a real sense a different poem
from *The Prelude* that we know. As we read it we see into Wordsworth's mind at that very period when his creative powers were at
their height, and watch its first searchings after the true history of his
inner life.

   Wordsworth never intended to publish his autobiography until
his great philosophical poem *The Recluse* was completed. But *The
Recluse* was never completed, and he came to realize that *The Prelude*
must stand on its own merits and that he must prepare it for posthu-
mous publication. Thus began a process of periodic revision which
ceased only with his life. The first two finished manuscripts were
made in the winter of 1805-6; the third was written probably between 1817 and 1819; the fourth round about 1828, correced in
1832, and completely overhauled in 1839; the fifth, which embodies these corrections, was the copy from which the text of 1850
was printed. The first three manuscripts are closely in harmony;
the fourth and fifth represent a thoroughly revised and altered
poem. Professor de Selincourt's edition gives us in admirably critical
form all the information that we need, and makes it possible for us
to see the poem in all the stages of its growth. The text of 1850 is

1 Clarendon Press.

printed page by page opposite that of 1805-6, and the relevant readings from other manuscripts appear in the *apparatus criticus*.

The general trend of the alterations can be confidently foretold by anyone who knows Wordsworth's way of tinkering with his text. In style, bald simplicity will give place to a more decorative, more obviously literary form. In thought, a tendency to revolutionary politics will be checked, and moral and religious conceptions will be conformed to a more orthodox pattern. These familiar processes can be traced, surely enough, in the successive texts of *The Prelude*.

Another change, proper to that poem, springs from a change in his personal life. When he wrote and dedicated the poem to Coleridge the two were on terms of closest intimacy. In 1810 an unhappy estrangement divided them, and the old loving friendship was never regained. Many altered or omitted passages in *The Prelude* bear silent witness to the change. The tender address to Coleridge, 'most loving soul', is altered to 'capacious soul'; his 'gentle spirit' becomes a 'kindred influence'. The daring phrase in which Wordsworth claims their close intellectual kinship, 'though twins almost in genius and in mind', is struck out. And, most telling of all, the allusion to Dorothy, 'thy treasure also', is changed to the less poignant 'dear to thee also'. Further, the whole manner of the poem is altered. He had addressed himself to Coleridge heart to heart.

> I speak bare truth
> As if to thee alone in private talk,

he writes. In revising he changes the intimate and personal form, substituting general for particular expressions, replacing the pronoun 'I' by impersonal constructions. In short, with a touch here and a new patch there, he turns what was a glorified private letter to Coleridge into a poetic confession, fit for the medium of cold print.

But the most vital changes lie deeper still; they touch what we should now call the psychology of the poem. The inspiration of Wordsworth's poetry had its vitalizing source in the power with which he realized a peculiar experience. The experience begins in sensation and ends in thought. It begins in such an adventure of the senses as that of his boyish birdsnesting:

                    Oh! when I have hung
Above the raven's nest, by knots of grass
And half-inch fissures in the slippery rock
But ill sustained, and almost (so it seemed)
Suspended by the blast that blew amain,
Shouldering the naked crag, oh! at that time
While on the perilous ridge I hung alone,
With what strange utterance did the loud dry wind
Blow through my ear! the sky seemed not a sky
Of earth – and with what motion moved the clouds!–[1]

(a passage whose power and significance is inexplicable; for what
can we say of those last bare words except that they 'carry alive into
the heart' something we have all heard with our ears and seen with
our eyes, yet never felt with so strange a thrill?).

  It ends in such thought as that of the famous invocation:

Wisdom and Spritit of the Universe!
Thou Soul that art the eternity of thought,
That givest to forms and images a breath
And everlasting motion, not in vain
By day or starlight thus from my first dawn
Of childhood dist thou intertwine for me
The passions that build up our human soul;
Not with the mean and vulgar works of man,
But with high objects, with enduring things, –
With life and nature –[2]

The core of the experience was an intense consciousness of Nature
passing through his senses to his mind; and the growth of that
consciousness, its action and reaction upon his inner life, is the
central theme of The Prelude. The experience was peculiar simply in
its intensity. So pure and strong was the life his senses led that it
passed, on a tide of feeling, into the life of his spirit. Here lies the
mystery which he calls, in a significant phrase, 'the incumbent
mystery of sense and soul'. What matters to us is not so much to
understand the experience as to realize it, not so much to solve the
mystery as to see where it lies. This is what the early Prelude helps us

1 [1850], I, 330–39.   2 [1805], I, 428–37.

to do. In it Wordsworth told the inner workings of his mind as nakedly and truthfully as he could; and the changes most to be deplored in his later text are those which overlay or obscure that naïve immediate expression. They generally mar the poetry; they always disguise the truth.

The poet, Wordsworth has said elsewhere, is one

Contented if he may enjoy
The things which others understand.

That was written in 1800. The early *Prelude* insists again and again on the primacy and self-sufficiency of feeling. Of his Cambridge days we read:

I lov'd and I enjoy'd, that was my chief
And ruling business, happy in the strength
And loveliness of imagery and thought.

In the final text these lines go out and a single line stands in their stead:

Content to observe, to admire, and to enjoy.

Again, of his unsophisticated childhood he first wrote:

I felt, and nothing else; I did not judge,

but rewrote:

I felt, observed, and pondered, did not judge.

That bold trust in feeling meant a belief also in the value of sensation out of which such feeling springs. Seeking to tell how in London, living amongst thousands of nameless human beings, he was at times overpowered by the consciousness of 'the unity of man,' he put it simply thus:

When strongly breath'd upon
By this sensation, whencesoe'er it comes
Of union or communion doth the soul
Rejoice as in her highest joy: for there,
There chiefly, hath she feeling whence she is,
And, passing through all Nature rests with God.

The conception came to him as a powerful sensation out of which grew a profound feeling. The physical image 'strongly breathed upon', and the naked language,

There chiefly, hath she feeling whence she is,
And passing through all Nature rests with God,

seem to spring straight out of the experience itself. In revising the lines he replaced the living fact by an intellectual statement about it:

The soul when smitten thus
By a sublime *idea*, whencesoe'er
Vouchsafed for union or communion, feeds
On the pure bliss, and takes her rest with God.

The simple truth about his inner life which he set out to tell in *The Prelude* was often strange and startling. Two sides of it strike the common-sense mind as particularly strange. Physical images have a power in the poet's inner life which the ordinary man only knows in delirium. And Wordsworth is conscious of two lives, or two levels of experience – the surface life to which he belongs with the rest of the world, and another life beneath this, in which, with a deep drop into himself, he seems to join the inner life of the whole universe. His earlier text deals boldly with these strange things. Poets, like lunatics and lovers – and, we might add, like children – differ from the rest of us in their power not only to see and hear images but to feel and think them. Thus breath, air or breeze is not for Wordsworth merely a symbol for spiritual life – it actually becomes it. His use of the image seems at first natural and innocent enough, as when he writes (in a cancelled passage) of the babe drinking in through its senses the tender passion of its mother:

Such feelings pass into his torpid life
Like an awakening breeze,

or of the 'gladsome air' (significantly altered later to 'absolute wealth') 'of my own private being'.

But under the image lay for Wordsworth a living fact. *The Prelude* opens with the blowing of a breeze 'from the green fields and from the sky' to greet him as he issues from the city. It does more than refresh him physically, for while it blows upon his body he feels within

A corresponding mild, creative breeze,
A vital breeze which travelled gently on
O'er things which it had made, and is become
A tempest, a redundant energy
Vexing its own creation.

That is, the air blowing from without passed within him and became
a spiritual and creative energy. Other passages in the early *Prelude*
tell in plain terms the same tale. Turning from his story of the
Revolution, he invokes once more the powers of Nature:

Ye motions of delight, that through the fields
Stir gently, breezes and soft airs that breathe
The breath of Paradise, and find your way
To the recesses of the soul!

To place beside these lines the version of 1850 is to measure how much
was lost in psychological truth when Wordsworth revised his poem:

Ye motions of delight, that haunt the sides
Of the green hills; ye breezes and soft airs,
Whose subtle intercourse with breathing flowers,
Feelingly watched, might teach man's haughty race
How without injury to take, to give
Without offence.

The bold fact of the first statement is omitted, the influence of the
breeze tritely moralized.

'Motions of delight' is an arresting phrase, and Wordsworth's use
of the word 'motion' is worth watching. Physical movement was
to him, as it is perhaps to every imaginative mind, stimulating in a
high degree. In Nature he was alive to the perpetual energy of
motion. The Solitary of *The Excursion* longs to surrender his body to
the elements,

and reckless of the storm
Be as a presence and a motion, – one
Among the many: here.

Wordsworth seems to find in motion the very essence of life. God
Himself, the divine principle in things, *is* motion:

> a motion and a spirit that impels
> All thinking things, all objects of all thought,
> And rolls through all things.

When he says:

> I felt a kind of sympathy with power,
> Motions raised up within me,

the word takes on a new meaning. If a breeze or a 'motion of delight' passes into the inner being, then a motion is a feeling as well as a physical movement. And so, indeed, he calls his first impulses of love towards man 'those motions of delight'; and again his early sensations of sympathy with Nature 'the first and earliest motions of my life'. These phrases occur in cancelled passages which now first see the light; but readers of Wordsworth are already familiar with 'those hallowed and pure motions of the sense' in the first book of *The Prelude*. The word in the sense of impulse or emotion was used by Shakespeare and by Milton, but was moribund in Dr Johnson's day.[1] Wordsworth's revival of it was necessary to his thought. It illustrates tellingly that fusion of physical with mental life, that direct, startling passage of image into thought or feeling, which he so freely expressed in his first draft of *The Prelude*. If the life of the spirit was motion and breeze, the suspension of that life was a deadly stillness. A cancelled passage, recalling his preoccupations with superficial interests at Cambridge, ends strangely thus:

> Hush'd, meanwhile,
> Was the under soul, lock'd up in such a calm,
> That not a leaf of the great nature stirr'd.

The soul lives a life of its own, shut away from our ordinary conscious life. Wordsworth even invents a new word for it, the under soul, a word of which the New English Dictionary gives no example before 1868. A still more surprising passage, which never found its way into a final draft of *The Prelude*, describes that state of mind, deeper than conscious thought, in which the individual is lost in the life of the whole universe:

[1] Cf. also his idea of 'truth' as

> a motion or a shape

Instinct with vital functions (*The Prelude*, VIII, 298).

                    I seemed to learn
That what we see of forms and images
Which float along our minds, and what we feel
Of action, and recognizable thought,
Prospectiveness, or intellect, or will,
Not only is not worthy to be deemed
Our being, to be prized as what we are,
But is the very littleness of life.
Such consciousness I deem but accidents,
Relapses from the one interior life
That lives in all things, sacred from the touch
Of that false secondary power by which
In weakness we create distinctions, then
Believe that all our puny boundaries are things
Which we perceive and not which we have made, –
In which all beings live with God, themselves
Are God, existing in one mighty whole,
As indistinguishable as the cloudless East
At noon is from the cloudless West, when all
The hemisphere is one cerulean blue.[1]

There is no escape from the meaning of this – God is in the soul
of man as He is in Nature. The only times when we truly live are
those in which, with no effort of will or intelligence, no consciousness
of forms or images, the soul merges into the life of the universe and
we *are God*. The great mind, Wordsworth says, is one

That is exalted by an underpresence,
The sense of God, or whatsoe'er is dim
Or vast in its own being.

Again, there is much significance in the word 'underpresence', altered
in another manuscript to 'underconsciousness', neither word recorded
in the New English Dictionary.
    The experiences here described have a character which he later
shrank from allowing them. They were involuntary; they had
nothing to do with his conscious will or intelligence. Again and
again he tampered with his early record, cutting out words that tell

1 Fragment found in an MS notebook.

of involuntary action in the mind – things happening of themselves –
and substituting other words either nugatory or expressly making
the mind itself the agent. Thus his gift as a poet, first described as an
'influx' vouchsafed to him, becomes an 'insight'. 'Motions raised
up within me' become 'motions not treacherous or vain'. Of the
vision on Snowdon in Book XIV he first wrote:

A meditation rose in me that night
Upon the lonely mountain when the scene
Had pass'd away, and it appear'd to me
The perfect image of a mighty mind,

but altered it significantly:

When into air had partially dissolved
That vision, given to spirits of the night
And three chance human wanderers *in calm thought
Reflected*, it appeared to me the type
Of a majestic intellect.

   Perhaps the most interesting piece of psychology in the early
Prelude – no trace of it remains in 1850 – is found in the lines leading
up to his midnight encounter with the old soldier in Book IV. He is
returning, tired from an evening's revelry, along a solitary mountain
road.

            On I went
Tranquil, receiving in my own despite
Amusement, as I slowly pass'd along,
From such near objects as from time to time,
Perforce, intruded on the listless sense
Quiescent, and dispos'd to sympathy,
With an exhausted mind, worn out by toil,
And all unworthy of the deeper joy
Which waits on distant prospect, cliff, or sea,
The dark blue vault, and universe of stars.
Thus did I steal along that silent road,
My body from the stillness drinking in
A restoration like the calm of sleep.
But sweeter far. Above, before, behind,

Around me, all was peace and solitude,
   I look'd not round, nor did the solitude
Speak to my eye; but it was heard and felt.
O happy state! what beauteous pictures now
Rose in harmonious imagery – they rose
As from some distant region of my soul
And came along like dreams; yet such as left
Obscurely mingled with their passing forms
A consciousness of animal delight,
A self-possession felt in every pause
And every gentle movement of my frame.[1]

Why did he strike the passage out? The mental exhaustion, the gradual restoration of the mind through the body, the involuntary images that rose as from some inner recess of his being, the consciousness of animal delight, make up a state which, reviewed in the cold light of reason, must have seemed to him confused, irrelevant to the purpose in hand. He was wrong. The passage is strictly relevant to his purpose. The sudden vision of the old soldier, still, uncouth, majestic, rising up as from another world, gets much of its sublime effect from its contrast with the mood that preludes it. This mood itself, described with an intimacy unparalleled elsewhere in Wordsworth's writings, belongs to that undefined borderland between the physical and mental life which rational minds distrust. What makes the passage important to us is that it lets us see into his mind in a state not rapt and mystical, but shallow and calm – a mood that reveals, as distinctly as clear water shows pebbles in a brook, the simple elements of sensation that underlie thought and feeling. Who but Wordsworth would have dared to say that dreamlike visions rising from some distant region of the soul are bound up with, if they do not actually spring from, 'a consciousness of animal delight'? Who, at any rate, could have dared to say so in the year 1798? From such passages 'the incumbent mystery of sense and soul' receives illumination.

From the experiences which they record sprang his philosophy or faith. And of this again the first *Prelude* gives a first-hand statement. Wordsworth's creed may be said in three words: God, Man, Nature.

1 375-99.

These three were divine: it might almost be said that they were one divinity. God was necessarily greatest, Man came next, and Nature, who had taught him to know the divinity in man, was last yet first, the source of his inspiration and first step in all his vital knowledge. When he first confessed his faith in *The Prelude* he had only to use these words, simply and passionately, and all his meaning was conveyed. He had only to speak, in the lines already quoted, of the soul that 'passing through all Nature rests with God,' and he had uttered the first article of his creed. The words were charged with power. What greater things can be said than God, Man, Nature? But the middle-aged Wordsworth who revised *The Prelude* had lost this vital sense. He was betrayed by the ineradicable weakness of civilized man; he had to explain, to rationalize, to moralize. Moreover, since he was not only a civilized man, but a devoutly religious Victorian Englishman, he had to translate his thought into the terms of an orthodox Christian creed. Thus the phrase 'to think with admiration and respect of man' becomes

> to think
> With a due reverence of earth's rightful lord
> Here placed to be the inheritor of heaven.

'God and Nature's single sovereignty' is amplified to

> presences of God's mysterious power
> Made manifest in Nature's sovereignty.

'Great God' gives place to 'Power supreme'! and in another context, ludicrously and lamentably, to 'How strange!' 'Living God,' simplest sublime address to the Deity, becomes 'righteous Heaven'! At the time when he wrote *The Prelude* Wordsworth's faith, in one aspect a simple form of pantheism, in another a Hegelian belief in the power of the human mind, bore little, if any, trace of dogmatic Christianity. If he gave it afterwards a carefully Christian colouring, was this only, to use his own phrase of a famous expunction in *Peter Bell*, 'not to offend the pious'? Or did it portend some vital change of mind?

To answer that question we must examine some of the patched places in *The Prelude* text.

In the early version of Book V, lines 11–14 ran:

> Hitherto
> In progress through this Verse, my mind hath look'd
> Upon the speaking face of earth and heaven
> As her prime Teacher, intercourse with man
> Established by the soveriegn Intellect
> Who through that bodily Image hath diffus'd
> A soul divine which we participate,
> A deathless spirit.

In revising this, he cut out the line which holds the essence of his meaning, 'A soul divine which we participate', and substituted an apologetic phrase to fill the gap, so that the triumphant passage now ends lamely thus:

> Who through that bodily image hath diffused,
> As might appear to the eye of fleeting time,
> A deathless spirit.

Again his apostrophe in Book X:

> Great God!
> Who send'st thyself into this breathing world
> Through Nature and through every kind of life,
> And mak'st man what he is, Creature divine,

is reworded:

> O Power Supreme!
> Without Whose care this world would cease to breathe,
> Who from the fountain of Thy grace doth fill
> The veins that branch through every frame of life
> Making man what he is, creature divine.

The early versions here show a vital difference in thought, not only in expression. The great God who sends Himself into the world through Nature, who diffuses through her 'a soul divine which we participate', is the God of the pantheist. What Wordsworth has ejected in the process of revision is the naked fact of the soul of man meeting God in Nature.

One more passage will throw light. He altered the lines

The feeling of life endless, the great thought
By which we live, infinity and God,

to

Faith in life endless, the sustaining thought
Of human being, eternity and God.

The verbal change is slight, but its import great. 'The feeling of life
endless', his own personal intuition, comes to be called 'Faith in life
endless', a faith which he shares with the Christian Church; the great
thought by which we live, infinity and God, becomes the Christian
thought of human immortality. Strange that the words 'infinity' and
'eternity' should mean the same thing with such a difference. The
truth is that he both changed and did not change. That central
experience, the merging of his soul with the divine soul in Nature,
remained the core of his religion, 'the masterlight of all his seeing';
but it came to him more and more rarely: he distrusted its sufficiency,
and he backed it up with the support of a traditional creed. Moreover,
he had no intention of offending the pious, or of being himself
misjudged. At no time of his life, except perhaps at the brief period
of disillusion after his return from France in 1793, was Wordsworth
a disbeliever in Christianity. 'There is no such thing as "natural
piety"', said Blake, commenting on Wordsworth's phrase, 'because
the natural man is at enmity with God'. But Wordsworth did not
think so. For him natural piety was not inconsistent with Christian
piety. The two creeds stood by him side by side: when one failed the
other helped. But they never quite merged. In spite of all the tinker-
ings to which his text was submitted, many bold and challenging
passages in *The Prelude* remain intact to vindicate the persistent
strength of his early thought. The *Prospectus* to *The Excursion* remains;
'*The Lines composed above Tintern Abbey*' remain. The passage which
is the core of that poem,

                    a sense sublime
Of something far more deeply interfused,
Whose dwelling is the light of setting suns,
And the round ocean and the living air,
And the blue sky, and in the mind of man:
A motion and a spirit that impels

All thinking things, all objects of all thought,
And rolls through all things,

is quoted by Coleridge as an expression 'in language but not in sense
or purpose' of a doctrine which he condemns with pain, the conception of God as the *anima mundi*. It was a poor compliment to Wordsworth to say that his language expressed what was not his sense and
purpose. Whatever his other faults, Wordsworth always meant what
he said.

Here, then, are two layers of thought, one superimposed upon but
not displacing the other, a passionate intuition of God in the universe
and a belief in the God of the Anglican Church: here, also, are two
modes of expression, the one naïve and immediate, fitting the utterance of strong personal feeling, the other dignified and general,
coloured by the language of a familiar creed.

In another direction his thought at once changed and did not
change. Everyone knows what Wordsworth thought of the human
mind. Hegel could go no further in exalting it than Wordsworth
went in his *Prospectus* to *The Excursion*:

For I must tread on shadowy ground, must sink
Deep – and, aloft ascending, breathe in worlds
To which the heaven of heavens is but a veil.
All strength – all terror, single or in bands,
That ever was put forth in personal form –
Jehovah – with his thunder, and the choir
Of shouting Angels, and the empyreal thrones –
I pass them unalarmed. Not chaos, not
The darkest pit of lowest Erebus,
Nor aught of blinder vacancy, scooped out
By help of dreams – can breed such fear and awe
As fall upon us often when we look
Into our Minds, into the Mind of Man –
My haunt, and the main region of my song.

Blake, speaking of this passage (to him so upsetting that it gave him
a stomach complaint of which he nearly died), asked, 'Does Mr
Wordsworth think his mind can surpass Jehovah?' This belief in the
greatness of the human mind is at the very centre of Wordsworth's

thought. As a young man he exulted almost to arrogance in the strength and power of his own mental life. In the early *Prelude* he uses such phrases as 'majestic thoughts', 'sovereignty within', 'religious dignity of mind', 'majesty of mind', 'majestic intellect'. In his revision these phrases are thrown out, or their fangs drawn. His 'majestic thoughts' become 'exalted thoughts'; 'sovereignty within' and 'religious dignity of mind' go out; 'majesty of mind' is displaced by 'a creed of reconcilement'; 'majestic intellect' becomes 'unfolding intellect'. A particular passage more closely scanned will show how his mind was working. It follows upon the account of his failure to fit into the student's life at Cambridge.

> But wherefore be cast down?
> Why should I grieve? I was a chosen Son.
> For hither I had come with holy powers
> And faculties, whether to work or feel:
> To apprehend all passions and all moods
> Which time, and place, and season do impress
> Upon the visible universe, and work
> Like changes there by force of my own mind.
> I was a Freeman: in the purest sense
> Was free, and to majestic ends was strong.
> I do not speak of learning, moral truth
> Or understanding; 'twas enough for me
> To know that I was otherwise endow'd.

The meaning of these lines is unequivocal. The holy powers in which he exulted were the powers of his own mind freely communicating with Nature and drawing thence mysterious strength. They had nothing to do with intellectual training or moral worth, still less with religion in the orthodox sense, which he does not so much as refer to.

The passage appears in our known text shorn of all its daring, and decorously touched with Christian thought:

> But wherefore be cast down?
> For (not to speak of Russian and her pure
> Reflective acts to fix the moral law
> Deep in the conscience, nor of Christian Hope

Bowing her head before her sister Faith
As one far mightier), hither I had come,
Bear witness, Truth, endowed with holy powers
And faculties, whether to work or feel.

Hope bows before Faith: both are expressly Christian. Reason is
tied to a moral function. Majesty, dignity, sovereignty, freedom,
give place to a studious humility of mind. And here once more we
touch a radical change in Wordsworth's thought. The pressure of the
years and crushing personal sorrows had taught him the inherent
weakness of human nature, a weakness from which neither mind nor
spirit was exempt. And so the Christian doctrine of humility went
home to his heart. When we find him after a magnificent eulogy
of man, 'as of all visible natures crown', adding the words 'though
born of dust and kindred to the worm', we are disgusted by what
seems an irrelevant concession. But the words, out of key as they are
with his earlier mood, were strictly relevant to his later position.
They stand for something not only sincerely thought, but passionately
felt. This will be acknowledged when we reflect upon some other
lines in his final text, themselves magnificent and, as we thought,
inevitable:

Dust as we are, the immortal spirit grows
Like harmony in music, –

which originally ran:

The mind of man is fram'd even like the breath
And harmony of music. –

with no reference to our dusty origin. The altered version vindicates
itself. 'Dust as we are, the immortal spirit grows . . .' Thought and
feeling have been transmuted into pure poetry. The question 'Did
Wordsworth mean what he says?' simply cannot be asked in the face
of it.

  In thought, then, the later *Prelude* records an inevitable change of
mind. The increasing rarity of certain passionate experiences of his
own lent force to his friends' warnings about the taint of pantheism;
and he omits, or rewrites in a Christian sense, lines that record those
passionate and possibly pantheistic experiences. Again, his exultant
pride in the greatness of the human mind gives place at times to a

truly Christian humility. At times only is that pride displaced. For here again, in certain passages, his earlier thought survives untouched. No terms could be stronger than these:

> Of genius, power
> Creation and divinity itself,
> I have been speaking, for my theme has been
> What passed within me.

Wordsworth could not help himself. When his religious thought flowed into the channel of Anglican doctrine he had to retouch his autobiography, and incidentally tamper with its poetry, in the spirit of that doctrine. But even in the interests of his creed he was wrong. If anyone has been converted to Christianity by *The Prelude* – and everyone who has really read it must have undergone conversion of some kind – it was not the Christianized passages that converted him, not the allusions to 'fountain of Thy grace', 'man inheritor of Heaven', 'Righteous Heaven', 'Power Supreme', but rather the poetry of a spiritual experience so intense, so pure and so profound that it holds the essence of all religion. The text of the early *Prelude* gives us that elemental experience freed from the gloss of later interpretation. And it shows us, further, how its roots lay, where Wordsworth did not shrink from finding them, in the sensuous or animal life which is our common heritage. The poets of our own era have attempted to explore this region of the senses, with something, perhaps, of Wordsworth's daring. But he knew things which they do not know; and he kept himself severely aloof from knowledge that he did not need. He was innocent, where they are sophisticated. His extraordinary purity of mind and heart kept strong and pure to and almost supernatural degree those senses of his to which, as he is never tired of telling us, he owed everything that mattered.

A. N. Whitehead

from *Science and the Modern World* 1926

We quickly find that the western peoples exhibit on a colossal scale a peculiarity which is popularly supposed to be more especially characteristic of the Chinese. Surprise is often expressed that a

Chinaman can be of two religions, a Confucian for some occasions and a Buddhist for other occasions. Whether this is true of China I do not know; nor do I know whether, if true, these two attitudes are really inconsistent. But there can be no doubt that an analogous fact is true of the west, and that the two attitudes involved are inconsistent. A scientific realism, based on mechanism, is conjoined with an unwavering belief in the world of men and of the higher animals as being composed of self-determining organisms. This radical inconsistency at the basis of modern thought accounts for much that is half-hearted and wavering in our civilization. It would be going too far to say that it distracts thought. It enfeebles it, by reason of the inconsistency lurking in the background. After all, the men of the Middle Ages were in pursuit of an excellency of which we have nearly forgotten the existence. They set before themselves the ideal of the attainment of a harmony of the understanding. We are content with superficial orderings from diverse arbitrary starting points. For instance, the enterprises produced by the individualistic energy of the European peoples presupposes physical actions directed to final causes. But the science which is employed in their development is based on a philosophy which asserts that physical causation is supreme, and which disjoins the physical cause from the final end. It is not popular to dwell on the absolute contradiction here involved. It is the fact, however you gloze it over with phrases. Of course, we find in the eighteenth century Paley's famous argument, that mechanism presupposes a God who is the author of nature. But even before Paley put the argument into its final form, Hume had written the retort, that the God whom you will find will be the sort of God who makes that mechanism. In other words, that mechanism can, at most, presuppose a mechanic, and not merely *a* mechanic but *its* mechanic. The only way of mitigating mechanism is by the discovery that it is not mechanism.

When we leave apologetic theology, and come to ordinary literature, we find, as we might expect, that the scientific outlook is in general simply ignored. So far as the mass of literature is concerned, science might never have been heard of. Until recently nearly all writers have been soaked in classical and renaissance literature. For the most part, neither philosophy nor science interested them, and their minds were trained to ignore it.

There are exceptions to this sweeping statement; and, even if we confine ourselves to English literature, they concern some of the greatest names; also the indirect influence of science has been considerable.

A side light on this distracting inconsistency in modern thought is obtained by examining some of those great serious poems in English literature, whose general scale gives them a didactic character. The relevant poems are Milton's *Paradise Lost*, Pope's *Essay on Man*, Wordsworth's *The Excursion*, Tennyson's *In Memoriam*. Milton, though he is writing after the Restoration, voices the theological aspect of the earlier portion of his century, untouched by the influence of the scientific materialism. Pope's poem represents the effect on popular thought of the intervening sixty years which includes the first period of assured triumph for the scientific movement. Wordsworth in his whole being expresses a conscious reaction against the mentality of the eighteenth-century. This mentality means nothing else than the acceptance of the scientific ideas at their full face value. Wordsworth was not bothered by any intellectual antagonism. What moved him was a moral repulsion. He felt that something had been left out, and that what had been left out comprised everything that was most important. Tennyson is the mouthpiece of the attempts of the waning romantic movement in the second quarter of the nineteenth century to come to terms with science. By this time the two elements in modern thought had disclosed their fundamental divergence by their jarring interpretations of the course of nature and the life of man. Tennyson stands in this poem as the perfect example of the distraction which I have already mentioned. There are opposing visions of the world, and both of them command his assent by appeals to ultimate intuitions from which there seems no escape. Tennyson goes to the heart of the difficulty. It is the problem of mechanism which appalls him,

'The stars,' she whispers, 'blindly run.'

This line states starkly the whole philosophic problem implicit in the poem. Each molecule blindly runs. The human body is a collection of molecules. Therefore, the human body blindly runs, and therefore there can be no individual responsibility for the actions of the body. If you once accept that the molecule is definitely determined to be what it is, independently of any determination by reason of the total organism of the body, and if you further admit that the blind run is settled by the general mechanical laws, there can be no escape from this conclusion. But mental experiences are derivative from the actions of the body, including of course its internal behaviour. Accordingly, the sole function of the mind is to have at least some of its experiences settle for it, and to add such others as may be open to it independently of the body's motions, internal and external.

There are then two possible theories as to the mind. You can either deny that it can supply for itself any experience other than those provided for it by the body, or you can admit them.

If you refuse to admit the additional experiences, then all individual moral responsibility is swept away. If you do admit them, then a human being may be responsible for the state of his mind though he has no responsibility for the actions of his body. The enfeeblement of thought in the modern world is illustrated by the way in which this plain issue is avoided in Tennyson's poem. There is something kept in the background, a skeleton in the cupboard. He touches on almost every religious and scientific problem, but carefully avoids more than a passing allusion to this one.

This very problem was in full debate at the date of the poem. John Stuart Mill was maintaining his doctrine of determinism. In this doctrine volitions are determined by motives, and motives are expressible in terms of antecedent conditions including states of mind as well as states of the body.

It is obvious that this doctrine affords no escape from the dilemma presented by a thoroughgoing mechanism. For if the volition affects the state of the body, then the molecules in the body do not blindly run. If the volition does not affect the state of the body, the mind is still left in its uncomfortable position.

Mill's doctrine is generally accepted, especially among scientists, as though in some way it allowed you to accept the extreme doctrine of materialistic mechanism, and mitigated its unbelievable consequences. It does nothing of the sort. Either the bodily molecules blindly run, or they do not. If they do blindly run, the mental states are irrelevant in discussing the bodily actions. . . .

So far as concerns English literature we find, as might be anticipated, the most interesting criticism of the thoughts of science among the leaders of the romantic reaction which accompanied and succeeded the epoch of the French Revolution. In English literature, the deepest thinkers of this school were Coleridge, Wordsworth and Shelley. Keats is an example of literature untouched by science. We may neglect Coleridge's attempt at an explicit philosophical formulation. It was influential in his own generation; but in these lectures it is my object only to mention those elements of the thought of the past which stand for all time. Even with this limitation, only a selection is possible. For our purposes Coleridge is only important by his influence on Wordsworth. Thus Wordsworth and Shelley remain.

Wordsworth was passionately absorbed in nature. It has been said of Spinoza, that he was drunk with God. It is equally true that Wordsworth was drunk with nature. But he was a thoughtful, well-read man, with philosophical interests, and sane even to the point of prosiness. In addition, he was a genius. He weakens his evidence by his dislike of science. We all remember his scorn of the poor man whom he somewhat hastily accuses of peeping and botanizing on his mother's grave. Passage after passage could be quoted from him, expressing this repulsion. In this respect, his characteristic thought can be summed up in his phrase, 'We murder to dissect.'

In this latter passage, he discloses the intellectual basis of his criticism of science. He alleges against science its absorption in abstractions. His consistent theme is that the important facts of nature elude the scientific method. It is important therefore to ask, what Wordsworth found in nature that failed to receive expression in science. I ask this question in the interest of science itself; for one main position in these lectures is a protest against the idea that the abstractions of science are irreformable and unalterable. Now it is emphatically not the case that Wordsworth hands over inorganic matter to the mercy of science, and concentrates on the faith that in the living organism there is some element that science cannot analyse. Of course he recognizes, what no one doubts, that in some sense living things are different from lifeless things. But that is not his main point. It is the brooding presence of the hills which haunts him. His theme is nature *in solido*, that is to say, he dwells on that mysterious presence of surrounding things, which imposes itself on any separate element that we set up as an individual for its own sake. He always grasps the whole of nature as involved in the totality of the particular instance. That is why he laughs with the daffodils, and finds in the primrose 'thoughts too deep for tears'.

Wordsworth's greatest poem is, by far, the first book of *The Prelude*. It is pervaded by this sense of the haunting presences of nature. A series of magnificent passages, too long for quotation, express this idea. Of course, Wordsworth is a poet writing a poem, and is not concerned with dry philosophical statements. But it would hardly be possible to express more clearly a feeling for nature, as exhibiting entwined prehensive unities, each suffused with modal presences of others:

Ye Presences of Nature in the sky
And on the earth! Ye Visions of the hills!
And Souls of lonely places! can I think
A vulgar hope was yours when ye employed
Such ministry, when ye through many a year
Haunting me thus among my boyish sports,
On caves and trees, upon the woods and hills,
Impressed upon all forms the characters
Of danger or desire; and thus did make
The surface of the universal earth
With triumph and delight, with hope and fear,
Work like a sea? . . .[1]

In thus citing Wordsworth, the point which I wish to make is that we forget how strained and paradoxical is the view of nature which modern science imposes on our thoughts. Wordsworth, to the height of genius, expresses the concrete facts of our apprehension, facts which are distorted in the scientific analysis. Is it not possible that the standardized concepts of science are only valid within narrow limitations, perhaps too narrow for science itself?

Wordsworth was born among hills; hills mostly barren of trees, and thus showing the minimum of change with the seasons. He was haunted by the enormous permanences of nature. For him change is an incident which shoots across a background of endurance,

Breaking the silence of the seas
Among the farthest Hebrides.

Every scheme for the analysis of nature has to face these two facts, *change* and *endurance*. There is yet a third fact to be placed by it, *eternality*, I will call it. The mountain endures. But when after ages it has been worn away, it has gone. If a replica arises, it is yet a new mountain. A colour is eternal. It haunts time like a spirit. It comes and it goes. But where it comes, it is the same colour. It neither survives nor does it live. It appears when it is wanted. The mountain has to time and space a different relation from that which colour has. In the previous lecture, I was chiefly considering the relation to space-time of things which, in my sense of the term, are eternal. It was necessary to do so before we can pass to the consideration of the things which endure.

Also we must recollect the basis of our procedure. I hold that philosophy is the critic of abstractions. Its function is the double one, first of harmonizing them by assigning to them their right relative status as abstractions, and secondly of completing them by direct comparison with more concrete intuitions of the universe, and there-by promoting the formation of more complete schemes of thought. It is in respect to this comparison that the testimony of great poets is of such importance. Their survival is evidence that they express deep intuitions of mankind penetrating into what is universal in concrete fact. Philosophy is not one among the sciences with its own little scheme of abstractions which it works away at perfecting and improving. It is the survey of sciences, with the special objects of their harmony, and of their completion. It brings to this task, not only the evidence of the separate sciences, but also its own appeal to concrete experience. It confronts the sciences with concrete fact.

The literature of the nineteenth century, especially its English poetic literature, is a witness to the discord between the aesthetic intuitions of mankind and the mechanism of science. Shelley brings vividly before us the elusiveness of the eternal objects of sense as they haunt the change which infects underlying organisms. Wordsworth is the poet of nature as being the field of enduring permances carrying within themselves a message of tremendous significance. The eternal objects are also there for him,

The light that never was, on sea or land.

Both Shelley and Wordsworth emphatically bear witness that nature cannot be divorced from its aesthetic values; and that these values arise from the cumulation, in some sense, of the brooding presence of the whole onto its various parts. Thus we gain from the poets the doctrine that a philosophy of nature must concern itself at least with these five notions: change, value, eternal objects, endurance, organism, interfusion.

We see that the literary romantic movement at the beginning of the nineteenth century, just as much as Berkeley's philosophical idealistic movement a hundred years earlier, refused to be confined within the materialistic concepts of the orthodox scientific theory. We know also that when in these lectures we come to the twentieth century, we shall find a movement in science itself to reorganize its concepts, driven thereto by its own intrinsic development.

It is, however, impossible to proceed until we have settled whether this refashioning of ideas is to be carried out on an objectivist basis or on a subjectivist basis. By a subjectivist basis I mean the belief that the nature of our immediate experience is the outcome of the perceptive peculiarities of the subject enjoying the experience. In other words, I mean that for this theory what is perceived is not a partial vision of a complex of things generally independent of that act of cognition; but that it merely is the expression of the individual peculiarities of the cognitive act. Accordingly what is common to the multiplicity of cognitive acts is the ratiocination connected with them. Thus, though there is a common world of thought associated with our sense-perceptions, there is no common world to think about. What we do think about is a common conceptual world applying indifferently to our individual experiences which are strictly personal to ourselves. Such a conceptual world will ultimately find its complete expression in the equations of applied mathematics. This is the extreme subjectivist position. There is of course the half-way house of those who believe that our perceptual experience does tell us of a common objective world; but that the things perceived are merely the outcome for us of this world, and are not *in themselves* elements in the common world itself.

Also there is the objectivist position. This creed is that the actual elements perceived by our senses are *in themselves* the elements of a common world; and that this world is a complex of things, including indeed our acts of cognition, but transcending them. According to this point of view the things experienced are to be distinguished from our knowledge of them. So far as there is dependence, the *things* pave the way for the *cognition*, rather than *vice versa*. But the point is that the actual things experienced enter into a common world which transcends knowledge, though it includes knowledge. The intermediate subjectivists would hold that the things experienced only indirectly enter into the common world by reason of their dependence on the subject who is cognizing. The objectivist holds that the things experienced and the cognizant subject enter into the common world on equal terms. In these lectures I am giving the outline of what I consider to be the essentials of an objectivist philosophy adapted to the requirement of science and to the concrete experience of mankind. Apart from the detailed criticism of the difficulties raised by subjectivism in any form, my broad reasons for distrusting it are three in number. One reason arises from the direct interrogation of our perceptive experience. It appears from this interrogation that we are *within* a world of colours, sounds and other sense-objects, related in space and time to enduring objects such as stones, trees and human bodies. We seem to be ourselves elements of this world in the same sense as are the other things which we perceive. But the subjectivist, even the moderate intermediate subjectivist, makes this world, as thus described, depend on us, in a way which directly traverses our naïve experience. I hold that the ultimate appeal is to naïve experience and that is why I lay such stress on the evidence of poetry. My point is, that in our sense-experience we know away from and beyond our own personality; whereas the subjectivist holds that in such experience we merely know about our own personality. Even the intermediate subjectivist places our personality between the world we know of and the common world which he admits. The world we know of is for him the internal strain of our personality under the stress of the common world which lies behind.

My second reason for distrusting subjectivism is based on the particular content of experience. Our historical knowledge tells us of ages in the past when, so far as we can see, no living being existed on earth. Again it also tells us of countless star-systems, whose detailed history remains beyond our ken. Consider even the moon and the earth. What is going on within the interior of the earth, and on the far side of the moon! Our perceptions lead us to infer that there is something happening in the stars, something happening within the earth, and something happening on the far side of the moon. Also they tell us that in remote ages there were things happening. But all these things which it appears certainly happened, are either unknown in detail, or else are reconstructed by inferential evidence. In the face of this content of our personal experience, it is difficult to believe that the experienced world is an attribute of our own personality. My third reason is based upon the instinct for action. Just as sense-perception seems to give knowledge of what lies beyond individuality, so action seems to issue in an instinct for self-transcendence. The activity passes beyond self into the known transcendent world. It is here that final ends are of importance. For it is not activity urged from behind, which passes out into the veiled world of the intermediate subjectivist. It is activity directed to determinate ends in the known world; and yet it is activity transcending self and it is activity within the known world. It follows therefore that the world, as known, transcends the subject which is cognizant of it.

The subjectivist position has been popular among those who have been engaged in giving a philosophical interpretation to the recent theories of relativity in physical science. The dependence of the world of sense on the individual percipient seems an easy mode of expressing the meanings involved. Of course, with the exception of those who are content with themselves as forming the entire universe, solitary amid nothing, everyone wants to struggle back to some sort of objectivist position. I do not understand how a common world of thought can be established in the absence of a common world of sense. I will not argue this point in detail; but in the absence of a transcendence of thought, or a transcendence of the world of sense, it is difficult to see how the subjectivist is to divest himself of his solitariness. Nor does the intermediate subjectivist appear to get any help from his unknown world in the background.

The distinction between realism and idealism does not coincide with that between objectivism and subjectivism. Both realists and idealists can start from an objective standpoint. They may both agree that the world disclosed in sense-perception is a common world, transcending the individual recipient. But the objective idealist, when he comes to analyse what the reality of this world involves, finds that cognitive mentality is in some way inextricably concerned in every detail. This position the realist denies. Accordingly, these two classes of objectivists do not part company till they have arrived at the ultimate problem of metaphysics. There is a great deal which they share in common. This is why, in my last lecture, I said that I adopted a position of provisional realism.

In the past, the objectivist position has been distorted by the supposed necessity of accepting the classical scientific materialism, with its doctrine of simple location. This has necessitated the doctrine of secondary and primary qualities. Thus the secondary qualities, such as the sense-objects, are dealt with on subjectivist principles. This is a half-hearted position which falls an easy prey to subjectivist criticism.

If we are to include the secondary qualities in the common world, a very drastic reorganization of our fundamental concept is necessary. It is an evident fact of experience that our apprehensions of the external world depend absolutely on the occurrences within the human body. By playing appropriate tricks on the body a man can be got to perceive, or not to perceive, almost anything. Some people express themselves as though bodies, brains and nerves were the only real things in an entirely imaginary world. In other words, they treat bodies on objectivist principles, and the rest of the world on subjectivist principles. This will not do; especially, when we remember that it is the experimenter's perception of another person's body which is in question as evidence.

But we have to admit that the body is the organism whose states regulate our cognizance of the world. The unity of the perceptual field therefore must be a unity of bodily experience. In being aware of the bodily experience, we must thereby be aware of aspects of the whole spatio-temporal world as mirrored within the bodily life. This is the solution of the problem which I gave in my last lecture. I will not repeat myself now, except to remind you that my theory involves the entire abandonment of the notion that simple location is the primary way in which things are involved in space-time. In a certain sense, everything is everywhere at all times. For every location involves an aspect of itself in every other location. Thus every spatio-temporal standpoint mirrors the world.

If you try to imagine this doctrine in terms of our conventional views of space and time, which presuppose simple location, it is a great paradox. But if you think of it in terms of our naïve experience, it is a mere transcript of the obvious facts. You are in a certain place perceiving things. Your perception takes place where you are, and is entirely dependent on how your body is functioning. But this functioning of the body in one place, exhibits for your cognizance an aspect of the distant environment, fading away into the general knowledge that there are things beyond. If this cognizance conveys knowledge of a transcendent world, it must be because the event which is the bodily life unifies in itself aspects of the universe.

This is a doctrine extremely consonant with the vivid expression of personal experience which we find in the nature-poetry of imaginative writers such as Wordsworth or Shelley. The brooding, immediate presences of things are an obsession to Wordsworth. What the theory does do is to edge cognitive mentality away from being the necessary substratum of the unity of experience. That unity is now placed in the unity of an event. Accompanying this unity, there may or there may not be cognition.

At this point we come back to the great question which was posed before us by our examination of the evidence afforded by the poetic insight of Wordsworth and Shelley. This single question has expanded into a group of questions. What are enduring things, as distinguished from the eternal objects, such as colour and shape? How are they possible? What is their status and meaning in the universe? It comes to this: What is the status of the enduring stability of the order of nature? There is the summary answer, which refers nature to some greater reality standing behind it. This reality occurs in the history of thought under many names, The Absolute, Brahma, The Order of Heaven, God. The delineation of final metaphysical truth is no part of this lecture. My point is that any summary conclusion jumping from our conviction of the existence of such an order of nature to the easy assumption that there is an ultimate reality which, in some unexplained way, is to be appealed to for the removal of perplexity, constitutes the great refusal of rationality to assert its rights. We have to search whether nature does not in its very being show itself as self-explanatory. By this I mean, that the sheer statement, of what things are, may contain elements explanatory of why things are. Such elements may be expected to refer to depths beyond anything which we can grasp with a clear apprehension. In a sense, all explanation must end in an ultimate arbitrariness. My demand is, that the ultimate arbitrariness of matter of fact from which our formulation starts should disclose the same general principles of reality, which we dimly discern as stretching away into regions beyond our explicit powers of discernment. Nature exhibits itself as exemplifying a philosophy of the evolution of organisms subject to determinate conditions. Examples of such conditions are the dimensions of space, the laws of nature, the determinate enduring entities, such as atoms and electrons, which exemplify these laws. But the very nature of these entities, the very nature of their spatiality and temporality, should exhibit the arbitariness of these conditions as the outcome of a wider evolution beyond nature itself, and within which nature is but a limited mode.

One all-pervasive fact, inherent in the very character of what is real is the transition of things, the passage one to another. This passage is not a mere linear procession of discrete entities. However we fix a determinate entity, there is always a narrower determination of something which is presupposed in our first choice. Also there is always a wider determination into which our first choice fades by transition beyond itself. The general aspect of nature is that of evolutionary expansiveness. These unities, which I call events, are the emergence into actuality of something. How are we to characterize the something which thus emerges? The name 'event' given to such a unity, draws attention to the inherent transitoriness, combined with the actual unity. But this abstract word cannot be sufficient to characterize what the fact of the reality of an event is in itself. A moment's thought shows us that no one idea can in itself be sufficient. For every idea which finds its significance in each event must represent something which contributes to what realization is in itself. Thus no one word can be adequate. But conversely, nothing must be left out. Remembering the poetic rendering of our concrete experience, we see at once that the element of value, of being valuable, of having value, of being an end in itself, of being something which is for its own sake, must not be omitted in any account of an event as the most concrete actual something. 'Value' is the word I use for the intrinsic reality of an event. Value is an element which permeates through and through the poetic view of nature. We have only to transfer to the very texture of realization in itself that value which we recognize so readily in terms of human life. This is the secret of Wordsworth's worship of nature. Realization therefore is in itself the attainment of value. But there is no such thing as mere value. Value is the outcome of limitation. The definite finite entity is the selected mode which is the shaping of attainment; apart from such shaping into individual matter of fact there is no attainment. The mere fusion of all that there is would be the nonentity of indefiniteness. The salvation of reality is its obstinate, irreducible, matter-of-fact entities, which are limited to be no other than themselves. Neither science, nor art, nor creative action can tear itself away from obstinate, irreducible, limited facts. The endurance of things has its significance in the self-retention of that which imposes itself as a definite attainment for its own sake. That which endures is limited, obstructive, intolerant, infecting its environment with its own aspects. But it is not self-sufficient. The aspects of all things enter into its very nature. It is only itself as drawing together into its own limitation the larger whole in which it finds itself. Conversely it is only itself by lending its aspects to this same environment in which it finds itself. The problem of evolution is the development of enduring harmonies of enduring shapes of value, which merge into higher attainments of things beyond themselves. Aesthetic attainment is interwoven in the texture of realization. The endurance of an entity represents the attainment of a limited aesthetic success, though if we look beyond it to its external effects, it may represent an aesthetic failure. Even within itself, it may represent the conflict between a lower success and a higher failure. The conflict is the presage of disruption.

The further discussion of the nature of enduring objects and of the conditions they require will be relevant to the consideration of the doctrine of evolution which dominated the latter half of the nineteenth century. The point which in this lecture I have endeavoured to make clear is that the nature-poetry of the romantic revival was a protest on behalf of the organic view of nature, and also a protest against the exclusion of value from the essence of matter of fact. In this aspect of it, the romantic movement may be conceived as a revival of Berkeley's protest which had been launched a hundred years earlier. The romantic reaction was a protest on behalf of value.

D. G. James

'Visionary Dreariness' from *Poetry and Scepticism*   1937

> It was, in truth,
> An ordinary sight; but I should need
> Colours and words that are unknown to man,
> To paint the visionary dreariness
> Which, while I looked all round for my lost guide,
> Invested moorland waste, and naked pool,
> The beacon crowning the lone eminence,
> The female and her garments vexed and tossed
> By the strong wind.

WORDSWORTH, *The Prelude*, Book XII

The passage in Book II of *The Prelude* in which Wordsworth writes of the activity of the imagination in the life of the child clearly derives its substance from Coleridge. The 'first poetic spirit of our human life' is Coleridge's 'primary imagination', the condition of perception. The mind of the child, we are told, is 'prompt and watchful, eager to combine in one appearance, all the elements and parts of the same object, else detached and loth to coalesce'.[1] The 'else detached and loth to coalesce' rings indeed of associationism, as well as of the doctrine of the imagination creative in knowledge which Kant asserted and Coleridge adopted. Wordsworth, indeed, was not a philosopher, either by inclination or natural ability; and we can allow for confusion in whatever of philosophical theories he undertook to present. In any case, what Wordsworth, despite confusion in his thought, was most clearly concerned to assert was the activity of the mind in knowledge, not a bare receptivity to associated elements. And in speaking of this task of primary creation in perception, Wordsworth again follows Coleridge, for when he says that the power of imagination

Doth like an agent of the one great Mind
Create . . .

1 This is, of course, almost a travesty of Coleridge's view, which did not suggest that the child is a more or less conscious creator.

we are hearing Coleridge's 'the primary imagination I hold to be . . . a repetition in the finite mind of the eternal act of creation in the infinite *I am*'.

Wordsworth, however, does not represent the imagination as working alone in this act of creation; other parts of the child's personality are involved; above all, his active response to his mother and those around him. The child is not an 'outcast' working alone. His creation of a world of objects is not his alone; the cooperation of society is necessary to complete the activity of his own original powers. The child 'claims manifest kindred with an earthly soul'; the 'discipline of love' is ever present; the flower 'to which he points his hand, too weak to gather it' is plucked for him; and he quickly learns the active and emotional responses to objects of those who live with him. And in saying this Wordsworth no doubt gives a fuller psychological account of the primary imagination than Coleridge. He is quite right in insisting on the importance of social cooperation, and in refusing to view the creativeness of the imagination in the making of its world as the activity of the isolated mind. It is in all strictness true that the child's affections for and dependence on others are of the most vital importance to the activity of the imagination. The entire life of the child is involved in its creativeness, and not merely an abstract faculty. The imagination, the primary organ of knowledge, is part and parcel of a personality reaching in a hundred ways to an environment of people, in what psychologists are accustomed to call 'intersubjective intercourse'. The knowledge of other minds and of objects as responded to by other minds, is made possible only through the affectionate ministration of his mother and others; without this life of action and emotional response the imagination could never obtain a foundation for its activity. This point is of the greatest importance for Wordsworth's scheme; it means that he viewed the imagination not as a power divorced from the full activities of life, but as dependent on them, the flower of personality in all its activities and responses, deriving its health from a total well-being of mind. He says in the second book of *The Prelude* that the imagination can only grow through the ministration of affection and love; and at the conclusion of the poem he says that intellectual love and imagination cannot act nor exist without each other, cannot stand 'dividually'.

In human life, Wordsworth tells us, the imagination grows from this humble beginning into the sublimest faculty of man, a faculty which he describes at length in two famous passages in *The Prelude*. Of imagination he says, at the end of the poem, that it is

> but another name for absolute strength
> And clearest insight, amplitude of mind,
> And reason in her most exalted mood.
> This faculty hath been the moving soul
> Of long labour: we have traced the stream
> From darkness . . .
>   . . . follow'd it to light
> And open day, accompanied its course
> Among the ways of Nature, afterwards
> Lost sight of it bewilder'd and engulph'd,
> Then given it greeting, as it rose once more
> With strength, reflecting on its solemn breast
> The works of man and face of human life,
> And lastly, from its progress have we drawn
> The feeling of life endless, the great thought
> By which we live, Infinity and God.[1]

And it is of the imagination in this last sense that he speaks in the other passage –

> Imagination! lifting up itself
> Before the eye and progress of my Song
> Like an unfather'd vapour; here that Power,
> In all the might of its endowments, came
> Athwart me; I was lost as in a cloud,
> Halted, without a struggle to break through.
> And now recovering, to my Soul I say
> I recognize thy glory; in such strength
> Of usurpation, in such visitings
> Of awful promise, when the light of sense
> Goes out in flashes that have shown to us
> The invisible world, doth Greatness make abode,

1 XIII, 168–84. This and all other quotations from *The Prelude* in this section are taken from the text of 1805.

There harbours whether we be young or old.
Our destiny, our nature and our home
Is with infinitude, and only there;
With hope it is, hope that can never die,
Effort, and expectation, and desire,
And something ever more about to be.[1]

Wordsworth, then, with Coleridge, viewed the imagination as an essential unifying agency in all perception; but it was also something more. For it is the imagination, 'so called through sad incompetence of human speech', which also gives order and unity to life through its sense of an infinitude which is beyond 'the light of sense'. The imagination, failing to apprehend nature and man as a self-contained whole, beholds the world as pointing beyond itself to an infinite unknown. In its 'struggle to idealize and unify' the imagination, starting from its beginnings in the perception of the child, advances to the sense of an infinitude and of 'unknown modes of being'. The highest reaches of the imagination are of a piece with the simplest act of perception, and issue from the demand for unity which is the life of the imagination. There is a passage in *The Prelude* in which Wordsworth develops this thought. It occurs after his description of his ascent of Snowdon, in which he describes the moon 'naked in the heavens' shining upon a huge sea of mist 'through which a hundred hills their dusky backs upheaved'; while from below

Mounted the roar of water, torrents, streams
Innumerable, roaring with one voice.[2]

In this scene Wordsworth beheld

The perfect image of a mighty Mind,
Of one that feeds upon infinity.

The resemblance between the scene and the 'mighty Mind' is then expounded. In the scene nature exhibited a 'domination upon the face of outward things'

So moulds them, and endues, abstracts, combines,
Or by abrupt and unhabitual influence
Doth make one object so impress itself

Upon all others, and pervade them so
That even the grossest minds must see and hear
And cannot chuse but feel.

The thought appears to be that in the scene before him the effect of
the moon was to create so strange and 'unhabitual' a spectacle that
the 'grossest mind' could not but be affected. The appearance of the
moon created a new and astonishing world. Such a creation by
nature of a strange and new world is the 'express resemblance',

> a genuine Counterpart
> And Brother of the glorious faculty
> Which higher minds bear with them as their own.

Here is Coleridge's 'secondary' imagination having expression in
verse. 'Higher minds'

> from their native selves can send abroad
> Like transformations.

They are 'ever on the watch', 'willing to work and to be wrought
upon';

> in a world of life they live,
> By sensible impressions not enthrall'd,
> But quicken'd, rouz'd and made thereby more apt
> To hold communion with the invisible world.
> Such minds are truly from the Deity.
> For they are Powers; and hence the highest bliss
> That can be known is theirs, the consciousness
> Of whom they are habitually infused
> Through every image and through every thought
> And all impressions. . . .

And hence, he adds, come 'religion, faith, sovereignty within, and
peace at will'. The creativity of the imagination in perception,
quickened in the life of the poet, leads on to, and is of a piece with,
the sense of a transcendent world. It was clearly Wordsworth's view
that the free development of the imagination is bound up with a
perception of the world as in itself fragmentary and unified only in
what is beyond itself. Such an imagination, operating in and through
'recognitions of transcendent power', is the condition of 'freedom'

and 'genuine liberty', of an abiding reconciliation of emotion and peace.

Such was, we may believe, the essence of Wordsworth's doctrine of the Imagination. But he did not continuously enjoy such an imaginative life; for at the time of the Revolution he had not integrated into his imaginative scheme recognition of the world's suffering, pain and evil. He responded to the Revolution with overwhelming enthusiasm; and the effect upon him of the attitude of the English Government, and then of the subsequent course of the Revolution, was catastrophic. It may appear surprising to us, when we consider the strongly religious character of his earlier imaginative life, that he should have been absorbed so completely in hopes of what he called

> Saturnian rule
> Returned, – a progeny of golden years
> Permitted to descend, and bless mankind.

Certainly his sense of life was not so clear-eyed as was that of Keats, who from the outset rejected any hopes of earthly happiness for mankind. Yet the fact remains that it seemed to Wordsworth that his view of life demanded, as a condition of its validity, 'Saturnian rule returned'. Shocked, therefore, by what happened, he felt that the failure of the Revolution was destructive of his imaginative life, and his confidence in what Keats was to call the 'truth' of the imagination. What happened, therefore, was a revulsion from the imaginative way of life and a search for a touchstone which could stand unshaken by circumstance. He therefore fell back upon the discursive intelligence, and endeavoured to create, by its exercise, a way of life and an attitude to the universe in which he might have a permanent confidence. Later, Wordsworth was to formulate what he came to think was the true relation of the discursive intelligence to the imagination. But this he did only after he had recovered his belief in the imagination. The faltering of his spirit before the facts of life which he experienced during the course of the 1790s found him unprepared by reflection on the relation of the imagination to the intellect; and he was all the more inclined to abandon the imagination because of the respect which, when at Cambridge, he had felt for mathematical inquiry. From such studies

                        I drew
A pleasure quiet and profound, a sense
Of permanent and universal sway,
And paramount belief.

And he goes on to say

            specially delightful unto me
Was that clear synthesis built up aloft
So gracefully.

He sets this 'clear synthesis' in opposition to the turgid condition in
which the mind is
                        beset
With images, and haunted by herself.

Hence, when the passionate strength of his imagination was weakened,
it was inevitable that his mind should revert to the clearness and
certainty of intellectual inquiry which formerly he had most intim-
ately known in the field of greatest abstraction, namely, mathematics.
He turned naturally at this juncture to the exercise of the intelligence,
but no longer to the intelligence in its activity of making

            an independent world
Created out of pure intelligence,

but to the intelligence which seeks to discover a 'clear synthesis' of
the world in its multiplicity, the concrete world of perception, feeling,
will, and also to arrive at clear principles of knowledge and behaviour.
In his first stage of doubt and despair he cheered himself by taking to
mind
                        those truths
That are the commonplaces of the schools . . .
Yet with a revelation's liveliness,
In all their comprehensive bearings known
And visible to philosophers of old.

But after the Terror he spoke

                        with a voice
Labouring, a brain confounded, and a sense,
Death-like, of treacherous desertion, felt
In the last place of refuge – my own soul.

And from this point on he could no longer cheer himself with the platitudes of ancient philosophy. If he was to recover, it would be, he then knew, by hard reflection compelled upon him by his own experience, by a philosophy sprung from the necessity of destroying, if might be, his sense of 'treacherous desertion' in his soul, and built up as a permanent bulwark against further collapse of his inner life.

> Evidence
> Safer, of universal application, such
> As could not be impeached, was sought elsewhere.

> What he needed were
> speculative schemes
> That promised to abstract the hopes of Man
> Out of his feelings, to be fixed thenceforth
> For ever in a purer element.

The result of this incursion into philosophy was disastrous – it gave him over, not to a 'clear synthesis', but to 'despair'.

> So I fared
> Dragging all precepts, judgments, maxims, creeds
> Like culprits to the bar; calling the mind,
> Suspiciously, to establish in plain day
> Her titles and her honours; now believing,
> Now disbelieving; endlessly perplexed
> With impulse, motive, right and wrong, the ground
> Of obligation, what the rule and whence
> The sanction; till, demanding formal *proof*,
> And seeking it in everything, I lost
> All feeling of conviction and, in fine,
> Sick, wearied out with contrarieties,
> Yielded up moral questions in despair.[1]

This rejection of philosophy was absolute, and there was no going back to it. No one ever had greater motive for philosophy than Wordsworth – it was a matter of life and death, an intellectual search behind which a passionate need was present. No doubt what training he had had in mathematics reinforced his sense of need in endeavour-

1 [1850, XI, 293–305, 1805 (X, 889–901) is a little different.]

ing to extract from philosophical reflection a degree of clarity, of 'clear synthesis' which philosophy is notoriously slow to supply, and set a standard of proof which he found philosophy incapable of sustaining. The demand for 'formal proof', arising both from his mathematical training and from the insistence of his personal need, was inevitably left unsatisfied. He might seek escape in abstract science

Where the disturbances of space and time –
Whether in matters various, properties
Inherent, or from human will and power
Derived – find no admission.

But this was merely escape, and he knew it. What certainties abstract science could supply were irrelevant to his need. Thus, with the total collapse of his belief in the 'holiness of the heart's imagination', and the exasperation and despair to which philosophy brought him, he was completely adrift. A crisis had arisen in which he was helpless. The imagination carried within it no criterion of its truth; philosophy could supply no criterion of its truth or afford proof of that for which he hungered. All effort, all conscious direction of his energies, was stopped. There was nothing more he could do. He could but abandon effort; and in that abandonment remain.

In the third book of *The Excursion* Wordsworth retells this story, at least in part, in the character of the Solitary. The Solitary in *The Excursion* is the Wordsworth of his crisis, and is sharply set over against the Wanderer who is the Wordsworth who was afterwards matured and confirmed in his belief in the Imagination. In the Solitary, the rejection of life has gone to extreme lengths, paralysing action. Imagination and intellectual inquiry are not for him –

Ah! What avails imagination high
Or question deep? –

and with this goes the extreme of despair –

Night is than day more acceptable; sleep
Doth, in my estimate of good, appear
A better state than waking; death than sleep:
Feelingly sweet is stillness after storm,
Thought under covert of the wormy ground!

The Solitary indeed, unlike Wordsworth, had known private grief; but it drove him to that state of agitated inquiry which was Wordsworth's after the Reign of Terror –

> Then my soul
> Turned inward, – to examine of what stuff
> Time's fetters are composed; and life was put
> To inquisition, long and profitless!
> By pain of heart – now checked – and now impelled –
> The intellectual power, through words and things,
> Went sounding on, a dim and perilous way!

From this condition he was restored by the hopes he fixed in the French Revolution; but the outcome was to plunge him more deeply than ever into the condition from which he had just escaped; a complete atrophy of his mental life set in.

> My business is,
> Roaming at large, to observe, and not to feel
> And, therefore, not to act – convinced that all
> Which bears the name of action, howsoe'er
> Beginning, ends in servitude – still painful,
> And mostly profitless.

The Borderers is the one considerable work which dates from this period in Wordsworth's life. It has, therefore, a great significance as an additional comment upon his inner life at this time. *The Borderers* is a tragedy, for these few years were indeed Wordsworth's 'tragic period'; and that he should have written what at no other period of his life he attempted to do – a tragedy – offers us the possibility of an illuminating comparison with those plays of Shakespeare which convey the condition of Shakespeare's mind when he, like Wordsworth, knew a sense of 'death-like, treacherous desertion'. For our present purpose it is of more immediate importance to notice how the story of *The Borderers* is connected with the story of Wordsworth's own life and of the story of the Solitary. Both Oswald and Marmaduke are men to whom a grave wrong has been done; the sense of 'death-like, treacherous desertion' has been theirs. Oswald and Marmaduke alike, through deception by others, have been made responsible for an innocent man's death. And the words of Marmaduke

> the firm foundation of my life
>
> Is going from under me;

and those of Oswald when, narrating his story to Marmaduke, he says

> for many days
>
> On a dead sea under a burning sky
>
> I brooded o'er my injuries, deserted
>
> By man and nature –

alike spring from the same condition which was also Wordsworth's condition. In all 'desertion' is the key word; an unfair, cruel blow had been struck at one utterly undeserving of it, who trusted and believed his environment. The Solitary, Oswald, and Marmaduke are all the Wordsworth of this time. Indeed, Oswald uses words which are identical with those of the Solitary after the death of his wife and children –

> three nights
>
> Did constant meditation dry my blood;
>
> Three sleepless nights I passed in *sounding on*,
>
> *Through words and things, a dim and perilous way.*

All three are men of nobility of imagination; all had known 'rainbow arches', 'highways of dreaming passion',

> What mighty objects do impress their forms
>
> To elevate our intellectual being.

Thence had they been brought back to

> The unpretending ground we mortals tread.

But while the Solitary, Marmaduke and Oswald are one in these respects, the response of each to this identical situation is different. In the Solitary there occurs a revulsion from feeling, and therefore from action, a permanent numbing of sensibility; in Oswald it leads to deliberate evil; in Marmaduke to resignation and the life of religion, 'in search of nothing this earth can give'.

There can be little doubt that it is Oswald who, though the villain of the piece, voices most of Wordsworth's thought and feeling of the time. In the play Wordsworth symbolizes his own state as one suffering an unjust blow struck at a trusting and confident nature.

Sensitive to the forms of nature, Oswald's disgust with humankind
struck at his sense of our high 'intellectual being'; what he now knew
of

The world's opinions and her usages

could not be reconciled in one personality with the life of the imagination and the contemplation of objects which 'impress their forms to
elevate our intellectual being'. The latter, 'a thing so great', must
'perish self-consumed'. Personality under these circumstances becomes
split in two, a condition which, in Oswald's case, resolved itself, so
far as it resolved itself at all, by a total rejection of moral sense. And
though in part his treatment of Marmaduke was animated by
resentment of a universe of experience which had betrayed him, a
resentment which he vented on the conspicuous virtue of Marmaduke,
it was also inspired by a certain inverted idealism, a pure assertion of
the will, which sought to issue in an enlargement of 'Man's intellectual
empire'. This pure, disinterested assertion of the will, concerned to
maintain itself in disregard of good, became in the heart of Oswald
a demand for pure freedom, free from the soft claims of shame,
ignorance and love.

We subsist
In slavery; all is slavery; we receive
Laws, but we ask not whence those laws have come;
We need an inward sting to goad us on.

That 'inward sting' had come to Oswald as it had come to Wordsworth. In the Solitary, Wordsworth later envisaged a person whom
the 'inward sting' had failed to goad into activity, leaving, after its
first pain, a permanent numbness, a lasting extension of the chilling
of life which he himself had for a while known. In Oswald, writing
from the midst of this period of his life, he envisaged the other
alternative, in which the sting became a 'goad'.

This condition of intellectual hate, of living in rebellion and a
pure assertiveness, which was to be in later years a theme for the
novels of Dostoyevsky, never, it is probable, took considerable
possession of Wordsworth's mind. It must, indeed, have occurred
with unusual vividness to his imagination – The Borderers shows that
it did. Yet over against Oswald is Marmaduke, embodying so different

an attitude from that of Oswald that if what we have is what Wordsworth actually wrote in the years 1795 and 1796,[1] we are compelled
to believe either that Wordsworth was never in the gravest danger
of the pure rebellion of Oswald, or that, at the time of writing, he
was recovering in some degree the previous condition of his mind.
It is true that Marmaduke, believing, at Oswald's prompting, in the
depravity of Herbert, reacted as Wordsworth at the time of the Terror
had done, with a despair which believed the 'world was poisoned at
the heart'; yet he was unable to say

> there was a plot
> A hideous plot, against the soul of man;
> It took effect – and yet I baffled it,
> In *some* degree.

Which he can say, a little priggishly indeed, because he killed Herbert,
not with his sword but by leaving him exposed to cold and hunger,
out of regard for a higher judgement than his own. And, instead of
a goad to enraged activity, his action becomes an inducement to the
way of religious humility and expiation –

> A man by pain and thought compelled to live
> Yet loathing life.

There are three issues of this experience which is represented differently in the guise of fiction in *The Borderers* and *The Excursion*, yet
in essence identical with that which Wordsworth himself suffered –
first a lasting atrophy of the imagination and intellectual life, secondly
a fierce effort to live a life in the greatest degree lawless, and thirdly
the way of religious humility. Wordsworth was to re-discover the
last. But, inevitably, he could not be the same; although, in all
essentials, he was to find again the attitude to life which he asserted
in the famous passage in Book VI, it had now become an attitude far
more inclusive, an imaginative grasp of life richer and more comprehensive than formerly it was. For where formerly it was a vision
of life irrelevant to and without knowledge of evil, crime and
suffering, it must now incorporate that knowledge into itself and be
reconciled with it. Wordsworth now knew the unmitigated reality

---

1 And we have Wordsworth's word for it that in all essentials it is.

of evil and pain. Somehow, before he could be a man again, these facts must become part of a single imaginative grasp of things. He had known the bitterness of mind of a Stavrogin, the extremity of revolt; to forget this and to ignore the facts and realities from which such a condition takes its origin would necessarily mean a loss of integrity and self-respect. If his imaginative life, as formerly he knew it, was to return, it must be inclusive of all his experience and to that degree must be changed. To be led back

> through opening day
> To those sweet counsels between head and heart
> Whence grew that genuine knowledge, fraught with peace –

was what was necessary to him, a 'genuine knowledge' which might occur out of, and as a reconciliation of, the conflict of head and heart. Formerly his strong imaginative life was a natural growth, unimpeded by perplexity and conflict. That condition, indeed, could not last; it was too simple, too easily come by. Terror in some form was bound to come. And having come, it destroyed, or at least overcast, the vitality of his imaginative vision; and his head, saturated with realizations which in his youth did not exist for him, was unable to give liberation. Out of this condition he could not release himself. The vitality and energies of the imagination do not operate at will; they are fountains, not machinery. And from his intellectual inquiry came no knowledge. Such a condition is, in a sense, final. There was no more that Wordsworth could do. Life was cut off from him,

> inwardly oppressed
> With sorrow, disappointment, vexing thoughts,
> Confusion of the judgment, zeal decayed,
> And, lastly, utter loss of hope itself
> And things to hope for!

Here is the nadir of descent from that view of the imaginative life of which he said

> With hope it is, hope that can never die
> Effort, and expectation, and desire,
> And something ever more about to be.

After reviewing the restoration of his imaginative vitality, Words-worth, although he has paid tribute to Dorothy and Coleridge for all they meant to him, insists upon the loneliness in which the im-agination is nourished –

Here keepest thou in singleness thy state:
No other can divide with thee this work:
No secondary hand can intervene
To fashion this ability; 'tis thine,
The prime and vital principle is thine
In the recesses of thy nature, far
From any reach of outward fellowship,
Else is not thine at all.[1]

This 'singleness of state' Wordsworth must have felt to an extreme degree during this period of his life, exhausted as he must have been by a sense of his own helplessness. Yet, in his helplessness, it was his early imaginative life which stood him in greatest stead; and what returned to him was not, at first, the joyous and abounding vitality of his earlier years, but recollection of two incidents which from this time on were to be a type of symbol very frequently throughout his poetry. It is worth while pausing to comment at length upon them; for, in looking back, he realized, through the memory of these incidents, that his imagination in years gone by had been acquainted with something of the desolation which in greater degree he had since known. Both the incidents relate to death, and to a natural scene associated in each case with death. In the first he describes how he had stumbled upon an old and mouldering gibbet, and saw, clearly preserved upon a stone, the name of a murderer who had been hanged there. He fled 'faltering and faint, and ignorant of the road'. In his terror he climbed to a point whence he saw

A naked pool that lay beneath the hills,
The beacon on the summit, and, more near,
A girl, who bore a pitcher on her head,
And seemed with difficult steps to force her way
Against the blowing wind. It was, in truth,
An ordinary sight; but I should need

1 XIII, 190–97.

Colours and words that are unknown to man
To paint the visionary dreariness
Which, while I looked all round for my lost guide,
Invested moorland waste, and naked pool,
The beacon crowning the lone eminence,
The female and her garments vexed and tossed
By the strong wind.

 The second incident, of identically the same quality, describes his
ascent to a crag from which he could see two roads, along either of
which he was feverishly and impatiently awaiting horses whereby
he might return home.

                              'twas a day
Tempestuous,dark, and wild, and on the grass
I sate half-sheltered by a naked wall;
Upon my right hand couched a single sheep,
Upon my left a blasted hawthorn stood.

Some days afterwards his father died; the event at once carried back
his imagination to

The single sheep, and the one blasted tree,
And the bleak music from that old stone wall.

And his imagination of the scene became for him a fountain whence
he drank. Wordsworth clearly attaches an enormous importance to
these two incidents; and to his recollection of them at this period of
his life. Recalled from a time when his imagination was strong and
growing, they had a peculiar significance for him now. They contained, he came to see, a dissolvent of his present condition, a 'reno-
vating virtue'. They had left 'power behind', and

              feeling comes in aid
Of feeling, and diversity of strength
Attends us, if but once we have been strong.

'If but once we have been strong.' Wordsworth recalled that no
once, but twice, he had been strong, and had found imaginative
vision in which strong feelings of revulsion and pain had been
absorbed or had purgation. What, then, was the secret of the power
of these incidents upon his troubled mind?

In the second incident, the scene came to have 'visionary dreari-ness' only after his father's death; his response to it while waiting for the horses was negligible – he was merely impatient to be gone. It became, in all truth, an object to his imagination only after sorrow had come. In the first, the desolate scenery had stirred him as he fled in terror from the thought of the hanged murderer. In both cases the scene was bare, wild, swept with wind and mist, untouched by gentleness or softness of colour; in both were features marked by a curious stillness; in the one, the naked pool, the beacon, the girl bearing a pitcher on her head; in the other, the sheep, the tree, the stone wall – all set around with tempest and vast expanse. It is this which, in each case, held his imagination, reconciled peace with tempest, calm with emotion, an 'emblem of eternity', an over-whelming sense of 'something ever more about to be'. It is no wonder that in the revulsion and numbness of mind at the time he recalled this experience –

> I should need
> Colours and words that are unknown to man
> To paint the visionary dreariness.

Here, we may be sure, more than even the ministrations of Coleridge and Dorothy, were places of power which on revealing themselves in the 'recesses of his nature', renewed his imagination. He knew then that he was no further changed

> Than as a clouded and a waning moon.

His past had reappeared to succour him. And from this time on his imagination, in all its variety of activity, centred around, as its highest objects of contemplation, images of a like type, men and women who knew the extreme of desolation and suffering, creatures of curious impassivity, who in the midst of 'dreariness' seem to be almost terrifying intimations of 'otherness'. In speaking of the restoration of his imaginative life he made special mention of the two incidents which we have quoted, incidents dating back to early years; but it is to be noticed that in the poem are recounted two other incidents, of a like kind, incidents which no doubt had been brought back vividly to his mind when he had realized the signifi-cance of the incidents relating to the gibbet and his father's death.

They are to be found in Book IV and Book VII. That in Book IV
describes a soldier whom he met on a road, in moonlight –

> He was alone,
> Had no attendant, neither Dog nor Staff,
> Nor knapsack; in his very dress appear'd
> A desolation, a simplicity
> That seem'd akin to solitude. Long time
> Did I peruse him with a mingled sense
> Of fear and sorrow. From his lips meanwhile
> There issued murmuring sounds, as if of pain
> Or of uneasy thought; yet still his form
> Kept the same steadiness; and at his feet
> His shadow lay, and mov'd not.[1]

Here, again, is desolation, and again a terrifying acquiescence:

> and when, erelong,
> I ask'd his history, he in reply
> Was neither slow nor eager; but unmov'd
> And with a quiet, uncomplaining voice,
> A stately air of mild indifference,
> He told, in simple words, a Soldier's tale. . . .

and throughout the telling of his story there was in all he said

> a strange half-absence, and a tone
> Of weakness and indifference, as of one
> Remembering the importance of his theme,
> But feeling it no longer.

In the seventh book Wordsworth describes a beggar whom he saw
in London, on his chest a label telling who the man was and his
story –

> My mind did at this spectacle turn round
> As with the might of waters, and it seem'd
> To me that in this label was a type,
> Or emblem, of the utmost that we know

[1] This and the three following quotations are taken from the 1805 version of
The Prelude.

Both of ourselves and of the universe;
And on the shape of the unmoving man,
His fixed face and sightless eyes, I look'd
As if admonished from another world.

So it is with the leech-gatherer 'from some far region spent'; in all alike is the extremity of suffering and desolation coupled with composure, unmoving and awful.

There can be no doubt that it was in the contemplation of such scenes and personages as this that Wordsworth's imagination reached its highest limit. He could never, to reiterate Keats, have seen these scenes and these men as he describes them had he not 'committed himself to the Extreme'; and certainly his ability to recall them from his past and to contemplate them mark the full restoration of his powers. It was not, indeed, that he effected such a restoration; his restoration was a gift to him from his early imagination which in its young strength had been able to encompass and grasp all that the scenes described in Book XII represented. In them sweet counsels between heart and head are re-established; a finality of desolation is incorporated into a supreme object of imaginative contemplation, reconciled with vision, and suggestive 'of unknown modes of being'. There is a sense in which, humanly speaking, such imaginative vision is final. It is the stage to which Keats's young Apollo had come when he cried –

Names, deeds, grey legends, dire events, rebellious
Majesties, sovran voices, agonies,
Creations and destroyings, all at once
Pour into the wide hollow of my brain
And defy me.

In all these passages the greatest dreariness and dereliction is melted into the visionary, and lost in it; suffering, known in the extreme, is invested, more than aught else could be, with the sense of something 'ever more about to be', so that the soldier, telling the story of his life, spoke as one who, 'remembering the importance of his theme', yet felt it no longer.

Once Wordsworth had reached this phase in the growth of his imagination, it became true of him that knowing too well the

importance of the story of human life and suffering, he felt it no
longer. For over the abyss hung the world of vision. It was not that
he became insensitive to the spectacle of human evil and pain, but
that over it lay suspended the firmament of otherness. The overwhelming sense of the unknown, the unforeseen, which visited him
when he had crossed the Alps, was now with him in his contemplation
of the deepest suffering and apparent dereliction. And in the attainment to this sense in the face of pain and destitution lay the full
restoration of his imaginative power. His imagination had now en-
compassed with the feeling of Infinity not only the world of nature,
but the world of man. The importance of that world he could never
indeed deny, or wish to deny; but he could 'feel it no longer' in the
same degree. 'So still an image of tranquillity, so calm and still'
could he now maintain in himself that

– What we feel of sorrow and despair
From ruin and from change, and all the grief
The passing shows of Being leave behind,
Appeared an idle dream.

In other words, Wordsworth had come to see the error which he
had made in thinking that his early view of the life of imagination
was bound up with a return of 'Saturnian rule'. Actually, as he
came to see, in recollecting those early days, his experience had
contained within itself the answer to the questions which in his
time of crisis he asked and could not answer. And indeed it was not
that his early imaginative powers were inadequate to meeting that
crisis; instead, he had allowed himself to become absorbed in a
passionate social idealism to a degree which blinded him to the power
and adequacy of his imagination to include in its synthesis the whole
world of human suffering. He thought, overwhelmed by a disappointment accompanied by a sense of human evil greater than anything he had known before, that his life was destroyed, and all
foundations for the future destroyed. But in reality, all that was
necessary was the exploration in memory of his former days of
imaginative vitality. 'The days gone by return upon me'; and those
days proved 'hiding-places' of his power. It was not that his imagination had failed him, but that he had failed his imagination. Natural
as it was that, when a very young man, he had abandoned himself to

revolutionary ardour, yet it was the recollection of his imaginative
experiences, above all those which were vitally associated with pain,
terror and sorrow, which saved him. Then he was able to see that his
imagination, which in his younger days could invest dreariness with
vision, might do so again. It was not that his revolutionary ardour
had been misplaced or mistaken; no one, I think, would judge that
it was. What had been misplaced was the effort, however unconsciously made, by his imagination, to circumvent the fact of evil
and suffering – the refusal to see them as inevitable to human life.
But the result of his revolutionary experiences was more than ever to
thrust them before his eyes, even to the point of paralysing his
powers. Then there was no escape; and he was delighted and surprised to find that in himself and 'days gone by' lay the power to
encompass all the degradation of human life with his imagination.
He was thus able to see the French Revolution as the 'weak functions
of one busy day' set over against the 'slowly moving years of time,
with their united force', the years of effort and suffering which even
no return of 'Saturnian rule' could blot out for an imagination which
in its contemplation of life seeks to maintain its integrity.

Within the soul a faculty abides,
That with interpositions, which would hide
And darken, so can deal, that they become
Contingencies of pomp; and serve to exalt
Her native brightness.

What had come to him was an extension of the power of imagination
which he had enjoyed in his youth. If he rejected that power for a
while, the circumstances of that rejection proved but 'contingencies
of pomp'. 'The sense of possible sublimity', which he had known
in the presence of nature, to which he felt the soul aspires

With faculties still growing, feeling still
That whatsoever point they gain, they still
Have something to pursue,

he now felt with, if possible, a still greater force, his mind 'swept, as
with the might of waters', in the presence of what is, humanly, a
total dereliction. The infinity of the soul's aspiration, so that however
far it moves and grows there is always a 'something', the vast un-

known dimly apprehended before it, became now the 'main theme of his song'; a 'something' so real that in comparison sorrow, despair, ruin, change and grief are but 'the passing shows of Being', an 'idle dream'. The triumph of his imagination, or better, the restoration to him of imaginative power, was the apprehension, however dim, of 'Infinitude' as the necessary complement and completion not only of the beauty of nature, but of the extremity of suffering. Now that this realization, or this imaginative grasp of reality, had been made in his mind, it was natural and indeed inevitable that the dogmas of Christianity should increasingly appear to his mind as a consummate conveyance of all that he had learnt; and his increasing humility before Christianity is surely a mark not of the decay, as is so often rashly thought, of his imagination, but of the consummation of it. His gratification in realizing that all that he had learnt, by 'proof upon the pulses', in the loneliness of his imagination, 'in singleness of state', was embodied in the tradition of Christianity must indeed have been tempered with a sorrowful and healthy humiliation. He was, indeed, no longer

Voyaging through strange seas of thought, *alone*;

he was no longer

> sounding on,
> Through words, a dim and perilous way;

he had found community. His greatest poetry is indeed the story and expression of his lonely voyaging. But if his imagination in those later days found adequacy and rest in forms of expression not his own, it is not for critics to assume, as they have been so quick to do, that his life degenerated at its source.[1]

Of the relation of poetry to religion we shall try to speak in a later chapter, and we shall have occasion to recur again to the effect upon his poetry of Wordsworth's Christianity. There is occasion, however,

1 Some time after the above was written, a reference in an article on A. C. Bradley in *The Times Literary Supplement* (23 May 1936), led me to read (what, to my shame, perhaps, I had not formerly read) Bradley's lecture on Wordsworth in *Oxford Lectures*. The reader who feels that in the above section I have over-emphasized one aspect of Wordsworth's imaginative life may be advised to read Bradley's remarkable lecture.

at this point to observe the attitude which, after the restoration of his mental health, Wordsworth adopted towards science, an attitude which showed that Wordsworth never arrived at a harmonized view of human experience. Holding the view of the imagination which I have tried to set out earlier in this essay, Wordsworth never tired of setting over against the direct creativity of the imagination

> that false secondary power
> By which we multiply distinctions, then
> Deem that our puny boundaries are things
> That we perceive and not that we have made.

In the same passage, immediately preceding that in which he writes of the imagination in the earliest years of the mind, we find the following lines, in which Coleridge is addressed –

> to thee
> Science appears but what in truth she is,
> Not as our glory and our absolute boast,
> But as a succedaneum, and prop
> To our infirmity.

It is difficult not to be puzzled by these lines, written by one who at a time of the greatest 'infirmity' sought a 'succedaneum' and a 'prop' in intellectual and scientific inquiry, and signally failed to find one. During that time he despaired, as we have noticed, of philosophy; science, by its very security 'from disturbances of space and time', might be an escape; but by its very irrelevance to his life, 'to human will and power', it could not conceivably help him. Whether, therefore, in the passage quoted he means by 'science' the discursive intelligence in all its operations, or physical science in a strict sense, it is difficult to see how he could write of it as a 'succedaneum' or 'prop'. For it was precisely as a succedaneum, something we fall back upon, a substitute source of power, that it had failed him. If his experience was an adequate guidance, it was neither our glory, absolute boast, succedaneum nor prop. Yet he continued to cleave to this sentimental view of science. In the fourth book of *The Excursion*, in other respects one of the very greatest pieces of Wordsworth's work, his attitude to intellectual inquiry is

childish and condescending, mistaken in thought and false in feeling.
Go, he says,

> demand
> Of Mighty Nature, if 'twas ever meant
> That we should pry far off yet be unraised;
> That we should pore, and dwindle as we pore,
> Viewing all objects unremittingly
> In disconnexion dead and spiritless ...
>   waging thus
> An impious warfare with the very life
> Of our own souls!

Certainly, if the exercise of the intelligence necessarily implied an
atrophy of imaginative powers, one could understand such an outburst. But it is only a superficial view of the intellectual life which
implies that this is so. Wordsworth writes in resentment of the life of
intellectual inquiry. But why? Wordsworth should surely have seen
that there is as urgent a practical and moral necessity to exercise the
intelligence to the full extent of its powers as to exercise the powers
of the imagination. And later, we find the following –

>   Science then
> Shall be a precious visitant; and then,
> And only then, be worthy of her name:
> For then her heart shall kindle; her dull eye,
> Dull and inanimate, no more shall hang
> Chained to its object in brute slavery ...[1]

nor –

> Shall it forget that its most noble use,
> Its most illustrious province, must be found
> In furnishing clear guidance, a support
> Not treacherous, to the mind's *excursive* power.

This is the height of nonsense. Such a condescending attitude to
science is merely silly; and condescendingly to justify science at all
by holding that it can, if it behaves itself nicely, give evidence and
support to the 'excursive power' is not only utterly mistaken but

1 IV, 1251–6.

false to Wordsworth's own experience. It is monstrous to seek to justify science and philosophy by any other than intellectual values; it is still more monstrous that Wordsworth should thus ignore all that his experience had most clearly taught him. Had he reflected a little more he would have seen, what indeed he should have seen from his own experience, that science is simply irrelevant to the problems of life. Wordsworth no doubt was right to give pride of place to the imagination; but it is merely an insult to science patronizingly to offer it second place, and that on condition that it furnishes 'clear guidance' and 'a support not treacherous' to the creative imagination. The fact is that science can no more offer clear guidance or reliable support to the imagination than it can offer false guidance or doubtful support to the imagination; and there was a time in Wordsworth's life when he saw this, compelled on him as it was by the very anguish of his experience. And equally his enjoyment of mathematics should have saved him from such mistaken condescension to the intellectual life. The Arab of his Cambridge dream was concerned to save mathematics as well as poetry from the general deluge. And there was no reason why Wordsworth should not combine in his reflection both a knowledge of the essential irrelevance of science and mathematics to the problem of life, and a recognition of their worth and joys. This, however, he failed to do, however nearly we may judge, in reviewing his story, he came to succeeding. He was right in his perception that what knowledge science can give is 'secondary' and abstract. But he was not true enough to his own experience to conclude with a recognition of what is, from the point of view of the imaginative life, the unimportance of scientific knowledge.[1] Had he gone the whole length of this realization he would not have been tempted to such a pompous patronage of science nor sought from science 'aids and supports'. The imagination he tells us in the Preface to the *Lyrical Ballads* is, in contrast to the detachment of science, part and parcel of our life 'as enjoying and suffering beings', the apprehension by personality, in action and

[1] That this is so is shown by the fact that the issue between a mechanistic and purposive view of the universe stands today precisely where it did when Socrates read the works of Anaxagoras. Similarly, despite a widespread illusion to the contrary, it is absurd to suggest that Freud's psychology has in the slightest degree affected the agelong conflict of freedom *versus* determinism.

emotion, of the world. 'If the time should ever come', he goes on to say, 'when what is now called science – shall be ready to put on, as it were, a form of flesh and blood, the Poet will lend his divine spirit to aid the transfiguration.' This is, indeed, eloquent; but such a transfiguration is as undesirable as it is impossible, an absurd fiction created for an eloquent argument more passionate than careful. He says rightly that science must seek to view all objects unremittingly

In disconnexion dull and spiritless;

but this 'deathly and bloodless' condition is for science a condition of its life; and to resent it, or wish it changed, is the merest peevishness. And equally foolish is it to expect science to offer 'props and stays'; for as Wordsworth himself recognized, science simply is not concerned with the values which are 'flesh and blood' to the life of personality. Though one hesitates to quarrel with a statement which has won such universal quotation and respect, it is nevertheless difficult to see how poetry is the 'breath and finer spirit of all knowledge', and how it is the 'impassioned expression which is in the countenance of all science'. At a later date Wordsworth was to deplore the viewing of things in 'disconnexion, dead and spiritless' and to urge that to do so is to 'wage an impious warfare on the soul'. The countenance of activity such as that would hardly bear the 'impassioned expression' which Wordsworth claims poetry to be. And Wordsworth cannot have it both ways. It is merely rhetoric to say that science is really a poetical affair. On the other hand, it is equally absurd to say, as Wordsworth says in *The Excursion*, that science is a kind of demoralizing 'prying'.

Wordsworth's mature view of human nature failed to embrace a clear comprehension of the relation of the imaginative to the intellectual life. But on the other hand, his perception of the relation of imagination to morality was clear and sure. Here at least he stood on sure ground. He grounded his moral sense in the contemplative life which gives release from immersion in action and emotion. And in *The Prelude*, at least (and he did not see fit to change it in the later version), it is the discipline of the contemplative life lived in intimacy with nature which he sets over against the formal discipline of religious observances as the condition of moral health. It is in the potency of 'a mere image of the sway' of solitude that the self which is the seat of true morality finds itself. The moral life, that is to say, flows naturally from the discipline of quietude. In such a discipline, he held, is the condition of a true morality, springing not from imposed precept, and proof therefore against 'shock of accident'. Such morality therefore cannot be sought for itself; it is a product of a life animated by

The universal instinct of repose
The longing for confirmed tranquillity

which is, indeed, the life of the imagination, craving peace

Not as a refuge from distress or pain
A breathing-time, vacation, or a truce
But for its absolute self.

And in such a life the forms of nature, a world of life at peace, are the paramount and lasting influence. Sought for their own beauty, they give the imagination freedom from the urgency of will and emotion, creating thereby 'stability without regret or fear'.
(141-69)

James Smith

'Wordsworth: A Preliminary Survey' *Scrutiny*, no. 7, 1938

Wordsworth's poetry is not only an extensive, it is a difficult country; and therefore, before attempting to cross it, I have thought it worth while to summarize what I imagine I know about it. Much of this may be legend, and I put it forward without any confidence that it is anything more; but a summary of legend is useful if, by internal confusion or apparent improbability, it brings home the amount of labour necessary to attain the truth.

And, first, the traps or pitfalls with which Wordsworth's poetry abounds. One of these is, I think, its mere amount, by which we should not allow ourselves to be unduly impressed. This may seem a slight temptation, but I am not sure that it is easy to avoid. Staying power is a comparatively rare thing, and even the appearance of it

moves at times to admiration. With Wordsworth it is an important
question, how much of it is mere appearance; and an answer can be
given only after going through a poem line by line, inquiring into
the significance of each. It is not sufficient to listen for the general
effect of a passage, which may be a sonorous cadence with a buzzing
of meaning in the background. Wordsworth was skilled in sounding
cadences, and with him as with any other poet meaning should be
either more or less than a buzz.

From *The Prelude* and the *Preface to the Lyrical Ballads* it is at least
probable that he looked on poetry as a sort of natural product, like
fruit and flowers; brought into being by nature rather than by man,
or by man only as nature works in him. Thus from one point of view
he might be said to shift responsibility for composition from his own
shoulders on to nature; from another, to arrogate to himself the
privilege of unrestrained fertility. As nature a hundred daisies for a
single oak, so he throws up a hundred insignificant verses for one of
substance. But towards them all, as towards the daisies and the oak,
he feels the sort of reverence due to the manifestations of a higher
power. He receives them into his collected works, and arranges
them in a cunning order to ensure that all shall be read; and in that
way he at least dissuades, if he does not intimidate, his critic from the
task of discrimination.

Secondly, we must take care not to be dazzled by his rhetorical skill
– 'rhetorical' is a word with a number of senses, but I use it, I believe,
in the best. It would be difficult to exaggerate this skill in Wordsworth, and the danger which results from it.

Nature, he seems to have thought, produces only the bare essence
of poetry, to which man must fit an outer garment of words and
metre; therefore a poet, if he would not be mute, must set himself
to acquire the knack of metre, as he would any other accomplishment. Wordsworth laboured early and long for this end. 'I have
bestowed great care upon my style', he said, 'and yield to none in the
love of my art.' From his use of the term elsewhere, it seems probable
that by 'art' and 'style' he means the power simultaneously to observe
the rules for lucid and grammatical English, and for any verse-form
in which he happened to be working. He practised and attained
proficiency in a great many: in the sonnet, and in the forms of
Spenser, Milton, Pope, Hamilton, Burns and Scott.

The sort of merit which he thus brought within his reach, and which it is important to recognize and name lest, remarkable as it is, it be mistaken for something yet more remarkable, is fairly clearly illustrated by his poem *Yew-Trees*. This is familiar, if for no other reason, for being quoted as an example of the grand style outside Milton. It may be so; but I do not think we can call it anything more than an exercise in Miltonics.

... those fraternal Four of Borrowdale,
Joined in one solemn and capacious grove;
Huge trunks! and each particular trunk a growth
Of intertwisted fibres serpentine
Upcoiling, and inveterately convolved;
Nor uninformed with Phantasy, ...

A brilliant exercise, but only brilliant. On re-reading I am sometimes halted by the line in which Time the Shadow, Death the Skeleton and the rest are said to 'meet at noontide'; there seems promise here of a complication of ideas; but if there is, it is soon untied. The ghostly company meet only for the unexpected purpose of united worship, or for the incongruous one of listening to the flood on Glaramara. The yew-trees themselves lack depth, and might well be figures in tapestry. Wordsworth, I should say, is not much interested in his images or his ideas, except as they serve to support certain rhythms; it is these which claim the greater part of his attention, and which, as with a sterile art, he exploits for their own sake.

Mastery over metre qualifies him to be a conversational poet – the sort of poet, that is, who flourished in a number of countries during the Renaissance, and in England in the early eighteenth century. At these places and periods a firm tradition of poetic performance permitted the treatment of an unusually wide variety of subjects at least as efficiently in verse as in prose, and often with the urgency and vividness of verse. A number of passages in *The Prelude*, like the description of his dame at Hawkshead or of the sights of London, reach a high level of excellence in this way. One of them, on the Terror, suggests that he might have maintained himself fairly consistently at the highest level, if he had been more secure of an audience; for poetry of this kind, to persist, depends on a society whose members continually stimulate and restrain. But the audience was lacking, and for various reasons he gradually withdrew into a more and more remote exile. In consequence, some of his later verse, which has been praised for its technical perfection, is no more than scholarly, it is directed, that is, at a distant, almost a disembodied audience. And some of the rest suffers from a lack of focus, as though it were directed at two widely differing audiences at once. This is the fault of the didactic part of *The Prelude*, where Wordsworth seems unable to convince himself that what he has to say is of itself such as to interest the reader. Therefore, by means of orotundity and ornament he seeks to provide an elegant diversion, to combine, as it were, the roles of Lucretius and of Dyer in *The Fleece*. The result is a compromise which I find intensely irritating, though it has been praised. But *The Prelude*, because of a multitude of ingredients, deserves more than one paper to itself.

A third kind of trap can be described in Wordsworth's own words. Readers of 'moral and religious inclinations', he says, 'attaching so much importance to the truths which interest them ... are prone to overrate the Authors by whom those truths are expressed and enforced. They come prepared to impart so much passion to the Poet's language that they remain unconscious how little, in fact, they receive from it.' The vocabulary is that of intellectualism; but what it expressed might serve as the basis for a distinction between more and less valuable responses to poetry.

Wordsworth often wrote, not only about joy in widest commonality spread, but about common joys. His subjects in themselves, and apart from any treatment he may give, are such as to evoke memories or aspirations in which it is pleasant, if not always profitable or proper, to indulge. If the opportunity for indulgence were offered alone, it might be immediately rejected; but its nature is masked – and this is the gravest danger; perhaps the last two kinds of traps, which I have taken separately, should be considered together – its nature is masked by the accompanying rhetoric. It is easy to be affected by the subject and by the style or metre of one of Wordsworth's poems, as by two separate things: the one appearing to dignify the other, because of their accidental association; but neither modifying the other – neither the metre imposing itself upon and ordering the subject, nor the subject filling out the cavities of the metre. And at the same time it is easy to assume that the poem as a whole is effective when the truth may be that as an integrated whole the poem does not exist. The point is a difficult and, I think, an important one, which will justify one or two illustrations.

Arnold's selection contains a number of not very striking poems; but the one of least merit is possibly that which begins;

Pansies, lillies, kingcups, daisies,
Let them live upon their praises;
Long as there's a sun that sets,
Primroses will have their glory;
Long as there are violets,
They will have a place in story:
There's a flower that shall be mine,
'Tis the little Celandine.[1]

The lilt, the tone, is that of a music-hall ditty; it is difficult to imagine how anyone with an ear sensitive to rhythm, with a feeling for more than the surfaces of words can have written it. As Wordsworth had both, the explanation may be the abdication of responsibility to which I have already referred. But how has the poem come to be approved? For it figures in other anthologies besides Arnold's – for example in the *Oxford Book of Regency Verse*. In the first place, the language is clear, the metre gives no occasion for stumbling; it has at least the negative virtues. And, secondly, the subject, or a large part of the subject, is humility, which is a popular quality; it inculcates the popular opinion that to be humble is to be happy, even to be merry; and finally, it harmonizes with the absentee or vacation cult of nature which was a force in English society and in English poetry from the middle of last century onwards. There was nothing that, in his better moments, Wordsworth despised more than he did this cult; there was nothing about which he wrote more lamely – or rather, when he can be taken to be writing about it, he is always at his lamest. Yet his choice of subjects is such, and his unfailing rhetorical skill, that he has imposed himself upon the cult, and figured as its canonized poet. In a similar way he has been the canonized poet of English and American institutions; and as recently as 1915, with the

1 *To the Small Celandine.*

publication of Professor Dicey's *Statesmanship of Wordsworth*, he was hailed with renewed conviction as the poet of patriotism. His sentiments on that topic were of course unexceptionable; and he dresses them out in a language which the percipient can take to be that of inner compulsion, of inspiration. Yet some of these patriotic effusions, as Mr Leavis has said, are no more than claptrap; the best probably should not rank as high as what I have called his conversational successes. It seems that patriotism, like religion, is not a safe theme for poetry, and that, for the reason quoted from Wordsworth, it is at least as difficult to compose.

The isolated appeal of the subject in passages like the above is on doubt too obvious for it nowadays to form a trap. But it was on account of their obviousness I chose them; it seemed to me they might help in a further discussion, of which the conclusion is not obvious at all. To what extent are we justified in acknowledging Wordsworth as a mystical poet, as is often done? Are we being deceived somewhat in the manner described – that is, are we responding to the subject by itself, and to certain tricks of style by themselves, rather than to a poem in which both are in alliance and unison? By 'mystical poet' I do not mean one who has intense experiences on the occasion of natural phenomena, nor one who is convinced of the importance of spirit in the life of man and in the affairs of this world. This is perhaps not an unusual meaning for the term, but I employ it in a narrower and, I hope, more useful sense. I mean by it a poet who has the sort of experience Wordsworth claims in one or two passages of *The Prelude* – that of a communion or a community with something outside and above the world, with a divine soul or with the highest truth.

The possibility that in these passages the subject may make an isolated appeal arises from the flattering nature of the belief that such communion is possible to a fellow man; and from certain comfortable consequences which seem to follow. Wordsworth may play upon these rather than convey the experience upon which, if the belief is true, it must ultimately be based.

I take as an example the passage in which he seeks to tell what happened to him when, writing an account of his experiences, he realized that once he had crossed the Alps.

And now recovering, to my soul I say
I recognize thy glory; in such strength
Of usurpation, in such visitings
Of awful promise, when the light of sense
Goes out in flashes that have shown to us
The invisible world, doth Greatness make abode,
There harbours whether we be young or old.
Our destiny, our nature and our home
Is with infinitude, and only there;
With hope it is, hope that can never die,
Effort and expectation and desire,
And something evermore about to be.[1]

Let me first note about this passage the ample warrant it provides for
all that has been said about Wordsworth's skill in rhetoric. Like
Milton, he knows how to draw out the sense variously from verse to
verse; or, as he puts it to Klopstock, to secure 'an apt arrangement of
pauses and candences, and the sweep of whole paragraphs'. Secondly,
the occasion seems not unsuitable for the display of such skill; an
attempt, it seems, is to be made to communicate something by its
nature difficult, if not incapable, of communication, upon which
therefore only a number of sallies can be made. If each is doomed to
be ineffectual, all of them together, and the variety of their points
of departure and return, may be not wholly without effect. 'Strength
of usurpation' and 'visitings of awful promise' corroborate each
other; and if it is not clear exactly how, inevitable lack of clarity is
part of what is to be conveyed. The figure of an invisible world made
visible by a flash of light which thereby extinguishes itself, as though
by a supreme effort, recommends for acceptance a difficulty for which,
even when accepted, there can be no hope of solution. And as the
passage goes on, a solution begins to appear less and less necessary:
the metre becomes more regular, the difficulty is not at all impossible,
it is even exhilarating to live with. The line 'With hope it is, hope
that can never die' encourages to aspiration; 'Effort and expectation
and desire' suggests an unremitting eagerness in the soul. The last
line, 'And something evermore about to be', is the most regular of
all.

1 [*The Prelude* (1805), VI, 531–42.]

The trouble is that it is too regular – too regular to be smooth. There is no peace about it, but a merciless beat; and with infinitude there should surely be peace. When we have reached this line the suspicion arises, I think, that Wordsworth is not in fact where a mystic should be – with infinitude, outside or above the world; but, rather, well within it. And, if so, some of the preceding lines need to be reconsidered, and our opinion on them to be revised. Aspiration can be unreservedly welcome only where, as with infinitude, there is certainty that it will be fulfilled; elsewhere 'hope that can never die' is but a euphemism for hope that has never lived. And elsewhere than with infinitude effort and expectation and desire are grim companions: that eagerness is unremitting is no guarantee that, in this world, it will not be baffled. If we turn our attention from the sound to the sense of the last line we see it to have the minimum of meaning: there is nothing in the future to which it will not apply. So far as we can talk of a future in eternity it is of a piece with the present and prophecy cannot arouse mistrust; but to a creature in time the mere idea of futurity cannot bring consolation, and confidence based upon it and nothing more is a poor thing. Loudly to proclaim such a confidence is a still poorer thing.

If we read over the passage with these and similar reflections in mind we discover I think that the rhetoric is not only skilful, it is too obviously skilful: it has no natural movement which, if we admire, we admire as concrete in the substance which moves; but rather a mechanical, to admire which we must abstract and even oppose it to the substance. 'How subtle the play of the levers!' we say, and all the time are thinking of the unexpectedness of such subtlety in dead matter. The poem is not alive, but an extremely cleverly constructed simulacrum; a robot put together, no doubt, for his purposes; but still not a poem.

It is sometimes said that, to judge with any security of a mystical verse, one should be a mystic oneself. That would, however, reduce the number of judges to such an extent that it is hardly likely to be true. It may be suggested that the question whether Wordsworth succeeded in conveying a mystical experience, and whether he had it, are two different questions, the one falling under biography, the other under criticism; and that the answers to them are not necessarily identical. Not that biography is irrelevant to criticism, to which it

can give valuable if extra-technical aid; and the biographical question,
it is true, might profitably be raised here. But it would require much
time and space; to analyse (among other things) the biographical
element in *The Prelude*, to compare it with the similar element in
Tintern (from which it seems to differ in not unimportant ways; as
though Wordsworth altered his views about his own experiences
as he grew older), and, finally, to compare that biography, according
to whatever view may prove more acceptable, with the history of
a mystic or mystics who are fairly widely acknowledged to be
such.

In default of such aid, it is perhaps advisable to consider somewhat
closely a second passage. I will choose the lines about *The Simplon
Pass*, as the most difficult ones I know to criticize satisfactorily. If, as
is only too likely, I cannot make clear my point about them and their
kind, perhaps I can at least make the difficulty clear; and that is a
sufficiently important matter.

The lines are as follows:

— Brook and road
Were fellow-travellers in this gloomy Pass,
And with them did we journey several hours
At a slow step. The immeasurable height
Of woods decaying, never to be decayed,
The stationary blasts of waterfalls,
And everywhere along the hollow rent
Winds thwarting winds, bewildered and forlorn,
The torrents shooting from the clear blue sky,
The rocks that muttered close upon our ears,
Black drizzling crags that spake by the wayside
As if a voice were in them, the sick sight
And giddy prospect of the raving stream,
The unfettered clouds and region of the heavens,
Tumult and peace, the darkness and the light –
Were all like workings of one mind, the features
Of the same face, blossoms upon one tree,
Characters of the great Apocalypse,
The types and symbols of Eternity,
Of first, and last, and midst, and without end.

I had better say at once, to prevent misunderstanding as far as I am able, that I think the greater part of this passage is very impressive indeed. I think it so impressive that I am disappointed perhaps more than I should be with the rest; but this, I think, distracts and divides the attention although it is short. It may also influence unfavourably the style of the whole.

In these lines Wordsworth, it seems to me, is trying to do not one thing but two; or rather, having done one thing and done it well, he goes on to another which perhaps by its nature cannot be so well done. Down to the last three lines he is concerned to express a feeling of surprise, almost vexation: like the thwarting winds he is bewildered and forlorn; while the woods, the waterfalls and the rocks about him threaten ruin and decay, they seem fixed for ever. They threaten destruction to one another, and even to the spectator – there are sick sights and giddy prospects – nevertheless there is and there will be no annihilation, only persistence. He finds escape from this bewilderment by, so to speak, living into the phenomena by which it is caused: in all of them he finds the working of a 'single mind', with which he can identify himself, or of which he can become a part. And then he sees that the stresses which they exert upon one another and upon himself, all of which he experiences in himself, serve only for their mutual support. This notion of immobility resulting where action and change might be expected occurs elsewhere in Wordsworth's best poetry, of some of which it is almost a mark; but in such work he rests in the notion as the only satisfaction which the circumstances can afford. Here, however, he takes a step further, and seeks a satisfaction which, so far springing from the circumstances, seems only to discount them. The bewilderment yields to or is transformed into a revelation, an apocalypse, and the ground for it is removed by degrading the woods, the water falls and the rocks from being themselves eternal into the types and symbols of eternity. And this eternity, rather than charged with a greater significance than what are said to be its symbols, seems empty of everything: it is dismissed in flat pentameter, the only content of which is the highest common factor of the many associations hanging about a scrap from the liturgy. In other words Wordsworth (I think) finally adopts an answer which has no particular relevance to, and is therefore an escape from, his immediate problem; which, as it might answer any problem, answers none, and is provided for him rather by talk about mysticism than by mysticism itself – by religiosity rather than religion: at least by a deadening, not a vivifying force.

Perhaps I exaggerate: but I think it is a danger that these last few lines, connected with their predecessors by the sweep of the metre, and offering the reader an alternative against which, in the context, he is least on his guard, may hinder him from entering into the full and difficult meaning of that context; and they may do so even when the alternative is rejected. How Wordsworth came to write in this mixed and broken way, if, as I think, he did so, is obviously a serious problem; it would almost seem that acute perception was something of which he had learnt to be afraid. Elsewhere there are traces of a similar fear; of which, of course, it would be a gross impertinence to speak in any tone of censure, not of regret. Perhaps also the phenomenon may be not unconnected with what has already been described as an abdication of responsibility in composition.

From a summary account of what may be the traps – the marshy lowlands, the hidden gulfs – in Wordsworth's poetry, I pass to an account which must be yet more summary of what seem to be its highlands. From a distance it is no less possible to be mistaken about these than about the former; and as they are of wider significance, I speak with greater diffidence.

It is, I think, a useful question to ask how Wordsworth first came to believe that he was a poet: a man, that is, in whom nature works so as to produce poetry. As he thought that nature, instead of repeating herself, provides for a development of the spirit or a gradual revelation of truth, it must have been because he felt he had something new within him.

Part of it was a peculiar sensitivity to nature, or a novel intimacy with her and her manifestations. When he was fourteen, he says, he became conscious 'of the infinite variety of natural appearances which had been unnoticed by poets of any age and country', and resolved 'to supply in some degree the deficiency'. But he was more than an observer: the other childhood experience must be remembered, that he sometimes felt himself slipping into 'an abyss of idealism'. He was part of what he saw, or what he saw was part of him. And as early as the *Descriptive Sketches* he speaks of 'abandoning the cold rules of painting' to consult both 'nature and his feelings'. From that date onwards he gives no mere lists of natural appearances, but groupings of them as they served to prompt a dominant emotion.

As long as what he calls the idealism persisted, or whenever it reasserted itself, this emotion was some degree of joy; for there was nothing other than himself by which he might be thwarted. It marks various well-known passages in *The Prelude*:

The sea was laughing at a distance; all
The solid mountains were as bright as clouds,
Grain tinctured, drenched in empyrean light;
And in the meadows and the lower grounds,
Was all the sweetness of a common dawn,
Dews, vapours and the melody of birds,
And labourers going forth into the fields.[1]

It is at its most exuberant in the spring poems of the *Lyrical Ballads*:

Love, now a universal birth
From heart to heart is stealing,
From earth to man, from man to earth;
– It is the hour of feeling.

One moment now may give us more
Than years of toiling reason:
Our minds shall drink at every pore
The spirit of the season.[2]

But exaggerations of this kind are themselves a criticism of the mood: as by its nature it is fleeting, it can be maintained for any length of time only by self-deception, to which one means is a loud boasting.

Already in his childhood Wordsworth had made such a criticism: 'idealism' he had recognized as an 'abyss', and to save himself had put out his hand. In doing so he was not repeating the Johnsonian experiment: his intention was not to refute a metaphysic, but to repeat a type of experience, that of being resisted, which for a time he had forgotten. Resistance, thwarting, comes from things outside himself, other than himself and the second new thing about his poetry

1 IV, 335–9.
2 *To My Sister*, 21–8.

is, I think, its preoccupation with *other things as other*. In various ways they threaten his equanimity, disturb his peace.

In his early years there seems to have been a rapid oscillation between the sense of joyous union and one of divorce from the external world; the latter giving rise to unhappiness, and at times to fear. A mountain pursued him 'with measured motion, like a living thing'; and 'after he had seen that spectacle' – these are his words:

... for many days my brain
Worked with a dim and undetermined sense
Of unknown modes of being; in my thoughts
There was a darkness, call it solitude
Or blank desertion, no familiar shapes
Of hourly objects ...
But huge and mighty Forms that do not live
Like living men moved slowly through the mind
By day and were a trouble to my dreams.[1]

From time to time he returns to this notion of opposition, of enmity – not only between himself, but between other people and the external world; and at times, as in *The Simplon Pass*, between the external occupants of the world. But it does not long remain the centre of his interest. Conceived of as enemies, other things are in a measure like himself, and in that measure reconciliation with them might be possible; it is in the measure in which they are unlike himself, in which they are other, that the fascination they exert is unescapable.

Are they real? he seems compelled to ask. They are so different that there is no quality, however abstract, he might split off from himself – not even the bare quality of being – in which they might partake. Either they exist exactly as he does, and are himself – but that is impossible; or they do not exist at all – but they obviously do. And as though to convince himself of the latter fact in a subtler manner than by clutching at a wall, he considers repeatedly in his verse the sort of realities which maintain themselves under apparently impossible conditions.

   ... the lifeless arch of stones in air
Suspended, the cerulean firmament

1 *The Prelude*, I, 418–27.

And what is; the river that flows on
Perpetually, whence comes it, wither tends
Going and never gone; the fish that moves
And lives as in an element of death.[1]

A rainbow he saw near Coniston, 'the substance thin as dreams',
nevertheless stood unmoved through the uproar of a storm,

Sustained itself through many minutes space
As if it were pinned down by adamant.[2]

And reflections in water occupy his attention either because of the
instability of the element on which they are traced – like that of
Peele Castle, which 'trembled, but it never passed away'; or because
of their apparent identity with the object reflected, from which,
nevertheless, they are other. Mr de Selincourt quotes an early version
of some lines in *The Excursion*:

Once coming to a bridge that overlooked
A mountain torrent, where it was becalmed
By a flat meadow, at a glance I saw
A two-fold image; on the grassy bank
A snow-white ram, and in the peaceful flood
Another and the same; most beautiful
The breathing creature; nor less beautiful
Beneath him, was his shadowy counterpart:
Each had his glowing mountains, each his sky,
And each seemed centre of his own fair world.
A stray temptation seized me to dissolve
The vision – but I could not.[3]

He had picked up a pebble, but dropped it unthrown. The passage
has many defects, but I quote it for one or two phrases – 'another
and the same', 'each had his glowing mountains', – and for the
conclusion. This suggests that the habit of contemplating things when
and in a way in which existence seems impossible has led to a respect
for them which is almost superstitious. When other things are fleeting

1 See de Selincourt's *Prelude*, 1926, p. 554 n.
2 p. 601 n.
3 See *The Excursion*, IX, 441.

they are capable of being destroyed; but that they are fleeting is a vindication of their reality as other, and this forbids destruction like a desecration.

Reflections in water retain form and colour; and, carrying analysis as far as it can go, Wordsworth seeks to know what they have which makes them to be other than their objects. What are the principles which render possible a multiplicity of things? which separate him from the external world, as objects in the external world are seperated from one another? The ultimate answer he gives is time and place, duration and extension: it is because the reflection of the ram is elsewhere than the ram itself that, apparently identical in all other respects, it is obviously different from the ram. And it is upon duration and extension, which, highly abstract as they are, yet seems the soil and sap of other reality, that the superstitious respect just noted finally bears. However confused his account of the experience when he realized that he had crossed the Alps, the experience was of an impressive kind; and, stripping the account of its references to eternal destiny, we see the experience to have consisted merely in the realization that, whereas he had been on one side of the Alps, he was now on the other. Or we might say that, as he does not contrast the two sides in respect of any of their qualities – their orientation, their contour or their covering – he realized there is diversity of place. It is this, and this alone, that 'wrapt him in a cloud'. That a mountain barrier arose between two particular places – that they were the *sides* of a mountain – was not his concern, for there rose between them another barrier which, if more ideal, is more impassable. It was erected by the very notion of space, of which the parts are by definition external to one another; each, for the rest, an *other*. The experience is perhaps more easily discerned behind a second passage from *The Prelude*, which describes an entry into London. At the time Wordsworth was not occupied by any ideas of the capital as a storehouse of tradition or magnificence, and his immediate surroundings did not invite attention – there were 'vulgar men' about him, and 'mean shapes on every side'. His senses and his memory were unheeded or asleep. But he was awake to the notion of the boundary, the imaginary line which sets up place against place, and by crossing which, from having been without London, he would find himself within.

The very moment that I seem'd to know
The threshold now is overpass'd . . . .
A weight of Ages did at once descend
Upon my heart.[1]

By a sort of intellectual vision he saw himself as having been *there*
and now being *here*, and this was sufficient to move him deeply.

Duration is marked and made manifest by events; and there are
passages in some of Wordsworth's poems which are perhaps only
too well known, in which the sole purpose seems to be to record that
something, no matter what, has happened. Throughout a number of
stanzas the metre is supported by little more than expletives, repeti-
tions and tautologies; our attention is claimed, it seems, only that it
may be cheated of an object – for the stanzas contain neither narration
nor description, and very little reflection. The reader is exacerbated
or wearied, though Wordsworth, presumably, is full of excitement:
so that when something finally happens, if only the prevarication of
a child or an old man's tears, it is hailed with relief.

Passages of this kind are little more than biographical or psychological curiosities: in them, Wordsworth is so fully occupied with
abstractions the he forgets the concrete business of living. But when
he returns he is the better qualified to face its problems, having a
keener eye for their elements. The external world, for example, he
sees quite clearly is not to be subdued or placated like an enemy; in
so far as it is external, it is there while we are here, then while we are
now: it is irreducibly *other* than ourselves, so that to stand in any
relation to it, to affect it, even to be aware of it, seems to imply a
contradiction. If we wish to give any account of it, we can employ
only adjectives which are the opposites of those which we apply to
ourselves: if we are active then it is immobile; if we are alive then it
is dead, as points in space are dead. Yet it is in such a world that he
finds himself, and with which he must come to terms, on pain of
a sense of desertion blanker than that to which he was first summoned
by the pursuing mountain.

His solution seems to be something like the following. He imagines
– but imagine is a weak word; he creates and it is a part of his own
experience – a kind of being in which both the external world and
himself can share. It combines the characters of both: internally it is

1 *The Prelude* [1805] VIII, 699–704.

active and striving, as he is, but looked at from outside it is immobile like the world. While for himself, that is, he renounces the possibility of action upon other things, he need not on that account feel cut off from them. They and he are united by the common possession of a hidden activity, in the knowledge of which he can feel, while among them, at home and at peace. If his spirit is sealed, so is that of the dead Lucy, so are rocks and stones and trees; and with dead things he has a sort of sympathy. The universe as thus apprehended has no very remote resemblance to *The Simplon Pass*: if it cannot quite properly be spoken of as a balance of stresses, it yet contains a number of stresses which, though they are active, produce no alteration. At these moments of apprehension Wordsworth describes himself as 'seeing into the life of things' or, elsewhere, as seeing 'the very pulse of the machine'. The word 'machine' is important, for it gives that sense of change within stability which I am trying to suggest. And the pulse is conveyed in verses, some of which are among the best he wrote, which describe ambiguous creatures like the horse

>   ... that stood
> Alone upon a little breast of ground
> With a clear silver moonlight sky behind.
> With one leg from the ground the creature stood
> Insensible and still – breath, motion gone,
> Hairs, colour, all but shape and substance gone,
> Mane, ears and tail, as lifeless as the trunk
> That had no stir of breath; we paused awhile
> In pleasure of the sight, and left him there
> With all his functions silently sealed up,
> Like an amphibious work of Nature's hand,
> A Borderer dwelling betwixt life and death.

The horse has one foot off the ground, and that it is clear he might move is one of the reasons for the pleasure which he gives; the other reason is that he is restrained from moving, or that he restrains himself. Similar to the horse in this way are the solitary beings whom Wordsworth met at night, or in almost permanently lonely places: like the discharged soldier, who remained 'fix'd to his place', 'at his feet His shadow lay, and moved not'. 'I wish'd to see him move,' exclaims Wordsworth, that he might be assured of the reality of the soldier; but when at last the soldier did so

> I beheld
> With ill-suppress'd astonishment his tall
> And ghostly figure moving at my side.[1]

Most carefully drawn of them all is the leech-gatherer, who is compared both to a 'huge stone', and to a 'sea-beast' – that is, he is capable of locomotion, but will not engage upon it. He is

> Motionless as a cloud ...
> That heareth not the loud winds when they call

– he does not hear, not in the sense that he is deaf, but that he will not obey –

> And moveth all together, if it move at all.

I do not know whether Wordsworth was acquainted with the doctrine of the school that all motion is by parts; whether or no, something of the kind has a share in the effect which is intended here. 'The cloud must move all together' – that is, it cannot be imagined to move, for if it did one part would be seen to take precedence of another; and yet it may move, for otherwise it would not have a share in being, in reality.

So far as I know, Wordsworth was quite new, and has remained unique, in concerning himself with 'being as such': the old phrase is convenient, in spite or because of its habit of bearing now the minimum, now the maximum of meaning. He explored the significance, or examined the experience, of being for other things, and this modified the experience of being for himself. It would be a mistake, I think, to see in this any influence of contemporary German thought: there is a difficulty about the dates. Wordsworth was not sympathetic to German thinkers, and the whole course of his dealing with the problem suggests that it was posed for him by what he lived through, rather than by what he read or what he heard in Coleridgean conversation. And as the achievement in this matter was his own, he used it as the starting-point for a new enterprise.

The problem of suffering, if he awoke to it later than to that of the external world, came in early manhood to occupy him no less

1 *The Prelude*, IV, 432-4.

Suffering = X

continually. The notion of being at which he arrived seemed to offer promise of a solution. For if suffering arises from thwarted effort, either to affect other things or to avoid being affected by them, it is a consequence of a creature's desire to operate beyond itself. And if this is renounced, as Wordsworth conceived it might and should be, suffering as the occasion of rebellion or complaint will cease. But is it humanly possible to carry renunciation to the point which may be necessary? It is conceivable that other things should close in to such an extent upon a creature that, if he yields to them, any inner activity left is too insignificant to be called human. There are three poems which are perhaps especially important by the answers they return to this question.

They are *The Leech-Gatherer*, *The Lesser Celandine*, and *Michael*. It will be possible to notice them only briefly.

When he comes across the leech-gatherer Wordsworth is a man of moods, and he generalizes from himself to the human race:

As high as we have mounted in delight,
In our dejection do we sink as low.

But the leech-gatherer, like the stone to which he is compared, knows no moods; he has few hopes, and such disappointments as come his way do not disturb him. Though the stock of leeches has dwindled, and they are to be found only by wandering alone about the weary moors,

   Yet still I persevere, and find them where I may.

He preserves a courteous and cheerful demeanour, even 'stately in the main'. Wordsworth marvels there should be 'in that decrepit man so firm a mind'; and contrasting the firmness with his own levity, which is at the mercy of other things, he accepts the implied rebuke.

The Lesser Celandine usually closes its petals against the foul weather:

But lately, one rough day, this Flower I passed
And recognized it, though an altered form,
Now standing forth an offering to the blast,
And buffeted at will by rain and storm.
I stopped and said with inly muttered voice,

'It doth not love the shower, nor seek the cold:
This neither is its courage nor its choice,
But necessity in being old.

The sunshine may not cheer it, nor the dew,
It cannot help itself in its decay.'

Other things have compelled the Celandine to forfeit the last scrap
of independence and dignity; therefore it can administer no rebuke –
it cannot be admired, but only deplored.

Nevertheless, it has had what might be considered its due of glory:
if it falls a victim, it is only to the forces of time and senility about
which, as nothing escapes them, there seems something equitable.
In *Michael* the shepherd and his family are involved in a similar fate
while still in their prime – for the old man is 'strong and hale' – and
although they have taken every measure to avoid it. Like the leech-
gatherer they make few claims on life:

Our lot is a hard lot; the sun himself
Has scarcely been more diligent than I;

they are 'neither gay perhaps, nor cheerful'; and if they have objects
and hopes, it is for 'a life of eager industry', for the continued
performance of the tasks which their ancestors performed before
them. Their only pleasure is 'the pleasure which there is in life itself',
that which is necessary to the pulse and implied in the spark of
consciousness. They are submissive to the natural course of things,
of which their tasks are almost a part; and, had circumstances
permitted, it might have been said of them as of their ancestors, that
when

At length their time was come, they were not loth
To give their bodies to the family mould.

They seek to preserve a submissiveness even to their abnormal
afflictions; and the hopes and fears which these cannot but provoke,
if wild, are immediately curbed. Each watches the other for signs
of strain:

                    the Old Man paused
And Isabel sat silent. . . .
. . . her face brightened. The Old Man was glad.

At night Isabel

Heard him, how he was troubled in his sleep:
And when they rose at morning she could see
That all his hopes were gone.

Here it is the ready confidence of the son which redresses the balance:

She said to Luke, while they two by themselves
Were sitting by the door, 'Thou must not go ...
For if thou leave thy Father he will die.'
The youth made answer with a jocund voice;
And Isabel, when she had told her fears,
Recovered heart.

But Luke, too, has his misgivings; and, when setting on his journey
he reaches the public way, he finds it necessary to 'put on a bold face'.
All is in vain; Luke is driven into exile, and Michael survives hardly
as a man but as an animal – by his brute strength.

His bodily frame had been from youth to age
Of an unusual strength

is the first thing we are told about him, and almost the last. He is,
moreover, a sick animal, able to perform some but not all of his instinctive tasks. When he visited the site of the projected sheepfold

He never lifted up a single stone.

The verse of the poem is a delicate thing. It has almost ceased to
beat, and seems maintained only by the flutter of tenuous hopes and
sickening fears.

                    the unlooked-for claim
At the first hearing for a moment took
More hope out of his life than he supposed
That any old man ever could have lost.

Wordsworth, who was so often an imitator, here speaks with his own
voice; and the verse is the contribution he makes to prosody. He
uses it rarely – elsewhere than in *Michael*, only, I think, in *Margaret*
and occasionally in *The Brothers*; but it should be taken as a measure
of his work. Against it the verse of *The Simplon Pass*, though very

different in intention, reveals itself as forced and harsh. As I believe I suggested, what is noble in *The Simplon Pass* is in a measure debased by the immediate context.

From *Michael* it appeared that the extinction of suffering is the extinction of humanity. To be sure of this lesson, it had been necessary for Wordsworth to experience suffering in an exquisite form, unadulterated in any way, as, for example, with the satisfaction of playing either to himself or to an audience. There is no audience in *Michael* except shepherds too close to the hero to do anything but 'feel pity in their heart'.

I do not know that any other poet has done quite the same thing; I do not think that Wordsworth did it either before or since. It is as though he exposed a nerve which, as it was too sensitive for the impressions it could not but receive, must immediately be deadened.

The conclusions of both *The Leech-Gatherer* and *The Lesser Celandine* suggest that something like this happened. Though both are less intense than *Michael*, neither maintains such intensity as it possesses to the end: suddenly both run down with a sickening whir – or, to change the metaphor, the music in both poems is broken by a discord. After the discovery of firmness in the leech-gatherer, Wordsworth does not prepare himself for any rigorous self discipline: he 'laughs himself to scorn':

'God', said I, 'be my help and stay secure;
I'll think of the Leech-gatherer on the lonely moor!'

In this jauntiness there is no relevance to his circumstances. It is as though he had become oblivious of these; as though they were now presented to the deadened nerve: and the jauntiness had opportunity to supervene from a disconnected part of his consciousness. In *The Lesser Celandine* the break is even more noticeable. It happens in the last line of a stanza:

'The sunshine may not cheer it, nor the dew;
It cannot help itself in its decay;
Stiff in its members, withered, changed of hue.'
And in my spleen, I smiled that it was grey.

To be a Prodigal's Favourite – then, worse truth,
A Miser's Pensioner – behold our lot!
O Man, that from thy fair and shining youth
Age might but take the things Youth needed not!

The word 'spleen' has a multitude of meanings, one of which might
be suitable to the poem; but there is no reason, other than a complete
abandonment of seriousness, why Wordsworth should smile. And
this would explain the final stanza, which is the sort of platitude with
which we dismiss an argument when we have not solved it, and when
it has come to weary us; or the copy book maxim with which we hand
over a vexing problem of conduct to chance for its decision. Wordsworth's maxim is not so much irrelevant to his problem as a denial
of the conditions which it presupposes. The Celandine cannot help
itself in its decay – 'if only it could!' observes the final stanza.

But, as though foreseeing the outcome of the solution attempted
in *Michael*, already in *Margaret* Wordsworth had prepared for another way of dealing with suffering. Unlike *Michael*, *Margaret* plays
to an audience, who are the author and the Wanderer; and like all
spectators of tragedy, in so far as mere spectators, they are in the role
of *tertius gaudens*. Evil to the actor is good to them. Some of the better
poems of the middle years – up to *Peele Castle* and beyond – are
devoted in part at least to affirming the belief that evil is in addition
and in some way good. The belief may be true, or may be necessary;
but as, without revelation or an augmentation of the faculties, it
cannot be comprehended without at least partly neglecting evil, the
poems, if they can be looked down on from no mean height, can
certainly be looked down on from *Michael*. Others of Wordsworth's
occupations were, with the help of the optimistic Hartley, refashioning his memories of the past so that they might support the belief
(and hence *The Prelude*, in passages like the two we have examined,
is of the nature of a palimpsest); or inditing scholarly poems and less
disinterested ones on behalf of patriotism, Anglicanism and the like.
Some of these have already received summary notice.

But an exploratory paper is no occasion to draw the lower con-
tours of Wordsworth's poetry. It is enough to indicate the high peaks;
for even about these – I hope I may be forgiven this last repetition –
a distant observer is likely to be mistaken.
(33–55)

J. S. Lyon

'The Diction of *The Excursion*', *The Excursion: A Study* 1950

The diction of *The Excursion* constitutes one of the most marked deviations of Wordsworth from his earlier practice and theory. It has long been recognized that in *The Excursion* the effort to approximate the real language of country people and to observe the prose order and choice of words has been largely abandoned.

There is really a surprising resemblance between many phrases in *The Excursion* and the 'poetic diction' of eighteenth-century poets that Wordsworth denounced in the famous Preface and Essay Supplementary to the Preface of *Lyrical Ballads*. The following list of some of the more striking examples will illustrate this correspondence. Wherever necessary for clarity, the example is followed by a parenthetical translation into 'the real language of men'.

Book	Line	Phrase
II	100	the fleet coursers they bestride
II	719	[the sun's] substantial orb
III	3	[falcons'] clamorous agitation
III	42	copious rains have magnified the stream
III	50	a semicirque of turf-clad ground
III	541	shining giver of the day diffuse (sun)
IV	180	visual orbs (eyes)
IV	450	the feathered kinds (birds)
IV	460	etherial vault (sky)
IV	858	blazing chariot of the sun
IV	1179	Athwart the concave of the dark blue dome (across the night sky)[1]
V	138	sacred pile (church)
VII	843	The forked weapon of the skies (lightning)
VIII	461	A reverend pile (parsonage)
IX	491–4	A hawk ... cleaves ... With correspondent wings the abyss of air.

These flowery circumlocutions would hardly be recognized as Wordsworthian, yet they are in the best tradition of poetic embellish-

1 Wordsworth speaks of 'the concave' of the sky three times in *The Excursion*.

ment and probably indicate a greater familiarity with both eighteenth-century poetry and books of style and rhetoric.

A similar extension of style is apparent in Wordsworth's choice of modifiers in *The Excursion*.

Book	Line	Phrase
III	17	spot so parsimoniously endowed
III	523	unendangered myrtle
III	974	conglobulated bubbles
IV	245	reiterated steps
IV	456	sedentary fowl
IV	793	contiguous torrent
IV	884	goat's depending beard
IV	1160	circumambient walls
V	84	copious stream
VII	193	unsedentary master
VII	620	fleece-encumbered flock
VII	745	indefatigable fox
VIII	66	Examples efficacious
VIII	450	commodious walk
VIII	557	capacious surface [of a smooth blue stone!]
IX	6	unenduring clouds

There are many other expressions in *The Excursion* which have this tone of verbose formality and which are not simple and plain. For example:

Book	Line	Expression
Passim		from out
I	49	nothing willingly
V	269	amusive
VI	18	what time [when]
VII	6	" " "
IX	781	peradventure

Occasionally words appear in *The Excursion* which seem distinctly prosaic. It is perhaps hazardous to call any particular word a prose word, because it is easy to imagine a Donne or a Dickinson making very successful poetic use of almost any word that may be suggested.

However, Wordsworth did not have their transforming skill, and therefore it is safe to say that the following words, among others, are distinctly prosaic in his hands. He used them only in *The Excursion.*

appendage	hatchment
cognizable	incalculably
connatural	preponderates
contiguous	presumptuousness
deciphered	self-disparagement
discomfitures	unambitiously
disencumbering	unobnoxious
disesteem	unstigmatized
disproportioned	

There are occasional archaisms in *The Excursion,* but they occur with no greater frequency than elsewhere in Wordsworth's poetry and therefore represent no significant factor in the development of his style from plainness to ornateness.

It is noticeable even in the lists already presented in this chapter that words of Latin derivation predominate over those of Old English derivation. This represents a real trend in Wordsworth's diction by the time of *The Excursion.* A study of 781 words which occur with significantly greater frequency in *The Excursion* than elsewhere in Wordsworth reveals that among such words those of Latin origin predominate over those of Old English origin in a ratio of approximately five to two, and a list of 717 words which occur only in *The Excursion* shows almost invariably Latin derivations. Conversely, in a list of 392 words which occur significantly less frequently in *The Excursion* than elsewhere in Wordsworth, Old English derivations are in the majority. The same proportions hold true for the lengths of these words and show a marked tendency on the part of Wordsworth to adopt and make use of more and more trisyllables and polysyllables and at the same time to depend less on monosyllables. Thus the vocabulary of *The Excursion* is made up of decidedly longer and more Latin words than is the vocabulary of his previous works, which accounts for the impression of sonorousness and verbosity made by the poem.

Another pronounced tendency of the diction of Wordsworth in

The Excursion is the increasing use of negative adjectives. Probably in an effort to lend depth or variety to his vocabulary, Wordsworth frequently used the negative form of an adjective of opposite meaning from the positive adjective which might be expected. In fact, there are over a hundred negative adjectives in *The Excursion* which occur nowhere else in Wordsworth, many of them exceedingly awkward. For example:

unambitious	unobnoxious
unavengeable	unredressed
uncountenanced	unsearchable
undistempered	unseconded
unelbowed	unsubstantialized
unescutcheoned	unvoyageable
unimprisoned	unwealthy

A similar increase in the use of hyphenated forms, also occasionally producing awkwardness, seems to result from a desire for greater accuracy and detail of description. Over 125 hyphenated forms were used by Wordsworth in *The Excursion* which occur nowhere else in his works.

It is interesting to notice in passing that in most of the tendencies discussed so far in this chapter the diction of *The Excursion* corresponds much more closely with that of *An Evening Walk*, *Descriptive Sketches*, and *The Borderers* than with that of the intervening works, which might indicate that in *The Excursion* Wordsworth was in some respects returning to the more detached, topographical, traditional diction of these early works.

Some of the shifts in diction apparent in *The Excursion* may reflect the changing interests of an older man. For example, words often associated with the security of later life, such as 'peace', 'rest', 'tranquillity', 'stillness', 'calm', 'comfort' and 'leisure', are increasingly used in *The Excursion*, as are words referring to death and the transience of life, and words showing an awareness of pain and misery. Words reflecting domestic concern are also more frequent: 'house', 'habitation', 'household', parent', 'husband', 'partner', 'matron', 'maternal', 'children' and 'little-one'. However, many of these increases are called for by the subject matter of the poem and their value as evidence of a changing Wordsworth must not be insisted upon.

The Excursion has been called 'a tissue of elevated but abstract verbiage', and one of the commonest criticisms of the poem has been that the diction is too abstract and lacking in the concrete sensuousness that usually characterizes poetry. Wordsworth, it is felt, has abandoned minute observation of nature and turned to metaphysical and political speculation. However, a careful survey of the diction of the poem reveals that Wordsworth was really continuing to extend his vocabulary among the minutiae of nature even while he was adopting more long and Latin words. For example, the following words he used only in *The Excursion*.

bind-weed	heath-plant	sweet-briar
carnations	heath-cock	trouts
chicken	knoll	vulture
currants	magpies	water-fowl
foot-path	mocking-bird	water-lily
fossils	snipe	whortle-berries
grasshoppers	stone-crop	willow-flowers

It is noteworthy that this list includes nine plants and seven birds, which testifies to Wordsworth's continuing study of and ever growing familiarity with nature. The following words occur with significantly greater frequency in *The Excursion* than elsewhere in Wordsworth.

air	leaf	shrub
beams	mountain	sods
cloud	oak	soil
dew	path	sun
dust	pool	tufts
echo	rill	turf
fowl	seas	vale
hound	seed	waves
insect	shade	wren
land	shadows	

These words also seem evidence of greater attention and enduring devotion to the small details of nature. To be compared with these are the nature words which the poet used less frequently in *The Excursion* than elsewhere.

birds	lake	rose
cataracts	moonlight	sands
fountain	morning	tempest
gleam	ocean	water
horse	pines	
island	river	

This list is so brief that one hesitates to draw inferences from it, but it is perhaps significant that a comparatively general word like 'birds' occurs less frequently, while the names of several specific birds are used for the first time, and that the poetically more conventional natural details – 'cataracts', 'tempest', 'fountain', 'moonlight', 'rose' – are relinquished, while the words used more in *The Excursion* are generally more concrete and detailed, apparently the result of closer observation and study.

Apart from nature words, *The Excursion* includes a great many concrete details, many of them as homely as anything in *Goody Blake*. Used only in *The Excursion*:

awning	cube	hemp
axle-tree	cupboard	hoe
bracelet	curd	knife
chimney-top	football	maps
chip	hay-field	quoit
copper	hay-makers	sofa

Used significantly more often in *The Excursion* than elsewhere:

bread	fire	roof
carpet	floor	shelf
cheek	limbs	sound
circle	lip	spade
coffin	liquid	veil
ear	loom	voice
eye	pillar	warmth
fabric	plough	wheel
finger	porch	

Thus it can be seen that the diction of *The Excursion* is not exclusively 'abstract verbiage'. Domestic details and details descriptive of physical man seem to be on the increase.

As a final bit of evidence that Wordsworth was not utterly given to high-flown abstraction in *The Excursion*, a sampling of the adjectives and verbs should be made.

Used only in *The Excursion*:

bare-headed	skyey
body-bending	thyme-besprinkled
brazen	ticked
cackling	turf-built
nibbled	whining
pelting	wormy
roof-high	

Used significantly more often in *The Excursion* than elsewhere:

cool	moist	tall
crooked	pale	tattered
crystal	rough	tremble
dark	rugged	vapoury
fanning	shaggy	wintry
flat	slender	wooden
hear	soft	

It is perhaps also worthy of notice that the words 'red', green', 'blue', 'grey', 'gold' and silver' occur more frequently in *The Excursion* than elsewhere, while only 'black' and 'yellow' are used less.

The diction of *The Excursion* shows Wordsworth extending his poetic vocabulary to include more long and Latin words, partly to meet the demands of a more difficult subject matter and partly in an effort to achieve a more stately, sonorous and varied style. The most surprising result of this tendency is the frequent resemblance of the diction of *The Excursion* to the 'poetic diction' of eighteenth-century poets against which he always inveighed so strenuously. The diction of *The Excursion* also offers some evidence of an effort by the poet to develop greater accuracy in description and to include more variety of concrete and sensuous detail. There are still many simple and homely words in his poetic vocabulary.

(124–30)

Donald Davie

from 'Diction and Invention: Wordsworth' *Purity of Diction in English Verse* 1952

Wordsworth was his own worst critic. Coleridge was right. The Preface to *Lyrical Ballads* is great literature; but it is great as a personal testament, not as criticism, or if as criticism, then as criticism at its most theoretical. It is not theoretical in the sense that Wordsworth did not know from personal experience what he was talking about. He did, of course; that is what is meant by calling it a testament. It is theoretical in the sense that it is wise about the nature and function of poetry and poetic pleasure, and foolish about poetic techniques.

To be particular, Wordsworth invites us to approach his poems by considering their diction; whereas most of those poems by-pass questions of diction altogether. For the question of diction only rises when a poem begs it. It is never perhaps indifferent, but it is often of little importance. In the eighteenth century this was generally acknowledged; Goldsmith, for instance, says that a chaste diction is less important in the sublime poem than in the pathetic. And it is notable that modern poets when they have approached the question, have been forced to the same distinction.[1] We may well be reluctant to reopen an old controversy which proved so often sterile; but we need 'sublime', or something like it, to classify the many poems which merely avoid questions of diction altogether.

We can do so sufficiently for the present purpose by exhuming another critical term which has fallen into disuse. I mean the notion of 'invention', or finding. There are poems which are poetic by virtue of the finding and conduct of a fable, over and above the poetry of their language. I am well aware of the dangers of this contention. It is always dangerous to divorce poetry from words and locate it in some air-drawn 'form'. Nevertheless, T. Sturge Moore is an example of the poet whose language is undistinguished, whose powers of invention, at least in his longer works, are strikingly poetic. We can call a poem 'sublime' when it displays powers of invention so conspicuously that considerations of diction, while never indifferent, are of only minor moment.

1 J. M. Synge, Preface to *The Plays and Poems of J. M. Synge* (ed. T. R. Hern) 1963, Methuen.

Now Wordsworth is a conspicuous example of a poet in whom invention is so powerful that diction hardly ever matters. De Quincey said as much in a fine passage[1] when he hailed Wordsworth as above all a discoverer of new or forgotten truths. And of no part of Wordsworth's work is this so true as of *Lyrical Ballads*. Wordsworth was technically incompetent at least until 1801, when he seems to have put himself to school with Chaucer, Shakespeare and Milton. By luck or genius (they amount to the same thing) he had before that hit upon some primitive forms which could just sustain what he had to say; and what he had found to say before that was so novel and surprising that it could carry the day. Even *The Brothers* and *Michael* are great in spite of, not because of, their language. And even so, luck failed him on occasions; for instance *The Two Thieves* of 1800 displays a nobly poetical conception (similar to *The Old Cumberland Beggar*) thrown away in an inappropriate form. The early poems, when they succeed, do so by virtue of invention; the language is as nearly irrelevant as it can be in poetry.

After the turn of the century Wordsworth emerges, through some uncomfortable experiments, as a highly accomplished poet. He creates not one style, but many, according to what he needs to do. There is the style of the political sonnets; the style of *The Prelude*; and the style of the Immortality Ode. There are others, but these are the most important. And each of these styles can be called a 'diction', in the sense of a private language, a distinctive vocabulary and turn of phrase. Wordsworth's own criticism had paved the way for this loose usage. And the shift in meaning is further obscured for us by the circumstance that some later poets, such as Arnold, made use of one or other of the Wordsworthian styles; so that we detect 'Wordsworthian diction' in other poets.

But this use of diction, to mean a private language, is the very opposite of the older one, by which it was 'the perfection of a common language'. It is only the latter of which one can say that it is pure or impure. And this is a diction which hardly ever appears in Wordsworth's work. The question of purity does not arise. Almost to the end what matters in Wordsworth is his invention, his astonishing discoveries about human sentiments. As he pieced his discoveries

1 *De Quincey's Literary Criticism* (ed. H. Darbishire, 1909), Oxford University Press, p. 234.

together into systems, he had to learn his trade and master techniques more elaborate and sophisticated than those which had served him in *Lyrical Ballads*. But at no time does the question of pure or impure diction enter into the matter.

After all, how could it? A pure diction embodies urbanity; a vicious diction offers to do that, and fails. But Wordsworth was not interested in urbanity, and had no faith in it; he pledged himself to its opposite, a determined provincialism. He spoke as a solitary, not as a spokesman; urbanity was none of his business, nor diction either. It is one way of explaining what went wrong with Wordsworth's poetry, in his later life, to say that as recognition came to him, he saw himself more and more as, after all, a spokesman of national sentiment.[1] No poet was less fitted, by training and temperament, for such a role; and no poet's art was so unsuitable for carrying it.

There are two or three exceptions. The most important is *The White Doe of Rylstone*. It is a poem which will never be popular, because it does without so many attractions incidental and usual in poetry. Alone of all Wordsworth's poems, it requires of the reader that he come to terms with the famous contention that "There neither is, nor can be, any essential difference between the language of prose and of metrical composition.' In the Preface to *Lyrical Ballads*, Wordsworth's views on diction are so ill considered that, to the reader baffled by *The White Doe of Rylstone*, they can still give little assistance. But they are far more pertinent to that poem than to any of the ballads.

The verse-form of *The White Doe* has been variously defined as derived from Scott and from Virgil. More probably, I think, the model was Samuel Daniel. A prefatory note to *Yarrow Visited* implies that Wordsworth read Daniel about the time he was reading Chaucer, soon after the turn of the century. Now Daniel was the poet selected by Coleridge, when he discussed Wordsworth's style, to exemplify the genuinely and culpably prosaic in verse:

Ten Kings had from the Norman Conqu'ror reign'd
With intermix'd and variable fate,
When England to her greatest height attain'd

1 Quite early in Wordsworth's career he began to produce patriotic sonnets on the Miltonic model, in which he aimed to express national sentiment. Some of these are widely admired; but it is an enthusiasm which I cannot share.

Of power, dominion, glory, wealth, and state;
After it had with much ado sustain'd
The violence of princes, with debate
For titles and the often mutinies
Of nobles for their ancient liberties.

For first, the Norman, conqu'ring all by might,
By might was forced to keep what he had got;
Mixing our customs and the form of right
With foreign constitutions, he had brought;
Mast'ring the mighty, humbling the poorer wight,
By all severest means that could be wrought;
And, making the succession doubtful, rent
His new-got state, and left it turbulent.

These are two of the stanzas quoted from Daniel by Coleridge; and
it would be hard to find in English poetry another passage so similar
as this from *The White Doe*:

It was the time when England's Queen
Twelve years had reigned, a Sovereign dread;
Nor yet the restless crown had been
Disturbed upon her virgin head;
But now the inly-working North
Was ripe to send its thousands forth,
A potent vassalage, to fight
In Percy's and in Neville's right,
Two earls fast leagued in discontent,
Who gave their wishes open vent;
And boldly urged a general plea,
The rites of ancient piety
To be triumphantly restored,
By the stern justice of the sword!
And that same Banner, on whose breast
The blameless Lady had exprest
Memorials chosen to give life
And sunshine to a dangerous strife;
That Banner, waiting for the Call,
Stood quietly in Rylstone-hall.

It seems likely that those who dislike *The White Doe* as prosaic can call upon the authority of Coleridge.

And yet the comparison is unjust. For if Wordsworth's verse has 'the virtues of good prose' (as Daniel's has), it has also a felicitous concentration that can only be called poetic. That Wordsworth's account of the reasons for the Rising of the North should tally with the findings of modern historians is interesting, but not so important as the consistency and conciseness of his treatment. A modern editor[1] has drawn attention to the propriety of 'inly-working', pithily characterizing the complicated discontents which were at work. Dynastic and personal quarrels lay behind the insurrection and were the cause of it at least as much as the stubborn adherence to the Old Faith. Wordsworth's acknowledgement of this colours his whole treatment, and gives an ironic aptness, for instance, to his account of the banner. Embroidered with the Cross and the wounds of Christ, it was to give 'life and sunshine to a dangerous strife'; 'sunshine' is played off against the 'inly-working', expressing the symbolic with the actual function of the flag, and throwing on the whole enterprise the shadow of divided loyalties and coming doom. More, the theme of the whole poem, the hard-won serenity of the abandoned lady, symbolized in her creature, the doe, is an example of just such 'inly-working'.

In the verse of *The White Doe of Rylstone*, Wordsworth achieved, as nowhere else in a poem of any length, a pure diction, a speech of civilized urbanity which can 'purify the language of the tribe'. Of course, the poem exhibits only one mode of such a diction, the mode proper to the peculiar purpose of historical narrative, and to the correspondent tone, neither elevated nor intimate, of the so-called 'mean style'. This is a staple verse and does not lend itself to purple passages, though Coleridge, who thought Wordsworth a poet of purple passages, claimed to find one. Throughout, the verse maintains one level of subdued excellence. There are impurities,[2] but they are

1 Comparetti, *The White Doe of Rylstone* (*Cornell Studies in English*, vol. 24), 1940.
2 An example of such 'impurity' may help – lines 720, 721:
Like those eight Sons – who, in a ring,
(Ripe men or blooming in life's spring . . .).
– where the second line is too 'literary'. Wordsworth tried to change it in 1827, but returned to this version in the 1837 text.

few. The verse of *The White Doe*, a poem which Wordsworth believed
to be 'in conception, the highest work he had ever produced', answers
to the programme announced in the Preface to *Lyrical Ballads*; but not
to the programme which Coleridge would have substituted. It is
notable, for instance, that the poem avoids personification and
generalization, those components of the diction which Wordsworth
rejected. Miss Comparetti has shown that *The White Doe* depends
upon an abstraction, upon the 'melancholy', not of Shakespeare and
Robert Burton, nor of Matthew Arnold, but of Thomson and Gray,
the Miltonic 'melancholy' which is strong and composed. The poem
depends on that notion; but, true to his principles, Wordsworth
eschews all reference to it as a personified abstraction, and embodies
it instead in the symbolic or emblematic figure of 'the doe'. By so
doing, he reaped just the benefits which he had promised himself.
For Melancholy had been handled so often by the decadent poets of
the sensibility-cult that in its form as a personified abstraction it was
unmanageable to any serious ends; Wordsworth, adopting a diction
which did not permit him to personify, was able to make the Miltonic
melancholy once again a respectable topic and a moral force.

I have called the doe 'a symbolic or emblematic figure'. One
hesistates to find in the doe the force of a symbol; and yet it is hard
to say that it is anything else. Wordsworth was right when he
compared it with the 'milk-white lamb' in *The Faerie Queene*. *The
White Doe* is a thoroughly Spenserian poem. For all the great difference between Spenser's opulent rhetoric and the sobriety of Wordsworth's language, although the structure has none of Spenser's
complexity, although Wordsworth does not think in Spenser's
terms, we infer a marked similarity between the ways of thought
and feeling which produced the two poems. Wordsworth speaks of
Una's lamb as 'that emblem'; and there is no need to quarrel about
terms. If the doe is symbolic, it is so as Una's lamb is, or Dryden's
hind, or the statue of Hermione in *The Winter's Tale*. These figures
seem to arise from conceptions dwelt upon so intently that they assume
at last a wraith-like substance and life. They are quite different from
such recognized 'symbols' as Perdita–Marina, the girl lost and found,
on Blake's Little Boy Lost, or Wordsworth's own man upon the moor
who stands or strides or sits, wreathed in mist, through poem after
poem. These others are the images which walk about the poet's

mind, asking to be explained. The poetry which uses them is a poetry of wise passiveness; the poetry which uses symbols of the other kind is a work of will, of contrivance and persistence, not a finding but a making.

The poem cannot be appreciated until we realize this effort of will behind it, and the internal tension which that produces. On a first reading it appears innocent of compression, concentration, contrast or irony. There seems to be no tension, whether in the eddying narrative or the fluent language. This impression must persist until the reader can cultivate an ear or a palate for diction, for a central purity; then the tension appears, in our awareness of the words that have been left out. Because the tone is less elevated, it is easy to miss the point that the poem is written in a choice language, as *The Deserted Village* is, or *The Task*. Once we appreciate that, the poem takes its place in the line of activity inaugurated by the *Ode to Duty*, or, even earlier, in *Resolution and Independence*. In these poems Wordsworth acknowledges that the first springs of his creativeness have dried up, and that what comes after can be no longer buoyant with invention, with new discoveries given, but must be worked for, with self-discipline. At least, this is the implication for his art of the changes Wordsworth announces in his morality. Will and duty are to take the place of idleness and spontaneity. Perhaps Wordsworth misjudged the situation or his own temperament: at any rate the new programme was much poorer than the old one, from the point of view of the poems it produced; and one is inclined to agree with Dr Leavis that 'The Wordsworth who in the *Ode to Duty* spoke of the "genial sense of youth" as something he happily surrendered had seen the hiding-places of his power close.'[1] But *The White Doe of Rylstone* seems to me one poem in which the new programme justified itself. The heroine is herself the embodiment of resolution, endurance, and the will kept at a stretch: for all her exclusively passive role (here is the paradox, the pathos, and most of the interest), the lady, by embracing that role as a duty, makes of it something active, resolute and noble. This is Wordsworth's original and compelling variation on the theme of Miltonic melancholy. And apart from this, regarded from the poet's point of view, *The White Doe* itself is similarly an achievement of resolution, effort and self-denying endurance. It is the most

1 *Revaluation*, Chatto & Windus, 1936, p. 183.

absolutely 'made' thing that Wordsworth ever produced. It is free-standing, in its own right; not, like *The Prelude* or, to a lesser degree, *The Excursion*, taking half of its strength along the cord which still connects the poem to its parent. *The White Doe* is impersonal and self-contained, thrown free of its creator with an energy he never compassed again. He tried again, but with little success, in *Laodamia*. (111-21)

F. W. Bateson

from *Wordsworth: A Re-Interpretation* 1954

Why did he write? In the complex of conscious and semi-conscious motives, was there one that can be distinguished as the efficient cause of Wordsworth's poetry?

Wordsworth's stock answer, repeated with greater and greater emphasis as his youth receded, was that he was a teacher, and that he wrote his poetry primarily in order to provide his readers with moral instruction. This is certainly the gist of the long letter that he wrote to John Wilson, who is perhaps better known as 'Christopher North' of Blackwood's, in 1802. Wilson had praised *Lyrical Ballads* for the accuracy with which human emotions were delineated there. But this account did not satisfy Wordsworth:

You have given me praise for having reflected faithfully in
my Poems the feelings of human nature. I would fain hope
that I have done so. But a great Poet ought to do more than
this: he ought, to a certain degree, to rectify men's feelings,
to give them new compositions of feeling, to render their
feelings more sane, pure, and permanent, in short, more
consonant to nature, that is, to eternal nature, and the great
moving spirit of things. He ought to travel before men
occasionally as well as at their sides.[1]

And as examples of the emotional education that the great poet must take his reader through, Wordsworth went on to mention the excessive admiration paid in the past to 'personal prowess and

1 Wordsworth to John Wilson, June 1802.

military success'. 'So with regard to birth, and innumerable other
modes of sentiment, civil and religious.' His own *Idiot Boy*, he added,
was intended to show that 'the loathing and disgust which many
people have at the sight of an idiot' is really only 'false delicacy'.

If we can trust the letter to Wilson the central doctrine preached in
the earlier poems is egalitarianism. They were written, apparently,
to convince the rich – 'Gentlemen, persons of fortune, professional
men, ladies, persons who can afford to buy, or can easily procure,
books of half-a-guinea price, hot-pressed, and printed upon superfine
paper'[1] – that they could learn a great deal from the private lives of
the poor. Wordsworth was no doubt exaggerating the didactic
elements in his poetry, but if not entirely convinced we can see today
that egalitarian propaganda was certainly one of the motives that
contributed to the writing of *Salisbury Plain*, *The Ruined Cottage* and
The Old Cumberland Beggar. It may also have operated in *Lyrical
Ballads*, though most of the ballads in the first edition were apparently
intended for the middle and lower classes rather than the rich. But
what about *Tintern Abbey*? Or the Lucy poems? Or *The Prelude*? In
so far as there is doctrine in these poems it is not, except incidentally
in *The Prelude*, the lesson of the Universal Heart but a form of
Pantheism that is being inculcated. And in preaching the Religion of
Nature Wordsworth did not address himself specifically to either the
rich or the poor. The people he was most concerned about were
those who live in towns, 'the obstreperous city', as he calls it in *The
Excursion*.[2] Love, he maintained in *The Prelude*, does not

> easily thrive
> In cities, where the human heart is sick.
> And the eye feeds it not, and cannot feed.[3]

It had been his special fortune, as he was at pains to point out, that
he had grown up

> Not with the mean and vulgar works of Man,
> But with high objects, with enduring things.[4]

With these convictions Wordsworth's poetic mission-field as the
prophet of nature was necessarily in the towns. It was the townsman

1 Wordsworth to John Wilson, June 1802.   2 Book IV, l. 369.
3 *The Prelude*, Book XII, ll. 201–3.   4 Book I, ll. 435–6.

and not the countryman who in fact read his poems, and to whom they are obviously primarily addressed. Unfortunately, however, as an early critic pointed out,[1] the prolonged access which they prescribe to nature in its grandest and wildest forms was only possible in the nineteenth century to the townsman with a large income. The urban rich could save their souls, the urban poor couldn't – a conclusion that is hardly compatible with the enthusiastic egalitarianism of the letter to Wilson.

Wordsworth never succeeded in resolving this logical contradiction between his belief in equality and his belief in the spiritual benefits to be obtained from an intimate communion with wild nature. When it was proposed to extend the railway line from Kendal to Windermere he resisted the proposal with all the eloquence he could then command (1844) in both verse and prose. But to the advocates of the extension who pointed out that the new railway would now enable the poor to enjoy the scenery of the Lake District he could only reply (in a letter to the *Morning Post*):

Rocks and mountains, torrents and wide-spread waters, and
all those features of nature which go to the composition of
such scenes as this part of England is distinguished for, cannot,
in their finer relations to the human mind, be comprehended,
or even very imperfectly conceived, without processes of
culture or opportunities of observation in some degree
habitual.'[2]

The admission, however, is fatal to a central thesis of *The Prelude* – that the basis of the good life is *unconscious* intercourse with natural beauty. Moreover the townsman who has to undergo preliminary 'processes of culture' and be provided with appropriate 'opportunities of observation' will at best only turn into another connoisseur of Picturesque Beauty, like the Reverend William Gilpin.

The honest answer to the projectors of the Kendal and Windermere Railway – that the privacy of the Lake District was a necessity for

1 George Brimley, *Essays*, pp. 129–30.
2 Wordsworth reprinted his two letters on this matter in the *Morning Post* in a pamphlet – *Kendal and Windermere Railway*, 1844. My quotation is from de Selincourt's edition of *Wordsworth's Guide to the Lakes*, 1906, p. 151, which reprints the pamphlet as Appendix II.

his own mental health – was one that Wordsworth himself could not give. It is not that he was a hypocrite, but he was a man exceptionally unaware of his own motives. At this very time, when by opposing the railway he was strenuously denying the poor opportunities already available to the rich, he used to hold forth 'with great animation' at Ambleside tea-parties, we are told, 'of the unfortunate separation between the rich and the poor in this country'.[1] Nor was this an isolated sentimentality; the long 'Postscript' that he added to the Prefaces of his poems in 1835 contains a thoroughly sensible and humane attack upon the New Poor Law. But Wordsworth's right hand did not know, and so could not understand, what his left hand was doing.

It will be apparent that this contradiction between the 'messages' Wordsworth meant his poetry to convey is one more example of the incompatibility of the Two Voices. The egalitarianism can be equated, roughly, with his 'Augustan' voice and the nature-mysticism with the 'Romantic' voice. Put into prose, in terms of conscious intentions, the dilemma could not be resolved. Each 'message' was valid up to a point, but the two half-truths, instead of adding up to a whole truth, a consistent and coherent philosophy of life, only cancel each other out. To overcome the contradiction it is necessary to go behind Wordsworth's various pronouncements about the function of his poetry to the personal motives, of which he himself was often only partly conscious, out of which all that is most genuine and original in it really emerges. In other words, if we are to look for an efficient cause of his poetry, the ultimate explanation for its being written at all, the place where we may hope to find it is not in his Prefaces, or in semi-public letters like those to Wilson or Fox, but in the recesses of his personality, the dark corners that were only partly explored even in *The Prelude*.

The boy's abysses of idealism present the problem in its simplest form. These 'Fallings from us, vanishings' are recorded with some equanimity in *Intimations of Immortality*, but it must not be forgotten that they very much alarmed Wordsworth in his early schooldays. The only way in which he found that he could rescue himself when drowning in the deep sea of subjectivity was to grasp a wall or a tree

1 'Reminiscences of Lady Richardson (1843)' are printed in *Memoirs of William Wordsworth*, 1851, II, 440.

or a gate. The sense of touch, consciously and almost desperately appealed to, provided the one effective means of return to the objective world. The touch is the most primitive of the senses, and in less acute crises the more sophisticated senses, particularly those of sight and hearing, were able to perform a similar function. Wordsworth's excitement when he discovered at the age of fourteen, how different the oak on the Hawkshead–Ambleside road looked at sunset was clearly a connected psychological phenomenon. The resolution that he made to record 'the infinite variety of natural appearances' may perhaps be regarded, from this point of view, as a more disciplined defensive strategy against the terrors of the subjective world, such as the 'huge and mighty Forms' who haunted him after he had stolen the Ullswater boat. (It will be remembered that, in addition to troubling his dreams for many days, those formidable ghosts also 'mov'd slowly through the mind By day'.) It is possible that the ultimate source of Wordsworth's passionate devotion to wild nature was the gratitude he felt to 'rocks and stones and trees' for saving him from this nightmare world. The hypothesis will help to explain the striking difference in poetic quality between the descriptions of Esthwaite Water and its surroundings and those of inherently more beautiful or more impressive scenery elsewhere. The sights and sounds of the country round Hawkshead included objects that he had in fact 'grasped', with one or other of the senses, when the nightmarish moods described in The Vale of Esthwaite had descended upon him. The later enthusiasm for the Picturesque was perhaps only a rationalization of the adolescent gratitudes. It is certainly significant that a scene exceptionally picturesque by ordinary standards – I am thinking of the magnificent sunset in the Alps so conscientiously described in Descriptive Sketches[1] – was insufficient in itself to induce poetry in Wordsworth. Such scenery was too impersonal, too objective. The brilliant catalogues in An Evening Walk of the sounds to be heard on Esthwaite Water before and after sunset are in a wholly different category. Here personal memories and associations have unconsciously given the impressionism another dimension. Although it is not always visible on the surface the poetry in these passages almost certainly derives its quality from the momentary

1 ll. 336–47.

union in Wordsworth of intense objective and subjective pressures – the eye that recorded and the emotion that was recollected.

In Wordsworth's second phase the background of subjective terror reappears in a different form. When he paid his first visit to Tintern in 1793 he was once again, in his relations with natural scenery,

> more like a man
> Flying from something that he dreads, than one
> Who sought the thing he loved.

But the 'something' had lost its vulgar supernatural quality. It is true there are Druids in the first version of Salisbury Plain, but they are much less alarming than the Druids of The Vale of Esthwaite. There is also an unpublished ballad fragment written at Racedown that is all about a ghost.[1] But the nightmare quality has gone. The subjectivity of this phase is not an abyss of idealism. Wordsworth did not need to grasp things now to assure himself of the reality of the outer world. It was rather what might be called a social subjectivity – the mood in which he 'Yielded up moral questions in despair'. The failure of his own plans and ambitions, his unintended desertion of Annette and Caroline, the war with France, and the degeneration of revolutionary idealism into Robespierre's Reign of Terror had combined to deprive him not only of a social function for himself but of a content to the very concept of society. And the return to sanity was by a process of sympathetic self-identification with other social outcasts. In the anti-social nightmare he was still able from time to time to 'grasp' the basic human traits exhibited by such companions in his misfortune as Peter Bell's original or the heroine of We are Seven. It cannot be an accident that, with only one or two important exceptions, all the poems Wordsworth wrote during the five years between the summer of 1793 and the summer of 1798 are concerned with social outcasts and misfits, whose natural goodness and purity are contrasted with the treatment they receive from an indifferent and inhuman social order. By identifying himself subjectively with dramatis personae as objectively different from himself as the hero and heroine of Salisbury Plain, the Margaret of The Ruined Cottage, the Cumberland Beggar, Poor Susan, Goody Blake, Simon Lee and

1 The MS. is in the so-called Racedown Notebook, now in the Wordsworth Museum, Grasmere.

the others he was able to overcome in himself the temptations to moral nihilism represented by Oswald in *The Borderers* and the wicked mother in *The Three Graves*. In the process of understanding them he was learning to understand and accept his own position in an ideal society.

The third phase is more complex and more difficult to define. A more minute analysis will be necessary not only because the egocentric period includes what are generally considered Wordsworth's greatest poems but also because of the remarkable extension of poetic range that it exhibits. In addition to the autobiographical poems like *Tintern Abbey* and *The Prelude* and such quasi-autobiographical poems as *Resolution and Independence*, *Intimations of Immortality* and the *Ode to Duty*, there are poems like *Michael* and *The Sailor's Mother* that seem at first sight to be reversions to the second phase, as well as more fanciful pieces like the Lucy series and *Ruth* that are different from either group. It is true that a biographical unity in this diversity is provided by Dorothy. Some of the poems are about her, others are devoted to topics that were especially congenial to her, and a great many are about that childhood period that Wordsworth felt he shared with his sister in a special sense. But, though Dorothy's presence or influence serves as a connecting link between these poems, it does not altogether account for the fusion of subjective and objective attitudes in them.

A clue is perhaps provided by the appearance of a new feature in Wordsworth's poetry during this phase. The new feature is the recurring metaphors. In the earlier poems the metaphors are generally conventional and commonplace, but in 1798 they suddenly attain an almost Shakespearian vigour. A characteristic example of the metaphors of this third phase is the image describing the impression Windermere made upon the young Wordsworth, as he and his friends returned from Bowness, in the second book of *The Prelude*:

> Oh! then the calm
> And dead still water lay upon my mind
> Even with a weight of pleasure, and the sky
> Never before so beautiful, sank down
> Into my heart, and held me like a dream.[1]

1 *The Prelude*, Book II, ll. 176–80.

The impact of nature on the passive consciousness was described, it
will be remembered, in similar gravitational imagery in *There was a
Boy*. But it is the active appreciation of natural beauty that is the real
theme of *The Prelude*, and this intimate cooperation between the
human subject and the natural object is expressed in Wordsworth's
poems of this period in images of eating and drinking. The images
recur so frequently that they must be considered symbolic rather than
merely metaphorical. There are three examples in *Tintern Abbey*
alone,[1] and similar images are to be found in some of the finest
passages in *The Prelude*. As a child, it will be remembered, he

> held unconscious intercourse
> With the eternal Beauty, drinking in
> A pure organic pleasure from the lines
> Of curling mist . . .[2]

There were also those mysterious sounds that he heard at night

> Thence did I drink the visionary power . . .[3]

And the gap in the mist on Snowdon that seemed to him

> The perfect image of a mighty Mind
> Of one that feeds upon infinity. . . .[4]

Other examples of eating and drinking images have already been
quoted earlier in this book.

The Wordsworthian religion of nature seems to be implicit in these
recurrent metaphors. Their primitive, infantile character, for one
thing, shows how personal and subjective it was. In order to define
his feelings in the presence of wild nature Wordsworth had to use some
of the earliest and simplest sensations known to man. In *Expostulation
and Reply* – which was written in June 1798, only a month or so
before *Tintern Abbey* – both weight and food images are associated,
not altogether surprisngly, with a kind of animism:

> Nor less I deem that there are powers,
> Which of themselves our minds impress,
> That we can feed this mind of ours,
> In a wise passiveness.

1 ll. 64, 80, 227.   2 Book I, ll. 589–92.   3 Book II, l. 330.
4 Book XIII, ll. 69–70.

These natural 'powers' reappear in several early drafts of *The Prelude* and its offshoots, such as *Nutting*, as 'Gentle powers' 'powers of earth', 'genii', 'beings of the hills', 'spirits of the springs', etc. They are certainly not entirely conventional, though Wordsworth would no doubt have denied them phenomenal existence. In some of the shorter poems the moon and the stars have also been animated in the same way. It seems difficult to deny to this phase what R. D. Havens has called 'a reversion to primitive ways of thinking' in Wordsworth.[1]

What was the psychological condition which this insistent primitivism reflects? It is possible that the instinctive regression to childhood should be seen as an unconscious attempt to return to the childish pre-sexual relationship with Dorothy; Wordsworth's conception of wild nature is certainly curiously sexless. Or perhaps it was simply a profound reaction against the fragmentary, disconnected mode of life into which he had drifted since he left Cambridge, whose dangers had now been dramatically illustrated when he and Dorothy found themselves in love? I go on using the word, because it is the right word to use, but I am not suggesting, of course, that there was a physical consummation. All that was 'Augustan' in Wordsworth wanted there not to be – and was terrified at its mere possibility. There is a curious tribute to Coleridge's beneficial influence at this period at the end of *The Prelude* (1850 text):

Thy kindred influence to my heart of hearts
Did also find its way. Thus fear relaxed
Her overweening grasp; thus thoughts and things
In the self-haunting spirit learned to take
More rational proportions. . . .[2]

The revival of the subjective terrors recalls the boy's abysses of idealism, and there is perhaps a parallel between Wordsworth's 'grasping' natural objects and 'eating' an animated nature to escape fear's 'overweening grasp'. The animism assumed 'More rational proportions' as Wordsworth began to re-establish the sense of personal continuity by a conscious technique of emotion recollected in tranquillity. The process consisted, essentially, in restoring to con-

1 *The Mind of a Poet*, John Hopkins Press, 1941, p. 84.
2 Book XIV (1850), ll. 281–5.

sciousness and order the periods and events of his personal life that were lurking haphazardly in the depths of his memory. Its master-piece, of course, is *The Prelude*, but the theme of personal continuity is to be traced in most of the great poems of this phase. It is certainly present, as we have seen, in 'There was a Boy'. Wordsworth's psychological objective is summed up in a fragment of Coleridge's that was written at this very time (*c.* 1803):

... There does not exist a more important rule nor one
more fruitful in its consequences, moral as well as logical,
than the rule of connecting our present mind with our past –
from the breach of it result almost all the pernicious errors in
our education of children and indeed of our general
treatment of our fellow creatures.'[1]

The mental continuity aimed at by both Wordsworth and Coleridge was organic rather than rational. The metaphor in *The Prelude*'s sub-title ('Growth of a Poet's Mind') – unlike the poem's title the sub-title is Wordsworth's own – was not by any means a dead one. Indeed, as the deliberate anti-rationalism of 'She dwelt among the untrodden ways' has demonstrated, the secondary power that multiplies distinctions represented for Wordsworth one of the principal agents of discontinuity. There is among the MSS. at Grasmere a most interesting unpublished essay by Wordsworth, apparently written at Goslar, which contrasts the weakness of merely rational decisions with the powers of habit on the mind. Its general trend can be gauged from the opening sentences:

I think publications in which we formally & systematically
lay down rules for the actions of man (?) cannot be too long
delayed. I shall scarcely express myself too strongly when I
say that I consider such books as Mr Godwyn's, Mr Paley's &
those of the whole tribe of authors of that class as impotent to
all their intended good purposes, to which I wish I could add
that they were equally impotent to all bad ones. ... I know
no book or system of moral philosophy written with
sufficient power to melt into our affections, to incorporate
itself with the blood & vital juices of our minds, & thence to

1 Alice D. Snyder, *Coleridge on Logic and Learning*, Yale University Press, 1929, p. 60.

have any influence worth our notice in forming those habits
of which I am speaking.[1]

As against Paley, the Christian rationalist, and Godwin, the rational
anarchist, Wordsworth was feeling his way in this third phase, the
last genuinely creative phase, to a religion and a political philosophy
based upon man's primal instincts. It was literally a matter of 'feeling'
his way, and feeling did not always prove a reliable guide. But,
whatever the failures in practice, his programme of psychic integration – of the unification of the sensibility, as Mr Eliot would call it –
must surely be commended. Instead of relying solely on the senses, as
when he was struggling in the abysses of idealism, or solely on the
emotions, as in his second phase, he was now trying to rebuild his
personality on the basis of an emotional life rooted in the senses.
The 'affections' were not enough. The disembodied affections had
led into the ecstatic, explosive intimacy with Dorothy. In future, as
in childhood, he would integrate the affections with 'the blood &
vital juices'.

Why did he write? The question has now received a partial answer.
The efficient cause, so far as the poetry had a single originating
source, was the impelling need Wordsworth felt to integrate the more
subjective or inward-looking and the more objective or outward-
looking aspects of his personality. The poetry, it turns out, was not
so much autobiography as a technique of self-preservation and self-
recreation.

As part of the process of re-establishing his own mental health
Wordsworth found himself dramatizing in verse a series of situations
that paralleled or symbolized the regimen on which he was embark-
ing on his own person. This homoeopathic procedure was primarily
an unconscious one. The character of the Female Vagrant, for
example, cannot have been created in order that Wordsworth might
have an opportunity to try out on paper, as it were, a possible attitude
to his own personal disasters. But, if he was not wholly aware of the
relationship between his life and his poetry, he must soon have discovered that there were interconnections between them. The dilemma
of his personal life was that solitude, even when mitigated by the

1 MS. JJ of *The Prelude*, Wordsworth Museum, Grasmere.

company of one or two intimates, carried with it the potential threat
of melancholia, the condition that Coleridge called Wordsworth's
'hypochondriacism', while its opposite, the social life of a city,
tended to smother and frustrate all that was most original and creative
in him. And the conflicting 'pulls', either to a solitary communion
with wild nature or to all-night arguments with fellow-intellectuals in
Cambridge, London or Bristol, are reflected in the bases of his poetry.
One might say that the periods of solitude or near-solitude provided
the subject-matter out of which the poems were finally composed,
whereas the form they took and the language in which they were
written reflect the urban 'pull' in Wordsworth. But even such a
differentiation of the Two Voices would be an oversimplification. It
is true that the diction and the syntax of Wordsworth's poetry conform, with a few exceptions, to the literary language of late eighteenth-
century London, but the total stylistic impression that his poems
leave, again with some exceptions, is very different from that of the
poetry of contemporary Londoners. The fact is something of a
commonplace, though it is not always realized that Wordsworth's
use of language is as different from that of his younger London
contemporaries as it obviously is from those of the older poets; as
different, for example, from Keats's as from Cowper's. The difference
seems to derive from Wordsworth's attitude to his audience – a
problem that has not received the critical attention it deserves.

As a preliminary to a definition of Wordsworth's poetic audience,
it will be worth while looking rather closely into two voices that are
to be heard in his poetry in quite a different sense from J. K. Stephen's.
In so far as poetry is read aloud or recited, it is dominated by the
spoken voice. But poetry that is written primarily to be read appeals
to an *unspoken* voice. The two voices are not mutually exclusive and
in some of Wordsworth's poems it makes little or no difference
whether they are read to one or one reads them to oneself. But this
is not generally true. One of the most important differences between
Wordsworth and the other major poets of the eighteenth and
nineteenth centuries is that whereas they wrote for the silent reader,
i.e. for the eye, he wrote most of his poems to be declaimed, i.e. for
the ear. It was only in revising his poems later that he took into account
the claims of the eye. This characteristic is the real explanation of the
heaviness of style, the occasional clumsiness and general lack of

verbal polish, that Tennyson hit off in the epithet *thick-ankled* ('Wordsworth seemed to him *thick-ankled*').[1] Tennyson *saw* his own poems as well as hearing them. The critical standards that he applied to Wordsworth's verse – he objected, for example, to the want of literary instinct shown in the repetition of the word 'again' four times in the first fourteen lines of *Tintern Abbey* – were those of a poet for whom a poem exists primarily on a piece of paper. It is something he can return to whenever he likes, touching up a rhythm here and a metaphor there, as the mood takes him. For Wordsworth, except in the process of revising his poems for a new edition (when the basis was generally either pasted-up sheets of an earlier edition or transcripts made by his women-folk), the poem existed primarily *in his head* – as a rhetorical whole, that is, of which the part could only be reached after all that had preceded it had been declaimed.

It is significant that, instead of lending his friends MSS. or printed copies of his poems, Wordsworth preferred to read them aloud or recite them. Emerson, who paid his first call on the Wordsworths in 1833, found the Rydal Mount ritual of recitation a little disconcerting:

He had just returned from a visit to Staffa, and within three days had made three sonnets on Fingal's Cave, and was composing a fourth when he was called in to see me. He said, 'If you are interested in my verses, perhaps you will like to hear these lines.' I gladly assented; and he recollected himself for a few moments, and then stood forth and repeated, one after the other, the three entire sonnets, with great animation. . . . This recitation was so unlooked for and surprising, – he, the old Wordsworth, standing apart, and reciting to me in a garden walk, like a schoolboy declaiming – that I at first was near to laugh; but recollecting myself, that I had come thus far to see a poet, and he was chanting poems to me, I saw that he was right and I was wrong, and gladly gave myself up to hear.[2]

Some of Wordsworth's other American visitors seem to have found it even more difficult to adjust themselves. The poet Bryant, for

1 *Tennyson. A Memoir. By his Son*, 1897, vol. II, p. 505.
2 *English Traits*, 1856, ch. i.

example, used to give amusing, if irreverent, imitations of the performance.

Wordsworth also read his poems aloud as effectively as he recited them. Hazlitt's *My First Acquaintance with Poets* contains a vivid account of the way he did it:

We went over to All-Foxden again the day following, and
Wordsworth read us the story of *Peter Bell* in the open air;
and the comment made upon it by his face and voice was
very different from that of some later critics! Whatever
might be thought of the poem, 'his face was as a book
where men might read strange matters', and he announced
the fate of his hero in prophetic tones.

Wordsworth makes it clear in his 1815 Preface that he expected his poems to be read aloud.

Some of these pieces are essentially lyrical; and, therefore,
cannot have their due force without a supposed musical
accompaniment; but, in much the greatest part, as a
substitute for the classic lyre or romantic harp, I require
nothing more than an animated or impassioned recitation,
adapted to the subject.

The poems, he adds, will not 'read themselves'. The reader is to be encouraged to contribute his own modulation of the music of the poem. It is clear that Wordsworth regarded the facial expressions and dramatic intonations with which he read or recited his poems as an essential part of their meaning. Without this or a similar accompaniment – that is, if it was read silently by the reader to himself – the poetry would fail to achieve its proper effect. It is probably true that the technical slovenliness to which Tennyson objected in *Tintern Abbey* would not be noticed, if the poem was declaimed with sufficient animation. And in poetry a slovenliness that is not noticed does not exist. It is our modern reading habits that are at fault here, not Wordsworth.

Wordsworth's habit of either reading his poems aloud or reciting them was a corollary of his habit of composing aloud. This was a practice that fascinated his humbler neighbours, and Rawnsley's *Reminiscences of Wordsworth among the Peasantry of Westmorland* is full of stories of the poet's 'bummings' and 'booings'. One of Rawnsley's witnesses, a half-farmer, half-hotelkeeper, remembered how alarming Wordsworth's powerful voice could make the process of composition:

... thear was anudder thing as kep' fwoaks off, he had a terr'ble girt deep voice, and ye med see his faace agaan for lang eneuf. I've knoan fwoaks, village lads and lasses, coming ower by t'auld road aboon what runs fra Gersmer to Rydal, flayt a'most to death there by t'Wishing Gate to hear t'girt voice a groanin' and mutterin' and thunderin' of a still evening. And he hed a way of standin' quite still by t'rock there in t'path under Rydal, and fwoaks could hear sounds like a wild beast coming fra t'rocks, and childer were scared fit to be dead a'most.[1]

If this anecdote is to be taken at its face value, it looks as if Wordsworth enacted his poems as he composed them. No doubt on such occasions he would have thought he was alone and could not be overheard. The performance on the grass terrace at Rydal Mount, as the Wordsworths' garden-boy remembered it, was a more staid affair altogether:

... he would set his heäd a bit forrad, and put his hands behint his back. And then he would start a bumming, and it was bum, bum, bum, stop; then bum, bum, bum reet down till t'other end, and then he'd set down and git a bit o' paper out and write a bit; and then he git up, and bum, bum, bum, and goa on bumming for long enough right down and back agean. I suppose, ya kna, the bumming helped him out a bit. However, his lips was always goan' whoale time he was upon the gres walk.[2]

The bits of paper are interesting. They do not come into the account given to Rawnsley by a one-time maid of the Wordsworths of the procedure indoors:

1 *Lake Country Sketches*, Dillon's, 1903, pp. 38–9.
2 pp. 15–16. An earlier gardener to interest himself in Wordsworth's methods of composition was one of the Beaumonts' employees at Coleorton who, unknown to Wordsworth, used to follow him round to 'catch the words I uttered'. (I.F. note to 'Though narrow be that old Man's cares', *Poetical Works*, edited by E. de Selincourt, vol. III p. 430.)

. . . Mr Wordsworth went bumming and booing about, and
she, Miss Dorothy, kept close behint him, and she picked up
the bits as he let 'em fall, and tak 'em down, and put 'em
together on paper for him. And you med . . . be very well
sure as how she didn't understand nor make sense out of 'em
and I doubt that he didn't kna much aboot them either
himself. . . .[1]

Rawnsley's witnesses must be taken with a grain or two of salt.
They had none of them read any of Wordsworth's poems, and they
regarded him as an eccentric, whose actions rarely had any rational
basis. Moreover their evidence, which was only collected in the
1870s, refers for the most part to the last twenty years or so of
Wordsworth's life.

But the earlier evidence is on the same lines. Coleridge told
Hazlitt that 'Wordsworth always wrote (if he could) walking up
and down a straight gravel-walk, or in some spot where the continuity of his verse met with no collateral interruption'.[2] This seems
to confirm the garden-boy's account, though it omits the bits of
paper (perhaps they were proofs or fair copies that Wordsworth
was only revising?). One early poem that we know was composed
orally was *Tintern Abbey*, which was not written down until the
Wordsworths had returned to Bristol after their short tour of South
Wales. Although there are 160 lines in it, and no rhymes to act as
mnemonic aids, 'Not a line of it was altered, and not any part of it
written down till I reached Bristol'. According to G. M. Harper, the
most exhaustive of Wordsworth's biographers, it was his regular
habit to retain hundreds of lines in his mind, often for many weeks,
before they were completed. When a poem had been completed
orally it was often dictated to Dorothy, as Wordsworth disliked
intensely the physical exertion involved in writing. There is a
tradition that Wordsworth dictated Books I and II of *The Prelude* to
her, while he paced up and down a still-existing path at Lancrigg
near Grasmere. An Irish yew has been planted to mark the spot
where Dorothy sat.[3] Although the account may not be literally true
– much of Book I was written down in Germany, many months

1 p. 7.
2 *My First Acquaintance with Poets.*
3 *William Wordsworth*, John Murray, 1916, vol I, p. 401; vol. II, p. 6.

before the Wordsworths settled at Grasmere – it probably gives a reliable idea of the way many of the poems got on to paper. One of the reasons why the Wordsworths aroused the suspicions of their neighbours in the Quantocks in 1797 was their habit of sallying forth with folding stools and notebooks. 'The man has Camp Stools', the busybody at Bath reported to the Home Secretary, 'which he and his visitors take with them when they go about the country upon their nocturnal or diurnal excursions, and has also a Portfolio in which they enter their observations, which they have been heard to say were almost finished.'[1] It would be nice to know what it was in reality that was 'almost finished'. Was it *The Ruined Cottage*? Had the 'Portfolio' been acquired so that Wordsworth could dictate the final version to Dorothy while they sat on the 'Camp Stools' at some picturesque spot discovered on their walks?

Ambulatory composition was Wordsworth's most usual method, but it was not his only method. Charles Greville, the diarist, who met Wordsworth at one of Henry Taylor's breakfast parties in 1831, was told that 'he never wrote down as he composed, but composed walking, riding, or in bed, and wrote down after'.[2] The number of poems composed on horseback is probably small. Wordsworth was a poor horseman and only borrowed or hired a mount on exceptional occasions. The one poem that is known to have been composed when riding is 'Among all lovely things my Love had been', which was not only composed on horseback (between 'the beginning of Lord Darlington's park at Raby and two or three miles beyond Staindrop') but is also a record of an earlier ride. The poems composed in bed provide a more interesting category. The time of composition was apparently the morning. In 1830 Wordsworth told some undergraduates at Trinity College, Cambridge, that some of his best thoughts came to him 'between sleeping and waking, or as he expressed it, in a morning sleep'. The observation was recorded in his diary by Henry Alford, one of the undergraduates, and arose out of a discussion of *Kubla Khan*, which Wordsworth thought Coleridge might have composed in the same half-awake state in

1 A. J. Eagleston, 'Wordsworth, Coleridge and the Spy', *Nineteenth Century and After*, August 1908.
2 See Edith C. Batho, *The Later Wordsworth*, Cambridge University Press, 1933, pp. 11–21.

which some of his own poems came to him.[1] Wordsworth certainly attached a special importance to 'the first involuntary thoughts upon waking in the morning'. He once told R. P. Graves, the Vicar of Ambleside, that they ought to be watched closely 'as indications of the real current of moral being'.[2]

Wordsworth always composed orally. Normally he composed aloud. There is some evidence that his voice rose and fell in the process of composition, as though he was reciting the poem before an imaginary audience. Only when the poem had been completed, unless it was an exceptionally long one, was it put into writing. Often it was not Wordsworth himself but his sister who actually wrote down the poem.

These are the principal conclusions that it seems reasonable to draw from the existing evidence as to Wordsworth's methods of composition. His nervous objection to putting pen to paper may explain some of the peculiarities, but it does not explain his preference for reading his own poetry aloud or reciting it. It certainly seems as though oral communication was, for him, the natural medium of poetry. When he defined the poet as 'a man speaking to men' it is possible, I think, that he was using the word 'speaking' in a literal sense, and that the audience he envisaged when composing was a real audience – composed of *auditors*. The relationship, however, was not that of an actor to a theatrical audience so much as that of a priest to a congregation of devotees. Hazlitt, who is confirmed in this matter by Emerson, noted the prevalence of *chant* in the way Wordsworth recited his poems, which 'acts as a spell upon the hearer, and disarms the judgement'. The choice of metaphor is significant. A chant that acts as a spell is an *incantation*. The complement of a spell-bound hearer is a spell-binding poet, an *enchanter*. The metaphor brings out once more the essentially primitive nature of Wordsworth's conception of poetry. He is the bard, the *sacer vates*, whose relationship with his little audience is infinitely more intimate and more profound than the causal liaison between the modern poet and his readers that is provided by printers, publishers and booksellers.

The highly charged, almost hysterical atmosphere within the original inner circle of the Wordsworths, the Coleridges and the

1 *Life, Journals and Letters of Henry Alford*, Rivington, 3rd edn., 1874, p. 62.
2 Christopher Wordsworth, *Memoirs of William Wordsworth*, vol. II, p. 481.

Hutchinsons is apparent in a curious letter that Wordsworth wrote to Sara Hutchinson on 14 June 1802, just a few months before he married Mary. Sara had complained that the leech-gatherer in an early version of *Resolution and Independence* was *tedious*, a criticism that provoked the following outburst:

You speak of his speech as tedious: everything is tedious
when one does not read with the feelings of the Author –
The Thorn is tedious to hundreds; and so is the *Idiot Boy* to
hundreds. It is in the character of the old man to tell his
story in a manner which an *impatient* reader must necessarily
feel as tedious. But Good God! Such a figure, in such a
place, a pious, self-respecting, miserably infirm and [word
illegible] Old Man telling such a tale!

The letter concludes by contrasting Sara's reaction to *Beggars*, a much less ambitious poem that Wordsworth had written earlier the same year: 'Your feelings upon the Mother, and the Boys with the Butterfly, were not indifferent: it was an affair of whole continents of moral sympathy.' Wordsworth had not had an opportunity, as far as is known, to read or recite either poem to the Hutchinsons, but the commentary provided by intonation or gesture was presumably not required in their case. Instead he could normally count on 'whole continents of moral sympathy' within this intimate inner audience. The rarity of its failure is proved by the intensity of his disappointment when on this one occasion it did occur.

Like most of the Romantic poets Wordsworth found it hard to say who it was exactly he wrote his poems for. At one time, as he confessed to Wrangham, it was his ambition to write poems which would find their way into the cottages and supplant the superstitious and indelicate chapbooks that were the staple literary fare of country people in his time – 'half-penny Ballads, and penny and twopenny histories'.[1] In the 1815 'Essay Supplementary to the Preface' it is the People whom he addresses – not 'that small though loud portion of the community, ever governed by factitious influence, which, under the name of the PUBLIC, passes itself, upon the unthinking, for the PEOPLE', but the People 'philosophically

1 Wordsworth to Francis Wrangham, 5 June 1808.

383 F. W. Bateson

characterized'. In this sense the People was that select body of cultivated readers who maintain the continuity of literature by familiariz-
ing themselves with the best poetry both of their own time and of
earlier periods. In the nature of the case, therefore, Wordsworth now
admits, an original poet 'must reconcile himself for a season to few
and scattered hearers'. The contradiction between the two aspirations
– a mass working–class audience on the one hand and on the other a
few isolated intellectuals – is perhaps partly bridged in the word
'hearers'. The oral poetry that Wordsworth wrote demanded an
audience of listeners who would cooperate with him in the process
of communication and transmission. The 1815 'Essay' is emphatic
that the poetic auditor must not be a merely passive participant, 'like
an Indian prince or general stretched on his palanquin, and borne by
his slaves'. Now the one place where a tradition of oral poetry
persisted in Wordsworth's time was the country, though 'half-
penny Ballads' were, it is true, a dying art-form at the end of the
eighteenth century. What Wordsworth seems to have been feeling
his way towards was a somewhat similar oral relationship among a
select body of middle–class intellectuals. It may even be claimed that
he did succeed in creating a modern equivalent of the primitive
ballad-audience. In the early Wordsworthians – Lamb, Hazlitt, John
Wilson, De Quincey, Sir George Beaumont, Haydon, Crabb Robinson, Henry Taylor and Talfourd are probably the best-known of
them – he found the sort of intimate and enthusiastic audience,
cooperative and yet critical, out of which the great traditional ballads
must have originally emerged.

It was a poet–audience relationship different in kind from that of
a Spenser, a Milton, a Dryden or a Pope, partly because of its oral
basis and partly because of its emotional overtones. To a typical
Wordsworthian Wordsworth was so much more than just another
good poet. The process of discovering his poetry was more like a
religious conversion, an experience from which the convert emerged
with the whole of his way of looking at the world permanently and
profoundly changed. In a striking passage in *Appreciations* Pater has
described those who had undergone Wordsworth's influence as being
'like people who have passed through some initiation, a *disciplina
arcani*, by submitting to which they become able constantly to
distinguish in art, speech, feeling, manners, that which is only con-

ventional, derivative, inexpressive'.[1] And in the case of the best of the Wordsworthians – De Quincey, for example – the description is scarcely an exaggeration. All that is most original and profound in De Quincey's criticism at any rate undoubtedly derives, as he himself acknowledged on one occasion, from 'many years' conversation with Mr Wordsworth'.[2]

But if Wordsworth was necessary to the Wordsworthians they were not less necessary to him. It is no accident, for example, that the first and best verion of *The Prelude* is addressed directly to Coleridge, or that *Michael* was written for and about Thomas Poole, or even that it was Sir George Beaumont's indifferent painting of Peele Castle which inspired the magnificent *Elegiac Stanzas*. And even when the connection is not explicit it is impossible not to be aware, in many of Wordsworth's greatest poems, of that original audience on whom the poem will first be tried out, whose suggestions and criticisms will be considered and very often accepted, and who will copy the MS. out and send it round to their friends.[3] Unfortunately, as he grew older, Wordsworth began to take this intimate inner public too much for granted and to concern himself more and more with the reading public in general. The way to reach this outer public created a difficult technical problem. How could the spoken voice be transposed into the non-spoken voice of the printed page? What substitutes could be found for the facial and vocal accompaniments he normally relied on to tap the moral sympathy latent in his more intimate audience? In the end the solution was provided by the Wordsworthians, who gradually taught the upper middle class how to read Wordsworth. Their eulogies and commentaries bridged a gap that was too wide for Wordsworth to make himself heard across orally. But Wordsworth did not realize this. Instead of relying on the missionary efforts of his disciples he tried, in later life, to meet the reading public half-way. Instead of restricting himself to the oral poetry that came naturally to him, and that he wrote so well, he

1 The passage occurs in Pater's well-known essay on Wordsworth, which was written in 1874.
2 'The Literature of Knowledge and the Literature of Power' (1823).
3 See the cancelled 'Advertisement' originally intended for the 1807 *Poems*: '... as several of these Poems have been circulated in manuscript ...' (W. Hale White, *A Description of the Wordsworth and Coleridge Manuscripts in the Possession of Mr T. Norton Longman*, 1897, p. 71).

began to write non-oral poetry, poetry for the eye. Worse still, instead of concentrating on the intimate inner public who formed his natural audience, he started to give the common reader what he thought the common reader needed. He began to *preach*. (The turning-point was perhaps at the end of 1802, when he began to contribute sonnets in aid of the war effort to the *Morning Post*.) Worst of all, he started revising his earlier poems to make them more palatable to the silent reader. The hours of labour Wordsworth devoted to giving poems composed orally and intended for oral recitation the finish and elegance demanded in poetry written for the eye would be impressive, if they had not been so disastrous. Of the thousands of alterations that he made in one edition after another, only a very few can be considered any improvement at all, and many are ludicrously inferior to the readings they displace. As a general rule it is best to read Wordsworth's poems in the earliest text available. The non-spoken voice that he worked so hard to acquire was a falsetto that should not be allowed to drown the simple sincerity of the spoken voice in which his great poetry was composed.

The potential danger in the relationship between Wordsworth and the Wordsworthians was that it might turn into that of a spiritual healer ministering to a congregation of sick souls. It is true that the man – partly because of his acquired hardness and worldliness and partly because of a certain awkward integrity that he never lost – never degenerated into a drawing-room prophet. The disciples were taken for a walk round Grasmere and given tea at Rydal Mount, their letters were answered, their poems were read, but the routine proceeded with a minimum of uplift and unction. Long before the man's death, however, the poet had tended to become dissociated from him, and throughout the nineteenth century the poet Wordsworth was regarded primarily as a healer. John Stuart Mill has testified in his *Autobiography* to the restorative properties of Wordsworth's poetry after an overdose of Utilitarianism, and there is a similar testimony by William Hale White in *The Autobiography of Mark Rutherford*. It will be remembered that Arnold's *Memorial Verses*, which were written immediately after Wordsworth's death and were intended as a sort of poetical obituary notice, also select 'Wordsworth's healing power' as the essence of his genius. Under its influence the desiccated victim of the Iron Time was able to 'feel' once again:

He found us when the age had bound
Our souls in its benumbing round;
He spoke, and loos'd our hearts in tears,
He laid us as we lay at birth
On the cool flowery lap of earth;
Smiles broke from us and we had ease.

The tributes ring a little hollowly today. The old healing power
has certainly lost most of its efficacy. And if to be a Wordsworthian
it is necessary, as Arnold says in the Preface to his selection from
Wordsworth, to read 'with pleasure and edification' everything
Wordsworth ever wrote, how many of us are prepared to be Wordsworthians? Will the mid-twentieth century imitate Arnold in reading
'the whole series of *Ecclesiastical Sonnets* [there are 132 of them], and
the address to Mr Wilkinson's spade, and even the *Thanksgiving
Ode*'?[1] In America, according to Lionel Trilling, Wordsworth is not
read at all now, except in the universities,[2] and in this country too,
his popularity has declined almost as catastrophically. Wordsworth
is in considerable danger of becoming a classic, like Spenser or
Jonson, to whom we pay our respects, but in whom our real interest,
if we are to be honest, is decidedly tepid. If his poetry is to be saved
from that shelf, it will perhaps be by our returning, as far as that is
possible for a twentieth-century reader, to the sort of relationship
to it that his original inner audience had to Wordsworth.

The basis of that relationship was a common plight. The middle-
class intellectuals who made up Wordsworth's circle of friends lived
the same sort of rootless, functionless, fragmentary existence that he
had led after his mother's death. The difference between them,
however, was not that of doctor and patient but simply of degrees
of sickness. And all the evidence now suggests that Wordsworth's
soul was not less sick than Coleridge's or Lamb's or Hazlitt's or
De Quincey's but more sick. What fascinated and inspired his friends
was Wordsworth's continually renewed struggle towards normality
and mental health *in spite of his greater sickness* – a struggle which is

1 Preface (1879), pp. xxv–xxvi.
2 'Wordsworth and the Iron Time', *Kenyon Review*, Summer 1950 (reprinted
in *Wordsworth Centenary Studies*, edited by G. T. Dunklin, Princeton University
Press, 1951).

reflected and worked out in his poems with meticulous if often unconscious honesty and sensitiveness.

The tragic interest of Wordsworth's case is the exceptional degree to which his inner life was predetermined by psychic forces outside his control and of which he was himself only dimly conscious. The recurrent pattern of crisis, psychological disintegration, and gradual convalescence which I have tried to define, is itself evidence of a character in which the area left for the free will and the conscious mind to control was exceptionally small. If I am right in thinking that the pattern repeated itself almost identically at least three times and in each case over a period of almost exactly six years, the special nature of Wordsworth's case included not only a general psychic rhythm, but a pre-determined time-scheme. But if Wordsworth was to a greater degree than most of us the victim of circumstance he was the least acquiescent of victims. At one time I thought of calling this book *The Heroic Victim*. The phrase sums up for me the final impression that I have carried away from a long and fairly close reading of Wordsworth's poems. So far from surrendering to the neurotic elements in his personality, as so many Romantic poets have done, Wordsworth's early life was one long desperate struggle against them. And whatever one's reservations about this or that poem the general direction of the poetry is undoubtedly towards sanity, sincerity, sympathy, gaiety – in a word, the humane virtues. What makes their successful realization in Wordsworth's best poems so exhilarating to the modern reader is his continuous consciousness of how hardly the successes have been won, how precarious the achievement is. There were no easy victories for him either as a man or a poet. The failures on the other hand, and there were plenty of them, are refreshingly obvious and blatant.

Wordsworth achieves greatness because his private struggles towards psychic integration have a representative quality. The poems generalize themselves, as they are read, into the reactions of the human individual fighting for its spiritual survival in a society that seems to have no place for it. And this makes him, with Blake, the first specifically modern English poet. The difference between Wordsworth and Blake and poets like Chaucer, Spenser, Milton, Dryden or Pope is, it is not too much to say, almost a difference of kind. Although the exact emphasis naturally varies, the earlier poets all shared with their audience both a belief in the validity of the literary tradition they inherited, and also an ultimate sense of obligation to the social order (religious–ethical as well as political–economic) in which they had grown up. Wordsworth and Blake did not accept either of these presuppositions. But Wordsworth's example was more important than Blake's for his contemporaries, and perhaps for us too, because Wordsworth, or a part of him, would have *liked* to believe in a literary tradition and an inherited social order. To survive all that was most genuine in him, his *daimon*, the conscience of his conscience, had to fight against the ever-present temptation to conformity and to learn to make its denials and refusals more and more uncompromising. It is, I think, this extremism in Wordsworth, the drastic and even shocking elements in both the man and the poet, that gives his struggle towards integration its heroic quality. Poems like *The Idiot Boy*, *We are Seven* and *Peter Bell* are not merely outside the literary tradition – Blake's poems are outside it too – they are written in a deliberate defiance of it. The gross, offensive non-literariness is an important part of their meaning. The revolutionary manner complements the revolutionary matter – which might be described as a series of demonstrations of the superior humanity of men and women who are either outside or at best only on the edge of ordinary organized society.

The progress to the repudiation of literature, as of society, was a gradual one. In the earlier poems, in which Wordsworth was still feeling his way to a non-literary technique, the effect is rather of a misapplication of the literary tradition. The new wine is uncomfortable in the old bottles, though they are still used. In his Hawkshead–Cambridge phase, when he was struggling back to normality primarily through a cleansing and renovation of the senses, Wordsworth was still using the verse-forms and diction of Gray and Goldsmith, if the poetry that emerged, when poetry did emerge, was really completely different from theirs. It is essentially eye-on-the-object, ear-on-the-noise poetry. In spite of the conscientiously artificial style the reader is made to see and hear physical objects as they are in themselves, as mere sights and mere sounds, wholly divested from the human or conventional associations they generally had for Gray and Goldsmith. The cattle in lines 58–60 of *An Evening Walk*,

When stood the shorten'd herds amid the tide,
Where, from the barren wall's unshelter'd end,
Long rails into the shallow lake extend;

may be compared with those in *The Deserted Village*, line 119,

The sober herd that low'd to meet their young;

or in the second line of *Elegy written in a Country Churchyard*. Words-worth's 'shorten'd herds' leaves a vivid impression on the mind's eye, whereas Goldsmith's 'sober herd' is a metaphor implying a comparison with some human assembly, and Gray's 'lowing herd' is a mere conventionality (cows do not low as a herd).

But Wordsworth did not find himself as a poet until after the crisis year 1792-3. In this phase the personal quest was not so much for sensuous reality as for emotional reality – a reality that he found in the healthy instincts and simple affections of the Female Vagrant, Margaret, Jack Walford, the old Cumberland Beggar, Poor Susan, Goody Blake and their successors. Except as figures of fun such humble souls had not found a place hitherto in the literary tradition, and Wordsworth's extremism is as evident in *Salisbury Plain* and *The Ruined Cottage*, in which low life is described in Spenserian stanzas and Miltonic blank verse, as it is in *Lyrical Ballads*, which bases itself on the sub-literary *genre* of the street-ballad. This literary extremism is is much less evident in *Tintern Abbey* and the poems written at Goslar and Dove Cottage, Superficially most of the poems of this period are a good deal less defiant of the literary decencies. But the decorum, as the analyses of 'There was a Boy' and 'She dwelt among the un-trodden ways' have demonstrated , was a merely superficial one. Under the surface the poetry is more uncompromising, more drastic-ally non-literary, even than *Lyrical Ballads*. And the reason for this is that the repudiation of society, which had been implicit in *An Evening Walk* and explicit in the poems written between 1793 and 1798, has now been extended and developed into an implicit repudia-tion of the whole human race. Wordsworth's egotism cannot be called misanthropy, it is nearer to solipsism. The author of the Lucy poems, *Intimations of Immortality* and *The Prelude* (the list is not intended to be complete) could only solve his personal crisis – the tragic discovery that he and his sister were passionately in love with each other – by eliminating every other human being except himself from his emotional life. The process was largely, though not, I think, wholly, an unconscious one, and a casual intercourse was, of course, maintained with friends and acquaintances, including Dorothy. He even got married and had a family. But nobody seems to have been able during those difficult years to make any real contact with the deeper levels of his personality. The intensity with which as a school-boy and an undergraduate he had looked out on to the physical world and the profound emotional hunger which he had felt for primitive human nature in his second phase were now diverted into recollection in tranquility, a process as selective as it was concentrated. Dorothy, for example, the innocent cause of the crisis, was excluded from Wordsworth's memories of the past. It is significant that she plays no part in the account of the Cockermouth years in *The Prelude*. She was also omitted from *Resolution and Independence*, though the actual historical meeting with the leech-gatherer had occurred in her company, and Wordsworth clearly used the record of it in her journal when writing the poem. It is the same with *Beggars* and 'I wandered lonely as a cloud' and a dozen other poems. But after the Lucy poems, in which her symbolic death was recorded, there was no place for her in the organs of Wordsworth's poetic imagination, and she was cut out like so much decayed tissue. The uncompromising ruthlessness of it is awe-inspiring, an act of necessary cruelty, inevitable but heart-breaking – to himself (there can be no doubt of it) even more than to Dorothy. So Agamemnon sacrificed Iphigenia. In the last analysis it is, I think, the absoluteness of this inner integrity above all that compels our reluctant admiration.

But the Heroic Victim was not granted a tragic end. Arnold's sardonic parable called *The Progress of Poesy* describes Wordsworth's later career accurately enough: the youth who found the spring becomes first of all the mature man who chops 'a channel grand' for a stream that is already exhausted (*The Excursion*), and finally the old man who rakes among the stones. Arnold fails, however, to make clear the moral of his parable. Was it that Wordsworth's genius exhausted itself in the intensity of the early struggles? or did he perhaps win through in the end to normality, a somewhat hard and selfish normality? In that case the 'dotages' would be the evidence not of failure but success. If the great poetry was the product of a moment-ary and precarious harmonization of the Two Voices, it could have no *raison d'être* when they were no longer audible separately. The imaginative fusions were the resolutions of pre-existing psychological tensions. In the absence of such tensions there would be no oppositions to balance, no discordancies to reconcile.

(175–203)

John Jones

from *The Egotistical Sublime* 1954

Like all books, this is a public thing made for men to stare at; and, while doubt and failure are in mind, mention should be made of the attempt to say something of speculative interest about thought and language, something that sprang out of Wordsworth's poetry and his scattered reflections upon poetry. When he was confronted with the vulgar eighteenth-century definition of language as the clothing of thought, Wordsworth replied that language is not thought's dress but its incarnation.[1] His more specific remarks about language are nearly always consistent with this statement of general principle, as, for example, his protest against the Augustan element in Byron's poetry:

the sentiment by being expressed in an antithetical manner, is taken out of the Region of high and imaginative feeling, to be placed in that of point and epigram. To illustrate my meaning and for no other purpose I refer to my own Lines on the Wye *Tintern Abbey*, where you will find the same sentiment not formally put as it is here, but ejaculated as it were fortuitously in the musical succession of preconceived feelings.[2]

Wordsworth rejects the notion that poets, or other men, think a thought and then look for an attractive way of presenting it. Language is not like that. What then, of the distinction between knowing what you think and knowing how to say it? Implicit in his remarks about language, and especially, in his reckless commendations of spontaneous

1 Reported by De Quincey, 'Essay on Style', *Works*, vol. X.
2 *Letters, 1811–20*, ed. de Selincourt, Oxford University Press, 1937, p. 790.

utterance, is the will to free the activity of thinking from association with the concept thought. The abstract question is for men like Coleridge: he is concerned in a practical way, as an empirical psychologist, with an activity which is certainly polymorphous – he would not have denied musical or mathematical thinking – but which in one of its forms is linguistic; and his knowledge of this kind does not tally with conventional descriptions.

He dislikes the dress metaphor because it suggests that language is independent of other things in a way that is untrue. It goes wrong at the start by implying that there are naked thoughts. However importunate the hubbub of life below the level of expression, only error can result from talking of thoughts arising, like Venus, from the sea of brute experience; for the false dichotomy of thought and word is immediately encouraged. This is partly a matter of chronology, of Wordsworth's testifying, as other artsists have done, that although you cannot start work until you know what you want to do, it is equally the case that you do not know what you want to do until you have done it: so the thought has no priority in time. But more important is his objection to the analogy of the body and its dress. Even if Venus-Thoughts were described as emerging fully clothed, he would still have been unsatisfied. You can do what you like with clothes, tell any story you please, and if language is a kind of clothing, all use of language is a playing with words.

As always, Wordsworth's ultimate problem is a moral and aesthetic complex. Language is moral because of the way in which it is bound to life: it is poetic for the same reason. His quarrel with the dress metaphor affords an introduction to this complex since the status of language is endangered in both connections when it is associated with adornment or even with working clothes. A moral-poetic responsibility is evaded by those who think of something ready made, waiting to be assumed. And so he challenged the divorce of language and life, the whole idea of poetic diction, the principles involved in Gray's famous statement that there is one language for art and another for nature. He believed in a single language, no further from the living heart of things than the breath that bears it.

For the tired slave, Song lifts the languid oar,
And bids it aptly fall:

the Sound Ode refuses to treat language as accessory to action: it is one of action's modes, and perhaps the most effective. The song that lifts the oar will also, in his own poetry, 'deal boldly with intellectual things'; he speaks of 'the intellectual power' that

through words and things,
Went sounding on, a dim and perilous way.

Language is in the world, pushing and being pushed against.

When he criticizes Byron's poetry for inhabiting the region of point and epigram, having forsaken that of imaginative feeling, Wordsworth is protesting against a retirement from the world, encouraged by the dress metaphor, which makes language unable to deal boldly with things. Projected as the conceptual currency of men, language becomes an abstract structure, impotent because of its isolation, the external instrument of analytic intelligence by means of which, the *Lyrical Ballads* maintains, 'We murder to dissect'. How can language be more than this? In his use of the incarnative metaphor Wordsworth strikes an attitude. There is here no contrast of living and inorganic natures, or of enduring form and its chance habit. Above all, there is nothing to be made and mended, no independent construction to be managed. The dress metaphor will not do. Nor will that variation of the dress metaphor in which we suppose our thoughts to be shrouded in a diaphanous linguistic film. This is to reduce language in a different way, by ignoring it. Wordsworth's own solution is to abandon the idea of structure for that of function, and in his poetry to embark on the activity of language.

I once believed that this poetry held a lesson for the modern philosophy of linguistic analysis. In Wordsworth's solitude and relationship and in the features of his landscape there is a conspiracy of inner and outer which might properly be called philosophical: one may find a public context for this private effort in the traditions of western thinking, and especially in the Cartesian dichotomy of thing and thought. Confidence in the relational power of language inspires his attempt, not to deny this dichotomy, but to make it metaphysically tolerable; while an extreme sensitiveness to the logical limits of language has led philosophy in this generation to turn its back on the possibility of metaphysics. But now, when the excitement that attends beginnings has died away, it seems to me that

Wordsworth has nothing to teach modern philosophers which can be turned by them to philosophical advantage. Many of them take no pleasure in the estrangement of philosophy and wisdom, do not suppose that language is a symbolic structure, abstract and determined like that of mathematics, or even wish that it were so. But the logical distress is real: within the terms of a cognitive discipline there is very little they can find to say.

It is true that Wordsworth places over against the discursive intellect a higher and still rational faculty which he calls

> clearest insight, amplitude of mind,
> And reason in her most exalted mood:

and in this thrusting beyond the logic of the understanding there is a genuine metaphysical passion, a thing tougher in its mental stuff than any cult of poetic sensibility. But this is not coincident with the profession of philosophy, and does not entitle us to throw him to very professional lions. With regard to his poetry of the supernatural, I think it would be misleading to speak of philosophy at all, Not that there is anything unclear about the visions which 'appeared in presence of the spiritual eye': but visions are visions, whereas the early work is of a quite different order. Here I wish to have it both ways: to claim enough of system to justify the title of Philosopher–Poet first given him by Coleridge, and also to avoid any joining issue with contemporary thought, even though this has become in one sense a matter of language, of which Wordsworth had a larger knowledge than philosophers.

His attitude to language is consistent with the sympathetic whole which I have called solitude and relationship. Language serves the principle of action and reaction, of sympathy or reciprocity, through participation. Hence his curious theory of the imagination as a confering or abstracting of properties so that the object may itself 'react upon the mind';[1] and hence the personal ambition to celebrate the mind's marriage to the world, to

> chant, in lonely peace, the spousal verse
> Of this great consummation: – and, by words
> That speak of nothing more than what we are,

1 *Preface*, 1815.

Would I arouse the sensual from their sleep
Of Death.[1]

The poet is more than a chronicler or commentator because his
language is woven into the texture of this process, as a function of it,
and not in the ordinary sense as a description. Reality and language
are a going concern.

The linguistic activity is therefore central, and at the same time
there is no problem of language, no *thing* about which to be perplexed. 'Where meditation was', from *The Pedlar*, is one of Wordsworth's concretized abstractions; and this Roman secret is the whole
secret. Wordsworth saw the world with a systematic eccentricity due
to his being born out of time in attitude to mental and physical. This
means, in respect of language, an instinctive grasp of history: he is
no more concerned about the difference between language and not-
language than the baby who uses his voice as the most effective way
of procuring the presence of his mother. The infancy of the race may
have been a little like that – the remote ancestor of the poet who
wished to deal boldly with things.

Born into time, Wordsworth said that language is the incarnation
of thought. Thought incarnate is not thought expressed, or there
would be no need to distinguish the word and the mathematical
symbol; but when he refuses to allow that thoughts are clothed in
words, he fears not so much a direct confusion with mathematics as
the reducing of language to a conceptual instrument, external to
those who use it. Language must have a corresponding inwardness
in order to enact the reciprocity of nature.

We begin, then, with the concretized abstractions: with the River
Duddon which has

No meaner Poet than the whistling Blast,
And Desolation is thy Patron-saint;

and Toussaint L'Ouverture, imprisoned for defying Napoleon:

There's not a breathing of the common wind
That will forget thee; thou hast great allies;
Thy friends are exultations, agonies,
And love.

1 Preface to *The Excursion*.

In both cases the abstract nouns are associated with the action of the wind, which in its double movement is the most important feature of the Wordsworthian landscape. This is what they mean.

Four-syllable abstract nouns in '-ion' are very common in Wordsworth's poetry, and usually, as here with 'exultations', they occupy the fourth to the seventh syllables of the decasyllabic line. *Tintern Abbey*, the supreme example of his blank-verse prosody, has three, all in this position. 'Visitation', an important word in *The Prelude*, of the same kind as 'Presence' and 'Power', appears three times in the 1805 version of Book I, and on each occasion it holds the middle of the line, immense, bare, a windlike echoing. Wordsworth often uses these nouns at a decisive point in his argument. This is true of

> the spousal verse
> Of this great consummation

which we have just noticed, and of the 'authentic tidings' of

> central peace, subsisting at the heart
> Of endless agitation

with which he concludes the account of the child listening to the shell in *The Excursion*. For this and for other reasons, Arnold should not have said that Wordsworth has no style.

The famous sonnet that begins:

> It is a beauteous evening, calm and free,
> The holy time is quiet as a Nun
> Breathless with adoration; ...

betrays his authorship in several ways. 'Adoration' is one sign. The simile is another, and the strange unviolence in which it relates very different natures, the woman and the hour. 'Holy' is certainly a kind of bond between them, but the essence of the thing is his unself-conscious movement from abstract to concrete. In his Westminster Bridge sonnet he says that the city

> doth, like a garment, wear
> The beauty of the morning. ....

To this a friend objected that he goes on to describe the city as 'silent, bare', thus contradicting himself. Wordsworth admitted this fault, and in a letter he altered the sonnet so as to omit the garment image.[1] But the alteration was never adopted. He felt that the image was necessary, and we can see why:

Earth has not anything to show more fair:
Dull would he be of soul who could pass by
A sight so touching in its majesty:
This City now doth, like a garment, wear
The beauty of the morning; silent, bare. . . .

It is needed to sustain, strengthen and illuminate the 'sight so touching in its majesty'. The weak physical metaphor of 'touching' gains sudden pathetic force through this association; and in the balancing of 'touching . . . majesty' with 'garment . . . beauty' the poem's nature is confirmed.

'Breathless', too, from the Holy Time sonnet, is characteristic of Wordsworth. There is unexpected tension and effort in the shift of stress to the first syllable, and the situation of the word allows its silent concentration to flood back through the line end pause. He makes a similar, though more obvious use of this pause in *The Prelude* account of the boy who hooted to the owls and then waited for them to answer him:

Then sometimes, in that silence, while he hung
Listening.[2]

Language takes time – time backwards as well as time forwards.

The poet of many short words has a very careful use of the single long word. The best of the Ecclesiastical Sonnets compares the outward forms of truth with a ruined tower,

      which royally did wear
Her crown of weeds, but could not even sustain
Some casual shout that broke the silent air,
Or the unimaginable touch of Time.[3]

One of his many lonely women wonders what has become of her son:
[Perhaps thou]

1 *Letters, 1831–40* (ed. de Selincourt), p. 812 [see p. 168].
2 Book V, l. 406.
3 *Mutability*.

> hast been summoned to the deep
> Thou, and all thy mates, to keep
> An incommunicable sleep.[1]

When he stole game from another boy's snare, Wordsworth heard, following him,

> sounds
> Of undistinguishable motion, steps
> Almost as silent as the turf they trod.[2]

In *Tintern Abbey* he speaks of the state

> In which the heavy and weary weight
> Of all this unintelligible world
> Is lightened.

All these words arrest the movement of the sense which is usually easy and swift, though in the last example laboriously slow; and while they are going on they give the means of new awareness through release from the poem's time scale. The murmured succession, the fearful patter, the prolonged striving, are different kinds of escape almost from language itself, to experience-worlds outside language.

These words are united in their negative form as well as in their length. Wordsworth carries his delight in negatives to the point of tiresome mannerism: there are too many double negatives, such as 'not unnoticed'; too much rhetorical piling of adjective on adjective – 'unchastened, unsubdued, unawed, unraised' – and pointless circumlocution – 'not seldom' and 'nor seldom' appear five times in the final text of *The Prelude*. But the roots of this practice run very deep; the balance of positive and negative is a mode of reciprocity, like echo and reflection in his landscape. It also shows the unmathematical nature of language. If two minuses make a plus, it is a special kind of plus: the negative form can be on its own account heart-piercing.

> Six weeks beneath the moving sea
> He lay in slumber quietly;
> Unforced by wind or wave
> To quit the Ship for which he died.[3]

---

1 *The Affliction of Margaret.*
2 *The Prelude*, Book I, l. 330.
3 *Sweet Flower, belike . . .*

Wordsworth believed that the problem of thought issuing into language had been considered too much in isolation, at the expense of language's impingement upon the very mentality of mind. In this he felt no logical embarrassment: the double movement was as evident to him as the principle of sympathy in nature, was in fact an aspect of that principle. We saw how, in *The Borderers*, a star once held a man from murder. Words have their corresponding authority; and it is the moral poetic duty of all who use them to command attention of the precise quality required, and to command it for true ends. Sometimes language will fail: here, as with Nature's unrequited love for Peter Bell, Wordsworth's optimism was always precarious.

The poet's command of attention has often been spoken of as an incantatory skill. This is peculiarly unsuited to Wordsworth's matter of fact and his reliance on daylight powers. Nor is the idea of controlled ambiguity in poetic statement much more serviceable; for it must not imply, in his case, intellectual deliberation. Nor is the thing experienced as ambiguity. In *The Prelude* he speaks of

> heights
> Clothed in the sunshine of the withering fern.[1]

This, the 1850 and final text, has no less than five forerunners.[2] The 1805 text speaks simply of 'the mountain pomp of Autumn', which is later expanded by reference to the colour of the hills under autumn sun:

> the beauty and pomp
> Of Autumn, entering under azure skies
> To mountains clothed in yellow robe of fire.

He may have had the colour of the vegetation in mind, as well as that of the sunlight, but he has not yet succeeded in saying so. In the fourth version he gives up the attempt to mention colour, and returns in effect to 1805. The 'golden fern' appears in his fifth version, which paves the way for the final confluence of sun and vegetation. Autumn is not mentioned because the season is already known from the context.

'Clothed in sunshine' is easy: so is 'clothed in the withering fern'.

1 1850, Book VI, l. 10.
2 *Wordsworth's 'Prelude'* (ed. de Selincourt), pp. 170–71.

But 'clothed in the sunshine of the withering fern' is odd, its oddness resting in 'of', and the different kinds of work it has to do. One might say that the word is ambiguous; but this would be a perverse way of expressing it, since the block-impression of the phrase is clear, even without knowing its history. We admit 'of' as we admit others of Wordsworth's busy prepositions: in their degree they are the stride of his thought.

'Every great and original writer, in proportion as he is great or original, must himself teach the art by which he is to be seen.'[1] I have applied Wordsworth's general rule to his own poetry, in the hope of showing a *fait accompli*; the art well taught, the attention commanded. This is an achievement shared by the concretized abstractions, the mental-physical imagery, the captive labours of the verb 'to be'; by the short words, the long words, and all the time and space of language. Shared, too, by language's humblest parts. 'And', more frequent in Wordsworth than in any poet, is the preserver of extreme structural simplicity through hundreds of lines of *Prelude* narrative: if the ice is thin, the skating is light and swift. 'And' helps to sustain the calm elevation of *Tintern Abbey*:

And the round ocean and the living air,
And the blue sky, and in the mind of man . . .

By its monotony, its insistence on the particular, 'and' develops Wordsworth's expository style, in common with other words of modest function – 'but', 'thus', 'therefore'. Notice, in *Tintern Abbey*, how the two cadences:

Therefore am I still
A lover of the meadows

and

Therefore let the moon
Shine on thee:

introduce a logical, knitted quality, cause the reader to glance behind and collect the poem for himself.

'Therefore' is a confidence trick and 'of' an ambiguity only if Wordsworth's view of language is rejected for one more congenial

1 *Letters 1806–11*, vol. X (ed. de Selincourt), p. 130.

because less fateful. Otherwise, following him to 'the great Nature that exists in works Of mighty Poets', we can share what seems to be a divine joke – that this poet should bear the name he does. (195–207)

Robert Mayo

'The Contemporaneity of the *Lyrical Ballads*', *PMLA*, vol. 69   1954

A fruitful but unfrequented approach to the *Lyrical Ballads* is through the poetry of the magazines. The volume unquestionably belongs to 1798, and seen in relation to the popular verse of that day, its contemporaneous features are very striking. We have been asked to consider too exclusively the revolutionary aspects of the *Lyrical Ballads*. Revolutionary they unquestionably were, but not in every respect. Except that they were much better than other poems published in 1798, the *Ballads* were not such a 'complete change' as some writers would have us believe. Even their eccentricity has been exaggerated. Actually, there is a conventional side to the *Lyrical Ballads*, although it is usually overlooked. It is by way of the general taste for poetry in the 1790s that this essay will approach the poems, and it will attempt to show that they not only conformed in numerous ways to the modes of 1798, and reflected popular tastes and attitudes, but enjoyed a certain popularity in the magazines themselves.

The general interest in poetry during the last decades of the eighteenth century, also, is a phenomenon which is largely ignored, although it is relevant in a number of ways to the new poetry of Southey, Coleridge, Wordsworth, Byron and Scott. Something is known of the popularity of such writers as Helen Maria Williams, Anna Seward, Erasmus Darwin, W. L. Bowles, 'Peter Pindar', Charlotte Smith, Henry James Pye, Mary Robinson and Mrs West; but except for Bowles they are usually dealt with summarily as a deservedly forgotten generation. For most historians they are the 'modern writers' whose 'gaudiness and inane phraseology' were repudiated by the Advertisement and the Preface of the *Lyrical Ballads*. But critical as Wordsworth was of his contemporaries, he cannot be completely dissociated from them. He belonged to their generation, and he addressed himself to their audience. Moreover, he was not insensitive to popular favour. He repeatedly asserted in 1798–9 that he had published the *Lyrical Ballads* to make money; *The Ancient Mariner*, with its 'old words' and 'strangeness', had hurt the sale of the volume, and in the second edition he 'would put in its place some little things which would be more likely to suit the common taste'.[1] This is a fairly appropriate description of some of the contents of the second edition.

The student who wishes to consider the coinage of 'the common taste' will find in the magazines of the late eighteenth century the richest and most accessible repository. There poetry enjoyed a more honoured place than any other form of imaginative writing, and poetry departments were an inevitable feature of such serials as the *Gentleman's Magazine*, the *Monthly Magazine*, the *Scot's Magazine*, the *European Magazine*, and the *Lady's Magazine* – to name only a few of the more popular. Together these five magazines alone published about five hundred poems a year; and their total monthly circulation in 1798 must have exceeded 25,000. At the same time a great number of lesser miscellanies in London, Edinburgh, Glasgow, Dublin and the provincial towns, sought to satisfy in the same way the general taste for verse. It was, in more than one sense, a period of poetic inflation. Seemingly, anything was acceptable for publication, provided it was not too long, and did not offend the proprieties. The average poetry department was a hodge-podge, which by and large provides a very effective measure of popular taste. Its effectiveness is owing to several factors: the great abundance and immediacy of the poetry printed; the flexible combination of both new and reprinted verse; and the prevailing reader–writer situation, in which amateurs wrote the kind of 'original' verse in which they were interested.

As a result of the accepted interpretation of the Parliamentary Act of 1710, magazines lay outside the usual restrictions of the copyright laws, and the poetry departments of most miscellanies like the *Lady's Magazine* and the *Universal Magazine* are therefore likely to contain a large number of reprinted poems, collected from new books of verse, reviews of such volumes, newspapers, poetical miscellanies and other magazines. Such poems were read by – or at least exposed

1 *The Early Letters of William and Dorothy Wordsworth, 1787–1805*, ed. Ernest de Selincourt, Oxford University Press, 1935, pp. 225–7.

to – thousands of readers, and their influence should be measured accordingly. Pieces like Bürger's *Lenore* and M. G. Lewis's *Alonzo the Brave* enjoyed a tremendous popularity in the magazine world, being caught up and carried from miscellany to miscellany until their total circulation must have reached many thousands. 'Because of the trash which infests the magazines', Wordsworth proposed that *The Philanthropist* (The *Monthly Miscellany* which he projected in 1794) offer *reprinted* poetry exclusively, 'from new poetical publications of merit, and such *old* ones as are not generally known'.[1] The *Lyrical Ballads*, we shall find, were promptly raided in this manner by half a dozen magazines, so that the general acquaintance with *Goody Blake*, *We are Seven*, and other poems in the volume cannot be gauged by the number of copies of the original publication in circulation.

At the same time that they helped themselves from outside sources the magazines also printed quantities of what was termed 'original poetry' – that is, new poems written by the editor or his acquaintances, by readers, or by professionals. Some of the more substantial miscellanies like the *Gentleman's Magazine*, the *European Magazine* and the *Monthly Magazine*, published 'original poetry' almost exclusively, and were willing to pay for it. *The Ancient Mariner*, for example, was first planned by the two poets as a joint contribution to the new *Monthly Magazine*, for which it was hoped that five pounds might be obtained. But many miscellanies were unwilling to remunerate writers, and sought rather to obtain contributions gratis from their army of readers. The number of amateur scribblers in the 1790s is legion, and they are mostly anonymous. They are also inveterate plagiarists, so that the first appearance of any poem in the magazines, no matter how it is signed, is always a matter of conjecture. The distinction between 'original', adapted and reprinted verses is never sure. The only certainty is that there is a confused and eddying flood of popular poetry flowing through the magazines from the middle of one century to the next – some old, some new, some written by hacks, much more written by amateurs, who endlessly copied the accepted masterpieces of the past and rang changes on the approved models of the day. The vast proportion of this verse literature is hopelessly mediocre, and deservedly forgotten, except that it provides the best available chart for the shifting currents of popular taste.

1 p. 122.

Through it we can partly understand the ground swell of popular favour which helped to raise the *Lyrical Ballads* to eminence in spite of hostile criticism from the Edinburgh reviewer and others.

The student who approaches the *Lyrical Ballads* by way of the magazines may be struck first by differences rather than by resemblances. To most of the verse of the poetry departments the *Ballads* seem to have little relation, except to represent a kind of recoil. It is easy to see what the poets were reacting against in the Advertisement. The 'common taste' of the miscellanies not only approved the 'gaudy' and 'inane'; it was in most respects extremely conservative, if not antique. There is in much of the magazine verse of the 1790s a literary lag of at least half a century. In his attacks on Pope, Gray, Prior and Dr Johnson in the 1802 Appendix Wordsworth was not exactly beating dead horses. These poets, together with Gay, Parnell, Thomson, Akenside and Thomas Warton, were still the accepted masters for many verse-writers, amateur and professional alike; and most of the hackneyed elegies, odes, occasional poems and so on which flooded the poetry departments of the miscellanies can only be described as the backwash of the Augustan era.

The insipidity of magazine poetry, however, is deceptive. It is not uniformly antique, and it is far from being homogeneous. Not all of the verses in the magazines are imitations of Gray's *Elegy*, Pope's *Pastorals* and *The Pleasures of Melancholy*. A persistent minority – original and reprinted alike – are occupied with new subjects of poetry and written in the new modes of the late eighteenth century. The *Monthly Magazine* in particular, after 1796, was the resort of many of the new poets, but actually their writings, and imitations of them, are likely to be encountered anywhere. With the poems of this minority the *Lyrical Ballads* have a great deal in common, and although the resemblances are often superficial, they are numerous enough to show that Wordsworth and Coleridge were not out of touch with contemporary modes. A great deal of effort has been admirably expended in the last twenty years in developing the background of the poets' thought, and in showing the organic relation of the ideas and attitudes expressed in the *Lyrical Ballads* to the larger movements of eighteenth century thought and taste. It remains still to suggest the many ways in which they also conform to the literary fashions of the 1790s. These we may attempt to describe roughly with respect first to 'content', and second, to 'form', although such a separation, of course, is quite artificial.

There are twenty-three poems in the first edition, and viewed in the light of what we now know of their authorship and composition the volume no doubt seems, as Legouis says, 'a somewhat random and incongruous assemblage'.[1] But the incongruities were certainly less likely to 'puzzle and disconcert' contemporaries than they do modern historians. None of the writers of the notices for the 1798 edition, at least, was sufficiently struck with this feature of the volume to remark upon it. They all presumed, without any visible effort, that the poems were of single authorship, and by and large seemed to feel that the collection was not greatly out of line with contemporary practice. It was a period of feverish poetical activity and mawkish experimentalism, and a good deal of the lack of unity which Legouis and others have found in the *Lyrical Ballads* is obviously the heterogeneity of the literary fashion. In fact, compared with Southey's *Poems* of 1797, the *Ballads* are anything but extraordinary in unevenness of style and miscellaneousness of contents. Southey's volume moves with amateurish abruptness from one manner and one subject to another, whereas the movement of the *Lyrical Ballads*, on the surface at least, is fairly simple. Once the Ancient Mariner has gone his way, the other verses in the volume follow a more or less familiar course for 1798. In general, the drift is in several directions only – towards 'nature' and 'simplicity', and towards humanitarianism and sentimental morality. Without discriminating too precisely between these categories, the reader of that day would tend to construe most of the contents of the *Lyrical Ballads* in terms of these modes of popular poetry, with which he was already familiar.

He would, for example, if the poetry departments of the magazines are any index, regard as perfectly normal a miscellany of ballads on pastoral subjects (treated both sentimentally and jocularly), moral and philosophic poems inspired by physical nature, and lyrical pieces in a variety of kinds describing rural scenes, the pleasures of the seasons, flora and fauna, and a simple life in the out-of-doors. Subjects drawn from 'nature', including both landscape and rural life, as many

1 Emile Legouis, 'Some Remarks on the Composition of the *Lyrical Ballads* of 1798', *Wordsworth and Coleridge: Studies in Honor of George McLean Harper*, Princeton University Press, 1939, pp. 3, 7.

writers have pointed out, were commonplace in the minor verse of the last years of the eighteenth century. Viewed in relation to this considerable body of writing, poems like *Lines Written in Early Spring, Lines Left upon a Seat in a Yew-Tree, Lines Written near Richmond* and *The Nightingale* are obviously not experimental in subject; nor in *form* either, as a matter of fact. Considered as a species of poetry, the 'nature' poems of the *Lyrical Ballads* were anything but surprising in 1798.[1] Novelty, of course, is a very complex and ephemeral quality in any poem or collection of poems, extremely difficult to isolate. It depends upon a thousand particulars, now vanished, which were once an unmistakable part of the literary climate. But the more one reads the popular poetry of the last quarter of the eighteenth century the more he is likely to feel that the really surprising feature of these poems in the *Lyrical Ballads* (as well as of many of the others) – apart from sheer literary excellence – is their intense fulfillment of an already stale convention, and not their discovery of an interest in rivers, valleys, groves, lakes and mountains, flowers and budding trees, the changing seasons, sunsets, the freshness of the morning and the songs of birds. This fact is a commonplace. Yet it is astonishing how often responsible Wordsworthians go astray in this respect, and tend to view Wordsworth and Coleridge as reacting with a kind of totality against contemporary fashions in verse. The question is not whether the *Ballads* were altogether conventional, which no one would attempt to affirm, but whether they were completely out of touch with popular taste. This was certainly the nineteenth century concep-

1 A representative list of 'Wordsworthian' titles from the magazines of 1788–98 is as follows: *The Delights of a Still Evening, Stanzas on a Withered Leaf, A Thought on the Vicissitudes of the Seasons, On the Singing of a Red-Breast Late in Autumn, Inscription for a Rural Arbour, Sonnet to the River Arun, Inscription for a Coppice near Elsfield, Sonnet Written during a Morning's Walk, To a Tuft of Violets, On the Month of May, On the Return to the Country, An Autumn Thought, The Lake of Wyndemere, Description of a Morning in May, Contemplation by Moonlight, To the Daisy, To the Primrose, Ode to the Cuckoo.* The exact citations will not be given, since there are literally hundreds of such poems. Underneath many of the 'nature' poems of the magazines is the familiar conviction that nature is beautiful and full of joy; that man is corrupted by civilization; that God may be found in nature; and that the study of nature not only brings pleasure, therefore, but generates moral goodness. The nature poetry of the *Christian's Magazine* (1760–67), for example, has numerous 'Wordsworthian' features.

tion of Wordsworth, who was viewed as a kind of prophet writing in the wilderness; and it is evidently still the view of some present-day critics and historians, who, struck by the phenomenal literary quality of the *Ballads*, tend to confuse one kind of change with another. They have perhaps been misled by the ambiguities of the Advertisement of 1798, which seems to claim more than it actually does.

For most modern readers, certainly, the most extraordinary poems in the first edition of the *Ballads* are the first and the last in the volume: *The Ancient Mariner* and *Tintern Abbey*. With respect to the first, there is no doubt about the literary unorthodoxy of the poem. Even though readers of 1798 would be well acquainted with traditional ballads, and modern imitations were common, some with 'antiqued' language and orthography, *The Ancient Mariner* was definitely anomalous. Opinion was confused as by no other poem in the volume. But *Tintern Abbey* was quite another story. Although this poem, with its particular set of values and methods of expression, must surely be recognized as a seminal poem in the literary revolution which is traced to 1798, it must have seemed in its day far from revolutionary. Only two of the nine notices of the first edition mentioned it at all (whereas seven of them remarked on *The Ancient Mariner*). Southey in the *Critical* and Dr Burney in the *Monthly Review* mingled praise of the poems with blame. Both found *The Ancient Mariner* 'unintelligible'; but at *Tintern Abbey* there was no sign of surprise or bewilderment. To Southey the poem seemed supremely normal, and he quoted a passage of forty-six lines. Dr Burney described it as 'The reflections of no common mind; poetical, beautiful, and philosophical.' He objected, it is true, to the pernicious primitivism of the poem. But this was no novelty in 1798, and there is no indication that he regarded the poem as otherwise aberrant. With good reason – for, as we know, 'poetical, beautiful and philosophical' verses written in connection with particular regions and landscapes were one of the commonest species of poetry, in the magazines and outside. For more than half a century popular poets had been evoking in a wide variety of metrical forms, roughly equivalent 'wild green landscapes' and 'secluded scenes', and then reflecting upon them in the philosophic manner of *Tintern Abbey*. Many of these lyrical meditations are rhapsodic in character, purporting to have been written immediately after the experience, or (like *Tintern Abbey*) on the very spot where the poet was moved to a spontaneous overflow of thought and feeling. Regarded solely in terms of the modes of eighteenth-century topographical poetry, surely *Tintern Abbey* is one of the most conventional poems in the whole volume. Yet one of the best of Wordsworth's present-day critics can still write in 1950, that 'it is hard to see in the *Lyrical Ballads* any literary influence at all except that of the ballads [that is to say, of Percy's *Reliques*]'.[1] The real novelty of *Tintern Abbey* lay where it still lies in all of Wordsworth's 'nature' poems – not in subject matter and forms, but in sheer poetic excellence – in their vastly superior technical mastery, their fulness of thought and intensity of feeling, the air of spontaneity which they breathe, and their attention to significant details which seem to the reader to have been observed for the first time.

The movement of many of the poems in the volume is likewise towards 'simplicity' – that is (in the words of a reviewer of the *Lyrical Ballads*) towards 'sentiments of feeling and sensibility, expressed without affectation, and in the language of nature'.[2] This was no less the vogue in 1798. The new poets of the day were everywhere striving for artless expressions of sensibility. Both Southey and Coleridge were well-known magazine poets in 1797, and recognized masters of 'simplicity'. *The Nightingale*, written by Coleridge for the *Lyrical Ballads* on one of the most approved subjects of popular poetry, is in many ways a perfect expression of 'simplicity' – in its mingled joyousness and melancholy, its appreciative pictures of 'nature', and its air of complete sincerity. This poem, together with many of the songs and ballads of the volume, would be recognized by readers, and *were* recognized by reviewers, as essays in this literary manner. Conversational informality and freedom from artificiality or affectation were hallmarks of 'simplicity' – so that the bald style of the ballads and, to some extent, the theory of diction advanced in the Advertisement would be likely to be taken as more or less aggressive attempts to achieve 'simplicity'. Dr Burney in the *Monthly Review* questioned whether verses so unembellished as some of the *Lyrical Ballads* could properly be ranked as poetry. But these poems were merely the fulfilment of a tendency which a great number of contemporary poets, without the benefit of Wordsworth and Coleridge's

1 Helen Darbishire, *The Poet Wordsworth*, Oxford University Press, 1950, p. 46
2 *Monthly Mirror*, VI, 1798, 224.

aesthetic and psychological theories, were already showing. To most
readers this feature of the volume would seem less a revolution,
therefore, than the excess of a new orthodoxy.

The strains of 'nature' and 'simplicity' in the *Lyrical Ballads* deeply
blend with those of humanitarianism and sentimental morality, as they
did in a great deal of popular verse. This aspect of the *Lyrical Ballads*,
of course, has long been recognized, and has been fully explored in
points of doctrine. What is striking about the volume, however, in
relation to popular poetry, is not merely the climate of thought and
feeling, but the landscape and the figures – the extent to which
conventional imagery and detail have been employed by the poets.
However much they may be rendered fresh and new by poetic treatment, it must be recognized that most of the objects of sympathy
in the volume belong to an order of beings familiar to every reader
of magazine poetry – namely, bereaved mothers and deserted females,
mad women and distracted creatures, beggars, convicts and prisoners,
and old people of the depressed classes, particularly peasants. For
nearly every character, portrait or figure, there is some seasoned
counterpart in contemporary poetry. It is true that there were other
species of unfortunates and social outcasts being similarly favoured
in the literature of the 1790s – namely, negro slaves, blind men,
prostitutes, exiles, foundlings and natural children. Nevertheless,
although the two poets avoid some, they do not avoid all the way-
worn paths of literary convention.

It has sometimes been recognized, for example, but more often
forgotten, that Wordsworth's lonely and forsaken women are in
some degree stereotypes. To say this is not to deny that such figures
may likewise have had some personal meaning for the author. Nevertheless it must be observed that they were perfectly in line with
contemporary taste, and did not receive in the *Lyrical Ballads* a
disproportionate amount of attention. Bereaved mothers and deserted
females were almost a rage in the poetry departments of the 1790s,
and Wordsworth's counterparts, although unquestionably more
interesting and endowed with some freshness, conform in numerous
particulars to the literary fashion. Some of the women in this numerous class of magazine poems have been seduced (like Martha Ray in
The Thorn); some have been abandoned by their lovers or husbands
(like Wordsworth's Mad Mother and Indian Woman); others (like

his Female Vagrant) have been rendered destitute by death, war, exile and other kinds of misfortune. Some are homeless wanderers with babes in arms; others haunt the places where their loved ones died, or expire where their hopes lie buried. The poems which they frequent are described variously as 'songs' 'complaints', 'fragments', 'ballads', 'plaintive tales' and so on (more will be said later about the *forms of* the *Lyrical Ballads*); the permutations run their full course within the approved conventions. But the subjects are all miserable, grief-stricken and unhappy women, they are objects of sympathy and (very commonly) of humanitarian feeling, and their suffering is frequently rendered with great 'simplicity' of manner and senti-ment.

One of the recognized consequences of desertion or of separation from a lover or husband, according to the conventions of popular poetry, was child-murder, as in *The Lass of Fair Wone* and *The Thorn*; others were death (as in the *Forsaken Indian Woman*), prostitution, loneliness and poverty (as in *The Female Vagrant*); still another was madness. Wordsworth's Mad Mother was not the first of her kind in the 1790s. Demented mothers and distracted sweethearts were a spectacle likely to be encountered any time in the columns of the popular miscellanies. In Dibdin's *Poor Peg*, the subject, 'Mad as the waves, wild as the wind', laments her lost lover, whose body is cast up by the waves at her very feet. In Southey's *Mary the Maid of the Inn*, a romantic ballad founded upon 'a fact, which had happened in the North of England', the mind of the once-lovely and confident maiden has been unhinged by the discovery that her 'idle and worthless' lover is a murderous brigand. In *Ellen, or the Fair Insane*, as in *The Mad Mother*, the interest of the reader is centred in the mental aberrations of the broken-hearted speaker. The ill-fated Ellen wanders in search of her lost lover who has taken his life in an envious fit. She vacillates wildly between the fear that he is lost to her forever and the illusion that he will come again. The poem is outrageously sentimental, whereas Wordsworth's is not; but it may surely be said of Pitt's as well as Wordsworth's (in the words of the Preface of 1800) that it 'has a worthy *purpose*' – that it, also, attempts 'to follow the fluxes and refluxes of the mind when agitated by the great and simple affections of our nature'. The special novelty of *The Mad Mother* for late eighteenth-century readers would lie not in its general intention, nor in its subject, nor in in its narrative method, but in its far greater degree of subtlety and its imaginative use of concrete detail, which give the poem some of its feeling of intensity. Poems about insanity and the plight of madmen, and poems illustrative of the mental processes of rude, simple or defective minds, were having a slight run in the 1790s. *The Idiot Boy*, *We are Seven*, and *Anecdote for Fathers* are related to this class of poems, some of which are in ballad metres and present a simple moral. Wordsworth's poems of this category, therefore, are not so much original in kind, as they are distinguished by a mature theory of psychology and a serious interest in 'manners and passions'.

The Idiot Boy, for example, is usually considered one of the extra-ordinary poems in the 1798 volume. There is considerable truth in this view. The poem, which is one of the showpieces of the collection, was somewhat daring, and it did not go unremarked by the reviewers. Five of the nine gave it particular mention. Opinion on the poem was sharply divided. Southey and Dr Burney, of course, were hostile. But neither treated the poem as a complete anomaly. Both associated it with other 'rustic delineations of the low life', like *The Thorn* and *The Mad Mother*, whose subjects though humble can be shown to be somewhat conventional. *The Idiot Boy* was unquestionably a surprising poem, but less so perhaps in 1798 than it seems to students today who move directly from the major 'pre-romantic' poets to Wordsworth and Coleridge. This fact is suggested by an analogue entitled *The Idiot* which appeared almost simultaneously with the first edition of the *Lyrical Ballads*, in the *Sporting Magazine* for October 1798. This ballad, like *Goody Blake and Harry Gill*, purports to be founded on fact. In the poem, 'Poor Ned, a thing of idiot mind,' was the only child of an aging and doting mother:

Old Sarah lov'd her helpless child,
  Whom helplessness made dear,
And life was happiness to him,
  Who had no hope nor fear.
She knew his wants, she understood
  Each half artic'late call,
And he was ev'rything to her,
  And she to him was all.

When death finally took Old Sarah, Ned tried vainly to awaken her, and then stood 'wond'ring by' as they wrapped the old woman in a shawl and carried her to the grave. After the funeral party departed, Ned lingered behind, dug up the coffin, and carried it back to the cottage. He placed the corpse in the old chair, eagerly built a blazing fire, felt her hand, scrutinized her face, and cried:

'Why, mother, do you look so pale,
  And why are you so cold?'

What *The Idiot* crudely attempts to express in the pathetic inability of the child to understand death (compare with *We are Seven*, written, incidentally, in the same metre). But there is also much that recalls *The Idiot Boy*: the background of village life; the relation between mother and child; the interest in mental processes; and the incongruous mixture of the grotesque and the pathetic.

Wordsworth's Female Vagrant, as we have noted, is a kind of forsaken woman. But her real place is in another category. Whatever the causes for her change of fortune may be, in her wandering life, her abject poverty, her anguish of soul, and her friendlessness she is one of a familiar class of outcasts, the female beggar; and through that class she is associated with the long procession of mendicants who infested the poetry departments of the *Lady's Magazine*, the *Edinburgh Magazine*, and other popular miscellanies in the last years of the eighteenth century. Some of the mendicant poems are merely portraits, which make blunt appeals to sympathy for the poor, the aged, and the unhappy (as does Wordsworth's *Old Man Travelling* – more subtly); but others are narrative poems, sometimes, like *The Female Vagrant*, told in the first person and emphasizing the contrast between past joy and present sorrow, the horrors of war and its consequences, man's treatment of man, and the indifference of society.

Many of the pariahs of the magazine poets are pathetically old and sick, and some of them are soldiers and sailors who have fallen on evil times. In various ways this class of poems makes contact with other verses in the *Lyrical Ballads*. Wordsworth's *Old Man Travelling* is not a mendicant figure, but he is poor. He would be viewed by contemporary readers as a study partly of old age, and partly of the effects of war, which were very much the literary fashion in the 1790s. In their suffering old age, both Simon Lee and Goody Blake in some degree

would also be familiar objects of sympathy; and, as in many of the
mendicant poems, the pathos is heightened in the former by contrast
with earlier felicity, in the latter by contrast with unfeeling prosperity.
The Ancient Mariner, of course, is a figure of a vastly different cut,
but even he is not completely unrelated to the anguished and homeless
old sailors of the poetry departments. No doubt some of the difficulites
readers had with this poem resulted from their trying to view it in
terms of this stereotype.

Goody Blake's crime against the property of Harry Gill is extenu-
ated by her unfortunate circumstances. It was this which offended
Dr Burney in the *Monthly Review* as much as the poem's tacit acceptance of the supernatural. But such was the enlightened attitude
towards crime which a definite minority of magazine poets had
already adopted. This poem, therefore, together with the two
poems in the *Lyrical Ballads* about prisons and prisoners, was quite in
conformity with contemporary taste and interest. Coleridge's *The
Dungeon* and Wordsworth's *The Convict* are both closely associated
with those poems in the magazines which were viewing prisoners as
special objects of sympathy and expressing the need for reform.[1] In

1 Cf. 'The Poor Debtor's Lamentation', *Argus, or General Observer*, 1796, p. 132;
'The Bastille, an Ode, by Mr Thelwall', *Biographical and Imperial Mag.*, vol. 2,
1789, pp. 313-15; 'The Prisoner's Lamentation', *Britannic Mag.*, vol. 2, 1795,
p. 335; 'Verses written in a Prison', ibid., vol. 4, 1796, p. 218; 'The Female
Convict, from Southey's Botany Bay Eclogues', *Cabinet Mag.*, vol. 1, 1797,
pp. 418-20; 'Lines Lately Written at Portsmouth, by a Botany Bay Convict',
Diary, or Woodfall's Register, 6 August 1789, p. 4; 'The Debtor, by the Late Sir
John Henry Moore, Bart.', *Freemason's Mag.*, vol. 1, 1793, pp. 74-5; 'Verses
on the State of English and Foreign Prisons', *Gentleman's Mag.*, vol. 58, 1788,
p. 638; 'The Complaint of a Transport in Botany Bay', ibid., vol. 62, 1972,
pp. 559-60; 'Eulogy on Mr Howard', *Hibernian Mag.*, 1792, p. 88; 'Lines
Written by a Gentleman during a Long Confinement in Paris', *Lady's Mag.*,
vol. 27, 1796, p. 374; 'Idyllium, the Prison, by Dr Darwin', *Monthly Mag.*,
vol. 1, 1796, p. 54; 'Botany Bay Eclogue, Edward and Susan, by W. T.
(Southey), Oxford', ibid., vol. 5, 1798, pp. 41-2; 'A Tribute to Howard.
Written for the Use of a School', *New Lady's Mag.*, vol. 6, 1791, pp. 93-4;
'Lines on the Foregoing, Addressed to Mrs G. W. Willson', ibid., vol. 6,
1791, p. 94; 'On the Necessity of Solitary Confinement in Gaols', *Scots Mag.*,
vol. 54, 1792, p. 76; 'Lines, Written in a French Prison, in 1794', ibid., vol. 60,
1798, p. 195; 'On the Death of the late Benevolent Mr Howard', *Town and
Country Mag.*, vol. 22, 1790, p. 379; 'The Bastille, a Vision . . . by H. M. Williams', *Universal Mag.*, vol. 86, 1790, p. 151; 'A Prison', ibid., vol. 94, 1794,

Coleridge's and Wordsworth's poems the wretched darkness, stagna-
tion, and spiritual poison of prison life are contrasted with the 'soft
influences' of mountain, wood, and water, and the 'benignant touch
of love and beauty' in the life out of doors. The ameliorative effects
of nature are precisely the theme of several of Southey's *Botany Bay
Eclogues*, published in 1797-8. The first of these, for example, printed
in the *Poems* of 1797, and reprinted by the next year in at least eight
magazines and reviews as *Elinor* or *The Female Convict*, is a dramatic
monologue in blank verse, spoken by 'an outcast, unbeloved and
unbewailed', wearing 'the livery of shame' on the 'savage shore' of
New South Wales. Like so many of the mendicants she is haunted by
memories of past felicity in her father's cottage in rural England (there
is a great deal in *The Female Convict* which recalls Wordsworth's
Female Vagrant) and also by the degradation which she subsequently
suffered in a life of prostitution and crime. But this is her consolation:
that in this 'barbarous clime', with its 'wild plains unbroken by the
plough', she may escape 'the comforts and the crimes of polished life'
and find a refuge where the healing ministrations of nature may
regenerate her soul. The death of John Howard, the English reformer,
in 1790 had brought a rash of poems about the conditions of prison life.
Wordsworth's *Convict*, in its first version, was printed in the *Morning
Post* for 14 December 1797, only a few months after Southey's
Female Convict had begun to enjoy a great vogue. It was a topical
poem.

For Legouis 'the chief inner novelty' of the *Lyrical Ballads* lies in
the 'philosophical undercurrent' of the volume – its 'protest against
the out-and-out rationalism of the day', as represented by Godwin's
Political Justice. 'The woes', he writes, 'that Godwin tries to cure by
appealing to the intellect, Wordsworth strives to alleviate by refining
the sense of pity. Sensibility stands with him in the place of mere logic.
He fights for the same cause as Godwin, but his weapons are feeling
and "the language of the senses".'[1] But surely the sentimental
humanitarian poems of the magazines had been fighting for the same
cause for a number of years, using the same weapons. Moreover, if the

---

p. 368. The last-named poem draws a contrast between the 'cool grot on
verdant mead' and the 'soul-appalling' prospect of the prison, with the
languishing captives 'left to perish' there.
1 'Remarks on the Composition of the *Lyrical Ballads*', pp. 8, 10.

Lyrical Ballads were a 'democratic manifesto', as Grierson and others have declared, they were one which had already begun to be somewhat dulled by repetition.[1]

Nevertheless, although *The Last of the Flock*, *Simon Lee*, and *Goody Blake and Harry Gill* were not the first poems to represent unhappy and suffering rural folk, these three poems – especially the last two – seem to represent significant novelties in the first edition of the *Lyrical Ballads*. In their bald and homespun style, but more particularly in their sympathetic fidelity to everyday rural life, there is 'nature and simplicity' of a different kind and intensity from that which is met with in the endless pastorals of the magazines. Their relation to these popular poems of country life is somewhat like the relation of the early Waverley Novels to the sentimental adventure stories of the Gothic school. Both Wordsworth and Scott professed a serious interest in 'manners and passions'. For the melodramatic clichés of the novels of terror, Scott was to provide effective equivalents in terms of Scotch life and history. Similarly, Wordsworth, for the stereotyped pathos and generalized poverty, hardship, and old age of magazine pastorals like *Old Oliver* and *The Unfortunate Cottager*, offered Simon Lee with his blind eye and swollen ankles, and the 'canty dame in *Goody Blake*, with her 'wither'd hand', stealthily filling her apron with twigs. There was little precedent for this 'sentimental naturalism' (so to speak) in magazine poetry, and it seems to have been these poems, as well as *The Idiot Boy*, which Wordsworth was defending in the Advertisement when he begged the reader to consider whether they did not afford 'a natural delineation of human passions, human characters, and human incidents'. The feeling of particularity in these two poems is likewise very strong. It is true that Wordsworth's rustics have important links with the peasants of Cowper, Crabbe, Burns and Fergusson, and with the

1 H. J. C. Grierson: '. . . in a deeper sense these ballads were a democratic manifesto . . . he (Wordsworth) will try what poetry can do to change people's hearts and enlarge their sympathy for man as man. He will not write heroics for the amusement of a corrupt society; he will write of simple folk in simple language. . . . Therefore Wordsworth seeks his subjects not among Godwinian intellectuals, but among forsaken women, old men in distress, children, and crazy persons, in whom these instincts and emotions show themselves in their simplest and most recognizable forms' (*A Critical History of English Poetry*, Chatto & Windus, 1947, p. 314).

humble subjects of the jocular and sentimental verse of popular poets like Charles Dibdin, Thomas Holcroft and 'Peter Pindar', but in relation to the vast majority of magazine poems, *Goody Blake* and *Simon Lee* represent a modest innovation.

So much for the *contents* of the *Lyrical Ballads*. Considered strictly in terms of subjects and sentiments, most of the poems in the 1798 edition, it is clear, would not seem anomalous or outlandish to contemporary readers. It is precisely in the direction of 'nature', 'simplicity', and sentimental humanitarianism that a minority of popular contemporary poets had already moved. And, in general, it may be asserted that what is true of the contents of the *Lyrical Ballads*, is true also of the *forms*. Except for the language and style of a few poems, supported by the theory of diction advanced in the Advertisement, and a few limited experiments with meter, the *manner* of the volume cannot be regarded as extraordinary (disregarding, of course, all considerations of merit). It was a period of great confusion with respect to traditional literary genres – a period which was witnessing widespread dislocations in literary taste, and a corresponding shift in opinion concerning the true nature of poetry and of poetic excellence. Among magazine poets, as has been said, many of the minor neo-classical kinds were still popular – the ode, the elegy, the eclogue, the hymn, the epigram, the monody, the pastoral and so on. At the same time, in keeping with the vital new interest in lyrical expression, there was a good deal of experimentation with short poetical forms of other kinds, of which the *ballad* was one of the most popular. (The *sonnet*, adopted by Wordsworth in 1802, was another.) On the whole the words *lyrical* and *ballad* in the title of the new volume of verse – whatever they may have meant when used in conjunction with one another – and even the word *experiments* in the Advertisement would be likely to invite rather than repel readers. And beyond, the *forms* which they found inside would represent a rupture only with what was antique in contemporary taste. Although they might find it difficult to define or differentiate all the various lyrical and narrative kinds which they were offered there, on the whole they would tend to view the collection as a recognizable assortment of poetical species. Ballads, complaints and plaintive tales, fragments, fables and anec-dotes, songs and pastorals, sketches, effusions and reflective poems, and occasional pieces of various kinds – these were common coin in the poetry departments in the years previous to 1798.

Let us consider first the *ballads* of the volume. They represent one of the ubiquitous species of magazine verse. Self-styled ballads are everywhere in the last years of the century. The term is used by itself and in such combinations as 'pastoral ballad', 'antique ballad', 'new ballad', 'Scotch ballad', 'American ballad', 'legendary ballad' and 'gypsy ballad'. We shall be disappointed, however, if we expect the poets of the magazines to help us to a clear understanding of the term 'lyrical ballad'. By 1798 almost anything might be called a 'ballad', and very often it was. The word, of course, suggested traditional balladry – the folk ballad, the poetry of the non-literary classes, the celebrated verses of Bishop Percy's *Reliques*. But it suggested also the broadside ballad – i.e. any verses of several stanzas which might be sung to a popular tune, or be sold in the streets – and, by extension, any song on a popular subject. In the magazines, therefore, any *narrative poem* in stanzas, or any *lyric* which hoped to appeal to a large circle of readers, or any combination of both, was likely to be termed a ballad. Half of the so-called 'ballads' which appeared in the *Gentleman's Magazine*, the *Lady's Magazine*, and the *Edinburgh Magazine* in the last years of the eighteenth century have no resemblance to the traditional balladry of the non-literary classes, nor do they even tell a story.

If these poems are 'ballads' so are Wordsworth's 'Lucy Poems' of the 1800 edition. They are all essentially 'subjective'.

The two kinds of ballads, 'objective' and 'subjective', narrative and lyrical, are found in profusion, often in adjoining columns, in British magazines of the eighteenth century; they are found side by side in Percy's *Reliques*; and they are found together in the *Lyrical Ballads* – in the poems with a definite narrative element like *The Ancient Mariner*, *Goody Blake* and *The Idiot Boy*, and in the lyrics like *Expostulation and Reply* and *Lines Written in Early Spring*, which are written in traditional ballad stanza (or something very close to it) and which affect a 'simple' popular style. Which poems are the 'lyrical ballads' proper, and which belong to the 'few other poems' of the title page? For Wordsworth and for most of his reviewers the ballads seem to have been the narrative poems of the volume, of which there are about nine. A 'lyrical ballad' (we infer from Wordsworth's remarks in the 1800 *Preface*) was a tale like *Goody Blake* 'told in a more impressive Meter than is used in Ballads' – presumably in his five, eight, and ten-line stanzas. But he was only one of many verse-writers in 1798 who were using lyrical meters with ballad stories; and actually readers would be prepared to regard as ballads a number of other poems in the volume, particularly since they were invited to expect ballads of a *lyrical* order. For one thing, there might be 'songs' in ballad meters. Viewed in terms of the practice of popular poets, consequently, the title of the *Lyrical Ballads* is ambiguous and confusing. Significantly in the final classification of his poems, Wordsworth abandoned the category 'lyrical ballad'.

It is customary to consider the 'lyrical ballad' as a kind of literary hybrid, invented by the poets for a somewhat special purpose, which modified significantly the traditional features of the ballad species. In the eyes of many historians it represents one of the significant experimental features of the 1798 volume. 'The poems were to be ballads,' C. H. Herford has written, with the air of explaining an ingenious innovation, 'telling their stories in the simple, seemingly artless way which both poets admired in the *Reliques*, and in *Lenore*; but they were to claim rank as poetry, as song, and thus the volume received the title *Lyrical Ballads*.'[1] But in addition to the error of construing the term *ballad* far too narrowly, this view of the intention of the poets overlooks the practice of a host of late eighteenth-century ballad writers, among them the author of *Lenore*, who sought to claim for their poems 'rank as poetry, as song', while 'telling their stories'. In some of these poems the narrative element is reduced to a mere scaffolding in which the 'lyrical' passage is, as it were, suspended – as, for example, in *Julia, an Ancient Ballad* of the *Lady's Magazine* for 1797. In this poem, written in the eight-line stanzas of *Goody Blake*, the 'hapless Julia' makes her way in the first stanza to her lover's grave; in the five succeeding stanzas she laments her loss directly in the familiar 'complaint' form; in the seventh we are told that she expires in grief. Technically, therefore, *Julia* is a narrative poem; in however elementary a form, it exhibits character in relation to action. But the real intention of the poem is obviously 'lyrical', however ineptly carried out. The poem is a 'lyrical ballad', although the term itself seems to have been invented by Wordsworth and Coleridge.

1 *Wordsworth*, 1930, p. 99.

A less extreme example than *Julia*, but one closer in its blending of
narrative and lyrical elements to some of Wordsworth's ballads, is
Laura, a Ballad, by a Young Lady of Fifteen, from the same magazine
a few months earlier. This poem describes an edifying episode in the
life of the 'youthful, rich and fair' heroine. She was accosted in 'a
beauteous bow'r' of flowers by a distressed cottager seeking aid for
her sick husband and dying children. The 'haughty Laura' spurned
these entreaties. But when she witnessed the charity of 'a rustic
miller', she felt shame for her harshness, and begged forgiveness of
the woman she had scorned.

Take, then, this purse; give me no thanks –
    I grieve I have no more;
That gen'rous rustic taught me now,
    What ne'er I knew before:

That riches are but lent to us,
    To lib'rally be given;
And, when in charity employ'd,
    It paves our way to heav'n.[1]

The moral of this fable, and the manner in which the incident is represented, recall Wordsworth's *Simon Lee*, and some of the other *Lyrical
Ballads*, though it is far more naïve in every respect. In the first place,
the poem tends constantly to linger on the 'lyrical' possibilities of the
moment: the 'beauteous bow'r' of Laura (fourteen lines), the complaint of the cottager (ten lines), Laura's feeling of remorse (twelve
lines), and so on. Secondly, the action itself turns on a trivial event
which has significance only in climate of sensibility. It is Laura's
emotion, her sudden insight into her selfishness, which is intended to
distinguish a situation otherwise commonplace. When Wordsworth
writes, in the 1800 *Preface*, 'Another circumstance ... distinguishes
these Poems from the popular Poetry of the day; it is this, that the
feeling therein developed gives importance to the action and situation,
and not the action and situation to the feeling,' he is probably thinking of *Alonzo the Brave, Osric the Lion*, and other 'idle and extravagant
stories in verse'. For many years, certainly, among writers of sen-

1 'Julia, an Ancient Ballad,' *Lady's Mag.*, vol. 28, 1797, p. 619; 'Laura, a
Ballad, by a Young Lady of Fifteen', ibid., vol. 27, 1796, pp. 566–7.

sibility, in prose and verse alike, it had been a fundamental tenet that feeling alone was what gave importance to action and situation. It is certainly true of poems like *Laura, Hannah* and *The Female Convict*. The only essential difference is that *Simon Lee* succeeds, whereas these poems fail. Perhaps that is what Wordsworth meant; or merely that *he* 'looked more steadily at his subject'.

The more one reads the minor poetry of the magazines from 1788 to 1798, the more it is impossible to escape the impression that the concept of the 'lyrical ballad' does not represent a significant innovation in 1798, nor as a term is it particularly appropriate to the contents of this volume of poems. Perhaps the title was chosen casually. Perhaps it was designed to be nondescript – uniting poems of diverse subjects and kinds. Perhaps it was meant to suggest that the poems might be popular, and promised that they would eschew the recherché and the ultra-refined. Certainly as titles went in the years before 1798, this one was likely to surprise nobody.

Writers everywhere in the magazines, as we have said, had been seeking to give their works an air of spontaneity by emphasizing their casual, extemporaneous qualities, an effort in which Wordsworth was to be eminently more successful. Many such poems are sonnets, which were the rage in the 1790s; but others are written, like Wordsworth's, in blank verse, in four-line stanzas of various kinds and in the regular eight-line stanzas of *Lines Written near Richmond*. A full metrical analysis of the *Ballads* in terms of popular versification is not contemplated here, since it would unnecessarily prolong this study, but by and large it may be affirmed that whatever the claims which have since been made for them, the *Lyrical Ballads*, on the surface at any rate, do not exhibit revolutionary or even surprising prosodic tendencies. On the whole the two poets appear to have been satisfied to adopt meters which were current in their own day. Only half a dozen of the twenty-three poems in the first edition could be considered experimental in this respect. In a few of the narrative poems, chiefly those written in ten-line stanzas, Wordsworth seems to have been trying to work out stanzaic patterns which would allow him to achieve more sustained effects than were possible in the four-line stanzas of *We are Seven* and *Anecdote for Fathers*. This may, in fact, be partly what he meant by 'lyrical ballad'. But it could hardly be represented as more than a very limited

kind of prosodic experiment. Not a single reviewer of the first
edition seems to have been struck with the metrical novelties of the
volume.

In short, whtever aspect of the *Lyrical Ballads* we examine, whether
it be the meters, the lyrical and narrative kinds, the subjects, attitudes
and themes of individual poems or groups of poems, we are struck by
the great number of particulars in which the volume conforms to the
taste and interests of some segments of the literary world in 1798.
This is not to deny that the merit of the work was phenomenal, that
it was 'original' in various respects (as reviewers said it was), and that
it was to be a leavening force of extraordinary power in the years to
come. From one point of view the *Lyrical Ballads* stand at the beginning of a new orientation of literary, social, ethical and religious
values; and they are unquestionably a pivotal work in the transition
from one century to the next. But from another point of view,
equally valid, they come at the end of a long and complicated process
of development, according to which a great deal in the volume must
have seemed to many readers both right and inevitable. Wayward
as the two poets were in some respects, in others they must have
seemed to be moving briskly with various currents of the day, and
thus assuring themselves of some kind of following among the reading
audience.
(486–522)

W. W. Robson

'*Resolution and Independence*', in John Wain (ed.), *Interpretations*
1955

'*Resolution and Independence*,' says Coleridge, 'is *especially* characteristic
of the author. There is scarce a defect or excellence in his writings of
which it would not present a specimen.' It is also characteristic of the
author in its method. Wordsworth chooses an episode which would
seem, abstractly described, to be of small transmissable significance.
His success lies in convincing us of the significance *he* found in it, one
essentially particular and personal. He imposes conviction by means
of that characteristic medium *through* which we are made to see and

judge all that Wordsworth wishes us to see and judge, and *of* which the figures and situations he presents seem so completely to be.

This medium is verse of a *timbre* we recognize at once as Words-worthian: the medium of *The Ruined Cottage* and *Hartleap Well* and *Michael*. *Resolution and Independence* perhaps belongs more fully with the first of these than with the other two; Wordsworth (we can divine without knowing any external facts about the personal crisis that underlies it) is more deeply involved in the experience he offers for our contemplation. The point can be made by remarking on the quality of those poems. When we compare, for instance, *Michael* with Crabbe's best work, we feel that Crabbe has the advantage. *Michael* is a very fine poem, finer than Tennyson's *Dora*; but in comparison with Crabbe, *Michael* and *Dora* go together. But *Resolution and Independence* is, in an important sense, more profoundly personal than *Michael* or *The Brothers*; or, to say this in more strictly literary terms, it is more immediate; though it is on a larger scale, it has the same immediacy, as it has substantially the same method, as the 'Lucy' poems. A comparison of it with Crabbe would not be helpful – except as showing how far removed is its structure and its significance from anything appreciable by the eighteenth century mind.

I said that *Resolution and Independence* was profoundly personal. Certainly it has biographical value – whether we judge its impulsion to have come chiefly from Wordsworth's worry about Coleridge, or about his own resolve to marry and settle down, or about his tendencies to recurrent depression. Certainly, too, it has its humani-tarian aspect, as an example of poetic 'field-work among rustics'; and in this aspect also it is very typical of its author. But *Resolution and Independence* is not the anecdote related, in faithful detail, in Dorothy Wordsworth's Journal. For one thing, Dorothy is not there; and, though William of course is there, that sober, prosaic individual with the traditionally northern virtues, a child of the English eighteenth century, common-sensical, pious and *bourgeois* (while Dorothy with her simple grace is like the heroine of *Persuasion*), he is only fully asserted, and vindicated, at the poem's close; the core of the poem is the 'unknown modes of being': and in calling this poem personal we are testifying primarily to an experience of them, and to Wordsworth's way of resolving and validating that experience.

Resolution and Independence is a poem, self-sufficient and existing in its own right. It is a poem describing a psychological event which issued in a moral judgement. Our judgement that it is a 'public' poem follows closely upon the judgement that this moral consequence – this more general significance – is felt to spring rightly and naturally from Wordsworth's own interpretation of the psychological event. In *Strange Fits of Passion* Wordsworth comes very close to offering only the statement of a vividly evoked psychological curiosity: there is a tacit admission of limited significance ('But in the Lover's ear alone'). *Strange Fits of Passion*, nevertheless, is also a poem; but it is clearly a border-line case; 'border-line' between the private and the public, or (the distinction is often much the same where Wordsworth is concerned) between the successful poem and the unsuccessful one. *Resolution and Independence*, which has really a similar method and subject-matter, implicitly claims more for itself than the shorter poem; it is conceived on a grander scale; and we are asked, in judging it, to apply to it – and apply it to – much more of our experience. Dorothy wrote gravely to an uncomprehending critic of the poem within the Wordsworth circle:

When you happen to be displeased with what you suppose
to be the tendency or moral of any poem which William
writes, ask yourself whether you have hit upon the real
tendency and the true moral, and above all never think that
he writes for no reason but merely because a thing happened
– and when you feel any poem of his to be tedious, ask
yourself in what spirit it was written (Letter to Sara and Mary
Hutchinson, June 1802).

The 'real tendency' and 'true moral' of *Resolution and Independence*, together with the 'spirit in which it was written', make it clear that *Resolution and Independence* was meant to be important and general. If we cannot find it to be either, its failure must be judged to be more than technical; nothing in the poem will survive that failure of intention. However, I address myself here to readers for whom the poem does not so fail; wishing to examine more closely the grounds and conditions of its success.

The poem seems to begin artlessly enough, with a series of statements, in the specious present, that might be casual remarks introducing a very different kind of poem, 'lyrical' and careless of before and after. The shift to the past tense in III, going with the introduction of the poet (who brings in, though for the moment he has forgotten about them, 'all the ways of men, so vain and melancholy'), changes our sense of what the poem is to be; III, though so fully in the happy key of I and II, makes it certain that this key cannot honestly be maintained. Nevertheless, the opening stanzas play their part in our final impression. The 'presentness' is quite right: as we can see if we turn them, for experimental purposes, into statements about the past. This *is* Nature – as Nature is when Nature is happy; and there is, too, anticipatory contrast, not only between the happiness of Nature and the sudden sadness of Wordsworth, but between the bright light, the pleasant sounds, the gay movement of living creatures, and the sudden bareness, silence and stillness of the setting in which we see the leech-gatherer. (Compare the effect of 'Runs with her all the way, wherever she doth run' with 'And moveth all together, if it move at all.') Finally, when we go back to that opening having taken the poem as a whole, it seems a kind of proleptic clarification; Wordsworth, in 'laughing himself to scorn', laughs himself back to a happiness which is felt to be still there. The simple patterning of statements, then, turns out to be less artless than we might suppose from considering those stanzas in isolation. But the 'artless' effect is important; there is, we feel, no arranging; the objects of delight simply presented themselves so, freshly and naturally, in their innocent irresponsibility; their 'mirth' is not to be distinguished from the spectator's delighted motions of identification. The nature of *his* satisfaction is made explicit enough in one of Wordsworth's own pieces of 'practical criticism':

The stock-dove is said to *coo*, a sound well imitating the note of the bird; but, by the intervention of the metaphor *broods*, the affections are called in by the imagination to assist in marking the manner in which the bird reiterates and prolongs her soft note, as if herself delighting to listen to it, and participating of a still and quiet satisfaction, like that which may be supposed inseparable from the continuous process of incubation (Preface to Poems, 1815).

What follows the opening verses reminds us, of course, of another shade of meaning in 'broods'.

The satisfactions of I–III – those of Nature indistinguishable from those of the poet ('with joy' in III can be taken differently with 'the hare that raced about' or 'I saw') – are explicitly associated with childhood ('as happy as a boy'); so that we cannot say, when we reach 'all the ways of men' at the end of III, whether the 'old remembrances' suggest to the poet the contrast between 'men' and Nature or the contrast between 'men' and boys; clearly intending to remind himself of the former, he succeeds all the more in reminding us of the latter. Thus in V the sky-lark, like the hare, is no doubt a 'Child of earth' irrespective of its age; so are human beings; but in view of what has gone before we are inclined to give a slight extra stress to 'Child'. It is commonplace that Wordsworth (as in *Tintern Abbey* and *The Prelude*) associates Nature with the Child; but the association here, taken with the emphasis laid on the problems of adult liviing in VI, introduces a *kind* of contrast with the Man unusual in Wordsworth. For the theme of *Resolution and Independence* is maturity; or rather, the recognition of a fact of moral experience without which there cannot be full maturity; that is, a successful emergence from the world of the Child.

But though the critical attitude towards a prolonged childhood is felt in the gloomy anticipations of V ('Solitude, pain of heart, distress and poverty') and the retrospect and self searchings of VI, the transition to the Poets in VII ('Poets' cannot be poets without an ability to recapture the emotions of the Child) states it, if not ambiguously, at any rate with some doubt. Chatterton – of whom Wordsworth, in his prose moods, had no very high opinion – was only a Boy ('It is wonderful', said Johnson, 'how the whelp has written such things') but 'marvellous'; 'The sleepless Soul' cannot mainly mean his insomnia due to guilt at being found out, it is the Poet's eternal alertness that is relevant here; 'perished in his pride' might imply a doubt about the moral legitimacy of Chatterton's suicide, but the line sounds triumphant in itself, and it leads into the quite unequivocal 'glory and joy' of Burns, which cannot be separated from his 'Following his plough' as a child of Nature. The fifth line 'By our own spirits we are deified' therefore comes in oddly – oddly when we ask ourselves just what, for all its familiarity, it means. It serves its purpose, however; without it, the stanza would run the risk of smugness ('We Poets'); just being a Poet, and young, and glad, is enough to bring on eventually 'despondency' and 'madness' (why 'madness', we might ask?). 'Our own spirits', however, brings in the essential criticism, and, through 'deified', prepares the way for the surprising 'madness', while retroactively qualifying 'pride', 'glory' and 'joy'; one's spirits here are one's genius, or one's conviction of it, but 'spirits' also suggests the dispositional 'genial faith' and the more ephemeral 'high spirits' (Burns's whisky, I'm afraid, is irrelevant); and the line condenses a fundamental criticism of Romantic poetry all the more effectively because embedded in a Romantic stanza.

VIII, the turning-point of the poem, gives us an immediate contrast, in its Wordsworthian tentativeness and embarrassed syntax, with the rhetorical, poetical verse of VII; the 'peculiar grace' and the 'eye of heaven', carrying a further criticism of 'deified': the Poet has disappeared from the centre of interest in this stanza, with its characteristic starkness; in the next, there is nothing human at the centre at all. Of the two famous similes which occupy IX, Wordsworth observes:

In these images, the conferring, the abstracting, and the modifying powers of the Imagination, immediately and mediately acting, are all brought into conjunction. The stone is endowed with something of the power of life to approximate it to the sea-beast; and the sea-beast stripped of some of its vital qualities to assimilate it to the stone; which intermediate image is thus treated for the purpose of bringing the original image, that of the stone, to a nearer resemblance to the figure and condition of the aged Man; who is divested of so much of the indication of life and motion as to bring him to the point where the two objects unite and coalesce in comparison (Preface to Poems, 1815).

Wordsworth indicates by what are in such a context themselves unusual metaphors ('stripped' and 'divested') the workings here of his metaphoric technique. It achieves an effect, after the explicit emotionalisms, the exhilarations and depressions ('joy' and 'dejection') in the first part of the poem, of an extraordinary dehumanization and spareness. 'Beside a pool bare to the eye of heaven' – that 'bare' is the keyword (cf. 'Couched on the bald top of an eminence').

Something existing by itself, obedient to its own mysterious laws, totally independent of the onlooker – this single figure now fills up the landscape that had formerly been so populous with 'blissful creatures'; that now, we realize for the first time, is a 'lonely place'. Instead of the metaphoric language 'clothing' the thought (as we should normally say) it seems to operate by a process of 'stripping' and 'divesting'. Even what might seem merely an ungainly Wordsworthianism, 'The oldest man he seemed that ever *wore* grey hairs', perhaps helps, by the negative suggestion of 'wore' to reinforce 'bare to the eye of heaven'. It is the mere existence of the old Man which is so impressive (speaking of an earlier version of this stanza, in which Wordsworth indulged his 'mystical feeling for the verb "to be" ' – 'By which the old Man *was*, etc.', the poet laid great stress on the importance, for his purposes, of the sudden unexplained appearance of this being in his primal simplicity). And it is this mere existence which the odd similes of IX cooperate to define. The first simile, indeed, if followed through strictly with an eye to its prose content, compares the old Man to something that only '*seems* a thing endued with sense'. The father-figure unquestionably is present but we do not yet know in which of his embodiments; he seems certainly to be 'from some far region sent', but we do not yet know just what his 'apt admonishment' will be: it might be something terrifying. The 'huge stone', 'Couched on the bald top of an eminence', so that we don't know how it got there, and the 'sea-beast crawled forth', while serving, as Wordsworth says, to establish the intermediate status of the old Man, are themselves directly evocative, and of something nearer terror than awe.

In X the old Man is still impressive, but is now a recognizable, if very Wordsworthian, human being, a character of *The Prelude*, with the 'more than human weight' of his past upon him. That 'more than human', while seeming to make a greater claim on our capacity for awe than the non-human similes of IX, actually makes less; it prepares us for the transition to XII–XV, the part of the poem that has been adversely criticized, but which is none the less not only justifiable but essential. The simile which concludes XI, while reminding us of the extreme difference between Wordsworth's sensibility and Shelley's, serves two purposes; its idiosyncrasy helps to reinforce the oddity of the previous similes of the stone and the

sea-beast, but, in being so much less disturbing, it induces our acceptance of the old Man as a simple, dignified and patient human figure,
a 'resigned solitary'; and in 'That heareth not the loud winds when
they call' we have both a direct evocation (again by negative suggestion) of the old Man, and a subtle hint of the imperious emotional
demand of the poet (compare XVII, 'Perplexed, and longing to be
comforted, My question eagerly did I renew'). The old Man is by now
a recognizable old Man – however cloud-like, he has more than a
figurative 'human weight': 'Himself he *propped*, limbs, body and
pale face, Upon a long grey staff of shaven wood' – 'propped',
taken with the simile that closes the stanza, is an important word,
helping as it does to counteract some part of the effect of 'cloud',
and giving a prosaic grounding to the summing-up line, 'And
moveth all together, if it move at all.'

The 'conversation' which follows brings forcibly to our attention
the criticism levelled at *Resolution and Independence*. Coleridge, in
illustration of his general thesis about Wordsworth, complains (in the
Biographia Literaria) of the incongruities of style; citing the contrast
between the diction of XVII and XIX on the one hand, and XVIII
('Yet still I persevere, and find them where I may') on the other.
Admittedly, he had an earlier, and still more prosy version of XVIII
in mind; as well as lines, later cancelled, such as

Close by a pond, upon the further side,
He stood alone; a minute's space, I guess,
I watched him, he continuing motionless;
To the pool's further margin then I drew,
He being all the while before me in full view.

('The metre', Coleridge had remarked a little earlier, 'merely reminds the reader of his claims in order to disappoint them.') But it
seems a very unintelligent reading of the poem as it stands that merely
finds in the manner of XII–XV and XIX–XX a Wordsworthian
lapse into prosaicism. The awkwardnesses have point; but a point that
cannot be brought out if one confines oneself to considering proprieties of diction. The mode of *Resolution and Independence* as a
whole has to be understood. *Resolution and Independence* is a poem
which casts some doubt on the theory, made current by I. A. Richards
in *The Principles of Literary Criticism,* that great poetry must in some

way immunize itself to irony, by 'containing' or neutralizing un-
sympathetic reactions, or by anticipating them. The corollary to this
theory, that great poems cannot be successfully parodied, is also made
to seem doubtful. For *Resolution and Independence* has been successfully parodied, by Lewis Carroll; and no doubt the parody, in its
final form (in *Through the Looking Glass*), makes a pointed comic
criticism of the poet's self-absorption and his tactlessness, and of the
poem's superficial inconsequence. But when you enjoy the parody
and take its point, you cannot feel that it damages the original. To
understand the mood and intention of *Resolution and Independence* is
to see why it is not an adverse or qualifying criticism to admit that it
contains no irony or humour, or that it is open to parody.

The justification for the banalities and gawkiness of the central
stanzas can be brought out by way of considering a parody of them
that does not, on the whole, come off, though it is amusing; the
earlier version (1856) of Lewis Carroll's *Looking Glass* parody. (Its
author thought that its 'appearance' must be 'painful . . . to the
admirers of Wordsworth and his poem of *Resolution and Independence*'.) The earlier version is much more severe on what, in speaking
of the 'White Knight' parody, I called Wordsworth's tactlessness;
what is burlesqued here is patronizing snobbery and a comically
brutal egotism and self-preoccupation.

I met an aged, aged man
  Upon the lonely moor:
I knew I was a gentleman,
  And he was but a boor.

(Yet compare 'But now a stranger's privilege I took'); Wordsworth's approach, and his handling of the spoken dialogue, are no
doubt comically ungainly, but the whole point is that the old Man
isn't a boor ('solemn order', 'lofty utterance', 'choice word and
measured phrase', 'a stately speech', etc.). And Wordsworth shows
no condescension towards him, rather a bewildered and at first only
half-comprehending respectfulness.

I did not hear a word he said,
  But kicked that old man calm,
And said, 'Come, tell me how you live!'
  And pinched him in the arm.

This has more point, in so far as it fixes upon the inanity of Words-worth's question. 'How is it that you live, and what is it you do?' *is* a flat line, and it does not cease to be flat when we see why it is there; but we need not find the poet's insistence ('My question eagerly did I renew') a complacent Wordsworthian indulgence of the kind here satirized. Wordsworth's personal need, his demand for reassur-ance, issuing in that oddly inappropriate question, is not so much for a reassurance *from* the old Man as for a reassurance *about* the old Man. When this is realized, the prosaicisms seem quite justified; they perform an essential function, in contrasting the public world of everyday human experience and human endurance with the inner world into which Wordsworth has taken the figure of the leech-gatherer, and made of it a quantity which cannot be apprehended without uncertainty and dread.

While he was talking thus, the lonely place,
The old Man's shape, and speech – all troubled me;

'Troubled' is the key word here. The significance of the old Man – one that is not finally grasped till the last stanza – is a very personal significance for the poet; there is no hint of anything like the self-indulgence of

I knew I was a gentleman,
　And he was but a boor

– whatever we might think about some other short poems of Words-worth. And we might notice that in the later version of the parody (in *Through the Looking Glass*) the 'Wordsworthian' becomes a sympathetic character (the White Knight) and many of the satiric touches are softened into Carrollian fantasy: so that many readers have enjoyed it without realizing that it is a parody at all.

The movement of the later part of *Resolution and Independence* may now be summarized. The old Man in XIII–XV, now seen in close-up, is a credible figure, with his endurance, and his simple dignity (the victim of 'an unjust state of society', Wordsworth remarked in a letter defending the poem). He stands for an important element in Wordsworth's own temperament and character; Walter Pater used the expression from XIV, 'grave Livers', to suggest the social and moral habit of Wordsworthian verse. We might say, indeed, that the poem as a whole gives us the two contrasting aspects of Wordsworth himself: his strength of character and prosaic simplicity in the leech-gatherer, his 'blank misgivings of a creature' and sense of 'unknown modes of being' in the poet-interlocutor. The conclusion of the poem gives us the reconciliation or 'resolution' of the two attitudes: an achieved integrity.

The way in which the Resolution is effected is characteristic. The mood of XVI – standing, as it does, in extreme and plainly deliberate contrast with XV – is of reversion to the experience of the stanzas in which the old Man first appears; he is an internalized figure, of uncertain significance:

And the whole body of the Man did seem
Like one whom I had met with in a dream.

His voice is 'like a stream Scarce heard'; the simile associates him again with the non-human. But by now we have, as we had not in IX, an alternative estimate of him to set against that. Wordsworth, we know, attached great importance to the trance-like condition described in XVI; but, even if we agree with Mr F. W. Bateson that he was mistaken in so doing, we can see the dramatic effect of the contrasting stanzas XV and XVI; the contrast, we note, is repeated in the juxtaposing of XVIII and XIX:

While I these thoughts within myself pursued,
He, having made a pause, the same discourse renewed.

The 'troubling' and uncertain significance of the old Man is one appropriate to the child's vision; the 'admonition' he represents to the child is morally ambiguous and disturbing. Recognition of the real nature of the 'admonition' – what the old Man really is and stands for – means achievement of 'so firm a mind'; the 'true moral' of the poem is not only that awareness of the greater suffering of others helps one to deal with one's own, but that *achieving* that awareness – that recognition of others' 'independence' of one's own fantasies, and of what one's fantasies make of them – is itself a moral discovery of the greatest importance: so that the last stanza comes with both a resolving and a validating effect. The old Man, existing in his own right, is himself a 'help' and 'stay' against the encroachments of fantasy; his solidity is guaranteed by the firmness and rectitude of that placid verse.

Resolution and Independence, then, has a structure, and it is this structure which makes it a successful and public poem. Properly viewed, the incongruities disappear, or seem to be functional; the artlessness and clumsiness serve to high-light, to dramatize a contrast which the poem intends to bring out (the 'Two Voices' in the same poem); they are intentionally set against a formal deliberateness of manner so noticeable that it suggests a stylization: one based upon a personal rehandling of the medium of Spenser – a poet with whom Wordsworth has much in common. (Wordsworth had been reading a Spenserian poem, Thomson's *Castle of Indolence*, about this time.)

The setting and presentation of the old Man may, indeed, show the influence of Spenser's Despair. But the significance of the leech-gatherer for Wordsworth is not only that he stands, of course, for something quite other than Despair, but that, in an important sense, he does not 'stand for' anything, but is just a normal and natural, though exceptionally dignified, patient and resolute, human being. This is quite as important as the more obvious 'message' of the poem; and plays quite a large part in the type-experience which the poem describes. But even if we take from it only the more obvious message (as Mr Empson puts it, 'The endurance of the leech-gatherer gives Wordsworth strength to face the pain of the world') we are taking what is certainly there, and what, even stated abstractly, is by no means contemptible.

> He had also dim recollections
> Of pedlars tramping on their rounds;
> Milk-pans, and pails; and odd collections
> Of saws, and proverbs; and reflections
> Old parsons make in burying grounds.

Shelley's smile is justified; but this element is essential to *Resolution and Independence*; it is part of the central Wordsworthian sanity and strength.

(117–28)

David Ferry

from *The Limits of Mortality: An Essay on Wordsworth's Major Poems* 1959

Certain 'obvious truths' about a band of gipsies are ignored in order that they may be used as part of a symbolic design that figures forth the relations of the poet's mind to the universe; a degree of emotion is invested in a field of daffodils which seems excessive if we consider them 'with relation to a fixed time and place'. The Romantic metaphysical poet of this sort is likely to view nature, then, not as a set of objects, events, conditions which are in themselves his final interest, his final subject matter, but as a *language to be read*, signposts to that metaphysical place to which he wants to go. Insofar as those signposts appear to give him right directions, he will celebrate them, they will seem to him to be holy. And what the objects of physical nature are to the metaphysical nature of which he wants to have experience, the 'surface' of his poems – its imagery and its feelings as expressed in tone and attitude – are to its 'deeper meanings', its ultimate subject matter, which is the celebration of the metaphysical, the eternal and one. Thus, if we read the poems from a more or less 'classicist' and common-sense point of view, as evaluations of this world seen with respect to time and place, we are likely to feel some dissatisfaction, to think that some obvious things about the condition of gipsies have been overlooked or that an excessive response is being made to mere daffodils. But if we read them as symbols of man's relations to the eternal, many of these dissatisfactions disappear. This is the principal habit of reading in which Wordsworth trains us.

But there are further considerations. If the natural world is for such a poet a system of signposts telling him the way to the place he wants to go to, he is likely to feel the sort of impatience with them that we often feel with signposts: if they tell us the way to get there, they also tell us that we have not gotten there yet. They are the sign of the incompleteness of our mission. And if the objects of this world are for Wordsworth signposts to eternity, they are more than that too, they necessarily have particular and individual complexities – he must to some degree see them with relation to a fixed time and place – and this is a cause of impatience too. This impatience is likely to be reflected, for example, in the poet's use of metaphor. The goldenness of the daffodils is first of all a quality which tells us that they are charming, but it is only after the poet has abstracted himself from that golden scene that the physical gold can be converted into a much more valuable gold, 'the wealth the show to [him] had brought'. In one sense the wealth is the same as the gold he saw in the daffodils at first, but in another it is what that mere physical prettiness had to be *transformed into*, after a rather complex abstractive and imaginative process. If the classical poet is like a miner, sifting through the ore of his experience for its real gold, the Romantic metaphysical poet of this sort is like an alchemist, transforming petty substance into gold. He is unlike most alchemists only in that the gold he achieves may be real gold, but he is like most alchemists in that the splendor of his achievement depends on the pettiness of what he begins with. And the word 'show', in the daffodils poem, illustrates this complexity too. The scene was a 'show' in the sense that it was the concrete embodiment of the metaphysical joy he was looking for; but it was 'only a show' in the sense that the physical scene was the appearance whose reality he was seeking and which he could find only after he had removed himself from that scene. The 'inward eye' with which at last he so truly sees is in one sense the outward eye functioning at its most profound, but in another sense it is the opposite of the out-ward eye and depends on its closing. . . . .

Such details illustrate very well the tension and in some respects the hostility between 'surface' and 'deeper' meanings in Wordsworth's poems, between symbols and what the symbols refer to, even as they illustrate the tension and in some ways the hostility between the physical and the metaphysical natures. An artist can never do entirely without the physical world, and a poet perhaps least of all. It is a condition of language that it involves willy-nilly all sorts of references and appeals not only to particular objects but to highly particularized emotions, and the complex ramifications of these are impossible for the poet utterly to resist. . . .

It is often as if the 'surface' meanings of the poems were a beautiful and intelligible message, apparent at once, and as if hidden in that message there were clues to a 'deeper' meaning, still more beautiful though in some way at odds with the message one had read at first. (10–12)

Though man and nature are distinct the relations between them are not passive or indifferent, like the relations of strangers. Man's attitude toward this nature in which there appears to be no death, though he knows it undergoes changes, must necessarily be complex. He will love it, but he is himself in a unique sense a creature of time, and even its agent. He will sometimes be discovered behaving according to the laws of his own kind, as an agent of time and therefore as a destroyer of natural things.

The beautiful poem called *Nutting* seems simple at first. One day, when he was a boy, Wordsworth went on a nutting expedition in the country. He came upon a peaceful grove of hazel trees, and though he enjoyed the calm and quiet of the scene for a while, eventually he went about his business of breaking the trees' branches for their produce. He was happy about having got so many of the hazelnuts but sorry that he had had to do damage to get them.

Certainly the first few lines encourage us to think of the experience as very simple:

>   – It seems a day
> (I speak of one from many singled out)
> One of those heavenly days that cannot die;
> When, in the eagerness of boyish hope,
> I left our cottage-threshold, sallying forth
> With a huge wallet o'er my shoulders slung,
> A nutting-crook in hand . . .

We are led to expect only an account of some childish innocent pleasure. The child's aged teacher had dressed him in his oldest clothes and off he went, 'o'er pathless rocks, | Through beds of matted fern, and tangled thickets, | Forcing my way.' The verse is leisurely and relaxed, even a little garrulous:

> Tricked out in proud disguise of cast-off weeds
> Which for that service had been husbanded,
> By exhortation of my frugal Dame –
> Motley accoutrement, of power to smile
> At thorns, and brakes, and brambles, – and, in truth,
> More ragged than need was.

But as soon as the verse tells how he came upon the glade, its quality changes astonishingly. As he stood surveying the 'virgin scene', he felt an anticipation like desire:

>   A little while I stood,
> Breathing with such suppression of the heart
> As joy delights in; and, with wise restraint
> Voluptuous, fearless of a rival, eyed
> The banquet. . . .

It is inaccurate to say only that he felt a sort of desire. Quite suddenly he *revealed himself* as having been a libertine all along, practiced and knowledgeable in the 'wise restraint' that enhances pleasures, 'voluptuous' and expert in it. 'Eyed' sounds sinister enough, and 'eyed | The banquet' suggests the habitual luxuriousness of all his tastes. He held back from taking his pleasure, not from any sense of decency or qualms of conscience or respect for the virtue of the glade, but entirely to make his later pleasure more delightful by postponing it awhile. He was able to do so because the absence of any rival, any other human being on the scene, gave him plenty of time. He was alone with his beautiful victim, the object of his desires, and she helpless before him, so he could afford to spend some time sitting beneath the trees, playing with the flowers, and allowing himself to pass into a sort of tranceful languor, in a bower

>   . . . beneath whose leaves
> The violets of five seasons re-appear ·
> And fade, unseen by any human eye;
> Where fairy water-breaks do murmur on
> Forever. . . .

The glade was enchanted ground, a fairy place, and a place where, though the changes and alterations of the seasons went on, they went on without any trouble, peacefully, the violets constantly and as it were invisibly renewing themselves under the fallen leaves, the brook murmuring on forever. It was as if he had been taken out of time. In this enchanted place he lay 'in that sweet mood when pleasure loves to pay | Tribute to ease,' and he was for the moment like the idle shepherd of the glade, the rocks his sheep, 'fleeced with moss' and 'scattered like a flock'.

He fell into a kind of dream of innocence and timelessness, all for the purpose of *postponing* his ravishment of the trees:

I heard the murmur and the murmuring sound,
In that sweet mood when pleasure loves to pay
Tribute to ease; and, of its joy secure,
The heart luxuriates with indifferent things,
Wasting its kindliness on stocks and stones,
And on the vacant air.

But 'luxuriates', and the irony in 'kindliness', warn us that he is still the libertine, and when he says '*that* sweet mood', he is assuming in us a practised libertinism like his own.

Suddenly he rose up out of his languor and 'dragged to earth both branch and bough, with crash | And merciless ravage.' Wantonly he destroyed the glade. (It is almost unnecessary to point out how the long, monosyllabic line shocks us at this point.) And the glade apparently accepted its destruction without a protest: the nook of hazel trees and the 'green and mossy bower,' though 'deformed and sullied' by him, 'patiently gave up | Their quiet being'. His feelings about what he had done were a curious mixture: he felt a sense of pain when he 'beheld the silent trees', but he was also 'exulting, rich beyond the wealth of kings'. The natural scene itself, which enjoys peace but can be destroyed, had a simpler response: it patiently gave up its quiet being.

The poem comes very quickly to an end, with three lines that seem quite inadequate, in tone and feeling, to the rest:

Then, dearest Maiden, move along these shades
In gentleness of heart; with gentle hand
Touch – for there is a spirit in the woods.

The lines seem to have missed the point or to have got only part of it, and so to have oversimplified the rest of the poem.

A child goes out on a day's expedition in the country, with his old schoolmistress' blessing and full of the 'eagerness of boyish hope', and turns out to be a sort of rapist and voluptuary in nature, the destroyer of the very peace and quiet he also enjoys. Surely the moral of this is not 'Keep off the grass!' or 'Don't pick the flowers!' Indeed, does the poem have a 'moral' at all? Does it do any good for him to tell the maiden to treat nature gently? Isn't the poem incredible, and incredibly foolish, if we insist on regarding it as a moral injunction rather than a dispassionate analysis of man's normal and ordinary relation to his natural environment – even as a symbol or allegory of that relation? How else are we to deal with the shocking juxta-position of the innocent and genial opening lines and the violent metaphor of lust and rapine with which his treatment of the glade is described? *All* men are like this in their relation to non-human nature, since *even* this innocent young child is a libertine and destroyer. The poem is able to look back on all this without making a moral judge-ment, and even to think of it as full of the charm of idyllic childish days, precisely because nothing can be done about it, since man and nature are there, as everywhere, demonstrating their usual and inescapable relationship. The inadequacy of the concluding lines is that they suggest a kind of judgement on the boy which is far too simple for the data. The judgement is merely arbitrary, because the boy's behavior was inevitable. It was the behavior of mankind.

Of course all this can be explained away by saying the sexual metaphor is 'literary' and literarily ironic, a way of emphasizing the innocence of the boy's behavior by pretending it is not innocent. But this would reduce the prevailing tone of the poem to a mere grand-fatherly pastoralism about his youth, and it conflicts with what we know of Wordsworth's usual metaphorical practice. We are supposed to feel that this experience of gathering hazelnuts was *really* the experi-ence of a voluptuary, though at the same time it was *really* only an experience of gathering hazelnuts; and that it was like all man's experience of nature, the type and symbol of a relationship between the boy as a human being and the natural scene, a relationship which could well be described by such a metaphor. It is the 'virginity' of the natural scene that he loves, not merely as the boy Wordsworth but as a human being. And by his very nature as such, to love that virginity is to desire to possess it, and to possess it is to destroy it.

This is the central paradox the poem depends on. Reading it this way, we can understand why nature made it difficult for him to find the glade, why it put pathless rocks and matted fern and tangled thickets in his way – because once he found it he had necessarily to destroy it. And we can understand as well one reason why nature so 'patiently gave up' its 'quiet being'; nature is here acting its necessary part in a fundamental relationship. Also, there is perhaps no reason for nature to mind being 'deformed and sullied', for nature has no sense, no conscience, with which to mind it. The conflict is all in the heart of the destroyer, who in possessing the glade feels himself 'rich beyond the wealth of kings'. Read in this way, the line is not at all ironic, since his wealth is in the possession of all nature, his possession symbolic and total. But it *is* ironic, since in possessing nature by destroying it he possesses nothing, and since nature will reassert her ancient and peaceful order when he is gone. And he also feels a 'sense of pain' upon beholding what he has done – not for any sentimental reasons but because he had valued exactly what he destroyed.

This can be understood in two ways. Man uses nature and makes his civilization out of natural things, and this use involves necessary acts of destruction. The child went out to gather hazelnuts, and by so doing practised to be a grown-up man; nutting is a useful activity, symbolic of adulthood, and the schoolmistress' approval of the child's expedition is justified, though the expedition will make him harm the glade. The other way to understand it is far more general, and I think more characteristic of Wordsworth. Man is – not by his 'civilization' and its useful acts but *by definition* – a destroyer of non-human nature, its definitive enemy. How he is so can best be understood by thinking of the poem as a kind of allegory of consciousness. The distinction between man and nature is a distinction between consciousness and un-consciousness of death. The human being is an agent of time. He alone, of all creatures, is self-conscious about his limitations in time, and when he brings that consciousness among things which do not have it, it is the equivalent of an act of violence against them. He is willy-nilly a destroyer or disturber of the calm of things, because he alone knows that he must die, and also that they must die. He introduces a sense of change and death where it was not before. His own feeling about this has to be complex, for it is a definition of him to say he is an agent of time, and he has to exult in his own definition; at the same time he grieves for what he has done, since peace and quietness, protection from destruction, are what he himself desires most, and therefore in ravaging the glade he has ravaged the object of his own desires.

It is not surprising that nature gives up its quiet being so patiently, since in doing so it is only playing its passive role in an essential relationship: its function is to 'bend with the remover to remove'. The natural scene – nonhuman nature – is perishable and unconscious of its own possibility, so it 'cooperates' in its own death or change. What does the flower care if it wither up and die?

But man cares. If he is the agent of time, carrying death and change everywhere with him, he is not always a willing or loyal agent. Time oppresses him; change is his tragedy, or at least his pathos, and he is always trying to find a way of escaping into the quietness of the eternal. So he is always trying to come to terms with the eternal nature, even while he is aware of (and thus 'destroying') the natural scene which is the metaphor for the eternal. He is double-natured, and he cannot avoid the implications of either side of himself. He is exiled from eternity, and his place of exile is time.
(22–7)

Jonathan Bishop

'Wordsworth and the "Spots of Time" ', *ELH*, XXVI   1959

The Prelude is at the center of our experience of Wordsworth; at the center of our experience of *The Prelude* are those 'spots of time' where Wordsworth is endeavoring to express key moments in the history of his imagination. Basil Willey[1] has suggested that we might isolate the genuine element in Wordsworth by collating these passages; this essay is an attempt in that direction.

Narrowly speaking, the 'spots of time' are the two incidents introduced by Wordsworth's own use of the phrase: 'There are in our existence spots of time, | That with distinct pre-eminence retain | A renovating virtue,'[2] that is, the little boy's encounter with the gibbet and his wait for his father's horses. Yet the poet's language implies that there were in fact many such 'spots' from which his mind could draw new strength, and every reader of *The Prelude* will at once associate with these two those other 'passages of life' which

[1] Basil Willey, *The Eighteenth-Century Background*, Chatto & Windus, 1940, p. 274.
[2] *The Prelude*, Book XII, 208–210 ff. References throughout are to de Selin-court's edition of the 1850 version Oxford University Press, 1926.

collectively establish the greatness of the poem. Using the phrase in a looser sense, the 'spots of time' must include the descriptions of Wordsworth's boyhood exploits as a snarer of woodcocks, a plunderer of bird's nests, a skater, a rider of horses, and such single events as the famous Stolen Boat episode, the Dedication to poetry, the Discharged Soldier, the Dream of the Arab-Quixote, the memory of the Winander Boy, the Drowned Man, Entering London, the Father and Child and the Blind Beggar, Simplon Pass, The Night in Paris, Robespierre's Death, and Snowdon. Some would wish to include the memories of childhood play at Cockermouth, and the moment under the rock when Wordsworth heard 'The ghostly language of the ancient earth' (Book II, 309), or such border-line cases as the Druid Reverie. But a list incorporating every moment of excitement in *The Prelude* would be unwieldly and tendentious. The passages I have named everyone can agree upon; they must form the major items in any argument which seeks, in whatever terms, to express a sense of the poem.

I will assume for the purposes of this article that my reader has in fact appreciated the power of these 'spots' and that I need not devote space to quotation and exegeses intended to establish their poetical existence. Let us agree that the job of introducing Wordsworth's excellences has been done, perhaps more often than is strictly necessary. I should like to raise here a question that emerges after we have made ourselves acquainted with the general limitations and strengths of *The Prelude*, and recognized the peculiar interest of the 'spots'. How do we get into them? What sense do these crucial experiences make as we go over them in our minds? What do they appear to be *about*?

The first thing that strikes us is the degree to which they tend to share common themes. Consider the way they commence: 'Oh, many a time have I, a five years' child' (Book I, 288); 'Not less when spring had warmed' (Book I, 326); 'And in the frosty season' (Book I, 425); 'many a time | At evening' (Book V, 365–6); 'When summer came, | Our pastime was' (Book II, 54–5); the opening lines set the date and the season of adventures many times experienced by the boy Wordsworth. This note of repetition recurs as each memory develops. Wordsworth is always conscious of movements; the river Derwent 'blends' and 'flows' and 'winds' and the young boy 'plunges', 'scours' and 'leaps'; and movement tends to become a rhythm of repeated actions: 'Basked in the sun, and plunged and basked again' (Book I, 291), or 'Scudding away from snare to snare, I plied' and 'sounds | Of indistinguishable motion, steps' (Book I, 313; 323–4). Motion often means climbing, the ascent of a road or crag or mountain, and when the protagonist himself does not rise, another participant in the experience may. Repeated action seems to be linked with the presence of animals; the boy Wordsworth ranges heights 'where woodcocks run' (Book I, 311); his skiff heaves 'through the water like a swan' (Book I, 376); the skating boys are a 'pack' and 'hare' (Book I, 437); even the ascent of Snowdon is diversified by the antics of a dog. Horses are especially prominent; they appear more or less importantly in Entering London, Robespierre's Death, The Dream (in the form of a dromedary), and the Gibbet and Waiting for Horses. Perhaps we are closest to the meaning horses have for Wordsworth in his recollection of mounted expeditions to the seashore, when 'Lighted by gleams of moonlight from the sea | We beat with thundering hoofs the level sand' (Book II, 136–7).

The presence of powerfully repeated action seems linked with another common element, the emergence of a solitary figure from a crowd. While skating the boy Wordsworth detaches himself from the games of his playmates to 'cut across the reflex of a star' (Book I, 450) as he says in a wonderful image, and the Dedication and his encounter with the Discharged Soldier each follow upon dancing parties from which Wordsworth is returning alone. There is a crowd to witness the drowned Man's rise from the lake, and to listen as the solitary flautist 'blew his flute | Alone upon the rock' (Book II, 169–70). Is there perhaps an analogy between the separation of an individual from a crowd and the theme of repeated action? Just as, at the climax of a 'spot', the protagonist detaches himself from his companions, so the rhythm of motion, rising to a height, often receives a check, a breaking in of new experience.[1] The skating memory illustrates this clearly:

1 We may recall that in dreams, crowds are often a symbolic personification of repeated impulses. The presence of a crowd may mean that the activity or wish in question has occurred many times. See for example Daniel E. Schneider, *The Psychoanalyst and the Artist*, Farrar, Straus & Girona, 1950, p. 32.

> and oftentimes,
> When we had given our bodies to the wind
> And all the shadowy banks on either side
> Came sweeping through the darkness, spinning still
> The rapid line of motion, then at once
> Have I, reclining back upon my heels,
> Stopped short
> (Book I, 452-8)

transferring the skater's motion to the cliffs around him, which wheel by him giddily. Similarly, the climax of the nest-plundering memory comes at the moment when, his own movement checked, the boy hangs on the face of the rock while wind and clouds move for him. More developed is the experience of the Winander boy, calling repeatedly across a lake; at moments as he 'hung | Listening', he felt 'a gentle shock of mild surprise' which 'carried far into his heart the voice | Of mountain torrents' exchanging for his proud shouts a heartfelt impression of the 'visible scene' (Book V, 381-4). Wordsworth was conscious of the importance of this formula in his mental life and twice instanced the Winander 'spot' as evidence that 'an act of steady observation, or ... expectation', suddenly relaxed, might carry to the heart whatever at that moment impressed the senses.[1] The most vivid example of reciprocation is the famous Stolen Boat memory. The boy rows his skiff out into the lake, his eyes fixed on a peak behind as a mark, 'lustily' enjoying his rhythmical motion through the water. Suddenly his own actions bring about another, vaster motion and a farther peak rises up behind his mark:

> I struck and struck again,
> And growing still in stature the grim shape
> Towered up between me and the stars, and still,
> For so it seemed, with purpose of its own
> And measured motion like a living thing,
> Strode after me
> (Book I, 380-85).

[1] The relevant autobiographical passages are most easily available in de Selincourt, p. 531, and R. D. Havens, *The Mind of a Poet*, John Hopkins Press, 1941, vol. II, 392.

Reciprocation has become retaliatory. His action is guilty; he has stolen the boat, and nature's reaction is correspondingly punitive. We may recall the 'low breathings' the boy heard following him when he stole birds from others' snares, and remember that there is often a degree of guilt attached even to innocent actions, running out into the fields is 'wantonness' and climbing after eggs 'plundering'. At the climax of the Stolen Boat episode the language seems to put us in touch with a more severe crime than theft; we read that, astonished, he 'struck and struck again' with his oars, as if an act more violent than rowing alone were meant.

The 'low breathings' just noticed may also remind us of the role moving air plays in the 'spots'. Wind is literally present as the boy scales the heights; it blows 'amain, | Shouldering the naked crag' (Book I, 334–5) where the birds' nests are found, and sweeps the skaters over the ice. Raised to its human equivalent the wind blows 'strange utterance', or, as personified Nature, 'breathes'. The recurrence of occasions on which sounds are heard over a watery surface seems linked with this half-human air. The Winander boy shouts across the lake, and church bells, voices, and echoes combine in an 'alien sound | Of melancholy' (Book I, 433–4) that resounds over the icy surface of the lake in the skating memory. In an interestingly linked series, the music of bird song from an island is echoed by 'that single wren | Which one day sang so sweetly' over ground wet from 'recent showers' (Book II, 118–20) and the climatic image of a boy sitting on an island blowing his flute over 'dead still water' (Book II, 171). In the memories of youth and adulthood we encounter, in place of natural sounds, a voice speaking words, inarticulate or cryptic, threatening or relieving. This sound or voice seems most often to occur at the extreme moment of the repeated action, to enunciate, as it were, the check or reversal which climaxes the experience; though in the case of the Winander boy, the voice is itself the repeated action. Perhaps the presence of something written, like the intial carved in the turf in the Gibbet episode, or the pamphlet in the Paris Night memory, or the 'books' carried by the Arab Quixote, are derivations from the commoner and more vivid image of an articulate cry.

Surfaces hide depths. The boy shouts over water, rows upon it, gallops beside it; he also bathes in it, and we are soon made aware of water as a powerful image of the apprehensive mind. The 'uncertain

heaven, received | Into the bosom of the steady lake' (Book V, 387–8)
is a famous and explicit image for the impression made upon the boy's
heart, and the sound of his companion's flute makes him feel that the

> calm
> And dead still water lay upon my mind
> Even with a weight of pleasure, and the sky,
> Never before so beautiful, sank down
> Into my heart, and held me like a dream
> (Book II, 170–75)

These words place the boy first under the water, then identify him
with it; imaginatively, he dissolves into the element that drowns him.
We recall Wordsworth's comparison of his effort to remember to

> one who hangs down-bending from the side
> Of a slow-moving boat, upon the breast
> Of a still water
> (Book IV, 256–8)

seeking to distinguish objects on the bottom.

This metaphor is dramatized in the Drowned Man[1] 'spot'. Walking

---

1 The image of the Drowned Man pursued Wordsworth throughout his
poetical career. The most important use of it outside *The Prelude* is in *Peter
Bell*, which employs this material on the scale of a full length narrative. In the
course of his adventure Peter finds himself staring at the surface of a river:

> Is it the moon's distorted face?
> The ghost-like image of a cloud?
> Is it a gallows there portrayed?
> Is Peter of himself afraid?

Peter faints, wakes and looks again:

> Thought he, that is the face of one
> In his last sleep securely bound!

With his staff Peter stirs the water and

> The man who had been four days dead,
> Head-foremost from the river's bed
> Uprises like a ghost!
> (de Selincourt, *Poetical Works*, ii, pp. 353–8).

While Wordsworth was on a tour of the continent in 1820 a young American
was drowned in a Swiss lake. Wordsworth felt himself obscurely responsible
for this incident: 'it was the misfortune' of the young man 'to fall in with a
friend of mine who was hastening to join our party'. In consequence he wrote
some worthless *Elegaic Stanzas* to comfort the parent (*P.W.*, iii, p. 193).

alone around a silent lake as a schoolboy Wordsworth had seen a heap of garments on the opposite shore, and the next day he watched as the body, grappled to the surface, 'bolt upright | Rose, with his ghastly face, a spectre shape | Of terror' (Book V, 449–51). A very similar figure, described in virtually the same terms, appears in the encounter with the Discharged Soldier. Wordsworth leaves a party, and starts home 'up a long ascent, | Where the road's watery surface, to the top | Of that sharp rising glittered. . . .' His reverie is suddenly interrupted by 'an uncouth shape.'

Stiff, lank, and upright; a more meagre man
Was never seen before by night or day.
Long were his arms, pallid his hands; his mouth
Looked ghastly in the moonlight
(Book IV, 37–96).

Can we connect these spectral figures with the ghostly retaliator who lurked in nature, whose 'low breathings' and 'steps' he heard behind him, the 'grim shape' whose 'head' 'upreared' behind the mountain horizon, and see him again in the 'blind Beggar, who, with upright face, | Stood, propped against a wall' (Book VII, 639–40) in one of the London memories? It seems relevant that the sight of this beggar made Wordsworth's mind turn 'round | As with the might of waters' and that he gazed 'As if admonished from another world' (Book VII, 643–9).[1] In these experiences the other world is literally beyond the limits of this; the grim shape emerges from behind the horizon, from under the surface of the water, at the crest of a road. To pass a boundary is to evoke the unknown. In Entering London he is riding on a vehicle surrounded by crowds when he suddenly becomes aware that 'The threshold now is overpast' (Book VIII, 549), as if these words were spoken to his inner ear; whereupon

---

1 One might pursue the theme of the Grim Shape through all those pictures of old men who fill Wordsworth's poems, and see them as diminished versions of a starker original, in which terror has been converted to pity and admiration, and the stiffness of death to stoic endurance. Florence Marsh has brought together some of the main images to be found in the whole body of Wordsworth's poetry. Her survey of the old man, sounds, water and buildings are relevant to my argument. See her *Wordsworth's Imagery*, Yale University Press, 1952, pp. 78–103.

A weight of ages did at once descend
Upon my heart; no thought embodied, no
Distinct remembrances, but weight and power, –
Power growing under weight
(Book VIII, 552-5).

Power growing under weight; the image expresses a paradoxical release of inner force complementing the very pressures which inhibit it, as if suffering authorized strength. Does not such language, echoed in so many of the 'spots', suggest that the moment of illumination is irresistibly followed by a punitive crushing, a death by a weight like that of water and all that water obscurely symbolizes? To be sure, Wordsworth tells us as often as not that such experiences are matter for self-congratulation, and perhaps ultimately they are, yet we should not allow his often rather sanctimonious afterthoughts to blur for us the clear drift of his language. The immediate experience is terror.

As we go over the 'spots', and recall the associated areas of Words-worth's other poetry, we come upon other evidences of a shared vocabulary. We notice how often key experiences take place in darkness, especially darkness qualified, perhaps at the moment of inner illumination, by the sudden presence of light; the role of the moon is worth following for its own sake through the whole body of Wordsworth's work. Trees, too, have a special meaning for him, though their place in the 'spots' seems less prominent than one might expect. Buildings, especially ruined buildings, do appear. Cocker-mouth Castle, 'a shattered monument' (Book I, 284), stood beside the river in which the 'five-year child' bathed; in the memories of Book II a bird sings in a ruined shrine; a chapel on an island is part of the scenery in Robespierre's Death; cottages, huts and tenements appear in other 'spots'. But moonlight, trees and even buildings seem relatively isolated images; to pursue them is to leave behind the context in which, if anywhere, they acquire a meaning. Our job as readers is less to establish the presence of individual items than to articulate the latent argument these recurrences suggest. What we seem to have are fragments of a drama, moments in a single action which has retired behind the reach of direct expression, leaving in our hands fragments of imagery. In what sentences will this vocabulary combine?

Perhaps a recapitulation will clarify. We seem to have in the 'spots' a repeated action, something a crowd does, or the protagonist does over and over, an action with guilty overtones, expressive of power and pride, rising as it proceeds to a boundary, there to be checked and retaliated upon from without, by counter-motion, or by a voice or the appearance of a grim shape, whose arrival precipitates an oppressive catastrophe. Is this rehearsal too abstract? Objections will arise, for many a 'spot' mixes or omits elements of this story: the relation between the protagonist and the grim shape, for example, is very changeable, in some memories reducing to identity. And many of the early memories never rise to a distinct crisis; we hear of customary actions, repeated experiences which stay, as it were, in the back of Wordsworth's mind, pleasant but indistinct. When something does happen, though, the event follows at a greater or lesser distince this curious pattern.

Wordsworth himself is not certain what to name these moments. They demonstrate the workings of 'unknown modes of being' (Book I, 393) as dreams do and we recall that the hills swirling about the skater calm down 'Till all was tranquil as a dreamless sleep' (Book I, 464), and that the music of the flute sinks into his heart to hold him 'like a dream' (Book II, 176). One of the major 'spots' of adult life is literally a dream; others are nearer hallucination (Paris Night) or vision (Snowdon). Wordsworth offers interpretations when he feels he can put the event satisfactorily into philosophic terms. The Snowdon experience appears to him 'The type | Of a majestic intellect' (Book XIV, 66-7), a symbol of the mind, a view which clearly embodies a real insight, yet the language in which the insight is elaborated, most readers will agree, is invincibly prosaic. The 'philosophic mind' can interpret, but only in abstract terms; the feelings embodied in the original mysterious event remain attached to the structure of the event itself.

Let us turn, with this caveat in mind, to a related group of 'spots' experienced in young manhood, and see how far the pattern we have been able to find may help us to disengage a meaning. Book X begins with Wordsworth returning to Paris in October 1792. He is on his way home, leaving Annette pregnant behind him. It is a moment of public tension. The king is in prison, and the massacres of September just past. Entering the city, Wordsworth crosses the empty square where men had died a few weeks before, looking on the sights 'as doth a man | Upon a volume whose contents he knows | Are memorable' (Book X, 58–60) but which he cannot read. He ascends to his bed in a 'large mansion', and with 'unextinguished taper' begins to read. The elements necessary to significant experience begin to combine, as he climbs out of the populous city to his lonely nocturnal eminence, lit by a single light, and broodingly works upon himself, recalling reasons why the massacres of the previous month must be followed by new terrors:

> The fear gone by
> Pressed on me almost like a fear to come.
> I thought of those September massacres,
> Divided from me by one little month,
> Saw them and touched: the rest was conjured up
> From magic fictions or true history,
> Remembrances and dim admonishments.
> The horse is taught his manage, and no star
> Of wildest course but treads back his own steps,
> For the spent hurricane the air provides
> As fierce a successor; the tide retreats
> But to return out of its hiding-place
> In the great deep; all things have second birth;
> The earthquake is not satisfied at once;
> And in this way
> (Book X, 71–85)

He works upon himself, piling images of retaliation one upon another, including as he goes references to horses, wind and sea, drugging himself to the point where a hallucinatory voice breaks in, crying 'To the whole city, "Sleep no more."' It is the cry of Macbeth after killing his king.

The next morning Wordsworth walks out to find a pamphlet being sold in the streets. This pamphlet reprints a speech made by a brave Girondist named Louvet, who, provoked by Robespierre's challenge had while

> no one stirred,
> In silence of all present, from his seat
> ... walked single through the avenue,

And took his station in the Tribune, saying,
'I, Robespierre, accuse thee!'
(Book X, 109-13)

This story accidentally repeats the formula of the previous night;
again we have a solitary man, separating himself from a crowd,
walking to an eminence, and again a voice challenges the bloody deeds
of a murderer. The ambiguity of the grammar allows us to make the
necessary connections: Wordsworth feels himself both as the utterer
of the cry and the murderer to whom it is directed.

   The depths of Wordsworth's imaginative involvement in the
political events that followed that night is easy to read in his own
actions. He returned to England in December 1792; in January
Louis XVI was executed. Typically, the poem does *not* mention this;
we hear instead of the 'shock' Wordsworth's moral nature felt when
England joined the allies against France. In the middle of January he
wrote his unmailed letter to the Bishop of Llandaff, accusing this
fellow north countryman, liberal and Cambridge man[1] of apostasy
from the revolutionary creed, and taking pains to defend the execution of the king. As the Terror commenced and gathered strength,
Wordsworth found himself nightly engaged with dreams of imprison-
ment and 'long orations, which I strove to plead | Before unjust
tribunals' (Book X, 411-12) like Louvet, with a terrifying sense of
impotence and desertion. His explanation for the atrocities is interesting; he believed them the result of a 'terrific reservoir of guilt' which
could no longer hold its 'loathsome charge' and 'burst and spread in
deluge through the land' (Book X, 477-80).

   These events and preoccupations serve as a chain of associations
to bind the Paris Night 'spot' to the next crucial experience. One
August day in 1794 he was walking on the sands of the Leven estuary.

1 Legouis (*The Early Life of Wordsworth 1770-1798*, Dent, 1897, pp. 226-7)
points out the parallels between Bishop Watson's position and Wordsworth's
without appreciating their meaning. The Bishop was the son of a Westmorland schoolmaster, a Whig and a liberal, known as a 'levelling
prelate' by his enemies and disliked by George III for his independence. He had
first approved of the Revolution, but the September massacres made him
doubt. Upon the execution of the King he determined to make a public
retraction. It is clear that Wordsworth was angry because the Bishop so nearly
expressed a strong part of Wordsworth's own mixed feelings from an analogous personal position.

As he admired the cloud effects he meditated upon memories of his
old teacher, whose grave he had that morning visited. He recalled
this worthy man's last remark to him, '"My head will soon lie low"
(Book X, 538); and wept a little, for Taylor had put him on the way
to be a poet.

As I advanced, all that I saw or felt
Was gentleness and peace. Upon a small
And rocky island near, a fragment stood
(Itself like a sea rock) the low remains
(With shells encrusted, dark with briny weeds)
Of a dilapidated structure, once
A Romish chapel, where the vested priest
Said matins at the hour that suited those
Who crossed the sands with ebb of morning tide.
Nor far from that still ruin all the plain
Lay spotted with a variegated crowd
Of vehicles and travellers, horse and foot,
Wading beneath the conduct of their guide
In loose procession through the shallow stream
Of inland waters; the great sea meanwhile
Heaved at safe distance, far retired.
(Book X, 553–68)

The elements of significance experience begin to combine. Here is
the wide surface, associated with the presence of water; here is a
crowd, including horses, a multiplicity of movement; here is an
island and on it a ruined building. The sea is benign; it 'heaves',
but at a distance. At this moment Wordsworth is accosted by a
stranger, who without prologue cries out '"Robespierre is dead"'
(Book X, 573).[1]
We may speculate that the shock of this news is compounded for
Wordsworth by the theme of his meditations, for he had just been
complacently enjoying a diminished version of an analogous experience. Taylor, his amiable foster father, had predicted a death, and the

1 In A²C he is a 'Horseman', See de Selincourt, *The Prelude*, p. 391 n. Havens
(*Mind of a Poet*, vol. I, p. 16) finds the detail about the ruined chapel on its
island an irrelevant interruption. With the pattern in mind, we can understand
why Wordsworth noticed and incorporated this detail.

prediction unexpectedly comes true for a man with whom Wordsworth has for many years felt a profound connection, a villain who acted out fantasies of murderous rebellion in which Wordsworth, it is not too much to say, half-consciously participated.

He is free to respond with joy; Robespierre has suffered the punishment of a regicide and Wordsworth may therefore allow himself some liberty from the apprehensions his conscience has burdened him with. 'Sleep no more' is no longer addressed to *him*. The image of the deluge is evoked again as he dissociates himself from the wicked who have been 'swept away' by the 'river of blood' (Book X, 584, 586) they had affected to direct. His mind takes him back to a more innocent moment on this very shore, when the implications of action were uncontaminated, and the deluges of metaphor were a real ocean, as 'Along the margin of the moon light sea – | We beat with thundering hoofs the level sand' (Book X, 602–3).

Such a paraphrase of the political 'spots' and the biographical material with which they are associated may bring out the additions these particular 'spots' make to the pattern. We notice that the grim shape of the earlier memories has become a definite human figure, who speaks articulate words, and that the criminal activity hinted at in some of the earlier memories has acquired, in the new context provided by political awareness, a definite outline. The violent death of a king and of his executioner is at the centre of Wordsworth's political preoccupations.

If with the clues suggested by these revolutionary memories we turn back to the private experiences with which Wordsworth explicitly linked his general remarks about the 'spots', we find this theme of violent death re-translated into terms which, we may feel, come closer to the emotional sources of Wordsworth's disquiet. Consider the Gibbet episode. As a very young child Wordsworth finds himself lost among barren hills, leading a horse. He stumbles upon a ruined gibbet:

The gibbet-mast had mouldered down, the bones
And iron case were gone; but on that turf,
Hard by, soon after that fell deed was wrought,
Some unknown hand had carved the murderer's name
(Book XII, 237–40)

Terrified, he runs away up a hill.

Faltering and faint, and ignorant of the road:
Then, reascending the bare common, saw
A naked pool that lay beneath the hills,
A beacon on the summit, and, more near,
A girl, who bore a pitcher on her head,
And seemed with difficult steps to force her way
Against the blowing wind
(Book XII, 247–53)

The event preserves several of the images we have noticed, including
wind, water, something written, a horse, a ruin and an ascent toward
a limit. The theme of murder is explicit. Yet the order in which the
images appear is broken. We may identify the initials on the turf with
the voice whose cry climaxes so many 'spots', but here it appears at
the beginning, rather than the end. And in place of a grim and ghostly
masculine shape we have a living girl. Can we read the extraordinary
concentration upon the separate images of pool, beacon and girl as
a displacement of feeling from the evidences of crime and punishment
to accidental concomitants of an experience too overwhelming to be
faced directly? The three static impressions have become symbols
which bear all the weight of a meaning not directly their own. Some
portion of that meaning presumably resides in the gibbet from which
the boy flees; we may gather hints of the rest when we recall that this
experience takes place at Penrith, that it is to be dated at a time close
to his mother's death, and that his later associations with the scene
were those of young love.[1]

   The Gibbet memory is immediately followed by the memory of
climbing a crag with his brothers to wait for the horses that would
take them all home from school for the Christmas holidays:

1 The naked pool reappears in *The Thorn*, a poem about a mother who has
murdered her child, either by hanging or drowning, it is not clear which. A
stanza of this poem brings us back to the 'spot' describing the drowned man:

Some say, if to the pond you go,
and fix on it a steady view,
the shadow of a babe you trace,
A baby and a baby's face.
(*P. W.*, ii, p. 248)

                    There rose a crag,
That, from the meeting-place of two highways
Ascending, overlooked them both, far stretched;
Thither, uncertain on which road to fix
My expectation, thither I repaired,
Scout-like, and gained the summit; 'twas a day
Tempestuous, dark, and wild, and on the grass
I sate half-sheltered by a naked wall;
Upon my right hand couched a single sheep, ·
Upon my left a blasted hawthorn stood;
With these companions at my side, I watched,
Straining my eyes intensely, as the mist
Gave intermitting prospect of the copse
And plain beneath.
(Book XII, 292–305)

The expectation depicted in these lines is not consummated then and there; Wordsworth breaks off, as he so often does in an important memory; it was, he says, days later that his anticipation was reciprocated unexpectedly by his father's death.[1] The feelings roused by this event revert upon the experience of waiting, fastening upon the 'single sheep, and the one blasted tree, | And the bleak music from that old stone wall' (Book XII, 319–20), making of these symbols to which, as he writes, he can repair to 'drink, | As at a fountain' (Book XII, 325–6). Is it an accident that these two 'spots' should be linked together and that the first should appear to deal with the child's fantasies about his mother, the other about the death of a father? Does the presence of a gibbet in the first memory suggest that, in fantasy though not in fact, the later event preceded the earlier? It is interesting that the 'spots' which Wordsworth chooses to illustrate his general theory of the restorative value of childhood memories should be the ones which

1 The experience is also described in an early poem, in such a way as to suggest that he received the news of his father's death while waiting on the crag. See *The Vale of Esthwaite*, Book II, 422–3 (*P. W.*, i, p. 279). Miss Moorman believes that *The Prelude* version is nearer the facts of the case. (*William Wordsworth: 1770–1803*, Oxford University Press, 1957, p. 68 n.). H. W. Garrod (*Wordsworth: Lectures and Essays*, Oxford University Press, 1923, pp. 207–8) believes the crag spot was written immediately after Wordsworth heard the news of his brother's death. If this is true the pathos of the episode is so much the more meaningful.

most directly concern family feeling, and that in both the weight of emotion shifts from the human occasion to associated images. Such memories bring us some distance from the public world of the political 'spots'; 'The hiding-places of man's power | Open; I would approach them' (Book XII, 279–80), but the threshold cannot be passed either by Wordsworth himself or by his readers.

This does not of course prevent us from essaying acts of interpretation: my own is implied in the manner in which I have paraphrased the 'spots' we have just been considering. The prevailing tendency among critics of Wordsworth has been to see the experiences the 'spots' record in quasi-mystical terms, to find their subject the relation of mind to nature and reality. Havens's massive study is perhaps the best representative of what can be done in this line. Yet there are obvious objections to linking Wordsworth with the mystics. The experiences recorded in the 'spots' are not impersonal, but private; in them Wordsworth, far from finding himself rapt from the world, discovers a special importance in the details of common life. He does not feel, as the mystic traditionally does, an unqualified joy, nor are claims made of insight into a supernatural reality; the claims that are made are imaginative and emotional. Indeed Wordsworth's *religious* life tends to be quite distinct from the 'spots', and to mean, psychologically, a state of affairs in opposition to the part of life they embody. The mystic rejects words; 'spots', as we have seen, are embodied in a special vocabulary. We have besides the negative evidence that Coleridge, who would have known, never thought of them as mystical.[1] If we stress the mystical dimension in these experiences we are forced to rule out certain 'spots' in favor of other,[2] yet if any one is important, they all are; if they vary, it is in poetical fullness an imaginative authority, not mystical purity. Is there perhaps a certain unconscious devaluation of the imagination on the part of readers who wish to make Wordsworth over into a thinker or mystic?

An analogous short-circuiting may be behind the desire to associate the 'spots' with a single period in Wordsworth's creative life. The boyhood memories of Books I and II were written at Goslar in 1798–9; the existence of MS. V proves this. But the speculation that the equally significant Snowdon 'spot' was written at the same time can

1 Havens admits this himself (Book I, p. 167).
2 Havens, Book I, p. 168.

be called no more than probable.[1] The same is true of the Gibbet. The Discharged Soldier is definitely early,[2] but Paris Night and Robespierre's Death were as far as anyone knows written in late 1804. The Simplon Pass experience, I shall argue in a moment, takes place in the act of composition, i.e. sometime in March or April 1804. The temptation to translate one's awareness of the literary and psychological equality of the spots' into bibliographical terms must, it seems to me, be resisted. Wordsworth's creativity was not limited to the Goslar period.[3]

My re-telling of the political and personal 'spots' makes plain the direction it seems to me most rewarding for the modern reader to go. We have a group of memories; these share a vocabulary of imagery, a vocabulary which seems to combine into a story, a story which, so far as it is interpretable, tells of the fears, curiosities, and guilt of childhood. The memories we have seem to acquire their special meaning from other and more remote sources; the repetition of language and situation becomes, once it is noticed, a clue to something father back.

A recent article in The Psychoanalytic Quarterly 'On Earliest Memories' is suggestive.[4] Its authors, in summing up professional work on this subject, point out how similar ones earliest memories are to dreams, how they are chosen, as it were, to represent one's life style. They 'reveal, probably more clearly than any other single psychological datum, the central core of each person's psychodynamics, his chief motivations, form of neurosis, and emotional problem'. Selected and distorted to express their possessor's 'nuclear emotional constellation',[5] they persist through life, less influenced by superficial experience than dreams. They are added to only through some major shift in the interior balance of power. Do we not have, in the 'spots', experiences to which these generalizations will apply? To be sure, there are obvious differences between the fragmentary recollections recorded in the autobiographical portion of Christopher Wordsworth's Memoirs, memories we can literally call 'earliest', and the

1 See de Selincourt, p. xxxv, and Havens, p. 638.
2 de Selincourt, p. xxxiii.
3 Nor was everything written at Goslar good. A VII, 721–29 is entirely dull stuff, and A VII, 21–37 merely cute.
4 Leon S. Saul, Thoburn R. Snyder, Jr and Edith Sheppard, 'On Earliest Memories', Psychoanalytic Quarterly, vol. 25, 1956, pp. 228–37.
5 pp. 229 and 230.

much more developed and expressed experiences, occuring at intervals well into adult life, which the 'spots' articulate. Yet we have seen that they share common themes. Can we suppose that we have, in Wordsworth, a mind with an extraordinary capacity to recreate, or have recreated for it, moments which embody the significance of its own life, as the ordinary mind can no longer do, once it has emerged from early childhood, except in the very much weaker and more ambiguous forms of dreams? Given a chance conjunction in Wordsworth's environment of certain elements which have an *a priori* significance for him, together with a state of mind under a sufficient condition of tension, waking experiences as vivid, symbolic and mysterious as a dream could overwhelm him, with all advantages of his waking mind at hand to help him articulate the event. Legouis quotes a saying of Landor that Wordsworth gives us the protoplasm of poetry, rather than poetry itself.[1] Perhaps, in Wordsworth's case, the distinction is not worth drawing. For it is precisely the most poetic moments which come closest to their creator's central concerns. We may even claim that *The Prelude* constitutes the record, half-concealed in a commonplace autobiographical structure, of a process which, in these days, we would call a self-analysis; the precipitate of an interior battle, a sequence of manoeuvres against the incomprehensible, fought out in the public domain of verse. To be sure, every artist, so far as he achieves an imaginatively convincing structure, embodies in that structure a dramatic self-illumination from which he may, merely as a man, profit: it is Wordsworth's special genius that he should have devoted himself so massively to the imagination taken in this sense as to be, virtually, the first and last of his line.[2] With all this held in mind I should like to forestall some of the criticisms my argument may have evoked in my reader by returning to the poetry, and address myself to two 'spots' in which the imagination as such explicitly figures.

1 Legouis, p. 317.
2 At this point Dr Leavis breaks in with an objection. Having noticed the 'spots' from something of the same position, he rejects the temptation to move on: 'If these "moments" have any significance for the critic . . . it will be established, not by dwelling upon or in them, in the hope of exploring something that lies hidden in or behind their vagueness, but by holding firmly on to that sober verse in which they are presented' (*Revaluation*, Chatto & Windus, 1947, p. 174). The distinction between honest criticism and vulgar psychologiz-

At one point during his first visit to France Wordsworth and his friend Jones found themselves climbing among mountains up a dubious path in pursuit of their guide. As they climb they meet a peasant, from whom they ask direction. He tells them they have crossed the Alps. Obscurely depressed by the news, they hurry downwards through a gloomy chasm, whose rocks, torrents, and tumult seem 'like workings of one mind, ... symbols of Eternity' (Book VI, 636, 639).

As it stands this is no more than a minor experience, though the descent into the chasm is vividly expressed and reminds the re-reader of the *Prelude* of the chasm in the Snowdon 'spot' from which the roar of water ascended. What makes this section of the poem extraordinary is an interruption in the description of this past event. As Wordsworth writes the words, 'we had crossed the Alps', the articulation of this old experience of passing a limit takes effect in the present; Wordsworth breaks off, filled with an immediate emotion. And here we see the heroic quality of the poet's mind; instead of allowing his feelings simply to be, his pen put down until the spasm passes, he sets out to express what he feels:

Imagination – here the Power so called
Through sad incompetence of human speech,
That awful Power rose from the mind's abyss
Like an unfathered vapour
(Book VI, 593–5).

The peasant's words were, he has just said, 'translated by our feelings'; a symbol was interpreted. As he reviews this event it suddenly acquires a double sense. Just as he and Jones had interpreted the peasant's remark once, so now, as he writes, Wordsworth finds himself 'interpreting' the meaning of the whole experience.[1] The

---

ing asks for the automatic bob and curtsy it commonly receives; no one wants to seem a bad amateur analyst. But is the apposition really exclusive? Don't we in fact, precisely by attending to the verse ('sober' seems an odd word to use about the 'spots') find words in which we can locate, impeccably, the cause for our curiosity? 'Holding firmly' need not mean 'holding exclusively' to anyone but a grammarian.

1 I am aware that 'here' is ambiguous: Wordsworth may mean either 'just now, as I was writing' or, more prosaically, 'at that moment, in 1791'. The chief argument for the first interpretation is, I suppose, the tone of the follow-

tone shifts and he speaks directly to a new companion: 'Imagination –' The imagination itself becomes as it were a solitary, a grim
shape of greater dignity than the literal peasant from which by
association it derives; an 'awful power', ghostlike, it rises, self-born
the dead father of the other 'spots' lurks here as an adjective.

> . . . unfathered vapour that enwraps.
> At once, some lonely traveller. I was lost;
> Halted without an effort to break through
> (Book VI, 595–7).

His forward movement as a writer is checked by a half-compre-
hended shock of recognition. He sees obscurely, why *not* checking
his climb over the mountain range was so moving. When is he
'halted'? Presumably right after he tried to start, that is, right after
writing the key word, 'Imagination'. May we speculate that he was
preparing to say something prosy *about* the imagination, something
analogous to the lecture he does read us in the last books of the poem,
when it came over him that the word was also a cry, a call to a person?
Whereupon there rose within him the reality of which, in its abstract
form, he was about to speak. The interior power holds him, enwraps
him, halts him; he is checked by the very power which, if he could
break through, would endow him with some scarcely imaginable
flow of strength. He is caught at the moment of psychic paradox; his
true self is his enemy.

A moment of silence follows the semi-colon; then, 'But. . . .'
There are several possibilities. 'I will make an effort? I *have* made an
effort and I give up? In any case?' The tense shifts to the present: this
is what he finds he can say: 'But to my conscious soul I now can say'
(Book VI, 598). We should not mistake the eighteenth-century
meaning of 'conscious' for the sense the word has now; but there
has been a shift of address, a movement, perhaps accompanied by a

---

ing lines. Wordsworth expresses his admiration in the present tense because he
is immensely relieved at being able to see the power in whose grip he has just
been as benign. I am glad to find myself in this matter on the same side as
Havens (Book I, 158) and Moorman (p. 139 and note). This passage is not the
only place where a present emotion finds its way into *The Prelude*. When he
recalls the 'bravest youth of France' marching to the frontiers, tears start to his
eyes. See *The Prelude*, Book IV, 263–9 and following.

loss, from the all-inclusive name 'Imagination' to the limited, traditional, 'conscious soul'. Is there also some dwindling of the original impact in the distance implied by *what* he says? ' "I recognize thy glory" ' is spoken from a place apart. The imagination, now the conscious soul, is 'recognized' as a legitimate ruler; yet the emotion in all its ambiguity is still alive, for it is the 'usurpation' accomplished by the imagination with its primitive strength that he goes on boldly to praise, following the fruitful inconsistency of the political metaphor with a more explicit paradox, a 'light' that goes out in a 'flash':

'I recognize thy glory:' in such strength
Of usurpation, when the light of sense
Goes out, but with a flash that has revealed
The invisible world, doth greatness make abode,
There harbours; . . .

From here on the development is firm, unqualified; the voice honors the reality he has experienced magnificently:

                    whether we be young or old,
Our destiny, our being's heart and home,
Is with infinitude, and only there;
With hope it is, hope that can never die,
Effort, and expectation, and desire,
And something evermore about to be.
Under such banners militant, the soul
Seeks for no trophies, struggles for no spoils
That may attest her prowess, blest in thoughts
That are their own perfection and reward,
Strong in herself and in beatitude
That hides her, like the mighty flood of Nile
Poured from his fount of Abyssinian clouds
To fertilize the whole Egyptian plain.
(Book VI, 603–16)

To feel intuitively and directly some portion of the meaning of the memory he is describing, to apprehend as a present experience what is symbolized by the breaking of a barrier is to release the associated stores of emotion as an overwhelming power, a power which Wordsworth with wonderful courage and, we can be sure, exact insight, immediately names the source of poetry itself, the efficient cause of the splendid lines on the page before us. The psychic reserves locked in the key experiences of his life are at rare moments available to a mind strong enough to face them, to address a lifetime to their articulation. At such times the mind may joyfully congratulate its own nature, and the flood of unconscious energies are, like those of the Nile, benign.

Floods, however, are not always fertilizing. Consider the other 'spot' which deals explicitly with the imagination, the famous dream of the Stone and the Shell. I don't want to spend time on the details of the dream as such; anyone who has come so far with me and recalls the story will understand the degree to which the adventure of the dream incorporates the vocabulary of the other 'spots', with its wide waste of sand, its movement, its grim shape in the form of a strange Arab, who rides a dromedary instead of a horse. This figure carries a stone, representing geometry and a shell standing for poetry. He presents the shell to the dreamer, who puts it to his ear, 'And heard that instant in an unknown tongue, | Which yet I understood, articulate sounds' (Book V, 93–4), prophesying destruction by deluge to the inhabitants of the world. Explaining that he intends to bury the two objects, which he calls 'books', the Arab races away, with the dreamer in chase. As he rides the Arab looks back; following his glance, the dreamer sees 'over half the wilderness diffused, | A bed of glittering light' (Book V, 128–9). He is looking at ' "The waters of the deep | Gathering upon us" ' (Book V, 130–31) Pursued by the 'fleet waters of a drowning world' (Book V, 137), the dreamer wakes in terror.

Let us look first at the shell.[1] The Arab tells the dreamer in so many

1 The other images in this dream all have an important history. The sea and the desert may be found, together or apart, in *The Affliction of Margaret* (*P.W.*, ii, p. 49); *To Enterprise* (*P.W.*, ii, p. 284); *The Solitary Reaper* (*P.W.*, iii, p. 77); *The Borderers* (*P.W.*, pp. 195–7); and in *The Prelude* itself, Book VI, 142–54. The shell image may lie behind the famous lines in the *Ode*:

Hence in a season of calm weather
Though inland far we be,
Our souls have sight of that immortal sea
Which brought us hither,

for how else can a 'soul' see the ocean from far inland? This is supported by *The Excursion*, Book IV, 1132–40, *The Blind Highland Boy* floats to sea on a words that it represents poetry, and though the allegory is a little stiff,[1] we need not hesitate to accept this interpretation as broadly correct. There are two facts about shells which make this interpretation exciting. First, they come from the sea. If the shell is a book of poetry, the sea from which it has its being must be the creative mind. We have seen how the experience of the imagination eventuated, in the Simplon 'spot', in an image of a fertilizing river: here, the destructive aspect of this image predominates, pursuing life to destroy it. Once again, the act of understanding an image is dangerous; as one handles the symbol one evokes the reality for which it stands; and this is as likely to mean destruction as renewed creativity. Comprehension too often means catastrophe. The real source from which catastrophe comes we learn when we consider the other fact about shells. When you hold one to your ear, the roar you hear is the tide of your own blood. The deluge, in other words, wells up from within.[2]

We may now paraphrase the dream as follows: 'If you choose poetry as a way of life, as you have done and are bound to do, you run the severe risk of being overwhelmed by the unconscious forces from which your poetry must derive its vital inspiration and the

huge shell (*P. W.*, iii, pp. 88–96), and Wordsworth himself comments on and defends his use of the shell image in an I.F. note. (*P.W.*, iv, pp. 397–8.)

1 The stiffness may be due to the fact that Wordsworth consciously or unconsciously borrowed this element from the 'studious friend' to whom the whole dream is assigned in the early versions of *The Prelude*. Jane Worthington Smyser has recently suggested ('Wordsworth's Dream of Poetry and Science,' PMLA, vol. 71, 1956, pp. 269–75) that the idea of two books, one representing science and the other poetry, originates in a dream of Descartes, perhaps told Wordsworth by his friend Beaupuy.

2 More than one reader of Wordsworth has made the connection between water and the imagination. See Geoffrey H. Hartman, *The Unmediated Vision*, Yale University Press, 1954, pp. 31–45; Kenneth MacLean, 'The Water Symbol in *The Prelude*', *University of Toronto Quarterly*, vol. 17, 1948, 372–89; and p. 447 above. The psychoanalytic interpretation of water symbolism is relevant here. Pools, oceans and floods are commonly associated with the mother. Is the experience of drowning then an inversion of terrors associated with the idea of birth and coitus? Marie Bonaparte's 'The Legend of the Unfathomable Waters', *The American Image*, vol. 4, August 1946, pp. 20–48 is worth looking at in this connnection. The most extravagant and still the most interesting pursuit of the subject I know is Sandor Ferenczi, *Thalassa*, trans. Henry Bunker, *Psychoanalytic Quarterly*, 1938.

463 Geoffrey H. Hartman

significant portion of its subject matter; if you lose your nerve, you
will find yourself "burying" your talent to escape the emotional
turmoil it brings upon you.'

As Wordsworth himself understood when he contemplated his
hopes for his poem,

> This is, in truth, heroic argument,
> ... which I wished to touch
> With hand however weak, but in the main
> It lies far hidden from the reach of words.
> Points have we all of us within our souls
> Where all stand single; this I feel, and make
> Breathings for incommunicable powers
> (Book III, 184–90).
> (45–65)

Geoffrey H. Hartman

from *Wordsworth's Poetry 1787–1814*   1964

The Solitary Reaper

Wordsworth records in *The Solitary Reaper* his reaction to an
ordinary incident. What others might have passed by produces a
strong emotional response in him, therefore the imperatives: Behold,
Stop here, O listen! His response rather than the image causing it is
his subject, yet he keeps the latter in mind and returns to it, especially
in the last stanza, so that our attention is drawn to a continuous yet
indefinite relationship between mind and image, each of which retains a certain autonomy.

To value Wordsworth's emotions is sometimes hard. Coleridge,
his most sympathetic critic, is surely right in saying that they may be
'disproportionate to such knowledge and value of objects described,
as can be fairly anticipated of men in general, even of the most
cultivated classes'.[1] Wordsworth quite consciously distinguished his
'lyrical' ballads from the popular poetry of the day by allowing
feeling to 'give importance to the action and the situation, and not

1 *Biographia Literaria*, 1818, ch. 22.

the action and situation to the feeling'.[1] Now this problem of the appropriateness or decorum of the poet's feelings may seem to be a rather simple one, to be resolved not *a priori* but by individual critical decision, or by these decisions in so far as they indicate a consensus. One might agree, for instance, that the feelings developed in *The Solitary Reaper* are appropriate and that the poem as a whole is a success, while those expressed in the stanzas on the daisy (already mocked by *The Simpliciad*) are too big for their subject. Wordsworth criticism, however, does not provide a consensus that effectively separates his mental or emotional bombast from appropriate lyrical effusion.

Today, for example, no objection is made to Wordsworth's lyric on the daffodils ('I wandered lonely as a cloud'). It seems as fine a poem as *The Solitary Reaper*. Yet Coleridge thought its last stanza excessive in its stated emotion,[2] and Anna Seward, a not unromantic bluestocking, waxes almost hysterical about it. 'Surely Wordsworth must be as mad as was ever the poet Lee,' she writes in her only extended comment on his poetry.[3]

Those volumes of his[4] . . . have excited, by turns, my
tenderness and warm admiration, my contemptuous
astonishment and disgust. The two latter rose to their utmost
height while I read about his dancing daffodils, ten thousand,
as he says, in high dance in the breeze beside the river,
whose waves dance with them, and the poet's heart, we are
told, danced too. Then he proceeds to say, that in the hours
of pensive or of pained contemplation, these same capering
flowers flash on his memory, and his heart, losing its cares,
dances with them again.

After dismissing the poem with the irony of paraphrase, she rises to the final thunder of invective: 'Surely if his worst foe had chosen to

1 Preface, 1800, to *Lyrical Ballads*.
2 *Biographia Literaria*, ch. 22.
3 *Letters of Anna Seward, Written between the Years 1784 and 1807*, 6 vols. Edinburgh, 1811, vol. 6, pp. 366–7. On 'Anna Seward and the Romantic Poets', see Samuel H. Monks, in E. L. Griggs (ed.), *Wordsworth and Coleridge: Studies in Honor of George McLean Harper*, Princeton University Press, 1939, pp. 118–34.
4 *Poems in Two Volumes* (1807).

caricature this egotistic manufacturer of metaphysic importance upon trivial themes, he could not have done it more effectually!' This is the same poem A. C. Bradley called 'a pretty thing' that 'could scarcely excite derision'; and which F. A. Pottle considers at length in *Wordsworth Centenary Studies* because of the very feature which so disturbed Anna Seward, the strange crescendo of those 'capering flowers'.[1]

Although there is no consensus, it is clear that a crux in Wordsworth criticism was established early. Anna Seward is not alone in her opinions. Contemporary opposition to Wordsworth and the Lake School, whether based on a principle of decorum, the doctrine of general nature, or deeply ingrained social and religious diffidence, tended to center on what Keats termed the 'egotistical sublime'. Keats's comment on this fault in Wordsworth[2] is significant in that it should repeat (in a finer tone, as it were) Anna Seward's objection and that Coleridge and Jeffrey should ally themselves in reprehending a new species of bombast that is laid to the poet's excessive involvement in random, personal experience.[3]

Wordsworth's egotism, however, would have been beneath notice had it not contained something precariously 'spiritual' which was not exhausted by his overt choice of scenes from low or rural life. Those who objected to Wordsworth often commended Burns,

1 A. C. Bradley, 'Wordsworth', *Oxford Lectures on Poetry*, Macmillan, 1909 p. 104; Pottle, 'The Eye and the Object', in G. Dunklin (ed.) *Wordsworth: Centenary Studies*, Princeton University Press, 1951, pp. 23–42. For other comments on the 'battle' of the Daffodils, see *Middle Years*, vol. 1, pp. 129, 149, 170.

2 Keats, letter to Richard Woodhouse, 27 October 1818; and letter to John Hamilton Reynolds, 3 February 1818.

3 Jeffrey, review of Crabbe's *Poems* in the *Edinburgh Review* of April 1808; cf. the many remarks by Hazlitt, as in a lecture of 1818 that might have influenced Keats. Members of the modern school of poetry, said Hazlitt, 'surround the meanest objects with the morbid feelings and devouring egotism of the writers' own minds. Milton and Shakespeare did not so understand poetry. They gave a more liberal interpretation both to nature and art. They did not do all they could to get rid of the one and the other, to fill up the dreary void with the Moods of their own Minds (the title of a section of Wordsworth's *Poems in Two Volumes*).' See also G. Steiner, 'Egoism and Egotism', in *Essays in Criticism*, vol. 2, 1952, pp. 444–52; A. Gerard *L'Idée romantique de la poésie en Angleterre*, 1955, pp. 252–6; W. J. Bate, *From Classic to Romantic*, Cambridge University Press, 1946.

Crabbe and even Robert Bloomfield, and the magazine poetry of the 1790s is full of compassionate subjects, rural themes and personal reflections.[1] Modest Christian sentiment was welcome, and to 'suck Divinity' (or even metaphysics) from daffodils[2] was too common a poetic indulgence to have roused the contemptuous disgust of a literary lady. What is so precariously spiritual about Wordsworth, and so difficult to separate from egotism, is the minute attention he gives to his own most casual responses, a finer attention than is given to the nature he responds to. He rarely counts the streaks of the tulip, but he constantly details the state of his mind. When Wordsworth depicts an object he is also depicting himself or, rather, a truth about himself, a self-acquired revelation. There is very little 'energetic' picture-making in him.[3]

I call this aspect of Wordsworth's poetry spiritual because its only real justification (which few of his contemporaries were willing to entertain) was that it carried the Puritan quest for evidences of election into the most ordinary emotional contexts. Wordsworth did

1 Anna Seward, while by no means without reservations concerning Bloomfield (author of *The Farmer's Boy*), gives the 'fidelity' of his 'pictures' warm praise (*Letters*, vol. 5, 383), and Jeffrey, while censuring Burns's 'rusticity', still contrasts his 'authentic rustics' with Wordsworth's (On the *Reliques* of Robert Burns, *Edinburgh Review*, January 1809). Robert Mayo in 'The Contemporaneity of the Lyrical Ballads', *PMLA*, vol. 69, 1954, pp. 486–522, has shown the degree to which the subjects, themes, and attitudes of Wordsworth poetry conformed to popular taste.

2 'Surely the Heathens knew better how to joyn and read these mystical Letters than we Christians, who cast a more careless Eye on these common Hieroglyphics, and disdain to suck Divinity from the flowers of Nature', *Religio Medici*, 1643, Pt. I, sec. 16.

3 Jeffrey again and again praises an author for his 'force, and truth of description,' for the 'selection and condensation of expression,' which are the great and simple standards of picturesque poetry. His comparison of Crabbe with Wordsworth expresses this pointedly: 'He (Crabbe) delights us by the truth, and vivid and picturesque beauty of his representations, and by the force and pathos of the sensations with which we feel that they are connected. Mr Wordsworth and his associates, on the other hand, introduce us to beings whose existence was not previously suspected by the acutest observers of nature; and excite an interest for them – where they do excite any interest – more by an eloquent and refined analysis of their own capricious feelings, than by any obvious or intelligible ground of sympathy in their situation' (*Edinburgh Review*, April 1808). On the importance of 'energetic' picture-making, see J. H. Hagstrum, *The Sister Arts*, Chicago University Press, 1958.

not himself talk of election or salvation but, as we shall see, of renovation (regeneration), and he did not seem to be directly aware of his Puritan heritage, although the *Poems* of 1807, which includes both 'I wandered lonely as a cloud' and *The Solitary Reaper*, shows a heightened intimacy with seventeenth-century traditions.[1] Failure or access of emotion (inspiration) *vis-à-vis* nature was the basis of his spiritual life: his soul either kindled in contact with nature or it died. There was no such thing as a casual joy or disappointment. Such 'justification by nature' was not, however, a simple matter, to be determined by one experience – Wordsworth's response is often delayed for a considerable time. His spirit may be 'shy,' or stirrings may rise from almost forgotten depths. It was on reading a sentence in a friend's manuscript (Wilkinson's *Tour in Scotland*) that the two-year-old memory of the solitary reaper returned to him;[2] and though the poem does not record this directly, it reflects an analogous fact, that the imagination was revived from an unsuspected source.

Anna Seward might have reached new heights of indignation had she known the religious and metaphysical effusion in Book VI of *The Prelude*, drawn from the poet when he remembers and interprets

---

1 Helen Darbishire's introduction and notes to her edition of the *Poems in Two Volumes* (Oxford University Press, 1914 and 1952) set forth Wordsworth's debt to seventeenth-century poetry. His particular relation to Puritanism, or 'left-wing' Protestant currents, has not, I believe, been fully considered. There is an interesting note on his relation to Methodism (in the broad sense of the word) in Arthur Beatty, *Representative Poems*, Doubleday, 1937, introduction, p. xxxi. Wordsworth knew such works as Richard Baxter's 'Self-Review', to which he refers in a note to the (1814) *Excursion*, Book IV, 131–2; but he may not have read it till reprinted in Christoper (later Bishop) Wordsworth's *Ecclesiastical Biography*, Rivington, 1810. Jeffrey, who had a keen nose for 'Methodist' enthusiasms, easily makes a connection in his review of *The Excursion* ('the mystical verbiage of the Methodist pulpit is repeated, till the speaker entertains no doubt that he is the chosen organ of divine truth and persuasion,' *Edinburgh Review*, November 1814). The second volume of H. N. Fairchild's *Religious Trends in English Poetry*, Columbia University Press, 1939–57, esp. pp. 149 ff., remains the best account of the religious temper of the times into which Wordsworth was born; Erich Thurmann, *Der Niederschlag der evangelischen Bewegung in der englischen Literatur*, Münster, 1936), though not concerned with Wordsworth has interesting sidelights on the vitality of the movement and the reactions to it (including that of the *Edinburgh Review*). Cf. also J. Crofts, *Wordsworth and the Seventeenth Century*, British Academy, 1940, a Warton Lecture which is still the vest evocation of Wordsworth's latter-day Puritanism.

2 *P.W.*, 3, pp. 444–5. Cf. *The Waggoner*, ll. 209–15, *P.W.*, 2, p. 204.

a mood fourteen years old. Religion cannot wait on such freaks of the heart. The heart's response, moreover, is always too great or too small; and since without this disproportion there is no such thing as man conscious of himself, we see how precarious Wordsworth's condition is, how inevitably linked to a self-consciousness that may seem egotistical. Yet I confess I am moved by a poet so faithful to his condition, so totally 'spiritual' that the most insignificant mood is weighed because it should be significant of something beyond itself, of some actual or hidden relation to the possibilities of self-renewal.

It is a dangerous half-truth, however, to connect Wordsworth's spirituality with habits of introspection spread abroad by such different movements as Protestantism, Rationalism and Rousseauism. No doubt, as Mme de Staël said, with her inexhaustible talent for charming vulgarization, while 'the ancients had, so to say, a corporeal soul whose motions were strong, direct and efficacious . . . the soul of the moderns, nourished by Christian repentance, has fallen into the habit of continually returning on itself'.[1] As important, however, as the shared fact of self-consciousness is the way each poet faces it. *The Solitary Reaper* is not a brooding analytic inquiry into the source of an emotion. The poet does not explain why he responded so strongly to the Highland girl but takes advantage of the strength of his response. After expressing the fact that he is moved, he allows the emotion its own life and delights in new accesses of thought and feeling. A poet, we read in the preface to *Lyrical Ballads*, 'rejoices more than other men in the spirit of life that i s in him'.

Neither is this the whole truth, for the poet's spirit, tinged by melancholy, is not completely free-moving. Some burden of mystery is present, linked to his initial mood. To take this mood as expressing nothing more than surprise is to dispel the mystery too quickly. Though the poem begins in surprise – an ordinary sight is modified by an unusual circumstance: the harvester is alone and her song heightens the solitude where communal and joyful activity was expected – surprise turns into something pensive, even elegiac. There

1 'Les anciens avaient, pour ainsi dire, une âme corporelle, dont tous les mouvements étaient forts, directs, et conséquents; il n'en est pas de même du coeur humain développé par le christianisme: les modernes ont puisé dans le repentir chrétien l'habitude de se replier continuellement sur eux-mêmes' (*De l'Allemagne*, Pt 2, ch. 11).

is an inward sinking, as if the mind, having been moved by the Highland girl, is now moved by itself. The mystery lies in that sudden deepening, or doubled shock.

I put this in the form of an impression but the text supports it. If the first imperative, 'Behold her, single in the field,' is addressed to the reader, the second, 'Stop here, or gently pass,' is certainly said also by the poet to himself. The inward sinking or turning – the reflexive consciousness – is quite clear. The poet himself is made to stop, reflect and listen, like a traveler who has come on the scene by chance. An image has 'singled' him out.[1]

At the end of the first stanza, moreover, we are still in the shadow of the mystery and uncertain why the poet is moved. His third imperative, 'O listen!,' again addressed either to an auditor or to himself, is followed by an explanation ('for the Vale profound | Is overflowing with the sound') which explains nothing. It would be inane if 'listen' did not suggest an activity more intense than hearing, and if 'overflowing' did not heighten the idea of strong emotional participation. Even the vale seems to be moved: and should not a passerby, therefore, stop and respond? It would be ungenerous not to enter into communion.

The question why the poet is moved is subordinated to the fact *that* he is moved, that his mind overflows under the influence of song. While the poem begins with a girl who is alone in her work and in her song, which is not expressly for others but which she sings to herself, she and her song reach across the valley to halt the traveler, who then resumes his journey with music in his heart. The last lines of the poem,

The music in my heart I bore,
Long after it was heard no more,

have a literal and an extended meaning, which collaborate to express response, repercussion, overflow. The poet heard the girl inwardly after he had passed out of actual range of hearing (the literal import),

1 The subdued pathos of the situation emerges more strongly when we consider the poem's genesis. Wordsworth has been *waylaid* by an image (either out of his past or out of his imagination), and now exhorts himself to attend it. The poem itself, of course, gives practically no hint that a mental traveler is speaking: this kind of consideration is a bonus of biographical study.

yet the 'long after' may be taken to reach to the moment of composition two years later. *The Solitary Reaper* is evidence that the song has survived in his heart.

The overflow of the poet's feelings, and the pleasure he takes in each new mood or thought, can be traced stage by stage. In the second stanza he has already traveled, as through a magic casement, beyond the immediate scene, and though he returns to the present in stanza three, it is only to begin a new 'dallying with surmise'.[1] Even the question on which he returns is significant. 'Will no one tell me what she sings?' is a sociable gesture revealing how the song has spread beyond itself to cause this appeal he whimsically makes. His new address to the reader blends outward-directed feeling and inward-going thought.

The third stanza, composed of two surmises, continues to advance *through* the solitary to the social.[2] Does the song, it is asked, 'flow' for sufferings associated with a historical or mythical past, or does it treat of familiar things, past, present and future? This return to the familiar, and from the fixed past to the more open 'has been, and may be again', is characteristically Wordsworthian and anticipates the 'something evermore about to be' toward which the poem tends. For in the final stanza, though Wordsworth gives up surmise and reverts to the indicative, his variations of the central word (sang, song, singing), his circling back to the figure of the girl at work (is she in a laboring or a thoughtful attitude?), and his first use of feminine rhyme ('ending' | 'bending') modify the matter-of-factness of the event. As the poet returns in thought from one solitary, the girl, to another, himself, and therefore uses the 'I' more overtly than before, the power for communion in so random an image, and its indefinite echo, are acknowledged. A finitude is removed from the verbs as from the action.

Thus Wordsworth, under the impress of a powerful feeling, turns round both it and its apparent cause, respecting both and never reducing the one to the other. By surmise he multiplies his moods, if not the phenomenon. His surmises have a pattern, which is to proceed through the solitary to the social and from stasis to motion,

1 Milton, *Lycidas*, l. 153.

2 Cf. Pottle, 'The eye and the object', in G. Dunklin (ed.), *Wordsworth: Centenary Studies*, Princeton University Press, 1951.

or to make these interchangeable. Yet everything stays in the realm of surmise, which approves, in any case, of such fluidity. Surmise is fluid in nature; it likes 'whether ... or' formulations, alternatives rather than exclusions, echoing conjecture (Keats's 'Do I wake or sleep?') rather than blunt determinateness. The actual is in some way the potential, and in *The Solitary Reaper* surmise has unobtrusively influenced even the rhythm and certain verbal figures. Such a line as 'Stop here, *or* gently pass' (my italics) is directed in theme and format against the purely determinate. The line contains, in fact, one of the many 'fluidifying' doublings of this poem ('Reaping and singing', 'cuts and binds', 'Things, and battles', 'Perhaps ... or'). Because the second phrase of each doubling is expanded thematically or in the number of syllables or by an equally subtle increment, the effect is that of expansion: 'cuts and binds' flows into 'and sings', and a parallel lengthening occurs in each stanza, whose symmetry is beautifully disturbed by the fourth line of six syllables, which expands into regular tetrameter at the end.

An exhaustive analysis of verbal effects is not necessary and may even distract us. The essential fact is that Wordsworth allows the sudden emotion (or, in the daffodil poem, sudden optical impression) to invade and renew his mind instead of reducing the emotion by an act of mind. Knowing that his relation to nature is as unpredictable as a relation of Grace – that whether or not he originally responded, and whether or not he responded fully, the encounter has a secret life that may later flash out and renew his feelings – Wordsworth adopts the stance of surmise which points to liberty and expansiveness of spirit. In *The Solitary Reaper* it is impossible to distinguish what originally happened from what happened to the mental traveler in the field of Wilkinson's prose. But however we construe the situation, Wordsworth's response reflects the importance of surmise both in his own and in Romantic lyricism.

I would like to deal briefly with the enlarged role of surmise in Romantic poetry by comparing Milton at his most Romantic with Wordsworth and Keats. Milton resorts to surmise when he wishes to 'interpose a little ease' during his lament for Lycidas. To make death seem less deadly he turns first to the old pastoral myth of sympathetic Nature and calls on the Sicilian Muse (the Muse of Bion, Theocritus, and others who originally used the myth) to bid all flowers mourn his friend. A gorgeous *anthology* follows, in which each flower is evocatively invoked (lines 133–51), but Christian honesty then compels Milton to dismiss this consoling picture as a dallying with 'false surmise' (line 153) and to proceed to a more painful conjecture that culminates in the truer 'ease' of Resurrection:

Ay me! Whilst thee the shores, and sounding Seas
Wash far away, where'er thy bones are hurl'd,
Whether beyond the stormy *Hebrides*,
Where thou perhaps under the whelming tide
Visit'st the bottom of the monstrous world;
Or whether thou to our moist vows denied,
Sleep'st by the fable of *Bellerus* old,
Where the great vision of the guarded Mount
Looks toward *Namancos* and *Bayona's* hold;
Look homeward Angel now, and melt with ruth:
And, O ye *Dolphins*, waft the hapless youth.
  Weep no more, woeful Shepherds weep no more,
For *Lycidas* your sorrow is not dead.

The 'surmise' might be thought an *ad hoc* invention of Milton's, but it is actually a specific rhetorical figure developed by him from Classical sources.[1] My purpose being prospective rather than retrospective, it is sufficient to indicate that he did use the surmise as a conscious and distinct figure of thought. His most striking use of it outside 'Lycidas' comes in *Paradise Lost* (Book I, line 740–46), where another 'false surmise' interrupts the narrative and tempts us with a charming pagan fable. Milton's pastoral evocation of Mulciber's fall from heaven, sheer mythopoeic embroidery of a hint from *The Iliad*, is immediately followed by the harsh disclaimer: 'thus they [the Pagans] relate | Erring. . . .' Yet while the fable is being told, our mind is released from the harsh pressure of a higher truth, and a meditative pause, not irreconcilable with Christian inwardness, calms the poem.[2]

1 Its classical radix is probably the 'Fallor? an . . .' construction (cf. Keats's 'Do I wake or sleep?'), which Milton uses in *Elegy* Book V, l.5, and in *Comus*, ll. 221–3. Merritt Hughes has pointed out its frequency in Latin poetry (e.g. Ovid, *Amores* 3.1.34, and Horace).
2 Cf. my 'Milton's Counterplot', *ELH*, vol. 25, 1958, pp. 1–12.

If *Lycidas* is compared with *The Solitary Reaper* and Keats's odes, it is apparent that surmise is no longer an exceptional figure of thought but an inalienable part of the poetry. The poem itself is now largely surmise, a false surmise perhaps, but the poet has nothing else to dally with, and the distinction is less between false and true than between surmise and surmise. This too is an unsatisfactory formulation of the difference, for the single projections add up to more than their sum: they revive in us the capacity for the virtual, a trembling of the imagined on the brink of the real, a sustained inner freedom in the face of death, disbelief, and fact.[1]

All is surmise in *The Solitary Reaper* except the startled opening: the poet's mind swings far from the present to which it keeps returning until raised to the virtue of the song it hears, apposing to the song the mind's own flowingness. In Keats's ode, however, there is from the outset a strong attempt to transcend surmise, to turn it into real vision, and his poems are this flight and faltering. Wordsworth's more leisurely procedure can lead to a dangerous prolixity rarely felt in Keats; through Keats's sharper vacillations, moreover, we once again feel 'the surmise' as a separate movement, although this separateness is not intellectual, as in Milton, but based on levels of imaginative intensity. Surmise, for Keats, is the middle-ground of imaginative activity, not reaching to vision, not falling into blankness. Stanza five of *Ode to a Nightingale*, which owes a specific debt to Milton's flower passage in *Lycidas*, and which by its profuse tenderness, and this reminiscence, anticipates an easeful death, is a perfect expression of the mood of surmise as such:[2]

1 J. M. Murry discusses Keats's use of 'speculation', which is close in meaning to 'surmise' (*Keats*, 4th edn, Oxford University Press, 1955, ch. 8). Keats joins the two words in a letter to Benjamin Bailey of 22 November 1817: 'have you never by being surprised with an old Melody – in a delicious place – by a delicious voice, felt over again your very speculations and surmises at the time it first operated on your soul'. (Louis Martz, in the last chapter of *The Poetry of Meditation*, Yale University Press, 1954, suggests there may be an intrinsic link between lyric poetry and the 'meditative style', pointing out, at the same time, that poetry like Wordsworth's is different from that patterned more deliberately on religious techniques of meditation.)

2 In the *Ode on a Grecian Urn*, similarly, only stanza 4 is free of the 'over-wrought' tempo of speculation: the poet almost comes to rest within his surmise.

I cannot see what flowers are at my feet,
Nor what soft incense hangs upon the boughs,
But, in embalmed darkness, guess each sweet
Wherewith the seasonable month endows
The grass, the thicket, and the fruit-tree wild. . . .

It might be useful to consider the Romantic lyric as a development of the surmise. We have no proper definition, formal or historical, of this kind of lyric, which disconcertingly turns all terms descriptive of mode into terms descriptive of mood. When we say, for example, that *The Solitary Reaper* is a blend of idyll and elegy we refer more to states of mind expressed by it than to formal genres. Though the surmise is not a genre originally, it a specific rhetorical form whose rise and modifications one can trace and which significantly becomes a genre in the Romantic period.

Yet the designation 'a lyric of surmise' would be too simple and artificial. In *The Solitary Reaper*, as in Keats's ode ('Darkling I listen . . .'), surmise is tinged by a *penseroso* element that sinks toward melancholy. Romantic lyricism, pensiveness and melancholy are interrelated, even if the exact nature of the relation has remained obscure. We know that surmise expresses the freedom of a mind aware of itself, aware and not afraid of its moods or potentialities – what darker burden, then, is expressed by this 'dewy' melancholy?[1]

These questions of mood, and the relation of mood to mode, are clarified by a strange line in Wordsworth's poem. 'Stop here, or gently pass' is a variant of apostrophes to the passing traveler found on gravestones or commemorative statues. 'Look well upon this statue, stranger', is the opening of one of Theocritus's *Inscriptions*. Again: 'Stand and look at Archilochus, the old maker of iambic verse.' This is sometimes coupled with the wish that soil or tomb lie lightly on the dead man: 'Blessed be this tomb for lying so light above the sacred head of Eurymedon.'[2] Wordsworth's poem is

---

1 E. M. Sickels's *The Gloomy Egoist*, Columbia University Press, 1932, is a valuable compendium of the melancholia of the Romantics. On the 'sentimental' (i.e. reflective-sad) character of modern poetry, cf. Schiller's *Über naive und sentimentalische Poesie* (1790).

2 *The Greek Bucolic Poets*, trans. J. M. Edmonds, Heinemann, 1928, p. 364 ff. Theocritus's 'epigrams' or 'inscriptions' were translated into English for Robert Anderson's edition of *The Works of the British Poets*, London, 1795, 13, 157–60.

linked to the epitaph, though we do not know immediately what valor or virtue it mourns, and though it is strange that a harvest scene should suggest this memento mori to the poet. The traveler – man, the secular pilgrim – is halted by an affecting image. And something peculiar in the image, or the suspension itself of habitual motion, or an ensuing, meditative consciousness, brings him into the shadow of death. That shadow is lightened or subsumed as the poem proceeds, and the unusual image pointing like an epitaph to the passer-by is transformed into a more internal inscription testifying of continuance rather than death: 'The music in my heart I bore, | Long after it was heard no more.'

The reflective stopping of the poet, which is like the shock of self-consciousness and may express it in a mild and already distanced form, is a general feature of Romantic lyricism and related to its *penseroso* or 'white' melancholy. The halted traveler, of course, does not always appear so clearly and dramatically. But a meditative slowing of time – a real deepening of mind-time or self-conscious-ness – is always present and often sharply announced, as in the first strong beats of 'My heart aches' (Keats) or the absoluteness of 'A sudden blow . . .' (Yeats). In Wordsworth's poetry local traditions of genre are still felt, and many of his poems are recognizably cognate with the Epitaph, or at least the Inscription: the latter is the most contemporary way of being Classical about Spirit of Place. One of Wordsworth's first genuinely lyrical poems is such an epitaph-inscription, namely the *Lines left upon a Seat in a Yew-Tree which stands near the Lake of Esthwaite*; and even the *Lines composed a few miles above Tintern Abbey*, with their specific registry of place and date and a distinctly elegiac and memorializing strain, carry some marks of the genre they transcend.[1]

Is there a more archetypal situation for the self-conscious mind than this figure of the halted traveler confronting an inscription, confronting the knowledge of death and startled by it into feeling 'the burden of the mystery'? Two problems remain, however, one of which is peculiar to Wordsworth and the other more general,

1 See below, chapter on the *Lyrical Ballads*, p. 151 ff. and notes, for further details concerning the influence of inscriptions on Wordsworth's poetry. Also my 'Wordsworth, Inscriptions, and Romantic Nature Poetry', *From Sensibility to Romanticism*, Oxford University Press, 1965.

touching on the Romantic as such. The first broaches again the mystery of the poet's initial response. That strangely intense response, never directly explained within the poem, is part of the frame or donnée of a situation now identified as an access – a new birth – of self-consciousness. 'No one,' says Willard Sperry, 'has come to the heart of Wordsworth's verse unless he is fully aware of the poet's quickened subjectivity in the presence of one or another of his chosen subjects from the outer world.'[1] But why should *this* scene have renewed or intensified his self-awareness?

Biography can enter here in a limited way. The original incident stems from a tour made in 1803; this tour elicited a number of poems gathered later under the title of *Memorials*, most of which are elegiac in mood, memorials in more than one sense. They include verses written at the grave of Burns, of Rob Roy, and of 'Ossian'. Others are ballads, and there are also commemorative sonnets and inscriptions.[2] The North Country, it appears, associated with Burns and the bards and ballad singers of old, was to Wordsworth a poetic ground as sacred as the 'South Country' (the Mediterranean) to other Romantics. The song of the Highland girl is probably an Erse ballad, whether composed long ago or contemporaneous with Burns. It should also be noted that *The Solitary Reaper* was not written till 1805, the year in which Wordsworth lost his brother, the year of the *Elegiac Stanzas* on Peele Castle, with the darkest lines, perhaps, that Wordsworth ever wrote: 'A power is gone, which nothing can restore; | A deep distress hath humaniz'd my soul.'

Though this context should be respected in some way, it cannot explain the poet's reaction to the solitary reaper unless his poem is melancholy simply by association and he has transferred to it his sadness on his brother's death, or his thoughts on dead poets, or even on the death of communal poetry in touch with 'nature'. All this may well be present, but unless we feel that the relation of mood to incident is incongruous, we must suppose these personal facts are subsumed like the genre of the epitaph itself, and that the true way to relate them to the poem is via the poem, which is their center rather than vice versa.

1 *Wordsworth's Anti-Climax*, p. 27.
2 See *Poems written during a Tour in Scotland*, volume 2 of *Poems in Two Volumes* (1807), and *P.W.*, 3, pp. 64–96.

Allowing, then, the poem to integrate the biography of the poet, we come on the following reason for its intense opening. The unusual solitariness and melancholy of the harvester may have suggested that the link between harvesting and joy – 'they that sow in tears shall reap in joy'[1] – is broken; that a natural order is reversed. The idea of reversal could have deepened under the pressure of the context already detailed. Wordsworth forebodes a betrayal, a harvest of death rather than life. 'In nature there is nothing melancholy', Coleridge had argued in a poem addressed to William and Dorothy[2] and which denies that the nightingale is, as Milton had said, 'most musical, most melancholy'. (Milton's description, says Coleridge, has only a dramatic propriety, being spoken in the character of '*il penseroso*'.) Yet the human nightingale Wordsworth hears in the Highlands is of this melancholy species: an alien note has entered her song, she is no 'skylark warbling in the sky', no 'happy Child of earth'.[3] She reminds the poet that there is no harvest except death or through death. This thought is almost explicit, some years before John Wordsworth drowned, in a poem already haunted by the apparent defeat or reversal of the promise of Nature. Wordsworth again reflects on a passage from scripture and implicitly compares his faith to that of the lilies of the field (Matthew 6):

My whole life I have lived in pleasant thought,
As if life's business were a summer mood;
As if all needful things would come unsought
To genial faith, still rich in genial good;
But how can He expect that others should
Build for him, sow for him, and at his call
Love him, who for himself will take no heed at all?

I thought of Chatterton, the marvellous Boy,
The sleepless Soul that perished in his pride;
Of Him who walked in glory and in joy
Following his plough, along the mountain-side;
By our own spirits are we deified:

1 Psalm 126:5, one of the psalms of exile.
2 *The Nightingale, a Conversational Poem* (1798).
3 See *Resolution and Independence* (1807).

We Poets in our youth begin in gladness;
But thereof come in the end despondency and madness.[1]

The poet's elegiac response to the Highland girl is, of course, converted into a consolation, an 'eternity structure'[2] of a kind. The song he hears spreads sociably from one person to another over great spaces of fantasy and solitude. It flows and overflows; it transcends the finitude of self and the fixity of self-consciousness. It continues secretly in the poet's heart, and its idea later revives the image that inspires the poem.

The larger question to be answered is whether self-consciousness and Wordsworth's lyricism are connected in an intrinsic and more than occasional way. May self-consciousness, as well as having a bearing on the subject or form of a particular poem, be related also to the very nature of poetry, at least of Wordsworth's poetry?

The startled, yet subdued, opening of The Solitary Reaper is, as we have seen, not fortuitous. In fact, the more typical a Wordsworth poem the more it arises 'from some incident which, for him, had a novel and arresting character and came on his mind with a certain shock; and if we do not get back to this through the poem, we remain outside it'.[3] This shock, though consonant with the ordinary mechanism of heightened awareness, may also be, as some poems indicate explicitly, a 'conversion' or 'turning' of the mind. 'My mind turned round,' Wordsworth can say, 'As with the might of waters.'[4] In the Lucy poem, Strange fits of passion, the moon dropping suddenly behind the cottage roof engenders as suddenly a thought of death, and if the poet mutes its implication (it is called 'fond and wayward') the thought has some truth, as the ensuing poems telling of Lucy's death suggest. Is Wordsworth aggrandizing the prophetic character of ordinary perception or subduing an extraordinary perception? In The Solitary Reaper, likewise, ordinary attention blends with a stronger awareness (call it imagination or revelation) as if the poet were afraid of distinguishing them too precisely.

We can understand the blending best if we suppose that the

---

1 Resolution and Independence, Stanzas vi and vii.
2 See G. Wilson Knight's 'The Wordsworthian Profundity' in The Starlit Dome, Methuen, 1941.
3 A. C. Bradley, Oxford Lectures on Poetry, p. 104.
4 The Prelude, Book VII, ll. 643–4.

'Behold' by which Wordsworth's attention is engaged or redirected signals the influx of an unusual state of consciousness which is quickly normalized. A Wordsworth poem is then seen to be a *reaction* to this consciousness as well as its *expression*. *The Solitary Reaper* may be viewed as the product of two kinds of consciousness, old and new, ordinary and supervening, which gather in tension around the precipitating image. This view introduces a dialectical factor and considers the poem as the synthesis of a mind in conflict with itself.

There is an episode, perhaps the most significant in *The Prelude*, which shows the poet in the actual grip of the special consciousness we are positing. There, too, a halted traveler appears. In 1804, describing how he and a friend crossed the Alps some fourteen years earlier, Wordsworth is usurped by something in his mind which is both a new interpretation of the episode and a new state of consciousness, and he records the fact in place:

Imagination – here the Power so called
Through sad incompetence of human speech,
That awful Power rose from the mind's abyss
Like an unfathered vapour that enwraps,
At once, some lonely traveller. I was lost;
Halted without an effort to break through.[1]

To this episode, considered in its context, we shall return in the second part of this book. An ecstatic passage follows (ending with line 616) in which Wordsworth does break through to resolve partially the stasis, for the usurping consciousness produces its own rush of verses, becomes its own subject as it were, and so retains momentarily a separate existence. Wordsworth calls this separate consciousness 'Imagination'.

It is a strange name to give it. Imagination, we are usually told, vitalizes and animates. Especially the Romantic Imagination. Yet here it stands closer to death than life, at least in its immediate effect. The poet is isolated and immobilized by it; it obscures rather than reveals nature; the light of the senses goes out. Only in its secondary action does it vitalize and animate, and even then not nature but a soul that realizes its individual greatness, a greatness independent of

[1] *The Prelude*, Book VI, ll. 592 ff. Unless I state otherwise, the 1850 *Prelude* is used.

sense and circumstance. A tertiary effect does finally reach nature, when the soul assured of inner or independent sources of strength goes out from and of itself.

However removed this episode is from *The Solitary Reaper*, the halting of the traveler in that poem is also more than part of the random context. It expresses a sudden consciousness and is quietly linked to a memento mori. The great difference, indeed, is that this consciousness blends at once and imperceptibly with a new state or rather motion of mind, stasis being replaced by an evolving sense of continuity, till the traveler proceeds on his journey. The supervening consciousness does not have an abrupt and strongly separate existence as in *The Prelude*, Book VI. There is a pause, the mind sinks toward an intimation of death, but the vital rhythm is restored almost at once, and only an echo of that pause remains, as in the desert image and Hebrides-silence of stanza two. The intitial halting, so quickly countervailed, is at the source of many Wordsworth poems, and it is time to identify its character precisely. Together with the poem that is at once its overflow and masking, it will tell us something significant about the relation of poetry to the mind.

A definition can now be offered. The supervening consciousness, which Wordsworth names Imagination in *The Prelude*, Book VI, and which also halts the mental traveler in the Highlands, is *consciousness of self raised to apocalyptic pitch*. The effects of 'Imagination' are always the same: a moment of arrest, the ordinary vital continuum being interrupted; a separation of the traveler-poet from familiar nature; a thought of death or judgement or of the reversal of what is taken to be the order of nature; a feeling of solitude or loss or separation. Not all of these need be present at the same time, and some are obliquely present. But the most important consequence is the poem itself, whose developing structure is an expressive reaction to this consciousness. The poem transforms static into continuous by a gradual crescendo which is the obverse of the fixating initial shock. The Highland girl, a single, lonely figure, startles Wordsworth into an exceptionally strong self-consciousness, yet no stark feelings enter a poem which mellows them from the beginning. The poem here is on the side of 'nature'[1] and against the 'imagination' which fathered

[1] The poem begins in a disturbance of the idea of nature or natural order, which is then subsumed.

it; it hides the intense and even apocalyptic self-consciousness from which it took its rise; it is generically a veiling of its source.

It may be objected that Wordsworth rarely associates imagination and apocalypse. His tendency, indeed, is to deny any intrinsic link between imagination and the supernatural.

Peter Bell was composed under a belief that the Imagination not only does not require for its exercise the intervention of supernatural agency, but that, though such agency be excluded, the faculty may be called forth as imperiously, and for kindred results of pleasure, by incidents within the compass of poetic probability, in the humblest departments of daily life.[1]

Yet here, as always, it is the evidence of the poems which is decisive; the prose, in fact, depends for its sense on the poetry. Wordsworth, in his comment on *Peter Bell*, is talking of the *already naturalized* imagination. His hope is that the imagination can be domesticated, that nature can satisfy a mind which seeks, or used to seek, the supernatural. Imagination is consciousness of self at its highest pitch (or an immediate imaginal reaction to this), but Wordsworth writes in the faith that Nature will suffice the energies of consciousness. The full story of how he arrived at that faith is given in *The Prelude*, from which I now choose one of the earliest passages to be composed, the story of the Boy of Winander. It shows Nature both fostering and modifying the growing self-consciousness of the child.

The Boy of Winander

The tumultuous mimicry of the Boy of Winander is interrupted by a pause which parallels the other haltings. The pause affects the youngster by gently foretelling, and already fashioning, a later state of mind. His relation to nature must change from glad animal movements to a calmer and more conscious love. The episode went originally with others from the poet's childhood found in Books I and II, and illustrated how the child is moved gently and unhurt toward the consciousness of nature's separate life, this being an early step in the growth of the mind.

1 Letter to Robert Southey, prefatory to *Peter Bell*, *P.W.*, 2, 331.

In *The Prelude*, Book V there is a slight displacement from this theme to accommodate it to the book's argument: as well as suggesting the gradualism of this process, Wordsworth supports the more general idea of how resourcefully nature educates a boy entrusted to her rather than to a human agency. She is not held to single expedients, to an unvarying course of generative or regenerative action. Her infinite resources mock the presumptuous followers of Rousseau, educators who treat children like engines, confining them by a timetable scheme of development and seeking to eliminate idleness and fruitful accidents.

In both versions of the episode, however, the idea that nature leads the child into consciousness of nature is accompanied by the idea that she forms the child the more deeply as her action is less consciously present to him. Wordsworth knows that there must be 'shock', but his doublings qualify the notion that shock is nature's only or primary means. By a beautiful diminuendo the awareness (of nature as Nature) seeded in that pause between the hootings becomes 'a gentle shock of mild surprise' and is followed by the further qualification, 'or . . . unawares'. The suggestion of 'Severer interventions, ministry | More palpable' (*The Prelude*, Book I, lines 355–6) is minimized.

By this mild guidance the Boy of Winander reaches a sense of nature's, and perhaps his own, separate life. But he dies before self-consciousness can fully emerge. The boy's death (no cause given) is related in a second paragraph, though the first indicates the fulfillment of a scheme that would lead him via consciousness of nature to consciousness of Self. A later comment of Wordsworth's shows that his theme was growth and immortality, not death: the binding of imagination by nature for the mutual benefit of both. 'Guided by one of my own primary consciousnesses,' he writes, 'I have represented [in this sketch] a commutation and transfer of internal feelings, cooperating with external accidents to plant, for immortality, images of sound and sight, in the celestial soil of the Imagination.'[1] In one of the early manuscripts, moreover, the Boy of Winander is identified as Wordsworth himself ('And when it chanced | That pauses of deep silence mocked *my* skill,' etc.),[2] so that the death of the

1 Comment published in 1815, see *The Prelude*, p. 547.
2 My italics; MS. JJ, *Prelude*, pp. 639–40.

Boy may have been an afterthought, strangely self-referring, and perhaps contrary to the episode's first intent. The episode is, in any case, contemporaneous with the Lucy poems, which also tell of a mysterious death and were composed in Germany during the early winter of 1798-9.[1]

As in *The Solitary Reaper*, therefore, we encounter a mysterious and supervening thought of death. The simplest explanation for it is that Wordsworth, sensitive to audience reaction, may have felt 'There was a Boy' needed a literal context. To publish it as it stood might crudely puzzle his readers: There was a Boy, and – what happened to him? For the original sketch is a lyrical ballad in that it emphasizes 'character' rather than 'incident', psychology rather than plot. As to its rhetorical form, it is merely an elaborate sentence. The completed sketch, however, nicely rounded by converting a figurative death into an actual, yields to the prevalent taste and becomes a beautifully extended epitaph (There was a Boy, and – he died).

Yet Wordsworth cannot squelch his own genius. The conventionalizing incident becomes a new shock to popular taste, as Jeffrey's reaction showed. Jeffrey did not see the point of Wordsworth standing dumbly, a full half-hour, at the boy's grave.[2] (Many, like-

---

1 The MS lead me to think that the second paragraph of 'There was a Boy' is a later addition, although there is insufficient evidence for any very firm judgement. The letter in which Wordsworth sent the original lines to Coleridge (probably in November 1798) is lost, and what is left of Coleridge's answering letter of 10 December 1798 (Griggs, *Collected Letters*, vol. I, pp. 452-3), at least does not indicate that the boy was said to die. In MS. JJ the second paragraph is not found, and the first paragraph, as I have indicated, is explicitly autobiographical; but in MS. 18a, a notebook of the same time, the paragraph is found, and the episode given a more impersonal setting.

2 'The sports of childhood, and the untimely death of promising youth, is . . . a common topic of poetry. Mr Wordsworth has made some blank verse about it; but, instead of the delightful and picturesque sketches with which so many authors of moderate talents have presented us on this inviting subject, all that he is pleased to communicate of *his* rustic child, is, that he used to amuse himself with shouting to the owls, and hearing them answer. . . . This is all we hear of him; and for the sake of this one accomplishment, we are told, that the author has frequently stood mute, and gazed on his grave for half an hour together!' ('On Crabbe's Poems', *Edinburgh Review*, April 1808). I have quoted most of the passage to indicate again the dominantly 'picturesque' aesthetic of Jeffrey.

wise, would not see the point of *Simon Lee* as the poet anticipated by humorously self-conscious interpolations.) Though rounding off his sketch and making an incident out of an inward action, Wordsworth injects a new emphasis on inwardness. The strange half-hour pause suggests that he looks not only at something external, a grave, but also at something within, his former heart. Thus the original meaning of 'There was a Boy' is retained (if we agree to weigh the elegiac implication of 'was'): the poet is mourning the loss of a prior mode of being but meditates on the necessity of a loss which leads into matured awareness. 'Other gifts have followed.'

This interpretation of the second paragraph accords with other considerations. The timing of the boy's death and the tone in which it is narrated remind us strongly of the Lucy poems. Both Lucy and the Boy of Winander die before consciousness of self can emerge wholly from consciousness of nature. (Of the Lucy poems it would be more exact to say before the poet's consciousness of Lucy's individuated and mortal nature can emerge.) It is as if the Boy of Winander were fated to reach a developmental impasse. Growing further into consciousness means a simultaneous development into death (i.e. the loss of a previous, joyfully unselfconscious mode of being), and not growing further also means death (animal tranquillity, absorption by nature). The space or ellipsis between paragraphs one and two, which should be compared to that between stanzas one and two of 'A slumber did my spirit seal', points to that impasse, or precarious transition. Now, in one sense, every mature human being does bridge it, and Wordsworth indicates as much by replacing the boy with himself: he *was* a boy like that, but has now become self-conscious and aware of mortality. In another sense, however, no one crosses that gulf, at least not intact: the survivor contemplates his own buried childhood.

The Boy of Winander, then, dies at a crossroads in human life. Instead of waking from consciousness of nature into consciousness of self, he falls like Sleeping Beauty into the gentler continuum and quasi immortality of nature. He will experience no discontinuity, no uprooting; the places of his birth and death could not be closer: 'Fair is the spot, most beautiful the vale | Where he was born; the grassy churchyard hangs | Upon a slope above the village school.'[1]

1 I quote from the version found in *The Prelude*, Book V, ll. 391–3.

Perhaps it is better thus to die into nature than to survive one's former self. The poet who stands at the child's grave knows that consciousness is always *of* death, a confrontation of the self with a buried self.

The poet at the grave is, in fact, a type of the halted traveler. Yet the crisis of recognition – the shock of self-consciousness – is once more elided. A forgetful gaze, a downward and inward look (the very emblem of surmise or meditation) displaces a naked peripety. Though the link between consciousness and discontinuity is established by an insidious lapse from tumult to silence to death, while the poet's 'full half-hour' gaze, by a similar crescendo-diminution, seems to lengthen the 'lengthened pause' that baffled the child, encompassing presences soon make themselves felt:[1] the churchyard in which Wordsworth stands overhangs the village school; the 'throned Lady' of the church sits atop her green hill forgetful of the grave at her feet, listening only to the rising sounds of children at play. The poet's ideal, stated clearly in *The Prelude*, Book V, line 425, is 'Knowledge not purchased by the loss of power'; and it is because the wages of knowledge are death that the other death, by which Nature takes the child to herself, appears merciful.

'Strange Fits of Passion . . .'

We turn again to a traveler. The first stanza of this Lucy poem differs in tone from the others: its 'fits' and 'dare' contrast with the understatement that follows and show that the poem is a 'lyrical' ballad, preferring mood to the ballad-mongers' stock-in-trade of supernatural or extraordinary incidents. 'To freeze the blood I have no ready arts.'[2]

1 In the first paragraph the implication of a discontinuity intrinsic to human development yet possibly fatal to it is practically submerged by the depiction of the beauties of nature enveloping the child. The paragraph starts with a broken phrase, 'There was a Boy', an elegiac opening accentuated by the syntactical break: on this short phrase the whole description hinges, like a countermovement dispelling a tragic thought almost before the words are out. We think not of death but of the continuous natural presences, of stars rising and setting, of the responsive owls, of the generous circle of influences. The version here discussed is that of the 1805 *Prelude*, Book V, lines 423 ff.; the version printed in the 1800 *Lyrical Ballads* ends with the poet gazing mutely at the boy's grave.
2 *Hart-Leap Well* (1800).

The poem ironically evades the broadside crudity announced in its prologue.

Yet Wordsworth's innovations are always more than rhetorical. We can say of him that he grounded rhetoric in the heart, as Yeats grounded (or felt he did) mythology in the earth. By its understatement and rhetoric of implication, the poem again rejects a naked rendering of the moment of self-consciousness (or of the peripety that could bring it on), though expressing a mind moving ever closer to it. The *point* of the experience is displaced, appearing as 'fond and wayward'.

The thought of death intervenes here in explicit form. It is no less mysterious, however, for being explicit: the relationship between it and the omen is not transpicuous. To take the moon's drop as the direct cause of the thought assumes that the lover has identified his beloved with the moon. This is exactly what he has done, but why he has been psychically able to establish a link between Lucy and the moon, and, again, between the moon's drop and Lucy's death (no thought of Lucy's dying haunts the poet consciously during that ride; 'When she I loved looked every day | Fresh as a rose in June'[1]) is not easily explained.

The moon is not a static symbol but part of an action. Its sudden drop punctuates a hypnotic progress. As the rider draws near the cottage, his eyes fixed on the moon, the moon also draws near the cottage. Lucy seems to be their common center. The hypnotic ride lasts from the second stanza to the fifth, in which the lines:

My horse moved on; hoof after hoof
He raised, and never stopped,

suggest a monotone and supernatural slowing[2] motion approaching yet never quite attaining its end, and the horse advancing, as it were, apart from the rider, who is somewhere else. At this point the moon's drop breaks the hypnosis, stops the action, and releases a presage of death.

1 The poem is quoted throughout this section in the revised (not the 1800) version.
2 The lines come after the word 'moon' in a rhyme position: moon ... moon, my horse 'moved on'; 'hoof after hoof'; notice also the accumulation of spirants (h) not quite elided, just articulate enough to force a slowing division (helped by the monosyllables) between the words.

At the climax, there is no consciousness intervening between horse and moon: a horse climbs on by itself toward a bright moon. The only way to interpret this ghostliness (or depersonalization) is to suppose that the sense of self has been elided, that rider and moon approaching the cottage in the infinity of a slowed moment express powerfully an obscure resistance: resistance to a concentering action that draws them together to one point, the 'point' of self. The dropping of the moon then snaps the poet into self-awareness and an oblique ('wayward') thought of death. As long as his movement toward the 'center' is gentle, a continuous motion rather than an abruptly achieved stasis, the poet dwells in a dream state in which the mortal self – that vulnerable point at the center of being – is forgotten and the illusion of deathlessness takes over. But when the dream ('Kind Nature's gentlest boon') is broken, self-consciousness returns, and with it the thought of death.

This interpretation should not destroy the poem as a love poem. Its subject remains a going out of the self toward the beloved, but the 'ek-stasis' is linked to a more general need of which love and poetry are the strongest results: 'a going out of our own nature', as Shelley says, 'and an identification of ourselves with the beautiful which exists in thought, action, or person, not our own'.[1] This identification is inherently incomplete: Lucy, by the very fact of being loved, is something more than herself, becomes a landscape even (the moon, 'those paths so dear to me'[2]), and may not appear as only a person. The unconscious yet natural transfer from Lucy to the moon (also a single figure, cf. 'Fair as a star, when only one | Is shining in the sky') already denotes the power of love to draw the self out of itself, though still toward an image which is incipiently a new fixation.

Tintern Abbey

The halting of the traveler in *Tintern Abbey* is felt more in the slowed rhythm and meditative elaboration of its first lines than as part of the casual frame. We begin with 'Five years have past', a phrase as quietly elegiac as 'There was a Boy', and again a countervailing movement is felt at once. It is expressed by a peculiar type of redun-

1 From his *A Defense of Poetry*, 1821.
2 'She dwelt among the untrodden ways' (1800).

dance and indicates resistance to abrupt progression. The feminine caesurae (winters, waters, murmur) plus echoing sound enrich our sense of inwardness and continuity. It is no single means that produces the lingering or 'lengthening' effect also present in The Boy of Winander passage, and which a metrical scholar might wish to analyse as an intensification of quantitative values. As in all blank verse it is the pace (or breathing) which most immediately affects us, and this depends in good part on the distribution of pauses, on subtle organic or meditative haltings. However precarious an amateur rhythmical analysis may be, I am tempted to say that in the opening verses of *Tintern Abbey*, as well as in other sections, there is a *wave effect* of rhythm whose characteristic is that while there is internal acceleration, the feeling of climax is avoided. For example, as the rhythm reaches toward a peak, the resistance of the verse becomes more pronounced, and we find heavier overflow lines, either early breaking (three and seven syllable) or later subsiding (seven and three syllable), while an already loose sentence may be loosed still more (lines 19 ff.). Even when many eddies of a loose sentence seem to build up to a quasi-climatic point, a further statement, sometimes an understatement, comes to relax them once more. We can rarely tell, in fact, whether the 'wave' is rising or falling:

> For I have learned
> To look on nature, not as in the hour
> Of thoughtless youth; but hearing oftentimes
> The still, sad music of humanity,
> Nor harsh nor grating, though of ample power
> To chasten and subdue.

Carried by a strong explicative particle and a negative, the first lines lead the reader to anticipate a forceful 'but': yet Wordsworth breaks the rhythm by a semicolon (a favorite check), and instead of introducing a second main verb, he lets the construction trail into the form of a loose sentence. 'Hearing' depends, despite the semicolon, on 'to look on nature' and introduces one long unbroken verse, immediately qualified by several phrases having the effect of eddies.

I connect this rhythm with the shying from peripety or abrupt illumination, here as in other poems. On the thematic level, however, it is linked in *Tintern Abbey* to a vacillating calculus of gain and loss, of hope and doubt: Wordsworth remarks in a note to the 1800 edition of *Lyrical Ballads* that though he did not venture to call his poem an ode, 'it was written with a hope that in the transitions, and impassioned music of the versification, would be found the principal requisites of that species of composition'. This note I have never seen entirely explained; it must mean that Wordsworth is distilling from the versification itself, and probably from the informal transitions of one verse paragraph to another, an emotional analogue to the *turn* and *counterturn* of the traditional Sublime Ode.

By this wavering rhythm the halted consciousness flows precariously into the continuousness of meditation. Wordsworth, though sensing his mortality – that nature can no longer renew his genial spirits – continues to go out of himself and toward nature. His sight gradually expands into communion. A sentence from *Tintern Abbey* may start with the first person yet end on 'all things'; and that which has moved the poet sometimes, somewhere, as a personal feeling, becomes a principle animating the world.

> And I have felt
> A presence that disturbs me with the joy
> Of elevated thoughts; a sense sublime
> Of something far more deeply interfused,
> Whose dwelling is the light of setting suns,
> And the round ocean and the living air,
> And the blue sky, and in the mind of man:
> A motion and a spirit, that impels
> All thinking things, all objects of all thought,
> And rolls through all things.

Thus the 'I hear', 'I see' and 'I have felt', these simple personal acts, open a sustained movement of surmise ranging through present, past, and future, and raising the indicative mood of the first paragraph to the freer optative of the last.

The individual mind, its shadowy self-exploration, is always felt in *Tintern Abbey*. Wordsworth journeys, by a typical descent, into landscape and mental landscape, to find at mutual depth an image of the 'sole self' (the Hermit). This *descensus*, or deepening of the mind, is prophetic in purpose. The living mind questions nature to find an omen of its destiny. The contrary of hope, for the religious man, is fear for his salvation; and for the man whose sense of separate and mortal being is especially strong, as with Donne and his 'sin of fear' (the last and greatest of these), or with Wordsworth and his subtler doubts, the labor of faith is to overcome that fear of an absolute death, of a final separation from the sources of renewal. In the last paragraph of *Tintern Abbey* the halted traveler faces once more these fears and tries to overcome them. Wordsworth turns from nature to Dorothy, and what could have been an inscription poem, written not far from a ruined abbey and addressed implicitly to the passing Stranger, is now directed to the person at his side, 'Thou my dearest Friend, My dear, dear Friend'. It becomes a vow, a prayer, an inscription for Dorothy's heart, an intimation of how this moment can survive the speaker's death. Binding the landscape, his memory of the landscape and of his sister, and even his sister's future mind, into a single skein of life, Wordsworth foresees the survival of his kind of fidelity to nature:

> Nor, perchance –
> If I should be where I no more can hear
> Thy voice, nor catch from thy wild eyes these gleams
> Of past existence – wilt thou then forget
> That on the banks of this delightful stream
> We stood together; and that I, so long
> A worshipper of Nature, hither came
> Unwearied in that service: rather say
> With warmer love – oh! with far deeper zeal
> Of holier love. Nor wilt though then forget,
> That after many wanderings, many years
> Of absence, these steep woods and lofty cliffs,
> And this green pastoral landscape, were to me
> More dear, both for themselves and for thy sake!

Death in the shape of a god-sent plague; a voice from the whirlwind; a still small voice; the inscription on a grave; a sudden calm; an image that waylays; such interpositions, mild or terrible, make a man stop, consider, remember his end and his beginning:

> Here must thou be, O Man!
> Strength to thyself; no Helper hast thou here;
> Here keepest thou thy individual state.[1]

1 *The Prelude* (1805) XIII, 188–90.

Wordsworth is as 'self-haunting' a spirit as Coleridge. Yet his imagination flowed with nature's aid back into nature. To join imagination
to what both Wordsworth and Spinoza call Intellectual Love is the
solitary work, the solitude-redeeming labor, of which the poet speaks
at the end of The Prelude.

The summons to self-consciousness is rarely presented by Wordsworth as violent and supernatural.[1] Anything in nature stirs him and
renews in turn his sense for nature. But this is already the perspective
of hope and salvation. It is sometimes forgotten that Wordsworth's
poetry looks back in order to look forward the better. The poet's
great hope lies in unviolent regeneration and nature appears to him
in the light of a hope which nature itself originally kindled. The story
of how nature came to be associated so strongly with this anti-
apocalyptic view of regeneration, and poetry with nature, is told in
the following pages. It is first considered synoptically, via several
crucial episodes in The Prelude, then studied chronologically, to do
fuller justice to the growth of a notion and the development of
a poet.

Jonathan Wordsworth

from The Music of Humanity: A Critical Study of Wordsworth's
Ruined Cottage   1969

In The Ruined Cottage ... the surface level is strongly realistic, and
the traditional associations are submerged. One reaches them not
through the language, or the details evoked, but through the repetition ('She is dead ...' 'She is dead ...') and conscious rhythmic
patterning. Wordsworth's lines at this point fall roughly into stanzas,
each embodying a single contrast between past and present:

1 Cf. with Tintern Abbey a contemporary analogue printed by Gentleman's
Magazine in 1808, but identified as lines 'written at the place [Finchale Abbey],
by a stranger, in the year 1784'. The lines hearken back to 'those awful days, |
When stern Religion with her iron rod | And frown terrific, humaniz'd the
soul' (Gentleman's Magazine, no. 78, p. 924). This kind of reluctant protestant
shudder at the older and sterner religion is quite different from Wordsworth's
consciousness of 'The still, sad music of humanity'.

> She is dead,
> The worm is on her cheek, and this poor hut,
> Stripped of its outward garb of household flowers,
> Of rose and sweetbriar, offers to the wind
> A cold bare wall whose earthy top is tricked
> With weeds and the rank spear-grass.
>
> She is dead,
> And nettles rot and adders sun themselves
> Where we have sat together while she nursed
> Her infant at her breast.
>
> The unshod Colt,
> The wandering heifer and the Potter's ass,
> Find shelter now within the chimney-wall
> Where I have seen her evening hearth-stone blaze
> And through the window spread upon the road
> Its cheerful light.
> (103–16)

To an extraordinary degree *The Ruined Cottage* seems to grow out of this particular passage. The quality of personal elegy – stylized, perhaps a little mannered, here – extends to the whole of the Pedlar's story. The symbolic contrasts both establish the setting of the poem, and by giving substance to the Pedlar's emotional opening remarks ('Oh Sir, the good die first . . .'), serve as an introduction to Margaret herself. The past comes to represent not only personal happiness, but usefulness, charity, outgoing love: the water from Margaret's well was given to all, her house was dressed in flowers, her fire threw its light outward on to the road, and so on.

But the passage goes further. It sets up the curious identification which is felt throughout the poem between Margaret and her surroundings. It is not a case of straightforward metaphor –

> Tho
> The Soul's dark Cottage, batter'd and decay'd
> Lets in new Light thro chinks that time has made.[1]

– not even of the implied symbol (in some sense Margaret is presum-

1 Edmund Waller, Of the last verses in the Book, 13–14.

ably the rose pulled from its sustaining wall, the young apple-tree that will be dead and gone 'ere Robert come again'), but rather of a fusion such as Wordsworth himself describes in his brilliant piece of Practical Criticism about the stone and the sea-beast in *The Leech Gatherer*:

The Stone is endowed with something of the power of life
to approximate it to the Sea-beast; and the Sea-beast
stripped of some of its vital qualities to assimiliate it to the
stone; which intermediate image is thus treated for the
purpose of bringing the original image, that of the stone, to
a nearer resemblance to the figure and condition of the aged
Man; who is divested of so much of the indications of life and
motion as to bring him to the point where the two objects
unite and coalesce in just comparison (1815 Preface).

Margaret, already dead, loses not her 'vital qualities' but her humanity itself: the word 'on' especially (The worm is *on* her cheek), reduces her almost brutally to an object. The cottage too is reduced in status ('this poor *hut*', where it was at first 'a ruined *house*'), but Wordsworth is asking for it a sympathy which is properly Margaret's. It is as if she can no longer feel, and the cottage is left to suffer in her place. Already it has been to some extent 'endowed with the power of life' (*naked*, staring walls), but now it seems that Margaret's flowers were its *garb*, that it has been *stripped*, and that its *cold, bare* wall is *tricked* with weeds (taking up the associations of 'garb') and positively offers itself to the wind.[1]

Two relationships between Margaret and her natural surroundings were suggested in the last chapter, one merely symbolic, the other of basic importance. But neither can be said to account fully for one's response as one reads, for instance,

The earth was hard,
With weeds defaced and knots of withered grass ...
(414-15)

and they are both, of course, irrelevant to descriptions of the cottage as opposed to the garden. The answer seems to be that one associates Margaret so strongly with the place in which she lived that as one

1 The sexual undertones are odd, and not very helpful.

actually reads one thinks of its deterioration as hers. How conscious
Wordsworth himself was of this effect it is difficult to say, but the
identification is shared by the Pedlar –

> You will forgive me, Sir
> But often *on this cottage* do I muse
> As on a picture, till my wiser mind
> Sinks, yielding to the foolishness of grief.
> (116–19)[1]

– and at times the transference of human characteristics is so clear
that one feels it must have been intended. It is the cottage that sinks to
decay bacause Robert has gone, the cottage that is bereaved and
sapped:

> Meanwhile her poor hut
> Sunk to decay; for he was gone, whose hand
> At the first nippings of October frost
> Closed up each chink, and with fresh bands of straw
> Chequered the green-grown thatch. And so she lived
> Through the long winter, reckless and alone,
> Till this reft house, by frost, and thaw, and rain
> Was sapped. . . .
> (476–83)

Even the syntax forces the identification on one:

'And so she lived . . . till this reft house . . .'.

  Whether conscious or not, the effect is beautiful; and it enables
Wordsworth to leave – or to get away with leaving – Margaret
herself almost uncharacterized. One knows the exact position of
stains left by the sheep on the cottage door, but in the early versions
of the poem there is no description of the heroine at all; and when in
1800–1802 one is added, it is quite impersonal, merely stressing
Margaret's love, and her potential for happiness, the two qualities
that make her story tragic.[2] To have given her individual traits

1 The identification is in fact implied by the very names which the poem was
given during the early period. In 1797–8 it could be either *The Ruined Cottage*
or *The Story of Margaret*, *The Tale of a Woman*.
2 The lines are found in MS. 2 of *Peter Bell* dating from 1800, and incorporated
in the text of *The Ruined Cottage* in MS. E. (1802).

might certainly have made her more memorable as a character, but as long as she does not become nebulous the poem gains in universality what it loses in surface interest.

It is of course a way of writing that has its dangers. One might for instance wish that the heroine Margaret most closely resembles were not Marty South of *The Woodlanders*:

> gladly reconciled
> To numerous self-denials, Margaret
> Went struggling on through those calamitous years
> With chearful hope.

(145-8)

The virtue is a little inhuman, and though the Pedlar may love Margaret as his own child, and passers-by bless her for her gentle looks, against this one has to set the oblique first reference – 'very soon | *Even of the good* is no memorial left', and its counterpart a few lines later: 'Oh Sir, *the good* die first'. Even these oddly impersonal allusions, however, are partly sympathetic in their effect, emphasizing not only Margaret's goodness, but the essential fact that she is dead. There are obvious disadvantages in anticipating the end of a story, but Wordsworth is not interested in suspense. Margaret's death guarantees the initial sympathy of the reader, and every subsequent reference to the setting of the poem, every implied contrast between past and present, helps to sustain it.[1]

Robert too is of great importance in this respect. His deracination is described as Margaret's never is, and the accumulated pathos is then brilliantly transferred to Margaret herself:

> Ill fared it now with Robert, he who dwelt
> In this poor cottage. At his door he stood
> And whistled many a snatch of merry tunes
> That had no mirth in them, or with his knife
> Carved uncouth figures on the heads of sticks,
> Then idly sought about through every nook
> Of house or garden any casual task

---

1 There is also the fact that the dead are permitted a virtue which would be intolerable in the living. Emphasis on Margaret's goodness, though it may seem sentimental in the Pedlar, is not in practice held against her.

Of use or ornament, and with a strange
Amusing but uneasy novelty
He blended where he might the various tasks
Of summer, autumn, winter, and of spring.
But this endured not, his good humour soon
Became a weight in which no pleasure was,
And poverty brought on a petted mood
And a sore temper. Day by day he drooped,
And he would leave his home, and to the town
Without an errand would he turn his steps,
Or wander here and there among the fields.
One while he would speak lightly of his babes
And with a cruel tongue, at other times
He played with them wild freaks of merriment,
And 'twas a piteous thing to see the looks
Of the poor innocent children. 'Every smile',
Said Margaret to me here beneath these trees,
'Made my heart bleed.'
(161–85)

Each separate detail implies frustration: the very fact that Robert is
at the door at all, his whistling in 'snatches', the carving of uncouth
figures, the idle seeking of work which makes no distinction between
use and ornament. Frequent paradoxes serve to imply the norm
when Robert had been as merry as his songs, when life had been
stable and seasonal, good-humour effortless and genuine. At first the
observations are reported with a flatness that adds to their effect, but
gradually the language becomes more emotional ('petted mood',
'sore temper', 'cruel tongue'), and one becomes aware of a speaking
voice beneath the poetry:

And 'twas a piteous thing to see the looks
Of the poor innocent children.
(182–3)

The Pedlar, of course, did not see the children's looks. His story
derives from Margaret, and at this moment of climax merges into
her actual words:

> 'Every smile',
> Said Margaret to me here beneath these trees,
> 'Made my heart bleed'.
> (183-5)

The transition into dialogue is almost imperceptible, as is the transference of the reader's sympathy from Robert, via the children, to Margaret herself. All the suffering is now hers. A passage that starts, 'Ill fared it now with Robert, *he* who dwelt ...' and makes no mention of his wife, that goes on to describe *his* deracination, *his* relationship with the children, ends by establishing *her* clearly as the central figure.

In the last resort *The Ruined Cottage* is a great poem because of Wordsworth's understanding of human emotion. It is the children's *smiles* that hurt most; the Pedlar, after hearing from Margaret of Robert's disappearance, is

> glad to take
> Such words of hope from her own mouth as served
> To cheer us both ...
> (276-8)

Margaret shows in her every act:

> The careless stillness which a thinking mind
> Gives to an idle matter.
> (382-3)

Very occasionally this preoccupation with emotion leads to short sightedness in terms of plot. The death of Margaret's younger child, though unexplained, is perfectly acceptable:

> And when
> I passed this way beaten by Autumn winds,
> She told me that her little babe was dead,
> And she was left alone.
> (434-7)

The reader's attention at this point is so completely centred on Margaret that the child barely exists in his own right, and no questions are asked.[1] It is the disappearance of the elder boy that is less convincing. Wordsworth's explanation is not crass in itself, as is the reference to 'the dissolute city' and Luke's 'evil courses' in *Michael*, but in the long run it is almost as inadequate:

While on the board she spread our evening meal,
She told me she had lost her elder child,
That he for months had been a serving-boy,
Apprenticed by the parish.
(344–7)

As always, Wordsworth's interest is in his hero's response to the situation, not in the situation itself; but it is doubtful whether the moment of pathos he creates is worth the consequences. The overstatement 'lost' at first seems to imply that the child is dead, and if this usefully suggests Margaret's own extreme reaction, it also draws attention to the real state of affairs. Wordsworth clearly wishes to remove the child completely, but does not even get him out of the parish. It is not a very serious fault, and might pass unnoticed but that a boy is introduced later in the story to help Margaret with her spinning of hemp, and one is forced to ask why not her own son.[2]

1 Except by De Quincey, who makes the child's death the occasion for one of his wittiest passages:

apart from the vicious mechanism of the incidents, the story is far more objectionable by the doubtful quality of the leading character from which it derives its pathos. Had any one of us the readers discharged the duties of coroner in her neighbourhood, he would have found it his duty to hold an inquest upon the body of her infant. This child, as every reader could depose . . . died of neglect, – not originating in direct cruelty, but in criminal self-indulgence. Self-indulgence in what? Not in liquor, yet not altogether in fretting. Sloth, and the habit of gadding about, were most in fault. The Wanderer himself might have been called, as a witness for the crown . . . (De Quincey, *Collected Writings*, ed. D. Masson, Edinburgh University Press, 1889).

2 The change in the 1814 text makes matters rather worse:
She told me . . .

That she had parted with her elder Child;
To a kind master on a distant farm
Now happily apprenticed. . . .
(1814 *The Excursion*, pp. 39–40).

Fortunately the bareness of the narrative leaves Wordsworth little
scope for carelessness of this kind, and his portrayal of emotion
almost always convinces. The result of telling the story largely in
terms of Margaret's surroundings is to throw unusual emphasis on to
the brief passages of straightforward narrative, and especially on to
the moments of dialogue and reported speech. Again and again
Margaret's words are used to pull together the implications of a descriptive passage and precipitate the emotion that has been building up.
The movement of the poem is in fact one of successive climaxes and
fallings away. 'Every smile . . . made my heart bleed' has been quoted,
and is of course followed by the deliberate slackening of tension
which ends Part One:

> At this the old Man paused
> And looking up to those enormous elms
> He said, ''tis now the hour of deepest noon. . . .'
> (185-7)

The Pedlar's first visit works up through an untypical passage of
suspense to Margaret's pathetic asking after Robert:

> I knocked, and when I entered, with the hope
> Of usual greeting, Margaret looked at me
> A little while, then turned her head away
> Speechless, and sitting down upon a chair
> Wept bitterly. I wish not what to do,
> Or how to speak to her. Poor wretch, at last
> She rose from off her seat, and then, oh Sir,
> I cannot tell how she pronounced my name.
> With fervent love, and with a face of grief
> Unutterly helpless, and a look
> That seemed to cling upon me, she enquired
> If I had seen her husband.
> (246-57)

The distance of the farm is clearly intended to meet criticism, but hardly
explains why the child was no comfort to his mother in her 'Nine [MS. D.
'Five'] tedious years'; while 'she had parted with' as opposed to 'she had lost',
and the stress on the farmer's kindness, play down the pathos which was
presumably the reason for the child's introduction.

The scene is brilliantly visualized and brilliantly described. Margaret's every movement at once heightens the expectation and delays its fulfilment. The last sentence especially, with its three successive clauses and the positioning of 'she enquired' at the end of the line, is a piece of superb story-telling as well as impressively flexible blank verse.

The Pedlar's second visit is the most lesisurely. Wordsworth has time at this stage for an elaborate transition-piece – 'I roved o'er many a hill and many a dale | With this my weary load. . . .' – and builds up to Margaret's appearance through the longest of his garden-descriptions. There is time also for the careful development of hints dropped earlier in the poem. Robert in his frustration had turned his steps towards the town without an errand, 'Wander(ed) here and there among the fields'. Now the Pedlar arrives to find Margaret away from home. A stranger passes with the comment that, 'she was used to ramble far'. 'Her solitary infant' cries inside the house. Margaret appears, and in a few lines of dialogue the wandering is shown to be a tragic searching for what she knows she cannot find:

'I perceive
You look at me, and you have cause. Today
I have been travelling far, and many days
About the fields I wander, knowing this
Only, that what I seek I cannot find.
And so I waste my time: for I am changed,
And to myself', said she, 'have done much wrong,
And to this helpless infant. I have slept
Weeping, and weeping I have waked. My tears
Have flowed as if my body were not such
As others are, and I could never die.
But I am now in mind and in my heart
More easy, and I hope', said she, 'that heaven
Will give me patience to endure the things
Which I behold at home.'
(347–61)

Again there is the taking up of an earlier hint, this time one that links the garden – descriptions to a direct statement of Margaret's feelings:

> I turned aside
> And strolled into her garden. *It was changed*.
> (312–13)

is picked up first in the Pedlar's objective comment on Margaret

> Her face was pale and thin, *her figure too*
> *Was changed*
> (338–9)

and now in her own words: 'for *I* am changed'. Wordsworth's poetry at this moment is at its most openly emotional, but it remains quite unsentimental. The repetition, alliteration, inversion of

> 'I have slept
> Weeping, and weeping I have waked.'

is beautiful in context, and consciously played off against the almost monosyllabic plainness and dignity of the lines that follow. This is not the greatest poetry in *The Ruined Cottage*, but it illustrates Wordsworth's complete control and delicate variation of rhythm: the withholding of 'Only', for instance, in

> 'About the fields I wander, knowing this
> Only, that what I seek I cannot find.'

or the insertion of 'my', which cheats the expectation and throws such emphasis on 'heart':

> 'But I am now in mind and in my heart
> More easy. . . .'[1]
> (358–9)

Controlled as Wordsworth's rhythms are, the emotional level is one that could not be sustained; and it is at this point that he inserts the Pedlar's strange and beautiful fantasy of Margaret's reawakening:

---

1 cf. *Tintern Abbey*, where the word 'in' is used to similar effect:

And the round ocean, and the living air
And the blue sky, and *in* the mind of man
(1798, 99–100).

Both cases can be dismissed as padding to fill out the line.

Sir, I feel
The story linger in my heart. I fear
'Tis long and tedious, but my spirit clings
To that poor woman. So familiarly
Do I perceive her manner and her look
And presence, and so deeply do I feel
Her goodness, that not seldom in my walks
A momentary trance comes over me,
And to myself I seem to muse on one
By sorrow laid asleep or borne away,
A human being destined to awake
To human life, or something very near
To human life, when he shall come again
For whom she suffered.
(362–75)

'I fear | 'tis long and tedious' jars, but the idea of Margaret's returning

To human life, or something very near
To human life . . .
(373–4)

is curiously moving, and it matters not at all that the 'something'
cannot be defined. The associations of suffering and a second coming
might seem to be Christian, but a tone nearer to romance or fairy
story has been evoked in 'By sorrow laid asleep *or borne away*', and
one is partly comforted partly by the vague presence of magic, more
perhaps by the fact that the normally sententious Pedlar should be
moved to these unWordsworthian imaginings. The beauty of the
repetition too softens and generalizes the anguish that has gone before.
The sharpness of Margaret's suffering disappears, and one is offered
instead a series of poignant detailed observations. Nothing could be
more simple or telling than:

And when she at her table gave me food
She did not look at me. Her voice was low,
Her body was subdued.
(378–80)

And yet the simplicity is carefully made. The placing of 'at her
table' in the middle of the line, as well as concentrating attention on

the actual scene, serves to break the too obvious prose-rhythm. Similarly, the end stop after 'low' allows Wordsworth the effect, without triteness, of a single line with heavy caesura:

Her voice was low, her body was subdued.

The balancing of phrase seems to require an Augustan precision in the final epithet – and yet, when it comes, 'subdued' has a rightness of an entirely different kind. Margaret's loss of vitality is tenderly evoked, but the word goes further than this in its implications. Margaret could relapse, as the Old Man Travelling has – 'He is insensibly subdued | To settled quiet' – into complete resignation and acceptance. At this stage of the poem it seems, in fact, that she will do so; and one takes 'subdued' almost as a transferred epithet, applying to the mind. It is in this mood of half-suppressed hopelessness that the Pedlar's visit ends. Sighs come on his ear, but there is 'no motion of the breast', 'no heaving of the heart'. Tears stand in Margaret's eyes as he kisses the child, but there is no return to the intensity of the earlier moments of dialogue.

  The Pedlar's third visit opens with the image of Margaret as the drooping flower, conventional enough but delicately implied where in *The Excursion*, Book IV, for instance, it is crudely explicit:

But the green stalk of Ellen's life was snapped
And the flower drooped; as every eye could see,
It hung its head in mortal languishment.
(1814, *The Excursion*, p. 295).

                    I returned
And took my rounds along this road again
Ere on its sunny bank the primrose flower
Had chronicled the earliest day of spring.
I found her sad and drooping.
(392–6)[1]

1 The word 'drooping' is used elsewhere in *The Ruined Cottage* of both Robert and the Pedlar, and clearly did not always have flower associations for Wordsworth, but cf. *The Prelude*, Book VII, 544–54:

    when the Fox-glove, one by one
Upwards through every stage of its tall stem
Has shed its bells . . .
            would Fancy bring

The pronoun 'her' allows a momentary doubt as to whether it is the flower or Margaret that is being referred to; but of course the line goes on 'She had learned | No tidings of her husband'. Again it is a restrained opening, and again Wordsworth is consciously working up towards a high-point of dialogue.

The tragic effect of *The Ruined Cottage* comes from an interplay between suffering and physical decline on the one hand, and hope on the other. Wordsworth builds up his picture of suffering in the early part of the poem, but stresses it little towards the end, where it might be expected to dominate. Hope follows the opposite course, hardly mentioned at first, but stressed at the end, so that it *seems* to grow stronger as Margaret herself grows weaker. It is in the central movement of the Pedlar's third visit that this change of emphasis occurs. Both the extent and the cause of Margaret's suffering are brought out in lines of poignant beauty:

>   Of her herbs and flowers
> It seemed the better part were gnawed away
> Or trampled on the earth. A chain of straw
> Which had been twisted round the tender stem
> Of a young apple tree, lay at its root;
> The bark was nibbled round by truant sheep.
> Margaret stood near, her infant in her arms,
> And, seeing that my eye was on the tree
> She said 'I fear it will be dead and gone
> Ere Robert come again.'
> (417–26)

Margaret has apparently given up hope of Robert's return, and no longer cares about encroaching Nature, which will finally lead to her death. In so far as *The Ruined Cottage* is a story of undeserved suffering, this is its climax.

Some Vagrant thither with her Babes, & seat her
Upon the Turf beneath the stately Flower
Drooping in sympathy. . . .

Later versions of *The Ruined Cottage* make the comparison between Margaret and the primrose more obvious, by changing 'Ere' to 'When'.
(127–41)

Christopher Ricks

'Wordsworth: "A Pure Organic Pleasure from the Lines" ',
Essays in Criticism, volume 21   1971

There is reason to think that Wordsworth was aware of a discussion
about the difference between poetry and prose in Erasmus Darwin's
Loves of the Plants; aware, too, 'almost certainly', of an article in the
Monthly Magazine for July 1796 on 'Is Verse Essential to Poetry?'[1]
Such arguments are ancient, and usually yield only to fatigue.
Robert Lowell has recently said, 'I no longer know the difference
between prose and verse.'[2] T. S. Eliot towards the end of his life
declared: 'I do not believe that any distinction between prose and
poetry is meaningful.'[3] That was in 1958; but thirty years earlier,
when the usual arguments were being rehearsed in *The Times
Literary Supplement*, Eliot had come up with a very suggestive
formulation: 'Verse, whatever else it may or may not be, is itself a
system of *punctuation*; the usual marks of punctuation themselves are
differently employed' (*TLS*, 27 September 1928).

The punctuation of which poetry or verse further avails itself is the
white space. In prose, line-endings are ordinarily the work of the
compositor and not of the artist; they are compositorial, not com-
positional. Without entering into some traditional problems of
distinction, and without claiming here[4] that it is line-endings alone
which importantly distinguish poetry (or at any rate such poetry as
is not also verse) from prose, one may at least urge that the poet has
at his command this further 'system of punctuation'. The white
space at the end of a line of poetry constitutes some kind of pause;
but there need not be any pause of formal punctuation, and so there
may be only equivocally a pause at all. A non-temporal pause?
Unless the rhythm or the sense or the formal punctuation insists

1 See W. J. B. Owen, *Wordsworth as Critic*, Oxford University Press, 1969,
pp. 17–20.
2 In an interview with D. S. Carne-Ross, *Delos*, vol. I, 1968.
3 Introduction to a translation of Valéry's *Art of Poetry*, 1958.
4 See my review of John Sparrow's *Visible Words*, Cambridge University
Press, 1969, in *Essays in Criticism*, April 1970. Geoffrey N. Leech's *A Linguistic
Guide to English Poetry*, Longman, 1969 has some good instances of the literary
effects created by lineation.

upon it, the line-ending (which cannot help conveying some sense of an ending) may not be exactly an ending. The white space may constitute an invisible boundary; an absence or a space which yet has significance; what in another context would get called a pregnant silence.

Just how much a line-ending may effect has been finely shown in two classic passages of literary criticism. Dr F. R. Leavis commented on two lines from Keats's *To Autumn*:

And sometimes like a gleaner thou dost keep
  Steady thy laden head across a brook . . .

'As we pass across the line-division from "keep" to "steady" we are made to enact, analogically, the upright steadying carriage of the gleaner as she steps from one stone to the next.'[1] The perfect steadiness of rhythm matches the simply steady movement of the syntax; the sense that such steadiness has to be achieved, that it is laden and not just casual, is enforced by the line-ending, across which – it stands for the unseen brook which we are *not* looking down at – the steady movement must be made.

Such a line-ending creates its effect mimetically and without recourse to any type of ambiguity. But a line-ending – and here the classic piece of criticism is by Donald Davie – may create its significance by a momentary ambiguity:

Then feed on thoughts, that voluntarie move
Harmonious numbers; as the wakeful Bird
Sings darkling, and in shadiest Covert hid
Tunes her nocturnal Note.
(*Paradise Lost*, Book III, 37–40)

The language is deployed, just as the episodes are in a story, so as always to provoke the question 'And then?' – to provoke this question and to answer it in unexpected ways. If any arrangement of language is a sequence of verbal events, here syntax is employed so as to make the most of each word's eventfulness, so as to make each key-word, like each new episode in a well-told story, at once surprising and just. The eventfulness of language comes out for instance in

1 'Mr Eliot and Milton', *The Common Pursuit*, Chatto & Windus, 1952, p. 17.

'Then feed on thoughts, that voluntarie move', where at
the line-ending 'move' seems intransitive, and as such
wholly satisfying; until the swing on to the next line,
'Harmonious numbers', reveals it (a little surprise, but a
wholly fair one) as transitive. This flicker of hesitation
about whether the thoughts move only themselves, or
something else, makes us see that the numbers aren't really
'something else' but are the very thoughts themselves, seen
under a new aspect; the placing of 'move', which produces
the momentary uncertainty about its grammar, ties
together 'thoughts' and 'numbers' in a relation far closer
than cause and effect.[1]

Before now pointing to the kinds of effect, subtle and various,
which Wordsworth achieved with line-endings, I need to suggest
some of the ramifications. For the use of line-endings can be a type
or symbol or emblem of what the poet values, as well as the instrument by which his values are expressed.

First, there is Wordsworth's commitment to those ample relationships which yet do not swamp or warp the multiplicities which they
accommodate.[2] No fragmentation into separateness; but also no
dissolution within a greedily engrossing unity. Such a commitment
asks an analogous literary feat: that the relationship between the line
of verse and the passage of verse be just such a relationship. The
poetic achievement is itself to embody the values to which the poet
has allegiance. The separate line of verse must not be too simply
separate, and yet it must have its individuality respected. Nothing
must be viewed 'In disconnection dead and spiritless' (The Excursion,
Book IV, 962). Everything must be free, 'Itself a living part of a live
whole' (The Prelude, Book III, 625). The might of poetry is, like that
of mind and world, a 'blended might',[3] something which overrides
'our puny boundaries' (The Prelude, Book II, 223).

'Beyond, though not away from': Geoffrey Hartman's shrewd

1 'Syntax and Music in Paradise Lost', in The Living Milton, ed. Frank Kermode,
Routledge & Kegan Paul, 1960, p. 73.
2 John Jones is invaluable here; see in particular pp. 32, 33, 47, 68, 84 and 85
of The Egotistical Sublime, Chatto & Windus, 1954.
3 See Poetical Works, ed. E. de Selincourt and H. Darbishire, vol. V, Clarendon
Press, 1949, p. 339.

paradox is therefore as apt to the verse as to the vision. Beyond, though not away from: such, after all, is the relation of tenor to vehicle within a metaphor, and such is the relation of verse-paragraph to verse-line, or of poem to verse-paragraph. Wordsworth said:

The Imagination also shapes and *creates*; and how? By innumerable processes; and in none does it more delight than in that of consolidating numbers into unity, and dissolving and separating unity into number (*Preface* to *Poems*, 1815).

'Consolidating numbers': the words cannot but bring to mind the other sense of *numbers*, 'harmonious numbers', that poetic imagination which consolidates numbers into unity by creating poetic numbers within poetic unity.

So it is not surprising that a characteristic Wordsworthian effect should be that in which line gives way to line with the utmost intangibility of division. James Smith has written exquisitely of *Michael*:

The verse of the poem is a delicate thing. It has almost ceased to beat, and seems maintained only by the flutter of tenuous hopes and sickening fears.

>   the unlooked-for claim
> At the first hearing for a moment took
> More hope out of his life than he supposed
> That any old man ever could have lost.

Wordsworth, who was so often an imitator, here speaks with his own voice; and the verse is the contribution he makes to prosody.[1]

Yet Wordsworth made more than one contribution to prosody

1 *Scrutiny*, vol. VII, 1938. A related point is excellently made by Jonathan Wordsworth (*The Music of Humanity*, Nelson, 1969, p. 139); he quotes *The Ruined Cottage*, 379-80:

She did not look at me. Her voice was low,
Her body was subdued;

and he remarks that 'The end-stop after "low" allows Wordsworth the effect, without the triteness, of a single line with heavy caesura: "Her voice was low | her body was subdued"'.

(even though we might agree with Mr Smith that this was his greatest); and similar considerations bear upon verse of a quite different tone and tempo.

> and oftentimes
> When we had given our bodies to the wind,
> And all the shadowy banks, on either side,
> Came sweeping through the darkness, spinning still
> The rapid line of motion; then at once
> Have I, reclining back upon my heels,
> Stopp'd short, yet still the solitary Cliffs
> Wheel'd by me, even as if the earth had roll'd
> With visible motion her diurnal round;
> Behind me did they stretch in solemn train
> Feebler and feebler, and I stood and watch'd
> Till all was tranquil as a dreamless sleep.
> (*The Prelude*, Book I, 478–89)

'Stopp'd short': yet these lines are about – and supremely evoke – the impossibility of stopping short. There can be no cutting off the sequential, and the verbal sequences themselves tell their tale. Within the first three lines, *and* comes twice (not to return for eight lines). Next, within three lines, *sweeping*, *spinning* and *reclining* (all continuing, yet with no such participles recurring thereafter). Next, within three lines, *Stopp'd*, *Wheel'd* and *roll'd* (with the 'Stopp'd short' unable to prevent the emergence of such a sequence, and with 'watch'd' waiting to appear three lines later). Last, *and* three times within the single line, embodying the perfect rallentando and diminuendo which chasten the childish expectation that it might be possible to stop short:

> Behind me did they stretch in solemn train
> Feebler and feebler, and I stood and watch'd
> Till all was tranquil as a dreamless sleep.

The pleasure which one takes – and the understanding which one gains – in such an evolution through a dozen lines is itself 'a pure organic pleasure from the lines'. Such verse is a triumphant vindication of the severe judgement which Wordsworth passed on Macpherson's Ossian:

In nature every thing is distinct, yet nothing defined into
absolute independent singleness. In Macpherson's work, it is
exactly the reverse; everything (that is not stolen) is in this
manner defined, insulated, dislocated, deadened, – yet
nothing distinct (*Essay, Supplementary to the Preface*, 1815).

It is characteristic of Wordsworth's sturdiness that he wanted to
know where he stood. Blank verse was (in Milton's words) to have
'the sense variously drawn out from one verse into another'. The
heroic couplet was to practise its natural determination. And any
mongrel verse was more than disapproved of by Wordsworth – it
physically and psychically disconcerted him:

I have, indeed, a detestation of couplets running into each
other, merely because it is convenient to the writer; – or
from affected imitation of our elder poets. Reading such
verse produces in me a sensation like that of toiling in a
dream, under the night-mair. The Couplet promises rest at
agreeable intervals; but here it is never attained – you are
mocked and disappointed from paragraph to paragraph
(letter to Hans Busk, 6 July 1819).

Second, there is Wordsworth's understanding of how easily one
sense may tyrannize over the others – and in so doing may moreover
fail to realize its own fullest potentialities.

> for I had an eye . . .
Which spake perpetual logic to my soul,
And by an unrelenting agency
Did bind my feelings, even as in a chain.
(*The Prelude*, Book III, 156–67)

The eye and the ear (and not only those two senses) must be reconciled
neither lording it over the other. And this too must have as its
counterpart and embodiment a literary achievement. Reading
should itself be a type of the proper relation of eye to ear; and the
poet's lines – the relationships which he creates between the single
line and its accommodating passage – must effect such a relationship
of eye and ear.

Did the printing press minister to a situation in which literature

itself could not but tyrannize through the eye? No, because of the
subtly complementary relationship of eye to ear as we read – or
rather, as we read such literature as is delicately aware. The fluidity
and suppleness of line-endings, especially in true blank verse (such
as must always remember the warning 'Blank verse seems to be
verse only to the eye'[1]), create an equivocal relationship to the eye;
a relationship which creates its own checks and balances. As Hartman
says, 'Wordsworth's later thought is constantly busy with the fact
that the eye is or should be subdued. . . . He now sees into the life of
things not by a defeat of the eye which drives it on, but rather "with
an eye made quiet by the power | Of harmony, and the deep power
of joy".'[2]

Since the verse is to epitomize such harmony and balance, it is
natural that the word *line* or *lines* should figure so often in Wordsworth's lines, sometimes with a covert metaphorical application to
the verse-lines themselves. Pope had used such a self-referring:

The spider's touch, how exquisitely fine!
Feels at each thread, and lives along the line.
(*Essay on Man*, I, 217–18)

'Line' there is not a mere repetition of 'thread'; by giving us both,
Pope ensures our noticing that the verse-line too is evoked, itself to
be as exquisitely fine, as feeling, as alive. Wordsworth evokes both
the line and the line-ending:

> Dreamlike the blending of the whole
Harmonious landscape; all along the shore
The boundary lost, the line invisible
That parts the image from reality;
(*Home at Grasmere*, 574–7)

The boundary is also that which we cross when we pass from one
'line' to another; the 'line invisible' is also that which separates one
line from another, 'invisible' because it is emblematized on the page
by the white space. Invisible, but not non-existent; there is no thing
solidly there, no formal punctuation, but there is nevertheless the
parting – by means of a significant space, a significant vacancy – of

1 Johnson's *Life of Milton*.
2 *Wordsworth's Poetry*, Yale University Press, 1964, p. 114.

one thing from another. Consider too the self-referring effect created in the skating episode by invoking 'The rapid line of motion'. And there is the disconcerting mixture of gains and losses – as so often – in the two versions of *The Prelude*, Book I, 588–93:

1805:

> even then,
> A Child, I held unconscious intercourse
> With the eternal Beauty, drinking in
> A pure organic pleasure from the lines
> Of curling mist, or from the level plain
> Of waters colour'd by the steady clouds.

1850:

> even then,
> I held unconscious intercourse with beauty
> Old as creation, drinking in a pure
> Organic pleasure from the silver wreaths
> Of curling mist, or from the level plain
> Of waters coloured by impending clouds.

1850 has the richly proleptic suggestion of 'impending', and it retains the crucial inaugurations of the last two lines, both *Of*. But it weakens the force of the other prepositions, removing *With* from the head of the line and *in* from the end of the line, thereby abolishing the engrossing energy of the enjambment: 'drinking in | A pure organic pleasure'. (The *1850* line-break at 'drinking in a pure | Organic pleasure' is altogether ineffectual.) But the superiority of *1805* is clearest in the change from 'the lines | Of curling mist' to 'the silver wreaths | Of curling mist'. On the one hand, the austerity of *lines* has been sacrificed to prettiness; on the other, a suggestiveness too has been sacrificed. For the word *lines* unobtrusively related Wordsworth's delight in 'the eternal Beauty' to his own beautiful lines which are here speaking; we were given a sense of what that 'pure organic pleasure' was, by experiencing its literary counterpart, a 'pure organic pleasure' of a literary kind, drinking it in from these very *lines*. It is a bad bargain which trades away both austerity and suggestiveness. Just for a handful of silver wreaths.

It is the placing of lines at the end of the line there which should especially alert us. A quiet paradox informs this stanza (added in 1815) of 'I wandered lonely as a cloud':

Continuous as the stars that shine
Or twinkle on the milky way,
They stretched in never-ending line
Along the margin of a bay:
Ten thousand saw I. . . .

Not literally a 'never-ending' line of daffodils, of course – any more than the line of verse itself is never-ending. Yet the fact that the verse-line is not brought to an end by punctuation, the fact that it opens into unending space, allows the other aspect of the paradox to impinge on us too. The effect of the lines would be quite different if they were re-punctuated:

Continuous as the stars that shine
And twinkle on the milky way,
They stretched in never-ending line.
Along the margin of a bay,
Ten thousand saw I. . . .

Third, there is Wordsworth's insistence that a proper surprise is something serene not crashing: 'a gentle shock of mild surprise' (*The Prelude*, Book V, 407). Life necessitates transitions, indeed it thrives on them, but a true transition is one which finds its spontaneity and its surprise somewhere other than in violence. Such transitions and transformations can be set by the poet before your very eyes; they can be the transitions and successions by which a line is taken up by a sequence of lines without being impaired, without ceasing to be itself. In Davie's words, 'a little surprise, but a wholly fair one'. The mutuality and reciprocity within the poem itself are witnesses to those mutualities and reciprocities which engaged Wordsworth's mind and heart, and they are to surprise not startle us. The transitions within the poem, from line to line, are to parallel the great transitions to which all life moves. One season gives way to another – gives way, but does not collapse or succumb; the seasons change, but with no sudden or brutal dismissal. 'The seasons came . . .' – and their coming leads naturally to the word 'inobtrusive' (*The Prelude*, Book

II, 307, 316). Or there is the coming of dawn. In what does the superiority of *1850* over *1805* consist in the following example?

1805:
But I have been discouraged; gleams of light
Flash often from the East, then disappear
(Book I, 134–5)

1850:
That hope hath been discouraged; welcome light
Dawns from the east, but dawns to disappear

The second line now itself *dawns*; the silent self-referring metaphor then tautens the whole line.

We may therefore wish to apply a word like *passage*, so aptly used by Hartman, to the passage of verse itself; everything that Hartman here says has its stylistic counterpart or obligation:

Change is not destruction, transition is not violence, and the
passage from one mode of being to another should resemble
the storm at the beginning of *Resolution and Independence*
which passes into the calm, sunny energies of a new day. . . .
    [Wordsworth's] aim [is] to render the advent of a new
season without defining it into absolute, independent
singleness. The passage from one season to another as from
one state of being to another is thought of as a gentle
transfer of energies (p. 203).

And such a gentle transfer of energies must be both effected and symbolized in the transfer of energies from one line to the next, in such a *passage*. 'Transformations can occur without injury' (p. 204): that they can do so is something which the transforming movement of the verse itself must not only state but epitomize.

Lineation in verse creates units which may or may not turn out to be units of sense; the 'flicker of hesitation' (Davie's term) as to what the unit of sense actually is – a flicker resolved when we round the corner into the next line – can create nuances which are central to the poet's enterprise. 'Again and again I must repeat, that the composition of verse', Wordsworth said, 'is infinitely more of an art than men are prepared to believe; and absolute success in it depends upon innumerable minutiae.'[1] Take the conclusion of one of the greatest passages in *The Prelude*:

>   in my thoughts
> There was a darkness, call it solitude,
> Or blank desertion, no familiar shapes
> Of hourly objects, images of trees,
> Of sea or sky, no colours of green fields;
> But huge and mighty Forms that do not live
> Like living men mov'd slowly through my mind
> By day and were the trouble of my dreams.
> (Book I, 420–27)

As we move forward through the lines, it seems that they are asserting, and not just intimating, that the huge and mighty forms do not live; then as we reach the next line, we realize that what may be being said is rather that they live but do not live as men live – or is it that they do not live whereas men do? The ambiguity is not removed by the 1850 punctuation, though the movement within the inaugurating line is thereby changed. And although the ambiguity would still exist if the lines were simply deployed as prose with no change of word-order, the ambiguity would then be less tangible, since there would not be the possibility (created by the line-ending and its non-temporal pause) that the unit of sense is conterminous with the line-unit, 'But huge and mighty Forms that do not live'. Redeployed as prose, the following 'Like . . .' would come too hard upon the heels of 'that do not live', and would hardly permit of much of a 'flicker of hesitation'.

The instance is a famous one, but none the worse for that, and certainly it is central to Wordsworth, since the question of whether such mighty forms do not live or whether they do indeed live but not as men live (rather as 'unknown modes of being') is one which his poetry never ceased to revolve. Indeed William Empson drew attention to the fugitive suggestiveness of the line-ending at this very point:

>   my brain
> Work'd with a dim and undetermin'd sense

[1] Letter to William Rowan Hamilton, 22 November 1831.

Of unknown modes of being;
(*The Prelude*, Book I, 418-20)

'There is a suggestion here from the pause at the end of the line that
he had not merely "a feeling of" these unknown modes but something like a new "sense" which was partly able to apprehend them –
a new *kind* of sensing had appeared in his mind.'[1]

The white space, then, may act somewhat as does a rest in music;
it may be a potent absence. One might give a new application to
Wordsworth's remark in the Preface to *Lyrical Ballads* that 'To these
qualities he [the poet] has added a disposition to be affected more
than other men by absent things as if they were present.' Like all
poets, Wordsworth creates meanings which take into account those
absent senses of a word which his verse is aware of fending
off:

I saw him riding o'er the Desert Sands,
With the fleet waters of the drowning world
In chase of him. . . .
(*The Prelude*, Book V, 135-7)

No reader but knows that 'fleet' there means *swift*; yet the pressure
within that very line of both 'waters' and 'drowning' is such as to
call up that *fleet* (of ships) which the sense positively precludes. That
other sense is thereby surmised and then ruled out, so that the total
effect of the word resembles *fleet, not – indeed not – fleet*. The adjective
'fleet' would be careless or perverse if it were not positively (rather
than forgetfully or wilfully) setting aside the other sense. Such is one
form which may be taken by the poet's 'disposition to be affected
more than other men by absent things as if they were present'. Or
what Wordsworth relatedly called 'The spiritual presences of
absent things' (*The Excursion*, Book IV, 1234).

and all
Their hues and forms were by invisible links
Allied to the affections.
(*The Prelude*, Book I, 638-40)

1 'Sense in *The Prelude*', *The Structure of Complex Words*, Chatto & Windus,
1951, p. 290. Empson's observation that the word *sense* comes very often at
the end of the line is one to which I owe a great deal.

And there on the page is such an invisible link: off the end of the line. The line-ending can thereby be both a type of and the instrument of all such kindly linkage.

Hartman has used the term *rites de passage*. The crossing from one line to the next must be of particular importance to a poet for whom crossing was so important. We think not only of Wordsworth crossing the Alps, but also of everything which he does with boundaries, and all which they meant to him. In James Smith's words:

He was awake to the notion of the boundary, the
imaginary line which sets up place against place, and by
crossing which, from having been without London, he
would find himself within.

The very moment that I seem'd to know
The threshold now is overpass'd . . .
A weight of Ages did at once descend
Upon my heart;
(*The Prelude*, Book VIII, 699–704)

True boundaries are numinous, and are to be distinguished from man-made categorizing; Wordsworth uses the line-ending here to crystallize his contempt:

       Thou art no slave
Of that false secondary power, by which,
In weakness, we create distinctions, then
Deem that our puny boundaries are things

– are *things*, whereas they are only fantasies or fictions? –

                        are things
Which we perceive, and not which we have made.
(*The Prelude*, Book II, 220–24)

The critic, then, will need to be alert to that stylistic potentiality, the line-ending, which furnishes a counterpart to such a concern with boundaries. Or with borderers; not just *The Borderers*, but much else in Wordsworth, such as the poised horse, 'A Borderer dwelling betwixt life and death'. Can there be such suspended animation within a poem? Yes, since the white space at the end of a line is such a suspension, between linguistic life (the words) and linguistic death (*empty* silence). One might apply (with a specific literalness which he did not intend) F. W. Bateson's perceptive remark that for Wordsworth 'the poetry lay *between* the words'.[1] Similarly, John Jones has noted how Wordsworth's solitaries are 'placed at the verge of life', and how his 'lonely buildings' are 'at the extreme of life'.[2] Such a verge, such an extreme, has its stylistic counterpart. It too can be fostered alike by beauty and by fear. On the one hand:

– Ah! need I say, dear Friend, that to the brim
My heart was full;
(*The Prelude*, Book IV, 340–41)

where the brim (itself the brim of the line) is delight, not peril. On the other hand:

To struggle, to be lost within himself
In trepidation, from the blank abyss
To look with bodily eyes, and be consoled.
(*The Prelude*, Book VI, 469–71, *1850*)

– where the sequence which leads up to abyss (which at the end of the line opens an abyss) is fearful, so that 'and be consoled' comes with the force of providential surprise.

   The metaphorical or mimetic possibilities are many, and Wordsworth is fertile and various. He may take as the defining term the line itself, rather than the ensuing space; and next do the opposite:

Even as a shepherd on a promontory,
Who, lacking occupation, looks far forth
Into the endless sea . . . .
(*The Prelude*, Book III, 546–8)

The line itself functions as a promontory, with the self-referring word concluding it and with the punctuation circumscribing it. And then the next line reverses the implications, with 'looks far forth' having to look forth across the space represented by the white space.

1 *Wordsworth: A Re-Interpretation*, Longman, 1954, p. 38.
2 *The Egotistical Sublime*, pp. 67, 103. Donald Wesling's chapter-title 'Images of Exposure' might also be applied in such a way (*Wordsworth and the Adequacy of Landscape*, Routledge & Kegan Paul, 1970).

The change from verse to prose would be the abolition of the implicit metaphorical enacting: 'looks far forth into the endless sea' lacks a dimension of enacting which operates in

> looks far forth
> Into the endless sea. . . .

Forth has one kind of relationship to its ensuing space; *promontory* has another. A third is represented by all those words which signify those great presences which are potent yet invisible: air, sky, space, wind, breath, echo, silence. Wordsworth finds a metaphorical dimension in relating them to that presence on the page which can be potent though invisible: the white space.[1] He therefore often places them at the ends of lines; we cannot see air or sky or space any more than we can see anything but absence at the end of the verse-line:

> From the great Nature that exists in works
> Of mighty Poets. Visionary Power
> Attends upon the motions of the winds
> Embodied in the mystery of words.
> (*The Prelude*, Book V, 618–21)

The varieties of visionary power are analogous, and more than analogous; there is an effect of mysterious rhyming, with *works*, *winds* and *words* ending three of the lines. And *winds* meets the invisible.

With such thoughts in mind, we may remember the best lines in *The Borderers*:

> Action is transitory – a step, a blow,
> The motion of a muscle – this way or that –
> 'Tis done, and in the after-vacancy
> We wonder at ourselves like men betrayed:

1 John Jones has said: 'Breath is also closely associated with urgent spiritual presence. Thus he describes the thought of an absent person as being like "an *unseen* companionship, a breath"' (*The Egotistical Sublime*, p. 99; much of pp. 96–104 has its bearing on my argument). I should also wish to apply David Ferry's remark: 'It is especially moving that one of the great representatives of our human powers of articulation should be himself a lover of silence' (*The Limits of Mortality*, Wesleyan University Press, 1959, p. 15).

Suffering is permanent, obscure and dark,
And shares the nature of infinity.
(Act III)

How superb is the match of sense and substance in the only line
which has no concluding punctuation.

'Tis done, and in the after-vacancy

and there the vacancy looms, an intersection of time and the timeless,
a miniature counterpart to the 'spots of time'. Of the ten instances of
vacancy in the Concordance, six come at the end of the line.[1]

What terror doth it strike into the mind
To think of one, blind and alone, advancing
Straight toward some precipice's airy brink!
But, timely warned, *He* would have stayed his steps,
Protected, say enlightened, by his ear;
And on the very edge of vacancy
Not more endangered than a man whose eye
Beholds the gulf beneath.
(*The Excursion*, Book VII, 491–8)

The line-endings (and would that this were more often the case in
The Excursion) are wonderfully exploited:

To think of one, blind and alone, advancing
(– advancing into space)

Straight toward some precipice's airy brink!
(– the airy brink at the airy brink)

But, timely warned, *He* would have stayed his steps,
(– with the comma staying the steps)

And on the very edge of vacancy
– with the vacancy opening before us. And all this woven through

1 A related, but significantly different, effect is achieved by surmising a
vacancy which is to be crossed before – instead of after – the word 'vacancy':

so wide appears
The vacancy between me and those days,
(*The Prelude*, Book II, 28–9)

– 'so wide appears': and there it appears.

a relationship of eye to ear which is itself a lesson in 'how to read' – protected, say enlightened, by our ears. Such verse superbly practises what Coleridge superbly preached:

The reader should be carried forward, not merely or chiefly by the mechanical impulse of curiosity, or by a restless desire to arrive at the final solution; but by the pleasurable activity of mind excited by the attractions of the journey itself. Like the motion of a serpent, which the Egyptians made the emblem of intellectual power; or like the path of sound through the air; at every step he pauses and half recedes, and from the retrogressive movement collects the force which again carries him forward (*Biographia Literaria*, ch. 14).

The metaphorical words may refer to the line itself or to the space itself; or they may refer to what the line-ending precipitates.

Blew mimic hootings to the silent owls,
That they might answer him; and they would shout
Across the watery vale, and shout again,
Responsive to his call, with quivering peals,
And long halloos and screams, and echoes loud,
Redoubled and redoubled, concourse wild
Of jocund din; and, when a lengthened pause
Of silence came and baffled his best skill,
Then sometimes, in that silence while he hung
Listening, a gentle shock of mild surprise
Has carried far into his heart the voice
Of mountain torrents; or the visible scene
Would enter unawares into his mind,
With all its solemn imagery, its rocks,
Its woods, and that uncertain heaven, received
Into the bosom of the steady lake.
(*The Prelude*, Book V, 373–88, *1850*)

1805 had its *pause* in the middle of the line ('That pauses of deep silence mock'd his skill'); *1850* lengthens the pause – but also removes it from simple clock-time – not only by adding the adjective 'lengthened' but by setting *pause* at the end of the line:

and, when a lengthened pause

The Concordance shows how often Wordsworth places the word 'pause' so that it pauses at the brink of the line. How often, too he places his indispensable word 'hung' or 'hang' there:

Then sometimes, in that silence while he hung

– and there is the silence before us, and he and we hang upon the brink of it. A dozen lines later, there is a literal counterpart which conveys its different sense of suspension:

Fair is the spot, most beautiful the vale
Where he was born; the grassy churchyard hangs
Upon a slope above the village school,

There can be no doubt as to how much of Wordsworth's deepest concerns depended from, hung from, some such way of speaking. The inquiry into the nature of the Imagination which Wordsworth pursues in his *Preface to Poems*, 1815, begins with three instances which depend upon *hangs* – from Virgil, Shakespeare and Milton: 'Here is the full strength of the imagination involved in the word *hangs*.'[1] Stephen Prickett[2] has drawn attention to 'the basic question why, for both Wordsworth and Coleridge, the most typical feature of these moments of insight is not the feeling of the Imagination at work in perception, but of its *suspension*'. And the poetry itself delights in such suspensions:[3]

        Oh! when I have hung
Above the raven's nest, by knots of grass
And half-inch fissures in the slippery rock
But ill sustain'd, and almost, as it seem'd,
Suspended by the blast which blew amain,

1 Milton's image of the fleet which 'Hangs in the clouds' had figured in a notable letter by Wordsworth to Sir George Beaumont, 28 August 1811.
2 *Wordsworth and Coleridge: The Poetry of Growth*, Cambridge University Press, 1970, pp. 141–2.
3 Wordsworth introduced more of them in *1850*. 'In my thoughts | There was a darkness' became 'o'er my thoughts | There hung a darkness' (I, 420–21; I, 393–4). 'The Moon stood naked' became 'The moon hung naked' (XIII, 41; XIV, 40).

Shouldering the naked crag; Oh! at that time,
While on the perilous ridge I hung alone, . . .
(*The Prelude*, Book I, 341–7)[1]

There is a variety of dispositions there for the crucial words *hung*,
Suspended and *hung*, and the dispositions answer to varieties of purpose. But the effect of the line-ending can be seen if we think about
that last line:

While on the perilous ridge I hung alone.

It is not Wordsworth's intention at this point (the tone has changed
within the lines) to convey peril; he seeks to convey also exultation,
an extraordinary nonchalance of security, and even (banal but newly
important, like much of his substance) the knowledge that the young
Wordsworth did not in fact fall off. The line, therefore, although it
speaks of *perilous* and *ridge* and *hung*, does not put any of them where
they could create a frisson; each of them is safely *within* the line, not
at its extremities, and the word *hung* has a significantly different
effect from that which it had six lines before. Compare these different
drapings of the words, the last three bogus:

 (i)   While on the perilous ridge I hung alone,
(ii)   Shouldering the crag; while on the perilous
       Ridge, all alone I hung
(iii)   Shouldering
      The naked crag; while on the perilous ridge
      I hung alone,
(iv)   Shouldering
      The crag, while on the perilous ridge I hung
      Alone,

Granted, the wording cannot be identical, and of course the rhythms
are altogether different; but we will not have a comprehensive feeling
for just what is being conveyed by

While on the perilous ridge I hung alone,

1 Donald Wesling speaks finely of the effect of *hung* here: 'it achieves the
almost visceral quality of danger at the end of an enjambing line' (*Wordsworth and the Adequacy of Landscape*, p. 38; see also p. 43).

unless we also sense how unprecipitously the line-ending is there being used, and how easily Wordsworth could have had it otherwise if he had wished.

Last of the important words which can act as a hinge for the line-ending – and different in kind from the others – is the word *end* itself. This too Wordsworth frequently deploys at the end of a line. And just as the word 'beginning' finds itself charged with paradox when we hear at the end of a poem 'In my end is my beginning', so the word *end* acts upon us differently according not only to the context but also to its placing within those units which may not be units of sense – those units which constitute poetry but not prose, and which make of poetry a medium which is more totally and persistently involved in effecting something through its recurrent sense of an ending.[1] Poetry is involved, more than prose, in persistently stopping and starting – and yet it must not be a thing of stops and starts.

Once again metaphors and puns may be effected through the placing within the line. As with the birds-nesting:

> Though mean
> My object, and inglorious, yet the end
> Was not ignoble.
> (*The Prelude*, Book I, 339–41)

There the strong sense – 'the aim' – is tempered, and saved from pomposity, by the play effected through the smaller sense of 'end'. Something more like a pun emerges here:

> Ah me! that all
> The terrors, all the early miseries,
> Regrets, vexations, lassitudes, that all
> The thoughts and feelings which have been infus'd
> Into my mind, should ever have made up
> The calm existence that is mine when I
> Am worthy of myself! Praise to the end!
> (*The Prelude*, Book I, 355–61)

1 Geoffrey Hartman has some characteristically brilliant and arcane thoughts on beginnings and endings in his essay 'The Voice of the Shuttle', *Review of Metaphysics*, vol. 23, 1969. Now in his *Beyond Formalism*, Yale University Press, 1970.

The effect of the disposition within the line ('end' at the end[1]) is to encourage us to take 'Praise to the end!' to mean 'Unending praise'. But the turn to the next line discloses a different asseveration:

> Praise to the end!
> Thanks likewise for the means!

The result there is a severe variety of wit. But Wordsworth can elicit quite different tones, as in the touching disposition of 'in the end' (at the end of the line but not, importantly not, at the end of the verse-paragraph) within some of the most touching lines he ever wrote:[2]

> ... Not in Utopia, subterraneous Fields,
> Or some secret Island, Heaven knows where,
> But in the very world which is the world
> Of all of us, the place in which, in the end,
> We find our happiness, or not at all.
> (The Prelude, Book X, 724–8)

Within the sequence there is a delicate contrast of two kinds of line-ending.

> But in the very world which is the world

– that (in the trice before it turns before our very ears and eyes into '... which is the world Of all of us') suggests the utter intransigence, as near as Wordsworth might ever get to impatience, of a tautology: with its weighty insistence 'the world which is the world'. (The absence of any punctuation makes it the more appropriate that a modern vulgarity expressing something of the same feelings might be 'the world which is the world – period'.) And then the next line deploys its ending quite differently: ending with 'in the end', and with the concluding (though not fully concluding) comma of a line which has three deliberating commas.

---

1 As again seven lines later.
2 The problem of tone in Wordsworth is brought home to me by Donald Wesling's hearing in these lines a 'jocular seriousness' (Wordsworth and the Adequacy of Landscape, p. 6). Nor can I agree with Mr Wesling (p. 26) that in Tintern Abbey the blank-verse lines 'in every way deny closure and pause' – not in every way, since this would deny the possibility of interplay between the way in which the line does indeed end and the way in which it doesn't.

Yet the metaphoric possibilities of the line-ending are not, of course, limited to any particular set of words, though they may most often inhere there.

But deadening admonitions will succeed

– we have at that stage no way of excluding from consideration the possibility that we are on the way to '. . . will succeed in damping the spirits, etc.'. It is only when we round the corner that we find the neutral sense of *succeed*:

> will succeed
And the whole beauteous Fabric seems to lack
Foundation,
(*The Prelude*, Book I, 225–7)

Of the more dispiriting possibility which momentarily supervened ('will succeed in doing something unfortunate'), we might remark:

What might have been is an abstraction
Remaining a perpetual possibility
Only in a world of speculation.

But it does remain that. And then after this faintly ambiguous line-ending, the next line hinges upon a line-ending which is free of ambiguity but which is beautifully mimetic:

And the whole beauteous Fabric seems to lack
– waiting, we pass through a spot of time

Foundation

– at which the foundation is found; the necessary continuance is founded. A weirdly serene enlisting of similar feelings occurs in the pregnant brevity which tells of the death of the young Wordsworth's parents:

The props of my affections were remov'd,
And yet the building stood, as if sustain'd
By its own spirit!
(*The Prelude*, Book II, 294–6)

– where the sustaining is invisible but active, is indeed spiritual, and is evoked by the invisible activity of the space.

A comparable mystery is evoked by the extraordinary line-ending (an enjambement which takes all the time in the world despite its necessity for proceeding apace):

> and I would stand,
> Beneath some rock, listening to sounds that are
> The ghostly language of the ancient earth,
> (*The Prelude*, Book II, 326–8)

It is not just that the sounds are the ghostly language of the ancient earth, though that is pregnantly mysterious enough; the basic mystery is that they exist at all, that they *are*:

> Beneath some rock, listening to sounds that are

– no other poet performs such miracles with the verb to be.

Such suggestions are transitory, but not the less telling for that. Let me cite Geoffrey Hartman's praise of surmises, and let me suggest that it is one function of line-endings to be so delicately fertile of surmises: 'They revive in us the capacity for the virtual, a trembling of the imagined on the brink of the real.' That brink can be the brink of the line-ending. Again, a perceptive comment by Herbert Lindenberger[1] could be complemented by a consideration of the stylistic minutiae which effect and reflect what he describes:

> One can discern a certain 'brinkmanship' in which
> Wordsworth engages, whereby he leads the reader to the
> edge of the abyss, only to reveal the saving hand of a higher
> power. His image of the boy virtually hanging from the
> cliff is, I think, emblematic of this habit.

What then is it, we could legitimately ask, which itself emblematizes this emblem?

> Oh! at that time,
> While on the perilous ridge I hung alone,
> With what strange utterance did the loud dry wind
> Blow through my ears! the sky seem'd not a sky
> Of earth, and with what motion mov'd the clouds!
> (*The Prelude*, Book I, 346–50)

1 *On Wordsworth's Prelude*, Princeton University Press, 1963, p. 222.

Again the felicities of space, with *wind* opening into vacancy; and with

    ... the sky seem'd not a sky

– it did not seeem to be a sky at all, with this effect drawing strength from the way in which *sky* is brought to the very edge, up against that free space which is as invisible as the sky or the wind but as existent and active. And then the sense is evolved and dissolved, and Wordsworth is seen to have been about to say something both more confined and less confined than that it didn't seem to be a sky at all:

>   the sky seem'd not a sky
> Of earth, and with what motion mov'd the clouds!

We cannot doubt the translatable sense: that the sky did not seem to be the sky which goes with our Earth. And yet there is – at the same time as we feel the Wordsworthian sublimity which inaugurates yet another of its great lines with *Of* – something audacious to the point of apparent wilfulness about such a use of the preposition. 'A sky of earth': it cannot but sound as if the sky might be made of earth. It is not just the ambiguity of *Of* which does this, but the ambiguity of *earth*, by which although the contrast with sky does in one direction insist that earth means the Earth, another implicit contrast with sky (its airiness) suggests the sense of the element earth, the least airy of the elements. Any competent creative-writing course would at once have deleted 'seem'd not a sky | Of earth', and urged the aspiring poet to think what he was about. But Wordsworth was, as so often, about strange things. The extraordinary vision glimpsed here, as of a calm vertigo, is one which delights in calling up a suggestion which it then has the power to exorcise: we are to entertain the phantasmal unimaginability of a sky of earth – to entertain it, and then with a wise relief to cleave to the other sense. Far-fetched? But less so than the supposition that Wordsworth simply did not notice how strangely misleading his wording could be, or simply was unable to think of a less misleading way of putting it.

    'A trembling of the imagined on the brink of the real': it is often at the brink that we shall see it happening.

My own voice cheer'd me, and, far more, the mind's

– what this leads us to expect is something like '. . . and, far more, the mind's own voice'. What we then meet is significantly like and unlike that.

> My own voice cheer'd me, and, far more, the mind's
> Internal echo of the imperfect sound;
> (*The Prelude*, Book I, 64–5)

The effect of the surmised sense is to make us consider the second line as in some sense a definition. What would it have meant to speak of the mind's own voice? For the mind's own voice, we are being given to understand, is in fact 'the mind's | Internal echo of the imperfect sound'. Another instance:

> The Poet, gentle creature as he is,
> Hath, like the Lover, his unruly times;
> His fits when he is neither sick nor well,
> Though no distress be near him but his own

– no distress but his own distress? – such surely is the expectation. And once again it is both met and modified.

> Though no distress be near him but his own
> Unmanageable thoughts.
> (*The Prelude*, Book I, 145–9)

For if we ask what the poet's 'own distress' would have been, we then find it defined for us in a way which both sets the poet among the rest of humanity in that it *is* a form of distress, and yet distinguishes him from most of humanity in that it is a specific form of distress: 'his own | Unmanageable thoughts'. Such is the form that the poet's own distress would take; the line-ending has been used to effect an exploratory definition which is half-riddling, and we may reflect that there is very little poetry as great as Wordsworth's which does not in some way tap, however subterraneously, the resources of the riddle.

Surmises are doubts, but they can be richly happy ones. As in the childhood pleasures of the river Derwent:

> Was it for this
> That one, the fairest of all Rivers, lov'd

– the pressure of 'fairest' is surely such as to make it at least possible
(I should say probable) that 'lov'd' will prove to be an epithet for the
river: 'the fairest of all Rivers, lov'd by us all with a love deeper
than etc.' Indeed, within twenty lines we are told of the river (and
the final word is strategically placed): 'He was a Playmate whom
we dearly lov'd.' And yet the verse-sentence evolves otherwise:

> Was it for this
> That one, the fairest of all Rivers, lov'd
> To blend his murmurs with my Nurse's song,
> (*The Prelude*, Book I, 271–3)

And yet the momentary uncertainty, that trembling of the imagined
on the brink of the real, is itself a pointer to the lines' meaning. For
it is of the nature of the word *lov'd* that it should evince reciprocity,
just as it is of the nature of the pathetic fallacy (the river 'lov'd to
blend his murmurs') that it should succeed in speaking the truth
when it reflects feelings that are truly existent. It is because the child
loved the river (as the line began by intimating) that it may be said
that the river 'lov'd | To blend his murmurs with my Nurse's song'.
And all this is blended there in Wordsworth's song.

There is an even more piercingly charming instance a few lines
later:

> For this, didst Thou,
> O Derwent! travelling over the green Plains
> Near my 'sweet Birthplace', didst thou, beauteous Stream
> Make ceaseless music through the night and day
> Which with its steady cadence, tempering
> Our human waywardness, compos'd my thoughts

– the expectations created by 'music' and 'cadence' urge us to take
'composed' as *fashioned* or *created*. But the sequence chooses another
emphasis:

> compos'd my thoughts
> To more than infant softness,
> (*The Prelude*, Book I, 276–82)

– at which we realize that the river did not so much compose his thoughts as compose them *to* serenity. But the momentary doubt (which would disappear in the immediate succession of prose: 'compos'd my thoughts to . . .') precipitates the pun: it points to what was for Wordsworth the essential relationship between *composition* and *composure*. Just as 'music' and 'cadence' lead mostly towards the sense of *composition*, so 'steady' and 'tempering' lead mostly towards the sense of *composure*. Wordsworth's point is the concurrence. It is, in the profoundest sense, composure (not disturbance) which is creative, which composes. (There is an analogous delicacy of doubt in the phrase 'make ceaseless music', where we are aptly uncertain whether the river makes as composer or as performer.) As John Jones says,

It remained a cardinal principle with him that only a happy man can write good poetry; and he attributed Coleridge's failure as a poet to his unhappiness, because of which 'he could not afford to suffer with those whom he saw suffer' (*The Egotistical Sublime*, p. 113).

The fluidity of water and of air was for Wordsworth a type of the perfect interrelationship. In some lines which are at once importantly like and importantly unlike Milton, he exults in the multifariousness of creation:

O'er all that leaps, and runs, and shouts, and sings,
Or beats the gladsome air, o'er all that glides
Beneath the wave, yea, in the wave itself
And mighty depth of waters.
(*The Prelude*, Book II, 425–8)

In these lines everything turns upon what is indeed the turn: the word *glides* at the end of the line. It beautifully takes up the preceding 'air' – and then with the turn into the next line we discover that *glides* is about movement through the water, not through the air. (Again the immediateness of prose would destroy this tiny suspension: 'that glides beneath the wave'.) The word *glides*, placed where it is, compacts the two elements without crowding them; it interfuses them, in a way which may remind us of a beautiful evocation in Wordsworth's *Guide to the Lakes*:

and could almost have imagined that his boat was suspended
in an element as pure as air, or rather that the air and water
were one.[1]

A supreme instance of such delicacy of doubt happens also to place
hung where Wordsworth most cared for it and with it:

> the moon to me was dear;
> For I would dream away my purposes,
> Standing to look upon her while she hung
> Midway between the hills, as if she knew

– as if she knew how much we loved her, how much we gazed and
worshipped her?

> as if she knew
> No other region; but belong'd to thee,
> Yea, appertain'd by a peculiar right
> To thee and thy grey huts, my darling Vale!
> (*The Prelude*, Book II, 196–202)

– and we find, with a gentle shock of mild surprise, that *knew* was
not as in *savoir* but as in *connaître*. Upon the brink of the real, there
trembled our imagining that the moon *knew*; the attribution of the
pathetic fallacy has seldom been made with such pathos, and the
rescinding of the fallacy has seldom been made with such gentleness.

Such stylistic reaching before and after might be brought into
relation with Walter Pater's words on Wordsworth's sense of past
and future:

He had pondered deeply, for instance, on those strange
reminiscences and forebodings, which seem to make our
lives stretch before and behind us, beyond where we can see
or touch anything, or trace the lines of connection.[2]

Trace the lines, yes.

1 Quoted by Herbert Lindenberger, *On Wordsworth's Prelude*, p. 82.
2 'Wordsworth' (1874), *Appreciations* (1889). Pater's words might be related
to Wordsworth's mild but piercing puns on *prospect*; most notably in *The
Old Cumberland Beggar*: 'one little span of earth | Is all his prospect'. (See too
The Prelude, Book II, 371 and Book III, 229.)

My final instance can be one where the power of Wordsworth's prepositions[1] allies itself to the sane suggestiveness of his line-ending:

How goodly, how exceedingly fair, how pure
From all reproach is yon ethereal vault,
And this deep Vale its earthly counterpart,
By which, and under which, we are enclosed
To breath in peace,
(*Home at Grasmere*, 640-44)

'By which, and under which': the distinction has the scrupulous assurance and authority of Wordsworth at his finest – the poetry's distinction is in its distinctions, at once firm and serene. And then 'enclosed' is not really enclosed at all, since although it brings the line to an end it opens directly into that free space which is a 'counterpart' of all free space:

By which, and under which, we are enclosed

We have only to make this line the end of its verse-sentence to find the word *enclosed* acting upon us quite differently:

By which, and under which, we are enclosed.

Too total an enclosing, this would then preclude our breathing in peace; would induct just that claustrophobia, that sense of being pinioned, which Wordsworth eschews – the vault of heaven, after all, is such that though it does indeed enclose us, it does so without coercion and with total freedom and airiness. The sense of an ending is perfectly taken up within the sense of a blending. At which point there dawns upon us the calm splendour of the ambiguity of 'breathe in peace'. Does it mean breathe *in peace* or *breathe in* peace? Both. Under the vault of heaven we can breathe *in peace* because what we *breathe in* is peace. The two meanings co-exist with perfect 'inobtrusive sympathies'; no strain, no pressure, but an interfusion which is limpidly and lucidly at ease. John Jones's useful phrase about 'Wordsworth's busy prepositions' would do less than justice to this instance, which is so active and yet so unbusy.

Such poetry both meets and makes high demands. In particular it

1 See my essay on 'The Twentieth-Century Wordsworth' in *Harvard English Studies* (1971).

asks that we take our time: in poetry such as Wordsworth's there is in the first place nothing more important that we should take. In such a spirit we many recall Wordsworth's anger: 'These people in the senseless hurry of their idle lives do not *read* books, they merely snatch a glance at them that they may talk about them.'[1] The obverse of his anger at such haste of pseudo-reading is his praise for the chastening dignity of the carver's slow art, at work upon a funeral inscription which is committed to reticence:

The very form and substance of the monument which has received the inscription, and the appearance of the letters, testifying with what a slow and laborious hand they must have been engraven, might seem to reproach the Author who had given way upon this occasion to transports of mind, or to quick turns of conflicting passion. . . .
(*Epitaphs; The Friend*, 22 February 1810)

The twentieth century is even more open to 'senseless hurry' than was the nineteenth century. Wordsworth urges us to take his time. (1-29)

1 Letter to Lady Beaumont, 21 May 1807.

Select Bibliography

Editions

Literary Criticism of William Wordsworth, edited by Paul M. Zall Lincoln, University of Nebraska Press, 1966.

The Poetical Works of William Wordsworth, 5 vols., edited by E. de Selincourt and H. Darbishire, Clarendon Press, 1959.

The Prelude, edited by E. de Selincourt; revised H. Darbishire, Clarendon Press, 1959.

The Prelude: A Parallel Text, edited by J. C. Maxwell, Penguin, 1971.

Prose Works of William Wordsworth, 3 vols., edited by A. B. Grosart, London, 1876.

Prose Works of William Wordsworth, 2 vols., edited by W. A. Knight, London, 1896.

Lyrical Ballads, edited by R. L. Brett and A. R. Jones, Methuen, 1963.

Bibliographies

James V. Logan, *Wordsworthian Criticism: A Guide and Bibliography*, Ohio State University Press, 1947. [Covering the period 1850–1944]

Elton F. Henley and David H. Stamm, *Wordsworthian Criticism 1945–1964: An Annotated Bibliography*, New York Public Library, 1965.

Letters and Biographies

The Early Letters of William and Dorothy Wordsworth, 1787–1805 (1935); *The Letters of William and Dorothy Wordsworth: The Middle Years*, 2 vols. (1937); *The Later Years*, 3 vols. (1939), edited by E. de Selincourt, Clarendon Press. Second edition of the Letters, Vol. 1, *The Early Years, 1787–1805*, revised by Chester L. Shaver; Vol. 2, *The Middle Years, 1806–11*, revised by Mary Moorman; Vol. 3, *The Later Years, 1812–50*, revised by Mary Moorman and Alan Hill; Clarendon Press, 1967.

G. M. Harper, *William Wordsworth: His Life, Works and Influence*, 2 vols., John Murray, 1916.

E. Legouis, *The Early Life of William Wordsworth, 1770–1798*, London, 1897.

Mary Moorman, *William Wordsworth: A Biography: The Early Years*,

Selected Criticism

1770–1803 (1957); *The Later Years, 1803–1850* (1965), Clarendon Press.

L. Abercrombie, *The Art of Wordsworth*, Oxford University Press, 1952.

M. H. Abrams, 'Wordsworth and the Eighteenth Century', in *The Mirror and the Lamp: Romantic Theory and the Critical Tradition*, Norton, 1958.

Irving Babbitt, 'The Primitivism of Wordsworth', in the *Bookman*, vol. 74, 1931.

W. Bagehot, 'Wordsworth, Tennyson and Browning; or, Pure, Ornate and Grotesque Art in English Poetry', 1864, in *The Collected Works of Walter Bagehot*, vol. 2, edited by N. St John-Stevas, Longman, 1965.

F. W. Bateson, *Wordsworth: A Re-Interpretation*, Longman, 1954.

Edith C. Batho, *The Later Wordsworth*, Cambridge University Press, 1933.

Arthur Beatty, *William Wordsworth: His Doctrine and Art in their Historical Relations*, Madison, 1922.

Harold Bloom, 'William Wordsworth', in *The Visionary Company*, Faber, 1962.

Cleanth Brooks, 'Wordsworth and the Paradox of the Imagination', in *The Well Wrought Urn*, Dennis Dobson, 1949.

Mary Burton, *The One Wordsworth*, University of North Carolina Press, 1942.

Colin Clarke, *Romantic Paradox*, Routledge & Kegan Paul, 1962.

Patrick Cruttwell, 'Wordsworth, the Public, and the People', in *Sewanee Review*, vol. 64, pp. 71–80, 1956.

John Danby, *The Simple Wordsworth*, Routledge & Kegan Paul, 1960.

Helen Darbishire, *The Poet Wordsworth*, Oxford University Press, 1950.

Helen Darbishire, *Introduction to Wordsworth's Poems in Two Volumes, 1807*, Oxford University Press, 1914, 1952.

Donald Davie, 'Syntax in the Blank Verse of Wordsworth's Prelude', in *Articulate Energy: An Enquiry into the Syntax of English Verse*, Routledge & Kegan Paul, 1955.

S. De Madariaga, 'The Case of Wordsworth', in *Shelley and Calderon*, Constable, 1920.

William Empson, 'Sense in *The Prelude*', in *The Structure of Complex Words*, Chatto & Windus, 1951.

David Ferry, *The Limits of Mortality: An Essay on Wordsworth's Major Poems*, Wesleyan University Press, 1959.

H. W. Garrod, *Wordsworth*, Clarendon Press, 1927.

Geoffrey H. Hartman, *Wordsworth's Poetry 1784–1814*, Yale University Press, 1964.

R. D. Havens, *The Mind of a Poet: A Study of Wordsworth's Thought with Particular Reference to* The Prelude, John Hopkins Press, 1941.

John Jones, *The Egotistical Sublime*, Chatto & Windus, 1954.

G. Wilson Knight, 'The Wordsworthian Profundity', in *The Starlit Dome*, Oxford University press, 1941.

Herbert Lindenberger, *On Wordsworth's Prelude*, Princeton University Press, 1963.

J. S. Lyon, *Wordsworth: A Re-Interpretation*, Yale University Press, 1950.

K. Maclean, *Agrarian Age: A Background for Wordsworth*, Yale University Press, 1950.

F. Marsh, *Wordsworth's Imagery*, Yale Univesity Press, 1952.

Josephine Miles, *Wordsworth and the Vocabulary of Emotion*, University of California Press, 1942.

W. J. B. Owen, *Wordsworth's Preface to Lyrical Ballads*, Rosenhilde & Bagge, 1957.

W. J. B. Owen, *Wordsworth as Critic*, Oxford University Press, 1969.

David Perkins, *The Quest for Permanence: The Symbolism of Wordsworth, Shelley and Keats*, Harvard University Press, 1959.

Abbie F. Potts, *Wordsworth's Prelude: A Study of its Literary Form*, Cornell University Press, 1953.

Herbert Read, *Wordsworth*, Cape, 1930.

C. Salvesen, *The Landscape of Memory*, Arnold, 1965.

N. P. Stallknecht, *Strange Seas of Thought: Studies in William Wordsworth's Philosophy of Man and Nature*, Indiana University Press, 1966.

A. W. Thomson, (ed.) *Essays Old and New: Wordsworth's Mind and Art*, Oliver & Boyd, 1969.

F. M. Todd, *Politics and the Poet: A Study of Wordsworth*, Methuen, 1957.

E. Welsford, *Salisbury Plain: A Study in the Development of Wordsworth's Mind and Art*, Blackwell, 1966.

Basil Willey, ' "Nature" in Wordsworth' in *The Eighteenth-Century Background*, Chatto & Windus, 1940.

C. Williams, 'Wordsworth', in *The English Poetic Mind*, Clarendon Press, 1932.

Jonathan Wordsworth, *The Music of Humanity: A Critical Study of Wordsworth's 'Ruined Cottage'*, Nelson, 1969.

Acknowledgements

For permission to use copyright material acknowledgement is
made to the following:

For the extract from *Oxford Lectures on Poetry* by A. C. Bradley to
Macmillan; for 'Wordsworth's *Prelude*' by Helen Darbishire to the
author; for the extract from *Science and the Modern World* by A. N.
Whitehead to Cambridge University Press and The Macmillan Com-
pany; for 'Visionary Dreariness' by D. G. James to George Allen and
Unwin Ltd; for 'Wordsworth: A Preliminary Survey' by James
Smith to Cambridge University Press; for 'The Diction of *The Ex-
cursion*' by J. S. Lyon to Yale University Press; for the extract from
Purity of Diction in English Verse by Donald Davie to Routledge &
Kegan Paul; for the extract from *Wordsworth: A Re-Interpretation* by
F. W. Bateson to Longman; for the extract from *The Egotistical
Sublime* by John Jones to Chatto & Windus; for 'The Contemporaneity
of the *Lyrical Ballads*' by Robert Mayo to the Modern Language
Association of America; for '*Resolution and Independence*' by W. W.
Robson to Routledge & Kegan Paul and Humanities Press; for the
extract from *The Limits of Mortality: An Essay on Wordsworth's Major
Poems* by David Ferry to Wesleyan University Press; for 'Wordsworth
and the "Spots of Time"' by Jonathan Bishop to The Johns Hopkins
Press; for the extract from *Wordsworth's Poetry 1787–1814* by Geoffrey
H. Hartman to Yale University Press; for the extract from *The Music
of Humanity: A Critical Study of Wordsworth's 'Ruined Cottage'* by
Jonathan Wordsworth to Harper & Row and Thomas Nelson and Sons.

Index

Index

Extracts included in this anthology are indicated by
bold page references

Penguin Critical Anthologies

Already published

Geoffrey Chaucer
Edited by J. A. Burrow

Charles Dickens
Edited by Stephen Wall

Henrik Ibsen
Edited by James McFarlane

Andrew Marvell
Edited by John Carey

Alexander Pope
Edited by F. W. Bateson and N. A. Joukovsky

Ezra Pound
Edited by J. P. Sullivan

Edmund Spenser
Edited by Paul J. Alpers

Wallace Stevens
Edited by Irvin Ehrenpreis

Jonathan Swift
Edited by Denis Donoghue

Leo Tolstoy
Edited by Henry Gifford

John Webster
Edited by G. K. and S. K. Hunter

Walt Whitman
Edited by Francis Murphy

William Carlos Williams
Edited by Charles Tomlinson

Forthcoming

W. B. Yeats
Edited by William H. Pritchard

Penguin English Poets

Instead of offering selections of the works of English and American poets, the Penguin English Poets will consist of the complete poems, in one or more volumes depending on the length of the *oeuvre*. The aim of the series is to provide a sound, readable text with helpful annotation which does not intrude on the text itself.

Already published

Robert Browning: The Ring and the Book
Edited by Richard D. Altick
Regents' Professor of English, Ohio State University

John Donne: The Complete English Poems
Edited by A. J. Smith
Professor of English Literature, University of Keele

Samuel Johnson: The Complete English Poems
Edited by J. D. Fleeman
Tutorial Fellow of Pembroke College, Oxford

Christopher Marlowe: The Complete Poems and Translations
Edited by Stephen Orgel
Associate Professor of English, University of California at Berkeley

Andrew Marvell: Complete Poems
Edited by Elizabeth Story Donno
Associate Professor of English, Columbia University

Sir Gawain and the Green Knight
Edited by J. A. Burrow
Fellow of Jesus College and Lecturer in English, University of Oxford

William Wordsworth: The Prelude: A Parallel Text
Edited by J. C. Maxwell
Reader in English Literature and Fellow of Baliol College,
University of Oxford

Pelican Biographies

Already published

Baudelaire
Enid Starkie

Joseph Conrad
Jocelyn Baines

Charles Dickens
Una Pope-Hennessy

John Keats
Robert Gittings

Mr Clemens and Mark Twain
Justin Kaplan

Scott Fitzgerald
Andrew Turnbull

Flaubert
Enid Starkie

Rudyard Kipling
Charles Carrington

Picasso
Ronald Penrose

Tolstoy
Henri Troyat

Prometheus: The Life of Balzac
André Maurois

H. G. Wells
Lovat Dickson

W. B. Yeats
Joseph Howe

Penguin Modern Poets